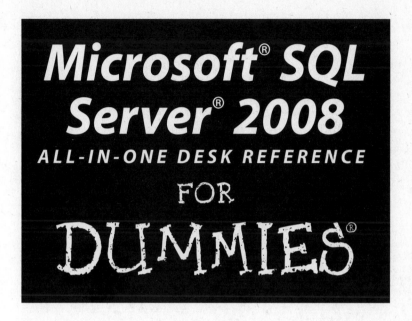

Microsoft® SQL Server® 2008
ALL-IN-ONE DESK REFERENCE
FOR DUMMIES®

by Robert D. Schneider and Darril Gibson

D1397287

WILEY

John Wiley & Sons, Inc.

Microsoft® SQL Server® 2008 All-in-One Desk Reference For Dummies®

Published by
John Wiley & Sons, Inc.
111 River Street
Hoboken, NJ 07030-5774

www.wiley.com

WILEY

About the Authors

Robert D. Schneider has more than 15 years of experience developing and delivering sophisticated software solutions worldwide. He has provided technical and business expertise on topics such as Service Oriented Architecture (SOA), database optimization, and distributed computing to a wide variety of enterprises in the financial, technology, and government sectors. Clients have included Chase Manhattan Bank, VISA, HP, SWIFT, Booz Allen Hamilton, and the governments of the United States, Mexico, Brazil, and Malaysia.

Robert is the author of *Optimizing Informix Applications, Microsoft SQL Server: Planning and Building a High Performance Database, MySQL Database Design and Tuning,* and *SQL Server 2005 Express For Dummies*. He has also written numerous articles on technical and professional services topics and has been quoted as a subject matter expert in publications worldwide. He can be reached at `Robert.Schneider@Think88.com`.

Darril Gibson has been a Microsoft Certified Trainer (MCT) for more than nine years, providing training on SQL Server (since SQL Server version 7.0) and a wide variety of other Microsoft technologies. He is currently contracted with the U.S. Air Force, providing extensive technical training to Air Force personnel in support of a major network operations support center. He holds nearly 20 current certifications and has been certified in each SQL Server version since SQL Server 7.0.

Darril is the author of *MCITP: SQL Server 2005 Database Administration All-In-One* and *MCITP: SQL Server 2005 Database Developer All-In-One*. He developed several video training courses for Keystone Learning on several certification topics including A+, MCSE, and Microsoft Exchange. He has also developed several courses teaching technical topics at the college and university level, and for U.S. government clients.

Dedication

To my family for their support, patience, and encouragement.
—Robert D. Schneider

To my loving wife of 16 years who I'm grateful to also call my best friend.
—Darril Gibson

Authors' Acknowledgments

The authors want to acknowledge the following people for their invaluable assistance in creating and publishing this work: Carole McLendon, Nicole Sholly, Kyle Looper, Brian Walls, Toni Settle, Joan K. Griffitts.

Publisher's Acknowledgments

We're proud of this book; please send us your comments through our online registration form located at `http://dummies.custhelp.com`.

Some of the people who helped bring this book to market include the following:

Acquisitions and Editorial

Project Editor: Nicole Sholly

Acquisitions Editor: Kyle Looper

Copy Editor: Brian Walls

Technical Editor: Damir Bersinic

Editorial Manager: Kevin Kirschner

Editorial Assistant: Amanda Foxworth

Sr. Editorial Assistant: Cherie Case

Cartoons: Rich Tennant
(www.the5thwave.com)

Composition Services

Project Coordinator: Katie Key

Layout and Graphics: Carl Byers, Reuben W. Davis, Ronald Terry

Proofreaders: David Faust, Jessica Kramer, Toni Settle

Indexer: Joan K. Griffitts

Publishing and Editorial for Technology Dummies

    Richard Swadley, Vice President and Executive Group Publisher

    Andy Cummings, Vice President and Publisher

    Mary Bednarek, Executive Acquisitions Director

    Mary C. Corder, Editorial Director

Publishing for Consumer Dummies

    Kathleen Nebenhaus, Vice President and Executive Publisher

Composition Services

    Debbie Stailey, Director of Composition Services

Contents at a Glance

Table of Contents

Introduction

*W*ith the release of SQL Server 2008, Microsoft continues its assault on its more established, higher-priced competition. This instance of SQL Server builds on its reputation as a powerful, yet easy-to-use relational database management system.

What's especially compelling about SQL Server is that it's available in different editions that all use the same underlying technology and architectural philosophy, yet are aimed at constituencies with different needs. Additionally, SQL Server offers a collection of well-integrated tools and assistants that streamline analysis, reporting, and integration responsibilities within the same framework.

About This Book

This book is designed to help you get productive with SQL Server 2008 as quickly as possible. Chances are that you already have enough on your plate, and wading through reams of database architecture and theory before figuring out how to use the product just isn't in the cards.

Here are some of the tasks you can accomplish with this book:

✦ Correctly choose the right version of SQL Server.

✦ Quickly install the product in your environment.

✦ Rapidly design a database and then communicate with it.

✦ Efficiently monitor, maintain, and protect your important data.

✦ Construct a solid, robust application to work with your information.

Foolish Assumptions

You don't need a PhD from MIT to derive value from this book. On the contrary, any exposure to the items on the following list goes a long way toward helping you make the most of the book's information. And if you don't currently have any experience, you will soon.

✦ **Relational database management systems (RDBMS):** This group includes Microsoft SQL Server 2005, Oracle, DB2, MySQL, Microsoft Access, and so on.

✦ **Relational database design theory:** If you're light in this area, don't worry: We show you how to design a relational database quickly, as well as some best practices to follow when doing so.

✦ **Structured Query Language (SQL):** Even if you're not familiar with SQL, or Microsoft's flavor (Transact-SQL), we show you how to construct queries and data modification statements.

✦ **Integration technology:** SQL Server now includes some simple but extremely powerful tools for associating its data with other sources of information. We show you how to pick the right integration tool and get productive quickly.

✦ **Business intelligence tools:** The Business Intelligence Development Studio (BIDS) is included as part of the SQL Server installation. If you've worked with Visual Studio, you're ahead of the game because it's the same environment. Even if BIDS is completely new to you, you learn enough to get around.

✦ **Reporting tools:** Many of the SQL Server Reporting Services are Web-based tools. If you've used a Web browser such as Internet Explorer (and who hasn't), you can get around most of these tools without any problem.

✦ **Software development tools:** To get the most from software development tools, you should understand one or more languages (such as C# or Visual Basic). However, in this book, you learn more about the possibilities with other languages rather than the details of how to implement other languages beyond T-SQL.

Conventions Used in This Book

When you peruse the book, you'll probably notice several typographical tips along the way. Designed to help you quickly orient yourself, they include **bold** for user entry, `monofont` for code and other computer output, and *italics* for new terms.

What You Don't Have to Read

It's not necessary to read this book from cover to cover, although we sure hope you'll want to. You can skip around because all the mini-books and associated chapters are designed to be stand-alone; they don't require you to build a foundation of knowledge from other chapters.

However, if you're an absolute newbie with SQL Server who is building a new application, you'll probably want to look at the early chapters on the product's architecture and infrastructure before moving on to the development section.

Also, if you're not one to pop the hood of your car to see how the motor works, you're likely to find yourself skipping the information called out by the Technical Stuff icons. Just as your car runs without you memorizing the workings of its transmission, you can derive a lot of value from SQL Server 2008 without knowing its internal architecture.

How This Book Is Organized

SQL Server 2008 All-in-One Desk Reference For Dummies is split into nine mini-books. You don't have to read it sequentially, and you don't even have to read all the sections in any particular chapter. You can use the Table of Contents and the index to find the information you need and get your answer quickly. In this section, we briefly describe what you find in each part.

Book 1: Essential Concepts

Before you get up-and-running with SQL Server 2008, you probably want to know what you're getting into. This mini-book provides you with a solid foundation upon which you can construct a productive SQL Server implementation. To begin, we tell you all about what's new in this version, along with guidance on how to select the right edition. A high-level overview of SQL Server's architecture and related tools follows. After that, it's time to itemize SQL Server's hardware and software requirements, followed by a detailed explanation of how to install the product. Finally, we show you how to use the powerful and flexible SQL Server Management Studio for all database design and administration tasks.

Book 11: Designing and Using Databases

You're probably itching to get started and to get the most from your SQL Server database. If that's the case, you'll want to spend some time exploring this mini-book. To begin, we show you how to create your SQL Server database from scratch. Because mistakes happen to the best of us, the next chapter focuses on how to modify an already existing database.

Databases are made up of tables, which themselves are made up of data; therefore, we devote a chapter to illustrating all the different types of information that you can store in SQL Server. With that important task out of the way, the next chapter dives into building new tables, followed by a chapter on how to maintain your tables after you've created them. We close this mini-book with an important discussion on how relationships and constraints can enhance performance while safeguarding your valuable information.

Book III: Interacting with Your Data

The first time a child peers into a candy store, he typically has one thought on his mind: How can I get in there and get some? Likewise, you might be peering at a database and wondering how you can get in there and get some. This mini-book shows you exactly what you need to do to retrieve your data. The primary tool used to retrieve data is the SELECT statement. It has many options you can use to fine-tune your queries so that you can retrieve exactly what you need and nothing more. SQL Server Management Studio (SSMS) also includes easy-to-use graphical user interface tools that can make your job much easier. They can even be used to build your SELECT statements just by pointing and clicking.

Book IV: Database Programming

Functions, triggers, and stored procedures all sound much scarier than they actually are. By understanding what programming objects are available and what objects you can create, you can jumpstart your database knowledge. Whether you know nothing about what's possible with database programming objects or you're an old hand with past versions of SQL, this mini-book gives you valuable insight into what you can achieve with SQL Server 2008.

Book V: Reporting Services

You know there's data in there. How can you get it out? This is a common challenge for database users. With SQL Server Reporting Services in SQL Server 2008, Microsoft has significantly improved the ability to get the data to the users' desktops by using familiar tools like Internet Explorer. For you sophisticated users, you can create report models and let them build their own reports based on their changing needs.

Book VI: Analysis Services

Your boss yells, "TMI" (Too Much Information). "Can't you get this database to tell me only what's important?" With SQL Server Analysis Services, you can. Very large databases sometimes contain too much data to be valuable. Decision makers need to be able to view the data in such a way that they can make educated decisions. To help, you can change the format of the data to give the decision makers actionable insight. By using SQL Server Analysis Services, you can reformulate the data into cubes using measures and groups. This mini-book provides a good overview of the capabilities of Analysis Services.

Book VII: Performance Tips and Tricks

No matter what level of performance you're currently receiving from SQL Server, there's always room for improvement, which is what this mini-book is all about. We get the ball rolling with some insight into how SQL Server's

Query Optimizer works, along with how you can help it to help you. Next up is a detailed review of the most effective monitoring tools to assist you on your performance optimization journey. After that, it's time to look at how to enhance your indexes, queries, and data modifications, followed by some SQL Server tuning suggestions.

Book VIII: Database Administration

The work of a database administrator never ends. This mini-book is meant to make this overloaded constituency's life easier. First up is some guidance on how to configure SQL Server for optimal maintainability. After that, it's time to see how to effectively perform major database administration tasks, followed by assistance on how to secure your SQL Server installation. Next is a deep dive into SQL Server's Integration Services, which are essential technologies for tying your database with other information silos. Because replication and partitioning are two effective techniques for improving performance and data distribution, we close this mini-book with a chapter dedicated to each of these concepts.

Book IX: Appendixes

First, we point out a group of handy resources where you can turn to obtain added information about making the most of SQL Server. The next section is meant to help you decipher some common problems that many administrators encounter. Finally, you find a practical listing of key terms that you'll commonly run into as part of your job.

Icons Used in This Book

What's a Dummies book without icons pointing you in the direction of really great information that's sure to help you along your way? This section briefly describes each icon we use in this book.

The Tip icon points out helpful information that is likely to make your job easier.

This icon marks a general interesting and useful fact — something that you might want to remember for later use.

The Warning icon highlights lurking danger. With this icon, we're telling you to pay attention and proceed with caution.

When you see this icon, you know that there's techie stuff nearby. If you're not feeling very techie, you can skip this info.

Where to Go from Here

Table 1-1 lists some common tasks, along with where you can get more details, to help you navigate more quickly.

Table 1-1	Key Tasks and Where to Find Them
Task	*Look At*
Installation requirements	Book I, Chapter 3
What's new in SQL Server 2008	Book I, Chapter 1
Overcoming common problems	Appendix B
Creating new databases	Book II, Chapter 1
Understanding SQL Server's data types	Book II, Chapter 3
Adding tables to your database	Book II, Chapter 4
Enabling the right network protocols	Book I, Chapter 4
Using views	Book III, Chapter 8
Web services and your database	Book IV, Chapter 5
Securing your database	Book VIII, Chapter 3
Referential integrity and your database	Book II, Chapter 6
Taking advantage of replication	Book VIII, Chapter 5
Using XML with SQL Server	Book III, Chapter 9
Integrating your database with other systems	Book VIII, Chapter 4
Implementing normalization	Book III, Chapter 1
Backing up your database	Book VIII, Chapter 2
Designing queries	Book III, Chapter 3
Building business intelligence solutions	Book VI, Chapter 2
Transact-SQL syntax	Book IV, Chapter 1
SQL Server's performance monitoring tools	Book VII, Chapter 2
Developing applications for SQL Server	Book IV, Chapter 4
Creating reports with Report Builder	Book V, Chapter 2
Optimal query techniques	Book VII, Chapter 3
Writing your own stored procedures	Book IV, Chapter 2
Integrating reports with SharePoint	Book V, Chapter 4
Performance-tuning SQL Server	Book VII, Chapter 4
Handy sources of information for SQL Server	Appendix A
Key terms and concepts	Appendix C

Book I

Essential Concepts

The 5th Wave   By Rich Tennant

"They're pushing the company into a new, hip direction and asked if we would pimp the storage system."

Contents at a Glance

Chapter 1: Introducing SQL Server 2008

In This Chapter

✔ **SQL Server 2008: An evolution, not a revolution**

✔ **More development productivity**

✔ **Improved integration**

✔ **Additional security and administrative options**

✔ **Understanding SQL Server's editions**

Before you take the plunge into SQL Server 2008, it's only natural for you to wonder what you're about to get yourself into. This chapter is all about discovering what distinguishes this version from its predecessor, SQL Server 2005, and helping you to identify the edition that will meet your needs. We begin by itemizing its new capabilities, grouped into the following categories:

✦ Development

✦ Integration

✦ Security

✦ Administration

After we cover these important topics, we move on to an exploration and explanation of the different SQL Server editions offered by Microsoft. Finally, if you're interested in a full architectural overview of SQL Server, keep reading: The next chapter offers a more holistic summary of its overall product design traits and philosophy.

SQL Server 2008: An Evolution, Not a Revolution

Once upon a time, if you wanted to store information on a computer, you had to write your own low-level, highly specialized program that organized this data and also made it possible to update and retrieve it. This process was very cumbersome, time-consuming, and error-prone. Eventually, a host of specialized companies sprang up to provide standardized, industrial-strength products known as databases. Even behemoths such as IBM joined the party with its own heavyweight, expensive database software products.

A *database* is a special kind of software application whose main purpose is to help people and programs store, organize, and retrieve information. This feature frees up application developers to focus on the business task at hand, rather than being responsible for supervising the intricacies of data management.

As more time passed, a new breed of database companies arose. With names like Oracle, Informix, and Sybase, these vendors (and many others) developed a particular kind of database, known as a *relational database.* Relational databases are particularly well designed for storing information in tabular format, which further helped software developers as they built a whole new class of enterprise applications.

Microsoft also entered the relational database fray some years back with the SQL Server database. Once thought of as a relatively lightweight database vendor, Microsoft has continually refined SQL Server to the point where it can compete for the largest and most complicated database-driven applications.

Whether you're upgrading from an existing SQL Server implementation or SQL Server 2008 represents your first foray into Microsoft's take on relational database management technology, you'll find that this product provides a nice balance between ease-of-use and powerful capabilities. For those who are new to Microsoft, what's especially compelling is the degree to which they've delivered full-featured, graphical, user interface–driven administrative tools; these intuitive assistants don't require you to switch to a cryptic command-line interface when the going gets tough. Administrators' lives are busy enough without having to master yet another confusing or cumbersome set of tools.

Comparatively, if you've invested time and effort learning earlier versions of SQL Server, such as SQL Server 2000 or 2005, you'll feel comfortable with this new release. The user interface, especially for SQL Server Management Studio, will be familiar. The product improvements can best be thought of as following more of an evolutionary, rather than revolutionary, approach.

Now that we've made that distinction, here's a look at some of what's new under the hood on the 2008 model.

Not all of these features are available in every edition of SQL Server 2008.

More development productivity

Microsoft's software architecture and database tools have always offered excellent integration and productivity. SQL Server 2008 amplifies the firm's "Developers, developers, developers, developers!" mantra. Here's how SQL Server 2008 has helped this important audience:

✦ **Language integrated query (LINQ):** Generally, developers use Structured Query Language (SQL) to construct and implement queries. LINQ makes it possible to use .NET programming languages (such as Visual Basic or C#) to issue these queries instead.

✦ **ADO.NET object services:** Microsoft offers Common Language Runtime (CLR) technology to facilitate the interplay between programming languages (such as C# and Visual Basic) and the SQL Server database engine. The ADO.NET framework streamlines application development and management using CLR-based objects.

✦ **Additional data types:** SQL Server 2008 supplements its already extensive catalog of data types with several new alternatives, including:

- **DATE:** Stores date-only details.

- **TIME:** Holds time-only data.

- **DATETIMEOFFSET:** Keeps track of time zone–based date and time details.

- **DATETIME2:** Enhancement of the already present DATETIME data type, capable of storing a bigger range of fractional seconds and years.

- **GEOMETRY:** You can use this new data type when the Earth's curvature is important to your application, such as when you need extreme accuracy or are calculating a long-distance path.

- **GEOGRAPHY:** A counterpart to the GEOMETRY data type, it allows you to easily track details about locations on a two-dimensional plane.

- **FILESTREAM:** This new data type lets you place large blocks of binary information directly onto an NTFS file system. This file system can be placed on less expensive storage devices, yet is still managed by SQL Server.

Improved integration

Integration of disparate components and technologies, as well as consolidating information into centralized data warehouses, have both become more important to customers over the past few years. To address these needs, SQL Server 2008 delivers additional capabilities, as follows:

✦ **Star join query optimizations:** Because data warehousing queries have distinct traits, SQL Server now sports improved query optimizations dedicated to streamlining these specialized queries.

✦ **MERGE SQL statement:** This new statement makes it easier for data warehousing-type operations to first determine whether a row exists and then perform an INSERT or UPDATE statement.

✦ **Change data capture:** By placing data alterations into dedicated change tables, SQL Server makes it easier than ever to update data warehouses with the most current information.

✦ **Persistent lookups:** SQL Server's excellent Integration Services (SSIS) can now handle very large tables even more efficiently.

Enhanced security

Of all the major relational database platforms, SQL Server has generally led the pack with regard to integrated operating system and database security. SQL Server 2008 builds on this secure foundation with additional improvements, as follows:

✦ **Enhanced encryption:** It's no longer necessary to code your applications to work around encryption. Instead, SQL Server now offers fully transparent data encryption. That is, your solutions don't require any special modifications to work with encrypted data: SQL Server handles all this for you.

✦ **More sophisticated key management:** An encryption solution is only as good as the keys that support it. SQL Server now includes support for third-party key management technologies, offering the administrator a broader range of choices.

✦ **Improved auditing:** It's easier than ever to set up and maintain auditing of your SQL Server instance. You can now use Data Definition Language (DDL) statements to simplify these tasks.

Streamlined administration

Because most database and system administrators are continually forced to do more with less, Microsoft has invested heavily in making SQL Server less of an administrative burden on these overstretched professionals. Here's a sampling of these advancements:

✦ **Resource Governor:** Runaway queries, undisciplined users, and other unpredictable performance drags have plagued the lives of database administrators for years. SQL Server now includes technology that lets you place limits on how your users consume valuable database resources.

✦ **Data compression:** SQL Server now features better, more integrated data compression. This helps save scarce disk space while lowering the amount of resources consumed when processing large blocks of data.

✦ **Better mirroring:** This technique, which helps improve performance as well as safeguard data, has become more sophisticated in SQL Server 2008. Performance is faster, and the database engine is better at gracefully recovering from damage to data pages.

✦ **Automatic page recovery from the mirror:** When a discrepancy arises between a primary data page and its mirrored counterpart, SQL Server is more adept at reconciling these differences without bothering the administrator.

✦ **Log compression:** Because transaction logs comprise a vital foundational component of SQL Server's mirroring architecture, anything that can reduce the amount of traffic between mirrored pairs can help improve performance. SQL Server 2008 now uses log compression to cut down on the amount of network traffic.

✦ **Policy-based management:** It can be very tedious to set up and maintain a comprehensive set of administrative guidelines, especially when there are many servers to look after. Policy-based management is Microsoft's strategy for centralizing these tasks in one place, and then deploying them to as many computers as necessary. The result is a reduced administrative burden, combined with a better, more consistent application of these policies.

Understanding SQL Server's Editions

To the average database administrator or application developer examining the various editions of SQL Server, it might seem that someone in Microsoft's products marketing department stayed up late thinking about ways to befuddle them. Fortunately, things aren't as confusing as they might appear at first glance. In this section, we give you some quick guidelines you can use to determine the right edition for your specific needs. Note that because this book covers such a broad range of functionality, we used the Enterprise edition to fully highlight SQL Server's capabilities.

✦ **Enterprise:** This is the flagship of the entire SQL Server 2008 family. It includes a host of features that make it a good choice for a mission-critical database server platform. Just a few of these benefits are

- *No limit on CPUs (other than that imposed by the operating system)*

- *Full data warehousing capabilities*

- *Enterprise-wide management tools*

- *Round-the-clock availability*

- *Superior security features*

- *High availability capabilities*

✦ **Standard:** With much of the feature set of its big brother, this edition is fine for the vast majority of database applications, especially those with a departmental rather than an enterprise scope. The main difference is that this edition is lighter in its business intelligence, high availability, data warehousing, and enterprise-wide management feature sets.

✦ **Workgroup:** Aimed at smaller, departmental applications, this powerful edition of SQL Server introduces some limitations that aren't likely to be issues for smaller computing environments. Some of these restrictions include

- *Hardware and database size constraints*
- *Diminished high availability*
- *Reduced business intelligence*

✦ **Compact:** The price is right for this edition: free. As you might surmise from its name, it's meant to support applications running on Windows Mobile devices, such as smart phones, Pocket PC devices, and set-top boxes. Independent Software Vendors (ISVs) are also able to distribute solutions based on this edition for no database charge.

✦ **Express:** This database offering is the simplest and easiest to use in the SQL Server 2008 product family. On top of that accolade, it's also free to download and redistribute (with some licensing restrictions).

This is the right edition if any of the following describe you:

- *A software developer (seasoned or brand-new) wanting to learn about relational databases.*
- *A packaged application provider looking to embed a free, yet sturdy, database with your solution.*
- *An end user with a lot of information to store, but not a lot of cash to buy a database.*

✦ **Developer:** Aimed at getting students and other budget-constricted individuals on board the SS SQL Server, this version offers all of the capabilities found in the flagship Enterprise, but with distribution licensing restrictions.

Chapter 2: SQL Server Architecture and Key Concepts

In This Chapter

✔ **The basics of relational databases**

✔ **Key SQL Server 2008 concepts**

✔ **A brief overview of administration, application development, business intelligence, reporting, and integration**

*W*hether you're a SQL Server veteran or new to this powerful, relational database management system, this chapter helps you understand what makes SQL Server 2008 tick. The chapter starts by examining the increasingly important role that relational databases play in modern information-processing solutions. Next up is how SQL Server is just one component in Microsoft's overall information access portfolio. The balance of the chapter takes you on a guided tour of the major architectural components of SQL Server 2008.

Relational Databases: The Heart of Modern Computing Solutions

Relational database management systems, which date back to the 1970s, show no signs of yielding their central role in most of today's data processing applications. In fact, the quantities and complexity of information entrusted to these technologies is expanding rapidly. Modern applications are voracious consumers of storage space. Users view relational databases as the repository of record for data that by its very nature requires high throughput combined with reliability and security guarantees. Video, music, geospatial, and information represented in other data formats all place enormous demands on any information-processing infrastructure.

As if this exponential growth in stored information wasn't enough, today's computing solutions are pushing boundaries in other dimensions. Users have come to expect their data be available to them on any device, such as handheld computers and Web browsers via a host of new, innovative applications. These requirements have driven technology providers, such as Microsoft, to expand the functionality of their offerings to meet incipient market needs. SQL Server 2008 represents the next step in the evolution of Microsoft's flagship database product line. However, it's not alone — other Microsoft technologies seamlessly interact with this database engine. These offerings along with SQL Server's ever-expanding architecture are the focus of the next portion of this chapter.

Understanding Key SQL Server 2008 Concepts

The relational database marketplace has been mature for several years. Established vendors now seek to differentiate themselves on price, functionality, and the degree to which their products integrate with other information-processing technologies. From a holistic, one-stop shop viewpoint, Microsoft offers one of the best and most compelling solutions on the market. SQL Server is part of a larger Microsoft philosophy best described as, "Your data: Any place, any time."

Microsoft's information access strategy includes SQL Server, along with these other products:

+ .NET
+ Visual Studio
+ BizTalk Server
+ Office

Technologies designed to work well with each other is what makes this product suite so appealing. In addition to this collaborative philosophy, Microsoft has also baked several key characteristics into SQL Server. Each of these attributes aims at making the jobs of the database designer, developer, and administrator easier. Here's a look at each of these in more detail.

Reliability

When a relational database is the core foundation of a solution, it's essential that users and administrators alike can count on the database server to be running, and any information entrusted to its care to be safely stored and retrieved. SQL Server offers a collection of features aimed at increasing the confidence of its users and managers. These range from highly configurable, efficient mirroring to technology that prevents runaway queries and the ability to add additional CPUs when needed without taking the database server down. Microsoft also offers what might be the most well-integrated set of performance monitoring and management tools on the market. To get a better idea of all that these tools can do for you, make sure to explore Book VII, Chapter 2.

Security

Microsoft hasn't ignored this often-neglected topic. SQL Server 2008 features numerous security-oriented capabilities. For example, transparently integrating encryption directly with all database objects is now possible. Therefore, writing integration-specific logic into your applications is no longer necessary. Instead, SQL Server handles all encryption-related tasks for both the developer and the administrator. This helpful behavior increases the likelihood that encryption is used in the first place. SQL Server also supports third-party key management solutions as well as more granular auditing and audit reporting.

Flexibility

To make SQL Server the central source of information for an enterprise, Microsoft has done an outstanding job of packaging a collection of highly capable supporting software alongside SQL Server. Ranging from integration to reporting to analysis services, these technologies all interact seamlessly and greatly simplify and streamline the workload facing an application developer or administrator. For the balance of this chapter, we point out many of these related offerings.

Administration

Throughout most of their history, relational database management systems have demanded that their database administrators be adept at writing and debugging scripts in order to automate most administrative tasks. The alternative has been to manually enter administrative commands one-by-one. Although this might have worked on stand-alone servers, it's no longer acceptable in today's highly distributed database implementations. To address these automation needs, Microsoft offers the SQL Server Management Studio. This rich environment, shown in Figure 2-1, lets the administrator perform all necessary tasks from within one interface. The result is that one administrator can look after many more servers than ever before.

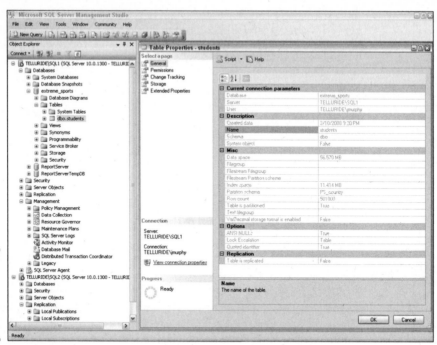

Figure 2-1:
The SQL
Server
Manage-
ment Studio.

If you're interested in becoming an expert in the SQL Server Management
Studio, make sure to look at Chapter 5 in this mini-book.

Application Development

SQL Server 2008, as was the case with several earlier incarnations, is tightly
coupled with Microsoft's flagship Visual Studio development product.
Although programmers are free to use any modern development technology,
they likely find that the combination of Visual Studio and SQL Server is hard
to beat from a productivity and functionality perspective. This interdepend-
ency goes far beyond traditional application programming paradigms, however, because Visual Studio is at the heart of many other types of SQL
Server-related projects. For example, Figure 2-2 shows the Visual Studio user
interface for creating a collection of different types of solutions.

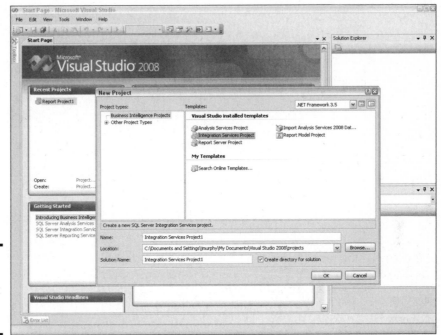

Figure 2-2:
Creating a
new project
in Visual
Studio.

Business Intelligence

In the not-too-distant past, only the largest enterprises could take advantage of the proven benefits from complex business intelligence analysis. The software and hardware necessary to run these computations was simply out of reach of most organizations. The past few years have seen the price of hardware and software fall at a steady pace, bringing these kinds of solutions to a new audience. Microsoft has done its part as well, delivering highly capable business intelligence technology in conjunction with its database framework. Known as SQL Server Analysis Services, these technologies, which seamlessly integrate with the Microsoft Office suite, make it possible to develop and deliver robust analytic solutions without the need for expensive software and consulting services. Figure 2-3 highlights how, again, the Visual Studio development environment is the foundation for developing a SQL Server–related solution. In this case, designing and creating a multidimensional cube.

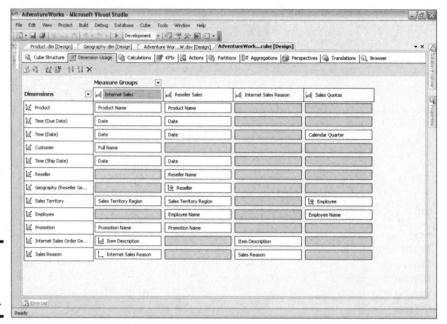

Figure 2-3:
Configuring
business
intelligence.

Reporting

SQL Server's Reporting Services (SSRS) aim to offering the IT organization a single source for creating, maintaining, and delivering reports on information stored in the database. Well-integrated with Microsoft Office, as well as SharePoint Server 2007, SSRS reduces the need to purchase and master third-party reporting solutions. Instead, application designers and developers can work within the same set of tools to deliver the information their users require. For example, Figure 2-4 shows the user interface for the Microsoft Report Designer.

Integration

Several new industries are addressing the ever-multiplying challenges of tying information together from multiple silos. Unfortunately, from the perspective of most IT organizations, this leads to purchasing and administering an increasing number of integration-related tools. Microsoft has gotten into the act as well by offering a set of technologies known as SQL Server Integration Services (SSIS) — a formidable challenger to the Extract, Transform, and Load (ETL) industry. What's especially attractive about Microsoft's offering is that there's no additional software to purchase; it's all part of SQL Server. It also uses Microsoft's field-tested approach to solving complex computing challenges via graphically based (rather than script-driven) tools. Figure 2-5, which shows the development platform in which you construct SSIS solutions, illustrates a rich graphical user interface.

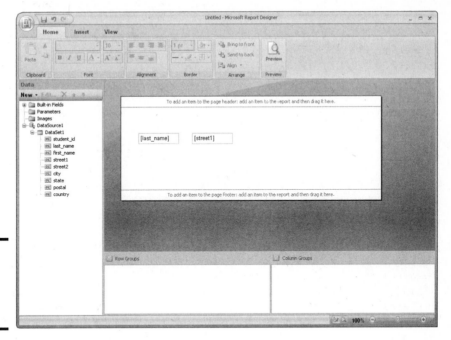

Figure 2-4:
The
Microsoft
Report
Designer.

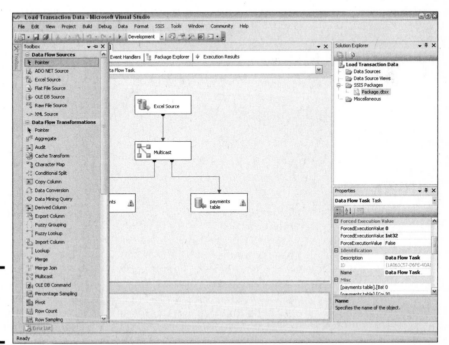

Figure 2-5:
Building an
SSIS
project.

Chapter 3: Getting Started, Getting Around

In This Chapter

✔ Hardware and software requirements

✔ Converting to SQL Server 2008

✔ Tools at your disposal

*I*f you're ready to get started on the road to a fully functional SQL Server environment, this chapter is for you. We get the ball rolling by telling you about the hardware and software foundations that you need to install the product. The next task is to examine what it takes to either upgrade from an earlier version of SQL Server or convert from an entirely different database platform. The chapter closes by taking you on a brief tour of the excellent tools included with SQL Server, along with some examples of situations where you're able to put them to work.

Hardware and Software Requirements

Although you might be tempted to pop in the DVD containing the SQL Server software, or point your browser at Microsoft's Web site and then immediately download and install the product, take a few minutes and determine whether your computer meets some minimal requirements. Otherwise, you might find that your installation efforts are for naught or that your SQL Server instance runs poorly (or not at all!). Fortunately, as the next chapter illustrates, Microsoft thoughtfully includes a system configuration check utility as part of the SQL Server installation. However, you can pass this test and still have a sluggish system, which is why you want to pay attention to the recommendations listed in this chapter.

Note: If you're curious about the installation experience, the next chapter gives that topic the rich treatment it deserves.

 Take the time to go through each of these major system readiness categories, making sure that you meet or exceed each of these prerequisites. Also, if you're installing SQL Server on multiple machines, remember that a machine acting as a central server will generally require faster and better hardware than one that primarily acts as a client. Finally, you need to have administrative privileges on the computer where you're installing SQL Server.

✦ **CPU:** To keep things moving, you need a CPU with at least a Pentium III-class processor running at a minimum of 1 GHz. For serious work, plan on employing a Pentium IV processor that offers at least 2 GHz.

✦ **Memory:** Because sufficient memory serves as the foundation of any well-performing relational database, make sure that you provide 1GB or more. Generally, just as you can't be too rich or too thin, you can't provide a relational database with too much CPU or memory; SQL Server will always use as much memory as it needs but not more.

✦ **Disk:** Given that relational databases use disk drives as their primary storage mechanism, it's always difficult to recommend a fixed value for the right amount of available disk capacity — every site and application is different. However, note that a full installation of SQL Server and related tools eats more than 2GB before any of your data arrives.

SQL Server ships in several editions for both 32- and 64-bit platforms. This can affect the exact hardware and software configuration that you need. In general, "more and faster" is better.

✦ **Operating system:** Microsoft gives you a fairly wide choice of operating systems (both 32-bit and 64-bit) that can run SQL Server. They include

- Windows Server 2008 (Standard, Data Center, Enterprise)

- Windows Server 2003 (Standard, Data Center, Enterprise)

- Windows XP Professional Edition

- Windows Vista (Ultimate, Home Premium, Home Basic, Enterprise, Business)

Be prepared to apply the latest service pack for your operating system; in many cases, SQL Server depends on these patches.

✦ **Supporting software:** Because it's built on top of some of Microsoft's newest technologies, SQL Server requires that you install some additional software components. These can include

- .NET Framework 2.0

- SQL Server Native Client

- SQL Server Setup support files

- Windows Installer 3.1

- Microsoft Data Access Components (MDAC) 2.8 SP1 or newer

- Internet Explorer SP1 or newer

SQL Server's installation logic is quite sophisticated; it generally obtains these components automatically for you as part of the installation process, assuming you're connected to the Internet.

Converting to SQL Server 2008

Unless you're building a brand new set of applications, chances are you have an existing database that will need to be converted to work with SQL Server 2008. This section shows you how to handle this important task. We've broken this portion into two segments: converting from an earlier version of SQL Server, and converting from a different relational database management system.

Before undertaking any major system or software upgrade, it's always wise to perform a complete backup of your information. The data you save may be your own!

Upgrading from earlier versions of SQL Server

Upgrading database software (and the data contained in it) is always a nerve-wracking experience. Luckily, if you're running an earlier instance of SQL Server (such as SQL Server 2000 or 2005), it's actually quite simple. You can even elect to have your SQL Server 2008 instance simultaneously running alongside the earlier edition.

Assuming that you want to upgrade the entire instance, here's how to get started:

1. **Obtain a copy of the product.**

   Most database administrators obtain a physical DVD containing the SQL Server product; there are also circumstances where it's available electronically. If you obtain a physical copy, place the media in your computer's DVD drive.

2. **Launch the SQL Server setup application.**

   The Setup.exe file is under the \Servers folder on your installation media.

3. **Accept the license terms and click Next.**

   The installation program obtains any necessary supporting software.

4. **Select the Upgrade from SQL Server 2000 or 2005 option in the SQL Server 2008 Installation Center dialog box.**

   The System Configuration Checker analyzes your computer to see if it's capable of running SQL Server 2008. If any problems occur, you're alerted here.

5. **Choose the instance you want to upgrade and click Next.**

   You can also instruct SQL Server on whether you want to upgrade the entire instance or just its shared components. Figure 3-1 shows how this dialog box appears:

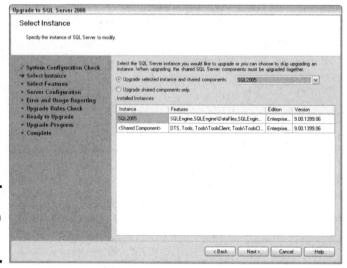

Figure 3-1:
Selecting an
instance to
upgrade.

6. **Review the features that will be upgraded and click Next.**

   Figure 3-2 shows the list of features that are being upgraded.

7. **Configure the accounts you want to run the SQL Server services and click Next.**

8. **When prompted, fill in details about how you want errors handled, and click Next.**

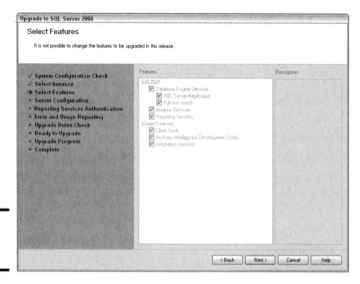

Figure 3-2:
Selecting
features.

9. **Run the Upgrade Rules Check wizard.**

SQL Server now executes a rules engine to ensure that your existing instance can be upgraded.

10. **Review the Ready to Upgrade page, and click Next.**

After you've given it the go-ahead, SQL Server upgrades your database to SQL Server 2008. You can monitor how things are going by watching the Progress page.

After the conversion is complete, you need to do a few more things to finish the job, including:

✦ **Refreshing usage counters.**

✦ **Updating statistics.** Book VII, Chapter 1 is where you can find out how to address these first two topics.

✦ **Registering your servers.** Check out Book IV, Chapter 6 for more about distributed environments.

✦ **Adjusting your configuration.** Book VIII, Chapter 1 shows you how to tweak your SQL Server configuration.

✦ **Rebuilding your full-text catalogs.** Book III, Chapter 8 includes an explanation of the care and feeding of SQL Server's full-text search capabilities.

On the other hand, if all you want to do is copy a database from an earlier version of SQL Server into a new instance, you can use the Copy Database Wizard to accomplish this task. Book VIII, Chapter 2 explains how to copy, export, and import databases.

Converting from a different database

Normally, the mere thought of converting between relational database platforms is enough to send shivers up the spine of even the most hardened database administrator. Fortunately, SQL Server 2008 offers several simple yet powerful tools to make migrating data less of a burden. I'll briefly describe two of these tools, along with criteria you can use to pick one of them.

SQL Server Import and Export Wizard

This utility (launched by right-clicking on the Management folder within the SQL Server Management Studio and selecting the Import Data menu option) allows you to import information easily into your new SQL Server instance. It's quite flexible and simple to use, and as shown in Figure 3-3, you can bring in data from a broad range of information storage formats, including:

- ✦ ODBC
- ✦ Oracle
- ✦ SQL Server
- ✦ Flat files
- ✦ Microsoft Access
- ✦ Microsoft Excel

If your existing database is on this list, then it's likely that this is the right tool to use to import information into SQL Server. Book VIII, Chapter 2 explores this topic in more detail.

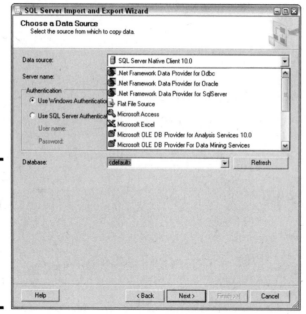

Figure 3-3: Available data source formats from the SQL Server Import and Export Wizard.

SQL Server Integration Services

These components are much more powerful, but significantly more complex to employ. They make it possible for SQL Server administrators and integration specialists to connect to and manipulate just about any data format out there. Figure 3-4 offers a brief glimpse into the kinds of sophisticated integration workflow available to you. Generally, if you're faced with a more complex or ongoing integration scenario, it's worthwhile to get to know this extremely capable technology.

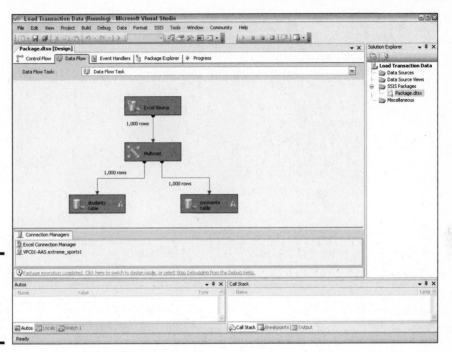

Figure 3-4:
Using SQL
Server
Integration
Services.

Tools at Your Disposal

The breadth and quality of SQL Server's supporting tools are often the deciding factors in helping an organization decide to standardize on this database product. In this section, we enumerate and briefly describe some of the most useful tools in the SQL Server arsenal. To make things clearer, the tools are separated into the following categories:

✦ Administration

✦ Performance

✦ Software development

Administration

For most professionals tasked with looking after a SQL Server instance, or developing new applications that rely on it, the SQL Server Management Studio is a tool that will soon feel comfortable. You can use it to perform just about any administrative task, as well as a host of additional operations. Figure 3-5 shows this valuable tool in action, configuring replication in this case.

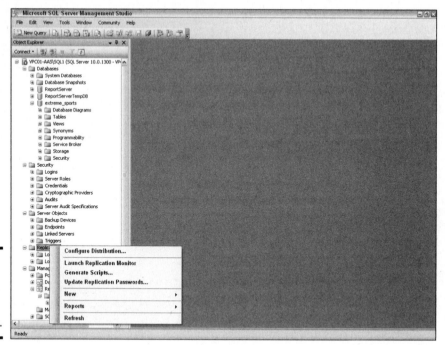

Figure 3-5:
The SQL
Server
Manage-
ment Studio.

In terms of tool coverage throughout the book, this technology is the star of the show: We use it to illustrate key concepts in just about every chapter.

Of course, Microsoft offers other tools of interest to administrators. For those readers who eschew these new-fangled administrative graphical tools, Microsoft offers the comfort of two old favorites: the SQLCMD character-based utility for entering direct SQL statements, and the Database Console Command (DBCC), which allows you to directly run a host of commands to find (and sometimes modify) details about the inner workings of SQL Server.

Performance

Using traditional, character-based, performance, metric-gathering tools while trying to isolate a system response problem has caused no end of problems for database administrators. Fortunately, SQL Server offers a broad range of graphical tools that you can use to more rapidly identify and fix performance problems.

To begin, Figure 3-6 illustrates a small sampling of the massive quantity of performance-related details that you can track with the Windows System Monitor.

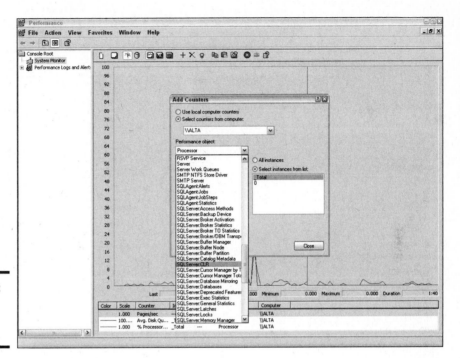

Figure 3-6:
Windows
System
Monitor.

SQL Server goes far beyond merely capturing performance-related information, however. It also offers a collection of tools and assistants that take a more proactive role in coaxing additional performance from your database server. Figure 3-7 illustrates output from the Database Engine Tuning Advisor.

You can use the SQL Server Profiler to get an even more detailed picture of what's happening during a critical database interaction. Figure 3-8 shows the depth of information delivered by this important utility.

Finally, if you need to take a harder line with database resource-gobbling miscreants, the new SQL Server Resource Governor allows you to block these troublemakers from bringing your system to its knees.

Note: If any of these performance tools pique your interest, make sure to spend some time examining Book VII, Chapter 2.

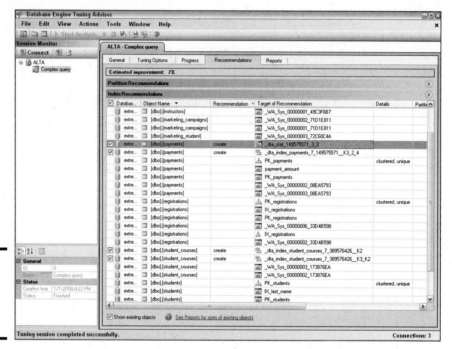

Figure 3-7:
Database
Engine
Tuning
Advisor.

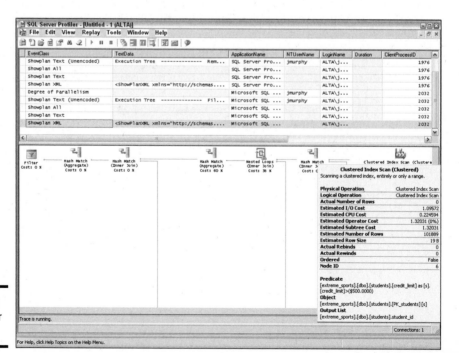

Figure 3-8:
SQL Server
Profiler.

Software development

Microsoft has done an excellent job in coupling SQL Server to the Visual Studio .NET platform. More so than with any other database platform, this combination means that developers have unprecedented productivity when building a SQL Server–based solution. This tight integration between Visual Studio and SQL Server extends beyond mere application development. In fact, it's the foundation for just about any type of solution that interacts with a database, including analysis, business intelligence, reporting, and integration. Figure 3-9 illustrates how Visual Studio .NET is the development environment for creating one of these types of projects.

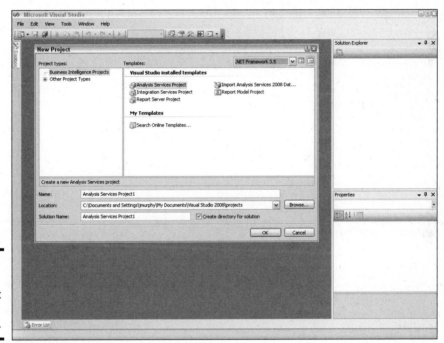

Figure 3-9:
Creating a new project in Visual Studio .NET.

Chapter 4: Setting Up SQL Server 2008

In This Chapter

✔ Installing SQL Server

✔ Creating an initial configuration

✔ Streamlining administration

*T*here was a time when installing and configuring a highly capable relational database management system meant clearing your calendar for a week, clearing your desk to hold a batch of weighty manuals, and clearing your mind in anticipation of a long and challenging job. Fortunately, that's no longer the case. However, installing and setting up a product like SQL Server 2008 does require some planning and preparation, which is what this chapter aims to tell you about.

We start by walking through the entire SQL Server installation process, pointing out several important things that you should do before, during, and after this crucial stage. After the product is installed, the next mission is to ensure that everything is shipshape. We then show you how to set your initial configuration parameters and how easy it is to make changes. The chapter closes with some guidance on establishing solid administration practices and policies.

Installing SQL Server

Deploying SQL Server 2008 on your computer is much less complicated than you might think. However, even if you have a screamingly fast server, completion can take some time; you probably have enough time to hit the gym, shower, and grab a sandwich after the actual file copying is underway.

SQL Server places some significant hardware and software requirements on your planned database platform. Take a look at Book I, Chapter 3 to get the scoop on these necessities before you get started.

When you determine your system is up to snuff and you're ready to get started, here's what to do:

1. **Run the `Setup.exe` application from your SQL Server installation CD.**

In many cases, inserting the media triggers the installation application to start automatically.

2. **If necessary, install the .NET Framework and accept its license terms.**

Assuming you have an Internet connection, SQL Server will automatically retrieve this software from Microsoft's servers.

3. **Review your options in the SQL Server Installation Center.**

As you can see in Figure 4-1, the SQL Server Installation Center offers several helpful paths, including hardware and software requirements, upgrade options, and SQL Server samples.

4. **Click on the Installation option from the SQL Server Installation Center.**

This brings up a new dialog box, shown in Figure 4-2 that offers a number of different installation trajectories, including new stand-alone installations, clustering configurations, upgrades, and so on. In this case, we're installing a new stand-alone instance of SQL Server.

As part of its standard installation process, SQL Server offers an extremely useful tool that inspects your computer's configuration to ensure that it's able to support the product. In many cases, you can still install the database even if your server is somewhat underpowered or otherwise not up to par. SQL Server simply warns you of this fact. Figure 4-3 displays output from this important check.

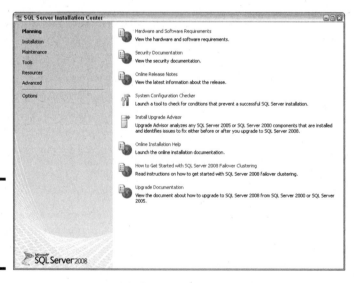

Figure 4-1:
The SQL Server Installation Center.

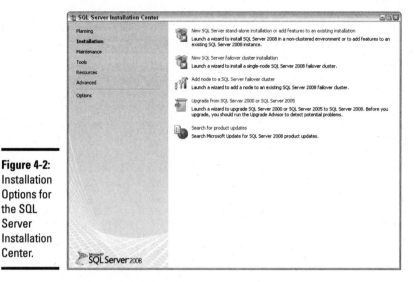

Figure 4-2:
Installation
Options for
the SQL
Server
Installation
Center.

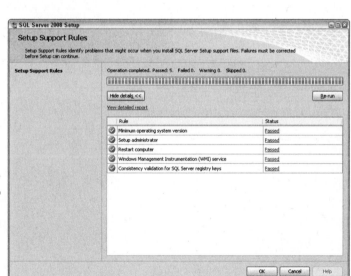

Figure 4-3:
Results from
the system
configur-
ation check.

5. **Fill in your license details and then click Next.**

After completing this step, SQL Server will automatically set up any
needed installation support files, as well as report on its Setup Report
Rules, as shown in Figure 4-4.

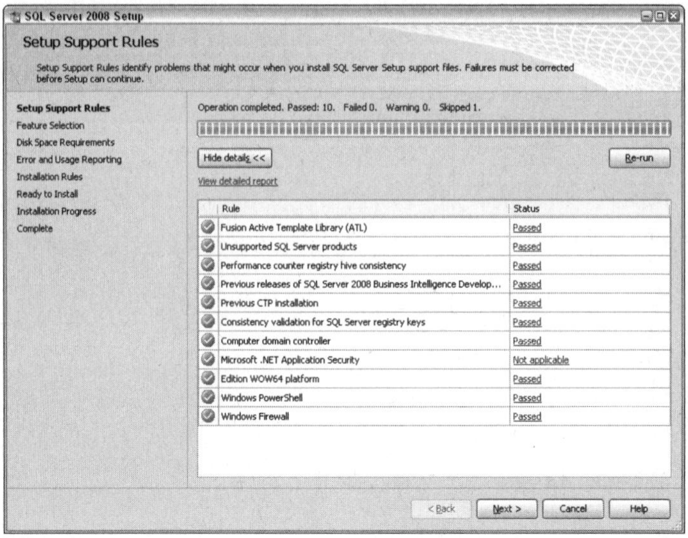

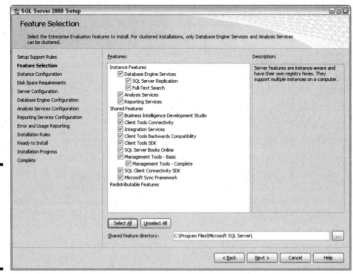

Figure 4-4:
Results from
the Setup
Report
Rules
check.

6. Review the results from the Setup Report Rules check and then click Next.

What you see next is the Feature Selection screen, where SQL Server allows you to specify where you want the product to reside. You can also choose which database and related features you want to enable. Figure 4-5 illustrates these options.

Figure 4-5:
Selecting
features for
this SQL
Server
instance.

7. **Select an installation directory, your desired features, and then click Next.**

   The Instance Configuration screen appears (shown in Figure 4-6), where you instruct SQL Server on what you want to call your instance and its root directory. If you don't specify a name, SQL Server suggests a default value.

8. **Review SQL Server's disk space requirements and then click Next.**

9. **Configure your SQL Server instance and then click Next.**

   SQL Server relies on a collection of Windows services to handle many of its key tasks. The Server Configuration screen, shown in Figure 4-7, is where you can associate usernames and passwords with these services, as well as identify how you want the services to be started. If you want, you can associate a single login with all the services.

   You must decide whether you want to employ a *local account* or a *domain account* (that is, one that's available across multiple computers) to run these services. For simplified administration, it's often wise to use a centrally administered domain account. On the other hand, if your environment has relatively few computers, a local account might be just fine.

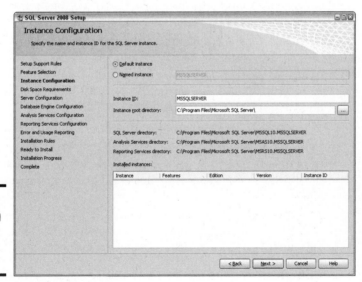

Figure 4-6:
Configuring
the SQL
Server
instance.

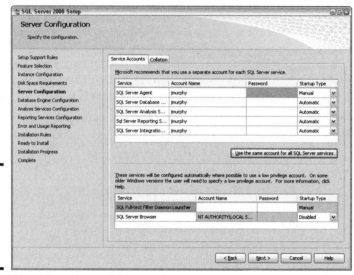

Figure 4-7:
Setting
usernames,
passwords,
and startup
options.

10. **Set up usernames, passwords, and startup options, and then click Next.**

The accounts you use must have passwords; SQL Server doesn't accept NULL values for these fields.

The Database Engine Configuration screen, which shows up next (see Figure 4-8), has three tabs:

- **Account Provisioning:** Here's where you dictate what security mode you want SQL Server to use, as well as login accounts for any administrators. Figure 4-8 highlights this tab.

  In most cases, the Windows Security Mode option provides the right blend of operating system and database security.

- **Data Directories:** Here's where you guide SQL Server on which directories to use for user databases, log files, temporary storage, and so on.

- **FILESTREAM:** SQL Server 2008 offers a high-performance data processing option that combines the speed and scalability of file system–based storage with the transactional integrity offered by a relational database. The FILESTREAM tab, shown in Figure 4-9, is where you elect to offer this capability, as well as determine its name and whether it should be accessible to remote clients.

11. **Configure SQL Server Analysis Services and then click Next.**

You're asked to associate a login with SQL Server Analysis Services (if you've elected to include this capability in your installation), as well as identify data, log, temporary file, and backup directories.

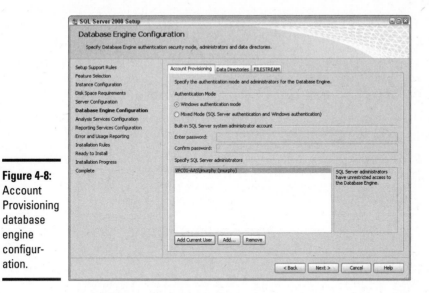

Figure 4-8:
Account
Provisioning
database
engine
configur-
ation.

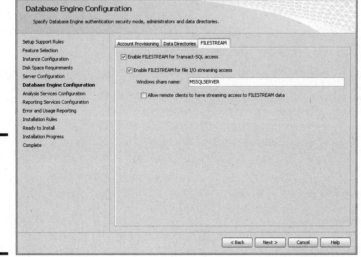

Figure 4-9:
FILE-
STREAM
database
engine
configur-
ation.

12. **Configure Reporting Services and then click Next.**

Figure 4-10 displays your choices for Reporting Services configuration (assuming that you've chosen to install this optional feature). Typically, it's simplest to accept the Native mode option, which gets the report server up-and-running as quickly as possible.

13. **Decide whether you want error and usage information sent to Microsoft and then click Next.**

SQL Server then runs a series of installation validation rules to ensure that everything will go smoothly when setting up your instance.

14. **Review the installation rules output and then click Next.**

Now you have a chance to review what you've asked SQL Server's installation program to do. Figure 4-11 highlights this itemization.

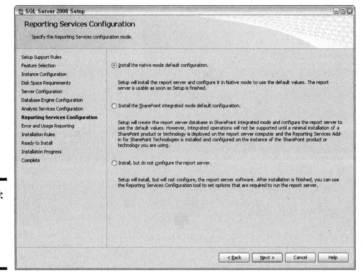

Figure 4-10: Reporting Services configuration.

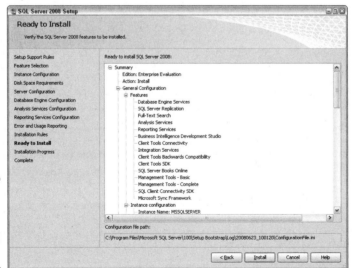

Figure 4-11: Viewing selected features and options.

15. **Review the proposed installation features and options and then click Install to launch the job.**

16. **Monitor the installation process.**

SQL Server keeps a running tally of everything that's happening during this process. Be patient — this can take quite a long time to finish. SQL Server also keeps detailed logs that provide insight into the entire installation process. These logs are grouped in the `Setup Bootstrap\Log` directory that's located beneath your SQL Server installation directory. Here's an example of the exciting details you find in these logs:

```
MSI (c) (D4:44) [14:59:16:008]: Client-side and UI is none or basic:
Running entire install on the server.
MSI (c) (D4:44) [14:59:16:008]: Grabbed execution mutex.
MSI (c) (D4:44) [14:59:16:018]: Cloaking enabled.
MSI (c) (D4:44) [14:59:16:018]: Attempting to enable all
disabled privileges before calling Install on Server
MSI (c) (D4:44) [14:59:16:018]: Incrementing counter to disable
shutdown. Counter after increment: 0
MSI (s) (68:C8) [14:59:16:028]: Grabbed execution mutex.
MSI (s) (68:EC) [14:59:16:028]: Resetting cached policy values
MSI (s) (68:EC) [14:59:16:028]: Machine policy value 'Debug' is 0
```

17. **Connect to your server.**

Think of this as a sanity check. Your goal is to establish a simple connection as proof that everything is installed correctly. The fastest way to do this is to launch the SQL Server Management Studio, available from the SQL Server 2008 menu.

Creating and Maintaining Configurations

You can put SQL Server to work right away, although you'll probably want to make several customizations and tweaks after you've completed your installation. In this section, we show you how easy it is to make changes. To begin, we show you how to employ the various communication protocols available to SQL Server. A brief exploration of configuring Reporting Services follows. After that, we provide some ideas on how to add or remove other features.

SQL Server communication protocols

Your database server is a social animal: It will happily chat with other users and computers, but only if you let it. For this part of the chapter, we show you how to enable and configure the various protocols that can make these conversations possible.

First, it's a good idea to understand what purpose a communication protocol serves. These standards make it possible for disparate database servers and clients to speak and understand each other. Multitudes of protocols are out there; here are the ones that work with SQL Server 2008:

✦ **TCP/IP:** This is, by far, the most popular communication protocol. In fact, it's the foundation of the Internet. Whenever you open a browser and connect to a Web site, TCP/IP is the underlying standard that makes it possible, and is probably the best choice for your database communication protocol.

✦ **Named pipes:** Generally used for both intra-machine and client/server communication, this protocol is less frequently found on Internet-based conversations. They are also somewhat less secure than TCP/IP.

✦ **Virtual Interface Adapter (VIA):** As a protocol that is reliant on specialized hardware, the odds are that most readers aren't likely to encounter VIA as frequently as they will TCP/IP or named pipes.

✦ **Shared memory:** You can guess from its name that this protocol relies on a fast, dedicated section of memory that SQL Server can use for communication between the database and any clients. However, there's one gotcha to shared memory: Client applications and processes must reside on the same computer as the database server, making this protocol somewhat irrelevant in a highly distributed environment.

Shared memory is the default protocol for the SQL Server Management Studio and other important tools when they're resident on the database server. Consequently, make sure not to disable this protocol.

Now that you're a wiz with SQL Server's myriad protocols, it's time to see how to enable or disable any of the ones we just listed.

1. **Launch the SQL Server Configuration Manager.**

You have two ways to make this happen. You can directly launch the SQL Server Configuration Manager, which you find in the Configuration Tools submenu of your root SQL Server menu.

You can also get to this user interface by right-clicking My Computer, choosing Manage, and then expanding the Services and Applications folder.

Regardless of how you launch it, the user interface is the same in both cases. The only difference is that in the former, you're running the utility stand-alone, while the latter displays it as part of Computer Management.

You have three paths to follow from here. They include

• **SQL Server Services:** Yet another way to start, stop, and disable your database services. For most installations, you see services dedicated to SQL Server's Analysis, Integration, and Reporting Services, as well as the database engine, agent, and browser.

- **SQL Server Network Configuration:** Where you enable, configure, or disable any of the four services we just listed, for inbound connections. This is the focus of the balance of this section.

- **SQL Native Client Configuration:** Where you specify how you want outbound (that is, from your database to other databases) protocols to work.

2. **Click the entry for your database server.**

   On the right, you see entries for each of the protocols.

3. **Right-click any protocol that you want to configure and then choose the Properties option.**

   In the case of TCP/IP, you have several properties at your disposal, including:

   - **Enabled:** This property asks a very simple question: Do you or don't you want this service to run?

   - **Keep Alive:** This sets how often SQL Server checks to ensure that an idle connection is still valid.

   - **Listen All:** This setting controls how SQL Server, your network, and your computer's network cards all work together. You can also switch to the IP Addresses tab for further configuration.

4. **When you're finished, click OK to save your changes.**

   If you change your mind, you can always return and modify your protocol settings.

Reporting services configuration

SQL Server's powerful reporting capabilities require little administrator intervention. However, if you do need to make configuration changes, it's very easy to implement these alterations.

1. **Launch the SQL Server Reporting Services Configuration Manager.**

   The best way is to launch it directly from the Configuration Tools submenu of your root SQL Server menu.

2. **Connect to the appropriate reporting server instance.**

   After you establish a session with the Report server, you see something similar to Figure 4-12.

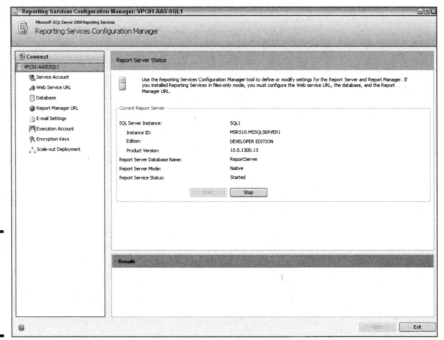

Figure 4-12:
Reporting
Services
Configur-
ation
Manager.

As shown in Figure 4-12, you have an extensive list of options available through this utility; here's a list, along with their purposes:

- **Service Account:** This dialog allows you to assign either a built-in account or an account of your choosing to run the report server service.

- **Web Service URL:** Where you set up the virtual directory, IP address, protocol, URL, and security options for Web service connectivity to your report server.

- **Database:** This dialog offers you the opportunity to switch the database that supports the report server.

- **Report Manager URL:** Because you can access the Report Manager via a browser, here's where you can set its address.

- **E-mail Settings:** A report server features e-mail notification capabilities; here's where you configure details about the account.

- **Execution Account:** This dialog is where you provide details for an account that you can use to connect to remote servers that hold images for your reports, or to servers that don't require credentials.

 To avoid security vulnerabilities, don't give this account any more permissions than necessary.

- **Encryption Keys:** Because Reporting Services take advantage of symmetric keys to encrypt sensitive reporting data, here's where you can back up, change, or restore these important keys.

- **Scale-out Deployment:** Reporting Services leverages additional computers to spread the processing load; you add or remove these servers here.

3. **Make your changes and then click Apply to save them.**

SQL Server features

In addition to configuring SQL Server's protocol portfolio, you're also free to adjust the exact set of features available to your database server by launching the SQL Server Installation Center. This utility should be familiar; you already used it to install the SQL Server product. You find it in the Configuration Tools submenu of your root SQL Server menu.

After you've finished making your feature changes, make sure to save them. In some cases, SQL Server requires you to restart the database engine.

Streamlining Administration

Even though SQL Server is now installed and configured to your liking, your work isn't quite done. In this section, we show you how to take advantage of SQL Server's handy wizard-driven tools to create and maintain well-thought-out administration plans and procedures. This happens to be a great time to take these steps, too. You're likely to be up to your ears in database and application creation tasks before you know it, and administration often takes a back seat to these more glamorous responsibilities. After reviewing this wizard, we veer into the more intricate world of SQL Server's policy-based management capabilities.

SQL Server Maintenance Plan Wizard

To get maximum value from this exercise, we show you how to automate a few vital administrative tasks all within one procedure. Here's what to do:

1. **Launch the SQL Server Management Studio.**

    You find it directly under the SQL Server menu.

2. **Connect to your new SQL Server instance.**

3. **Expand the Management folder.**

4. **Right-click the Maintenance Plans folder and then choose the New Maintenance Plan option.**

This launches the Maintenance Plan Wizard, which is an extremely easy-to-use tool to create and administer maintenance activities. Figure 4-13 shows the initial dialog box for the wizard.

5. **Provide a name and description for your new maintenance plan.**

6. **Decide whether you want to run administrative jobs separately or together.**

   In this example, we gather everything into one batch.

7. **Set a schedule by clicking the Change button, or simply run the job on demand.**

   SQL Server offers a powerful scheduling tool for this purpose. Figure 4-14 shows its broad-reaching capabilities.

8. **When you're finished setting the schedule, click OK to close the scheduling dialog box and then click Next.**

   This wizard allows you to automate a collection of important administrative responsibilities, as shown in Figure 4-15. If you're unsure about the purpose of a given task, just highlight it, and a brief description appears at the bottom of the screen.

9. **Select the administrative tasks you want performed by marking the check boxes. When finished, click Next.**

10. **If you've chosen more than one task, tell SQL Server in which order they should run and then click Next.**

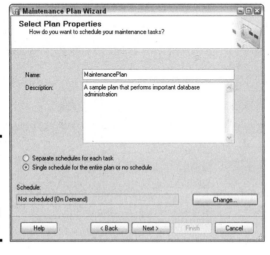

Figure 4-13:
Mainte-
nance Plan
Wizard
initial dialog
box.

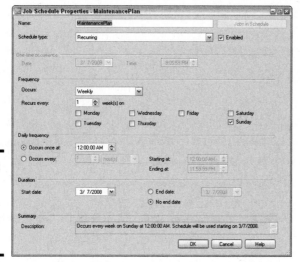

Figure 4-14:
Mainte-
nance Plan
Wizard
scheduling
dialog.

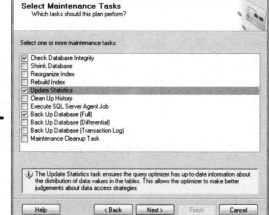

Figure 4-15:
Selecting
tasks for
the Mainte-
nance Plan
Wizard.

11. **For each administrative task, decide which databases should participate and then click OK.**

You can include

- *All databases*
- *System databases*
- *All user databases*
- *One or more databases from the available instances on your server*

12. **Depending on the specific administrative task, fill in any additional required details.**

For example, Figure 4-16 shows the dialog box that SQL Server displays to configure the backup task. If you're curious about the whole topic of backup and recovery, make sure to drop by Book VIII, Chapter 2.

13. **Tell SQL Server how you want it to report on the outcome of the administrative tasks and then click Next.**

You can have the report written to a file, or even e-mailed to you.

14. **Review your selections and then click Finish.**

Figure 4-17 shows the result of your hard work.

15. **If you've set a formal maintenance schedule, await your results. If not, run the job manually by launching it from the Maintenance Plans folder.**

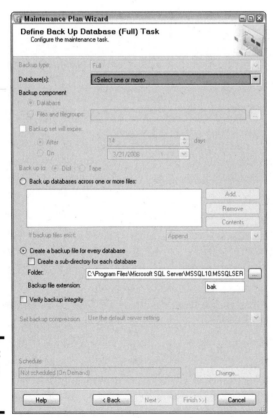

Figure 4-16:
Configuring
backup
options.

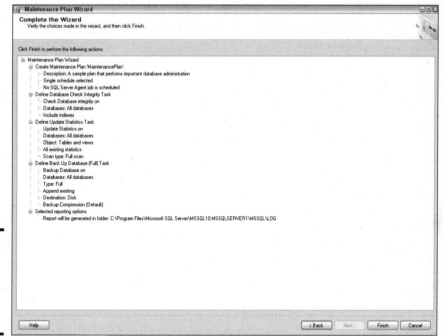

Figure 4-17:
Proposed
activity for
the Mainte-
nance Plan
Wizard.

Policy-based management

Database administrators tasked with looking after multiple servers, each
hosting hundreds of tables and other database objects, often find themselves overwhelmed by the number of administrative responsibilities they
face. This is especially true when their organization requires that they
implement a variety of sophisticated database administration policies and
procedures.

Microsoft recognizes the plight of the modern administrator and attempts to
ameliorate the situation by offering a feature-rich, graphically driven set of
tools to automate the amount of tedious, error-prone, and manual adminis-
tration-related tasks. Collectively known as *policy-based management,* using
these tools is a much saner way of administering complex environments.

The remainder of this chapter gives you a high-level overview of policy-
based management, including its architecture and key terms and concepts.

As is the case with many of SQL Server's more-advanced capabilities, you
would do well to experiment with a sample database before trying out your
ideas on a production environment.

Architecture

SQL Server's policy-based management is made of three primary components:

+ **Policy management:** Policy administrators (generally the same people who administer the entire SQL Server instance) are responsible for creating and maintaining policies. A *policy* is nothing more than a set of centrally governed, standardized rules for controlling SQL Server's behavior.

+ **Explicit administration:** A policy administrator chooses one or more database objects to see if they comply with the rules stated in a given policy.

+ **Execution modes:** These offer several different mechanisms to run a policy. They include

  - *On Demand:* Run manually by an administrator

  - *On Change – Prevent:* This automated approach uses SQL Server's data definition language (DDL) triggers as the mechanism for preventing policy violation.

  - *On Change – Log Only:* This automated approach takes advantage of SQL Server's event notification mechanism to log policy violations.

  - *On Schedule:* This approach uses the automated SQL Server Agent to check for, and log, policy violations.

Key terms

Now that you've gotten a brief overview of some of the architectural underpinnings of SQL Server's policy-based management capabilities, it's time to gain some insight into some key terms that you're likely to encounter.

+ **Managed target:** Database objects that you wish to enforce policies on. Typical targets are databases, tables, indexes, and so on.

+ **Facet:** Behaviors or attributes of a managed target. Look at Figure 4-18. On the left side of the screen is a partial list of facets under the Facets folder; the right side displays a particular focus on the facets related to the Database managed target.

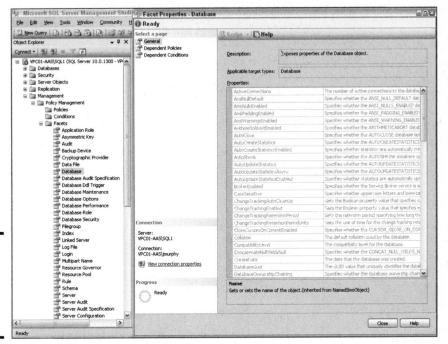

Figure 4-18:
A list of
facets,
along with
database
properties.

+ **Policy-based management policy:** This is the combination of a condition and its expected behavior.

+ **Policy category:** To help organize their policies, administrators are free to create and maintain their own categories and then assign policies to these categories.

+ **Effective policy:** It's not enough to simply define a policy; this term refers to a policy that is actually being actively enforced on valid managed targets.

Setting up and maintaining your own policies

As you're about to see, it's easy to create and sustain your own customized policies. For this example, imagine that your organization has an enterprise-wide rule that all database tables must take advantage of clustered indexes to boost performance and preserve data integrity. Unfortunately, some database analysts and application developers periodically forget this imperative. To figure out which tables are in violation, you *could* explore each database and all included objects. However, with dozens of SQL Server instances, hundreds of databases, and thousands of tables, this wouldn't be fun. Why make things harder than they need to be? Instead of performing this tedious task yourself, you can elect to put the power of SQL Server's Policy-based management system to work. Here's what to do.

Policy-based management is a rich topic: It could easily fill its own book. As is the case with many of SQL Server's more powerful capabilities, it's always best to experiment with a sample database before trying things out on production data.

1. **Launch the SQL Server Management Studio.**

2. **Expand the Management folder.**

3. **Expand the Policy Management folder.**

You'll notice subfolders for Policies, Conditions, and Facets. For the purposes of this example, we use an existing facet. Of course, you're always free to create your own customized facets.

4. **Right-click the Conditions folder and then choose the New Condition option.**

Think of the condition as one or more questions that we're going to ask SQL Server to evaluate. In this case, we're going to ask it to tell us whether a table has a clustered index.

5. **Fill in the details about the condition.**

You'll need to provide a name for the condition, as well as which facet to use. In this example, shown in Figure 4-19, we're using the Table facet.

6. **Define your condition's expression(s) and then click OK when you're finished.**

Here's where you tell SQL Server what you'd like it to check. With dozens of facets, each containing dozens of fields that can be evaluated, there are tons of details to explore. In this case, displayed in Figure 4-20, we've asked SQL Server to evaluate the @HasClusteredIndex field to see if it's true. You're also free to define your own edit criteria by clicking the ellipses button to the right of the Value column.

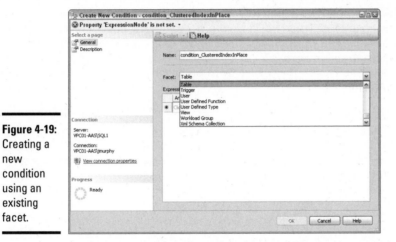

Figure 4-19:
Creating a
new
condition
using an
existing
facet.

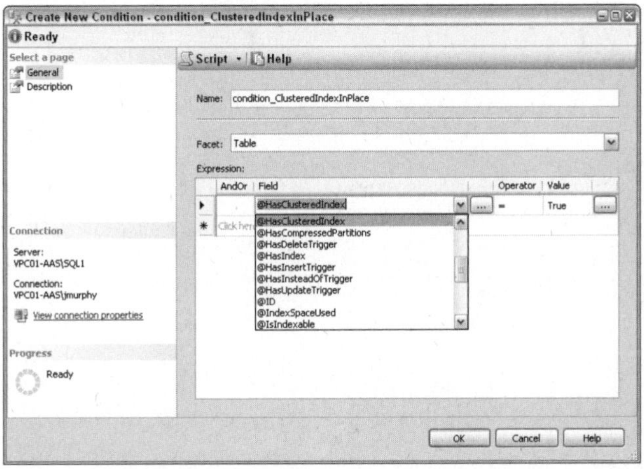

Figure 4-20:
Adding an
expression
to a new
condition.

7. Right-click the Policies folder and then choose the New Policy option.

This brings up a dialog box where you define the new policy, and then associate it with one or more conditions.

8. Setup your policy and then click OK when you're finished.

Here's where you define the policy's name, as well as associating it with the conditions you'd like it to check. You can also dictate whether you want the policy to run automatically or manually. Figure 4-21 shows the association between this policy and the condition we created in Step 6. You're also able to set restrictions on which server(s) should be subject to this policy.

9. **Right-click the new Policy and then choose the Evaluate option.**

This launches a full check of the policy. After a few moments, SQL Server displays a results dialog box like the one shown in Figure 4-22. By examining the contents of this dialog box, we can see that several tables do not comply with this rule. Depending on the type of rule we've created and violation encountered, we may then be able to correct the problem by simply clicking the Configure button.

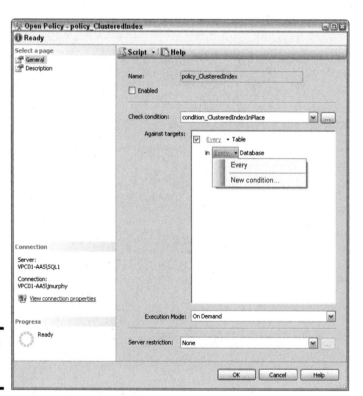

Figure 4-21: Defining a new policy.

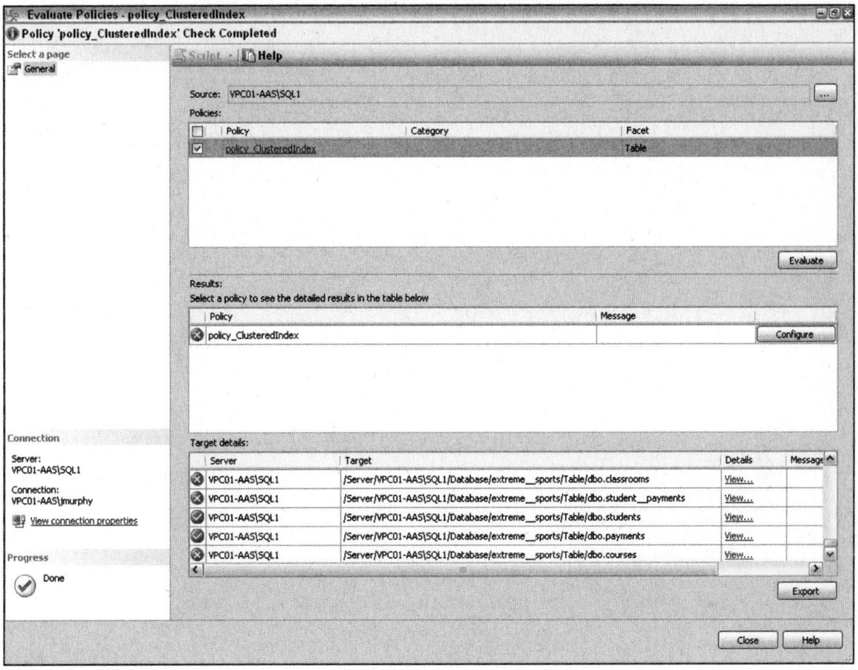

Figure 4-22:
Viewing
results from
a policy
evaluation.

Chapter 5: Using SQL Server Management Studio

In This Chapter

✔ Introducing SQL Server Management Studio: the DBA's best friend

✔ Getting to know the menu structure and icons

✔ Discovering Object, Template, and Solution Explorer

✔ Performing queries

*T*he average IT professional must be a master of multi-tasking. Because the demands of their jobs never end, wise database administrators, architects, and developers search for enhanced productivity wherever they can find it. That's where the SQL Server Management Studio comes in. Provided alongside every edition of SQL Server (even the free SQL Server 2008 Express), it's an excellent graphical query and administrative tool, especially when compared with those offered by other major, relational database vendors.

No matter your interaction with SQL Server, this chapter helps you see how this versatile tool can make life easier for you. To help you navigate, we begin by providing a 35,000-foot overview of its main menu structure and major icons. We then quickly dive in to what you can learn about your SQL Server instance by interacting with the Object Explorer. Next, we briefly touch on the Template Explorer and the Solution Explorer. The chapter closes with a detailed examination of how to run queries within the SQL Server Management Studio.

Although many character-based utilities are also at your disposal (most of them legacies from earlier versions), as time goes by you'll probably find yourself performing the majority of your database design and administrative tasks within SQL Server Management Studio. *Note:* We periodically refer to these other tools throughout the book, so if you prefer these types of utilities, stay tuned for these topics as well.

To launch the SQL Server Management Studio, simply choose it from the Microsoft SQL Server 2008 menu.

Menu Structure and Icons

SQL Server Management Studio follows the standard style and structure for Windows menus. Here's a quick summary of each major menu:

✦ **File:** Here's where you connect to database servers, create new projects or open existing ones, and save your work.

✦ **Edit:** If you've used any Windows-based software, you'll be comfortable on this menu. It allows you to select, copy, and paste text as well as search for terms within your files. You can also set helpful bookmarks.

✦ **View:** This menu allows you to switch among all the major SQL Server Management Studio objects, including all the explorers and toolbars.

If you're looking for a particular window or tool that seems to have disappeared, carefully explore the View menu, and you should be able to locate it.

✦ **Tools:** SQL Server ships with some extremely useful assistants designed to help you analyze and optimize performance. You'll find links to these tools on this menu. You're also free to link external tools, set preferences, and customize SQL Server Management Studio's behavior.

✦ **Window:** You come to this menu whenever you want to cycle among your open SQL Server windows or configure how they're displayed.

✦ **Community:** No database is an island. Visit this menu to connect to other SQL Server developers and administrators.

✦ **Help:** When all else fails, drop by this menu to search for assistance.

A collection of helpful icon-based shortcuts is near the top of the screen; you'll probably use the New Query icon most frequently. These icons are explored in more detail later in this chapter.

Note: You can often view important attributes of a given object (such as a database, table, connection, stored procedure, and so on) by enabling the Properties window. To do so, just select it from the View menu.

Object Explorer

The *Object Explorer* serves as a dashboard that provides a concise, yet content-rich, set of information about each of the databases under your control, and is the place where most administrators spend the majority of their time. Figure 5-1 shows an expanded view of this vital interface.

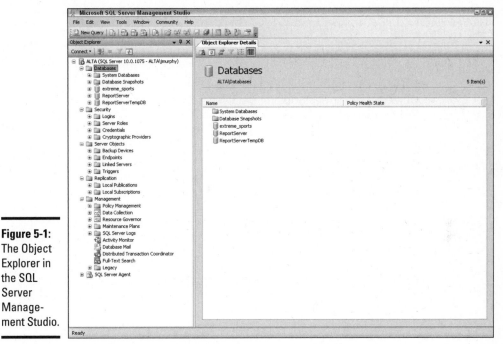

Figure 5-1:
The Object
Explorer in
the SQL
Server
Manage-
ment Studio.

The following list looks at each of the major Object Explorer sub-folders:

✦ **Databases:** Open this folder to get a comprehensive list of all the databases in this instance. You'll see SQL Server's system databases, as well
as any databases that you've created. You can then expand each database entry to see its internal structures, such as tables, views, stored
procedures, and so on. This folder and its children will occupy the
majority of your time.

✦ **Security:** You set up server-wide security options here. *Note:* Database-
specific security is configured within the Databases folder.

✦ **Server Objects:** This folder contains a collection of resources for diverse
subjects, such as system backup, services, other server linkages, and
triggers.

✦ **Replication:** This highly useful capability allows you to distribute your
data among multiple systems, as well as subscribe to information from
remote computers. You manage these options in this folder.

✦ **Management:** Administrators will spend an inordinate amount of time in
this folder. All your SQL Server logs, your data warehouse management,
the performance-optimizing Resource Governor, and other essential
administrative tools are here.

✦ **SQL Server Agent:** People tasked with looking after SQL Server's day-to-day operational activities will be very interested in this folder. You can monitor the status of jobs, manage operator access, maintain proxies, and view error logs here.

You can obtain additional information about most entries found in the Object Explorer by choosing the Object Explorer Details option from the View menu.

Template Explorer

If you'd like to benefit from Microsoft's philosophy of making database administration easier, be sure to check out the Template Explorer. It contains dozens of examples of common database maintenance and interaction scripts. To display the Template Explorer, choose it from the View menu within SQL Server Management Studio.

Figure 5-2 shows a small sampling of available templates (located on the right side of the screen), as well as a specific example of the template for creating a new table.

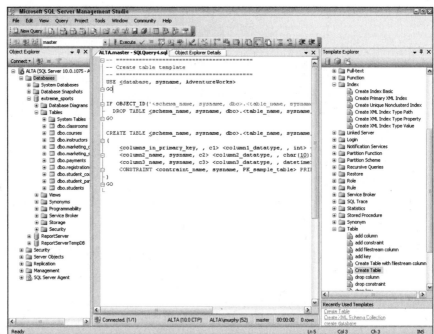

Figure 5-2:
The Template Explorer and sample in the SQL Server Management Studio.

To choose a template, simply double-click it. After the template is displayed, all you need to do is provide each placeholder a value. A quick way to provide each placeholder a value is to click the Specify Values for Template Parameters icon, which you find along the top row of icons. This opens a handy dialog box, as shown in Figure 5-3.

As if this collection wasn't helpful enough, you're also free to modify the existing templates and create your own. To modify a template, simply right-click the template and choose the Edit option. Remember to save your work when you finish changing the template. To create a template, just right-click anywhere in the Template Explorer and choose the New option. This opens a blank dialog box where you're free to enter your own SQL.

TIP

When creating a brand new template, consider using an existing template as a model. Just remember to save the template with a new, distinct name, or you'll overwrite the existing template.

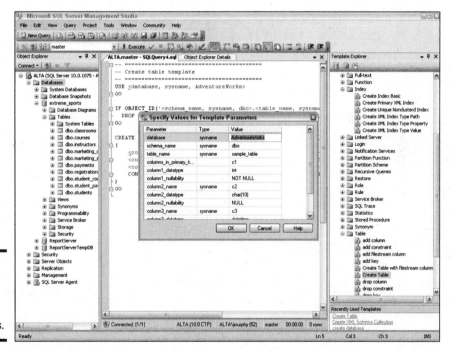

Figure 5-3:
Specifying
values for
template
parameters.

Solution Explorer

This component is meant to help you easily organize and visualize the elements used to create a database-oriented project. To begin creating a project, choose File⇨New Project. You're then presented with a dialog box asking what kind of project you wish to create. For the purposes of this illustration, we chose a SQL Server Scripts project and added a simply query to the endeavor.

With the project underway, you can evaluate the Solution Explorer's view, shown in Figure 5-4, by choosing View⇨Solution Explorer in the SQL Server Management Studio.

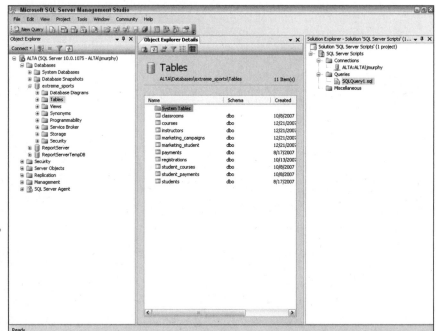

Figure 5-4:
The Solution Explorer in SQL Server Management Studio.

Running Queries

If your job is to design, develop, or administer a SQL Server database, you'll be very interested in this section. We show you how to take advantage of the SQL Server Management Studio's rich query capabilities. To begin, we take you on a brief tour of query-specific user interface features. After that, we illustrate some sample queries.

Although this section is titled "Running Queries," you can perform any database interaction (such as updates, deletions, creating tables, and so on) using these capabilities.

Query-specific user interface features

As shown in Figure 5-5, many icons for designing queries are at your disposal.

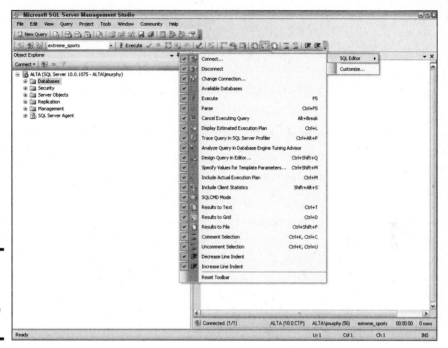

Figure 5-5:
SQL Server
Manage-
ment Studio
icons.

Here's a quick list of these icons, along with a simple summary of each one:

✦ **Connect:** Request a connection to a specific SQL Server instance.

✦ **Disconnect:** End your connection with this SQL Server instance.

✦ **Change Connection:** Switch connections to another SQL Server instance.

✦ **Available Databases:** Presents a list of accessible candidate databases.

✦ **Execute:** Run your SQL statement.

✦ **Parse:** Have SQL Server check your syntax and identify any errors.

✦ **Cancel Executing Query:** Stop a long-running query in its tracks.

✦ **Display Estimated Execution Plan:** Instruct SQL Server to tell you how it plans to process your statements.

✦ **Trace Query in SQL Server Profiler:** Show the progress of your SQL statements, with a particular focus on performance.

✦ **Analyze Query in Database Engine Tuning Advisor:** Help identify performance bottlenecks in your query.

✦ **Design Query in Editor:** Launch the SQL Server Query Designer.

✦ **Specify Values for Template Parameters:** Provide runtime values for your templates.

✦ **Include Actual Execution Plan:** Display the road map SQL Server followed to provide your results.

✦ **Include Client Statistics:** Display performance and other metrics.

✦ **SQLCMD Mode:** Emulate this character-based utility.

✦ **Results to Text:** Send the output of your query to plain text.

✦ **Results to Grid:** Use a grid format for your query's output.

✦ **Results to File:** Publish the product of your query to a text file.

✦ **Comment Selection:** Render selected lines of your query inoperative.

✦ **Uncomment Selection:** Enable processing of selected lines of your query.

✦ **Decrease Line Indent:** Move your query text to the left.

✦ **Increase Line Indent:** Move your query text to the right.

Creating a query

Queries are at the heart of most database interaction. In this section, we show you how to create and run a simple SQL query. If you're not comfortable with this concept yet, stay tuned. The next part of this chapter shows you how to take advantage of some very helpful graphical assistants to get you the results that you desire.

Here's how to get started on your query:

1. **Launch SQL Server Management Studio.**

2. **Connect to the appropriate SQL Server instance.**

3. **Click the New Query icon to bring up the query workspace.**

Make sure to select the appropriate database from the drop-down box in the upper-left of your screen.

4. **Enter your SQL statement(s), and click the Execute button.**

Here's where you discover yet another great productivity tool built in to SQL Server. *IntelliSense,* built in to many of Microsoft's development platforms, provides context-sensitive auto-completion capabilities to help speed things. For example, in Figure 5-6, IntelliSense has presented a list of possible candidates for the SELECT statement.

After you've executed your query, any results are displayed directly in the bottom half of the window, as shown in Figure 5-7.

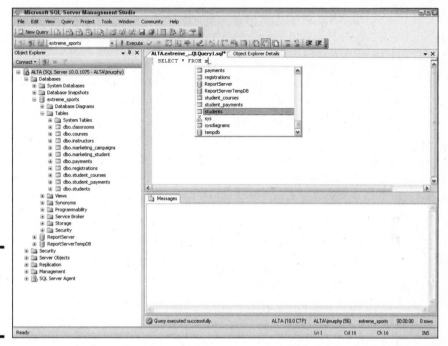

Figure 5-6:
IntelliSense
helping to
complete a
query.

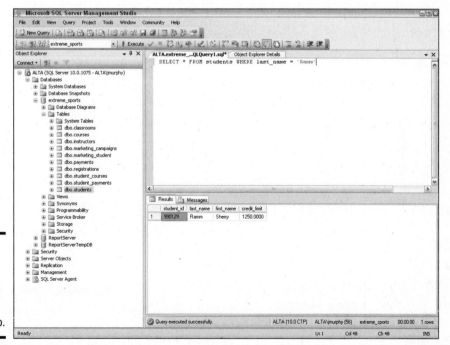

Figure 5-7:
Query
results in
SQL Server
Manage-
ment Studio.

Using the Query Designer

If you need to interact with your database but aren't an SQL whiz, never fear. In addition to the collection of superb examples found in the Template Explorer, you can always take advantage of the SQL Server Management Studio Query Designer to construct powerful queries and other database interactions.

Assuming you have the SQL Server Management Studio already running and have selected the New Query option, you need to

1. **Click the Design Query in Editor icon, found just above the query window.**

   This opens the SQL Server Query Designer, along with the Add Table dialog box, as shown in Figure 5-8.

2. **Select one or more tables for your query. Hold down the Ctrl key to make multiple selections.**

3. **While you choose tables, click the Add button to place these tables in the Query Designer.**

   If any foreign key relationships are configured, SQL Server automatically displays these important interactions in the Query Designer, as shown in Figure 5-9. It also creates a basic SQL statement that highlights the relationship among these tables.

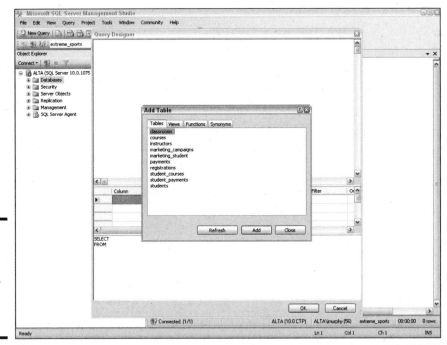

Figure 5-8:
The initial dialog box for the SQL Server Query Designer.

In addition to choosing one or more tables for your new query, you're also free to select from existing views, functions, and synonyms.

4. **After you've chosen all of your tables, click the Close button to remove the Add Table dialog box.**

5. **Select the columns you want to display from each table by placing a check mark next to the column name.**

   If you want to display all the columns, check the asterisk box. While you're adding tables and columns, you can watch the SQL statement in the bottom of the window include your requirements.

6. **After you've finished identifying tables and columns, your next task is to decide whether you want any sorting or filtering criteria. Use the drop-down boxes in the grid of chosen columns.**

   Figure 5-10 shows a simple join query with a filter and sort request.

7. **When all your work is finished, click OK to close the Query Designer.**

   SQL Server writes the automatically generated SQL statement into the query window, as shown in Figure 5-11.

   You're now free to run the query and see your results. Of course, you can also make modifications to the query if conditions change.

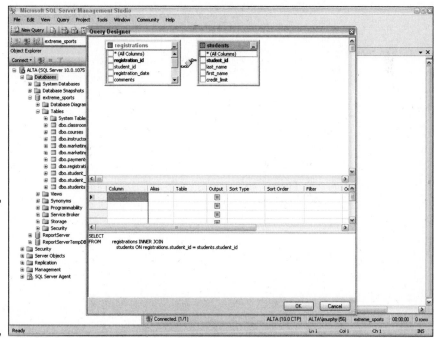

Figure 5-9:
Initial tables and relation- ships in SQL Server Query Designer.

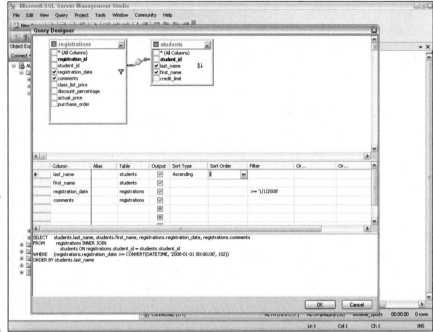

Figure 5-10:
Initial tables and relationships in SQL Server Query Designer.

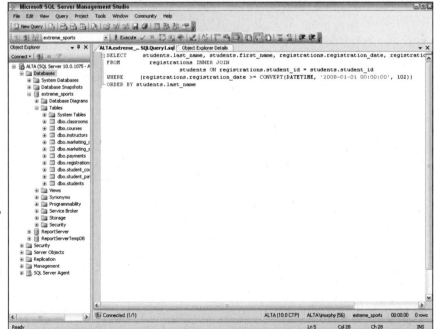

Figure 5-11:
The generated SQL query in SQL Server Query Designer.

You can save this query for future reference by simply clicking the floppy disk icon.

If you'd like a more complete picture of the Query Designer, visit Book III, Chapter 3. If you're curious about how to set and use query options, Book III, Chapter 4 answers your questions.

Book II

Designing and Using Databases

Creating a new database.

Contents at a Glance

Chapter 1: Setting Up a Database

In This Chapter

✔ System databases: the heart of your SQL Server environment

✔ Connecting to a database server

✔ Selecting an existing database

✔ Understanding the major database objects

✔ Creating a new database

*W*hen you want to store data in SQL Server, your first responsibility is to define a database that will serve as a container for your information. Your next task is to create the tables where the actual data will reside, along with any restrictions on what you can place in these tables. Finally, by defining relationships among your information, you help SQL Server ensure good data integrity and protect your business rules.

In this chapter, you get started on this road. To begin, you discover how the built-in system databases each have an important job to perform. With that out of the way, you find how to connect to a database server, and then see all its existing databases. After that, we tell you about the primary database objects you're likely to encounter. Finally, you get the hang of creating new databases by using the powerful SQL Server Management Studio tool, which allows you to perform all the database management tasks we describe throughout the chapter. Because you might have other preferences when it comes to data management tools, we also show you some different approaches you can take to achieve the same results.

System Databases

SQL Server ships with four built-in databases. Also known as *system databases*, these information repositories each play a significant role in keeping your data organized and tidy. Here's a brief look at them:

✦ **Master:** As you might guess from the name, this database means business: It keeps track of everything about your other databases, including where to find them, how they're configured, and even how to start up the database server. It also knows your security and other login settings.

✦ **Model:** SQL Server uses this database as a guideline for any new database that's created on your system.

✦ **Msdb:** Here's where the SQL Server Agent keeps track of its workload, such as scheduled jobs, alerts, Service Broker tasks, and database mail.

✦ **Tempdb:** This database fills the important job of serving as a temporary repository for transient information from both user tasks as well as internal SQL Server work. As you might imagine, it fills with all sorts of stuff over time. Luckily, every time you restart the database engine, SQL Server re-creates a fresh, empty copy of this database.

Figure 1-1 shows how system databases appear in the SQL Server Management Studio.

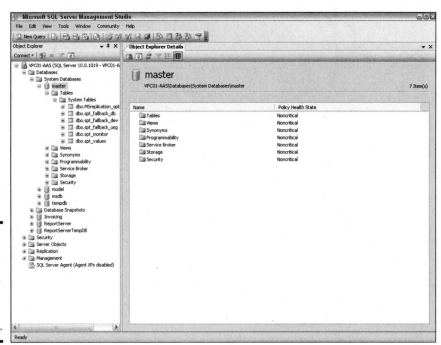

Figure 1-1:
System databases in the SQL Server Management Studio.

Connecting to a Database Server

Before you can interact with the information kept in a database, you first need to connect to the instance of a database server that holds that data. Here are the simple steps you need to follow:

1. **Launch the SQL Server Management Studio.**

2. Fill in the details on the Connect to Server dialog box.

This dialog box appears automatically whenever you launch the SQL Server Management Studio. If you don't see it or have closed it by mistake, just click the Connect button at the top of the screen, and it will reappear.

3. Choose the Database Engine option.

This opens the Connect to Server dialog box, as shown in Figure 1-2. Here's where you choose the specific database instance you want.

Figure 1-2:
Connecting
to a server
from the
SQL Server
Manage-
ment Studio.

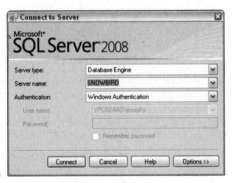

4. Choose a server from the Server Name drop down menu.

5. Select an authentication method.

Your choices here are:

- **Windows Authentication:** In this case, SQL Server inherits your login information from when you logged in to the Windows operating system.

- **SQL Server Authentication:** Choose this method when you have a separate login for the database itself, in addition to the username and password that you provide when signing in to the computer.

6. (Optional) Click the Options button and fill in any other connection properties if you like.

In most cases, the default connection options should suffice. However, here's what these settings mean if you want to experiment:

- **Connect to Database:** This allows you to choose a specific database on the server in question. You can browse all the available user and system databases if you like.

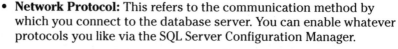

- **Network Protocol:** This refers to the communication method by which you connect to the database server. You can enable whatever protocols you like via the SQL Server Configuration Manager.

The default protocol for a local SQL Server connection is shared memory; it's also the fastest for this type of connection. If you're connecting to a remote server, you can use named pipes as well as TCP/IP. In most cases, it's wisest to simply use the default setting.

- **Network Packet Size:** This setting tells SQL Server how many bytes you want to include in each message package sent between a database client and SQL Server.

- **Connection Time Out:** This tells SQL Server how long you want to wait before giving up on establishing a new connection.

If you know that your network infrastructure is sluggish, consider raising this parameter from its default value. On the other hand, if you're confident in a speedy connection to your database, then a lower value makes more sense.

- **Execution Time Out:** After you're connected, this parameter instructs SQL Server how long you want to let a long running database operation continue before bailing out.

If you plan to run an operation that takes a long time (such as a major update or large insert job), don't make this setting too small, or you run the risk of aborting a valid transaction in the middle.

- **Encrypt Connection:** With an encrypted connection, all traffic between SQL Server and its client is scrambled to protect it from outside snooping. However, this defense comes at a price: a small amount of extra processing workload to handle encryption's overhead. Hence, if you're confident that your conversation is over an already-secure connection, you can leave this option unchecked. On the other hand, if you want this added protection, you can enable encryption at the server, and all traffic is handled accordingly no matter what settings are in place on the client.

Exploring an Existing Database

Before you start creating new databases, you probably want to check out some of the system databases that we just described, or perhaps an already-existing user database. Here's how to discover more about the databases in your SQL Server instance:

1. **Launch the SQL Server Management Studio.**

2. **Connect to a specific database server.**

   We just described how to do this in the previous section of this chapter.

3. **Expand the Databases folder.**

   Here's where you get a list of all available databases on this server. You can find out more about each database by expanding its folder. If you're interested in this topic, stay tuned because it's up next.

4. **Click on the database you want to explore.**

Understanding the Major Database Objects

When you're connected to your database server and a specific instance of a database, you see all sorts of interesting objects. Figure 1-3 shows these objects from the SQL Server Management Studio. *Note:* This sample database doesn't ship with SQL Server; we created it as an example.

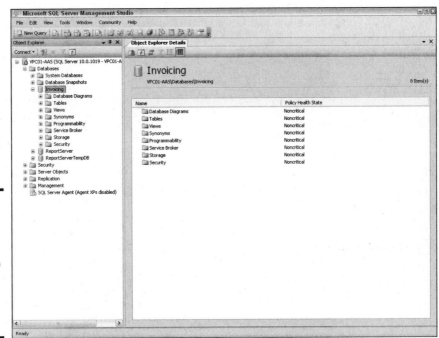

Figure 1-3:
The SQL Server Management Studio displaying major database objects.

Here's what each one contains:

✦ **Database Diagrams:** Here's where you get a graphical view of your information, including the relationships you've defined among objects in your database.

When you first expand this folder, SQL Server might ask you for permission to create the necessary internal objects to support database diagramming. These diagrams are very helpful, so it's a good idea to answer yes to this question.

✦ **Tables:** The contents of this folder are divided between system tables, which are provided for and looked after by SQL Server, and user tables. Each table further breaks down into columns and indexes.

✦ **Views:** *Views* are virtual tables, composed of information from one or more real tables. If you expand this folder, you see a list of both system and user-defined views. Opening a particular view yields a list of the columns that make up that view.

✦ **Synonyms:** These are substitute names for objects in your database.

✦ **Programmability:** Here's where you can get a list of all your system and user-defined stored procedures, including their input and output parameters. You can also find out about your functions, assemblies, triggers, rules, and so on via this tree entry.

✦ **Service Broker:** This technology offers powerful communication, messaging, and other distributed processing capabilities.

✦ **Storage:** Take a look in this folder if you like to see details about full-text catalogs and any database partitioning schemes and functions that might be in place.

✦ **Security:** This folder itemizes all the users who have access to your database.

To get the latest-and-greatest view of everything about your SQL Server instance, right-click the Object Explorer tree and choose Refresh.

Creating a New Database

It's time to construct a brand new database of your own. It's very easy, thanks to the SQL Server Management Studio. Here's all that you need to do:

1. **Launch the SQL Server Management Studio.**

2. **Connect to the appropriate SQL Server instance.**

3. **Expand the connection's entry in the Object Explorer view.**

4. **Highlight the Databases folder.**

5. **Right-click this folder, and choose New Database.**

A dialog box that lets you specify the new database's name appears, as well as a collection of properties about the new database.

6. **Fill in the General page.**

This page contains vital settings, including:

- **Database Name:** No mystery here — this is what you want to call your database.

- **Owner:** This is the login for the user who possesses the database. *Note:* You must first create this login in SQL Server; trying to assign an operating system-based user ID directly won't suffice. You can type in a name or browse from the list of potential logins.

- **Use Full-text Indexing:** SQL Server offers powerful search features that make it easy to locate information from massive quantities of text-based data. Check this box if you want to enable these capabilities. In general, unless you're sure that you'll never need it, it's smart to switch on this feature.

- **Data File Details:** These important parameters control the name, size, association, growth rates, and location of the file that holds your data. Table 1-1 illustrates what these settings mean, and how to set them optimally.

- **Log File Details:** Just as Data File Details allows you to configure key settings for the data file, here's where you do the same for your log files. See Table 1-1 for more details.

Book II
Chapter 1

Setting Up a
Database

Table 1-1	File Parameters
Parameter	*Purpose*
Logical name	Associate a meaningful, unique name for the file.
File type	Decide whether it holds data or transaction log information.
File group	Assign the file to a larger group of similar files, generally for administration.
Initial size	How large you want the file to be from inception.
Autogrowth	Whether you want the file to grow automatically.
Path	Where you want the file placed on disk.
File name	SQL Server generates this for you, using the logical name.

Figure 1-4 shows what this important dialog box looks like.

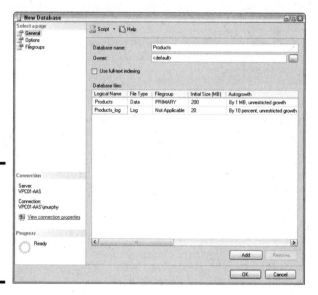

Figure 1-4:
General
settings
when
creating a
new
database.

7. (Optional) Fill in the Options page.

Take a deep breath, because you can configure more than 20 settings.
Alternatively, you could simply elect to go with the defaults. In either
case, if you'd like to know more about what these settings do, check out
Table 1-2.

Table 1-2	**Database Creation Options**
Parameter	*Purpose*
`ANSI NULL Default`	If you don't explicitly specify `NULL` behavior when you create a table, this setting determines whether the default value for any columns will be `NULL` (when the parameter is set to `ON`), and `NOT NULL` (when the parameter is set to `OFF`).
`ANSI NULLS Enabled`	If you disable this parameter, any time SQL Server compares two values that are both `NULL`, it will return `TRUE`. Otherwise, it returns `UNKNOWN`.
`ANSI padding Enabled`	This setting will no longer be present in newer versions of SQL Server, so don't plan to use it.
`ANSI warnings Enabled`	If switched on, you receive a warning message if an aggregation function (such as `SUM`, `AVG`, and so on) encounters a `NULL` value.

Parameter	Purpose
Arithmetic Abort Enabled	If this option is chosen, any arithmetic error causes an active transaction to roll back.
Auto Close	If selected, this causes SQL Server to take a database offline when the last user exits. **Note:** You need to bring the database back online manually if you select this option.
Auto Create Statistics	When enabled (which is the default) this lets the SQL Server Query Optimizer create the metrics it needs to keep better track of data distribution patterns. This helps improve the quality of the Optimizer's decisions.
Auto Shrink	Enable this option if you want SQL Server to tidy your database files automatically over time. However, you need to either back up your transaction log or use the Simple recovery model for this to work.
Auto Update Statistics	This option lets SQL Server fill in the blanks on any missing statistical information.
Auto Update Statistics Asynchronously	This setting determines whether SQL Server can update its internal statistics in the background.
Close Cursor on Commit Enabled	This setting determines what happens when you commit or rollback a transaction. When set to ON, SQL Server closes any open cursors in such an event.
Concatenate Null Yields Null	This parameter decides what happens when you try to combine a NULL value with a string. When the setting is ON, and you include a NULL value in your concatenation, SQL Server treats the entire product as NULL.
Cross-database Ownership Chaining Enabled	This handy setting lets you decide whether you want to allow ownership permissions to span multiple databases.
Database Read-Only	As you might expect, enabling this setting prevents the database from being modified.
Date Correlation Optimization Enabled	This parameter lets you order SQL Server to create and manage statistical information for any columns that have a foreign key relationship and are composed of the DATETIME data type. These statistics generally improve joining and other cross-table performance.

(continued)

**Book II
Chapter 1**

**Setting Up a
Database**

Table 1-2 *(continued)*

Parameter	Purpose
Default Cursor	This parameter determines the default scope of your cursors. Your choices here are LOCAL, or GLOBAL, but you can override this setting when you create your cursor.
Numeric Round-Abort	You use this setting to receive warnings and to generate errors whenever SQL Server loses precision for the results of a numeric operation.
Page Verify	This important parameter guides SQL Server in maintaining details about the health of its data and index pages. It's a good idea to leave this setting at the default of CHECKSUM.
Parameterization	Your options here are SIMPLE, or FORCED. If you want all queries in the database to be parameterized, use the FORCED option. Otherwise, the default value of SIMPLE leaves this determination up to the query developer.
Quoted Identifiers Enabled	Setting this option to ON allows you to use double quotation marks as enclosures for delimited identifiers.
Recursive Triggers Enabled	Here is where you tell SQL Server whether you want to allow recursive firing of AFTER triggers. Unless you're very comfortable with the implications of recursive triggers, it's a good idea to leave this setting at its default value of OFF.
Restrict Access	This option lets you determine the scope of access to your database. Your choices are MULTI_USER, SINGLE_USER, and RESTRICTED_USER. For most normal database operations and applications, you likely want to use the default value of MULTI_USER.
Trustworthy	This important setting lets SQL Server know whether it should consider this database as secure and uncompromised. If SQL Server knows that the database is trustworthy, it grants it access to sensitive resources.
File name	SQL Server generates this for you, by using the logical name.

Figure 1-5 shows these parameters.

8. (Optional) Fill in the Filegroups page.

For now, use the default value shown on this dialog. However, if you're building a large or complex database, you definitely want to check out the next chapter, because we describe this important database architectural concept in more detail.

Figure 1-6 displays these settings.

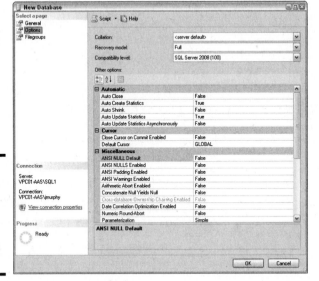

Figure 1-5: Additional settings when creating a new database.

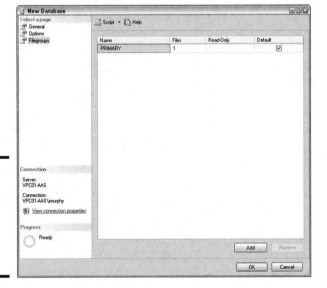

Figure 1-6: Filegroup settings when creating a new database.

9. **When finished, click OK.**

SQL Server dutifully creates your database.

With all these parameters to consider, it's natural for you to worry about the implications of making a mistake at this stage. Have no fear because in the next chapter you discover how to change the configuration for an existing database.

Using SQLCMD to Create a Database

If you prefer the crisp picture of a black-and-white television over color, trust slide rules more than computers, and haven't traded in your vinyl LPs for those newfangled CDs, you'll probably be first in line to use the SQLCMD tool — a very helpful utility that allows both batch and interactive access to SQL Server. Here, we show you how to use it to create a new database, as well as run an existing SQL script.

1. **Open a command prompt.**

Choose Run from the Windows Start menu, and enter **cmd**. You can also choose Programs➪Accessories➪Command Prompt from the Windows Start menu. When you see the friendly command prompt, it's time to launch SQLCMD.

2. **Enter** SQLCMD **at the command prompt, passing in the proper parameters.**

This can get a bit confusing. SQLCMD is rather picky about the exact syntax that it deigns appropriate to run. This isn't surprising when you realize that it supports more than two dozen parameters. Table 1-3 highlights a small group of key parameters.

Table 1-3	Key SQLCMD Parameters
Parameter	*Purpose*
S	Specify the server that you want to connect to
U	Provide your username
P	Provide your password
D	Which database to use (if any)
I	The SQL script file (if any)

If you get in hot water, you can always ask SQLCMD for help:

```
SQLCMD /?
```

3. Enter your SQL, ending your statement with GO.

After you're in SQLCMD, you have an interactive command prompt at your disposal. Figure 1-7 shows a very simple example of how to create a database via direct SQL entry in SQLCMD.

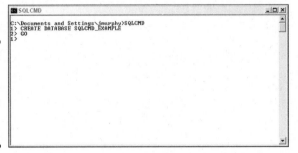

Figure 1-7:
Creating a new database by using SQLCMD.

4. Alternately, run your script from the command line.

One nice feature of SQLCMD is that it lets you run SQL script files without any user intervention. For example, here's how we ran a script file from the command line (Step 2 above) along with the parameters we provided:

```
SQLCMD -S dbserver -U Nicole -P Sierra -d WestBay -i
    build_abc.sql
```

Make sure that your script file is in the right directory; SQLCMD won't be able to find it otherwise. Alternatively, provide a full path to the file.

Scripting Your Database

When your database is set up and configured just the way you like, SQL Server offers a handy feature — *scripting* — that lets you re-create and then configure the database much more quickly in the future. Here's how you can take advantage of scripting:

1. Launch the SQL Server Management Studio.

2. Connect to the appropriate SQL Server instance.

3. Expand the connection's entry in the Object Explorer view.

4. Expand the Databases folder.

5. **Right-click the database you want to script and choose Script Database As⇨CREATE To⇨New Query Editor Window.**

You can also select to save the results to a file or the Clipboard. For this example, we show you the script in a query window, which you can see in Figure 1-8. In reality, you probably want to save the script to a file.

You can use the script any time you want to rebuild your database. This is especially helpful when you're experimenting with new databases.

What's especially nice about scripting is that you can use it for all sorts of administrative tasks, not just creating new databases.

Don't be afraid to experiment with scripting. In fact, after you start taking advantage of scripts, you'll probably find that your overall productivity increases along with your understanding of how to interact with SQL Server.

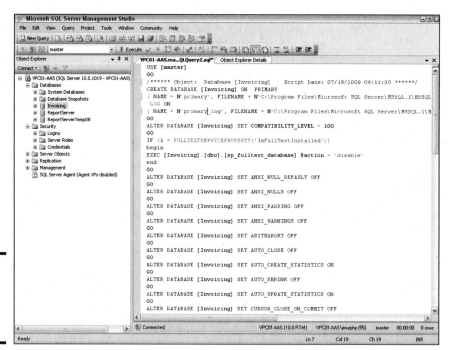

Figure 1-8:
Scripting a
CREATE
DATABASE
statement.

Chapter 2: Care and Feeding of Your Database

In This Chapter

✔ Renaming your database

✔ Viewing and modifying database properties

✔ Deleting a database

When it comes to creating and maintaining databases, with SQL Server very little is set in stone. That is, you nearly always have a second chance to make things right, which gives you the flexibility you need to make changes. In fact, sometimes you might even need to go as far as deleting a database.

No matter what brought you to this chapter, you'll soon see how easy it is to make modifications, whether trivial or significant, to your databases. To start, you get the story on renaming a database. Next up is changing database configuration parameters to tweak your data storage engine's behavior. Finally, you walk through the exact steps necessary to delete a database.

Renaming a Database

After you have a database in place, renaming it is easy:

1. **Launch the SQL Server Management Studio.**

2. **Connect to the appropriate SQL Server instance.**

3. **Expand the connection's entry in the Object Explorer view.**

4. **Expand the Databases folder.**

5. **Right-click the database name that you want to change and choose Rename.**

6. **Enter a new name for the database and press Enter.**

TIP

Make sure to update any external objects that might reference this database by name, such as scripts, programs, stored procedures, and so on.

Changing Database Parameters

SQL Server offers several settings for the database administrator. Many of these parameters are system-wide; others are narrower in their scope and relate to a single database. It's this latter group of variables that we show you how to view and configure. To make things clearer, we've organized this section to match the property pages that hold all these settings.

Regardless of the individual setting you want to modify, you need to follow the same series of steps to make this happen:

1. **Launch the SQL Server Management Studio.**
2. **Connect to the appropriate SQL Server instance.**
3. **Expand the connection's entry in the Object Explorer view.**
4. **Expand the Databases folder.**
5. **Right-click the database that you want to change and choose Properties.**
6. **Select the appropriate properties page.**

   You have a choice of eight properties pages. We describe each one in a moment.

7. **Make your changes and then click OK.**

Figure 2-1 shows you the General properties page.

We assume that you want to use the SQL Server Management Studio to make these changes; it's much easier that way. Comparatively, if you're more of a script or command-line person, you can use the SQLCMD utility instead.

Look at the parameters found on each of the properties pages. As shown in Figure 2-1, these properties can be grouped either alphabetically or in categorized order. To make things clearer, we follow the categorized approach.

REMEMBER

Because many of these properties fall under the umbrella of database maintenance, you find much more detailed descriptions and step-by-step instructions throughout Book VIII, which is devoted to administration.

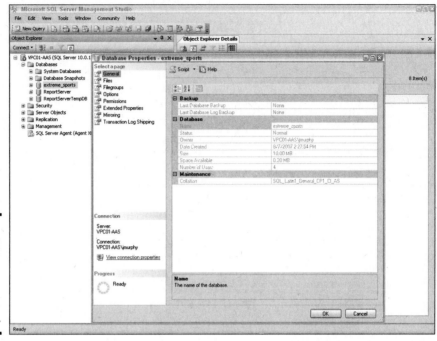

**Book II
Chapter 2**

**Care and Feeding
of Your Database**

Figure 2-1:
The General
properties
page in the
SQL Server
Manage-
ment Studio.

General

If you're interested in a high-level overview of your database, including its
size, backup status, and other key indicators, take a look at this important
properties page.

We explore each of the major categories found on this page. *Note:* Everything you see on the General properties page (refer to Figure 2-1) is read-
only. Think of it as a set of important metrics that tell you details about the
health of your database. Based on what you find here, you can then take
action on some of the other properties pages.

✦ **Backup:** As a database administrator, one of your most important
  tasks is to back up your vital information continually. This category of
  properties keeps you apprised of when these important jobs were most
  recently run. As you can see in Figure 2-1, the database administrator
  (yours truly) hasn't been doing his job!

✦ **Database:** Turn here to get insight into a collection of administrative
  metrics, including the overall size of the database, the number of users
  that have been created for it, and the amount of available space.

✦ **Maintenance:** This category contains only one property: the collation
  sequence used for this database. This setting guides SQL Server in

figuring how to properly manage and sort your information. You determine this property when creating the database. It's based on your expectations about the regional characteristics (for example, Western European, Asian, and so on) of your location and data.

Files

This crucial properties page, as shown in Figure 2-2, is where you physically lay out your information on disk. Additionally, this is where you determine whether full-text indexing will be available for this database. We describe full-text indexing in much more detail in Book III, Chapter 9. For now, think of full-text indexing as a series of internal structures and search optimizations that SQL Server offers you to make locating text-based information much easier. Full-text indexing is optional, which is why there is a check box on this page. Some administrators might not want to offer this capability because their specific applications aren't focused on large blocks of text, and consequently won't need this type of functionality.

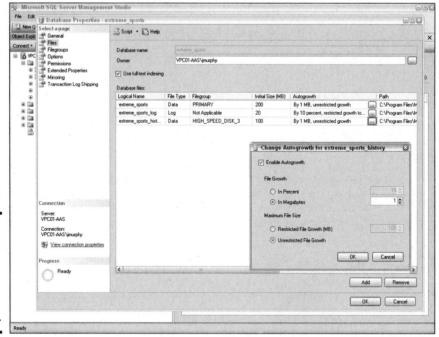

Figure 2-2:
The Files properties page in the SQL Server Management Studio.

Options available to you on this page include

✦ **Database Ownership:** In SQL Server, each database can be owned by different logins, which can be a person, an application, or even a Windows Group. Here's where you make that determination.

✦ **Database File Information:** For database administrators reading this book, we can guarantee that you'll spend a lot of time focusing on these settings. In looking at Figure 2-2, you might notice that information is distributed between two file groups. We discuss the purpose of file groups in a moment, but other important settings found here include file names, locations, and the initial size for your data and log files.

✦ **Autogrowth Settings:** Unless you're publishing a read-only database, or one that will never experience expansion, you want to pay particular attention to the Autogrowth settings on this properties page. As shown in Figure 2-2, you have fine control over exactly how your files grow, as well as whether their growth is unrestricted.

Filegroups

One way to squeeze additional performance and data security from your SQL Server technology is to distribute information onto multiple disk drives. With today's fast processors and highly tuned disk controllers, this division of labor often pays handsomely. You can use filegroups to organize your data and log files logically. For example, as shown in Figure 2-3, we created a new filegroup named HIGH_SPEED_DISK_3. As you might guess from the clever name, we intend to use this file group to store information on a brand-new, shiny, high-speed disk.

If you look back at Figure 2-2, you see that we took advantage of this new file group when creating an additional file that stores historical information.

Options

If you like to tinker with your database engine, this is the page for you. You find more than two dozen parameters, each of which can have a significant impact on SQL Server's performance and behavior. Many of these parameters are itemized in the previous chapter. For now, look at each major group of categories. Take a moment to examine Figure 2-4 to see where each of these categories fits in the overall scheme of things.

You begin your options odyssey by controlling the collation model for this database. With choices ranging from Albanian through Vietnamese, you're sure to find the right collation setting to meet your needs.

With that important determination out of the way, your next decision relates to the recovery model that you want SQL Server to follow. For most sites, the Full model is the right choice. Next, select the compatibility level that you wish SQL Server to follow. For most sites, chances are you simply want to be compatible with the most recent version of the product.

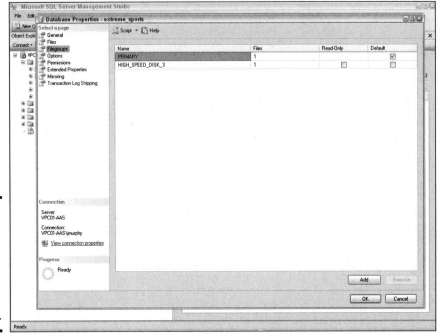

Figure 2-3:
The
Filegroups
properties
page in the
SQL Server
Manage-
ment Studio.

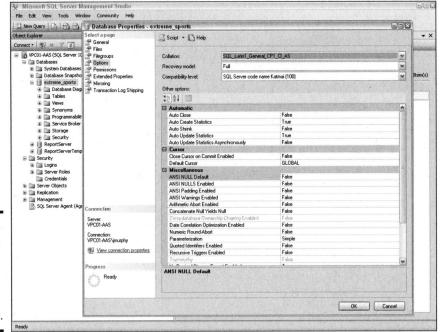

Figure 2-4:
The Options
properties
page in the
SQL Server
Manage-
ment Studio.

Here are the major categories in the Other Options portion of this page:

✦ **Automatic:** This category hosts a collection of settings that helps the SQL Server Optimizer do a better job, and efficiently manages disk space.

✦ **Cursor:** Here's where you can instruct SQL Server on what type of cursor you want to be the default, as well as what should happen to your cursor when a COMMIT operation is executed.

✦ **Miscellaneous:** Here you find a collection of properties that don't fit anywhere else. Ranging from required ANSI behavior to arithmetic configuration to trigger management, there's something for everyone in this category.

✦ **Recovery:** SQL Server gives you the option to configure its recovery mode. However, unless you have a good reason, it's probably a better idea to leave this setting alone.

✦ **State:** A few properties that affect how others might access your database.

**Book II
Chapter 2**

Care and Feeding of Your Database

Permissions

Book VIII, Chapter 3 is devoted to the important topic of how to secure your SQL Server database. At this point, our main goal is to show you the power and flexibility at your disposal when configuring your security settings. For example, Figure 2-5 shows a small sample of the number of explicit permissions that you can set, in this case for a guest user.

These settings are meaningful in the context of the database itself. You can also set additional security properties at the table, view, procedure, or other object level.

Security and permissions is one area where trial-and-error is your friend, as long as you plan and do it right. For example, before implementing a full security scheme, why not create a sample database (including some tables, realistic data, and users) and then conduct some security experiments? This hands-on experience will be much more valuable to you than attempting to translate what you read on a printed page into your organization's reality.

Extended properties

To help database administrators and developers in their ongoing efforts to build and maintain high-quality information systems, SQL Server offers the ability to create your own customized properties. For example, you might want to keep track of the database schema's revision history. You could easily create an extended property that serves as a common repository for all database administrators to log any schema changes, along with the date and any relevant comments.

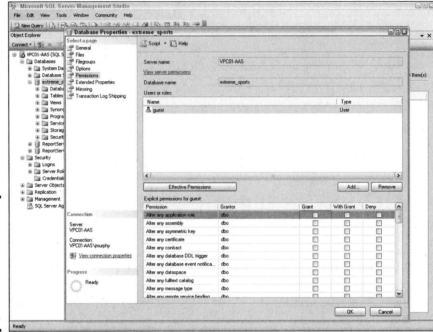

Figure 2-5:
The
Permissions
properties
page in the
SQL Server
Manage-
ment Studio.

Mirroring

It's never a good idea to put all of your eggs (or data) in one basket. SQL
Server offers mirroring as a way to increase data availability while protecting
your information. Briefly, *mirroring* entails either the database server or
operating system making more than one copy of your data and placing this
data on different disk drives.

Book VII, Chapter 4 explores mirroring and its effect on data security and
performance.

Transaction log shipping

We close out the database parameters section with a collection of variables
that helps you implement a redundant database strategy. Log shipping is a
superb way of keeping information in sync across a widely distributed network of computers. The result is greater system availability, better flexibility,
higher performance, stronger data protection, and enhanced disaster protection. Figure 2-6 shows a sampling of the settings at your disposal when
tuning your transaction log backup settings.

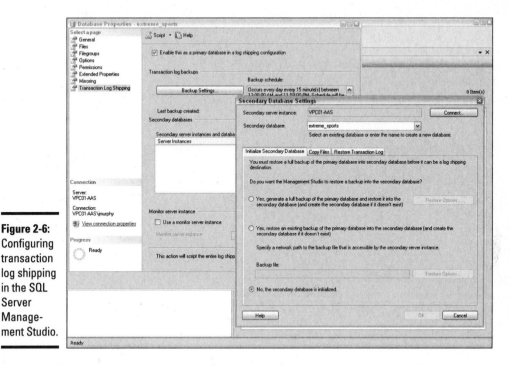

Book II
Chapter 2

Care and Feeding
of Your Database

Figure 2-6:
Configuring
transaction
log shipping
in the SQL
Server
Manage-
ment Studio.

Deleting a Database

When the time comes to say goodbye to a database, all you need to do is

1. **Launch the SQL Server Management Studio.**

2. **Connect to the appropriate SQL Server instance.**

3. **Expand the connection's entry in the Object Explorer view.**

4. **Expand the Databases folder.**

5. **Right-click the database that you want to remove and choose Delete.**

Renaming and dropping databases can be hazardous to your applications'
health. It's a good idea to create a backup before making changes of this
magnitude. The sanity you save may be your own.

If your database employs mirroring, log shipping, replication, and so on,
you will need to remove these settings prior to successfully dropping your
database.

Chapter 3: Data Types and How to Use Them

In This Chapter

✔ Understanding major data types

✔ Choosing the right data type for the job

✔ Getting to know SQL Server's expanded data storage options

✔ Creating your own data types

✔ Setting data types on new or existing columns

SQL Server provides you with many options when it comes to creating and storing information. In this chapter, you get a good picture of all these choices. To begin, we explore each of the major data types along with any related sub-types. As part of reviewing all these data types, you find out how to determine the right data type for the job.

Even if you're already familiar with most major data types, you'll be pleasantly surprised to learn how many new classes of information can be stored and tracked in SQL Server. We spend the subsequent part of the chapter looking at some of these new data types and taking advantage of them to build more productive database applications. After that, you discover that you can even define your own data types if you're so inclined. Finally, we show you how to use the SQL Server Management Studio and the SQLCMD utility to set data types on new or existing columns.

Traditional Data Types

If you have any experience with relational databases, you probably already know and love this first batch of data types. Many of them have been used to store information for decades, and more than 2 dozen are now at your disposal. To help you understand these types better, it's a good idea to group them into several major classifications, which is what we show you in this section.

Before we get started, first look at how you can get a full picture of all the data types at your disposal. Again, we turn to the trusty SQL Server Management Studio to help.

1. **Launch the SQL Server Management Studio.**

2. **Connect to the appropriate SQL Server instance.**

3. **Expand the connection's entry in the Object Explorer view.**

4. **Expand the Databases folder.**

5. **Open the folder entry for your database.**

6. **Expand the Programmability folder.**

7. **Expand the Types folder.**

You see a list of all the data types at your disposal. To begin, you can see all the *system data types.* In other words, these are the data types that ship with SQL Server, organized into the following folders:

✦ **Exact Numerics**

✦ **Approximate Numerics**

✦ **Date and Time**

✦ **Character Strings**

✦ **Unicode Character Strings**

✦ **Binary Strings**

✦ **Other Data Types**

A collection of other folders is here as well. These folders hold information about data types that you, the SQL Server administrator, can define, along with information about XML schema stored in your database.

Figure 3-1 shows how system data types appear in the SQL Server Management Studio.

Each database is able to have its own set of unique data types. This is because you can create types that are localized to a given database.

For the balance of this chapter, we discuss each of these data types and show you how to create data types that serve your needs.

If you're ever unsure about what you can store in a data type, open the folder as described previously and place your mouse pointer over the data type. SQL Server will then tell you, via a ToolTip, how you can use that data type.

Figure 3-2 shows an example of this helpful advice.

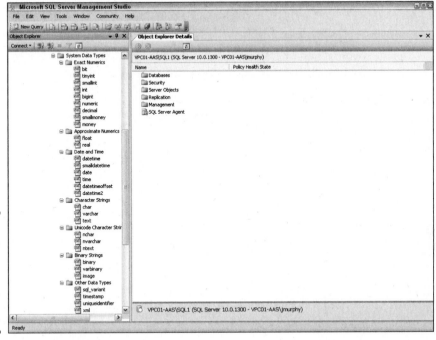

Figure 3-1:
System data types, as seen in the SQL Server Management Studio.

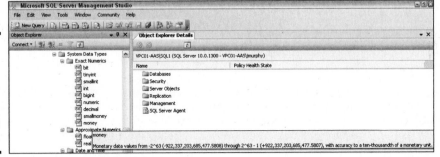

Figure 3-2:
The SQL Server Management Studio guidance on a data type.

Numeric data types

If you can represent your information with a number, these are probably the right data types to store it. However, if math wasn't your favorite subject during school, don't worry, because we show you how to select the appropriate numeric data type to solve your information storage challenge.

INTEGER types

As a database designer, the INTEGER family of data types gives you a great deal of flexibility when setting up a column. Integers hold *whole* (in other words, non-fractional) numbers. Table 3-1 highlights the range and storage requirements of each member of this family.

Table 3-1	Integer Types, Ranges, and Storage Requirements		
Type	*Range*	*Storage*	*Power of 2 equivalent*
bigint	−9,223,372,036,854,775,808 to 9,223,372,036,854,775,807	8 bytes	-2^{63} through $2^{63}-1$
int	−2,147,483,648 to 2,147,483,647	4 bytes	-2^{31} through $2^{31}-1$
smallint	−32,768 to 32,767	2 bytes	-2^{15} through $2^{15}-1$
tinyint	0 to 255	1 byte	2^{8}

Deciding on the appropriate INTEGER type is actually quite simple. All you need to do is figure what range of data is likely to be stored in that column, and then simply select the appropriate INTEGER type. Take a look at the following segment of SQL code:

```
CREATE TABLE INT_EXAMPLE
(
    AGE TINYINT,
    NUMBER_OF_EMPLOYEES SMALLINT,
    CITY_POPULATION INT,
    . . .
)
```

In this example, we chose TINYINT for AGE because it's unlikely to find someone older than 255 years. Comparatively, the NUMBER_OF_EMPLOYEES could be in the tens of thousands, so we chose SMALLINT, whereas the population of a city could be anywhere up to 2 billion (although we wouldn't want to live in that city!).

BIT

This data type is actually a specialized kind of integer. You use it to store 0, 1, or NULL. Another way to think of it is as a great candidate to hold values that could be either true or false. For example, in the following SQL statement, we use BIT to help keep track of whether a customer is up-to-date on her payments:

```
CREATE TABLE BIT_EXAMPLE
(
    PAYMENTS_CURRENT BIT,
    . . .
)
```

When we insert or modify a row in this table and request a value of 'TRUE', SQL Server converts it to a 1. On the other hand, a value of 'FALSE' is represented with a 0.

In this first example, we insert a value of 1 ('TRUE') into the table:

```
INSERT INTO BIT_EXAMPLE VALUES ('TRUE')
```

Next, we insert a value of 0 ('FALSE'):

```
INSERT INTO BIT_EXAMPLE VALUES (0)
```

When using TRUE or FALSE in SQL statements, remember to enclose the value with single quotes.

DECIMAL types

In this section, we provide some of the more esoteric types of numeric data. Each of the following data types can store decimal-based information.

DECIMAL and NUMERIC

Choose either of these data types when you're sure about the precision and scale of the information you want to track. For example, say you want to store numeric information in your database, and you know that there will be eight digits, with three to the right of the decimal. Here is how you define your column:

```
CREATE TABLE DECIMAL_EXAMPLE
(
    EXCHANGE_RATE DECIMAL(8,3),
    . . .
)
```

Precision and *scale* are the terms used to describe the overall size of these numbers along with the number of digits to the right of the decimal. In this example, the precision is eight, and the scale is three. SQL Server's default precision is 18, with a maximum of 38.

If you try to insert a value that exceeds the column's capacity, SQL Server dutifully reports an error:

```
Msg 8115, Level 16, State 8, Line 1
Arithmetic overflow error converting numeric to data type numeric.
The statement has been terminated.
```

FLOAT and REAL

In the previous section, you see how the DECIMAL and NUMERIC data types can be used when you know the exact size of the numbers stored in your database. However, you don't always know this detail, which brings us to these next two data types.

FLOAT and REAL are useful when you're not exactly sure how large (or small) a number is that you want to track, but you do know that you need a lot of flexibility. A helpful way to think of FLOAT is as a database representation of scientific notation. SQL Server gives you tremendous latitude when storing information in a column defined as FLOAT or REAL. ***Note:*** REAL is simply a synonym for FLOAT(24), which means 24 available bits of precision to store the mantissa in scientific notation.

Table 3-2 summarizes the range of data that you can store by using either of these two data types.

Table 3-2		FLOAT and REAL Storage Details			
Type	*n*	*Precision*	*Storage Size*	*Minimum*	*Maximum*
float[(n)]	1–24	7 digits	4 bytes	−1.79E + 308	1.79E + 308
	25–53	15 digits	8 bytes	−1.79E + 308	1.79E + 308
real		7 digits	4 bytes	−3.40E + 38	3.40E + 38

MONEY and SMALLMONEY

Designed to keep track of everyone's favorite commodity, these two data types differ only in the scale of information that they contract and the amount of data storage required.

For the MONEY data type, you can store a range of data between −922,337,203,685,477.5808 and 922,337,203,685,477.5807. SQL Server requires 8 bytes to keep track of this gargantuan range of data. For those of you with a little less cash in your pockets, you can take advantage of the SMALLMONEY data type. This allows you to track a range of information between −214,748.3648 214,748.3647, and uses four bytes.

Character data types

If your data contains any of the letters A through Z, or punctuation characters, these data types are just what the doctor ordered to store your information. We look at each of these in more detail. For those of you who are concerned about using SQL Server in support of multi-byte languages, such as Chinese or Japanese, we also explain how Unicode fits into this equation.

CHAR

If there were an award for most popular data type, CHAR would most likely be the winner. You typically use this data type when you know for sure that your character-based information is a fixed size, up to 8,000 characters in length. Of course, you run the risk of wasting storage space if most of the entries in a CHAR column are smaller than the specified size.

For example, the following snippet of SQL shows creating a CHAR field with a length of 30 bytes:

```
CREATE TABLE CHAR_EXAMPLE
(
    FIRST_NAME CHAR(30),
    . . .
)
```

**Book II
Chapter 3**

For each row, SQL Server stores 30 bytes of data for FIRST_NAME, regardless of whether all the bytes are used.

The multi-byte partner for CHAR is NCHAR, which stands for National Character. You use the NCHAR data type when you expect to store Unicode-based multi-byte data. NCHAR can store up to 4,000 bytes of information.

**Data Types and
How to Use Them**

VARCHAR

As you might expect, things are rarely so cut and dried in the real world. In many cases, you simply can't assume that each record in the table will have exactly the same length for a character-based column. Fortunately, SQL Server allows you to hedge your bet through the VARCHAR data type.

You use this data type when you cannot be certain of the size of each of the entries for a given column, and you want to conserve disk space. Of course, with disk space becoming ever cheaper, this may not be a concern. However, VARCHAR still adds value even if disk space is free, so we look at it in more detail.

Using the previous example, suppose that you aren't sure exactly how many bytes each FIRST_NAME requires. In this case, you could specify that the column be created with a variable length of up to 30 bytes:

```
CREATE TABLE VARCHAR_EXAMPLE
(
    FIRST_NAME VARCHAR(30),
    . . .
)
```

For any entries that are smaller than 30 bytes, SQL Server uses only the required amount of storage. Of course, if an entry is greater than 30 bytes, SQL Server truncates it beyond the 30th byte. To get around that possibility, make the column as big as you think its data could ever be or simply use the MAX directive when creating the table:

```
CREATE TABLE VARCHAR_EXAMPLE
(
    FIRST_NAME VARCHAR(MAX),
    . . .
)
```

By specifying MAX, you tell SQL Server that it should allow as much storage as possible for a given entry for this column. In fact, this amount is enormous, far beyond what you're ever likely to use.

If you expect a need to store multi-byte, variable-length character information, use the NVARCHAR data type.

Use MAX when you expect that one or more entries for a given VARCHAR column might exceed 8,000 bytes (or 4,000 bytes if the column is defined as NVARCHAR).

TEXT

Prior to SQL Server 2008, you used this data type to store character-based information that exceeded the capacity of the CHAR or VARCHAR data types. However, Microsoft has signaled that this data type isn't going to be supported in the future, so don't plan to use it for any new database applications. Instead, consider using the VARCHAR, NVARCHAR, or VARBINARY data types, making sure to specify the MAX size so that SQL Server can digest all the information you send its way.

Date and time data types

In addition to all their well-known talents, relational databases (such as SQL Server) do an outstanding job storing, maintaining, and searching on date and time-based information.

When you want to track a specific point in time (potentially, down to the millisecond), you use either the DATETIME or the SMALLDATETIME data type, depending on the accuracy that you need. The range of information you want to store also helps determine the appropriate data type.

SMALLDATETIME

This data type allows you to store information from January 1, 1900, through June 6, 2079, and is accurate to one minute. SQL Server uses two 2-byte integers to store this information.

DATETIME

This data type has a much larger range of storage and is much more accurate. To begin, it allows you to track dates from January 1, 1753, through December 31, 9999. It's accurate to within $3\frac{1}{3}$ milliseconds. However, this range and accuracy comes at a price because SQL Server requires twice the storage than it does for the SMALLDATETIME type.

DATETIME2

This is an instant of a DATETIME, including the year, month, day, hour, minute, second, and fraction of a second.

DATETIMEOFFSET

This is akin to the DATETIME2 type, except this type includes the time zone, and stores the information relative to Greenwich Mean Time (UTC).

DATE

If you want to store just the year, date, and month for a date range between January 1, 1 A.D., and December 31, 9999, this is the type for you.

TIME

This data type is used to store an instant of time, including its hour, minute, second, and fraction of a second, using a 24-hour clock.

The SMALLDATETIME data type is the right choice for most business-oriented applications, unless you need a very wide range of dates, extreme accuracy, or both.

Binary data types

If you like your database to store pictures, music, sounds, or other types of non-structured information (including some very large chunks of data), one of SQL Server's binary data types is the right choice.

BINARY

You use this data type when you're confident that you know the size of the binary information that you want to store in a given column in SQL Server. The maximum amount that you can store in this type of column is 8,000 bytes.

VARBINARY

Comparatively, you might not know how large the binary information is that you want to track. In this case, try using this data type, which allows you to store binary information of up to 8,000 bytes.

After looking at the capacity of both the BINARY and VARBINARY data types, you're forgiven for wondering whether you can store realistic binary information in your database. After all, music files and pictures are much larger than 8,000 bytes. Not to worry because you can specify a much larger size for the VARBINARY data type by providing the MAX instruction when creating your table.

For example, the following SQL statement creates a table to hold various types of binary information:

```
CREATE TABLE BINARY_EXAMPLE
(
    FIXED_BINARY BINARY,
    VARIABLE_BINARY VARBINARY,
    VIDEO VARBINARY(MAX),
    MUSIC VARBINARY(MAX)
)
```

In this example, the first column holds a batch of binary data that can be no longer than 8,000 bytes. The second column also holds binary information, but because we aren't sure of the exact size of this data, we elected to use VARBINARY. The final two columns are designed to hold much larger sets of binary information. In fact, you can safely store a little more than 2 gigabytes of data in a specific column for each row (depending on disk storage availability, of course).

IMAGE

This data type, which in spite of its name is not limited to images, is not going to be present in future versions of SQL Server. Therefore, if you need to store binary data of this type, use the VARBINARY data type. For most images, you probably want to provide the MAX directive when defining your VARBINARY column.

Other data types

Here, we get into more-esoteric types of information. SQL Server is equally adept at storing this type of data.

UNIQUEIDENTIFIER

In many data storage solutions, situations occur where it's necessary to guarantee uniqueness of a specific value. It's not enough to guarantee that the value is the only one of its kind on a single database; sometimes you even need to make sure that the value is unique across different systems. Fortunately, you can take advantage of the UNIQUEIDENTIFIER data type to guarantee a distinct value for a given row. You can even assign this data type to a variable in a program.

SQL Server relies on this data type to help guarantee the integrity of important internal operations, such as merge and transactional replication. As you can imagine, these values can be quite large because they must be distinct. For example, here's what one of these unique identifiers looks like:

```
9A1237DB-01AA-B238-FF3C-3AD9B93A11DC
```

Book II
Chapter 3

In terms of generating such a value, take advantage of the NEWID function, and SQL Server will create a unique identifier value for you. For example, look at the following sequence of SQL. A new table is defined, and then two rows are inserted into the table by using this helpful function:

```
CREATE TABLE UNIQUE_ID_DEMO
(
    UNIQUE_ID UNIQUEIDENTIFIER
)
INSERT INTO UNIQUE_ID_DEMO VALUES (NEWID())
INSERT INTO UNIQUE_ID_DEMO VALUES (NEWID())
```

Data Types and
How to Use Them

Here's what SQL Server inserted to the table:

```
F75AA7FD-6759-4037-B6D8-3096842D3359
0FCDD613-071A-47BD-83C0-7D266F57F910
```

TIMESTAMP

SQL Server maintains an internal counter that is updated every time a row is inserted or updated into a table. Known as a TIMESTAMP data type (which is synonymous with the ROWVERSION data type), this counter comes into play whenever there is a column defined with that data type for a given table.

This can be very helpful when trying to determine whether any columns in a given row have been changed. For example, suppose that you create a table and define one of the columns as TIMESTAMP. From this point, SQL Server automatically maintains values in that column. Any time a given row is either inserted or updated, the database engine automatically changes the TIMESTAMP column's value for that row. You can then keep track of this value, and if it changes, you can be sure that one or more columns in that row have also changed.

Enhanced Data Types

SQL Server 2008 offers many new types of data storage options. Although you might not be familiar with these, they can be very helpful when constructing a database-driven application. We look at each of them in more detail.

XML

You've been able to use SQL Server to hold this type of data for some time. However, it's only in the recent past that the native database capabilities have reached the maturity necessary to take full advantage of this powerful method of storing information. Providing an in-depth explanation of XML is beyond the scope of this book; however, it's a good idea to get some understanding of what you can accomplish with this exciting technology.

Specified in the late 1990s, XML has mushroomed into a very popular method for storing and working with information. It provides a structured, text-based approach to organizing data. Unlike many earlier file formats and data structures that were often proprietary, closed, and required special software, you can use any text editor or word processor to create and edit XML information. Today, many modern applications and tools support XML as well, including packages like Microsoft Office and, of course, SQL Server.

XML advantages

When compared with alternative means of representing and interchanging information, XML offers some compelling benefits, including:

✦ **Standards-based:** The XML standard was created and is maintained under the auspices of the Worldwide Web Consortium (W3C). Additionally, numerous standards bodies have in turn created their own XML-derived standards from this underlying specification.

✦ **Multilanguage:** Today, it's no longer acceptable for any commercial application to be hard-coded for only one language. Global organizations need to track information regardless of its native language. XML supports *Unicode,* meaning it can encode information in any language.

✦ **Plain text storage:** By storing its information in open, plain text files, rather than locking it inside proprietary formats, XML makes it easy for you to apply a broad range of technologies to work with your data.

✦ **Robust and easily enforced syntax:** Don't be fooled by XML's openness and ease of use; there are very specific syntax and formatting rules to which any XML-based information must adhere. These rules are what make it possible for XML data to interoperate so easily.

✦ **Vendor and platform independence:** When choosing a technology standard, the last thing most customers want is to have that standard tampered with by vendors who might not have their best interests at heart. Because of this, XML is particularly well suited in protecting you from the vagaries and machinations of hardware and software vendors.

A few relatively minor drawbacks to XML do exist. Chiefly, they revolve around the somewhat cumbersome nature of supporting non-text information (such as video, music, and other binary data) within an XML document. In addition, some believe that the parsing and manipulation of XML data is too expensive and leads to degraded performance. Finally, an XML document with many levels of nested data can be very hard for a person to read and understand.

XML structure

What does XML look like? Take a peek at the following small example of a purchase order:

```xml
<?xml version="1.0" encoding="UTF-8"?>
<PO Identifier="RR89291QQZ" date_generated="2006-30-Dec"
    application="Optimize v4.3">
  <Customer>
     <Name>Soze Imports</Name>
     <Identifier>21109332</Identifier>
     <reg:Instructions xmlns:reg="http://www.samplenamespace.com/importexport">
        <reg:Restrictions>Not subject to export control</reg:Restrictions>
        <reg:Duties>Not subject to duties</reg:Duties>
     </reg:Instructions>
  </Customer>
  <Creator>Michael McManus</Creator>
  <Product quantity="1" price="9.99">GG2911</Product>
  <Product quantity="6" price="54.94">TK3020</Product>
  <ship:Shipment xmlns:ship="http://www.samplenamespace.com/shipping">
     <ship:ShipDate>6/10/2007</ship:ShipDate>
     <ship:Instructions>Contact Mr. Hockney in receiving</ship:Instructions>
     <ship:Instructions>Fax bill to Mr. Kobayashi</ship:Instructions>
  </ship:Shipment>
</PO>
```

Confused? Don't be. The best way to make sense of an XML document is to look at it line by line, starting here:

```xml
<?xml version="1.0" encoding="UTF-8"?>
```

This first line is the *XML declaration,* which includes details about the XML version as well as any language encoding. In this case, it supports version 1.0 of the XML standard, and it's encoded with Unicode.

```xml
<PO Identifier="RR89291QQZ" date_generated="2006-30-Dec"
 application="Optimize v4.3">
 ...
</PO>
```

We said to look at XML on a line-by-line basis, yet we show you the second and very last lines. The reason for this is that the entire document is wrapped by the <PO...> and </PO> tags, known as the *start tag* and *end tag,* respectively. Everything between those two items refers to the purchase order, identified by PO in this case. Tags like this represent an *element.* You can nest elements as well; in fact, most XML data consists of elements deeply nested within higher-level elements. In this case, the PO element is the highest-level element. Everything that you see between the start tag and end tag is *content.*

The Identifier, date_generated, and application entries on the line above are *attributes,* which are additional details about an element. For example, the purchase order's date_generated attribute is set to December 30, 2006. All attributes must be enclosed in either single or double quotes.

Continuing, you see a nested element — Customer — whose start tag is <Customer> and end tag is </Customer>. This element contains two nested elements — Name and Identifier.

```
<Customer>
   <Name>Soze Imports</Name>
   <Identifier>21109332</Identifier>
   <reg:Instructions xmlns:reg="http://www.samplenamespace.com/importexport">
      <reg:Restrictions>Not subject to export control</reg:Restrictions>
      <reg:Duties>Not subject to duties</reg:Duties>
   </reg:Instructions>
</Customer>
```

It also contains an Instructions nested element. This element and those nested within it appear to be a little confusing, though. What's going on? Looking at the XML document listed earlier in the chapter, you might wonder how your computer can keep things straight when handling XML from different sources. For example, what happens if you receive purchase orders from two different organizations that use different element names and attributes that actually mean the same thing? Conversely, what happens if they use identical element names and attributes that mean different things?

This is where *namespaces* come to the rescue. Typically available for consultation and review via the Internet, they are assemblages of element type and attribute names that help establish order and clear confusion. By providing a solid point of reference, namespaces also assist when merging smaller subsets of XML documents.

In this case, the document includes a link to a namespace server:

```
<reg:Instructions xmlns:reg="http://www.samplenamespace.com/importexport">
```

By specifying this namespace server, we instruct any applications that might use this XML document that any elements or attributes prefixed with reg need to consult the namespace server for details about those data types. You'll see reference to a second namespace server a little later.

Here's an example of an element that has no nested elements:

<Creator>Michael McManus</Creator>

However, it's nested within the purchase order element.

You can see additional Product elements:

<Product quantity="1" price="9.99">GG2911</Product>
<Product quantity="6" price="54.94">TK3020</Product>

These elements have their own attributes: quantity and price.

Finally, the document contains a Shipment element that contains nested ShipDate and Instructions elements:

```
<ship:Shipment xmlns:ship="http://www.samplenamespace.com/shipping">
    <ship:ShipDate>6/10/2007</ship:ShipDate>
    <ship:Instructions>Contact Mr. Hockney in receiving</ship:Instructions>
    <ship:Instructions>Fax bill to Mr. Kobayashi</ship:Instructions>
</ship:Shipment>
```

To clear up confusion with the earlier reference to Instructions, there's a link to another namespace server:

```
<ship:Shipment xmlns:ship="http://www.samplenamespace.com/shipping">
```

That's it. You now know how to parse an XML document.

FILESTREAM

We told you about binary data types a little earlier in this chapter. If you've had much experience with this type of information, you might be a little uncomfortable storing it in a relational database because of performance, storage, or other concerns. However, you do probably want to leverage and benefit from the transactional capabilities of a database. SQL Server 2008 offers a new data type that helps address these concerns, while still giving you access to all the power of a relational database.

This new data type, known as FILESTREAM, allows you to place large blocks of binary information onto the file system. This file system can be placed on less expensive storage devices, yet it's still managed by SQL Server. You have all the database's transactional and other referential integrity capabilities at your disposal.

**Book II
Chapter 3**

**Data Types and
How to Use Them**

SQL_VARIANT

Sometimes, your data cannot make up its mind. In certain cases, information might be represented with numbers, and other times with letters. As another example, sometimes, one of the date-based data types represents date information; other times, a string represents it. This problem often arises when you're receiving externally generated information but need to place it into your own SQL Server database. You could perform all sorts of complex calculations and analysis to determine the appropriate data type, or you could take an easier way out. In this context, the easier way out is the SQL_VARIANT data type.

In a nutshell, one particular column defined as SQL_VARIANT can correctly store values of several data types, including INT, DECIMAL, CHAR, BINARY, and NCHAR. It's particularly useful when you're not 100 percent sure of the information that will be placed into your database. However, it isn't foolproof and can't store specific types of data such as XML, variable-length fields, and user-defined fields.

If possible, try to define your columns with the appropriate native data type or a specific user-defined data type. The SQL_VARIANT data type, although highly flexible, introduces complications that you probably don't want to manage unless absolutely necessary.

Spatial data

The past few years have witnessed the rise of a tremendous array of exciting, innovative applications that sport geography-based features. These include online mapping systems, Global Positioning System (GPS) applications, and other innovative solutions that incorporate details from the physical world.

To help support this new class of applications, SQL Server 2008 introduces enhanced data types specially focused on spatial information, thereby letting you manage location-based data. Although a deep dive in to their capabilities is beyond the scope of this book, we take a brief look at these new data types. Before beginning, it's important to understand that, at a high level, there are two ways to think of spatial data. You can think of a particular point on Earth from the perspective of a globe, using that point's latitude and longitude to identify the unique location. This method of spatial identification takes the curvature of the Earth into account. Another way to think of a location is as shown on a map, which doesn't factor in any curvature considerations.

GEOGRAPHY

You use this data type when the Earth's curvature is important to your application, such as when you need extreme accuracy or are calculating a long-distance path. To store this information effectively, you need to provide more location identifying details than you do with the GEOMETRY data type.

GEOMETRY

This data type suffices for most spatial applications. For example, suppose you want to calculate driving directions between two points. The curvature of the Earth isn't important in this calculation, so you can probably take advantage of the GEOMETRY data type. It allows you to track details about locations easily on a two-dimensional plane and doesn't require all the details necessary to populate a column that's assigned the GEOGRAPHY data type.

Creating Your Own Data Types

In the previous sections of this chapter, we show you quite a number of different data types. Some are quite simple and some are rather complex. However, if none of these types is an exact fit to solve your problem, you can create specialized data types via the SQL Server, user-defined type feature.

You can use the CREATE TYPE statement to define personalized alias data types. This essentially creates a synonym for the data type, which can be very useful when building your database.

For example, suppose your project has multiple database designers and that each of them is responsible for building some tables that will track addresses. Furthermore, imagine that you want to standardize all your address fields as variable length and character-based to hold up to 60 bytes (VARCHAR(60)).

You could rely on each designer to adhere to your request, but you're likely to be sorely disappointed. The odds are that each designer will implement his or her own interpretation of what an address should be. Some will choose fixed character fields, while others will use the VARCHAR type but at a different length than the 60 that you require.

Using the CREATE TYPE statement, here's how to enforce consistency for these fields:

```
CREATE TYPE ADDRESS FROM VARCHAR(60) NOT NULL
```

Now, your designers can use ADDRESS whenever they create a table that needs to track address information:

```
CREATE TABLE shipping_info
(
    ShippingID INT PRIMARY KEY NOT NULL,
    StreetAddress ADDRESS,
...
)
```

When SQL Server reports on your table, it will helpfully provide the ADDRESS alias as well as the fact that this translates to a VARCHAR(60).

As is usually the case with SQL Server, if direct entry of SQL isn't your bag, you have the freedom and flexibility to use the SQL Server Management Studio to do the dirty work. For example, here's how to create a new user-defined data type using this tool:

1. **Launch the SQL Server Management Studio.**

2. **Connect to the appropriate SQL Server instance.**

3. **Expand the connection's entry in the Object Explorer view.**

4. **Expand the Databases folder.**

5. **Open the folder entry for your database.**

6. **Expand the Programmability folder.**

7. **Expand the Types folder.**

8. **Right-click User-Defined Data Types and choose New User-Defined Data Type.**

    This opens a dialog box where you can provide key details about your new type. These details include:

    - *The schema that will house the data type*
    - *The data type's name*
    - *The underlying data type for this new type*
    - *The data type's numeric precision (if applicable)*
    - *Whether or not you want to allow NULL values*
    - *A default value binding for this data type*
    - *A rule binding for this data type*

9. **When you're finished, click OK to complete your work.**

Figure 3-3 shows the dialog box in more detail.

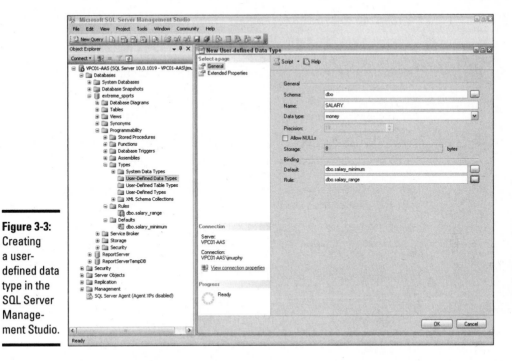

Figure 3-3:
Creating
a user-
defined data
type in the
SQL Server
Manage-
ment Studio.

You can even use SQL Server Management Studio to create your own user-defined table types. These are useful when creating stored procedures and other such programmable constructs. If you're curious about this capability, we cover it in more detail in Book IV, Chapter 2.

Assigning a Data Type

After you've identified the appropriate data type, you probably wonder how you actually request to use it. Here are two examples of choosing a data type when creating or modifying a table. If you're interested in this topic in more detail, peek at Chapter 4 of this mini-book.

First, the SQL Server Management Studio is a great tool that you can use to create and maintain your database and associated objects. Here's how to use it to create a new table and set a column's data type:

1. **Launch the SQL Server Management Studio.**

2. **Connect to the appropriate SQL Server instance.**

3. **Expand the connection's entry in the Object Explorer view.**

4. **Expand the Databases folder.**

5. **Right-click the Tables folder and choose New Table.**

That's all there is to it. You now see a dialog box that allows you to start entering details about your table. Here's how to select a data type:

1. **For each column in your table, enter a unique name.**

2. **Choose from one of the data types shown in the drop-down box.**

3. **When you've finished itemizing your new columns, save the table.**

Figure 3-4 displays the dialog box. The user-defined data type of SALARY uses the underlying MONEY data type.

Figure 3-4:
Selecting a data type in the SQL Server Management Studio.

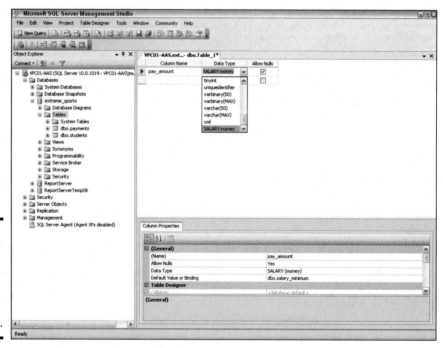

Second, if character-based utilities are more your style, you can use the SQLCMD utility to create and maintain your tables, setting data types in the process. Here's how to do that:

1. **Open a command prompt.**

Choose Start➪Run and enter **cmd**. Alternatively, you can choose Programs➪Accessories➪Command Prompt. When you see the friendly command prompt, it's time to launch SQLCMD.

2. **Enter** SQLCMD **at the command prompt, passing in the proper parameters.**

If you get in hot water, you can always ask SQLCMD for help:

```
SQLCMD /?
```

3. **Connect to the appropriate database.**

```
USE EXTREME_SPORTS
GO
```

In this case, you're connecting to the EXTREME_SPORTS database.

4. **Enter your SQL, ending your statement with GO.**

After you're in SQLCMD, you have an interactive command prompt at your disposal. Figure 3-5 shows an example of creating a table with many different data types via direct SQL entry in SQLCMD.

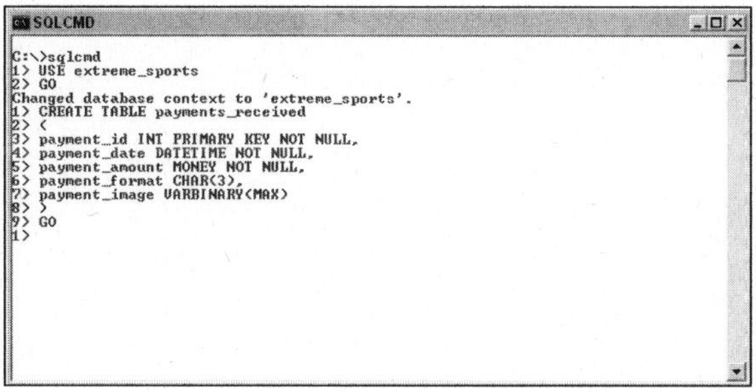

Book II
Chapter 3

Data Types and
How to Use Them

Figure 3-5:
Creating a
new table
by using the
SQLCMD
utility.

Chapter 4: Constructing New Tables

In This Chapter

- ✔ Building a new table
- ✔ Setting table properties
- ✔ Creating views
- ✔ Generating table maintenance scripts

*I*n a relational database, tables are at the center of the action. *Tables* store all your data, and serve as the primary interface to any applications or user interactions. In this chapter, you get a good idea about how to create your own set of tables. After you define how you want your tables to be structured, SQL Server offers many settings that you can use to tweak the behavior of these tables and their columns.

SQL Server does a great job of protecting your information. However, you can go the extra mile by taking advantage of a database concept known as *constraints.* In the next part of this chapter, we briefly show you how to take advantage of constraints to increase the integrity of your data. Views are another useful database capability, so we examine how to create them by using the SQL Server Management Studio.

Finally, because no one likes to hand enter code or reinvent the wheel, SQL Server offers helpful scripting capabilities that allow you to automate common database maintenance tasks, such as creating new tables. You'll see how to generate scripts quickly to help save time whenever you need to create or maintain a table.

Building a New Table

Before we get started, it's worth pointing out that, for this chapter, we spend most of the time in the SQL Server Management Studio. If you're inclined to use the character-based SQLCMD utility instead, it's no problem. We also show you how to use this utility to create new tables.

To begin, here is how you start the SQL Server Management Studio and prepare it to create new tables:

1. **Launch the SQL Server Management Studio.**

2. **Connect to the appropriate SQL Server instance.**

3. **Expand the connection's entry in the Object Explorer view.**

4. **Expand the Databases folder.**

5. **Right-click the Tables folder and choose New Table.**

That's all there is to it. You see a dialog box containing a grid that allows you to start entering details about your table. Figure 4-1 shows you how this empty dialog box appears.

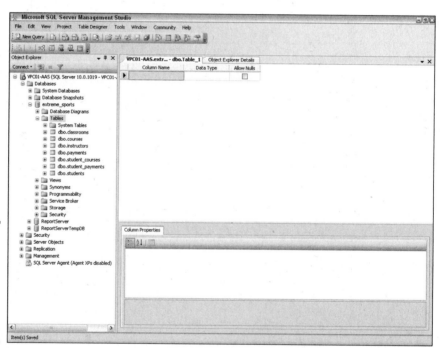

Figure 4-1:
Creating a new table in the SQL Server Management Studio.

After this dialog box is in front of you, here's what you do to create your table:

1. **For each column in your table, enter a unique name.**

After you've done this naming, the bottom half of the dialog box contains many configurable settings for this column, as shown in Figure 4-2. We spend a fair amount of time examining each of these settings.

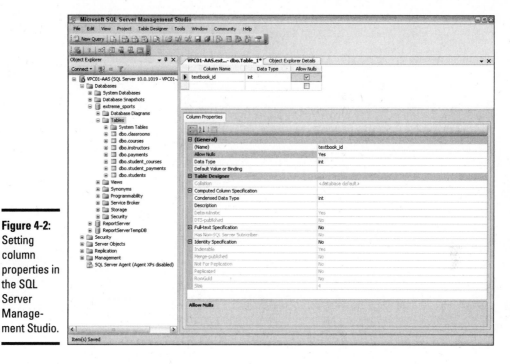

Book II
Chapter 4

Constructing
New Tables

Figure 4-2:
Setting
column
properties in
the SQL
Server
Manage-
ment Studio.

2. Pick from one of the data types shown in the drop-down box.

If you're curious about these data types, check out the previous chapter, where we describe them in much more detail. If you want only a brief explanation of each data type's purpose, see Table 4-1.

Table 4-1	SQL Server Data Types
Data Type	*Holds*
Bigint	Integers between –9.22 billion and 9.22 billion.
Binary	Fixed-length binary data, up to 8,000 bytes in size.
Bit	1 or 0 (also known as TRUE or FALSE).
Char	Fixed-length non-Unicode character data, up to 8,000 bytes in size.
Datetime	A timestamp between January 1, 1753, and December 31, 9999.
Decimal	Numbers with fixed precision and scale, ranging from –10^38 to 10^38.
Float	Floating-point data. Can have an enormous range.
Image	Variable-length binary data. Can be up to 2GB in size.

continued

Table 4-1 *(continued)*

Data Type	Holds
Int	Integers between –2.1 billion and 2.1 billion.
Money	Decimal numbers between –922 trillion and 922 trillion.
Nchar	Fixed-length Unicode character data, up to 4,000 bytes long.
Ntext	Variable-length Unicode data. Can be up to 2GB in size.
Numeric	Numbers with fixed precision and scale, ranging from –10^38 to 10^38.
Nvarchar	Variable-length Unicode character data. Can be very large if space permits.
Real	Floating-point data. Can have an enormous range.
Smalldatetime	A timestamp between January 1, 1900, and June 6, 2079.
Smallint	Integers between –32,768 and 32,768.
Smallmoney	Decimal numbers between –214 thousand and 214 thousand.
Text	Variable-length non-Unicode data. Can be up to 2GB in size.
Timestamp	Generates automatic, unique binary numbers.
Tinyint	Integers between 0 and 255.
Uniqueidentifier	Creates a system-wide unique identifier (GUID).
Varbinary	Variable-length binary data. Can be very large if space permits.
Varchar	Variable-length non-Unicode character data. Can be very large if space permits.
XML	Up to 2GB of XML-based data.

If all these data types aren't enough for you, you can create specialized data types via the SQL Server, user-defined type feature. If you want to examine this in detail, see Chapter 3 of this mini-book.

3. **Decide if you want the column to permit NULL values.**

   If so, mark the Allow Nulls check box.

4. **Set properties for this column.**

   You can sort this list either alphabetically or by category. Here's an alphabetical list of all the properties that you can set or view for a given column, along with what they mean and how to use them:

   • **Allow Nulls:** This determines whether a column can store NULL (that is, non-existent) values. Certain types of columns, such as primary keys, aren't permitted to hold NULL values.

   • **Collation:** Because SQL Server can store information from multiple languages, this setting (which can be set as defaults for the server, database, and column, respectively) determines what rules the database server follows when retrieving and sorting this data. For example, if you know that your database holds only Western European language-based data (for example, English, French, and so on), you might elect to have SQL Server use a specialized set of rules for those languages. Comparatively, if your database contains Asian language characters, you might choose Asian-focused guidelines. In most cases, you enable this setting at the server or database level.

- **Computed Column Specification:** SQL Server allows you to specify computational rules that are executed at runtime. For example, as shown in Figure 4-3, we've created three columns that track financial details about a class: `class_list_price`, `discount_percentage`, and `actual_price`. The `actual_price` field has no data type listed. That's because SQL Server takes the `class_list_price` field and subtracts the `discount_percentage` value from it, yielding the `actual_price` value. We provide this formula when defining the column. We also enable the `Is Persisted` setting, which instructs SQL Server to store these results in the database.

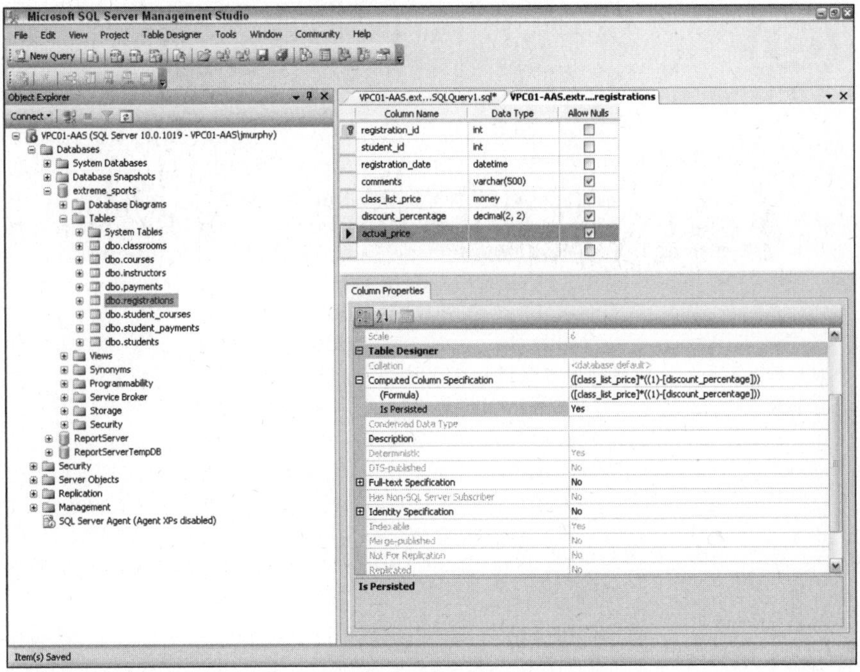

Figure 4-3: Creating a computed column in the SQL Server Management Studio.

- **Condensed Data Type:** This field uses the same format for choosing a field's data type as you find in the SQL CREATE TABLE statement.

- **Data Type:** This describes the format of the column and the information it can store. You can specify this value from the grid or from within this drop-down box. Previously, in this chapter, I describe all the data types at your disposal.

- **Default Value or Binding:** This handy feature can be used to fill a column with data even if the user never provides any information. For example, suppose that you're building a database to track new customers. As part of your workflow, you want to keep an eye on their credit limits. By using a default value of $100 for the customer's credit limit column, you're telling SQL Server to give all customers an initial credit in that amount. Of course, users can modify this value later, or even when creating the record; the default value setting simply ensures that something meaningful is placed in the table from the start.

- **Description:** As you might expect from the name, this is where you can provide details about this column, such as its purpose.

If you're building an application that will be maintained by others, don't be shy about describing your thinking when designing the database. It might make someone else's job much easier in the future.

- **Deterministic:** As you read previously, SQL Server allows you to create columns whose data is computed. In other words, rather than you explicitly entering data in this type of column, SQL Server fills it for you based on values returned from a function or from calculating results from other columns. The deterministic property refers to whether the function that populates this column returns the same result every time it's called with a given set of parameters (yes, it's deterministic). If the function returns differing results (even when it receives the same parameters), it isn't deterministic. For example, if a column is populated by calling the getdate() system function, it's non-deterministic because this function returns a different value every time it's called.

- **DTS-published:** Reports on whether this table has been published as part of the SQL Server Data Transformation Service functionality. If you're interested in this topic, we dedicate Book VIII, Chapter 4 to helping you understand your numerous SQL Server integration options.

- **Full-text Specification:** This specialized type of indexing supports a rich set of text-based queries. The previous chapter shows how to set up the underlying structures necessary for full-text indexing for your entire database. Additionally, Book III, Chapter 9 explains how to take advantage of this helpful feature. For now, take a look at Figure 4-4.

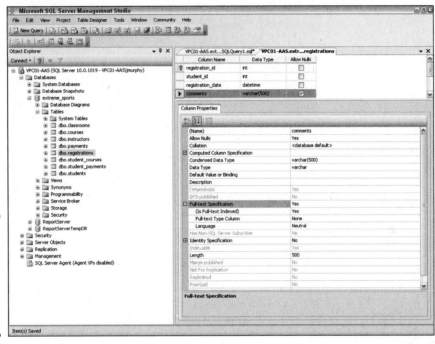

Figure 4-4:
Specifying a
full-text
index in the
SQL Server
Manage-
ment Studio.

We have created a full-text index on the `comments` field. This makes
it much easier for users and applications to conduct rich queries
that fully exploit SQL Server's full-text search capabilities.

If you want to create a full-text index on a particular column, you
need to permit this capability at the database level and define the
full-text catalog. To enable full-text indexing, right-click the database
name, choose Properties, and then Files. At the top of this page,
select the Use Full-text Indexing check box and click OK.

- **Has Non-SQL Server Subscriber:** If this table has been published
  (see more about replication later in this list), this field specifies
  whether a non-SQL Server database is a subscriber to its information.

- **Identity Specification:** Every table should have a unique primary
  key. This helps speed access to the database and protects your information's integrity. Sometimes, however, you're unable to locate a
  unique value within your data. This is where identity columns can
  come to your rescue. In a nutshell, SQL Server takes over the job of
  generating unique, integer-based values for you. This gives you all
  the benefits of a unique primary key without the headache of trying
  to come up with your own logic for creating its value. When you
  create an identity column (only one per table, please), you tell SQL

Server what you want its seed to be (that is, what the initial value is), and what its increment is (how many numbers are skipped between rows). Generally, unless you have some other numbering rules in mind, it's a good idea to start out with an identity seed of 1 and an identity increment of 1.

For example, Figure 4-5 shows that we asked SQL Server to enable the identity feature for the `registration_id` field. Furthermore, we requested that the initial value for this identifier be 1, and that each new row have this value incremented by 1.

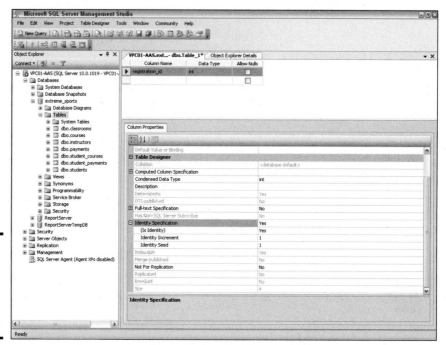

Figure 4-5:
Enabling
the identity
specifi-
cation for
a column.

- **Indexable:** Tells you whether this column is a candidate for indexing. *Remember:* Non-deterministic columns aren't capable of being indexed.

- **Length:** This is the number of bytes that you want the column to consume for its storage. This field only displays for columns that have data types where administrators can specify the number of bytes to use. For example, it displays for a column defined as type `CHAR`, but not for one defined as `INT`.

- **Merge-published:** SQL Server offers three types of replication: transactional, merge, and snapshot. This field indicates whether this table has been replicated by using the merge-published style, which is most commonly employed in Server-Client types of replication configurations.

- **Not for Replication:** States whether replication for this table is permitted. If you're interested in using replication to set up a high-performance, secure distributed computing environment, read Book VIII, Chapter 5.

- **Replicated:** States whether this table is replicated.

- **RowGUID:** This acronym stands for the row Global Unique Identifier. You use it when you need to guarantee a unique value across multiple SQL Server databases, even if they're running on different systems. To take advantage of this helpful feature, you set the data type for a column to UNIQUEIDENTIFIER. You then switch the RowGUID flag to Yes. SQL Server then generates these values and places them in your column. It also uses the NEWID() function as the default value for the column. *Note:* You can only have one RowGUID column per table.

- **Size:** This is the number of bytes of storage that the column will consume. This is a read-only field; you cannot edit it.

5. **When you're finished entering columns, click the disk icon to save your work.**

   If you haven't chosen a name for your table, SQL Server prompts you for one at this point. After that, your table is ready to use!

Additional Column Options

If the options in the previous section aren't enough to keep you busy, SQL Server offers even more choices. Simply right-click the column grid; the menu shown in Figure 4-6 appears.

These are all important options, so we take a brief look at each one.

✦ **Set Primary Key:** Relational databases like SQL Server rely heavily on primary keys. They use these internal structures to speed access to your information and protect its integrity. If you're interested in primary keys, take a look at the next chapter, where we delve in to this important concept in much more detail.

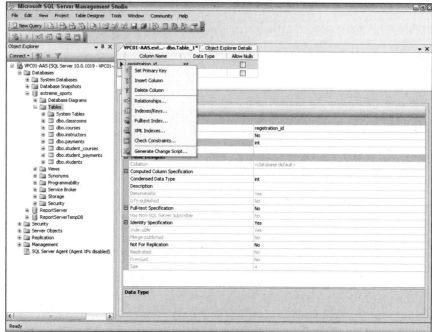

Figure 4-6:
The context-sensitive menu from the column grid in the SQL Server Management Studio.

For now, know that you can use this option to select columns as a primary key. ***Remember:*** You can have only one primary key per table, but primary keys can consist of more than one column. In Figure 4-7, we marked the `registration_id` field as the primary key. SQL Server places a handy key icon in that column's row in the grid. Additionally, we requested that this field have the identity property. Its starting value and incremental value are both set to 1.

✦ **Insert Column:** As you might surmise from its name, choose this option to create a new blank column.

✦ **Delete Column:** No mystery here. Select this option to remove an existing column.

✦ **Relationships:** Figure 4-8 shows the dialog box that's displayed when you choose the Relationships menu option. We associated the `student_id` column from this table to its source in the student table. This is a *foreign key relationship.* Relationships are so important that we dedicate an entire section to them. See Chapter 6 of this mini-book.

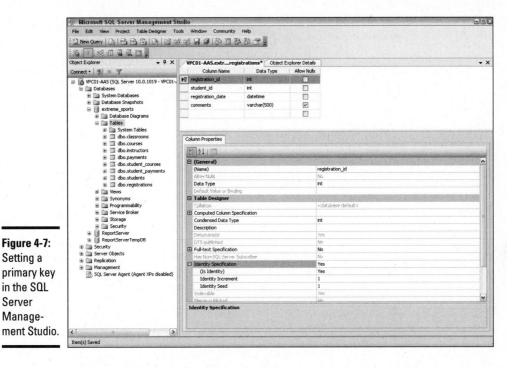

Figure 4-7:
Setting a primary key in the SQL Server Management Studio.

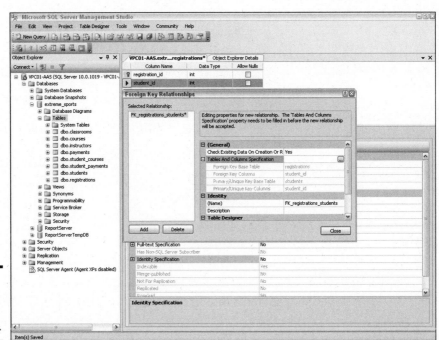

Figure 4-8:
Setting a foreign key relationship.

✦ **Indexes/Keys:** If your database application is running slowly, there's a good chance you don't have these important internal structures configured correctly. Book VII, Chapter 3 is dedicated to high-performance database access. In that chapter, you find all sorts of indexing tips and tricks. At this point, Figure 4-9 shows that we elected to create an index on the registration_date column, which makes both searching and sorting on that column much faster.

✦ **Fulltext Index:** Here's where you can create new full-text indexes, as well as set and view additional properties.

✦ **XML Indexes:** As discussed at length in Chapter 3 of this mini-book, XML is a new and exciting way of storing and interacting with information of any type. Figure 4-10 shows that we created a new column of type XML. We associated this purchase order data with an internal schema, although, we could have just as easily specified our own schema. Additionally, we instructed SQL Server to treat the information contained in this column as a full XML document, rather than a subset of a document. In Book III, Chapter 9 you discover much more about how to invoke queries against XML-based information.

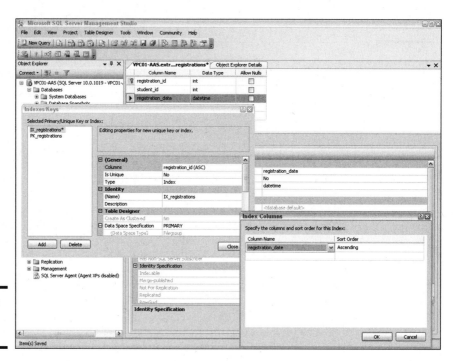

Figure 4-9:
Creating
an index.

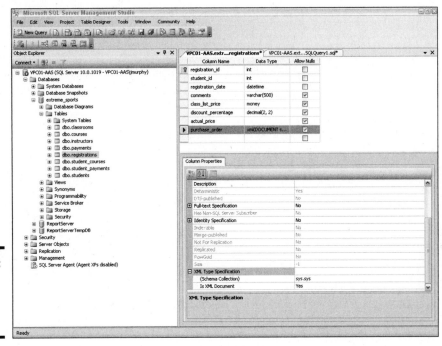

Figure 4-10:
Creating a
new XML-
based
column.

✦ **Check Constraints:** Think of this capability as a guardian for your data-base. Chapter 6 in this mini-book describes some of the very important uses of Check Constraints. For a specific example of a constraint in action, Figure 4-11 shows that we created a check constraint on the `discount_percentage` column.

In a nutshell, our organization's policy is that discounts range from a low of 0 percent to a high of 10 percent. By placing a check constraint on this column, we ensure that no deliberate or accidental violations of our policy occur.

✦ **Generate Change Script:** Even though everything you've seen so far is graphical in nature, SQL Server also allows you to generate scripts that you can run later to perform the same work you did via the graphic tool. Figure 4-12 shows a script that we generated performing all the work dis-cussed in this section.

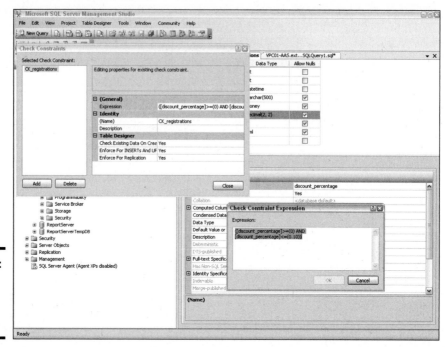

Figure 4-11:
Placing a
check
constraint
on a table.

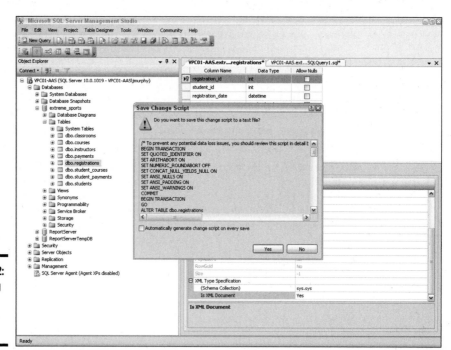

Figure 4-12:
Generating
a script of
table
changes.

Viewing Table Properties

It's only natural to be curious about your tables, whether they're new or have been working for five years. Finding these details is a cinch by using the SQL Server Management Studio. Here's how to discover more about your tables:

1. **Launch the SQL Server Management Studio.**

2. **Connect to the appropriate SQL Server instance.**

3. **Expand the connection's entry in the Object Explorer view.**

4. **Expand the Databases folder.**

5. **Expand the Tables folder, and then right-click the table you want to examine.**

6. **Choose the Properties option from the menu.**

The Table Properties dialog box opens, as shown in Figure 4-13.

**Book II
Chapter 4**

**Constructing
New Tables**

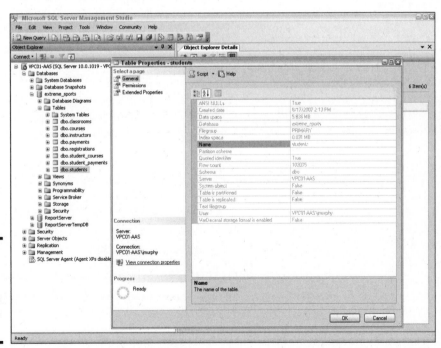

Figure 4-13:
The properties page for the students table.

Three pages of properties are at your disposal. The first page (shown in Figure 4-13) is a collection of general properties about the table. This is probably the page that you will consult most often when trying to understand the status of a given table.

The next page, Permissions, is where you track and set access rights to this table. The final page, Extended Properties, is where you define and maintain your customized properties, which you can enlist to better understand and manage your tables.

Creating Views

Although they're not tables per se, views have many of the same behavioral traits and features of tables. You can find much more about views in Book III, Chapter 8; however, it's worth a small detour at this point to see how to use the SQL Server Management Studio to create and inspect these helpful structures.

At its core, a view appears to be a virtual table that is made of one or more underlying tables. In fact, views can even include other views, functions, and synonyms. Database designers create views to help address many common challenges, such as

✦ Simplifying complex queries

✦ Working around security requirements

✦ Abstracting underlying database structures

✦ Reducing traffic between application server and database server, or the user and database server

After you create a view, it's available to be used by other users and applications. Sophisticated database-driven applications often utilize views heavily. Here's how to create a view and set its properties in the SQL Server Management Studio:

1. **Launch the SQL Server Management Studio.**

2. **Connect to the appropriate SQL Server instance.**

3. **Expand the connection's entry in the Object Explorer view.**

4. **Expand the Databases folder.**

5. **Right-click the Views folder and choose New View.**

You're presented with a dialog box, as shown in Figure 4-14.

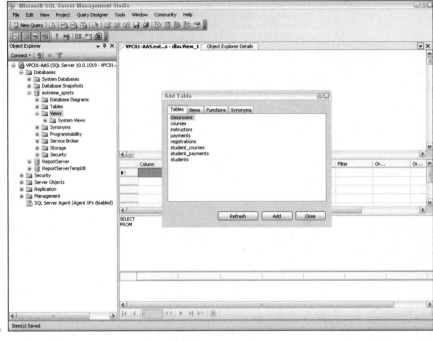

**Book II
Chapter 4**

**Constructing
New Tables**

Figure 4-14:
The preliminary dialog box for creating a view in the SQL Server Management Studio.

6. Select the tables that will make up your view.

You can hold down the Ctrl key to select multiple choices. In this case, we create a view that returns a list of all students and the courses for which they are registered. This makes use of the `students`, `courses`, and `student_courses` tables. *Note:* Previously, we created primary and foreign keys for each of these tables. In a moment, you see why this is so important.

7. When you've finished making your selection, click the Add button.

At this point, you can switch to the Views, Functions, or Synonyms tab to include those types of objects in your view.

8. When you've finished choosing the objects that will make up your view, click Close.

Figure 4-15 shows the three tables that make up the view, along with a column selector and the actual SQL statement.

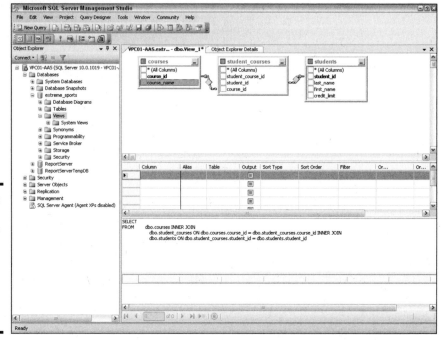

Figure 4-15:
The initial
relationship
diagram,
column
selector,
and SQL
statement
for a view.

The SQL statement shows that SQL Server has used the foreign key relationships set up earlier to figure how to join all these tables to create the view. Here's a great example of why it's wise to spend some time thinking about (and logically organizing) your underlying database structure. Over time, it pays off repeatedly.

All that remains is to check off the columns that we want to appear in the views output. Figure 4-16 shows the view just before we're ready to create it. We've successfully hidden all the internal identifying fields from the user; all they'll see is meaningful data. This is a great example of how a view can simplify complex underlying structures.

9. When you're satisfied with your work, click the disk icon to save it.

SQL Server prompts you for a name for your new view.

Try to use something meaningful when naming your view. It's also a good idea to prefix the view name with something that identifies it as a view. A capital V is always a good candidate.

SQL Server executes the SQL statement and constructs the view. After the view is created, you can easily examine it inside SQL Server Management Studio. All you need to do is expand its entry in the Views folder. Figure 4-17 shows the newly created view.

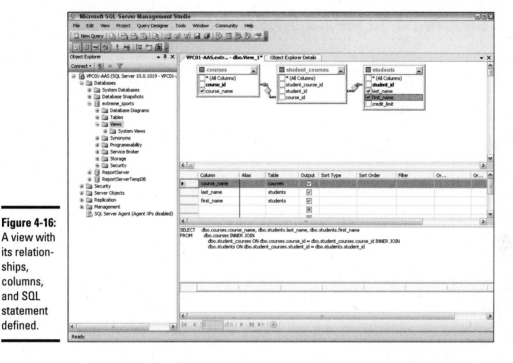

Figure 4-16:
A view with its relationships, columns, and SQL statement defined.

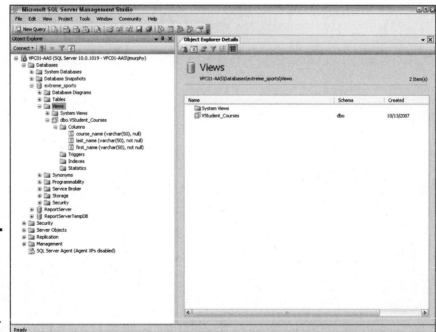

Figure 4-17:
Exploring a view in the SQL Server Management Studio.

Creating a Table via SQLCMD

If you're old school, and prefer to use character-based utilities rather than these newfangled graphical management environments like the SQL Server Management Studio, Microsoft hasn't forgotten you. The SQLCMD utility allows you to interactively enter SQL statements or run a predefined SQL script.

Here's how to use this utility to create a new table:

1. **Open a command prompt.**

Choose Start⇨Run and entering **cmd**. Alternatively, you can choose Programs⇨Accessories⇨Command Prompt. When you see the friendly command prompt, it's time to launch SQLCMD.

2. **Enter** SQLCMD **at the command prompt, passing in the proper parameters.**

This can get a bit confusing: SQLCMD is rather picky about the exact syntax that it deigns appropriate to run. This isn't surprising when you realize that it supports more than two dozen parameters. Table 4-2 highlights a small group of key parameters.

Table 4-2	Key SQLCMD Parameters
Parameter	*Purpose*
S	Specify the server that you want to connect to
U	Provide your username
P	Provide your password
D	Which database to use (if any)
I	The SQL script file (if any)

If you get in hot water, you can always ask SQLCMD for help:

```
SQLCMD /?
```

3. **Enter your table creation SQL, ending your statement with** GO.

After you're in SQLCMD, you have an interactive command prompt at your disposal.

If you can't live without your database scripts, consider using the SQL Server Management Studio as a friendly and powerful script development environment. You can use this tool to graphically set table and column options, and then generate a script that can be edited and modified to your heart's content.

Chapter 5: Looking After Your Tables

In This Chapter

- ✔ **Getting a list of your tables**
- ✔ **Determining dependencies**
- ✔ **Modifying a table**
- ✔ **Viewing table properties**
- ✔ **Deleting a table**

*W*ith your database and all related tables created, you might think it's time to sit back, relax, and put your feet up on the desk: Everything is on autopilot from here. Perhaps you're right; everything might be fine in your world. However, reality rarely plays out this way. There's a good chance that you'll periodically need to modify some tables. It's also likely that you'll need to delete a table from time to time. If nothing else, you'll at least want to get a comprehensive list of all the tables in your database.

This chapter is about taking good care of your tables after you've created them. To begin, we show you how to get a list of all the tables present in a database, view their data, and make sense of the details about each one. This is where you see how to determine whether there are any dependencies to consider. After you have a list of all your tables, you find out how to view and understand the characteristics of a given table. Next, we walk you through the often-necessary task of deleting a table. Finally, because you may be more of a command-line administrator, we show you how to achieve all these tasks by using the SQLCMD utility.

Getting a List of Your Tables

Here's how to use the SQL Server Management Studio to come up with this important list:

1. **Launch the SQL Server Management Studio.**
2. **Connect to the appropriate SQL Server instance.**

3. **Expand the connection's entry in the Object Explorer view.**

4. **Expand the Databases folder.**

5. **Expand the Tables folder.**

That's all there is to it. You have a full list of all the tables present in a database. Figure 5-1 shows this list, along with details about a specific table.

In reviewing Figure 5-1, you might notice that the entries are divided between system tables and user tables. As you might expect from the name, system tables are maintained by SQL Server for your benefit.

There should rarely, if ever, be a reason for you to modify a system table. Look, but don't touch!

Let's take a look at each of the folders underneath a given table. Figure 5-2 shows this list, along with details about a specific table.

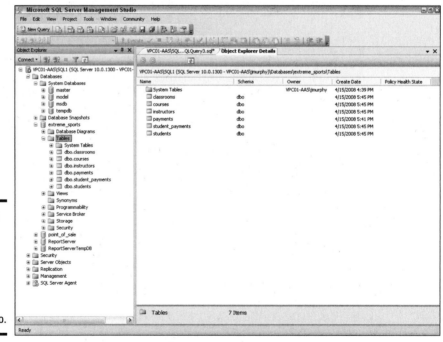

Figure 5-1:
A list of tables as shown in the SQL Server Management Studio.

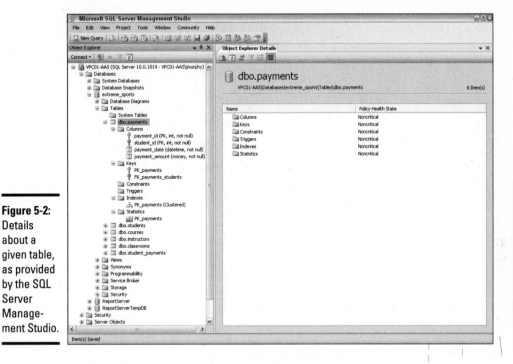

Book II
Chapter 5

Looking After
Your Tables

Figure 5-2:
Details
about a
given table,
as provided
by the SQL
Server
Manage-
ment Studio.

Each of these folders contains important details about the table, so we
spend a moment examining what they mean:

✦ **Columns:** A listing of all the columns that you've defined for this table,
along with their data type and size.

✦ **Keys:** The columns that have been defined either as primary or foreign
keys.

✦ **Constraints:** Limitations that you place on the table to protect its
integrity.

✦ **Triggers:** Specialized blocks of code that execute when a certain operation is undertaken on a table.

✦ **Indexes:** Database structures that help protect information while speeding access to it.

✦ **Statistics:** Metrics about the table to help the SQL Server Query
Optimizer do its job better.

Determining Dependencies

Dependencies refer to the interrelationships among objects in your database.
A foreign key relationship is the most commonly encountered dependency.

As your database grows in size, it can be difficult to keep track of exactly which objects depend on other objects. Compounding this confusion is that these interdependencies often cascade throughout the database.

Fortunately, SQL Server makes it easy for you to untangle this potentially complicated picture. Here's how to do it:

1. **Launch the SQL Server Management Studio.**

2. **Connect to the appropriate SQL Server instance.**

3. **Expand the connection's entry in the Object Explorer view.**

4. **Expand the Databases folder.**

5. **Expand the Tables folder.**

6. **Right-click the table you want to examine and choose View Dependencies.**

You see a new dialog box that allows you to view both objects that depend on this table and objects upon which this table depends. Figure 5-3 shows an example of what this looks like.

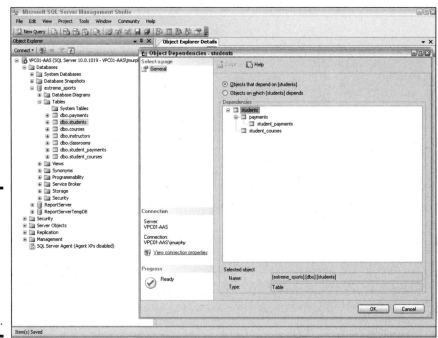

Figure 5-3: Dependencies for a given table displayed in the SQL Server Management Studio.

In this case, you can see that the `payments` and `student_courses` table depend on the `students` table. But wait, there's more! Expanding the `payments` table shows that the `student_payments` table also depends on the `students` table. Knowing these details helps you understand the potential ramifications of any database alterations. It's better to know this up front, rather than having to repair damage later.

Viewing the Table's Contents

Sometimes, the best way to understand what's going on in a table is to look at what's stored in it. Navigate to the table in question (as we describe earlier in the chapter), right-click it, and choose the Open Table menu option. You're presented with a list of records, as shown in Figure 5-4.

You have a full set of navigation options within this window. You can even create new rows if you like.

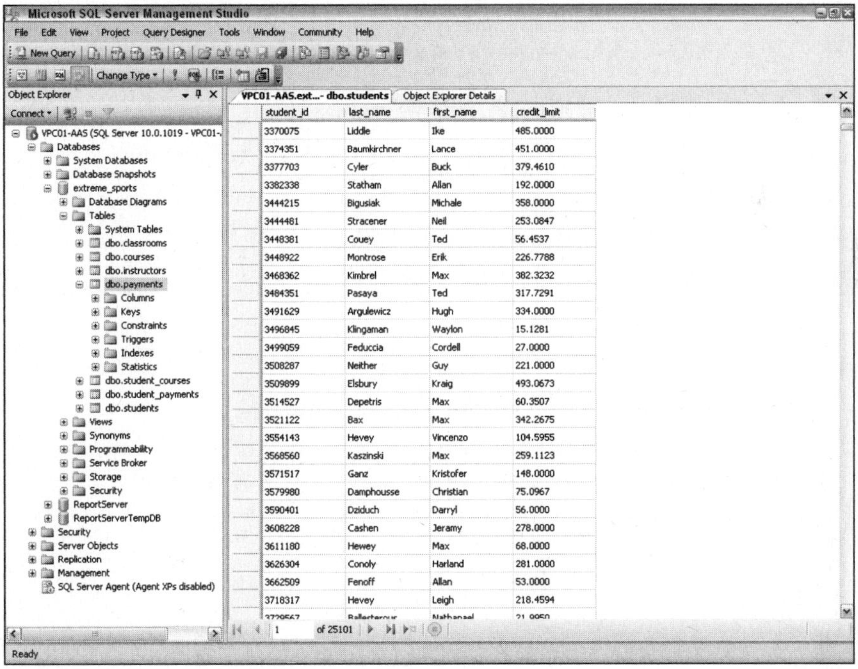

Figure 5-4: Viewing a table's contents in the SQL Server Management Studio.

Modifying a Table

Now that you've seen how to get a full list of all your tables and see their data, it's time to check out how easy it is to change them. These types of alterations can include

✦ Renaming the table

✦ Renaming a column

✦ Adding one or more columns to the table

✦ Changing a data type for a given column

✦ Changing a column's properties

✦ Removing one or more columns from the table

✦ Modifying properties for the table

We take a look at how to do each of these tasks. Because the SQL Server Management Studio is such an excellent tool, we use it as the primary mechanism to make these alterations. The initial steps that you need to follow for any modification are

1. **Launch the SQL Server Management Studio.**

2. **Connect to the appropriate SQL Server instance.**

3. **Expand the connection's entry in the Object Explorer view.**

4. **Expand the Databases folder.**

5. **Expand the specific database folder where your table resides.**

6. **Locate the table you want to change.**

Viewing a script for the table

Although the SQL Server Management Studio allows you to perform most administrative tasks without the need for programming, it's nice to know exactly what's going on underneath the covers. Here's how you can get a better understanding of the Data Definition Language (DDL) that SQL Server generates to build your table.

If you've followed the steps listed previously to locate the table, highlight the table name, right-click, and then choose Script Table AS⇨CREATE TO⇨ New Query Window. You're presented with a script window, as shown in Figure 5-5.

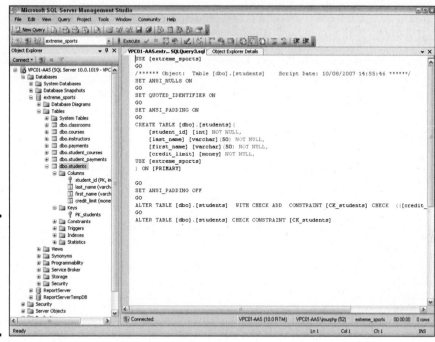

Book II
Chapter 5

Looking After Your Tables

Figure 5-5:
Viewing the DDL for a table in the SQL Server Management Studio.

Renaming the table

After you've identified the table that you want to rename, click once on the table name. This places you into rename mode. All you need to do now is enter the new name of the table, and press Enter. If you get cold feet and don't want to make this change after all, simply press Esc, and your alteration will be aborted.

Renaming a column

Changing the name of a column is easy. Continuing from the previous list of steps, here's what you need to do:

1. **Expand the table's entry.**

2. **Expand the Columns folder.**

3. **Right-click the column you want to change.**

4. **Choose Rename.**

5. **Enter the new name for the column.**

6. **When you're finished, press Enter to save your change.**

Adding one or more columns to the table

Sometimes, you discover that you need to add columns to an existing table. This is generally no problem, but you should be aware that adding new columns might affect other users and applications that were unprepared for this change. In any case, with the table located as described at the start of this section, follow these simple steps to include additional columns:

1. **Expand the table's entry.**

2. **Right-click the Columns folder.**

3. **Choose New Column.**

   This opens a dialog box where you can add as many new columns as you like. Check out Figure 5-6 to see what this looks like.

4. **When you're finished making changes, click the floppy disk icon to save your changes.**

As we mention earlier, adding new columns to a production database requires some thought. Applications that expect a certain set of columns might find themselves confused (and broken) if additional columns are on a table.

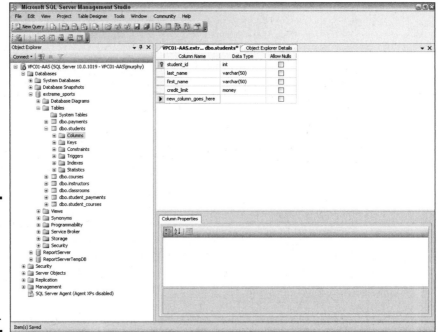

Figure 5-6:
Adding new columns for a table in the SQL Server Management Studio.

Changing a data type for a column

During database design and development, it's common for a database administrator to feel the need to change the data type for a given column. Perhaps you initially defined a column to hold numeric data, but after thinking things over, you realize that it might actually contain character-based information after all. Fortunately, it's easy to change an already-existing column's data type.

Assuming you've already followed the steps listed previously to locate the table in question, here's how to make this modification:

1. **Expand the table's entry.**

2. **Expand the Columns folder.**

3. **Right-click the column that you want to change.**

4. **Choose Modify.**

This opens up a dialog box where you're presented with a list of all the columns for the table.

5. **Choose the new data type from the data type drop-down box.**

6. **When you're ready to save the modified table, click the floppy disk icon.**

SQL Server carefully guards its data integrity. If you attempt to change a column's data type to one that doesn't make sense, SQL Server reports an error and blocks your change. For example, look at the following error message we received when we tried to change a column from character-based to numeric when there was non-numeric information in that column:

```
'students' table
- Unable to modify table.
Conversion failed when converting the varchar value
'Ramm' to data type int.
```

Changing a column's properties

As we describe in Chapter 4 of this mini-book, SQL Server sports numerous configurable properties for its tables and columns. Here's how to change those properties for an existing column. Assuming you've already navigated to the table in question (as described earlier in this chapter), just follow these steps:

1. **Right-click the table.**

2. **Choose Design.**

This opens a panel that shows you all the columns in the table.

3. Highlight the column whose properties you want to change.

The bottom portion of this panel now lists a collection of properties for this column, as shown in Figure 5-7. If you're interested in what all these properties mean, see Chapter 4 in this mini-book.

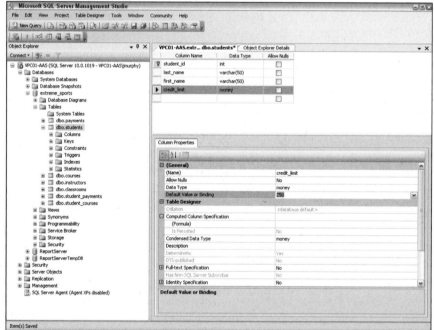

Figure 5-7: Changing a column's properties in the SQL Server Management Studio.

4. Make your changes to whatever properties you like.

In this case, we're setting the default credit limit to $250.

5. When you're ready to save the new properties, click the floppy disk icon.

Removing a column

With the table located in the SQL Server Management Studio, follow these simple steps to remove columns:

1. Expand the table's entry.

2. Open its Columns folder.

3. Right-click the column you want to delete.

4. Choose Delete.

This removes the column from the table. However, if deleting a column causes a referential integrity or other internal database constraint violation, you'll receive an error from SQL Server stating that your changes aren't possible. For example, look at the following message that we received when we tried to delete a column that was referenced in a foreign key:

```
Drop failed for Column 'student_id'. (Microsoft.SqlServer.Smo)
An exception occurred while executing a Transact-SQL statement or batch.
(Microsoft.SqlServer.ConnectionInfo)
The object 'PK_students' is dependent on column 'student_id'.
The object 'FK_student_courses_students' is dependent on column
'student_id'.
The object 'FK_payments_students' is dependent on column 'student_id'.
ALTER TABLE DROP COLUMN student_id failed because one or more objects
access this column. (Microsoft SQL Server, Error: 5074)
```

**Book II
Chapter 5**

Looking After
Your Tables

Making significant changes to a production database, such as modifying table names, adding or removing columns, and switching data types, isn't something that you undertake lightly. There are implications with regard to already-written applications, scripts, and so on. Think carefully before making any of these types of alterations. Of course, you'll also want to make a backup of your database before starting down this path.

Understanding table properties

If you're interested in even more than a table's columns, keys, and constraints, you might want to look at its properties. Assuming you've already followed the steps listed earlier in this chapter to locate the table in question, here's how to do that:

1. Highlight the specific table's entry in the list of tables.

2. Right-click the table name.

3. Choose Properties.

This opens an informative dialog box, as shown in Figure 5-8.

Three pages are available to you here:

✦ **General:** Holds all the system-defined properties for this table.

✦ **Permissions:** Tracks security and access rights for the table.

✦ **Extended Properties:** Shows administrator-defined properties for the table.

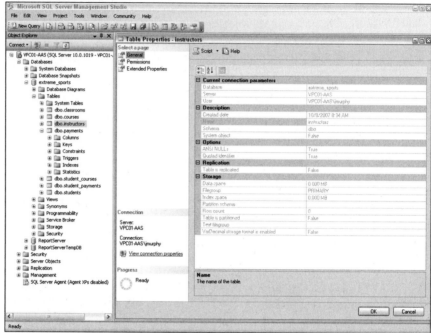

Figure 5-8:
Viewing a
table's
properties in
the SQL
Server
Manage-
ment Studio.

Here's a deeper look at the major classes of properties shown on the General page. If you're interested in security topics, we cover that important matter in Book VIII, Chapter 3.

You can sort the properties alphabetically or by category. For now, look at them by category. You can make changes to only the Permissions and Extended Properties pages; the General page is read-only.

✦ **Current Connection Parameters:** Here's where you can find the database name, server, and current user.

✦ **Description:** Covers details about the table's name, when it was created, the schema to which it belongs, and whether it's a user or system table.

✦ **Options:** States whether the table was created with ANSI NULL and whether the quoted identifier behavior is enabled.

✦ **Replication:** Is this table part of a replication scheme?

✦ **Storage:** Provides information about the number of rows in the table, the amount of disk space consumed, file groups, partitioning, and so on. As an administrator, you'll probably be most interested in this section.

Deleting a Table

When the time comes to bid farewell to a table, follow these simple steps and it will be gone from your life forever (unless you've made a backup, in which case the table has achieved immortality — and you still have a copy of the backup).

1. **Launch SQL Server Management Studio.**

2. **Connect to the appropriate SQL Server instance.**

3. **Expand the connection's entry in the Object Explorer view.**

4. **Expand the Databases folder.**

5. **Expand the Tables folder.**

6. **Highlight the table you want to delete.**

7. **Press Delete.**

If the table is part of a relationship, and removing the table violates the terms of the relationship, SQL Server reports an error and blocks the deletion of this table. For example, take a look at the error message we received when we erroneously tried to delete a table that others depended upon:

```
Drop failed for Table 'dbo.students'. (Microsoft.SqlServer.Smo)
An exception occurred while executing a Transact-SQL statement or batch.
(Microsoft.SqlServer.ConnectionInfo)
Could not drop object 'dbo.students' because it is referenced by a FOREIGN KEY
constraint. (Microsoft SQL Server, Error: 3726)
```

Before deleting a table, try viewing its dependencies to see what impact your change might have. We describe how to do that a little earlier in this chapter. Conveniently, SQL Server puts a handy button on the dialog box just before you actually delete the table.

Altering a Table via SQLCMD

If you're not a fan of graphical utilities like the SQL Server Management Studio, never fear. The SQLCMD utility allows you to interact directly with your database until your heart's content by using a character-based interface.

Here's how to use this utility to make a table modification. For this example, we're renaming a table and then adding a new column.

1. **Open a command prompt.**

Choose Start⇨Run and enter **cmd**. Alternatively, you can choose Programs⇨Accessories⇨Command Prompt. When you see the friendly command prompt, it's time to launch SQLCMD.

2. Enter SQLCMD **at the command prompt, passing in the proper parameters.**

This can get a bit confusing. SQLCMD is rather picky about the exact syntax that it deigns appropriate to run. This isn't surprising when you realize that it supports more than 2 dozen parameters. Table 5-1 highlights a small group of key parameters.

Table 5-1	Key SQLCMD Parameters
Parameter	*Purpose*
S	Specify the server that you want to connect to
U	Provide your username
P	Provide your password
d	Which database to use (if any)
i	The SQL script file (if any)

If you get in hot water, you can always ask SQLCMD for help:

```
SQLCMD /?
```

3. Enter your SQL, ending your statement with GO.

After you're in SQLCMD, you have an interactive command prompt at your disposal. Figure 5-9 shows a very simple example of altering a table by using direct SQL entry in SQLCMD.

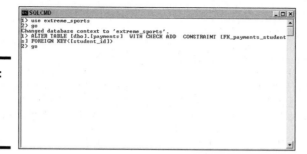

Figure 5-9:
Altering a
table by
using
SQLCMD.

Chapter 6: Understanding Relationships

In This Chapter

✔ **Why relationships are important**

✔ **Types of relationships**

✔ **Creating relationships**

✔ **Maintaining relationships**

✔ **Managing relationship errors**

Chances are, the store where you picked up this book has an entire section devoted to understanding and improving relationships. You can probably find all sorts of helpful information about bettering your relationships with parents, children, friends, neighbors, and co-workers. In this chapter, we add another relationship that you must consider: the relationship among your SQL Server data.

To begin, we show you why relationships are so important in any modern database management system. Next, you see the different types of relationships that are commonly found in SQL Server (or any other current relational database management system for that matter). With that out of the way, you find out how to use the tools provided by SQL Server to define and maintain these relationships. Finally, because all relationships have problems from time to time, the chapter closes by showing you what happens when a relationship goes bad.

Relationships: Making Data Meaningful

As you might surmise from the category name for these types of products — relational database management systems — relationships play a big part in their overall design philosophy. When these products appeared on the scene in the 1970s, their new architecture caused quite a stir. Until that point, data management software had structured its information in a variety of different ways. Certain products used a hierarchical structure, whereas others followed a more network-like approach. Although it's beyond the purpose of this book to go into database history, it's important to note that these earlier architectures were significantly more cumbersome for developers and end-users to navigate, locate results, and make sense of what was stored in these repositories. They also frequently led to significant data redundancy and made developing applications significantly more labor-intensive than we're used to these days.

Unlike these earlier approaches, relational databases separate information into distinct structures known as tables. Each table holds information of a similar type. For example, a Customers table would be expected to hold information about an organization's clients. Comparatively, a Payments table would be a likely candidate to store details of a customer's financial transactions.

This new architecture is both simpler and more elegant than the technologies it supplanted. The proof is in the pudding: Relational databases have enjoyed robust growth for more than 20 years, and are now the de facto standard for storing information. However, these new technologies also require that designers carefully consider the relationships among each of these tables.

Continuing the example of a Customer and Payments table, what would happen if a record existed in the Payments table, yet there was no corresponding customer? In older database management systems, details about customers and payments are often stored together in the same physical structure, making this type of scenario much less likely.

Consequently, designers and architects have given a great deal of thought to all possible relationships, and how they should be defined in the relational database world. In the remainder of this chapter, you get a list of all the major relationship types, and then see how to use SQL Server's graphical and character-based tools to define and maintain these relationships.

Relationship Types

In this section, we look at each of the relationship types that you're likely to encounter in SQL Server, along with the purpose of each relationship. Before we get started, it's useful to have a real-world example to help illustrate each type of relationship. We use this scenario when we create the relationships with SQL Server's tools.

After years working for The Man, you've decided that it's time to take control of your destiny and go into business for yourself. After a bit of soul-searching, you decide to follow your heart and open an extreme sports training school. However, without proper IT infrastructure, you know that you, your bungee cord, and your street luge gear will be back at The Man's doorstep before too long. Because you know that relational databases do an outstanding job of keeping track of vital information, you decide to use SQL Server as the core of your IT environment.

In examining the type of information you're likely to need to store in support of your new business, you identify the following major objects:

✦ **Student**

✦ **Student classroom feedback**

✦ **Class**

✦ **Payment**

✦ **Instructor**

You decide that each of these objects needs its own table. For the purpose of this example, don't worry about adhering to relational database design principles to the letter.

Now that you've established a new business, look at how each type of relationship affects this example.

One-to-one

In this type of relationship, two given objects are bound at the hip: They have one, and only one, relationship — with each other. It's worth pointing out that these types of relationships are quite uncommon in the real world, as well as in most relational database applications. However, to illustrate this example, assume that a specific class can be taught by one (and only one) instructor, and that an instructor can teach one (and only one) class. Again, this isn't terribly realistic, but we hope it highlights the point.

One-to-many

If a one-to-one relationship is distinguished by its rarity, a one-to-many relationship is known as a much more common situation. In this context, a given object can have many associated objects of the same type. For example, one student can make many payments, but a payment can be made by one (and only one) student.

Many-to-many

As you might guess from looking at the relational database model, it can be quite complicated to represent a situation where many objects relate to many other objects. For example, many students can attend many different classes at one time. Fortunately, as you'll soon see, relational databases let you create many-to-many tables that help store details of these complex relationships.

Constraints

While not relationships per se, constraints are often the mechanisms that allow you to help enforce and maintain these associations. When you build a database application, you're responsible for making sure that no bad data gets into your database. If you fail, there's a good chance that you (or your users) might make a bad decision because what's stored in your database won't accurately reflect reality. Constraints are how you define, at the database level, rules that help protect your database from data anomalies. We look at some of the major constraints that you have at your disposal.

Primary keys

By defining a primary key constraint, you're telling SQL Server that the values contained in one or more columns must be unique across all rows. In addition to protecting your data's integrity, a primary key constraint is a great help to database performance. By using the primary key, SQL Server can find a row almost instantaneously. In our extreme sports training school scenario, you'd likely define or generate a primary key for each of the objects.

For example, you would likely place a primary key on the `students` table. This would typically be a machine-generated numeric identifier that you could use to uniquely identify a given student. Comparatively, if you don't expect many attendees to your new school, you could also create a primary key on the combination of each student's first name and last name. However, after your school started growing, two students with the same first and last names would cause your database and associated applications to have difficulty distinguishing between these two students.

Foreign keys

Most relational database applications spread their knowledge among multiple tables. Each table ordinarily holds a specialized type of data. In the sports training school example, you can see dedicated tables for students, their classes, payments, teachers, and so on.

Here's where things can get tricky. If you're not careful, your application could delete a student's main data without deleting any associated information, such as student feedback, future course attendance, and so on. Alternatively, you could create a payment record but omit creating a student record. You've damaged your data's integrity in both of these cases. Foreign key constraints are specifically designed to prevent these unhappy situations from ever occurring.

When you place a foreign key constraint on two or more tables, you're telling SQL Server to intercept any attempts, deliberate or otherwise, where your data's integrity can be compromised. For example, by placing a foreign key on the payments table that references the students table, you instruct SQL Server to ensure that any records that are added to the payments table have a corresponding student record.

The really nice thing about this constraint is that your application code no longer serves as the last line of defense for your database's integrity. Of course, you want your applications to follow good data integrity rules, but it's comforting to know that SQL Server is also on the job.

CHECK

Think of CHECK constraints as bits of application logic that you place on your tables to guarantee that they reject any attempts to violate a business or other data rule that you want to enforce. For example, suppose that you don't want any payment information entered unless the payment is greater than $50. In this case, you would place a CHECK constraint on the payments table to validate that the amount entered exceeded your required threshold. If the amount was less than the constraint, the user would receive an error message, and the database's integrity would be preserved.

What's especially handy about check constraints is that you can place multiple constraints on the same table. Continuing the sports training school example, not only do you want payments less than $50 to be rejected, but you also want to block any single payments greater than $5,000. In this case, you would simply add a second CHECK constraint to your payments table, and SQL Server would sort out the details to ensure that neither of these two rules is violated.

UNIQUE

This is very similar to a primary key constraint, but unlike primary keys, UNIQUE constraints let you place a NULL value in the column. However, you generally define a UNIQUE constraint when you already have a primary key in place, but also want to enforce non-duplication on another column.

A realistic example of UNIQUE versus PRIMARY KEY constraints would occur when you define the student_id column as the primary key for the students table, and then require that the e-mail address for the student be unique.

NOT NULL

This constraint helps ensure that any database applications provide data for one or more of your columns. If you attempt to enter an empty (that is, NULL) value on a column that has a NOT NULL constraint, SQL Server will intercept the call.

You certainly would want to ensure that your students' first and last name fields had to have a value associated with them. In this case, you would demand that both of these columns have the NOT NULL constraint placed on them when the table is defined. From that moment, any attempts to enter a new student record with a blank first name or last name will result in an error. What's also great about this is that the constraint works all the time, even for existing records that are then modified.

Creating Relationships

In the previous section, we show you all the different relationships that your data can have. In this section, it's time for you to actually create and maintain these important constructs.

You have two main options when it comes to defining and then preserving relationships: the SQL Server Management Studio and direct SQL entry. Because both these techniques are equally valuable, we show you both.

The SQL Server Management Studio and relationships

When it comes to quickly and clearly defining new tables and all associated relationships, it's pretty hard to beat the SQL Server Management Studio. In this section, we look at how easy it is to perform these important tasks.

To begin, follow these steps to open the SQL Server Management Studio and its table designer:

1. **Launch the SQL Server Management Studio.**

2. **Connect to the appropriate SQL Server instance.**

3. **Expand the connection's entry in the Object Explorer view.**

4. **Expand the Databases folder.**

5. **Expand the folder entry for the database where you want to create the table.**

6. **Right-click Tables, and choose New Table.**

This opens a dialog box where you can interactively create your new table. We cover this subject in-depth in Chapter 4 of this mini-book. For now, pay special attention to the relationship aspect of creating a new table. By selecting the Table Designer menu option, the SQL Server Management Studio offers you a collection of options for defining important relationship, index, and other key settings. Figure 6-1 shows how these menu options initially appear.

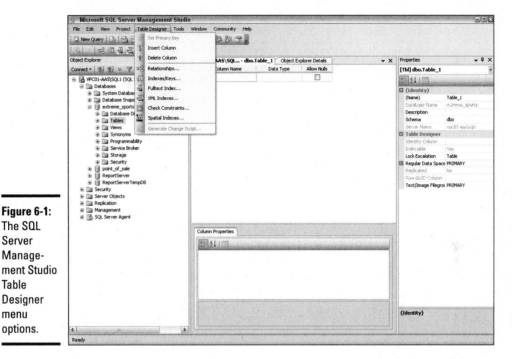

Figure 6-1:
The SQL
Server
Manage-
ment Studio
Table
Designer
menu
options.

Next, we begin filling in columns, along with filling in their data types and filling in whether NULL values are permitted. You can right-click any column to receive a context-sensitive menu for setting relationships, indexes, and so on. For example, Figure 6-2 shows that we want to set a primary key on the student_id column.

Figure 6-3 shows how the table looks when the primary key constraint is in place.

With the primary key set, it's time to set some additional restrictions on the table. One area that concerns you is that extreme sports students don't have a lot of money at their disposal. The best way to go out of business quickly is to extend excessive amounts of credit to your customers, especially when they might not be able to pay.

Rather than requiring each of your application developers to make a credit determination on their own, you decide to track each student's credit limit in the database by adding a new column (credit_limit) to the students table. However, you don't want an overzealous salesperson to grant a new student higher credit than your company's policy allows. Consequently, you want SQL Server to do the enforcement for you. This is where a CHECK constraint can be very helpful.

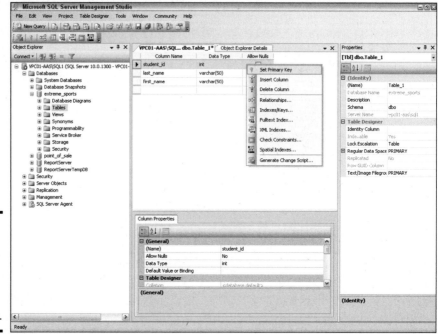

Figure 6-2:
Setting a
primary key
in the SQL
Server
Manage-
ment Studio.

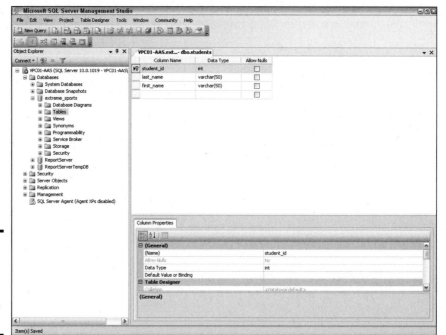

Figure 6-3:
A primary
key defined
for the
students
table.

It's easy to place a CHECK constraint on a table. All you need to do is choose the Check Constraints option from the Table Designer menu. This opens a dialog box, as shown in Figure 6-4.

With this dialog box displayed, here's how to place a CHECK constraint on a specific column:

1. **Click the Add button.**

   This opens a dialog box where you can enter in the details of your new constraint. Figure 6-5 shows this new dialog box.

2. **Click the Expression field and then click its ellipsis. Enter the syntax for your new CHECK constraint.**

   Figure 6-6 shows the syntax for placing a limit of 1,000 on each student's credit.

3. **Provide any additional details.**

   You can set your own name, or simply use the one provided by SQL Server. You can also specify how you want the constraint to be enforced.

Book II
Chapter 6

**Understanding
Relationships**

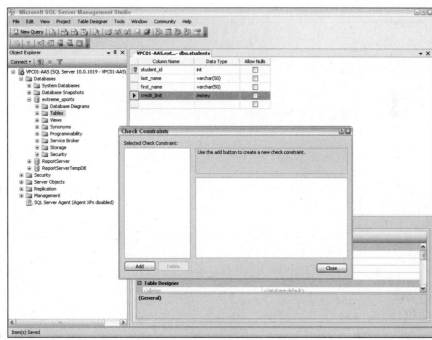

Figure 6-4:
The initial
Check
Constraints
dialog box in
the SQL
Server
Manage-
ment Studio.

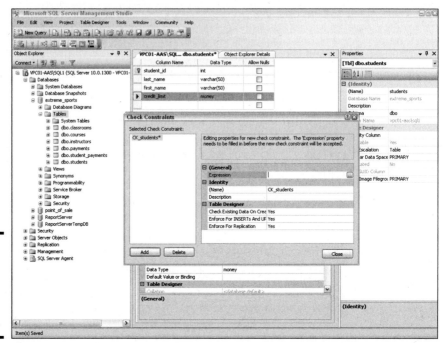

Figure 6-5:
The property sheet for CHECK constraints.

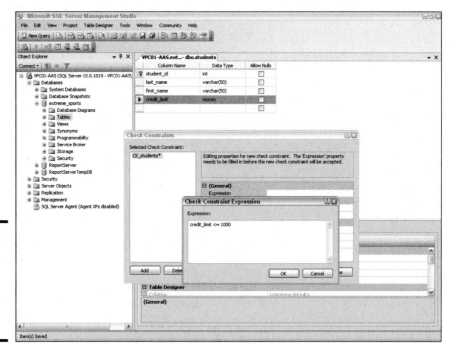

Figure 6-6:
Setting a CHECK constraint on a specific column.

4. **When you're finished, click** `Close`.

You can create as many constraints as you like. However, remember that you need to save the table itself, or all your hard work defining CHECK constraints will be lost.

That's all there is to it. Your table now has a CHECK constraint in place.

Of course, data doesn't exist in isolation; it's time to see how to tie the students table with the other tables that depend on its information. For this example, you set up a foreign key relationship between the payments table and the students table.

To begin, Figure 6-7 shows a newly created payments table. Only the primary key is defined at this point.

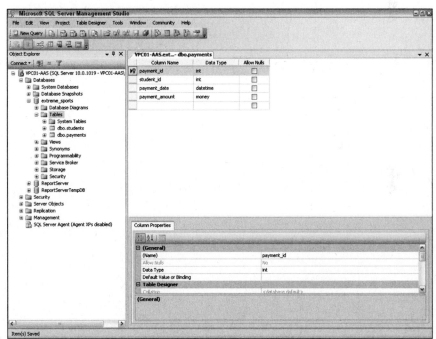

Figure 6-7:
The payments table with a new primary key in place.

It's now time to create the foreign key that will reference the students table. Assuming you already have the SQL Server Management Studio running, and have selected the database and table in question, here's how to make this happen:

1. **Choose Table Designer⇨Relationships.**

An empty dialog box opens.

2. **Click the Add button.**

A partially filled dialog box opens where you specify how you want to set up your relationship. Figure 6-8 shows this dialog box.

3. **In the dialog box, expand the `Tables and Columns Specification` field.**

4. **Click on the newly visible ellipsis.**

You define the tables and columns that will make up your foreign key relationship.

5. **Select the appropriate table and column entries from the drop-down boxes.**

In this example, you're setting a foreign key relationship between the `students` table (`student_id`) and the `payments` table (`student_id`). Figure 6-9 shows this dialog box filled in correctly.

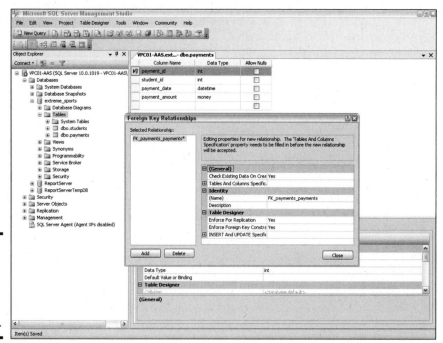

Figure 6-8:
A dialog box for setting up a foreign key relationship.

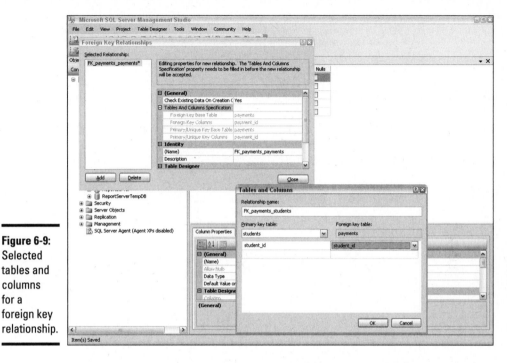

**Book II
Chapter 6**

**Understanding
Relationships**

Figure 6-9:
Selected
tables and
columns
for a
foreign key
relationship.

6. **Click OK to close this dialog box, and then click Close in the parent
dialog box.**

7. **Remember to save your work by clicking on the disk icon.**

As a sanity check, SQL Server displays a message to alert you of your
impending changes, and the tables that will be affected. Figure 6-10 displays how this warning appears.

You've made several important changes to your database. Fortunately,
it's easy to check your work. Figure 6-11 shows details about both the
students and payments table.

The expanded tree view shows that the students table has both a primary
key and a CHECK constraint in place, and the payments table has a primary
key and a foreign key.

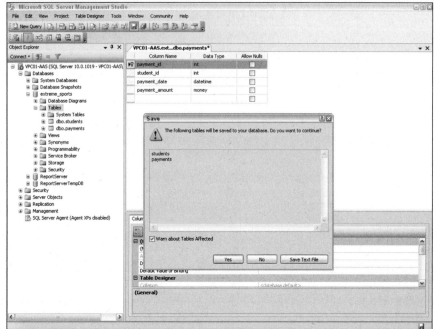

Figure 6-10: Confirmation from SQL Server prior to creating the relationship.

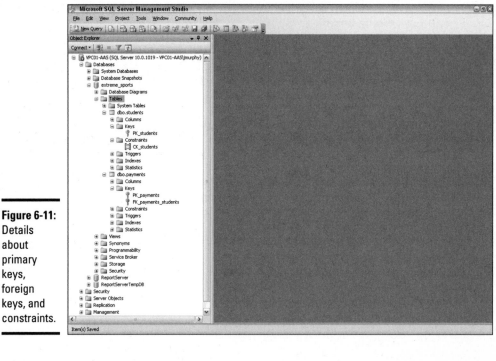

Figure 6-11: Details about primary keys, foreign keys, and constraints.

SQL and Relationships

If you would rather roll up your sleeves and enter your SQL by hand, here's how to do it. For the purposes of this example, we assume that you're using the SQLCMD utility. You're also free to use the direct SQL entry features of the SQL Server Management Studio.

1. **Open a command prompt.**

   Choose Start➪Run and enter **cmd**. You can also choose Programs➪ Accessories➪Command Prompt. When you see the friendly command prompt, it's time to launch SQLCMD.

2. **Enter** SQLCMD **at the command prompt, passing in the proper parameters.**

   This can get a bit confusing. SQLCMD is rather picky about the exact syntax that it deigns appropriate to run. This isn't surprising when you realize that it supports more than 2 dozen parameters. Table 6-1 highlights a small group of key parameters.

Table 6-1	Key SQLCMD Parameters
Parameter	*Purpose*
S	Specify the server that you want to connect to
U	Provide your username
P	Provide your password
D	Which database to use (if any)
I	The SQL script file (if any)

Book II
Chapter 6

Understanding
Relationships

   If you get in hot water, you can always ask SQLCMD for help:

   ```
   SQLCMD /?
   ```

3. **Enter your SQL, ending your statement with** GO.

For example, here's what the SQL looks like to create the students table and place a CHECK constraint on the credit_limit column:

```
CREATE TABLE [dbo].[students](
    [student_id] [int] NOT NULL,
    [last_name] [varchar](50) NOT NULL,
    [first_name] [varchar](50) NOT NULL,
    [credit_limit] [money] NOT NULL
    CONSTRAINT [CK_students1] CHECK(([credit_limit]<=(1000))),
) ON [PRIMARY]
```

Managing Relationship Errors

Relationships are one place where many database applications typically run into trouble. In this section, we look at a few of the most common error conditions that can arise, along with how SQL Server protects your data.

Despite of all the integrity protections we're about to show you, deleting an entire database will override any of the table level safeguards enforced by SQL Server. Consequently, use extreme caution when deleting databases; these rules will not step in and save you.

Primary key violation

Primary keys are what SQL Server uses to locate a given record quickly based on a unique value. Here's some SQL that creates a table and defines its primary key:

```
CREATE TABLE [dbo].[STUDENTS]
(
    [STUDENT_ID] [int] PRIMARY KEY NOT NULL,
    [LAST_NAME] [varchar](50) NOT NULL,
    [FIRST_NAME] [varchar](50) NOT NULL,
    [STREET1] [varchar](50) NOT NULL,
    [STREET2] [varchar](50) NULL,
    [CITY] [varchar](50) NOT NULL,
    [STATE] [char](4) NOT NULL,
    [COUNTRY] [varchar](50) NOT NULL,
    [PHONE] [varchar](20) NULL,
    [EMAIL] [varchar](50) NULL,
)
```

Suppose that you insert a new row as follows:

```
INSERT INTO STUDENTS VALUES (2291,'JONES','BOB','2454 LEGION STREET',
    'APT 21', 'PHOENIX', 'AZ', 'USA', 555-555-5555, 'bob@demo.com')
```

So far, so good. However, your application logic is a little sloppy, and you attempt to insert another row with the same student_id. SQL Server doesn't like this one bit, and stops your operation dead in its tracks:

```
Msg 2627, Level 14, State 1, Line 1
Violation of PRIMARY KEY constraint 'PK__students__0EA330E9'. Cannot insert
duplicate key in object 'dbo.students'.
The statement has been terminated.
```

As an application developer, it's vital that you stay aware of primary keys. It's very common for developers to duplicate manually generated primary keys unintentionally, which causes all sorts of excitement at runtime.

However, a better way to create primary keys is by using identity columns. See Chapter 4 in this mini-book if you're curious about this handy way of maintaining primary keys.

Foreign key violation

Foreign keys are an important tool that SQL Server uses to keep information stored in multiple tables in sync. Continuing with the `students` table example, imagine that you store financial transaction information in a `payments` table as follows:

```
CREATE TABLE [dbo].[PAYMENTS]
(
    [PAYMENT_ID] [int] NOT NULL,
    [STUDENT_ID] [int] NOT NULL REFERENCES STUDENTS,
    [PAYMENT_DATE] [datetime] NOT NULL,
    [PAYMENT_AMOUNT] [money] NOT NULL
)
```

**Book II
Chapter 6**

**Understanding
Relationships**

In this case, the `student_id` column in the `payments` table serves as a foreign key to the `students` table. Its job is to ensure that every row in the `payments` table has a corresponding student record in the `students` table.

You can trigger foreign key violations in a number of ways. For example, suppose you try to add a new payment record when there is no corresponding student record. SQL Server squawks and doesn't permit you to damage the database's integrity:

```
Msg 547, Level 16, State 0, Line 1
The INSERT statement conflicted with the FOREIGN KEY constraint
"FK__PAYMENTS__STUDE__1367E606". The conflict occurred in database
"extreme_sports", table "dbo.students", column 'student_id'.
The statement has been terminated.
```

Conversely, if you attempt to delete a row in the `students` table without first deleting any corresponding `payments` records, SQL Server will also block this potentially damaging operation:

```
Msg 547, Level 16, State 0, Line 1
The DELETE statement conflicted with the REFERENCE constraint
"FK__PAYMENTS__STUDE__164452B1". The conflict occurred in database
"extreme_sports", table "dbo.PAYMENTS", column 'STUDENT_ID'.
The statement has been terminated.
```

These protections extend to graphical tools as well. For example, suppose that you use the SQL Server Management Studio and try to drop the `students` table without first removing associated `payment` records. Figure 6-12 shows that SQL Server is still on the job.

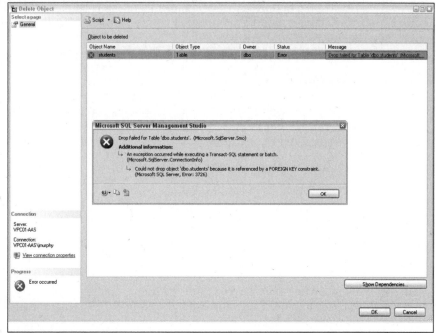

Figure 6-12:
The SQL
Server
Manage-
ment Studio
blocking a
foreign key
violation.

CHECK constraint violation

CHECK constraints are designed to let the database engine help enforce business or other information rules. As described earlier, suppose that you place a CHECK constraint on the credit_limit column in the students table. This constraint's job is to prevent anyone from having a credit limit greater than 1,000. If you try to create or update a record that exceeds this limit, here's what SQL Server will say:

```
Msg 547, Level 16, State 0, Line 1
The INSERT statement conflicted with the CHECK constraint "CK_students".
The conflict occurred in database "extreme_sports", table
"dbo.students", column 'credit_limit'.
The statement has been terminated.
```

Your database's integrity remains safe; no business rules have been broken.

NOT NULL violation

Some bad things can happen if someone erroneously creates records that have empty columns. Fortunately, you can easily prevent this nastiness by mandating that these columns be created with the NOT NULL constraint.

If someone then attempts to insert or update a row with NULL values where they're not allowed, here's the message that SQL Server will return:

```
Msg 515, Level 16, State 2, Line 1
Cannot insert the value NULL into column 'first_name', table
'extreme_sports.dbo.students'; column does not allow nulls. INSERT fails.
The statement has been terminated.
```

Again, SQL Server foils rogue or sloppy applications in their attempts to damage your data's integrity.

Book III

Interacting with Your Data

The 5th Wave By Rich Tennant

DATASUK
Service & Support

"Please answer the following survey questions about our company's performance with either, 'Excellent', 'Good', 'Fair', or 'I'm Really Incapable of Appreciating Someone Else's Hard Work.'"

Contents at a Glance

Chapter 1: Using Proper Normalization Techniques

In This Chapter

- ✔ Normalizing your database
- ✔ Removing repeating groups
- ✔ Insuring each column is dependent on the whole primary key
- ✔ Removing transitive dependencies
- ✔ Improving performance

Databases took a great leap forward when Edgar F. Codd defined the first three normal forms in his 1970 paper "A Relational Model of Data for Large Shared Data Banks." Over the years, many more normal forms have been defined, but even today, the first three normal forms are the most commonly used. Today's popular Relational Database Management Systems (including SQL Server 2008) are based on the relational model first identified by Codd.

Normalizing Your Database

Normalizing a database is dividing tables into their simplest forms and creating relationships between the tables. Instead of a single table of many columns to hold all your data, you can create multiple tables and spread the data between them in a logical manner.

Tables are connected to each other by creating relationships. Relationships between tables are primarily created between the primary key in one table and a foreign key in another table.

A *primary key* is a column within a table that is used to uniquely identify each row within that table. Primary keys are usually numbers, but you might see them as a combination of characters and numbers in some databases. Allowing the system to generate primary keys automatically is easiest, but developers might sometimes choose to do this within their database application.

Foreign keys are used to relate one table to another table and can be a combination of numbers and letters. A foreign key is in the related column and matches the same format (numeric, character, or a combination) of the primary key in the related table.

Book II, Chapter 4 covers relationships between tables in-depth, including the different types of relationships, how to create relationships, and maintaining relationships.

By normalizing a database, many problems can be prevented. Consider a company that sells products to customers. Information on each customer is maintained in a database, including a name, address, phone number, and e-mail address. In a non-normalized database (one single table), you could have multiple problems when you try to query or modify this data. These problems include:

✦ **Duplication of data:** In a non-normalized database, a customer's information might have to be entered every time he makes a purchase, storing the customer's data in an Orders table. The result is duplication of work. Additionally, odds are very low that this information would be entered the same way each time. Consider how many different ways employees might enter the name, Brandie Johansen, or a city, such as San Francisco (SF, San Fran, SFO, and so on). A normalized database prevents the duplication of work and the associated typos.

✦ **Update problems:** If a customer's address needs to be updated but the customer's personal data has been entered in multiple places, the update has to occur in multiple places within the database. If the update isn't done in multiple places, then the data will be inconsistent — correct in some places and incorrect in others.

✦ **Query problems:** Data in a database that isn't normalized is difficult to retrieve. Additionally, the data that is retrieved can't be relied on as being the most accurate. Consider the problem where a customer's data is stored in the Orders table and must be repeated for every order. If the customer moved, the only place where the customer's address is accurate is in the last order. If the address is retrieved from anywhere else, it would be incorrect.

Although as many as eight normal forms are sometimes listed, the most commonly used normal forms are the first three.

✦ **First normal form:** The table has no repeating groups, and each column is atomic. (*Atomic* doesn't mean explosive; instead, it means the columns are reduced to the smallest possible value. More about that in the upcoming "Atomicity" section.)

✦ **Second normal form:** Each column is dependent on the entire primary key. The second normal form applies only when a table has a composite primary key.

✦ **Third normal form:** Each column is directly dependent on the primary key. That is, non-primary key columns aren't directly dependent on other non-primary key columns.

The normal forms are progressively stricter for each higher normal form. The third normal form is stricter than the second normal form. The second normal form is stricter than the first normal form. Additionally, higher normal forms must comply with lower normal forms. If a table is in the second normal form, then by definition it's also in the first normal form.

First Normal Form: No Repeating Groups

The *first normal form* states that no repeating elements or groups of elements can exist within the tables. Additionally, it states that each column is atomic. These rules can be summarized as:

✦ **More than one value is not allowed in any cell** (a repeating group within a column). A column for the product purchased, can include only one product purchased. Two products can't be in the same column.

✦ **More than one column is not used to define the same piece of data** (a repeating group across columns). If more than one product is purchased, it's not in the same table as Product1, Product2, and so on.

✦ **Columns must be atomic.** Data within a column is broken down into the smallest meaningful element. A Name column would be divided into three columns as First Name, Middle Name, and Last Name.

No repeating groups within a column

A *repeating group* within a column is a group where more than one value is included in a single column.

For example, consider a table used to record sales information. For every sale, the table owner desires to record the customer's name, the date, and the item purchased.

Violating the first normal form, a table similar to Figure 1-1 could be created. Three columns (ItemDescription, ItemQty, and ItemPrice) have repeating groups. The customer purchased two books, and both book descriptions are in the ItemDescription column. Additionally, both quantities are in the ItemQty column, and both prices are in the ItemPrice column.

OrderID	CustomerName	SaleDate	ItemDescription	ItemQty	ItemPrice
100	Gibson	12/24/2007 ...	T-SQL Book, Rose Gardening book	1,1	34.99, 19.99
NULL	*NULL*	*NULL*	*NULL*	*NULL*	*NULL*

Creating the database this way defeats many of the strengths of a database. Creating queries to identify how many specific books have been sold, how many books have been sold in a specific price range, or the average price of books sold is quite difficult.

To comply with this portion of the first normal form, each column can have only one piece of data, such as only one item description in the ItemDescription column, only one item quantity in the ItemQty column, and only one price in the ItemPrice column.

However, limiting data entry to only one value per column won't be enough to fix this problem.

No repeating groups across columns

A *repeating group across columns* is a group where multiple columns are added to the table for the same group of data. Say a beginning database developer wanted to solve the problem from the previous example.

Instead of allowing more than one value in any column, he might choose to add additional columns to the table.

Figure 1-2 shows how this might be done. Because the table has repeating groups across columns, it's still violating the first normal form. A second column for ItemDescription, ItemQty, and ItemPrice has been added as ItemDescription1, ItemQty2, and ItemPrice2.

OrderID	CustomerName	SaleDate	ItemDescription	ItemQty	ItemPrice	ItemDescription2	ItemQty2	ItemPrice2
100	Gibson	12/24/2007 ...	T-SQL Book	1	34.9900	Rose Gardening	1	19.9900
NULL	*NULL*	*NULL*	*NULL*	*NULL*	*NULL*	*NULL*	*NULL*	*NULL*

This approach doesn't work from a practical sense because if a customer wanted to purchase 3 products (or 30 products), you couldn't add enough repeating groups across the columns to meet each possible condition.

Can you imagine a grocery store that limits customers to only two product purchases at a time? "Sorry. Please come back tomorrow for your next two items."

No. That's no way to run a business and that's no way to create a database in the first normal form.

A solution to this problem is to create two or more related tables. A possible solution is shown in Figure 1-3 where the repeating groups are taken from the first table and added to a related column named OrderDetails. The two tables are related on the OrderDetailsID column.

Figure 1-3:
Creating two tables to solve the problem of repeating groups.

The OrderDetails table has columns to describe the product, the quantity, and the price. Because the OrderDetails table is related to the Orders table, you can have as many rows in the OrderDetails table as needed. Each of the rows in the OrderDetails table would have the same OrderID value relating them to a single order in the Orders table.

The icons on the connector between the two tables further define the relationship. The small key icon indicates one. The infinity icon (°) indicates many. The Orders and OrderDetails are related in a one-to-many relationship. In other words, any order can have many order detail rows, each referring to a purchased item, such as a book, a magazine, a pen, and so on.

Atomicity

Atomic values are values that can't be reduced to a smaller meaningful value. For example, a `name` value could include someone's entire name (first name, middle initial, and last name), such as Harry J. Potter. However, this value isn't atomic because the name isn't reduced to the smallest meaningful values.

For a name, the smallest meaningful values would be the first name, the middle name (or middle initial), and the last name. Table 1-1 shows how you separate a name into smaller atomic values.

Table 1-1	Separating a Name into Atomic Values	
FirstName	*MiddleInitial*	*LastName*
Harry	J.	Potter

Why is this atomic? The term *atomic* comes from a time when it was believed that atoms were the smallest particle and that they couldn't be reduced to anything smaller. Of course, today, we know the atom can be split.

Applying this concept to the first normal form, values within a column can't be split into a smaller meaningful value.

You don't break down the names into the smallest *possible* values — a column for every letter in the name. How ridiculous is that? Instead, you break down the column into the smallest *meaningful* values — the different parts of a name.

Atomic value columns make it much easier to create queries based on the individual attributes of a name. For example, you can easily search based on the first name or last name, and just as easily create queries that alphabetically order the output based on the first name or last name.

Second Normal Form: Dependent on the Whole Key

The *second normal form* states that the table must be in the first normal form and each column must be dependent on the *entire* primary key. The second normal form comes into play only on tables that have more than one column designated as the primary key. Having more than one column as the primary key is also known as a *composite key.*

If a table doesn't have a composite key (only one column is designated as the primary key), and the table is in the first normal form, then it's automatically considered to be in the second normal form.

Comparatively, if a table has a composite primary key, is in the first normal form, and has columns that aren't dependent on each of the columns in the primary key, then it's not in the second normal form.

For example, consider Figure 1-4. Only the OrderDetails table has a composite key (composed of the OrderID and ProductID columns). Because the Orders and Products table both have only one column in the primary key, they're automatically considered compliant with the second normal form as long as they're in the first normal form.

Figure 1-4:
OrderDetails
isn't
compliant
with the
second
normal form.

For the OrderDetails table to be compliant with the second normal form, each of the non-primary key columns (ItemQty and Manufacturer) must be fully dependent on the entire primary key (both OrderID and ProductID columns). The ItemQty is fully dependent. It's identifying how many of the products (ProductID) are being ordered on this order (OrderID).

However, the Manufacturer column isn't dependent on the entire primary key. The manufacturer is dependent on the product (ProductID) but not on this current order (OrderID).

Moving the Manufacturer column from the OrderDetails table to the Products table makes it compliant with the second normal form.

Third Normal Form

A table in *third normal form* must be in the second normal form and every non-primary key column must be non-transitively (or directly) dependent on only the primary key. In other words, if any non-primary key columns are directly dependent on other non-primary key columns, then the table isn't in the third normal form.

The difference between the second normal form and the third normal form is sometimes lost on people learning about normal forms for the first time. The biggest difference is that the second normal form focuses on the primary key as a composite key and requires non-primary key columns to be dependent on the whole primary key, not just a part of it. The third normal form states that non-primary key columns must be dependent on the primary key and not other non-primary key columns. That is, columns must be dependent on the whole key (second normal form) and nothing but the key (third normal form).

Consider Figure 1-5, which isn't in the third normal form because of the CustomerPhone column. The CustomerPhone column is directly dependent on the CustomerName column for meaning. Because this customer placed this order, then the phone number is indirectly associated with the primary key of OrderID, showing a transitive relationship between the CustomerPhone and the OrderID.

Think about the salesperson filling in the data for this order. For a customer that placed 50 orders, the phone number needs to be entered 50 different times. In a perfect world, the phone number is entered the same way every 50 times, but more than likely, some typos might occur.

To make the Orders table compliant with the third normal form, you need to create a Customers table and put the associated customer data into the table.

As shown in Figure 1-6, the CustomerName and CustomerPhone columns have been replaced with a CustomerID column. Additionally, instead of just the customer name and phone number, the Customers table holds all associated customer data.

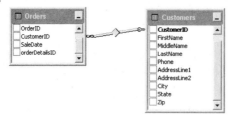

Denormalizing Your Database

Denormalizing a database is deliberately adding redundant data to a database to improve performance. Although Online Analytical Processing (OLAP) databases are highly denormalized, it's not uncommon for an Online

Transaction Processing (OLTP) database to have some level of denormalization designed to improve the performance of specific queries.

OLTP databases have a high level of transactions (UPDATE, INSERT, and DELETE statements). OLAP databases are highly queried (SELECT statements), but have very little, if any, transactions. Adding redundant data in an OLTP database has a performance cost because any updates to the redundant data must be made in multiple places. Because an OLAP database is rarely updated, the redundant data doesn't add any additional maintenance costs.

For a simple example of denormalization in a database, imagine that you have a Products table that includes the columns shown in Figure 1-7. This table is normalized.

Figure 1-7:
A normalized Products table.

Imagine that management has recently become very interested in the cost of on-hand inventory. On a weekly basis, and often on a daily basis, queries are run that identify the total value of on-hand inventory.

Every row in the Products table must be examined. Multiplying the OnHand inventory column by the ProductCost column calculates the on-hand cost of each individual product. To calculate a total value of on-hand inventory, each multiplied value is then added together.

If you have 200 products, this isn't a big deal. However, if you have more than 2 million products, running this query takes a lot of time and processing power, which might interfere with other processes on your server.

You can improve the performance of this query by denormalizing this table. The table can be denormalized by adding an OnHandCost column. The value of this column would be calculated by multiplying the OnHand value with the ProductCost column. An UPDATE trigger can be used to recalculate the value of the column any time the OnHand or ProductCost columns are changed.

You can also create the OnHandCost column as a computed column in the table definition. By default, a computed column is a virtual column. Whenever I hear "virtual," I think, "Ah, it doesn't really exist." That's exactly the case with a computed column. Whenever the data is retrieved, it calculates the value on the fly.

However, it is possible to mark a computed column as "persisted." A persisted computed column does exist in the table. When either the OnHand or the ProductCost values change, the persisted column would be recalculated.

UPDATE statements to the OnHand or ProductCost columns take a little longer because the extra column must be calculated; however, you'll never be updating these columns on 2 million rows at the same time.

Because the value of the OnHandCost is in the table for each row, the query that returns this information on two million rows runs much quicker. The calculation doesn't need to be done on each of the 2 million rows each time the query is run because the calculation is stored within the table.

Chapter 2: The SQL Server Optimizer

In This Chapter

✔ Knowing what the Optimizer can do for you

✔ Understanding the Optimizer

✔ Using execution plans

✔ Creating and maintaining statistics

*F*or speed and performance of any database management system, an *optimizer* identifies the best method to run queries. The best method includes identifying the best indexes to use and the most efficient methods of retrieving, joining, and sorting the data.

SQL Server uses its optimizer to evaluate and choose the best indexes and methods for individual queries. All queries are submitted to the optimizer, which in turn checks a variety of variables to create the best possible query plan. The query plan can be observed as text or in graphical mode by looking at the execution plan.

The most important thing you can do to support the optimizer is to ensure that statistics are automatically created and automatically maintained on all your indexes.

Why You Need the Optimizer

The SQL Server Optimizer (also called the Query Optimizer) has undergone several improvements through the years. In the days of SQL Server 6.5, a database administrator needed to tweak queries constantly by providing SQL Server an endless assortment of hints, such as which index to use or which type of join to use.

Although using hints helped the database management system (DBMS) perform better, they were a lot of work. The database administrator needed to fully understand the data and the database activity. In a dynamic database, the queries often had to be monitored while the data changed to determine whether the hints needed to be changed.

Currently, the Optimizer can analyze queries and quickly create a query plan without hints. Although hints can still be used, their use is generally discouraged except in the most advanced applications. The Optimizer automatically analyzes many aspects of the queries to create the query plan. Additionally, because the Optimizer optimizes queries when they're executed, the query plan can change when the data changes.

For example, you might want to optimize a Sales database query that pulls data from the Orders, OrderDetails, and Products tables. By analyzing the execution plan, you could determine the best indexes to use and provide hints in the query. Over time, the data changes, the indexes change, and the statistics for the indexes change. Therefore, instead of an optimal query, you have a very slow-running query because the indexes you picked are no longer the best indexes for this query.

However, even if hints aren't provided, the Query Optimizer can analyze the query and the elements of the database to determine the best possible query plan. Additionally, the same query can run later with a different query plan, based on the best possible query plan for that moment.

How the Optimizer Works

Query Optimizer analyzes an executed query and creates several possible query plans for the query. For each query plan, the Optimizer determines the estimated cost to run each query. The query plan with the smallest cost is then used to run the query. The query plans aren't actually run to determine the cost but instead are just estimated. Estimated costs derive from input and output requirements of the query, CPU requirements, memory requirements, and more.

Figure 2-1 shows how the Optimizer works. A query is submitted to the database management system. After the query is *parsed* (verified that the syntax is correct), it's sent to the Optimizer. The Optimizer analyzes the query and the database to determine different indexes to use and different join methods.

The Optimizer then creates several query plans. For each of these plans, it determines an estimated cost. The query is then compiled using the query plan with the lowest estimated cost — a *cost-based optimization.*

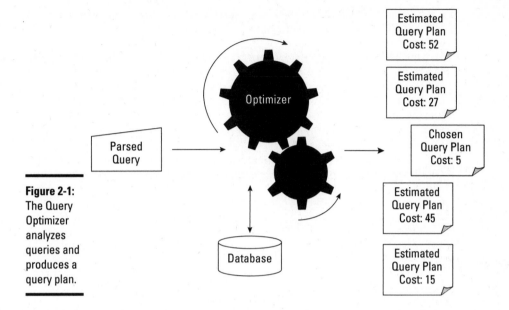

Figure 2-1:
The Query
Optimizer
analyzes
queries and
produces a
query plan.

The cost of a query

Within SQL Server 2008, query plans are evaluated based on the costs. Costs aren't dollars, but instead refer to time used to access resources. The cost is given in seconds but because cost is an estimated value, it doesn't equate to actual seconds. Instead, think of the cost as a measurement for comparison. When a query is issued, query plans are created. One query plan could be estimated to complete in one second, and a second query plan could be estimated to complete in three seconds. The Optimizer compares these measurements and chooses the quicker plan (in one second).

For every query run on SQL Server, the Optimizer strives to use the least amount of resources possible. This goal equates to having the lowest cost, or taking the shortest amount of time.

The following resources have an associated cost and are evaluated in the cost of a query:

✦ CPU or processor

✦ Memory usage

✦ Input/output operations

✦ Disk buffer space

✦ Disk storage time

Each of these resources is assigned an estimated cost. All the costs are added to identify an estimated total cost of the query.

For simple queries with a very small cost, it's possible for only a single query plan to be created and used. For example, if the first query plan created for a simple query is estimated to complete in 8 milliseconds, the Optimizer could use this query plan instead of creating multiple plans and picking the best one. Spending another 30 milliseconds to find a query plan that could run 1 or 2 milliseconds quicker isn't cost effective.

The Optimizer utilizes a sophisticated costing code to determine the actual cost based on a number of variables. The costing code considers

✦ How large the tables are

✦ What indexes are available

✦ How useful the indexes are for this query

✦ The best join methods

✦ The usefulness of statistics

Examining a query plan

A query plan can be viewed as text by using the SET SHOWPLAN_TEXT option. Viewing the query plan provides you a better understanding of how the queries are being run, and what indexes are being used.

The following steps show how to view a query plan:

1. **Launch SQL Server Management Studio (SSMS) by choosing Start⇨All Programs⇨Microsoft SQL Server 2008⇨SQL Server Management Studio.**

2. **On the Connect to Server screen, click Connect.**

3. **Click the New Query button to open a new query window.**

4. **Enter the following query into the query window and press the F5 key to execute it:**

    SET SHOWPLAN_TEXT ON

When turned on, the SHOWPLAN_TEXT option remains on for the rest of the session until it's turned off. While it's on, you can't get results from queries other than the query plan. To turn off the SHOWPLAN_TEXT option, enter the following query and execute it by pressing the F5 key: SET SHOWPLAN_TEXT OFF.

5. **Change the output from a grid format to a text format by right-clicking within the query pane and choosing Results To⇨Results To Text.**

The resulting query plan will be easier to view in a text format than in a grid format.

6. **Enter a query against a database on your system.**

If you have AdventureWorks2008 installed on your SQL Server, use the following query:

```
USE AdventureWorks2008;
GO
SELECT * FROM HumanResources.Employee
```

The query plan for the SELECT statement is in the text following the third StmtText line.

```
|--Compute
 Scalar(DEFINE:([AdventureWorks2008].[HumanResources]
 .[Employee].[OrganizationLevel]=[AdventureWorks2008]
 .[HumanResources].[Employee].[OrganizationLevel]))
     |--Compute
 Scalar(DEFINE:([AdventureWorks2008].[HumanResources]
 .[Employee].[OrganizationLevel]=[AdventureWorks2008]
 .[HumanResources].[Employee].[OrganizationNode].GetL
 evel()))
         |--Clustered Index
 Scan(OBJECT:([AdventureWorks2008].[HumanResources].
 [Employee].[PK_Employee_BusinessEntityID]))
```

This simple query plan merely states to use a clustered index scan when retrieving the data for this query. The clustered index is named PK_Employee_BusinessEntityID and is in the AdventureWorks2008 database, in the Human Resources schema, in the Employee table.

Queries that are more complex have more complex query plans. The following query accesses the data from a view named vEmployee based on a more complex query:

```
SELECT * FROM HumanResources.vEmployee
```

Although this query of the vEmployee view looks very similar to the previous query of the Employee table, the resulting query plan shows the complexity of the view. The query plan for the view includes a variety of indexes (clustered index scan, clustered index seek, and index scan), and different join methods (nested loops and hash matches).

Listing 2-1 shows the resulting query plan. I've bolded each of the methods chosen by the Query Optimizer (such as nested loops, hash match, and so on).

Listing 2-1: Query Plan for the Query of the vEmployee View

```
|--Nested Loops(Left Outer Join, OUTER REFERENCES:([p].[BusinessEntityID],
[Expr1030]) WITH UNORDERED PREFETCH)
     |--Hash Match(Right Outer Join,
HASH:([pnt].[PhoneNumberTypeID])=([pp].[PhoneNumberTypeID]),
RESIDUAL:([AdventureWorks2008].[Person].[PersonPhone].[PhoneNumberTypeID] as
[pp].[PhoneNumberTypeID]=[AdventureWorks2008].[Person].[PhoneNumberType].
[Phone
     |    |--Clustered Index Scan
(OBJECT:([AdventureWorks2008].[Person].[PhoneNumberType].[PK_PhoneNumberType_
PhoneNumberTypeID] AS [pnt]))
     |    |--Nested Loops(Left Outer Join, OUTER
REFERENCES:([p].[BusinessEntityID], [Expr1029]) WITH UNORDERED PREFETCH)
     |         |--Nested Loops(Inner Join, OUTER
REFERENCES:([sp].[CountryRegionCode]))
     |         |    |--Hash Match(Inner Join,
HASH:([sp].[StateProvinceID])=([a].[StateProvinceID]))
     |         |    |    |--Clustered Index Scan
(OBJECT:([AdventureWorks2008].[Person].[StateProvince].[PK_StateProvince_Sta
teProvinceID] AS [sp]))
     |         |    |    |--Nested Loops(Inner Join, OUTER
REFERENCES:([bea].[AddressID], [Expr1028]) WITH UNORDERED PREFETCH)
     |         |    |         |--Nested Loops(Inner Join, OUTER
REFERENCES:([p].[BusinessEntityID], [Expr1027]) WITH UNORDERED PREFETCH)
     |         |    |         |    |--Nested Loops(Inner Join, OUTER
REFERENCES:([e].[BusinessEntityID], [Expr1026]) WITH UNORDERED PREFETCH)
     |         |    |         |    |    |--Clustered Index Scan
(OBJECT:([AdventureWorks2008].[HumanResources].[Employee].[PK_Employee_Busin
essEntityID] AS [e]))
     |         |    |         |    |    |--Clustered Index Seek
(OBJECT:([AdventureWorks2008].[Person].[Person].[PK_Person_BusinessEntityID]
AS [p]),
SEEK:([p].[BusinessEntityID]=[AdventureWorks2008].[HumanResources].[Employee].
[BusinessEntityID] as [e].[
     |         |    |         |    |--Clustered Index Seek
(OBJECT:([AdventureWorks2008].[Person].[BusinessEntityAddress].[PK_BusinessE
ntityAddress_BusinessEntityID_AddressID_AddressTypeID] AS [bea]),
SEEK:([bea].[BusinessEntityID]=[AdventureWorks2008].[P
     |         |    |         |--Clustered Index Seek
(OBJECT:([AdventureWorks2008].[Person].[Address].[PK_Address_AddressID] AS
[a]),
SEEK:([a].[AddressID]=[AdventureWorks2008].[Person].[BusinessEntityAddress].
[AddressID] as [bea].[AddressID]) ORDERED FO
     |         |    |--Clustered Index Seek
(OBJECT:([AdventureWorks2008].[Person].[CountryRegion].[PK_CountryRegion_Cou
ntryRegionCode] AS [cr]),
SEEK:([cr].[CountryRegionCode]=[AdventureWorks2008].[Person].[StateProvince].
[CountryRegionCode] as [sp].[Cou
     |         |--Clustered Index Seek
(OBJECT:([AdventureWorks2008].[Person].[PersonPhone].[PK_PersonPhone_Busines
sEntityID_PhoneNumber_PhoneNumberTypeID] AS [pp]),
SEEK:([pp].[BusinessEntityID]=[AdventureWorks2008].[Person].[Person].[Busine
ssEntityID] a
     |--Clustered Index Seek
(OBJECT:([AdventureWorks2008].[Person].[EmailAddress].[PK_EmailAddress_Busin
essEntityID_EmailAddressID] AS [ea]),
SEEK:([ea].[BusinessEntityID]=[AdventureWorks2008].[Person].[Person].[Busine
ssEntityID] as [p].[BusinessEntityID]))
```

This query plan allows you to peer into the inner workings of the Query Optimizer. Of course, you may be wondering, "Why would I ever want to peer in there?" Sometimes you might just want to know whether the Query Optimizer is using an index you've created.

For example, you might have created a composite index that included the address lines, city, state, and postal code columns in the Person.Address table specifically to optimize this query. Now you want to ensure that the index is being used. Based on the query plan, you can verify whether the index is or isn't being used. The Person.Address table includes a composite index named:

```
IX_Address_AddressLine1_AddressLine2_City_StateProvinceID_PostalCode
```

Because the index isn't named in the query plan, you know it isn't being used by this query. You could either modify the index to make it more useful or delete it to eliminate the overhead required to maintain the index.

You can easily become overwhelmed with the quantity of data in a query plan. However, most of the data can be ignored. You typically use this to verify only that a specific index you've created is being used in this query plan.

For example, you could use the Database Engine Tuning Advisor to identify and create the best indexes to create for specific queries. Later, you might want to verify that the indexes you created are still being used. By viewing the query plan, you can easily determine whether the indexes are being used. If not, it's probably time to run the Database Engine Tuning Advisor again.

**Book III
Chapter 2**

**The SQL Server
Optimizer**

Using Execution Plans to Figure Out What's Happening

Execution plans are graphical representations of a query plan. You view an execution plan to determine how the query optimizer is building the query. Execution plans are often easier to view and interpret than the all-text query plans. They also provide a lot more information on the cost of a query.

To display an execution plan, perform the following steps:

1. **Launch SQL Server Management Studio (SSMS) by choosing Start⇨All Programs⇨Microsoft SQL Server 2008⇨SQL Server Management Studio.**

2. **On the Connect to Server screen, click Connect.**

3. **Click the New Query button to open a new query window.**

4. **Right-click in the query window and choose Include Actual Execution Plan.**

   You can also choose Display Estimated Execution Plan from the same menu as Include Actual Execution Plan. The estimated plan displays immediately based on the Optimizer's best guesses. The actual plan appears after the query runs and shows the actual times for the query and each sub element.

5. **Enter a query into the query window.**

   If you have AdventureWorks2008 installed, use the following query:

   ```
   USE AdventureWorks2008;
   GO
   SELECT * FROM HumanResources.Employee;
   ```

6. **Press F5 to execute the query.**

7. **Click the Execution Plan tab to view the execution plan.**

   As shown in Figure 2-2, the execution plan has four nodes with the majority of the work done in the Clustered Index Scan node.

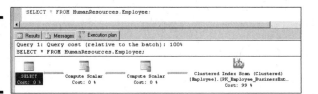

Figure 2-2:
A basic execution plan.

Execution plans are read from top to bottom, right to left. In this simple query, the first part of the plan is the clustered index scan, and the last part of the query is the SELECT statement.

Additionally, execution plans can easily become quite complex. Figure 2-3 shows the resulting execution plan from a query on the HumanResources. vEmployee view in the AdventureWorks2008 database. The details can't be read on this graphic, but you can see that the execution plan is composed of 18 different nodes. When analyzing this query, you drill down into the icon at the top right, and read from top to bottom and right to left.

Each of the steps has associated costs, which represent the steps' portion of the total cost. When you hover over the icon of an individual step, a ToolTip graphic appears showing the costs associated with that step.

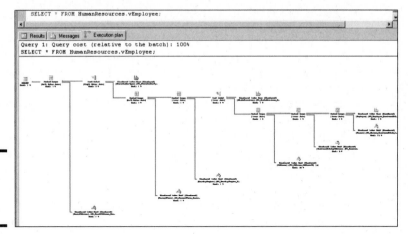

Figure 2-3:
A complex execution plan.

Figure 2-4 shows a ToolTip for one of the Clustered Index Scan nodes within the execution plan. The information that appears in the ToolTip is dependent upon the operation performed by the node.

Figure 2-4:
The Clustered Index Scan ToolTip from the execution plan.

Clustered Index Scan (Clustered)
[Employee].[PK_Employee_BusinessEnt...
Cost: 99 %

Clustered Index Scan (Clustered)
Scanning a clustered index, entirely or only a range.

Physical Operation	Clustered Index Scan
Logical Operation	Clustered Index Scan
Actual Number of Rows	290
Estimated I/O Cost	0.0075694
Estimated CPU Cost	0.000476
Number of Executions	1
Estimated Number of Executions	1
Estimated Operator Cost	0.0080454 (99%)
Estimated Subtree Cost	0.0080454
Estimated Number of Rows	290
Estimated Row Size	828 B
Actual Rebinds	0
Actual Rewinds	0
Ordered	False
Node ID	2

Object
[AdventureWorks2008].[HumanResources].[Employee].
[PK_Employee_BusinessEntityID]

The following list describes the information that appears in the ToolTip:

✦ **Physical Operation:** Indicates the operation that will be used to implement the specified logical operation. Physical and logical operations (see the following bullet) are sometimes the same. Common physical operators are sort, nested loop, hash match, clustered index seek, clustered index scan, and index scans.

✦ **Logical Operation:** Conceptually describes what operation needs to be performed. Common logical operators are sort, inner join, clustered index seek, clustered index scan, outer join, and index scans.

✦ **Actual Number of Rows:** No surprise here. This identifies the number of rows returned from the query.

✦ **Estimated I/O Cost:** The estimated total input/output cost for this node (in seconds). Input/output cost is typically referring to disk activity but can also include memory activity.

✦ **Estimated CPU Cost:** Estimated cost of all processor activity for this node (in seconds).

✦ **Estimated Operator Cost:** The total cost (in seconds) of this node. This is the sum of the I/O cost and the CPU cost.

✦ **Estimated Subtree Cost:** The cost of this node and all nodes preceding it (to the right of this node).

✦ **Estimated Number of Rows:** The number or rows produced by this node.

✦ **Estimated Row Size:** Estimated size of the row (in bytes) produced by this node.

✦ **Actual Rebinds:** Physical operators that initialize a connection with the data, collect the data, and then close. A *rebind* is the number of times the physical operator resets and repeats the initialize phase.

✦ **Actual Rewinds:** *Rewind* indicates that the inner result set for a join query can be reused (and a rebind isn't necessary).

✦ **Ordered:** Either true or false. If true, it indicates the data is ordered, such as alphabetically or numerically in ascending or descending order. For example, a clustered index would be ordered when first accessed, but might not be ordered after being merged with results of other nodes.

✦ **Node ID:** A number identifying a node. Nodes are numbered from left to right and from top to bottom (not right to left, as you would read the nodes) and start with the number 0.

Client Statistics: Helping the Optimizer Do Its Job

The Optimizer uses statistics to help it create estimated query plans. Statistics within SQL Server work the same way as they do in other applications.

For example, consider an orange buyer purchasing a truckload of oranges. The price of oranges varies depending on how sweet or how acidic the oranges are, so the first thing she needs to do is determine how sweet the oranges are. She can do this in one of two ways:

+ Take a sample from every orange on the truck and measure the sweetness and acidity.

+ Remove a statistical sampling of oranges and measure the sweetness and acidity of the sample.

Bet that the latter choice is picked. By calculating the average and deviation of the sample of oranges, accurate predictions of the entire truckload of oranges can be made.

The Optimizer uses statistics when trying to determine the usefulness of available indexes. When determining the usefulness of an index, the Optimizer must determine two things:

+ **What's the density of this index for this query?** A low density is desired.

+ **What's the selectivity of this index for this query?** A high selectivity is desired.

Understanding the density of an index

Density refers to the number of duplicate rows in a column.

Consider a business that does business in Virginia Beach, Virginia. More than 90 percent of the customers live in Virginia Beach. The other 10 percent of the customers live in nearby cities or are tourists from around the country.

The business has a database with a table named Customers. On the Customers table, an index has been created on the City column. If the following query were executed, the Optimizer would not use the index on the City column because the index is too dense.

```
SELECT *
FROM Customers
ORDER BY City
```

On a Customers table with 10,000 entries, about 9,000 entries are identical. Using the index would not increase the performance of the query.

However, this same index might be useful for another query. The following query retrieves a list of customers who do not live in Virginia Beach.

```
SELECT *
FROM Customers
WHERE City <> 'Virginia Beach'
ORDER BY City
```

By using the index, the entire table of 10,000 rows can quickly be whittled to only 1,000 rows. With the index, the Optimizer is able to reduce the amount of data that needs to be searched to only 10 percent of the total. In this case, the index isn't considered dense for the query.

Understanding the selectivity of an index

Selectivity is the number of rows returned by a query. The goal is to be *highly selective* (return the least number of rows).

Primary keys are created to enforce uniqueness on a table. With a primary key, every row is guaranteed to be *unique* (one of kind without any duplicates).

A query that retrieves a single row based on the primary key is highly selective. For example, the following query would return a single row based on the primary key of CustomerID:

```
SELECT *
FROM Customers
WHERE CustomerID = 1
```

Using statistics

How does the Optimizer know whether an index has either high selectivity or low density and should be included in a query plan? Consider the earlier example of the Customers table with 10,000 rows.

The same as the earlier example of the orange buyer who had two choices to determine the sweetness of the oranges, the Optimizer also has two possible choices to determine the usefulness of the indexes:

+ Look at each of the 10,000 rows and make a determination on the selectivity and density.

+ Look at a statistical sample of the 10,000 rows and make a determination on the selectivity and density.

For speed and performance, the Optimizer chooses the latter. Statistics are automatically created on indexes by default, and the Optimizer has these available for use.

With a 10,000-row Customers table, the index would also be 10,000 rows, but the statistics would be considerably less. The distance between rows in the statistics in the index is referred to as *steps*.

For example, on an index with 10,000 rows, the database management system might choose to create 300 statistics samples. When you do the math, 10,000 / 300 = 33.33, which rounds up to 34. With this example, the statistics would be created with the following data from the index:

✦ The first row of the statistics is always the first row of the index.

✦ Middle rows for the statistics are every 34th row after the first.

✦ The last row of the statistics is always the last row of the index.

Therefore, if the Optimizer needs to determine whether the index is useful for a given query, instead of having to search through 10,000 rows to determine the selectivity and density, it has to search through only 300 rows.

Automatically creating and maintaining statistics

One of the most important concepts to remember with statistics is to let the system do the work. As long as statistics are created and maintained by the system, you won't have to do anything else on the majority of databases.

Statistics are set to be automatically created and updated by default with the following two settings:

✦ **Auto Create Statistics:** This setting specifies that the Optimizer automatically create any missing statistics during optimization of a query. Statistics could be missing if they weren't created when the index was created, or they were deleted afterward.

✦ **Auto Update Statistics:** This setting specifies that SQL Server will automatically update statistics. If the Optimizer evaluates statistics that it determines are out of date, the Optimizer automatically updates them. Statistics can become out of date when the underlying data changes significantly.

If you suspect that statistics aren't being maintained on a database, check the properties of the database with these steps:

1. **Launch SQL Server Management Studio (SSMS) by choosing Start⇨All Programs⇨Microsoft SQL Server 2008⇨SQL Server Management Studio.**

2. **On the Connect to Server screen, click Connect.**

3. **Browse to your database in the Databases container.**

4. **Right-click your database and choose Properties.**

5. **In the Database Properties dialog box, select the Options page.**

As shown in Figure 2-5, Auto Create Statistics is set to True, and Auto Update Statistics is set to True. These are the defaults for both settings.

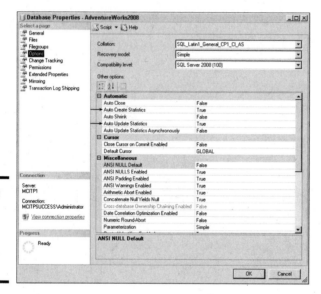

Figure 2-5:
Database
properties
showing
statistics
settings.

Chapter 3: Using the Query Designer

In This Chapter

✔ **Launching the Query Designer**

✔ **Creating queries with the Query Designer**

✔ **Editing queries within the Query Designer**

✔ **Exporting results**

✔ **Exporting queries**

Databases are great sources of information, but retrieving the data can be a challenge. Thankfully, SQL Server 2008 includes the Query Designer — a great GUI (Graphical User Interface; pronounced *GOO-ee*) — that makes creating and modifying queries easy. With a little pointing and clicking, you can create queries to access, and even modify, any data in your database.

This chapter shows you how to use the Query Designer to create and edit queries. With the queries created, you can execute them to access your data, export the result set, and then save your queries.

Creating a New Query

A *query* is a request for data; it's how you ask questions of the database. For example, suppose you want to retrieve a listing of everyone in the database by first name, last name, and e-mail address. You can create and execute a query to retrieve a listing of this data.

As with most work in SQL Server 2008, you start in the SQL Server Management Studio (SSMS).

With SSMS open, the first step is to launch the Query Designer. As with most tools in Microsoft products, you can achieve your objective by using multiple methods. The following steps show one method of accessing and using the Query Designer:

1. **Using the SSMS Object Explorer, browse to the AdventureWorks sample database within the Databases container.**

2. **Right-click the AdventureWorks2008 database and choose New Query to open a new query window.**

   A blank query window opens, and the SQL Editor toolbar appears, as shown in Figure 3-1. Because you create this query window from the AdventureWorks2008 database, queries in this window default to AdventureWorks2008 unless you change the context on the SQL Editor toolbar.

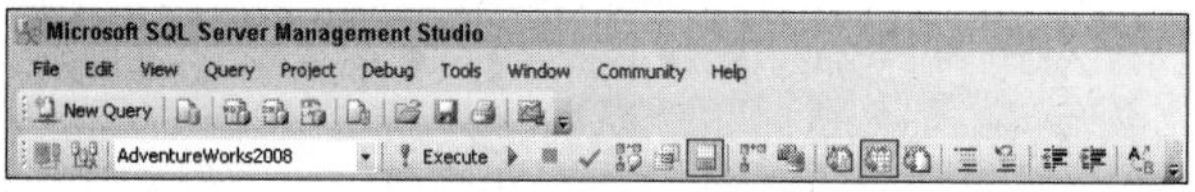

Figure 3-1:
The SQL Editor toolbar with context set to the Adventure Works database.

Microsoft SQL Server Management Studio

File   Edit   View   Query   Project   Debug   Tools   Window   Community   Help

New Query

AdventureWorks2008   Execute

You can also click the New Query button to open a new query window. However, you're often prompted to connect to the server, and instead of setting the context to the AdventureWorks2008 database, the context is set to the Master database. Unless you change the database from Master to AdventureWorks2008, your queries are executed against the Master database, not AdventureWorks2008.

3. **Right-click anywhere in the blank query window and choose Design Query in Editor.**

   The Query Designer opens, and the Add Table dialog box appears. All the tables in the AdventureWorks2008 database appear in the Add Table dialog box.

4. **Select the Person(Person) table, click the Add button, and then click Close in the Add Table dialog box.**

   Three panes are open in the Query Designer. The top pane holds the Person (Person) table, the middle pane is blank, and the bottom pane is beginning to build your query.

5. **In the Person(Person) table, select the check boxes next to the FirstName, LastName, and Title columns.**

   You have to scroll down to see all the columns.

As you select each of the columns, the bottom two panes are changing. In the bottom pane, your query is built as:

```
SELECT FirstName, LastName, Title
FROM Person.Person
```

6. **With your query built, you can now execute it. Click OK to return to the query window.**

The query you built in the Query Designer now appears in the query window.

7. **Click the Execute button on the SQL Editor toolbar.**

At the bottom of the screen, you see the results listed in the AdventureWorks2008 database — more than 19,000 rows of people and addresses.

Instead of using the Query Designer, you could have typed in the query from scratch. Alternatively, you could have copied the query from somewhere and pasted it into the query window. It doesn't matter how the query gets into the query window; when the query is there, you can execute it.

Exploring the Query Designer

The Query Designer has three or four panes depending on how the Query Designer is launched. When launched from the query window, only three panes appear. When launched from the Views container (we show you how in a moment), it includes a fourth pane. Figure 3-2 shows the Query Designer with all four panes.

✦ **Diagram pane (shown with the Person(Person) table):** This pane provides a graphical display of the selected tables. If multiple tables are included, it shows the relationships among the tables. It also allows you to pick the specific columns that you want to appear in your query.

✦ **Criteria pane (shown with FirstName, LastName, and Title columns):** This pane allows you to specify options for your query, such as which rows to display or the order of the output.

✦ **SQL pane (shown with SELECT statement):** Your SQL statement appears here as you make your selections in the Diagram and Criteria panes.

✦ **Results pane (the bottom pane with the results of the query):** After your query is created, you can execute it and see the results here, but only if you access the Query Designer via the Views container.

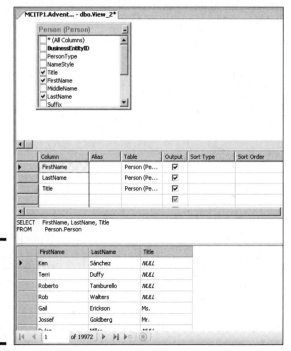

Figure 3-2:
The Query
Designer
with four
panes
showing.

Any of the four panes can be made visible or invisible. For example, after selecting the tables and columns in the Diagram pane, you can make the pane invisible so that you have more room to work with on your screen. Simply right-click the Query Designer and choose Pane. You can select Diagram, Criteria, SQL, or Results, to toggle the visibility of each of these panes. The only exception is when you're working in the Query Designer from the query window. In this view, the Results pane is dimmed and not selectable.

The Query Designer allows you to build more than simple SELECT queries. Generally, the SELECT query allows you to ask questions of the database. However, you can also create INSERT, UPDATE, and DELETE queries in the Query Designer.

An INSERT query allows you to add data to the database, such as when you hire a new employee. An UPDATE query allows you to modify data, such as a different phone number or e-mail address for an existing employee. A DELETE query allows you to delete rows, such as when an employee wins the lottery and quits the job.

Launching the Query Designer via the Views container

Earlier in this chapter, we show you how to create your first query by launching the Query Designer from the AdventureWorks database and using the New Query button. The Query Designer has more capabilities than those we've explored so far; however, it has two significant limitations when launched from the query window:

✦ **Queries can't be executed from within the Query Designer:** You must exit the Query Designer before you execute the query and see your results.

✦ **Queries can't be easily modified:** If your results aren't what you want, you must launch the Query Designer again and start over.

To overcome these limitations, launch the Query Designer from the Views container. When launched from the Views container, the Query Designer is sometimes referred to as the Views Designer. Your query is built the same way and, if desired, you can copy the query from the Query Designer and paste it into the query window.

In the following steps, you launch the Query Designer from the Views container, and create a query to retrieve a listing of the employee names and titles.

1. **With SSMS open, use the Object Explorer to browse to the Databases | AdventureWorks2008 | Views container.**

It looks similar to Figure 3-3.

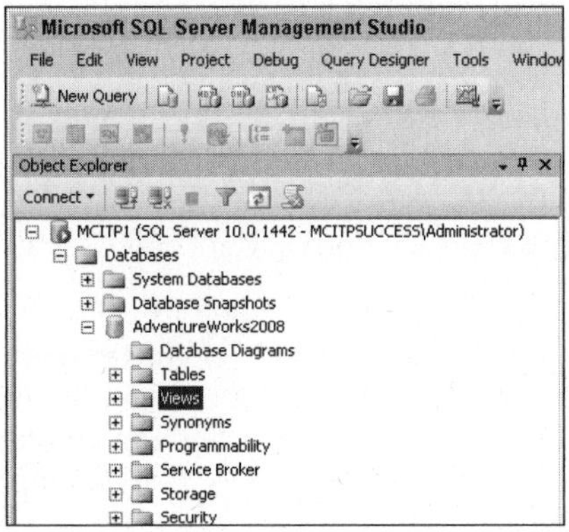

Figure 3-3: Using Object Explorer to browse to the Views container.

Book III
Chapter 3

Using the
Query Designer

2. **Right-click Views and choose New View.**

   The Query Designer opens, and the Add Table dialog box appears. Below the standard toolbar, you might also notice an additional toolbar — the View Designer toolbar.

3. **Select the Person(Person) table and click Add. Select the Employee (HumanResources) table and click Add. Click Close.**

   The Query Designer is open with your two tables (Person and Employee). Click the title of either table to drag and drop within the Diagram pane.

   The connector between the two tables identifies the relationship. The relationship has been defined on the BusinessEntityID (primary key) in the Person table and the BusinessEntityID (foreign key) in the Employee table. The connector has a key symbol on both sides. These icons indicate a one-to-one relationship between the two tables.

4. **Scroll through the columns in the Employee table.**

   The Employee table doesn't have any names or titles. AdventureWorks2008 is designed so that you see only the names of people in the Person table. Because you added the Employee table, however, your SQL statement now includes an INNER JOIN.

5. **Select the check boxes next to the FirstName, LastName, and Title columns in the Person(Person) table.**

   The SQL pane shows that your query is built similar to how it was built earlier. A significant difference is that each column name (FirstName, LastName, Title) is prefaced with the name of the table you selected the column from (Person.Person). Because you now have more than one table in your query, the tables are specified with the column name. Your query looks like the following code:

   ```
   SELECT Person.Person.FirstName, Person.Person.LastName,
          Person.Person.Title
   FROM HumanResources.Employee
     INNER JOIN Person.Person
     ON HumanResources.Employee.BusinessEntityID =
        Person.Person.BusinessEntityID
   ```

   Aren't you glad you didn't have to type that in?

   The T-SQL code generator in the Query Designer occasionally gets a little rambunctious and adds additional lines, such as AND Person. Person.BusinessEntityID = HumanResources.Employee. BusinessEntityID. If more than one identical comparison is added, it can be deleted. Only one of the comparions is needed.

6. With the query created, you can execute it. Choose Execute SQL from the Query Designer drop-down menu. (You can also press Ctrl+R on your keyboard or click the red exclamation mark on the View Designer toolbar.)

After executing the query, the results — a listing of 290 employees — appear in the Results pane.

7. To narrow your search, add filters. Below the Filter column to the right of LastName, type Shoop **and then press Enter.**

Your text changed to =N'Shoop'. The N indicates Shoop is displayed in Unicode characters. Your SQL statement is modified by adding a WHERE clause.

8. Execute your query by clicking the Execute SQL button (the red exclamation mark on the toolbar).

Your query returns a single row for Margie Shoop.

9. Right-click the SQL pane and choose Select All. Right-click again and choose Copy.

Your query is on the Windows clipboard. If desired, paste it into a query window and run it from there.

10. Right-click AdventureWorks2008 in the Object Explorer and choose New Query. Right-click the query window and choose Paste.

11. Click the Execute button to run this query in the query window.

Editing Your Query

You can modify any query that you create. If you're like most people, you probably won't get your query perfect the first time you try. Instead, the process involves a lot of editing — one of the reasons why the View Designer (the Query Designer accessible from the Views container) is so valuable.

Queries created in the View Designer can be tweaked (and ran) as many times as you like until it's exactly how you want. After you're happy with the results, copy your query and paste it into the query window.

Modifying queries within the query window is also possible. For example, say you create the following query by using the Query Designer from the query window. The query provides a listing of names and titles for all employees in AdventureWorks2008.

```
SELECT Person.Person.FirstName, Person.Person.LastName,
      Person.Person.Title
FROM HumanResources.Employee INNER JOIN
      Person.Person ON
    HumanResources.Employee.BusinessEntityID =
      Person.Person.BusinessEntityID
```

However, now the boss has asked you to include job titles. To do this, you could return to the Query Designer and re-create the entire query from scratch. However, being familiar with the database, you know that the JobTitle column is in the HumanResources table. You can add that column to the column list. You also have to add a comma after the Person.Person.Title column.

```
SELECT Person.Person.FirstName, Person.Person.LastName,
      Person.Person.Title, HumanResources.Employee.JobTitle
FROM HumanResources.Employee INNER JOIN
      Person.Person ON
    HumanResources.Employee.BusinessEntityID =
      Person.Person.BusinessEntityID
```

Likewise, if the boss asks for the columns to be in a different order, such as Last Name first, you can cut and paste the column names into the exact order you want. The query window works similar to any basic text editor.

You can filter the data differently by using the filter in the Query Designer. By specifying different search conditions, you can retrieve different data. Some of the possible search conditions are

✦ **IN:** Allows you to specify a list of possibilities. For example, `IN (Shoop, Smith, Jones)` returns a listing for any matches in the list.

✦ **LIKE:** Allows a search based on only partial matches. The `%` symbol is used as a wildcard. `LIKE S%` returns the matches that begin with S. `LIKE %S` returns the matches that end with S.

✦ **BETWEEN:** Allows a search based on a range. For example, `BETWEEN A and C` returns a list with anything that starts with A, B or C.

✦ **IS NULL (or IS NOT NULL):** Allows you to return a listing based on whether a specific column is `NULL`. For example, typing **IS NULL** in the EmailAddress filter would cause the query to return only rows where the EmailAddress had a `NULL` value.

To see how these filters work within the Query Designer, follow these steps:

1. **With SSMS open, use the Object Explorer to browse to the Databases | AdventureWorks2008 | Views container. Right-click Views and choose New View.**

2. **Select the Person(Person) table and click the Add button. Click Close.**

3. **Select the check boxes next to the FirstName, MiddleName, LastName, and Title columns.**

4. **In the Filter column that's next to LastName, type** Shoop **and press Enter. Click the Execute SQL button (the red exclamation mark) to execute your query. Click the close button.**

   Your query returns two rows — the only two rows that have an exact match of Shoop in the LastName column.

5. **Change the Filter column to** IN(Shoop, Smith, Jones) **and press Enter. Execute the query.**

   Your query returns 189 rows — the rows with a last name of Shoop, Smith, or Jones.

6. **Change the Filter column to** Like S% **and press Enter. Execute the query.**

   Your query returns 2,130 rows — the rows that have a last name that starts with S.

7. **Change the Filter column to** BETWEEN A and C **and press Enter. Execute the query.**

   Your query returns 2,116 rows — the rows that have a last name that starts with A, B, or C.

8. **Remove the filter in the LastName column by highlighting it and pressing the Delete key. In the Filter column next to MiddleName, type** NULL **and press Enter. Execute the query.**

   Notice that the word NULL in the filter is changed to IS NULL. Your query returns 8,499 rows — the rows that have NULL for the middle name.

You can create some sophisticated queries by using the Query Designer. By making some slight editing changes, you can change your query to give you exactly what you (and your boss) need from the database.

Exporting Your Query or Results

Both queries and results of queries can be exported or saved for later.

Say the sales department staff regularly asks you to retrieve a listing of all the sales to a specific customer; however, the customer they're interested in is different each time they ask. You can create a query each time, pull it up, edit it, and retrieve exactly the information you need.

Queries are saved as SQL scripts with the `.sql` extension. By double-clicking an SQL query file, the SQL script opens in a new query window in SSMS. (Similar to how Microsoft Word opens when you double-click a document with a `.doc` extension.)

So far, you've ran the queries, but no one (other than you) has seen the results. By saving the results to a file, you can give them to others. For example, you can share the results in an e-mail attachment. How the results are saved is dependent on how they're displayed.

You can save results of queries in three different ways. Each choice is selected via a button on the SQL Editor toolbar, or by choosing one via the Query⇨Results To menu item. The choices are:

✦ **Results to Grid:** The grid is the default output. It's similar to a Microsoft Excel Worksheet grid, with each data item having its own cell. The output can be saved to a comma-separated value file (CSV), which can be easily read by Microsoft Excel or a text editor.

✦ **Results to Text:** The output is in a text format, using tabs to align the columns. The output can be saved as a report file (RPT), which can be read by any text editor.

✦ **Results to File:** As soon as a query is run, you're prompted for a name to save the results to a file. It creates the report file, which can be read by any text editor.

Saving the query

In this section, you give saving a query a try. First, you build a query with the Query Designer to retrieve all the sales for a given customer. Then, you save the query so that you can easily call it again.

1. **With SSMS open, use the Object Explorer to browse to the AdventureWorks database.**

2. **Right-click the AdventureWorks2008 database and choose New Query.**

3. **Right-click the query window and choose Design Query in Editor.**

The Query Designer appears with the Add Table dialog box visible.

4. **Scroll to the SalesOrderHeader(Sales) table. Select it and click the Add button.**

5. **Select the check boxes next to the CustomerID, OrderDate, and TotalDue columns.**

6. **In the Filter column to the right of CustomerID, type** 11001 **and click OK.**

The following query is in the query window.

```
SELECT CustomerID, OrderDate, TotalDue
FROM Sales.SalesOrderHeader
WHERE (CustomerID = 11001)
```

7. **Click the Execute button to execute the query.**

8. **To save the query, press Ctrl+S.**

   The Save File As dialog box appears.

9. **Browse to the root of c:\ and click the New Folder button. In the New Folder dialog box, type** SQLScripts **so you have a C:\SQLScripts folder.**

10. **In the File Name box, type** CustomerSales.sql **and click the Save button.**

    That's it. You saved your query. You can open it again anytime you want.

11. **Click the X in the upper-right to close the query window.**

Saving the results

Saving the results is as easy as saving the query. Use the following steps to open the query you just saved and save the results of the query. When saving the file, you have two choices:

+ Comma-separated value file (CSV) format

+ Report file (RPT) format

In the following steps, you retrieve the script you created in the previous steps and run it. With the results showing, you save them in a comma-separated value format and a report format.

1. **With SSMS open, choose File⇨Open⇨File.**

2. **In the Open File dialog box that appears, browse to the C:\SQLScripts folder and select the CustomerSales.sql script you created in the previous section, "Saving the query." Click Open.**

   Your script is open. However, by default, the Master database is selected. If you ran the script against the Master database, it would fail. You need to change this to point to the AdventureWorks2008 database.

3. **Choose the AdventureWorks2008 database from the database drop-down menu on the toolbar.**

   As shown in Figure 3-4, the database listing is in alphabetical order. With the Master database showing, you have to scroll to the AdventureWorks database.

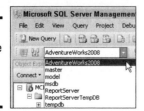

Figure 3-4:
Selecting the
Adventure
Works2008
database.

4. To query information on a different customer, change the CustomerID of 11001 to 11050. Click the Execute SQL button to execute your query.

You can change the CustomerID to whatever customer you're interested in. The point is that you don't have to re-create the entire query.

5. Right-click the Results pane and choose Save Results As.

6. In the Save Grid Results dialog box that appears, browse to the C:\SQLScripts folder. Type Customer11050 **in the File Name box and click Save.**

The results are saved as Customer11050.csv (a comma-separated value file).

7. Change the Results pane to show the data as text. Choose Query⇨Results To⇨Results to Text. Press F5 to rerun the query.

Alternately, you could press Ctrl+T to change it to text. Regardless, the results should be displayed in text in the Results pane.

8. Right-click the Results pane and choose Save Results As.

9. In the Save Results dialog box that appears, browse to the C:\SQLScripts folder and type Customer11050 **in the File Name box.**

The results save as Customer11050.rpt (a report file that can be read by any text editor).

Chapter 4: Setting Query Options

In This Chapter

✔ **Configuring query options with performance and control parameters**

✔ **Selecting formatting options for result sets**

*W*hen executing queries in the SQL Server Management Studio (SSMS) query window, you have the capability to modify how these queries execute by using the Query Options page. Two categories of query options can be manipulated:

✦ **Execution:** You can select General, Advanced, and ANSI standard options to use when executing your queries.

✦ **Results:** You can select various formatting options depending on whether you want your results in a grid format or a text format.

Configuring Query Options with Performance and Control Parameters

The Execution options allow you to specify many different parameters for your query. Parameters are specified on three separate pages:

✦ **General:** Basic query settings, such as how many rows can be returned.

✦ **Advanced:** Many advanced settings, such as those that can be configured with SET statements, are selectable on this page.

✦ **ANSI:** Transact-SQL is *ANSI compliant* — it can be configured to comply with ANSI specifications. The ANSI settings allow you to modify the specifications to either comply with ANSI specifications, or work according to business rules.

To access the Query Options dialog box, follow these steps:

1. **Launch SQL Server Management Studio (SSMS) by choosing Start⇨All Programs⇨Microsoft SQL Server 2008⇨SQL Server Management Studio.**

2. **Click the New Query button to open a new query window.**

3. Right-click the query window and choose Query Options.

You can also select the Query drop-down menu and choose Query Options. The Query Options dialog box appears, as shown in Figure 4-1. The Query Options dialog box defaults to Execution | General.

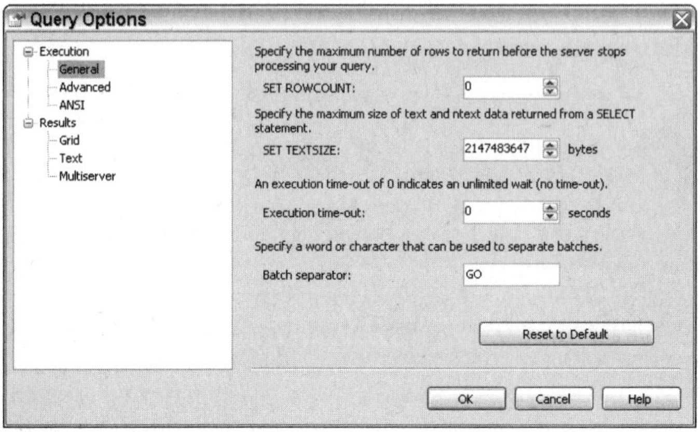

Figure 4-1:
The General settings of the Query Options dialog box.

General: Configure basic query options

The General settings allow you to select some basic options for the query.

✦ **SET ROWCOUNT:** Limits the number of rows for your query. For example, if you want only five rows returned, you set this to 5. When set to the default of 0, all rows from the query are returned.

✦ **SET TEXTSIZE:** Specifies the number of bytes displayed in text data types (varchar(), nvarchar(), text, and ntext). A default of 2GB (2,147,483,647 bytes) supports the large value data types — varchar(max) and nvarchar(max) but doesn't affect the XML data type. For example, if a column has 400 bytes of data but the summary is contained in the first 50 bytes, the text size can be limited to only 50 bytes.

✦ **Execution Time-out:** Specifies the number of seconds to wait before canceling the query. The default of 0 indicates that the query won't time-out. If your database is experiencing many locks, set a time-out to stop the query.

✦ **Batch Separator:** In Transact-SQL, GO (the default) is used to separate batches within a script. You might need to run a script that was created in something other than T-SQL that uses a different batch separator. Instead of changing the script, change the batch separator here.

Without a batch separator, the database engine runs the script from beginning to end. However, some lines within a script must run separately. For example, a script that creates a database and tables within the database must be run as separate batches. The partial script might look like the following code:

```
USE Master;
GO
CREATE Database MyDatabase;
GO
CREATE table . . .
```

✦ **Reset to Default:** Click this button to restore the defaults. You can also click this button to see what the defaults are.

Advanced: Configure advanced execution settings

By selecting Advanced in the Query Options dialog box, you access the advanced execution settings. Most of these are useful when troubleshooting performance issues with a query. Figure 4-2 shows the Advanced settings that can be configured.

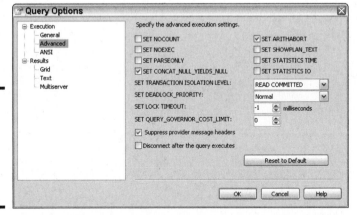

Figure 4-2: The Advanced settings of the Query Options dialog box.

Although manipulating these settings in the Query Options dialog box affects the query window, many of these same settings are commonly used in scripts and stored procedures to affect the environment when the script or stored procedure runs.

Any setting that begins with SET (which we describe in the following list) can be included within code. By searching SQL Server Books Online, you can find the exact syntax. For example, entering **SET NOCOUNT** into SQL Server Books Online finds the article for this command and shows the syntax is:

```
SET NOCOUNT { ON | OFF }
```

You can access Books Online by choosing Start⇨All Programs⇨Microsoft SQL Server 2008⇨Documentation and Tutorials⇨SQL Server Books Online.

✦ **SET NOCOUNT:** Normally, when a query runs, the Messages tab in the result set indicates how many rows were retrieved. The count can be suppressed by checking this box. If your result set is very large, suppressing the count might help performance. The setting is cleared by default.

✦ **SET NOEXEC:** Causes the batch to be compiled but not executed. Use this when you want to validate both the syntax and the objects (such as table names) within a batch. Unlike PARSEONLY, the NOEXEC setting verifies that the objects exist in the database (and the spelling is accurate). The default is cleared.

✦ **SET PARSEONLY:** This setting verifies the syntax of the script. Pressing the blue Parse button (✓) on the toolbar performs the same function. The Parse button is next to the Execute button (! Execute) on the toolbar. The default is cleared.

✦ **SET CONCAT_NULL_YIELDS_NULL:** With this set (the default), any time a query concatenates one value with another and one of the values is NULL, the result is NULL. For example, if the first name, middle name, and last name columns in a table are *concatenated* (logically joined together) and the middle name is NULL, then the entire name is interpreted as NULL.

✦ **SET ARITHABORT:** With this set (the default), arithmetic errors (such as divide by zero errors) cause the query to terminate. Clearing the check box causes NULL to be returned for values (whenever possible) instead of an error.

This setting interacts with SET ANSI_WARNINGS in the ANSI settings. If both settings are selected (the default), arithmetic errors cause the faulty query to terminate. However, if other queries are included in the batch the faulty queries still run. If SET ARITHABORT is selected but SET ANSI WARNINGS isn't selected, the entire batch is terminated.

✦ **SET SHOWPLAN_TEXT:** Setting this check box causes a query plan to be returned instead of the results of the query. (The Query Optimizer creates the query plan.) You use this setting to determine whether specific indexes are being used. For example, the following output was created after turning on this setting for a query. The clustered index on primary key BusinessEntityID is being used for the query.

```
StmtText
-----------------------------------------------------------------
SELECT *
FROM HumanResources.Employee
WHERE BusinessEntityID = 1

StmtText
-----------------------------------------------------------------
 |--Compute Scalar
   (DEFINE:([AdventureWorks2008].[HumanResources].[Employee].[Organizat
   ionLevel]=[AdventureWorks2008].[HumanResources].[Employee].[Organiza
   tionLevel]))
      |--Compute Scalar
   (DEFINE:([AdventureWorks2008].[HumanResources].[Employee].[Organizat
   ionLevel]=[AdventureWorks2008].[HumanResources].[Employee].[Organiza
   tionNode].GetLevel()))
         |--Clustered Index Seek
   (OBJECT:([AdventureWorks2008].[HumanResources].[Employee].[PK_Employ
   ee_BusinessEntityID]),
   SEEK:([AdventureWorks2008].[HumanResources].[Employee].[BusinessEnti
   tyID]=CONVERT_IMPLICIT(int,[@1],0)) ORDERED FORWARD)
```

✦ **SET STATISTICS TIME:** Activating this setting displays the number of milliseconds required to parse, compile, and execute each statement. You use this to capture basic time statistics of queries. This is cleared by default.

✦ **SET STATISTICS IO:** Activating this setting displays statistics on input/output activity for the query. It indicates the scan count (number of scans performed for the query), logical reads (number of pages read from cache), physical reads (number of pages read from the disk), and read-ahead reads (number of pages placed into cache for the query). This setting is cleared by default.

✦ **SET TRANSACTION ISOLATION LEVEL:** This setting can be used to control the locking and row versioning behavior of a query. For most databases, multiple users can read the data at the same time. However, if one user wants to modify that data, it's *locked* — other users can't access it until the modification is complete. This prevents *dirty reads* — reading modified data that hasn't been committed and might not be committed.

Occasionally, in advanced applications, the default behavior is modified to improve the performance of the database. By default, the READ COMMITTED transaction isolation level is set. The transaction isolation levels that can be selected via this property page are

- **READ COMMITTED:** Only data that has been committed to the database can be read within this query.

- **READ UNCOMMITTED:** Data that has been changed by one transaction (but not committed yet) can be read by this transaction.

**Book III
Chapter 4**

**Setting Query
Options**

- **REPEATABLE READ:** Data being modified by this transaction can't be read or modified by any other transaction.

- **SERIALIZABLE:** This is the most restrictive transaction isolation level. Data being read or modified by this transaction can't be read or modified by any other transaction.

✦ Modifying the transaction level is typically done only in very large databases. Changing the transaction level causes side effects with data, such as dirty reads, non-repeatable reads, phantom reads, and lost updates. This is typically done only within a stored procedure using the SET TRANSACTION ISOLATION LEVEL setting. By using the SET statement, the SNAPSHOT TRANSACTION ISOLATION LEVEL can be set, but it can't be set via the Query Options dialog box.

✦ **SET DEADLOCK_PRIORITY:** The default of this setting is Normal. By changing it to Low, your query loses any deadlock conflict and is terminated.

Deadlocks occur when the database engine recognizes that two different processes are waiting on a resource (such as rows within a table) that is locked by the other process. For example, Maria can run a query that locks the Sales table and then tries to access the Customers table. At the same time, Jose locks the Customers table and tries to access the Sales table.

Maria's Activity	Jose's Activity
Transaction started.	Transaction started.
Transaction accesses and locks Sales table.	Transaction accesses and locks Products table.
Transaction tries to access Products table.	Transaction tries to access Sales table.

The processing is deadlocked at this point. Jose can't access the Sales table until Maria releases it. Maria won't release the Sales table until she can access the Products table that Jose has locked while waiting for the Sales table. Thankfully, SQL Server 2008 recognizes the deadlock condition and terminates one of the processes. The default of Normal for the DEADLOCK_PRIORITY sets the priority the same for all transactions. The newest transaction is designated the deadlock victim and is terminated.

✦ **SET LOCK TIMEOUT:** This setting specifies how long (in milliseconds) your query waits for locks to be released. When set to –1 (the default), queries wait as long as necessary. A value of 0 causes queries to terminate with an error message as soon as a lock is encountered.

✦ **SET QUERY_GOVERNOR_COST_LIMIT:** This setting prevents long-running queries from running. Before a query runs, the Query Optimizer parses and optimizes it and determines an estimated cost in seconds. If the estimated cost is greater than this setting (also in seconds), then the query doesn't run. The default of 0 allows all queries to run no matter how long they're estimated to take.

✦ **Suppress Provider Message Headers:** SQL Server 2008 interacts with many different data sources by using database providers, such as Microsoft SQL Native Client OLE DB Provider and Microsoft OLE DB Provider for Oracle. Providers often return messages that can be useful when troubleshooting queries that are failing at the provider level. Activate this setting to see these messages; it's off by default.

✦ **Disconnect After the Query Executes:** This setting causes the connection with the server to close after a query executes. Subsequent queries will fail until the connection is reestablished. Use this setting when you're working on a production server that is running close to capacity and limited resources are available.

✦ **Reset to Default:** Click this button to restore the defaults. You can also click this button to see what the defaults are.

ANSI: Configuring ANSI parameters

ANSI (American National Standards Institute) adopted a standard for the SQL language in 1986 and then updated it in 1992. The standard adopted in 1992 is commonly referred to as the *SQL-92 standard.*

Additionally, the International Organization for Standardization (ISO) adopted an SQL standard formally known as ISO 9075 and published as the *ISO/IEC SQL-92 standard.* The settings in this section are sometimes referred to as ANSI SQL-92 standards, and at other times referred to as ISO settings. Within SQL Server 2008, both standards are the same.

ISO isn't an acronym for International Organization for Standardization. (If it was an acronym, it looks like I'm confused and should have listed it as IOS.) As an international organization, it was recognized that its name would be represented differently in different languages. The founders adopted the organization's short name of ISO from the Greek word *isos,* meaning equal.

By setting various ANSI parameters, you can cause SQL Server 2008 to mimic the functionality of the ANSI SQL-92 standard for SQL. The SQL-92 standard was created so that the SQL language would be standardized between different versions of SQL. However, many subtle differences exist among the different versions of SQL. Microsoft uses Transact-SQL, which includes its own subtle differences.

The ability to modify these parameters is useful if you're using scripts that were created from another version of SQL.

For example, a script written for an Oracle database could be copied and pasted into the query window, but it would function a little differently. Specifically, because an Oracle database uses explicit transactions, every INSERT, UPDATE and DELETE statement needs to be committed with a COMMIT TRANSACTION statement.

Because SQL Server 2008 uses implicit transactions, every INSERT, UPDATE and DELETE statement automatically commits to the database when it's executed. Extra COMMIT TRANSACTION statements that are required with the Oracle script are interpreted as errors within SQL Server 2008 unless the SET IMPLICIT_TRANSACTIONS check box is selected or the SET IMPLICIT TRANSACTIONS ON statement is executed at the beginning of the script.

Figure 4-3 shows the ANSI standard settings that can be selected for SQL Server 2008. If SET ANSI_DEFAULTS was selected, all the check boxes would be selected.

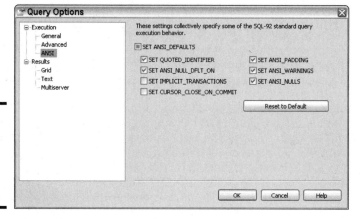

Figure 4-3:
The ANSI settings of the Query Options dialog box.

✦ **SET ANSI_DEFAULTS:** By selecting this check box, all the check boxes on this page will be selected. By default, this box is dimmed, indicating that some ANSI defaults are selected, but not all of them. Clicking it once clears the ANSI defaults; clicking it again sets them all.

✦ **SET QUOTED_IDENTIFIER:** This setting allows identifiers (names of objects) to be identified with quotation marks. Within T-SQL, objects are commonly identified with brackets ([ ]). However, the identifier marks can be omitted if the name of the object isn't a reserved word and has no spaces within it. For example, if you have an Employees table and the SET QUOTED_IDENTIFIER check box is selected, a `SELECT` statement could be written in three ways:

```
SELECT * FROM Employees
SELECT * FROM [Employees]
SELECT * FROM "Employees"
```

+ The marks (quotes or brackets) used to identify objects are *delimiters.* Delimiters are required if a name includes spaces, such as [Employee Address], or is a reserved word, such as a table named [Table] in a furniture business' database.

+ **SET ANSI_NULL_DFLT_ON:** When a table is created or altered, you can create columns and specify whether `NULL` data is allowed. If specified as NOT NULL, data must be entered into the column. If specified as NULL, data can be omitted, and a `NULL` value can be stored in the column. With this setting selected (the default), columns that aren't defined as NOT NULL default to a definition of NULL.

+ **SET IMPLICIT_TRANSACTIONS:** Within T-SQL, any `INSERT`, `UPDATE`, or `DELETE` statement commits when it's executed — *autocommit mode.* Other versions of SQL are written so that `INSERT`, `UPDATE`, and `DELETE` statements aren't committed until a `COMMIT TRANSACTION` statement is executed. For example, the following statement demonstrates autocommit mode. It executes and commits immediately within SQL Server 2008:

```
DELETE FROM Employees WHERE BusinessEntityID = 1
```

However, ANSI-92 SQL statements don't automatically commit until a `COMMIT TRANSACTION` statement is executed. The same statement written to the ANSI-92 specification is written as follows:

```
DELETE FROM Employees WHERE BusinessEntityID = 1
COMMIT TRANSACTION
```

This setting is cleared by default. Select it when using a script that was written for a database that uses implicit transactions instead of auto-commit transactions.

+ **SET CURSOR_CLOSE_ON_COMMIT:** A cursor is an in-memory representation of data that can be examined and manipulated on a row-by-row basis. Within T-SQL scripts, cursors remain open until they're explicitly closed (with the `CLOSE` and `DEALLOCATE` statements) or until the connection to the database is closed. Selecting this setting causes cursors to close when a transaction using the cursor is committed. It's not selected by default.

+ **SET ANSI_PADDING:** With this setting on (the default), trailing blanks in `varchar(n)` data types, and trailing zeros in `varbinary(n)` data types aren't trimmed but instead stored exactly as they're entered. If not selected, trailing blanks in `varchar(n)` data types and trailing zeros in `varbinary(n)` data types are trimmed.

Book III Chapter 4

Setting Query Options

The storage of char(n) and binary(n) data types is the same whether this setting is selected or not. If the inserted data is smaller than the column, trailing blanks are used for char(n) columns, and trailing zeros are used for binary(n) columns.

This setting is applied only when a column is created. After the column is created, the stored values are based on the setting when the column was created. Microsoft recommends this setting always be on. The ability to turn off this setting will disappear in future versions of Microsoft's SQL Server. Use of the SET statement to turn off this setting has been deprecated.

Deprecated features should not be used. When Microsoft deprecates a feature, it's giving notice that this feature will probably not be supported in the next version of the product. It's very possible that many users are using a deprecated feature, which is why the feature isn't discontinued completely; instead, it's being retained for backward compatibility. For example, the DUMP statement was deprecated in SQL Server 2005. The DUMP statement is no longer supported in SQL Server 2008.

✦ **SET ANSI_WARNINGS:** When this setting is on (the default), warnings and errors are reported according to ANSI standards.

• When on, warnings are generated anytime NULL values are calculated in aggregate functions (such as SUM, AVG, MAX, MIN, and COUNT). NULL values are ignored in aggregate functions, and the warning provides only a reminder.

For example, if you want the average weight of five products that had weights recorded as 1, 3, 5, NULL, and NULL, you get two possible answers depending on how the NULL values are interpreted. If NULL values are ignored, the calculation is (1 + 3 + 5) / 3, which equals a value of 3. If NULL values are assumed to be 0 (a dangerous assumption), the calculation is (1 + 3 + 5 + 0 + 0) / 5, which equals an incorrect value of 1.8.

Warnings display in the Results tab of the query window, as shown in Figure 4-4.

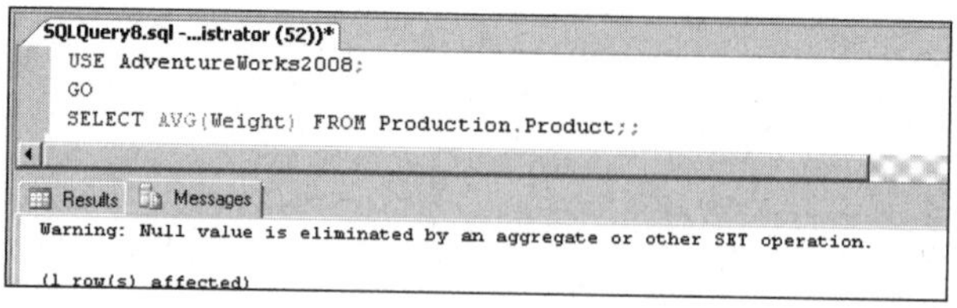

Figure 4-4:
A warning displays when a calculation includes NULL values.

```
SQLQuery8.sql -...istrator (52))*
    USE AdventureWorks2008;
    GO
    SELECT AVG(Weight) FROM Production.Product;;
◄
 Results   Messages
Warning: Null value is eliminated by an aggregate or other SET operation.

(1 row(s) affected)
```

- Divide by zero and arithmetic overflow errors within a T-SQL statement cause the statement to roll back with an error message. If this setting isn't selected, the errors are interpreted as NULL values whenever possible, and the statement continues.

- This setting interacts with SET ARITHABORT in the Advanced settings. If both settings are selected (the default), arithmetic errors, such as divide by zero errors, cause the faulty query to terminate. However, if other queries are included in the batch, they still run. If SET ARITHABORT is selected but SET ANSI WARNINGS isn't selected, the entire batch is terminated.

✦ **SET ANSI_NULLS:** When selected (the default), NULL values can be tested by using only the IS NULL or IS NOT NULL functions. A comparison using the equals (=) or not equals (<>) operators always evaluates to false because the value of NULL is unknown.

Consider a new employee named Addison. Is Addison a male or a female? You don't know. Certainly, if you saw Addison, you could tell, but by seeing just the name, you simply don't know.

Imagine Addison fills out paperwork as a new employee but doesn't check the gender block, and you enter the data into the database. When it comes to the gender block, instead of entering male or female, you could leave the gender blank, and it would be entered as NULL. With this setting selected, you could check for NULL values in the gender block with the following query:

```
SELECT * FROM HumanResources.Employee
WHERE Gender IS NULL
```

In contrast, the following statement wouldn't work; instead, it would always evaluate to false. This can be misleading. The query would succeed, though zero rows would always be returned, even if some of the rows had a NULL value in the Gender column.

```
SELECT * FROM HumanResources.Employee
WHERE Gender = NULL
```

The ability to turn off this setting will disappear in future versions of Microsoft's SQL Server. Use of the SET statement to turn off this setting has been deprecated and shouldn't be used.

✦ **Reset to Default:** Click this button to restore the defaults. You can also click this button to see what the defaults are.

Selecting Results Formatting Options

Outputs of queries can be displayed or saved directly to a file. Right-click the query window, select Results To, and select one of the following options:

✦ **Results to Text:** Displays results in a text format. The format of the text output can be modified by right-clicking the query window, selecting Query Options | Results | Text.

✦ **Results to Grid:** Displays in a grid format (the default). The format of the grid output can be modified by right clicking in the query window, selecting Query Options | Results | Grid.

✦ **Results to File:** Saves directly to a file. Files are saved in a report file (RPT) format that can be opened by a text editor.

Whether the output is sent to a grid or text format, you have several options available in the Grid and Text settings of the Query Options dialog box. Unlike the Execution options, which affect how the query runs, the Results options affect only how the results are displayed.

The following steps demonstrate how to modify the query output:

1. **Launch SQL Server Management Studio (SSMS) by choosing Start⇨All Programs⇨Microsoft SQL Server 2008⇨SQL Server Management Studio.**

2. **Click the New Query button to open a new query window.**

3. **Enter a query into the query window.**

If you have AdventureWorks2008 installed, use the following query:

```
USE AdventureWorks2008;
GO
SELECT * FROM HumanResources.Employee;
```

4. **Click the Execute button (! Execute) to execute the query.**

Pressing F5 also executes the query. The query results are displayed in the grid format.

5. **Right-click the grid and choose Save Results As.**

6. **In the Save Grid Results dialog box, type** EmployeeList **in the File Name box. Click Save.**

This saves the results as a comma-separated value file (CSV) that can be opened by a text editor or Microsoft Excel.

7. **Right-click the query window and choose Results To⇨Results to Text.**

8. **Press F5 to execute your query again.**

The query is displayed in a text format instead of a grid format.

9. **Right-click the text and choose Save Results As.**

10. **In the Save Results dialog box, type** EmployeeList **in the File Name box. Click Save.**

    This saves the results as an RPT file that can be opened in any text editor.

11. **Right-click the query window and choose Results To⇨Results to File.**

12. **Press F5 to execute your query again.**

    The results aren't displayed; instead, the Save Results dialog box appears.

13. **In the Save Results dialog box, type** EmployeeListFile **in the File Name box. Click Save.**

    This saves the results as an RPT file that can be opened in any text editor.

14. **Right-click the query window and choose Results To⇨Results to Grid.**

15. **Right-click the query window and choose Query Options.**

    Alternatively, you can select the Query drop-down menu and choose Query Options.

16. **Select Results | Grid.**

    As shown in Figure 4-5, this page allows you to modify the output of the grid results. You can leave this display open while you read the next section.

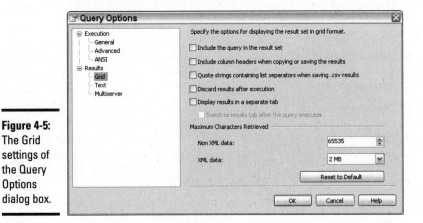

Figure 4-5:
The Grid settings of the Query Options dialog box.

Configuring the grid output

When results are configured to display in the grid format, select Query Options | Results | Grid (shown in Figure 4-5) to modify how the results are displayed.

+ **Include the Query in the Result Set:** Selecting this option causes the query to be included in the result set. The query is shown in the Messages tab. It's cleared by default.

+ **Include Column Headers When Copying or Saving the Results:** Checking this box causes the headers to be included when the results are copied to the Clipboard or saved in a file. It's cleared by default.

+ **Quote Strings Containing List Separators When Saving .csv Results:** Selecting this option causes values to be enclosed in quotes when the value includes a comma.

A comma-separated value file (CSV) has several values separated by commas. For example, a file with an EmployeeID and a Skills column might be saved as:

```
1, SQL Server 2008
```

That works fine as long as the employee has only one skill. However, what if the employee has multiple skills, such as SQL Server 2005 and SQL Server 2008? When a comma separates these two skills, it looks like three columns.

```
1, SQL Server 2005, SQL Server 2008
```

Instead, you can select this option to cause quotes to surround the skills. The EmployeeID of 1 doesn't have any quotes around it because that column has only one value and doesn't include a comma.

```
1, "SQL Server 2005, SQL Server 2008"
```

+ **Discard Results After Execution:** Selecting this setting discards the query results immediately after the query has run, freeing memory. It's cleared by default.

+ **Display Results in a Separate Tab:** Selecting this setting causes the results to be displayed in a separate tab. After running a query, the display (shown in Figure 4-6) has one tab for the query and one tab for the results. Additionally, the Messages tab appears in the figure because the Include the Query with the Result Set option has been selected, and the query is configured to send Results to Grid.

+ **Switch to Results Tab After the Query Executes:** If the Display Results in a Separate Tab option is selected, then this option becomes available. If selected, it causes the view to switch to the Results tab after the query is run.

Figure 4-6:
Results
shown in a
tabbed
format.

✦ **Maximum Characters Retrieved, NonXML Data:** You can enter a
number from 1 through 65,535 to specify the maximum number of characters that display in each cell in the results set. Be aware that setting
the font to a larger size might prevent all the characters from being displayed. The default is 65,535.

✦ **Maximum Characters Retrieved, XML Data:** Choices are 1MB, 2MB (the
default), 5MB, or unlimited. The XML data type supports data up to 2GB
in size. Use Unlimited to ensure you retrieve all the XML data.

✦ **Reset to Default:** Click this button to restore the defaults. You can also
click this button to see what the defaults are.

Configuring the text output

When results are configured to display in the text format, select Query
Options | Results | Text to modify how the results are displayed.

Figure 4-7 shows the default options for the Text settings of the Query
Options dialog box.

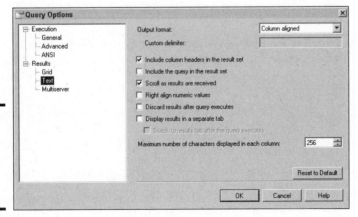

Figure 4-7:
The Text
settings of
the Query
Options
dialog box.

✦ **Output Format:** By default, the output is formatted as column aligned with spaces used to pad the results. Other formatting options are

  • *Comma Delimited:* A comma is used to separate the columns.

  • *Tab Delimited:* A tab is used to separate the columns.

  • *Space Delimited:* A space is used to separate the columns.

  • *Custom Delimiter:* Any desired character can be used to separate the columns.

✦ **Include Column Headers in the Result Set:** Checking this box causes the headers to be included when the results are copied to the Clipboard or saved in a file. It's cleared by default.

✦ **Include the Query in the Result Set:** Selecting this option causes the query to be included in the result set. The query is shown in the results tab prior to the actual results.

✦ **Scroll as Results Are Received:** Checking this box causes the display to focus on the bottom rows when they are returned. When cleared (the default), the focus stays on the first rows returned.

✦ **RightAlign Numeric Values:** Selecting this check box causes numeric values to be right aligned. Use this when you're reviewing numbers with a fixed number of decimal places.

✦ **Discard Results After Query Executes:** This setting discards the query results immediately after the query has run, freeing memory. It's cleared by default.

✦ **Display results in a separate tab:** Selecting this setting causes the results to be displayed in a separate tab. After executing a query, two tabs for the query are available: one tab for the query, and one tab for the results.

✦ **Switch to Results Tab After the Query Executes:** If the Display Results in a Separate Tab option is selected, then this option becomes available. If selected, it causes the view to switch to the Results tab after the query is run.

✦ **Maximum Number of Characters Displayed in Each Column:** By default, any column can display only 256 characters. If more characters are available, they're truncated in the result set. This column can be set to a maximum of 8,192 characters.

✦ **Reset to Default:** Click this button to restore the defaults. You can also click this button to see what the defaults are.

Configuring the multiserver output

You can also configure how results are displayed when they are retrieved from more than one server. Select Query Options | Results | Multiserver to modify how the results retrieved from more than server are displayed.

Figure 4-8 shows the default options for the Multiserver settings of the Query Options dialog box:

✦ **Add Login Name to the Results:** When set to true, this will add a column that includes the name of the login used to retrieve the results. Depending on how the query is executed and how the servers are configured, this could be different logins for different servers within the same query. This selection is set to False by default so a login column name will not appear.

✦ **Add Server Name to the Results:** When set to true, queries will include a column including the name of the server that provided the result row. It is set to True by default.

✦ **Merge Results:** Setting this to true will cause results from different servers to be merged into a single result set. This setting is set to True by default.

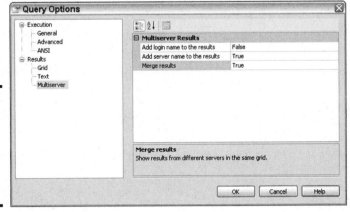

Figure 4-8:
The Multiserver settings of the Query Options dialog box.

Chapter 5: Searching for Information

In This Chapter

- ✔ Installing AdventureWorks2008
- ✔ Retrieving data by using single table queries
- ✔ Retrieving data by using multi-table queries
- ✔ Filtering information to retrieve only what you need

*A*dventureWorks2008 is a robust database created by Microsoft to demonstrate many features and examples within SQL Server. However, Adventure Works2008 isn't very useful unless it's installed; therefore, the first order of business in this chapter is to install AdventureWorks2008.

With AdventureWorks2008 installed, you can start writing SELECT statements against it to retrieve data. You can use the Query Designer to make the creation of your SELECT statements easier, and then fine-tune them within the Query Editor to retrieve exactly what you want.

By using this combination of tools, creating queries against one or more tables is easy — even when you're using sophisticated filtering techniques with the WHERE clause.

Using AdventureWorks2008

Since the release of SQL Server 2005, Microsoft has included a comprehensive database named AdventureWorks that's designed to demonstrate many of the capabilities of SQL Server. AdventureWorks is based on a fictitious company — Adventure Works Cycles. AdventureWorks was modified for the release of SQL Server 2008 and renamed AdventureWorks2008.

References to AdventureWorks can be found throughout SQL Server 2008's documentation, including:

- ✦ SQL Server Books Online
- ✦ SQL Server Tutorials
- ✦ SQL Server Samples

We focus on the Online Transaction Processing (OLTP) version of Adventure Works in this book; however, several versions exist. These include:

✦ **AdventureWorks:** The Adventure Works Cycles OLTP sample database.

✦ **AdventureWorksLT:** A *light,* or simple, version of the Adventure Works Cycles OLTP database.

✦ **AdventureWorksDW:** The Adventure Works Cycles Data Warehouse and the Analysis Services database project.

✦ **AdventureWorksDBScripts:** The data files and scripts that can be used to build both the Adventure Works Cycles OLTP database and the Adventure Works Cycles Data Warehouse.

Some of the samples in this book (especially those in this chapter) use the AdventureWorks2008 OLTP database. If you don't have AdventureWorks2008 installed on your system, follow the steps in this section to add it to SQL Server 2008.

To verify if AdventureWorks2008 is installed, follow these steps:

1. **Launch SQL Server Management Studio (SSMS) by choosing Start⇨All Programs⇨Microsoft SQL Server 2008⇨SQL Server Management Studio.**

2. **On the Connect to Server screen, click Connect.**

3. **Open the Databases container within Object Explorer.**

   If AdventureWorks is installed, your display looks similar to Figure 5-1. If AdventureWorks isn't installed, you won't see a database named Adventure Works2008 in the Databases container. You need to obtain and install it.

Figure 5-1:
Verifying the Adventure Works2008 database is installed.

Obtaining AdventureWorks2008

AdventureWorks2008 can be installed from a downloadable Windows Installer file (MSI). Type **"download adventureworks"** into your favorite search engine to quickly find a link to the downloadable file.

You can also go to Microsoft's CodePlex site. CodePlex is Microsoft's open source project hosting Web site where numerous code samples can be found. Use the following URL for the SQL Server database samples:

```
http://www.codeplex.com/MSFTDBProdSamples
```

Click the Releases tab to find a listing of downloadable links for the different AdventureWorks databases. Locate and download the OLTP version for SQL Server 2008.

You'll notice that a 32-bit (x86) and a 64-bit (x64) version is available. Download the version that matches your platform. For example, I'm running SQL Server 2008 on a 32-bit platform, so I would download the 32-bit file: `SQL2008.AdventureWorks_OLTP_DB_v2008.x86.msi`.

Different versions of AdventureWorks exist — at this writing, SQL Server 2005 and SQL Server 2008. Although SQL Server 2008 supports all versions, many people have experienced frustration when they installed Adventure Works for SQL Server 2008 onto an SQL Server 2005 system. AdventureWorks for SQL Server 2008 wouldn't install. You can install SQL Server 2005 onto SQL Server 2008, but you won't have all the features. Microsoft has since renamed AdventureWorks for SQL Server 2008 to AdventureWorks2008 to help avoid some frustration. Installing the version of AdventureWorks that matches your SQL Server version is best.

Book III
Chapter 5

Searching for
Information

Installing AdventureWorks2008

You install AdventureWorks2008 from the downloadable Windows Installer file. Download a copy of AdventureWorks2008 (see the earlier "Obtaining Adventure Works2008" section) and then follow these installation steps. AdventureWorks 2008 requires FILESTREAM to be installed and enabled to successfully install. If you want to take advantage of the full-text capabilities within AdventureWorks 2008, Full Text Search must also be installed. You can install Adventure Works2008 without installing and enabling Full Text Search, but not without installing FILESTREAM.

1. **Launch SQL Server Management Studio (SSMS) by choosing Start⇨All Programs⇨Microsoft SQL Server 2008⇨SQL Server Management Studio.**

2. **Right-click the server instance and select Properties. Select Advanced.**

3. **If the Filestream Access Level is set to Disabled, change it to Full Access Enabled. Click OK to close the Property page. If prompted to restart SQL Server, restart it at this time. Leave SSMS open.**

4. **Launch Windows Explorer and locate the AdventureWorks2008 installer file.**

5. **Double-click the AdventureWorks2008 installer file to begin the installation.**

6. **On the Welcome page, click Next.**

7. **On the License Agreement page, ensure you agree with the agreement and click the I Accept the Terms in the License Agreement check box. Click Next.**

8. **On the Custom Setup page, change the Restore AdventureWorks DBs setting to Will Be Installed on Local Hard Drive. Accept the other defaults and then click Next.**

9. **On the Database Setup page, review the information.**

   Note: This page provides a warning indicating that both FILESTREAM and Full-Text Search must be installed for AdventureWorks to install successfully. Full-Text search is enabled by default and you enabled FILESTREAM in earlier steps.

10. **On the Database Setup page, ensure your SQL Server instance is selected and click Next.**

11. **On the Ready to Install page, click Install.**

12. **When the installation completes, click Finish.**

13. **Return to SSMS. Right-click the Databases node and click Refresh.**

   The AdventureWorks2008 database can be seen in the Databases container.

Microsoft has provided a lot of documentation on the AdventureWorks database in SQL Server Books Online. If you want to find out more about Adventure Works, check out these articles: "AdventureWorks Sample OLTP Database," "AdventureWorks Data Dictionary," "SQL Server Objects in AdventureWorks," and "Schemas in AdventureWorks."

Retrieving Data from a Single Table

The simplest query is one that retrieves data from a single table. It doesn't require any join statements; instead, it uses a simple SELECT statement querying only one table.

A SELECT statement is one of several Data Manipulation Language (DML) statements. The SELECT statement reads data only, but doesn't modify it. Other DML statements are:

✦ **INSERT:** Adds new rows to a table.

✦ **UPDATE:** Modifies existing rows in a table.

✦ **DELETE:** Removes rows from a table.

By understanding the SELECT statement in detail, the other DML statements become much easier to grasp.

Using IntelliSense

One of the great features of SQL Server 2008 is the introduction of IntelliSense. When you're writing a query, IntelliSense identifies what commands are acceptable and provides you appropriate choices.

For example, you could have your query window pointed at AdventureWorks2008. Your plan is to type in the following query:

```
SELECT * FROM HumanResources.Employee
```

However, after you type in the H (as in SELECT * FROM H) an IntelliSense popup window appears, showing you all the possible choices. Because you entered an H, it displays the choices starting with H. Pressing the Tab key, the spacebar, or the Enter key selects the choice you want (in this case, HumanResources).

HumanResources fills in. Type in a period and all the objects in the HumanResources schema appear. Select Employee, press Return, and you're done.

SQL developers have wanted this feature for a while, and there's been a collective cheer heard in database dens around the world now that it's appeared. You see IntelliSense popups appear while you type your queries. Feel free to use them whenever you can.

Running a query in the SSMS query window

The SQL Server Management Studio includes a query window that can be used to build and execute queries. To access the query window, follow these steps:

1. **Launch SQL Server Management Studio (SSMS) by choosing Start⇨All Programs⇨Microsoft SQL Server 2008⇨SQL Server Management Studio.**

2. **On the Connect to Server screen, click Connect.**

3. **Click the New Query button.**

   This opens a query window.

4. **Enter the following script within the query window:**

   ```
   USE AdventureWorks2008;
   GO
   SELECT *
   FROM Production.Product
   ```

5. **To execute the script, click the Execute button (! Execute) on the toolbar.**

   Pressing F5 also executes the script. The result of the script appears in the Results pane at the bottom of the query window.

The first line in Step 4, USE AdventureWorks2008, causes the query window to point to the AdventureWorks2008 database. That is, it sets the context of the query window to the AdventureWorks2008 database. The context can also be set to a database by choosing the database from the database drop-down menu.

Figure 5-2 shows how the selected database can be changed in the drop-down menu. By clicking the down arrow to the right of the display, the desired database can be selected. After the database is selected, it doesn't need to be reselected. Subsequent queries use the context of the selected database until it's changed again.

Figure 5-2:
Selecting the Adventure Works2008 database.

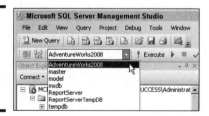

Building Queries with the SELECT statement

The SELECT statement is the T-SQL statement used to retrieve data from a database. The basic syntax of a SELECT statement is

```
SELECT column list
FROM table (or view)
```

A *column list* is a list of columns to retrieve. Only columns that are in the table in the FROM clause can be listed. To retrieve all the columns, the asterisk (*) is used as a wildcard.

For example, suppose you want to retrieve all the columns from the Person.Person table in the AdventureWorks2008 database. The following SELECT statement could be used:

```
SELECT *
FROM Person.Person
```

The name of the table is Person, and the Person table is contained in the Person schema, also referred to as the Person namespace. If the schema name is omitted, it defaults to the currently connected user's default schema. This is often dbo. In other words, this script:

```
SELECT * FROM Person
```

is interpreted as:

```
SELECT * FROM dbo.Person
```

Modifying the column list

If not all the columns are desired from a table, a column list can be provided. Each column name must match the actual column name in the table and be separated with a comma.

For example, the following query can be used to retrieve a listing of people in the Person table with just their first, middle, and last names.

```
SELECT FirstName, MiddleName, LastName
FROM Person.Person
```

Although the order of this list matches the order of the columns in the table, that isn't necessary. Pick the order of your columns based on your needs. For example, if you need the last name first, build your query to look like the following:

```
SELECT LastName, FirstName, MiddleName
FROM Person.Person
```

**Book III
Chapter 5**

**Searching for
Information**

Using aliases in the column list

Aliases are commonly used in the column list to provide an output that's easier to read. By adding aliases, the header of the result set changes. A column alias doesn't affect the data at all.

For example, the previous query could be rewritten as follows:

```
SELECT LastName AS [Last Name],
       FirstName AS [First Name],
       MiddleName AS [Middle Name]
FROM Person.Person
```

Brackets surround the alias. In this context, the brackets are *delimiters* — needed because the alias has a space. If the alias didn't have a space, the delimiter could be omitted.

Likewise, the AS preceding the alias can be omitted. Commas separate the column list, so text that comes after the column name is interpreted as an alias. The following script performs the same as the previous script. The comments (preceded by --) show what has changed.

```
SELECT LastName [Employee Last Name], -- the word AS omitted
       FirstName AS [First Name],
       MiddleName AS Middle -- Delimiters [] omitted
FROM Person.Person
```

Figure 5-3 shows the result of this script. The header of each column has been modified to match the alias as Employees Last Name, First Name, and Middle.

Figure 5-3:
Result of
query
showing
use of AS.

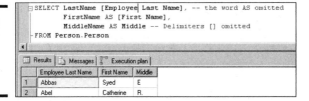

Building queries with the Query Designer

One of the challenges when working with large databases is knowing the data well enough so that you can easily build your queries. Not only do you need to know the names of the tables, but you also need to know the names of the columns. Additionally, you must spell them exactly how the designer of the database spelled them. Not always an easy task!

However, by using the Query Designer, you can build basic queries graphically and then modify them to meet your needs. To build a query with the Query Designer, follow these steps:

1. **Launch SQL Server Management Studio (SSMS) by choosing Start⇨All Programs⇨Microsoft SQL Server 2008⇨SQL Server Management Studio.**

2. **On the Connect to Server screen, click Connect.**

3. **Click the New Query button.**

This opens a query window.

4. **Right-click the query window and choose Design Query in Editor.**

The Query Designer appears with the Add Table dialog box showing. Tables are listed alphabetically by the table name. In parenthesis, the schema that the table belongs to is listed. For example, the Person.Person table is listed as `Person(Person)`.

5. **Select the Person(Person) table and click Add. Click Close.**

6. **In the Person(Person) table, select the LastName, FirstName, and ModifiedDate columns by clicking the check box next to each column name. Click OK.**

This creates the following query in the query window:

```
SELECT LastName, FirstName, ModifiedDate
FROM    Person.Person
```

7. **Press F5 to execute the query.**

8. **Modify the query by adding the middle name and aliases so that the query looks like the following SELECT statement. The changes are shown in bold.**

```
SELECT LastName AS [Last Name],
        FirstName AS [First Name],
  MiddleName AS Middle,
        ModifiedDate AS [Modified Date]
FROM Person.Person
```

9. **Press F5 to execute the query.**

The query created in the previous steps is very similar to the queries created earlier in this section. However, it was largely created by pointing and clicking, making it much simpler. Instead of typing the query, the Query Designer can be used to get you started, and then you can modify the query as necessary to meet your needs.

For more details on the Query Designer, take a look at Chapter 6 of this mini-book.

**Book III
Chapter 5**

**Searching for
Information**

Retrieving Data from Multiple Tables

Multi-table queries are queries that retrieve data from multiple tables in a single SELECT statement. The results from one table are joined with the results from another table. The INNER JOIN operator is used to identify the tables to be joined, and the ON operator identifies the column that the tables are joined on.

By using the INNER JOIN statement, you can include columns from multiple tables in the column list. In order for the output to have meaning, the joined tables must have an existing relationship — the INNER JOIN operator joins the tables on this relationship.

For example, Figure 5-4 shows the Person.Person and HumanResources. Employee tables from the AdventureWorks2008 database (shown as Person(Person) and Employee(HumanResources) in the Query Designer). These tables are related by the primary key of BusinessEntityID in the Person table and the foreign key of BusinessEntityID in the Employee table.

The primary key is used within a table to ensure that each row is unique. The foreign key in one table references the primary key in another table, creating the relationship between the two tables.

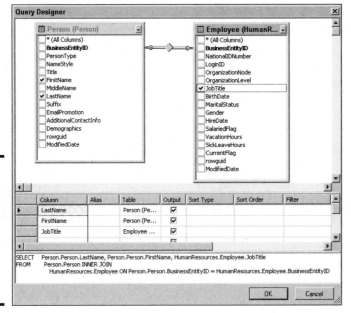

Figure 5-4:
The Person and Employee tables from the Adventure Works2008 database.

The primary key and foreign key relationship between the tables is what allows you to join the two tables in a SELECT statement. For example, if you want a listing of employees by name, you can join the two tables and retrieve the data. In other words, the join allows you to identify all the people in the Contact table that are also in the Employee table.

We simulate some data, shown in Figure 5-5, for two tables named Contact and Employee. The Contact table has ContactID's of 1 through 5, but the Employee table has ContactID's of 1, 3, and 5 only.

An INNER JOIN of these two tables on the ContactID table results in rows that have only matching ContactID columns in both tables.

The ContactID's of 1, 3, and 5 exist in both tables, so these rows are in the result set. The Contact ID's of 2 and 4 exist in the Contact table but not in the Employee table, so they're omitted.

Contact Table

ContactID	LastName	FirstName
1	Achong	Gustavo
2	Abel	Catherine
3	Abercrombie	Kim
4	Acevedo	Humberto
5	Ackerman	Pilar
. . .		

Employee Table

EmployeeID	ContactID	Login
1	1	adventure-works\gustavo
2	3	adventure-works\kim
3	5	adventure-works\pilar
. . .		

Figure 5-5: Simulated data from tables named Contact and Employee.

Joining two tables

Tables are joined by using both the INNER JOIN and the ON clauses. Although this can be typed in, you can also use the Query Designer to build the query for you. The following steps can be used to retrieve a listing of names and phone numbers for employees:

1. **Launch SQL Server Management Studio (SSMS) by choosing Start⇨All Programs⇨Microsoft SQL Server 2008⇨SQL Server Management Studio.**

2. **On the Connect to Server screen, click Connect.**

3. **Click the New Query button.**

   This opens a query window.

4. **Right-click the query window and choose Design Query in Editor.**

   The Query Designer appears with the Add Table dialog box showing.

5. **Select the Person(Person) table and click Add. Select the Employee(HumanResources) table and click Add. Click Close.**

6. **In the Person(Person) table, select the LastName, and FirstName columns by clicking the check box next to each column name. Click OK.**

   This creates the following query in the query window, though it might be formatted a little differently:

   ```
   SELECT  Person.Person.LastName,
           Person.Person.FirstName
   FROM    Person.Person
   INNER JOIN
      HumanResources.Employee
   ON
      Person.Person.BusinessEntityID =
   HumanResources.Employee.BusinessEntityID
   ```

7. **Press F5 to execute the query.**

   This returns a result set of about 290 rows.

The first part of the query is the same as it is when you're retrieving data from one table:

```
SELECT  Person.Person.LastName,
        Person.Person.FirstNameFROM    Person.Person
  . . .
```

If you run only this part of the query though, you retrieve more than 19,000 rows of people in the Person.Person table. That's not what you want. Instead, you want a listing of only the employees.

By adding the JOIN statement and the ON clause, the retrieved data is limited to only the contacts that are also in the employee table.

```
. . .
INNER JOIN
  HumanResources.Employee
ON
 Person.Person.BusinessEntityID=
 HumanResources.Employee.BusinessEntityID
```

Immediately after the JOIN clause, the name of the joined table is listed. Then the ON clause limits the query based on the matches in the primary key and foreign key relationships.

The column list of the query doesn't need to include columns from all the tables mentioned in the joins. In the preceding example, the query included columns from only the Person table, and not from the Employee table. However, the Employee table is still needed because the join is on the BusinessEntityID column from both tables.

Using table aliases

Repeating entire tables in a query can be large and cumbersome. Many times, you see table aliases used to make the queries a little easier to read. *Aliases* are just one or two letters used to shorten the name of the table.

Table	Possible Aliases
Person.Person	p or pp
HumanResources.Employee	e, hre, or emp
Address	a

The alias is defined when the table is identified. However, the alias is seen often in the column list of the SELECT statement, before it's defined.

For example, your previous query is rewritten here with table aliases.

```
SELECT p.LastName,p.FirstName
FROM   Person.Person AS p
INNER JOIN HumanResources.Employee AS e
ON p.BusinessEntityID = e.BusinessEntityID
```

The table alias for the HumanResources.Employee table is shortened to just an e. The Person.Person table is shortened to just a p. With the definition in place, the one-letter alias is used anywhere the table name is needed.

SQL Server recognizes the alias, whether it's defined with or without AS. You might see AS omitted in many queries. The following query works exactly the same:

```
SELECT p.LastName,p.FirstName
FROM    Person.Person p
INNER JOIN HumanResources.Employee e
ON p.BusinessEntityID = e.BusinessEntityID
```

Exploring join variations

Very often, you see INNER JOIN shortened to JOIN. Both work exactly the same. For example, the previous query is written often as follows:

```
SELECT p.LastName,p.FirstName
FROM    Person.Person p
JOIN HumanResources.Employee e
ON p.BusinessEntityID = e.BusinessEntityID
```

Although INNER JOIN is the most common join, other joins exist. All the common joins are listed here:

✦ **INNER JOIN** (often shortened to JOIN): Rows with matching values on the specified column from both tables are returned.

✦ **LEFT OUTER JOIN** (often shortened to LEFT JOIN): All the rows from the left table (the first table in the query) are returned. Additionally, rows with matching values on the specified column from both tables are returned.

✦ **RIGHT OUTER JOIN** (often shortened to RIGHT JOIN): All the rows from the right table (the second table in the query) are returned. Additionally, rows with matching values on the specified column from both tables are returned.

✦ **FULL OUTER JOIN** (often shortened to FULL JOIN): All the rows from both tables are returned.

✦ **CROSS JOIN:** Creates a Cartesian product equal to the number of rows in the left table times the number of rows in the right table.

Joining more than two tables

Adding additional tables works similarly to joining two tables. Depending on how many tables you add, these can become complex rather quickly. Therefore, Query Designer becomes very valuable in creating the basic SELECT statement.

For example, say you want to create an employee listing with the employee's name and address information. The first thing you need to know is where the information is contained.

Within the AdventureWorks2008 database, names are in the Person.Person table, employees are in the HumanResources.Employee table, Employee addresses are in the Person.Address table, and the state is in the Person.StateProvince table.

Figure 5-6 shows the six tables needed for a query returning employee names and addresses. The AdventureWorks2008 database is highly normalized, resulting in the need to join so many tables. The Employee table ensures that only employees are included in the query. The Address and StateProvince tables include the address. The BusinessEntityAddress table is the junction table providing the many-to-many relationship between the BusinessEntity and Address tables. Lastly, the Business Entity table provides the link to the Person table. This figure shows the relationships between each of the tables.

Figure 5-6: Related tables needed for an employee name and address query.

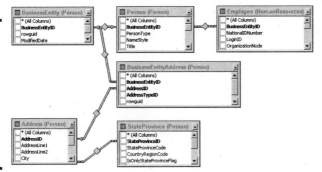

On the surface, the data needed is rather simple — employee names and addresses. However, looking at the required tables, it'd be easy to become overwhelmed if you had to create the queries from scratch. The Query Designer comes to the rescue again.

The following steps show how to create the query:

1. **Launch SQL Server Management Studio (SSMS) by selecting Start⇨All Programs⇨Microsoft SQL Server 2008⇨SQL Server Management Studio.**

2. **On the Connect to Server screen, click Connect.**

3. Click the New Query button.

This opens a query window.

4. Right-click the query window and choose Design Query in Editor.

The Query Designer appears with the Add Table dialog box showing.

5. Add the five needed tables.

   a. *Select the Person(Person) table and click Add.*

   b. *Select the Address(Person) table and click Add.*

   c. *Select the StateProvince(Person) table and click Add.*

   d. *Select the Employee(HumanResources) table and click Add.*

   e. *Select the BusinessEntity(Person) table and click Add.*

   f. *Select the BusinessEntityAddress(Person) table and click Add. Click Close.*

6. On the Person(Person) table, select the check boxes next to the LastName and FirstName columns.

7. On the Address(Person) table, select the check boxes next to the AddressLine1, AddressLine2, and City columns.

8. On the StateProvince(Person) table, select the check box next to the StateProvinceCode column.

9. On the Address(Person) table, select the check box next to the Postalcode column. Click OK.

At this point, you've built your multiple table query. It looks like the following code:

```
SELECT  Person.Person.LastName,
        Person.Person.FirstName,
        Person.Address.AddressLine1,
        Person.Address.AddressLine2,
        Person.Address.City,
        Person.StateProvince.StateProvinceCode,
        Person.Address.PostalCode
FROM    HumanResources.Employee INNER JOIN
            Person.Person ON
        HumanResources.Employee.BusinessEntityID =
            Person.Person.BusinessEntityID AND
        HumanResources.Employee.BusinessEntityID =
            Person.Person.BusinessEntityID AND
        HumanResources.Employee.BusinessEntityID =
            Person.Person.BusinessEntityID AND
        HumanResources.Employee.BusinessEntityID =
            Person.Person.BusinessEntityID AND
        HumanResources.Employee.BusinessEntityID =
            Person.Person.BusinessEntityID AND
```

```
HumanResources.Employee.BusinessEntityID =
  Person.Person.BusinessEntityID INNER JOIN
Person.BusinessEntity ON
Person.Person.BusinessEntityID =
  Person.BusinessEntity.BusinessEntityID
  INNER JOIN
Person.BusinessEntityAddress ON
Person.BusinessEntity.BusinessEntityID =
Person.BusinessEntityAddress.BusinessEntityID
  INNER JOIN
Person.StateProvince INNER JOIN
Person.Address ON
Person.StateProvince.StateProvinceID =
  Person.Address.StateProvinceID AND
Person.StateProvince.StateProvinceID =
  Person.Address.StateProvinceID ON
Person.BusinessEntityAddress.AddressID =
  Person.Address.AddressID
```

10. **Press F5 to execute the query.**

On the last INNER JOIN, the Query Designer added several AND clauses. However, these AND clauses are identical to the ON clause verifying that the BusinessEntityID is the same in multiple tables and the StateProvinceID is the same in both the Address and StateProvince tables. These clauses can either be left in or deleted. The results are the same.

Additionally, with all these schema and table names included, the query is long and cumbersome. To clean up the query, eliminate the unneeded AND clauses and use table aliases. The following query is an example of the cleaned up query:

```
SELECT p.LastName,
       p.FirstName,
       Person.Address.AddressLine1,
       Person.Address.AddressLine2,
       Person.Address.City,
       Person.StateProvince.StateProvinceCode,
       Person.Address.PostalCode
FROM   HumanResources.Employee AS e INNER JOIN
       Person.Person AS p ON
       e.BusinessEntityID = p.BusinessEntityID
         INNER JOIN
       Person.BusinessEntity AS be ON
       p.BusinessEntityID = be.BusinessEntityID
         INNER JOIN
       Person.BusinessEntityAddress AS bea ON
       be.BusinessEntityID = bea.BusinessEntityID
         INNER JOIN
       Person.StateProvince AS sp INNER JOIN
```

```
Person.Address AS pa ON
sp.StateProvinceID = pa.StateProvinceID ON
bea.AddressID = pa.AddressID
```

Filtering Information

Very often, you need to narrow your search of rows within a table to specific information. In other words, instead of retrieving all the rows, you want to retrieve specific rows based on specific search criteria.

For example, you might be asked for the e-mail address of a person named Dobney. You know the information is in the Person.Person table and Person.EmailAddress tables. You could run the following query and tediously look through the 19,000 entries until you found Dobney.

```
SELECT p.LastName, p.FirstName, e.EmailAddress
FROM Person.Person as p INNER JOIN
    Person.EmailAddress as e
    ON p.BusinessEntityID = e.BusinessEntityID
```

Or, you could add a WHERE clause that filters the query based on the LastName column. The following query returns a single row.

```
SELECT p.LastName, p.FirstName, e.EmailAddress
FROM Person.Person as p INNER JOIN
    Person.EmailAddress as e
    ON p.BusinessEntityID = e.BusinessEntityID
    WHERE p.LastName = 'Dobney'
```

In this query, the database engine examines the LastName column in every row in the Person table. If the last name is Dobney, then the row is added to the result set. If multiple rows include the last name of Dobney, then each row is included in the result set.

The syntax of the WHERE clause is

```
WHERE column name <search condition>
```

Multiple search conditions are possible. These are in different categories:

✦ **Comparison operators:** Using equal and not equal comparisons, such as =, <, and so on.

✦ **String operators:** Using LIKE and NOT LIKE

✦ **Logical operators:** Using Boolean logic operators, such as AND, OR and NOT.

+ **Range operators:** Using BETWEEN and NOT BETWEEN to search for ranges of data (such as between 1 and 10).

+ **NULL operators:** Using IS NULL and IS NOT NULL to search for NULL or NOT NULL data.

The following sections cover these different operators in more depth by using the AdventureWorks.Production.Product table. This table holds 504 rows of product information, including name, color, cost, prices, inventory, selling start dates, and selling end dates.

Comparing values

Comparison operators are probably the most commonly used in the WHERE clause. They allow you to search for exact matches by using the equal (=) operator and inequalities with different inequality operators. The supported operators are

=	Equal
<	Less than
>	Greater than
< =	Less than or equal
> =	Greater than or equal
! =	Not equal. The exclamation mark is expressed as Not.
<>	Not equal.
! <	Not less than. The exclamation mark is expressed as Not.
! >	Not greater than. The exclamation mark is expressed as Not.

When comparing string values, the string must be enclosed in a single quote. The following example retrieves a listing of all the products with a color of blue. The column is Color, and the value is Blue, so blue must be enclosed in single quotes.

```
SELECT *
FROM Production.Product
WHERE Color = 'Blue'
```

Similarly, you can easily find all the products that aren't the color blue with the following query. The only thing that has changed is that the equal (=) operator is replaced with the not equal (! =) operator.

```
SELECT *
FROM Production.Product
WHERE Color ! = 'Blue'
```

Numerical data is compared without any quotes. The following query retrieves a listing of all the products that have a price greater than $100.

```
SELECT *
FROM Production.Product
WHERE ListPrice > 100
```

Dates are compared with single quotes. The format of the date value needs to match the format of the date in the column for this to produce accurate results. The format of the date value is based on the collation, and the majority of databases in the United States have a format of yyyy/mm/dd. Additionally, date values should include the slash (/) to separate the year, month, and day.

The following query retrieves all the products that the company began selling on or after September 1, 2001.

```
SELECT *
FROM Production.Product
WHERE SellStartDate > = '2001/09/01'
```

Looking for strings

The LIKE and NOT LIKE operators allow you to search for specific patterns of string data. Although the comparison operators (such as = and !=) are effective at identifying exact matches for string or text data, they're limited. The LIKE and NOT LIKE operators give you a lot more flexibility.

When searching for string data, wildcards can be used. The LIKE and NOT LIKE operators support four wildcards:

% The percent sign is used in place of zero or more characters.

As an example, LIKE 'd%' causes a match for any data that starts with d and ends with zero or more characters.

_ The underscore character is used in place of a single character.

As an example, LIKE 'd_' causes a match for any data that starts with d and ends with one more character.

[ ] Brackets are used to represent a single character within a range.

For example, LIKE '[d-f]%' causes a match for any data that starts with d, e, or f and ends with zero or more characters.

[^] Brackets with the ^ symbol are used to represent a single character *not* within a range.

For example, `'[^d-f]%'` causes a match for any data that doesn't start with d, e, or f and ends with one or more characters.

The LIKE and NOT LIKE operators aren't case sensitive or case insensitive on their own. Instead, they're dependent on the collation of the data being queried. If the collation of the data is set to case sensitive, then a comparison of LIKE `'d%'` returns data that only begins with a lowercase d. Data with an uppercase D isn't returned. However, the same query on a database with the collation set to case insensitive returns data that begins with either a lowercase d or an uppercase D.

The following queries show how the LIKE and NOT LIKE operators are used within queries. This first query returns a listing of products that have a color that starts with a B — either black or blue.

```
SELECT *
FROM Production.Product
WHERE Color LIKE 'B%'
```

The following query returns a listing of products that have a product number starting with an H, a second letter, then a dash, and anything after the dash. In other words, the product numbers start with two letters and a dash, and the first letter is an H. The underscore is used to represent the second letter.

```
SELECT *
FROM Production.Product
WHERE ProductNumber LIKE 'H_-%'
```

The following is an example of a query that uses the brackets. It returns a listing of all the products that have product numbers that begin with a, b, c, or d.

```
SELECT *
FROM Production.Product
WHERE ProductNumber LIKE '[a-d]%'
```

A similar query using brackets but not using a dash for the range is shown in the following code. It returns a listing of products that begin with only e or k, not the range of e to h.

```
SELECT *
FROM Production.Product
WHERE ProductNumber LIKE '[ek]%'
```

**Book III
Chapter 5**

**Searching for
Information**

The ^ character can be added to queries with brackets to change the query to return only rows that don't match. Although the previous query returned only four rows, the following query returns 500 rows.

```
SELECT *
FROM Production.Product
WHERE ProductNumber LIKE '[ek]%'
```

Adding Boolean logic to your query

Logical operators are used within the query to mix and match how the search criteria are interpreted. The logical operators supported in T-SQL are

✦ **AND:** An AND expression evaluates to TRUE if all the conditions are true.

✦ **OR:** An OR expression evaluates to TRUE if any one of the conditions are true.

✦ **NOT:** Negates any Boolean expression. Evaluates to TRUE if Boolean expression is FALSE. Evaluates to FALSE if Boolean expression is TRUE.

Searching for multiple expressions with AND

By using the AND operator, multiple expressions are combined. Data is returned only if *all* expressions evaluate to TRUE.

For example, you might be looking for a list of products that are less than $200 but greater than $100. The expressions are

✦ ListPrice < 200: There are 315 rows where this is TRUE.

✦ ListPrice > 100: There are 214 rows where this is TRUE.

For every row in the table, the query looks at the ListPrice and returns only those rows that meet both expressions.

The actual query for this AND statement is listed in the following query. It returns 25 rows.

```
SELECT *
FROM Production.Product
WHERE ListPrice < 200
  AND ListPrice > 100
```

The order of the expressions doesn't matter because each expression (list price < 200 and list price > 100) only evaluates to TRUE or FALSE for each row.

The expressions in logical operators don't need to compare the results for the same column. For example, you might be looking for a list of products that are the color blue and have a price greater than $100. The following query retrieves the desired results:

```
SELECT *
FROM Production.Product
WHERE ListPrice > 100
  AND Color = 'Blue'
```

You can add as many AND statements as desired in your query. You simply add AND and another expression. The following query looks for prices between $100 and $200 and the color black:

```
SELECT *
FROM Production.Product
WHERE ListPrice < 200
  AND ListPrice > 100
  AND Color = 'Black'
```

Searching for one of many possibilities with OR

The OR operator looks for one of two or more possibilities. Only one of the listed possibilities in the OR operator needs to be true.

For example, you might be looking for products with the word *Mountain* or *Road* in the name. The expressions would be

✦ `Name LIKE '%Mountain%'`: There are 94 rows where this is TRUE.

✦ `Name LIKE '%Road%'`: There are 103 rows where this is TRUE.

The following query shows how these expressions are combined in a query. It returns 197 rows.

```
SELECT *
FROM Production.Product
WHERE Name Like '%Mountain%'
   OR Name Like '%Road%'
```

As with the AND operator, the OR operator compares values in different columns. The following query adds a search for the color blue to the previous query:

```
SELECT *
FROM Production.Product
```

```
WHERE Name Like '%Mountain%'
   OR Name Like '%Road%'
   OR Color = 'Blue'
```

Looking for the negative with NOT

The NOT operator changes the value of TRUE to FALSE, or changes the value of FALSE to TRUE.

For example, if you're looking for a product less than $200 and any color but blue, you could use the following query:

```
SELECT *
FROM Production.Product
WHERE ListPrice < 200
   AND NOT Color = 'Blue'
```

You might recognize that this query could be written differently and still achieve the same results. Instead of using the Boolean NOT, you could use the not equal (!=) operator.

```
SELECT *
FROM Production.Product
WHERE ListPrice < 200
   AND Color != 'Blue'
```

This is true of many queries. More than one method often exists to achieve the results. When you find one that works, use it.

Combining logical operators

You can also mix and match the logical operators within a query.

When using multiple logical operators, it's important to understand the order of precedence. In other words, if you're using AND, OR, and NOT operators in the same query, know that one is evaluated first. The order of precedence is

> AND evaluates first
>
> OR evaluates after AND
>
> NOT evaluates last

Why is order of precedence important? Consider order of precedence in math that you probably learned in grade school. The equation 3 + 4 * 5 is evaluated differently depending on which calculation you do first. In math, the order of precedence is multiplication first, then addition. Therefore, 3 + (4 * 5), or 3 + 20, is 23. If the addition is done first, the answer is different: (3 + 4) * 5, or 7 * 5, is 35.

The order of precedence is modified by adding parenthesis around Boolean expressions. For example, the following query causes the OR expressions to be evaluated first, and then the AND expression:

```
SELECT *
FROM Production.Product
WHERE (Name Like '%Mountain%'
    or Name Like '%Road%')
    AND ListPrice < 200
```

The previous query returns 53 rows. Without the parenthesis, it returns 117 rows.

Searching for ranges of data

The BETWEEN and NOT BETWEEN operators are used when searching for ranges of data. They work identical to combining AND with the > = and < = comparison operators.

For example if you're looking for a list of products with a price range of $100 to $200, then you could use the following query:

```
SELECT *
FROM Production.Product
WHERE ListPrice BETWEEN 100 AND 200
```

The biggest point to remember about the BETWEEN operator is that it's inclusive. In other words, it includes both values. The previous query includes the values of $100 and $200 in the results. The same query written with comparison operators would be

```
SELECT *
FROM Production.Product
WHERE ListPrice < = 200
  AND ListPrice > = 100
```

The NOT operator returns the data that isn't in the given range.

Searching for nothing and the unknown

Very often, you need to search for NULL data. It's important to remember that the value of NULL is unknown, so a comparison operator (such as =) can't be used to check for the value of NULL. Instead, you need to use the IS NULL and IS NOT NULL functions to accurately check for NULL data.

For example, if you want to retrieve a listing of products where the color was left as NULL, you could use the following query:

```
SELECT *
FROM Production.Product
WHERE Color IS NULL
```

This query returns 248 rows. The NOT operator can be added to return a listing of all the rows that have a color entered.

```
SELECT *
FROM Production.Product
WHERE Color IS NOT NULL
```

A common mistake is trying to use the equal (=) operator (for example, WHERE Color = NULL) when checking for NULL. Although the query succeeds without an error, it gives the wrong results. It returns zero rows.

Chapter 6: Organizing Query Results

In This Chapter

✔ Using ORDER BY to sort your results

✔ Grouping results with GROUP BY

To add a little extra to your queries, you can add the ORDER BY and GROUP BY clauses to your SELECT statements.

ORDER BY can be used to ensure that data is returned in a specific order, such as alphabetically by name, or numerically by a number. The GROUP BY clause can be used to provide summary data by using aggregate functions, such as SUM and AVG.

Using ORDER BY to Sort Your Results

Often, you need your data returned in a certain order, such as alphabetically or based on a number (say, sales figures). The only way to ensure your data is returned in a certain order is by using the ORDER BY clause within a SELECT statement.

The basic syntax of an ORDER BY clause is shown in the following code:

```
USE AdventureWorks2008;
GO
SELECT * from Person.Person
ORDER BY LastName
```

The ORDER BY clause follows the column list, the WHERE clause, and any joins in the SELECT statement. This returns an alphabetical listing of all the people in the Person.Contact table.

The following steps show you how to create and run a query with the ORDER BY clause. These steps assume you have AdventureWorks2008 installed on your system.

If you don't have the AdventureWorks2008 database installed on your system, download and install it before continuing. To find the file, go to the Microsoft CodePlex Web site (`www.codeplex.com/MSFTDBProdSamples`) and click the Releases tab. Full details on how to install AdventureWorks2008 is covered in Chapter 5 of this mini-book.

1. **Launch SQL Server Management Studio (SSMS).**

Choose Start⇨All Programs⇨Microsoft SQL Server 2008⇨SQL Server Management Studio.

2. **On the Connect to Server screen, click Connect.**

3. **Click the New Query button to create a new query window.**

4. **Enter the following code in the query window:**

```
USE AdventureWorks2008;
GO
SELECT * from Person.Person
ORDER BY LastName
```

The USE AdventureWorks2008 line with the GO statement sets the context to the AdventureWorks2008 database. The SELECT statement retrieves all the rows from the Person.Person table and orders the data by LastName.

5. **Execute the code by pressing the F5 key or by clicking the Execute button.**

6. **(Optional) Leave the query window open so that you can enter other code shown in this chapter.**

Results can also be filtered. For example, you might want only a listing of people whose last names start with A. The following code could be used. The query lists the results alphabetically for the second and subsequent letters.

```
SELECT * from Person.Person
WHERE LastName LIKE 'A%'
ORDER BY LastName
```

The ORDER BY clause comes after the WHERE clause.

Order your results in ascending or descending order

You can also specify how your results are ordered. Two choices exist:

✦ **Ascending:** Orders the query alphabetically from A to Z or numerically from lowest to highest. It's the default, so it doesn't need to be specified. Ascending can be shortened to ASC. The following code shows a query with ASC added to specify ascending order.

```
USE AdventureWorks2008;
GO
SELECT * from Person.Person
WHERE LastName LIKE 'A%'
ORDER BY LastName ASC
```

✦ **Descending:** Orders the query alphabetically from Z to A or numerically from the highest to the lowest. Descending can be shortened to DESC, as shown in the following query:

```
USE AdventureWorks2008;
GO
SELECT * from Person.Person
WHERE LastName LIKE 'A%'
ORDER BY LastName DESC
```

Using TOP to limit the number of rows

Sometimes you need to limit the number of rows. For example, you might be interested in knowing which customers have had the highest purchases and which salespeople have had the highest sales. The following query gives you this information:

```
SELECT CustomerID, SalesPersonID, TotalDue
FROM Sales.SalesOrderHeader
```

However, this query returns 31,465 rows, which is a little difficult to digest.

Instead, you can limit the number of rows. The TOP expression allows you to limit the number of rows in two ways:

✦ **TOP *<number>*:** With this method, you enter a number, such as 10, to limit the number of rows returned to the number you specify.

✦ **TOP *n* PERCENT:** With this method, you limit the number of rows returned to a percentage of the number of rows that would be returned without the TOP clause.

In the following two query examples, the order is changed to descending by using the DESC keyword. The TotalDue column is numerical; therefore, if it's in ascending order it's listed from lowest to highest. To show the top sales, the result needs to be listed in descending order so that the results are listed from highest to lowest.

The syntax for both methods is shown in the following code. The data is being retrieved from the Sales.SalesOrderHeader table. This is similar to the information you might find on an invoice, such as who placed the order, who took the order, and a total. The Sales.SalesOrderDetails (which isn't included in the query) includes the actual line items of what's been ordered.

```
SELECT TOP 10 CustomerID, SalesPersonID, TotalDue
FROM Sales.SalesOrderHeader
ORDER BY TotalDue DESC
```

The previous query returns 10 rows.

```
SELECT TOP 10 PERCENT CustomerID,
        SalesPersonID, TotalDue
FROM Sales.SalesOrderHeader
ORDER BY TotalDue DESC
```

This query returns 3,147 rows (10 percent of 31,465).

Grouping Results with GROUP BY

The GROUP BY clause can be used in a SELECT list to provide summary data. GROUP BY is most often used with aggregate functions. *Aggregate functions* are those that work on a group of data and return a single result. Some of the common aggregate functions you use with GROUP BY clauses are

✦ **SUM:** SUM adds all the values in a group and returns the result. Only numbers can be added.

✦ **AVG:** AVG provides an average of the values in a group by adding all the non-null values and dividing the sum by the number of values added. NULL values aren't included in the computation. Only numbers can be averaged.

✦ **MIN:** MIN (minimum) identifies the lowest value item within the column. NULL values are ignored. MIN works with numbers, text, and dates.

✦ **MAX:** MAX (maximum) identifies the highest value item within the column. NULL values are ignored. MAX works with numbers, text, and dates.

✦ **COUNT:** COUNT returns the number of rows in a table or result set. COUNT(*) includes the NULL and duplicate values in the result. COUNT(*expression*) returns the number of items in a group that match the expression (such as a column name) ignoring NULL and duplicate values. Because COUNT is used to count rows, it works on any data type.

Aggregate functions often work on numbers. Within SQL Server 2008, numbers are stored in numeric data types, such as tinyint (tiny integer), smallint (small integer), int (integer), bigint (big integer), decimal, money, smallmoney, float, and real.

The generic syntax of the GROUP BY clause is

```
SELECT column list
FROM table name
GROUP BY column
```

Because AdventureWorks2008 is populated with data that can easily be used with aggregates, the examples in this section use the AdventureWorks2008 database.

If you don't have the AdventureWorks2008 database, follow the procedures in Chapter 5 of this mini-book to install it on your system.

Grouping results into summary rows

Imagine that someone asks you for the sales that a particular salesperson had for the year 2001. One way you could retrieve this information is with the following statement:

```
SELECT SalesPersonID, TotalDue
FROM Sales.SalesOrderHeader
WHERE Year(OrderDate) = '2001'
  AND SalesPersonID = 280
```

This method returns 20 rows. All you have to do is get out your calculator and add the TotalDue column 20 times. For error-prone fingers, this method simply won't work. There must be a better way. That better way is by using the GROUP BY clause, as shown in the following steps:

1. **Launch SQL Server Management Studio (SSMS).**

   Choose Start⇨All Programs⇨Microsoft SQL Server 2008⇨SQL Server Management Studio.

2. **On the Connect to Server screen, click Connect.**

3. **Click the New Query button to create a new query window.**

4. **Enter the following code in the query window.**

   ```
   USE AdventureWorks2008;
   GO
   SELECT SalesPersonID, TotalDue
   FROM Sales.SalesOrderHeader
   WHERE Year(OrderDate) = '2001'
     AND SalesPersonID = 280
   ```

   The USE AdventureWorks2008 line with the GO statement sets the context to the AdventureWorks2008 database. The SELECT statement retrieves the 20 rows.

5. **Execute the code by pressing the F5 key or by clicking the Execute button.**

6. **Modify your code by adding the SUM aggregate in the column list and the GROUP BY clause. Execute the code by pressing the F5 key.**

```
SELECT SalesPersonID, SUM(TotalDue) AS [Total Sales for
    2001]
FROM Sales.SalesOrderHeader
WHERE Year(OrderDate) = '2001'
  AND SalesPersonID = 280
GROUP BY SalesPersonID
```

This query returns a single row.

7. **To retrieve the total sales for all salespeople in 2001, modify the WHERE clause so that the data isn't filtered based on a particular salesperson.**

```
SELECT SalesPersonID, SUM(TotalDue) AS [Total Sales for
    2001]
FROM Sales.SalesOrderHeader
WHERE Year(OrderDate) = '2001'
  -- AND SalesPersonID = 280
GROUP BY SalesPersonID
```

The AND SalesPersonID = 280 line is commented out of the query with two dashes (– –). Comment lines aren't evaluated by the query. Eleven rows are returned with this query — one for each salesperson who had a sale in 2001. Several sales that weren't attributed to any particular salesperson are identified with NULL as the SalesPersonID.

8. **Add the ORDER BY clause to your query to order the result set by the SalesPersonID.**

```
SELECT SalesPersonID, SUM(TotalDue) AS [Total Sales for
    2001]
FROM Sales.SalesOrderHeader
WHERE Year(OrderDate) = '2001'
  -- AND SalesPersonID = 280
GROUP BY SalesPersonID
ORDER BY SalesPersonID
```

The ORDER BY clause is after the GROUP BY clause.

9. **Leave the query window open in SSMS.**

Using the HAVING clause to filter your results

The HAVING clause allows you to filter the results of the GROUP BY clause. It's similar to the WHERE clause in a query.

As a reminder, the WHERE clause can be used to filter the results. In the previous example, the following query filtered the result so that data from only 2001 was used and only for the salesperson with the SalesPersonID of 280:

```
SELECT SalesPersonID, TotalDue
FROM Sales.SalesOrderHeader
WHERE Year(OrderDate) = '2001'
  AND SalesPersonID = 280
```

Instead of retrieving all 31,465 rows from the Sales.SalesOrderHeader table, the results were filtered to only 20.

Similarly, the HAVING clause can filter the results of the GROUP BY clause. For example, in the previous steps, the following query provided summary sales data for all salespeople who had sales in 2001.

```
SELECT SalesPersonID, SUM(TotalDue) AS [Total Sales for 2001]
FROM Sales.SalesOrderHeader
WHERE Year(OrderDate) = '2001'
GROUP BY SalesPersonID
ORDER BY SalesPersonID
```

This query returned 11 rows from the AdventureWorks2008 database. Imagine that the company pays bonuses to salespeople who have sales over $1 million. Instead of providing a listing showing sales data for all salespeople, you're asked to provide a listing of only salespeople who had sales over $1 million. The following query adds the HAVING clause to provide this information:

```
SELECT SalesPersonID, SUM(TotalDue) AS [Total Sales for 2001]
FROM Sales.SalesOrderHeader
WHERE Year(OrderDate) = '2001'
GROUP BY SalesPersonID
HAVING SUM(TotalDue) > 1000000
ORDER BY SalesPersonID
```

This query reduces the result set to only 6 rows.

Any of the numeric comparison operators in the WHERE clause (<, >, =, BETWEEN, and so on) can also be used in the HAVING clause. For example, if you want a listing of salespeople who didn't meet a sales quota of $1 million, you could modify the HAVING line to:

```
HAVING SUM(TotalDue) < 1000000
```

Chapter 7: Modifying Your Data

*M*ost databases are *dynamic* — that is, the data changes. The exception is an archive database that holds historical information. Rewriting history is not a good idea!

Three primary commands are used to change data in a database: INSERT to add data, UPDATE to modify data, and DELETE to remove data. Each of these commands is called a Data Manipulation Language (DML) command. In this chapter, we cover the basics of INSERT, UPDATE, and DELETE.

Using DML Commands

Data Manipulation Language (DML) commands are used to add, modify, and remove rows from tables. The DML commands can also be referred to as DML statements. The three DML commands supported in SQL Server 2008 are

✦ **INSERT:** Used to add rows to a table. A single INSERT statement can be used to add a single row, or multiple rows.

✦ **UPDATE:** Used to modify data in a table. An UPDATE statement can be used to modify a single column in one or more rows, or multiple columns in multiple rows. The WHERE clause is used to specify which rows to modify. If the WHERE clause is omitted, all the rows in the table will be modified.

✦ **DELETE:** Used to remove rows from a table. A single DELETE statement can be used to remove one or more rows from a table. The WHERE clause is used to specify which rows to modify. If the WHERE clause is omitted, all the rows in the table will be removed.

DML commands can be included within T-SQL batch files or stored procedures. Additionally, DML triggers can be created to respond to each of these DML commands.

For example, an UPDATE DML trigger can be configured on a table to capture and log any changes to the data within the table. Therefore, whenever an UPDATE command is issued against the table, in addition to the UPDATE, the UPDATE trigger will also fire.

Triggers are covered in more depth in Book IV, Chapter 3.

Adding Data to Your Database

The INSERT command is used to add rows to either tables or views.

Some general rules and guidelines to follow when adding data with the INSERT statement are

✦ **NULL data:** If a column is specified as NOT NULL, then the INSERT must include data for the column.

✦ **Data type:** The data type of the inserted data must match the data type of the column. In other words, if you try to add text data into a numeric column, the INSERT will fail.

✦ **Constraints or rules:** If the INSERT violates a constraint or rule on the table, the INSERT will fail. For example, if a constraint specifies that a credit rating column can have values between 1 and 5 only, then an INSERT with a value of 9 will fail.

✦ **Multiple columns:** Multiple columns can be added by using a single column list and multiple values lines.

The basic syntax of the INSERT command is

```
INSERT INTO tableName
       (column list,,,)
VALUES (value,,,),
       (value,,,)
```

In past versions of SQL Server, you had to add a column list for every value line. If you were adding 100 rows to a table with each row populating only some of the columns, you'd have to use 100 column lists. It looked similar to this:

```
INSERT INTO tableName
       (column list,,,)
VALUES (value,,,),
       (column list,,,)
VALUES (value,,,),
       (column list,,,)
VALUES (value,,,),
```

In SQL Server 2008, you can use one column list to identify the columns in each of your value lines. It might not seem like much, but if you're forced to repeat the values list 100 times, this change is enough to get many database professionals to stand up and yell, "Wooo Hoo!"

The column list is optional if data is inserted in the same order as the table definition. In other words, if your table has two columns (LastName and FirstName), you can omit the column list.

However, be aware that the first value in your values list will be entered as LastName and the second value will be entered as FirstName. If you mix up the order, the database isn't smart enough to know to switch them back.

Use the following steps to create a database named Sales, a table named Contacts within the database, and then to add some data to the Contacts table.

1. **Launch SQL Server Management Studio.**

Choose Start⇨All Programs⇨Microsoft SQL Server 2008⇨SQL Server Management Studio.

2. **Create a new query window by clicking the New Query button.**

3. **Create a database named Sales and a table named Contacts by using the following T-SQL code:**

```
USE Master;
GO
CREATE DATABASE Sales;
GO
USE Sales;
GO
CREATE TABLE Contacts (
 ContactsID int NOT NULL,
 LastName varchar(50) NOT NULL,
 FirstName varchar(50) NULL,
 Phone varchar(30) NULL
 )
```

Book III
Chapter 7

Modifying Your Data

The ContactsID and the LastName columns are both defined as NOT NULL. When adding data to the table, these columns must have data included in the VALUES clause.

4. **Add two rows of data into the Contacts table with the following INSERT statement:**

```
INSERT INTO Contacts
        (ContactsID, LastName, FirstName, Phone)
VALUES (101, 'Stooge', 'Larry', '757-555-1234'),
        (102, 'Stooge','Moe', NULL);
SELECT * FROM Contacts;
```

The column list specifies all the columns in the table. Because of this, all the columns must be specified in the values list even though the phone number for Moe isn't included.

In the previous code, the SELECT statement is used to show the result of the INSERT statement. The * indicates that all columns should be displayed. Because no WHERE clause is included, all the rows will be displayed.

5. **Add another row of data into the Contacts table with the following INSERT statement:**

```
INSERT INTO Contacts
VALUES (103, 'Stooge', 'Curly', '757-555-1235');
SELECT * FROM Contacts;
```

In this INSERT statement, the column list is omitted. As long as the values list includes the data in the same order as the columns are defined in the table, this statement will work.

6. **Add another row of data into the Contacts table with the following INSERT statement:**

```
INSERT INTO Contacts
VALUES (104, 'Stooge', NULL, NULL);
SELECT * FROM Contacts;
```

In the preceding code, you omitted the column list and used NULL for the last two columns.

Modifying Data in your Database

The UPDATE statement is used to modify existing data in a table or a view.

Some general rules and guidelines to follow when adding data with the UPDATE statement are

✦ **NULL data:** If a column is specified as NOT NULL then the UPDATE statement can't change the data to NULL.

✦ **Data type:** The data type of the modified data must match the data type of the column. In other words, if you try to modify numeric data with text data, the UPDATE will fail.

✦ **Constraints or rules:** If the UPDATE violates a constraint or rule on the table, the UPDATE will fail. For example, if a constraint specifies that a credit rating column can have values between 1 and 5 only, then an UPDATE with a value of 0 will fail.

The basic syntax of the UPDATE statement is

```
UPDATE tableName
SET columnNameA = value, columnNameB = value,,,
WHERE columnName = value
```

The column values are set to their new values in the SET clause. Notice that multiple columns can be changed in a single UPDATE statement. Additional column names and their new values are separated with a comma.

A WHERE clause is used to filter the data. In other words, the WHERE clause is used to identify specifically which rows to update. If the WHERE clause is omitted, all the rows are updated the same way.

Use the following steps to modify data in a table with the UDPATE statement:

1. **Launch SQL Server Management Studio.**

Choose Start⇨All Programs⇨Microsoft SQL Server 2008⇨SQL Server Management Studio.

2. **Create a new query window by clicking the New Query button.**

3. **If you haven't created the Sales database, the Contacts table, and added data to the Contacts table, then enter and execute the following code; otherwise, skip to Step 4.**

```
USE Master;
GO
CREATE DATABASE Sales;
GO
USE Sales;
GO
CREATE TABLE Contacts (
 ContactsID int NOT NULL,
 LastName varchar(50) NOT NULL,
 FirstName varchar(50) NULL,
 Phone varchar(30) NULL
)
INSERT INTO Contacts
      (ContactsID, LastName, FirstName, Phone)
VALUES (101, 'Stooge', 'Larry', '757-555-1234'),
      (102, 'Stooge', 'Moe', NULL),
      (103, 'Stooge', 'Curly', '757-555-1235'),
      (104, 'Stooge', NULL, NULL);
SELECT * FROM Contacts;
```

4. **Modify the phone number of 'Moe' from NULL to '757-555-1212' with the following UPDATE statement:**

```
UPDATE Contacts
SET Phone = '757-555-1233'
WHERE FirstName = 'Moe';
SELECT * FROM Contacts;
```

5. **Use the following code to change the value of two columns with the UPDATE statement:**

```
UPDATE Contacts
SET FirstName = 'Baby', Phone = '757-555-1233'
WHERE ContactsID = 104;
SELECT * FROM Contacts;
```

6. **Imagine all the stooges moved in together, and they now have the same phone number. Use the following UPDATE statement without a WHERE clause:**

```
UPDATE Contacts
SET Phone = '757-555-1233';
SELECT * FROM Contacts;
```

Removing Data from Your Database

The DELETE statement is used to remove rows from a table or view.

Some general rules and guidelines to follow when removing data with the DELETE statement are

+ **Foreign keys:** If a row is referenced in another table with a foreign key constraint, the DELETE statement will fail. For example, a Sales table might be related to a Customers table by a foreign key in the Sales table referencing a primary key in the Customers table.

  If a customer is deleted from the Customers table, an orphan is left in the Sales table — a sale would point to a non-existent customer. This situation isn't allowed, and the DELETE fails.

+ **WHERE:** The WHERE clause identifies which rows will be deleted. The WHERE clause works the same in a DELETE statement as it does in a SELECT statement. Support for all the same operations works the same in both commands.

  Caveat Coder (Coder Beware!). If the WHERE clause is omitted, all the rows in the table will be deleted. Needless to say, this may ruin your day.

If you wish to delete all the rows in a table, the TRUNCATE TABLE command is usually used instead of the DELETE command. TRUNCATE TABLE is quicker and more efficient, although it doesn't log as much information in the transaction log and can't be rolled back.

The basic syntax of the DELETE command is

```
DELETE FROM tableName
WHERE VALUE = value
```

Use the following steps to create a populated database and then delete some rows from a table:

1. **Launch SQL Server Management Studio.**

Choose Start⇨All Programs⇨Microsoft SQL Server 2008⇨SQL Server Management Studio.

2. **Create a new query window by clicking the New Query button.**

3. **If you haven't created the Sales database, the Contacts table, and added data to the Contacts table, then enter and execute the following code:**

```
USE Master;
GO
CREATE DATABASE Sales;
GO
USE Sales;
GO
CREATE TABLE Contacts (
 ContactsID int NOT NULL,
 LastName varchar(50) NOT NULL,
 FirstName varchar(50) NULL,
 Phone varchar(30) NULL
)
INSERT INTO Contacts
        (ContactsID, LastName, FirstName, Phone)
VALUES (101, 'Stooge', 'Larry', '757-555-1234'),
        (102, 'Stooge', 'Moe', NULL),
        (103, 'Stooge', 'Curly', '757-555-1235'),
        (104, 'Stooge', NULL, NULL);
SELECT * FROM Contacts;
```

4. **Use the following code to delete the contact with the ContactsID of 104:**

```
DELETE FROM Contacts
WHERE ContactsID = 104;
SELECT * FROM Contacts;
```

This deletes only the one row where the ContactsID is equal to 104.

5. **To delete more than a single row, the WHERE clause can be used to select a range. Enter and execute the following code to delete the contacts with the ContactsID of 102 and 103.**

```
DELETE FROM Contacts
WHERE ContactsID > 101 AND ContactsID < 110;
SELECT * FROM Contacts;
```

6. **You can also omit the WHERE clause to delete all the rows in the table.**

   ```
   DELETE FROM Contacts;
   SELECT * FROM Contacts;
   ```

   The SELECT statement displays zero rows because they've all been deleted.

7. **Add some data to the Contacts table with the following command:**

   ```
   INSERT INTO Contacts
           (ContactsID, LastName, FirstName, Phone)
   VALUES (105, 'Stooge', 'Larry', '757-555-1234'),
          (106, 'Stooge', 'Moe', NULL),
          (107, 'Stooge', 'Curly', '757-555-1235'),
          (108, 'Stooge', NULL, NULL);
   SELECT * FROM Contacts;
   ```

8. **Use the following DELETE statement with a complex WHERE clause to show how you can narrow your DELETE statement:**

   ```
   DELETE FROM Contacts
   WHERE LastName = 'Stooge' AND FirstName IS NULL;
   SELECT * FROM Contacts;
   ```

Only one row is deleted: the row that has the last name of Stooge and NULL for the first name.

When checking for NULL values, the IS NULL function is used. If the WHERE clause is rewritten as WHERE FirstName = NULL, the desired row wouldn't be deleted.

Chapter 8: Taking Advantage of Views

In This Chapter

✔ **Connecting information with views**

✔ **Creating views**

✔ **Retrieving and modifying views**

✔ **Managing views**

✔ **Giving a view the boot**

*V*iews are powerful objects in SQL Server that allow you to focus on exactly what you want to see within a database. They can be used to show just a few specific columns from a table, or multiple columns from two or more tables.

While views sound a little magical at first, they're really quite simple. If you can create a query, you can create a view.

Tying Information Together with Views

A *view* allows you to access specific columns easily from one or more tables with a simple query.

Views provide two significant benefits:

✦ **Simplify data retrieval:** Although the query creating the view can be quite complex, the query that retrieves the data from the view is very simple. It looks like this:

```
SELECT *
FROM ViewName
```

✦ **Maintain security:** If permission is granted on the view, permissions to the underlying table(s) aren't needed to retrieve data from the view. At the same time, permission to the underlying table can be expressly denied.

A view doesn't actually hold any data; instead, it's a *virtual table*. Each time data is requested from a view, it actually retrieves the data from the underlying tables.

Figure 8-1 shows an Employees table. The table includes personal data, such as name and phone number. It also shows data that is much more private, such as Social Security number and salary.

Figure 8-1:
A Contact table including salary and SSN data.

If you want someone to have access to a phone listing of employees, you could create a query for them and allow them to run the query whenever they want to access the data.

The query would look like this:

```
SELECT FirstName, LastName, Phone
FROM Employees
```

Even for a simple requirement, such as a phone listing, the query can look quite intimidating to someone unfamiliar with T-SQL. However, if a vwEmpPhone view is created, the query required to retrieve the data from the view looks like this:

```
SELECT *
FROM vwEmpPhone
```

The view hides the complexity.

Additionally, the view hides the secure data. Figure 8-2 shows a partial result of the query on the view. Notice the absence of any other columns, such as salary and social security number. The view can help keep this private data secure.

Figure 8-2:
Partial listing from vwEmp Phone query.

FirstName	LastName	Phone
Gustavo	Achong	398-555-0132
Catherine	Abel	747-555-0171
Kim	Abercrombie	334-555-0137
Humberto	Acevedo	599-555-0127
Pilar	Ackerman	1 (11) 500 555-0132
Frances	Adams	991-555-0183
Margaret	Smith	959-555-0151
Carla	Adams	107-555-0138
Jay	Adams	158-555-0142
Ronald	Adina	453-555-0165
Samuel	Agcaoili	554-555-0110

Creating a View

Views can be created in two ways:

+ **View Designer:** The graphical interface available in SQL Server Management Studio (SSMS) allows you to create views rather easily with a point-and-click interface.

+ **Transact-SQL:** If you created a query and then want to convert it into a reusable view, you can do so with a couple extra lines of code.

Creating a view with the View Designer

The *View Designer* is a valuable tool included within the SQL Server Management Studio (SSMS). With View Designer you can easily create sophisticated views against one or many tables in your database.

Exploring the View Designer

Follow these steps to open the View Designer:

1. **Launch SQL Server Management Studio (SSMS).**

Choose Start⇨All Programs⇨Microsoft SQL Server 2008⇨SQL Server Management Studio.

2. **On the Connect to Server screen, click Connect.**

3. **Using the SSMS Object Explorer, browse to the Databases | AdventureWorks2008 | Views container.**

4. **Right-click the Views container and choose New View.**

The View Designer appears with the Add Table dialog box on top.

5. **Select any table and click Add. Click Close.**

The View Designer, shown in Figure 8-3, is now fully visible. The View Designer has a toolbar and four panes that you use when building and testing your query.

The four panes within the View Designer are

+ **Diagram pane:** The top pane shows a diagram of the tables that have been added for the View.

+ **Criteria pane:** The second pane from the top shows the columns that have been selected from the tables and the tables they've been selected from. The Criteria pane also allows other query criteria to be added to the view.

Toolbar   Diagram pane

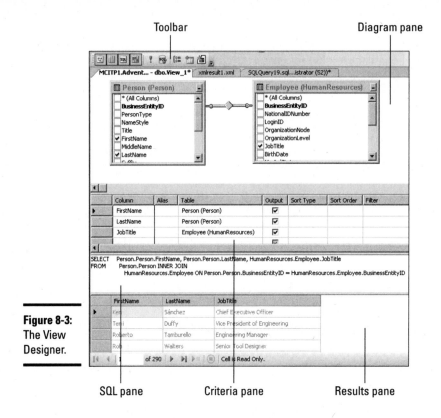

Figure 8-3:
The View
Designer.

SQL pane   Criteria pane   Results pane

✦ **SQL pane:** While the view is created, the SQL statement for the view is shown in the SQL pane. You can identify it by the SELECT statement.

✦ **Results pane:** After the view is executed, the results of the query are shown in the bottom pane.

The View Designer toolbar also appears when the View Designer is activated. In Figure 8-3, it's shown above the View Designer on the far left of your toolbar.

The toolbar items (shown from left to right in Figure 8-3) are

✦ **Show Diagram Pane:** Toggles the Diagram pane. That is, clicking this causes the Diagram pane to show or disappear.

✦ **Show Criteria Pane:** Toggles the Criteria pane.

✦ **Show SQL Pane:** Toggles the SQL pane.

✦ **Show Results Pane:** Toggles the Results pane.

✦ **Execute SQL (red exclamation mark):** Causes the SQL statement to execute and populate the Results pane with the results of the query.

+ **Verify SQL Syntax:** Parses the SQL statement to verify that it's syntactically correct.

+ **Add Group By:** Advanced feature. Adds Group By columns in the Criteria pane and adds a GROUP BY clause to the SQL statement.

+ **Add Table:** Opens the Add Table dialog box.

+ **Add New Derived Table:** Advanced feature. Adds T-SQL syntax to add a derived table to the SELECT statement.

Creating a view in the View Designer

The following steps show how to create a view to include name and phone numbers of employees in the AdventureWorks2008 database.

If you don't have the AdventureWorks2008 database installed on your system, download and install it before beginning these steps. Find this file by going to the Microsoft CodePlex site (www.codeplex.com/MSFTDBProdSamples) and clicking on the Releases tab. Full details on how to install Adventure Works is covered in Chapter 5 of this mini-book.

1. **Launch SQL Server Management Studio (SSMS).**

Choose Start➪All Programs➪Microsoft SQL Server 2008➪SQL Server Management Studio.

2. **On the Connect to Server screen, click Connect.**

3. **Using the SSMS Object Explorer, browse to the Databases | AdventureWorks2008 | Views container.**

4. **Right-click the Views container and choose New View.**

The View Designer appears with the Add Table dialog box on top.

5. **In the Add Table dialog box, select Person (Person) and click Add. Select Employee (HumanResources) and click Add. Click Close.**

6. **In the Person (Person) table, select the check boxes next to the FirstName, LastName, and Title columns.**

Watch the changes in the Criteria and SQL panes as you select these columns. Feel free to uncheck them and recheck them to observe the actions.

7. **Click the Execute SQL button (red exclamation mark) to observe the results of this query.**

8. **To save this view, press Ctrl+S.**

9. **In the Choose Name dialog box, type** vwEmployees **and click OK.**

The view is created and can be executed.

10. **Click the New Query button to create a new query window. If the Connect to Server dialog box appears, click Connect.**

11. **Ensure that the AdventureWorks database is chosen in the Databases drop-down box.**

   If the Connect to Server dialog box appeared, this defaulted to Master.

12. **In the new query window, enter the following query:**

   ```
   SELECT * FROM vwEmpEmployees
   ```

13. **Press F5 to execute the query.**

   This retrieves a listing of 290 employees.

Creating a view with T-SQL

If you already created a query that you want to convert to a view, it's sometimes easier to do so with Transact-SQL statements.

T-SQL provides three Data Definition Language (DDL) statements that can be used to create, modify, and delete objects, such as views. The three DDL statements that are used with objects are

✦ **CREATE:** Creates objects that can be reused.

✦ **ALTER:** Modifies existing objects.

✦ **DROP:** Deletes existing objects.

For example, imagine that you create the following query to retrieve a listing of employees and their phone numbers:

```
SELECT p.FirstName, p.LastName, p.title
FROM Person.Person p
INNER JOIN HumanResources.Employee e
ON p.BusinessEntityID = e.BusinessEntityID
```

The query might work fine for you, but a co-worker might have trouble typing in and executing the query. He asks if you can make it simpler for him. You respond, "Sure, no problem. I can make it into a view."

Use the following steps to create the view with a T-SQL statement:

1. **Launch SQL Server Management Studio (SSMS).**

   Choose Start➪All Programs➪Microsoft SQL Server 2008➪SQL Server Management Studio.

2. **On the Connect to Server screen, click Connect.**

3. **Click the New Query button to create a new query window.**

4. **Choose the AdventureWorks2008 database in the Databases drop-down box.**

   This normally defaults to the Master database.

5. **Enter the following query in the query window:**

```
SELECT p.FirstName, p.LastName, p.Title
FROM Person.Person p
INNER JOIN HumanResources.Employee e
ON p.BusinessEntityID = e.BusinessEntityID
```

6. **Execute the query by pressing F5 to ensure it works as you expect.**

   You receive 290 rows of data.

7. **Modify the query so it looks like the following code. The new code is in bold.**

```
CREATE VIEW vwEmployee
AS
SELECT p.FirstName, p.LastName, p.Title
FROM Person.Person p
INNER JOIN HumanResources.Employee e
ON p.BusinessEntityID = e.BusinessEntityID
```

8. **To verify that you have successfully created the query, execute the following statement.**

```
SELECT * FROM vwEmployee
```

   You receive 290 rows of employee data.

Using a View

If a view has been created, it can be used to retrieve and modify data. Remember though, the view is only a virtualized table. A view doesn't hold any actual data; instead, it retrieves and modifies data in underlying tables.

The AdventureWorks2008 database includes several views that have already been created. You can create your own views (as shown in the previous section), or you can use the existing views to retrieve and modify data in the underlying tables in the AdventureWorks2008 database.

Retrieving data with a view

The AdventureWorks2008 database includes a vEmployee view in the HumanResources schema. It includes name, phone, address information, and more by joining nine different tables.

This data can be retrieved with SQL Server Management Studio (SSMS) or T-SQL statements.

Retrieving view data using SSMS

Imagine you need to use one of the existing views to retrieve the phone number for Terri Duffy, one of the employees of AdventureWorks2008. The following steps show how to retrieve the information with SQL Server Management Studio (SSMS):

1. **Launch SQL Server Management Studio (SSMS).**

Choose Start⇨All Programs⇨Microsoft SQL Server 2008⇨SQL Server Management Studio.

2. **On the Connect to Server screen, click Connect.**

3. **Using the SSMS Object Explorer, browse to the Databases | AdventureWorks2008 | Views container. Select the HumanResources.vEmployee view.**

4. **Right-click the HumanResources.vEmployee view and choose Select Top 1000 Rows.**

The view executes, and the results from the view appear in a tabbed window in SSMS.

5. **Scroll to the record holding Terri Duffy's name.**

It's record 2 on our system, but it might be different on yours if records have been modified.

6. **With Terri Duffy's record selected, scroll to the right to locate her phone number.**

Figure 8-4 shows a partial listing of the view results. Terri Duffy's record is selected, and the display is scrolled to the right to show her phone number.

7. **Leave the SSMS query window open for the next set of steps.**

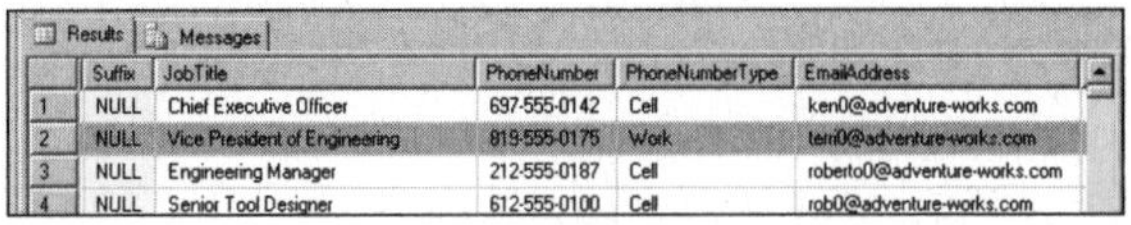

Figure 8-4:
Viewing employee data with the vEmployee view.

	Suffix	JobTitle	PhoneNumber	PhoneNumberType	EmailAddress	
1	NULL	Chief Executive Officer	697-555-0142	Cell	ken0@adventure-works.com	
2	NULL	Vice President of Engineering	819-555-0175	Work	terri0@adventure-works.com	
3	NULL	Engineering Manager	212-555-0187	Cell	roberto0@adventure-works.com	
4	NULL	Senior Tool Designer	612-555-0100	Cell	rob0@adventure-works.com	

Retrieving view data using T-SQL

Imagine you need to use one of the existing views to retrieve the e-mail address for Barry Johnson, one of the employees of AdventureWorks. The following steps show you how to retrieve the information with a query window in SQL Server Management Studio (SSMS):

1. **With a query window open in SSMS, enter the following code and execute it to ensure the AdventureWorks database is selected.**

    ```
    USE AdventureWorks2008
    ```

    Press F5 to execute the query.

2. **Enter the following query to retrieve all the data from the vEmployee view.**

    ```
    SELECT *
    FROM HumanResources.vEmployee
    ```

    Press F5 to execute the query. Figure 8-5 shows the partial results of this view. The retrieved data is identical to the data retrieved when opening the view in the previous steps. However, instead of being displayed in a full tabbed window, the data is displayed in the Results pane of the query window. In Figure 8-5, the results are scrolled to record 49 (Barry Johnson) and scrolled to the right to show his e-mail address.

Figure 8-5:
Results of
querying the
vEmployee
view with a
SELECT
statement.

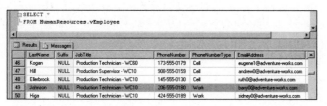

3. **Modify your query with a WHERE clause to show only the record of employee Barry Johnson.**

    The following query shows the new query with the changes in bold:

    ```
    SELECT *
    FROM HumanResources.vEmployee
    WHERE FirstName = 'Barry'
        AND LastName = 'Johnson'
    ```

4. **Leave SSMS open.**

Modifying data with a view

In addition to retrieving data with a view, it's also possible to modify the data in a view. This is much easier to do with SSMS, but it can also be done with a T-SQL UPDATE statement.

Modifying view data using SSMS

When data is retrieved with the Open View command from the right-click menu, the data can also be modified within this same display.

Imagine that an employee named Guy Gilbert has changed his phone company and now has a new phone number. You're asked to update the phone number in the AdventureWorks database. You know the phone number is held in the vEmployee view, so you plan to use this view to update the phone number.

1. **Using the SSMS Object Explorer, browse to the Databases |
   AdventureWorks2008 | Views container. Select the
   HumanResources.vEmployee view.**

2. **Right-click the HumanResources.vEmployee view and choose Edit Top
   200 Rows.**

   The view executes, and the results from the view appear in a tabbed window in SSMS.

3. **Verify Ken Sanchez's record is the first record in the view. Scroll to
   the right of the screen and click the box holding his phone number.**

4. **On Guy Gilbert's record, change the phone number from
   697-555-0142 to 697-555-1111. Press Return.**

5. **Leave SSMS open.**

The data is updated as soon as you press Enter. If you open a new query window and select the data from the view, you will see that the new phone number is displayed.

Modifying view data using T-SQL

Data can also be modified in a view with the T-SQL UPDATE statement. The basic syntax of the UPDATE statement is:

```
UPDATE TableName or ViewName
SET columnName = newValue
WHERE columnName = Value
```

Because the basic purpose of the primary key is to ensure uniqueness of the rows, the WHERE clause often uses the primary key to identify the specific row to be identified.

For example, imagine that you're asked to change Mary Baker's phone number from 283-555-0185 to 283-555-5810. The following steps would be used:

1. **With SSMS open, ensure the AdventureWorks database is chosen in the database drop-down box.**
2. **Enter the following query to retrieve all the data from the vEmployee view.**

   ```
   SELECT *
   FROM HumanResources.vEmployee
   WHERE LastName = 'Baker'
   ```

   Figure 8-6 shows the results of this query. It returned two records — the only records that exist in the view with the last name of Baker. Mary Baker's BusinessEntityID is 104.

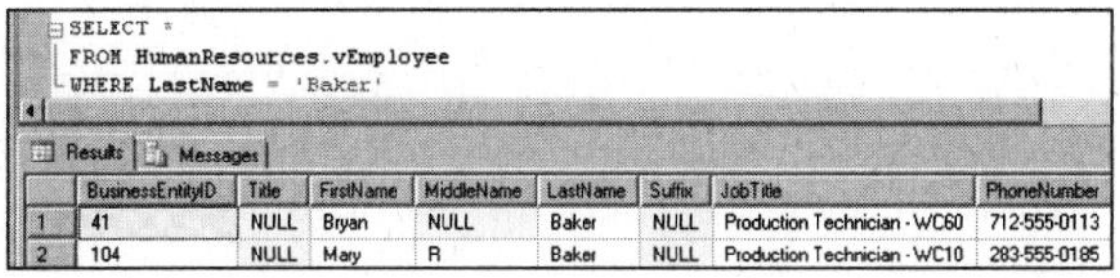
SELECT *
FROM HumanResources.vEmployee
WHERE LastName = 'Baker'
Results
Messages
BusinessEntityID | Title | FirstName | MiddleName | LastName | Suffix | JobTitle | PhoneNumber
1 | 41 | NULL | Bryan | NULL | Baker | NULL | Production Technician - WC60 | 712-555-0113
2 | 104 | NULL | Mary | R | Baker | NULL | Production Technician - WC10 | 283-555-0185

Figure 8-6: Results of querying the vEmployee view with a SELECT statement.

3. **Modify the `SELECT` statement to return only Mary Baker's record.**

   The following query shows the change in bold:

   ```
   SELECT *
   FROM HumanResources.vEmployee
   WHERE BusinessEntityID = 104
   ```

4. **Press F5 to execute the statement and verify that only Mary Baker's record is returned.**
5. **Change the query from a `SELECT` statement to an `UPDATE` statement with the following query. Press F5 to execute the query.**

   ```
   UPDATE HumanResources.vEmployee
   SET PhoneNumber = '283-555-5810'
   WHERE BusinessEntityID = 104
   ```

6. **Verify the change has occurred with the following query:**

   ```
   SELECT *
   FROM HumanResources.vEmployee
   WHERE BusinessEntityID = 104
   ```

Maintaining a View

Things change. People's needs change. And yes, views can change. When you first create a view, it's probably perfect. As people's needs change, though, that view might no longer meet their needs. Often, it takes only a minor change to make it perfect again.

Modifying a view is referred to as modifying the *view definition*. The view definition is the statement used to create or alter the view, starting with CREATE VIEW or ALTER VIEW. View definitions can be modified with the View Designer or the T-SQL ALTER statement.

To modify a view, you need an existing view. Although AdventureWorks has many views included, you might not want to modify one of them. The following step creates two copies of an existing view that you can then modify in the View Designer and with T-SQL statements.

1. **Launch SQL Server Management Studio (SSMS).**

Choose Start➪All Programs➪Microsoft SQL Server 2008➪SQL Server Management Studio.

2. **On the Connect to Server screen, click Connect.**

3. **Using the SSMS Object Explorer, browse to the Databases | AdventureWorks2008 | Views container. Select the HumanResources.vEmployee view.**

4. **Right-click the HumanResources.vEmployee view and choose Script View As➪CREATE To➪New Query Editor Window.**

A new query window appears with the view definition for the HumanResources.vEmployee view.

5. **Delete the last two lines in the query.**

Scroll to the bottom of the query window. The last two lines of the query start with GO and EXEC sp_addextendedproperty. This is an advanced feature that allows you to set extended properties but isn't needed for our example.

6. **Change the name of the view from vEmployee to vEmployeeViewDesigner by changing the CREATE VIEW line.**

```
CREATE VIEW [HumanResources].[vEmployeeViewDesigner]
```

7. **Press F5 to execute the script and create the view.**

8. **Change the name of the view from vEmployeeViewDesigner to vEmployeeTSQL by changing the CREATE VIEW line.**

   ```
   CREATE VIEW [HumanResources].[vEmployeeTSQL]
   ```

9. **Press F5 to execute the script and create the view.**

10. **Leave SSMS open.**

You now have two new views — vEmployeeViewDesigner and vEmployeeTSQL. You can modify and delete these views without affecting the AdventureWorks2008 database.

Modifying a view with the View Designer

Imagine that you need to change the view so that the address information is no longer included. Part of what you need to know is what tables hold the address information. In addition to removing the columns from the view, the tables holding the address information can also be removed from the view.

The tables that hold address information in the view are shown here with their associated aliases:

Alias	Table Name
ea	HumanResources.EmployeeAddress
a	Person.Address
sp	Person.StateProvince
cr	Person.CountryRegion

In Chapter 5 of this mini-book, you discover that aliases are used for table names to make queries easier to read. The full table name is spelled out in the JOIN clause, and the alias is identified immediately afterward with the AS keyword.

The full SQL query used to create this view is shown here with the address information in bold:

```
SELECTe.BusinessEntityID, p.Title, p.FirstName, p.MiddleName,
    p.LastName, p.Suffix, e.JobTitle, pp.PhoneNumber,
    pnt.Name AS PhoneNumberType, ea.EmailAddress,
    p.EmailPromotion,
    a.AddressLine1, a.AddressLine2, a.City,
    sp.Name AS StateProvinceName, a.PostalCode,
    cr.Name AS CountryRegionName, p.AdditionalContactInfo
FROM HumanResources.Employee AS e INNER JOIN
    Person.Person AS p
    ON p.BusinessEntityID = e.BusinessEntityID INNER JOIN
    Person.BusinessEntityAddress AS bea
```

```
ON bea.BusinessEntityID = e.BusinessEntityID INNER JOIN
Person.Address AS a
ON a.AddressID = bea.AddressID INNER JOIN
Person.StateProvince AS sp
ON sp.StateProvinceID = a.StateProvinceID INNER JOIN
Person.CountryRegion AS cr ON cr.CountryRegionCode =
sp.CountryRegionCode LEFT OUTER JOIN
Person.PersonPhone AS pp
ON pp.BusinessEntityID = p.BusinessEntityID LEFT OUTER
JOIN
Person.PhoneNumberType AS pnt
ON pp.PhoneNumberTypeID = pnt.PhoneNumberTypeID LEFT OUTER
JOIN
Person.EmailAddress AS ea
ON p.BusinessEntityID = ea.BusinessEntityID
```

The following steps show how to modify the view by removing these tables and the associated columns for these tables from the view:

1. **Select the HumanResources.vEmployeeViewDesigner view.**

Using the SSMS Object Explorer, browse to the Databases ǀ AdventureWorks2008 ǀ Views container.

2. **Right-click the HumanResources.vEmployeeViewDesigner view and choose Design.**

3. **Right-click the a table (which is the Person.Address table) and choose Remove.**

All the columns selected from this table are removed from the column list. This includes AddressLine1, AddressLine2, City, and Postal Code.

4. **Right-click the ea table (which is the HumanResources. EmployeeAddress table) and choose Remove. Right-click the pnt table (which is the Person.PhoneNumberType table) and choose Remove.**

5. **Right-click the sp table (which is the Person.StateProvince table) and choose Remove. Right-click the pp table (which is the Person. PersonPhone table) and choose Remove.**

6. **Right-click the cr table (which is the Person.CountryRegion table) and choose Remove. Right-click the bea table (which is the Person. BusinessEntityAddress table) and choose Remove.**

The only two tables remaining are the e table (which is the HumanResources.Employee table) and the p table (which is the Person.Person table). The query has been simplified to the following:

```
SELECT e.BusinessEntityID, p.Title, p.FirstName,
    p.MiddleName,
        p.LastName, p.Suffix, e.JobTitle,
        p.EmailPromotion, p.AdditionalContactInfo
FROM    HumanResources.Employee AS e
INNER JOIN Person.Person AS p
    ON p.BusinessEntityID = e.BusinessEntityID
```

In addition to removing the tables, you can also uncheck the columns that you no longer want. For example, if the AdditionalContactInfo was no longer desired in the view, the check box next to this column in the p table (Person.Person table) could be deselected, and the column would be removed from the View.

7. **Press Ctrl+S to save the HumanResources.vEmployeeViewDesigner view.**

You have saved the modified view. The last step is to test the view to ensure that it does what you want.

8. **Right-click the HumanResources.vEmployeeViewDesigner view and choose Select Top 1000 Rows.**

A new tabbed window appears in SSMS, and the results of the view appear. Verify that the address information is no longer contained in the view.

9. **Leave SSMS open.**

Modifying a View with T-SQL

For simple changes to a view, you might want to modify it by using T-SQL Data Definition Language (DDL) statements. The view can be created with the CREATE DDL statement. After the view is created, it can be modified with the ALTER DDL statement.

For example, suppose that you want to remove the AdditionalContactInfo column from the HumanResources.vEmployeeTSQL view that you created earlier in this section. The following steps show you how this is done:

1. **Select the HumanResources.vEmployeeTSQL view with the SSMS Object Explorer.**

Browse to the Databases | AdventureWorks2008 | Views container.

2. **Right-click the HumanResources.vEmployeeTSQL view and choose Script View As⇨ALTER To⇨New Query Editor Window.**

A new query window appears with the view definition for the HumanResources.vEmployeeTSQL view. The definition is shown with the ALTER VIEW statement.

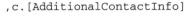

3. **Find the line that holds the AdditionalContactInfo column and delete it.**

   It's the last line before the FROM clause and looks like this:

   ```
   ,c.[AdditionalContactInfo]
   ```

   This line begins with a comma, which is often done with scripts so that the line can be removed or commented out (by using two dashes) without affecting the line before it.

4. **Press F5 to run this script and modify the definition of the view.**

5. **At the bottom of the query window, enter the following code:**

   ```
   SELECT *
   FROM HumanResources.vEmployeeTSQL
   ```

6. **Highlight only the SELECT statement that you just entered and press F5 to run it.**

   Your view runs.

   If you scroll to the last column, you see that the AdditionalContactInfo column no longer appears. The last column is the CountryRegionName.

Deleting a View

When a view is no longer needed, you might choose to remove it from the database. Views can be removed by using two methods:

✦ SQL Server Management Studio (SSMS): Views can be deleted.

✦ T-SQL Script: Views can be dropped.

We know it seems that one word could be used to define this simple concept of removing a view instead of both *deleted* and *dropped*. T-SQL has long used the terms *dropping objects* and *deleting data*. For example, a table or view is dropped, but rows within a table are deleted. However, in SSMS, the designers chose to use *delete* to remove objects.

Deleting a view using SSMS Object Explorer

To delete a HumanResources.vEmployeeViewDesigner view with the SSMS Object Explorer, follow these steps:

1. **Launch SQL Server Management Studio (SSMS).**

   Choose Start➪All Programs➪Microsoft SQL Server 2008➪SQL Server Management Studio.

2. **On the Connect to Server screen, click Connect.**

3. Using the SSMS Object Explorer, browse to the Databases |
   AdventureWorks2008 | Views container.

4. Select the HumanResources.vEmployeeViewDesigner view.

5. Right-click the view and choose Delete.

6. On the Delete Object dialog box, click OK.

7. Leave SSMS open.

Dropping a view using T-SQL

To drop a view named HumanResources.vEmployeeTSQL with T-SQL statements, use the following steps:

1. In SSMS, click the New Query button to create a new query window.

2. Ensure the AdventureWorks database is chosen in the database drop-
   down box.

3. Enter the following query to retrieve all the data from the vEmployee
   view.

```
DROP VIEW HumanResources.vEmployeeTSQL
```

Chapter 9: Advanced Query Topics

In This Chapter

✔ **Protecting your data**

✔ **Exploring full-text search**

✔ **Discovering outer joins**

✔ **Querying XML data**

Sometimes you need to go beyond the basics and use some advanced methods to interact with your data. In this chapter, you discover some of those advanced methods.

Transactions are often used in stored procedures and can be very valuable when you want to control the success (or failure) of changes to your data. *Full-text queries* allow you to search text-type data with more power than the simple LIKE clause. The INNER JOIN statement retrieves data based on matches between two tables, but sometimes you want a listing of everything in one of the tables regardless of matches in the other table; OUTER JOIN statements allow you to do just that.

Moreover, XML data is becoming increasingly important in the storage of data due to its ease of use between platforms. When you start storing XML data, you'll want to be able to retrieve and modify it. The XML methods used to retrieve and modify XML data are demonstrated in the last section of this chapter.

Using Transactions to Protect Your Data

A *transaction* is a group of database statements that are combined into a single unit of work. Transactions are used to ensure multiple statements either succeed or fail as a whole.

The three primary commands used with transactions are

✦ **BEGIN TRANSACTION:** The BEGIN TRANSACTION marks the beginning of a transaction. No data modifications issued from this point are committed to the database until a COMMIT TRANSACTION command is issued.

✦ **COMMIT TRANSACTION:** The COMMIT TRANSACTION implies that all commands after the BEGIN TRANSACTION command have succeeded and the data needs to be written to the database. Up to this point, the data changes have been logged in to the transaction log but not actually written to the database.

✦ **ROLLBACK TRANSACTION:** The ROLLBACK TRANSACTION command causes all data modifications after the BEGIN TRANSACTION command to be undone. They're not written to the database.

Most databases today (including SQL Server 2008) use a transaction log to track changes to the database. Figure 9-1 shows how the transaction log fits into the process. Any data modifications (such as INSERT, UPDATE, and DELETE) are written to the transaction log first, and then written to the database. Normally, data modifications are written to the database almost immediately. When a transaction is used, the modifications aren't written to the database until a COMMIT TRANSACTION is received.

Figure 9-1:
Modifications are recorded in the transaction log first.

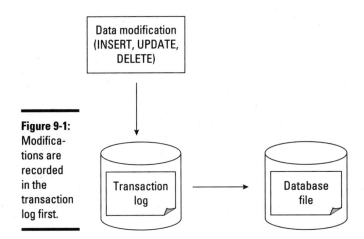

Consider this scenario. You're at the ATM to withdraw money. You put your card in, enter your PIN, and then enter how much money you want. The ATM checks your account and gives you the money. However, just before it debits your account, the power shuts off. You have your money, but the account hasn't been debited.

Is this acceptable? Maybe for you it is, but not for the bank. More than likely, though, the algorithm used for the ATM debits your account first and then gives your money. Therefore, the possibility exists that the ATM debits your account, the power fails before giving your money, and you don't get your money. This might not be acceptable to you!

Both examples are prevented by using a transaction. The two major events (giving your money and debiting your account) are enclosed within a transaction, and if one event fails, the transaction causes both events to fail.

Pseudocode for this example looks like this:

```
--Code to verify account and specify money desired.
BEGIN TRANSACTION
 -- Code to debit account
 -- Code to give money
COMMIT TRANSACTION
```

Understanding implicit and explicit transactions

Transactions are referred to as either implicit or explicit.

✦ **Implicit:** An *implicit* transaction is a command (such as INSERT, UPDATE, or DELETE) that doesn't use a BEGIN TRANSACTION, but it's *implied*. Further, a COMMIT TRANSACTION command isn't needed. If the command completes without an error, it's written to the transaction log and then, shortly afterwards, written to the database. Most modification commands in SQL Server are implicit transactions.

✦ **Explicit:** An explicit transaction is one where both BEGIN TRANSACTION and COMMIT TRANSACTION commands are used. Explicit transactions are primarily used when you want to ensure that multiple commands either succeed or fail as a whole.

Our focus in this section is on explicit transactions.

**Book III
Chapter 9**

Creating a transaction

In the following steps, you create a table within a database that you use for testing. You then use transactions to modify the table and use another query window to see the results.

**Advanced Query
Topics**

1. **Launch SQL Server Management Studio (SSMS).**

   Choose Start➪All Programs➪Microsoft SQL Server 2008➪SQL Server Management Studio.

2. **On the Connect to Server screen, click Connect.**

3. **Click the New Query button to create a new query window.**

4. **Enter and execute the following statement to create a database. The command can be executed by pressing the F5 key or clicking the Execute button.**

   ```
   CREATE DATABASE TranPractice
   ```

5. **Enter and execute the following statement to create a table named Customers within the TranPractice database:**

   ```
   USE TranPractice;
   GO
   CREATE TABLE Customers(
   ```

```
CustomerID int NOT NULL,
LName varchar(50) NOT NULL,
FName varchar(50) NULL,
Street varchar(50) NULL,
City varchar(50) NULL,
State char(2) NULL,
Zip varchar(10) NULL,
Phone char(13) NULL
)
```

6. **Enter and execute the following command to add two rows of data in the Customers table:**

```
INSERT INTO Customers (CustomerID, LName, FName)
VALUES (101,'Bunny', 'Bugs'),
       (102, 'Runner', 'Road')
```

The VALUES line allows multiple rows to be added without having to redefine the columns in the INSERT line. This is one of the little improvements in SQL Server 2008 that makes geeks like us want to stand up and shout, "Wooo Hooo!" The feature wasn't available in SQL Server 2005; instead, each VALUES line had to have an INSERT line.

7. **View the data you entered by executing the following query:**

```
SELECT * FROM Customers
```

Only the first three columns (CustomerID, LName, and FName) have data. The rest of the columns are NULL.

8. **Create a transaction without committing by executing the following query:**

```
BEGIN TRANSACTION
   UPDATE Customers
   SET STATE = 'VA'
   WHERE CustomerID = 101
```

Although this indicates that the query completed successfully, it hasn't been committed to the database.

9. **Enter and execute the following command to view the changes you entered:**

```
SELECT * FROM Customers
```

Again, although this looks like the changes have been completed, the changes haven't been committed. Instead, the changes are being read from the transaction log.

10. **Roll back the transaction by entering the following command:**

```
ROLLBACK TRAN
```

TRANSACTION can be reduced to just TRAN. Therefore, ROLLBACK TRANSACTION can be shortened to ROLLBACK TRAN. Likewise, you can reduce BEGIN TRANSACTION to BEGIN TRAN and COMMIT TRANSACTION to COMMIT TRAN.

11. **View the contents of the Customers table by entering and executing the following command:**

```
SELECT * FROM Customers
```

The data in the State column has reverted to NULL.

12. **In contrast, the results of the command are visible if a COMMIT TRANSACTION statement is added to our original transaction. Execute the following command:**

```
BEGIN TRAN
  UPDATE Customers
  SET STATE = 'VA'
  WHERE CustomerID = 101
COMMIT TRAN
```

13. **View the contents of the Customers table by entering and executing the following command:**

```
SELECT * FROM Customers
```

The State column's data now appears in the table.

Performing error checking

Transactions commonly have error checking within them to determine whether the transaction should be committed or rolled back. Two ways to do this are with the TRY ... CATCH block and by using logic.

Using the TRY ... CATCH block

The TRY ... CATCH block allows your code to try certain statements. If they fail, then the code within the CATCH block runs.

The following pseudocode shows how the TRY ... CATCH block is written.

```
BEGIN TRY
  BEGIN TRAN
    -- Code for your transaction
  COMMIT TRAN
END TRY
BEGIN CATCH
  -- output an error message
  ROLLBACK TRAN
END CATCH
```

**Book III
Chapter 9**

**Advanced Query
Topics**

The transaction is enclosed in the TRY block. If no errors are encountered, the transaction is committed. If errors are encountered, the execution of the TRY block is terminated, and the CATCH block runs.

Using logic to check for errors

Transactions can also be used with programming logic. In other words, you can use decision statements, such as IF or CASE, to make a decision to either commit or roll back the transaction.

Although you can use IF and CASE statements within a transaction, the TRY . . . CATCH blocks are the preferred method of error handling with T-SQL and the .NET languages. Still, you might see some IF and CASE statements within existing code.

The following code shows one way this could be done:

```
BEGIN TRANSACTION
  UPDATE Customers
    SET STATE = 'VA'
    WHERE CustomerID = 101
  IF @@ERROR <> 0
    ROLLBACK TRAN
  Update Customers
    SET STATE = 'CA'
    WHERE CustomerID = 102
  IF @@ERROR <> 0
    ROLLBACK TRAN
COMMIT TRANSACTION
```

The @@ERROR function returns a 0 if the code succeeds without any errors. If an error occurs, it returns the number of the error.

Finding Information with Full-Text Search

The full-text search capability allows you to add significant functionality when searching text-type data. Without enabling full-text search, you can use the LIKE clause in SELECT statements. However, LIKE limits searches to only exact pattern matches. Full-text searches allow you to do much more. For example, you can search for

✦ **One or more words (simple term):** Both single words and entire phrases can be searched. For example, both *duck* and *ducks in a pond* can be searched. Even *Duck, the roller coaster is going through the tunnel* can be searched.

✦ **Inflectional forms of words (generation term):** Inflectional forms of words include different tenses of a verb and singular and plural forms of a noun. For example, a search on *ride* would also search *riding* and *rode;* a search on *mouse* would also search *mice.*

✦ **Synonyms (thesaurus):** The same as a thesaurus, this search returns similar words. For example, a search on *fun* would return matches for *amusing, enjoyable, entertaining, pleasurable,* and *cool.* SQL Server 2008 includes a thesaurus file in XML format.

✦ **Words or phrases that are close to each other (proximity term):** For example, you might want to search for beauty products that include *skin* near *firming* in the description. You wouldn't necessarily want a description that states at the beginning, "Don't let this product touch your skin," and at the end of the description states, "the firming agent takes about 3 hours to fully set."

✦ **Words or phrases that begin with certain text (prefix term):** For example, you might want to search for any words that begin with *macro.* This would return words and phrases, such as *macro photography, macro economics,* or even *macro paycheck.* The asterisk (*) is used as a wild card; to search for words that begin with macro, you would use *macro*.*

The term you want to search on is specified in the CONTAINS clause, which is used in full-text searches. This is demonstrated in the upcoming "Using full-text queries" section.

Full-text searches are limited to text-type data in the following data types:

✦ **Char, varchar, and nvarchar:** These data types store simple text-based data.

✦ **Varbinary(max):** Entire documents (such as a Word document or a PDF file) can be stored in a `varbinary(max)` column. Filters are used to query the `varbinary(max)` column based on the type of file that's stored in the column.

The `varbinary(max)` data type was introduced in SQL Server 2005. It was designed to replace the `image` data type that was deprecated in SQL Server 2005. Although the `image` data type is still supported for backward compatibility in SQL Server 2008, its use is not recommended.

Enabling full-text search capabilities

The three steps needed to enable Full-text search on a database are

1. **Enable full-text search on the database:** This is enabled by default. Often, you simply need to verify that it's enabled by using the DATABASEPROPERTYEX command, as shown in the following SELECT statement:

   ```
   SELECT
       DATABASEPROPERTYEX('databaseName','IsFullTextEnabled
       ')
   ```

   If not enabled, use the sp_fulltext_database system stored procedure to enable it, as shown in the following T-SQL statement.

   ```
   EXEC 'databaseName'.dbo.sp_fulltext_database @action =
       'enable'
   ```

2. **Create a full-text catalog on the database:** The full-text catalog holds full-text indexes. Full-text indexes cannot be created without a full-text catalog. Often, a single full-text catalog holds all full-text indexes, but it's possible to create multiple catalogs to separate large indexes. The generic code that you can use to create a full-text catalog is

   ```
   CREATE FULLTEXT CATALOG catalogName AS DEFAULT
   ```

   AS DEFAULT causes any full-text indexes to be created in this full-text catalog by default.

3. **Create one or more full-text indexes:** Full-text indexes are created on specific text-based columns within a table. The generic code that you can use to create a full-text catalog is

   ```
   CREATE FULLTEXT INDEX ON tableName(columnName)
   KEY INDEX tablePrimaryKey
   ```

The following steps demonstrate how to create a database, verify that full-text capabilities are enabled, create a full-text catalog, and create a full-text index:

If Full-Text Search isn't installed, you'll receive an error message on Step 8. You can go through the setup process from the installation DVD and add Full-Text Search as an added feature. Click the link for New SQL Server Stand-alone Installation or Add Features for an Existing Installation. Follow the installation wizard and select Full-Text Search as an added feature.

1. **Launch SQL Server Management Studio (SSMS).**

   Choose Start⇨All Programs⇨Microsoft SQL Server 2008⇨SQL Server Management Studio.

2. **On the Connect to Server screen, click Connect.**

3. **Click the New Query button to create a new query window.**

4. **In the query window, enter and execute the following text to create a database named FTExample.**

   ```
   CREATE DATABASE FTExample
   ```

5. **Enter and execute the following code to create a table in your new database:**

   ```
   USE FTExample;
   GO
   CREATE TABLE Employees(
       EmployeeID int NOT NULL,
       LName varchar(50) NOT NULL,
       FName varchar(50) NULL,
       Skills varchar(300) NULL,
    CONSTRAINT [PK_Employees] PRIMARY KEY CLUSTERED
      (
       EmployeeID ASC
      )
    )
   ```

   A primary key (named PK_Employees) is created on the EmployeeID column. The full-text index requires a primary key.

6. **Verify full-text search is enabled on your database by entering and executing the following statement:**

   ```
   SELECT DATABASEPROPERTYEX('FTExample',
       'IsFullTextEnabled')
   ```

   Your display should return a single row with a single column. 1 indicates that full-text is enabled. 0 indicates that it isn't enabled. Because full-text is enabled by default on new databases, it will be a 1.

7. **Create a full-text catalog on your database by executing the following code:**

   ```
   CREATE FULLTEXT CATALOG FTCatalog AS DEFAULT
   ```

8. **Create a full-text index on the Skills column of the Employees table.**

   ```
   CREATE FULLTEXT INDEX ON Employees(Skills)
   KEY INDEX PK_Employees
   ```

   The index is being created on the Skills column and is using the PK_Employees primary key.

9. **Leave the query window in SSMS open for the next set of steps.**

In the next set of steps, you populate the table and perform a full-text query.

Using full-text queries

Full-text queries are performed by using one of four predicates. A *predicate* is an expression that evaluates to true, false, or unknown. An evaluation of unknown occurs when trying to evaluate a null condition.

- **CONTAINS:** CONTAINS allows searches on specific words or phrases, words or phrases near each other, inflectional terms, prefixes, and synonyms.

- **CONTAINSTABLE:** CONTAINS TABLE works similar to CONTAINS but returns two extra columns (RANK and KEY). RANK returns the relevance of the row compared to other rows returned. KEY is typically the primary key value of the row returned. For example, if a search returned a skill for an employee with an EmployeeID of 101, the KEY would be 101.

- **FREETEXT:** FREETEXT is designed to search for values that match the meaning of the given text but not necessarily the exact words. FREETEXT is less precise than CONTAINS. It allows you to enter a string of words, such as a full sentence or even a paragraph, and it returns similar matches.

- **FREETEXTTABLE:** FREETEXTTABLE is similar to FREETEXT, but it returns the data as a table with two extra columns (RANK and KEY). The RANK and KEY columns work the same in the FREETEXTTABLE as they do in the CONTAINSTABLE.

The following steps populate the Employee table created in the previous steps, "Enabling full-text search capabilities," and use the CONTAINS clause to return matches:

1. **Return to the SSMS query window left open in the previous steps.**

2. **Enter and execute the following INSERT statement to add data to your Employee table:**

   ```
   USE FTExample;
   GO
   INSERT INTO Employees (EmployeeID, LName, FNAME,
       Skills)
   VALUES
   (101, 'Holmes', 'Sherlock','Sleuth, detective, boxer,
       swordsman, impersonator'),
   (102, 'Doyle', 'Conan', 'physician, writer, story-teller,
       sold books, author'),
   (103, 'Watson', 'John', 'physician, biographer,
       confidante, rugby player')
   ```

3. **Enter and execute the following query to identify any employees that have "physician" listed as one of their skills. This is a simple full-text search.**

   ```
   SELECT FName, LName, Skills
   FROM Employees
   WHERE CONTAINS(Skills, 'Physician')
   ```

   This returns two rows: John Watson and Conan Doyle.

It does take some time to populate the full-text index. If you're quick on the keyboard, the previous query might take a little while before it completes. If you run the query a second time, it runs without the pause.

4. **Enter and execute the following query to identify any employees that have skills starting with the letter A. This search is using a prefix.**

```
SELECT FName, LName, Skills
FROM Employees
WHERE CONTAINS(Skills, '"A*"')
```

This returns one row. Conan Doyle has *author* as a listed skill.

5. **Enter and execute the following query to identify any employees that have selling skills.**

This search looks for the inflectional values of sell (sell, sold, and selling).

```
SELECT FName, LName, Skills
FROM Employees
WHERE CONTAINS(Skills, ' FORMSOF (INFLECTIONAL, sell) ')
```

This returns one row. Conan Doyle has *sold books* as a listed skill.

Understanding Outer Joins

The primary method used to join two tables is an `INNER JOIN`, often shortened to `JOIN`. However, `OUTER JOINS` also exist, such as `RIGHT OUTER JOIN`, `LEFT OUTER JOIN`, and `FULL OUTER JOIN`.

✦ **RIGHT OUTER JOIN (RIGHT JOIN):** The `RIGHT OUTER JOIN` displays all the rows from the table on the right (the second table mentioned in the query) and only those rows that have matches in the table on the left.

✦ **LEFT OUTER JOIN (LEFT JOIN):** The `LEFT OUTER JOIN` displays all the rows from the table on the left (the first table mentioned in the query) and only those rows that have matches in the table on the right.

✦ **FULL OUTER JOIN (OUTER JOIN):** The `FULL OUTER JOIN` displays all the rows from both tables.

All the `JOIN` operations join two or more tables. When more than two tables are joined, the Query Optimizer joins two tables at a time and then uses the result from that join to join to another table. This process continues until all the tables are joined.

**Book III
Chapter 9**

**Advanced Query
Topics**

The example queries in this section run against the AdventureWorks database. Use the steps in Chapter 5 of this mini-book to check whether AdventureWorks is installed. If not, install it.

Using an INNER JOIN

Although the INNER JOIN is discussed in the "Creating a New Query" section of Chapter 3 in this mini-book, it's listed here for easy comparison with the outer joins. The INNER JOIN displays only rows that have a matching column in both of the tables listed in the JOIN operation.

The basic syntax of an INNER JOIN is shown in the following code:

```
SELECT columnList
FROM table1 INNER JOIN table2
  ON columnFromTable1 = columnFromTable2
```

The relationships between tables are primarily created by using foreign key to primary key references. Foreign key to primary key references can be used in JOIN statements.

For example, you might want to retrieve a listing of all the AdventureWorks2008 employees with their first name, last name, and title.

The name and title data is in the Person.Person table. Employees are listed in the HumanResources.Employee table. The relationship between the two tables is created on the BusinessEntityID column. With this knowledge, you can create a query that joins the two tables on the BusinessEntityID column.

```
SELECT FirstName, LastName, Title
FROM Person.Person AS p
INNER JOIN HumanResources.Employee AS e
ON p.BusinessEntityID = e.BusinessEntityID
```

Aliases are commonly used in JOIN statements to shorten the amount of typing necessary. In the preceding query, the Person.Person table is identified with the alias of "p" by using the AS clause. The HumanResources.Employee table is identified with the alias of "e".

The previous query returns only those rows that have matching BusinessEntityID columns in both tables.

Using RIGHT OUTER JOIN

The RIGHT OUTER JOIN returns a listing of all the rows in the right table, and only those rows that have matches in the specified column in the left table.

The basic syntax of a RIGHT OUTER JOIN is shown in the following code:

```
SELECT columnList
FROM table1 RIGHT OUTER JOIN table2
  ON columnFromTable1 = columnFromTable2
```

Notice that table2 is to the right of the JOIN clause. It's referred to as the right table.

Say, you want a listing of all salespeople along with their assigned territory. If you perform an INNER JOIN, salespeople who are unassigned to territories aren't listed. However, a RIGHT OUTER JOIN can be used to list all the salespeople, and if they aren't assigned to a territory, the territory is NULL.

```
SELECT t.Name, p.BusinessEntityID
FROM Sales.SalesTerritory t
RIGHT OUTER JOIN Sales.SalesPerson p
ON t.TerritoryID = p.TerritoryID
ORDER BY t.Name
```

The previous listing orders the result by the territory name, which causes NULL territories to be listed first.

Using LEFT OUTER JOIN

The LEFT OUTER JOIN returns a listing of all the rows in the left table, and only those rows that have matches in the specified column in the right table.

The basic syntax of a LEFT OUTER JOIN is shown in the following code:

```
SELECT columnList
FROM table1 LEFT OUTER JOIN table2
  ON columnFromTable1 = columnFromTable2
```

Notice that table1 is to the left of the JOIN clause. It's referred to as the left table.

For example, you might want a listing of all job candidates and include those that have also become employees. All the job candidates are in the HumanResources.JobCandidate table. Employees are in the HumanResources. Employee table. The following script will work:

```
SELECT j.JobCandidateID, j.BusinessEntityID, j.Resume
FROM HumanResources.JobCandidate j
LEFT OUTER JOIN
HumanResources.Employee e
ON j. BusinessEntityID = e. BusinessEntityID
ORDER BY j. BusinessEntityID DESC
```

The JobCandidate table is listed to the left of the JOIN clause (the first table listed), so all the rows from this table are listed. Next, only those rows in the Employees table that have a matching BusinessEntityID in both tables are listed.

Further, the result is ordered by the BusinessEntityID in descending order so that actual employees are listed first. Lastly, job candidates that have NULL for the BusinessEntityID (non-employees) are listed.

Using FULL OUTER Join

A FULL OUTER JOIN returns rows from both tables. It doesn't care whether there are matches or not.

The basic syntax of a FULL OUTER JOIN is shown in the following code:

```
SELECT columnList
FROM table1 FULL OUTER JOIN table2
  ON columnFromTable1 = columnFromTable2
```

If no matching rows on the JOIN exist, the column would be NULL. This allows you to use a WHERE clause to filter your results to columns that don't exist in either table.

For example, if you're trying to identify products that weren't sold, you could use the following query. It adds a WHERE clause to look for any rows that are NULL in the right table (SalesOrderDetail).

```
SELECT p.ProductID, p.Name, s.ProductID, s.SalesOrderID
FROM Production.Product p
FULL OUTER JOIN Sales.SalesOrderDetail s
ON p.ProductID = s.ProductID
WHERE s.ProductID IS NULL
```

Querying XML Data

Microsoft has added significant support for XML data in recent versions of SQL Server. XML data can be stored in the XML data type or in the nvarchar(max) data type. Both data types can support data as large as 2GB.

XML data is simple text data that uses XML tags. For example, you could have product data defined with XML tags such as the <Product> </Product> tag. Within the opening and closing product, you can next add additional tags, such as <ProductID> <ProductID>, <ProductName> </ProductName>, and so on. You can use an XML schema to define the XML tags, or use XML tags without a schema.

If stored using the XML data type, XML methods can be used to query and modify the XML data taking advantage of the native XML format. In SQL Server 2008, the following XML methods exist:

+ **Query:** The query XML method can query a single node from an XML document.

+ **Value:** The value XML method can retrieve a single value from an XML document.

+ **Exist:** The exist XML method is used to determine if a certain value exists within an XML document.

+ **Nodes:** The nodes XML method is used to retrieve multiple values from an XML document. It is commonly used to display XML data in a table format as rows and columns. This is also referred to as *shredding* an XML document.

+ **Modify:** The modify XML method is used to make changes to an XML document.

Both the nvarchar(max) and XML data types can store XML documents as large as 2GB. The difference is that the nvarchar(max) data type can store and retrieve the XML documents as a single document only. XML methods can't be used if the data is stored as nvarchar(max).

Using the query XML method

The query XML method uses the XQuery language to retrieve values from within an XML document. The basic syntax is

```
Query('XQuery')
```

The XQuery language can be quite complex. We keep the next example simple to show you how to retrieve a single value.

In the following query, an XML instance is created named @myXML that holds contact information. Then, the query method is used against the XML instance to retrieve specific information.

```
--Declare the variable for the XML instance
DECLARE @myXML xml
--Create the XML instance
SET @myXML = '
<Root>
  <Contact ContactID="101" ContactName="Homer Simpson">
   <ContactInformation>
     <email>Homer@springfield.com</email>
     <Cell>1-123-555-1234</Cell>
   </ContactInformation>
```

```
    </Contact>
    <Contact ContactID="102" ContactName="Marge Simpson">
     <ContactInformation>
       <email>Marge@springfield.com</email>
       <Cell>1-123-555-5678</Cell>
     </ContactInformation>
    </Contact>
</Root>'
--Use the query method to query the XML instance
SELECT @myXML.query('/Root/Contact/ContactInformation')
```

The result of this query is returned as an XML snippet. As shown in Figure 9-2, the XML snippet is returned as a hyperlink. By clicking on it, another window opens showing the XML data in the result.

Figure 9-2:
Result
returned
from the
query XML
method.

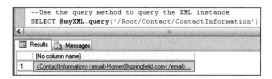

The following XML snippet shows what is returned by the XML query. The following text shows the XML snippet. All of the information in the ContactInformation node (e-mail address and cell phone number) is returned.

```
<ContactInformation>
  <email>Homer@springfield.com</email>
  <Cell>1-123-555-1234</Cell>
</ContactInformation>
<ContactInformation>
  <email>Marge@springfield.com</email>
  <Cell>1-123-555-5678</Cell>
</ContactInformation>
```

If the query is modified to include the email node, only the e-mail data is returned, as shown in the following code:

```
SELECT @myXML.query
    ('/Root/Contact/ContactInformation/email')
```

The result from the modified query is

```
<email>Homer@springfield.com</email>
<email>Marge@springfield.com</email>
```

Using the value XML method

The value XML method also uses the XQuery language to retrieve values from within an XML document. However, instead of returning the data as an XML data type, the value method allows you to specify the data type of the result.

Basic syntax for the value XML method is

```
value (XQuery, SQLType)
```

The following query uses similar code as the query method. It creates variables, creates an XML instance, and then retrieves a single value from the XML instance. The result is returned in a column value, not an XML document.

```
--Declare the variable for the XML instance
DECLARE @myXML xml
--Declare the variable to hold the contact ID value
DECLARE @ContactID int
--Create the XML instance
SET @myXML = '
<Root>
   <Contact ContactID="101" ContactName="Homer Simpson">
    <ContactInformation>
      <email>Homer@springfield.com</email>
      <Cell>1-123-555-1234</Cell>
    </ContactInformation>
   </Contact>
   <Contact ContactID="102" ContactName="Marge Simpson">
    <ContactInformation>
      <email>Marge@springfield.com</email>
      <Cell>1-123-555-5678</Cell>
    </ContactInformation>
   </Contact>
</Root>'
--Retrieve value of ContactID for the 2nd row [2]
SET @ContactID =  @myXML.value
      ('(/Root/Contact/@ContactID)[2]', 'int' )
--Display the value
SELECT @ContactID
```

The result of this query is shown in Figure 9-3. The data is in a column format as if a regular row was queried.

Figure 9-3:
Result
returned
from the
value XML
method.

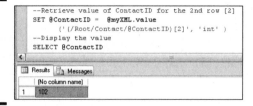

```
--Retrieve value of ContactID for the 2nd row [2]
SET @ContactID =  @myXML.value
        ('(/Root/Contact/@ContactID}[2]', 'int' )
--Display the value
SELECT @ContactID
```

	(No column name)
1	102

Using the exist XML method

The `exist` XML method returns a value indicating whether the queried data exists in the XML instance. Possible results from an `exist` query are

- ✦ **1:** Indicates True. The data exists in at least one node.
- ✦ **0:** Indicates False. The data doesn't exist in the XML instance.
- ✦ **NULL:** Indicates that the XML instance is NULL.

Basic syntax for the `value` XML method is

```
exist (XQuery)
```

Using the previous example with the XML instance that included Homer Simpson and Marge Simpson's contact information, you can use the `exist` method to determine if Homer Simpson exists in the XML instance.

```
--Declare the variables for the XML instance and the exists
    bit
DECLARE @myXML xml
DECLARE @dataExists bit
--Create the XML instance
SET @myXML = '
<Root>
  <Contact ContactID="101" ContactName="Homer Simpson">
   <ContactInformation>
     <email>Homer@springfield.com</email>
     <Cell>1-123-555-1234</Cell>
   </ContactInformation>
  </Contact>
  <Contact ContactID="102" ContactName="Marge Simpson">
   <ContactInformation>
     <email>Marge@springfield.com</email>
     <Cell>1-123-555-5678</Cell>
   </ContactInformation>
  </Contact>
</Root>'
--See if Homer Simpson exists in the XML instance
SET @dataExists =
    @myXML.exist('/Root = ("Homer Simpson") ')
```

```
--Display the value
SELECT @dataExists
```

The result is a 1 because Homer Simpson exists within the XML instance.

This code searches the entire XML instance because it searches from the root. If you know that the name occurs in only one specific node (such as ContactName), you can optimize the query to search only that node. The following code shows how the optimized query would look:

```
SET @dataExists =
    @myXML.exist('/ContactName = ("Homer Simpson") ')
```

Using the nodes XML method

The nodes XML method is commonly used to shred XML. In other words, it retrieves XML values from an XML instance and displays the values in a table format with rows and columns.

Basic syntax for the nodes method is

```
nodes (XQuery) as Table(Column)
```

For example, you might want to create a listing of names, e-mail addresses, and cell phone numbers from an XML instance. The following code uses the value and query methods to retrieve the relevant data from the XML instance and display it in a table format using the nodes method

```
--Declare the variables for the XML instance
DECLARE @myXML xml
--Create the XML instance
SET @myXML = '
<Root>
  <Contact ContactID="101" ContactName="Homer Simpson">
   <ContactInformation>
     <email>Homer@springfield.com</email>
     <Cell>1-123-555-1234</Cell>
   </ContactInformation>
  </Contact>
  <Contact ContactID="102" ContactName="Marge Simpson">
   <ContactInformation>
     <email>Marge@springfield.com</email>
     <Cell>1-123-555-5678</Cell>
   </ContactInformation>
  </Contact>
</Root>'
--Retrieve the nodes
SELECT
  MyTable.cols.value('@ContactName', 'varchar(35)') AS Name,
```

```
MyTable.cols.query('ContactInformation/email') AS [E-
   Mail],
MyTable.cols.query('ContactInformation/Cell') AS [Cell
   Phone]
FROM @myXML.nodes('/Root/Contact') MyTable (cols)
```

Figure 9-4 shows the result of this query. The `value` method used to retrieve the name shows the data as a simple text string, while the `query` method used in the email and Cell columns displays the data with the XML tags (though still in their own columns).

Figure 9-4:
Shredded
XML using
the nodes
method.

Using the modify XML method

If you need to modify XML data within an XML instance (such as in an XML data type), use the `modify` method.

The basic syntax is

```
modify (XML_DML)
```

In T-SQL, Data Manipulation Language (DML) statements are used to insert, delete, and update data. XML_DML is a variation of DML used specifically for XML. Instead of `INSERT`, `DELETE`, and `UPDATE`, XML_DML uses `INSERT`, `DELETE`, and `REPLACE`.

In the following example, you change the e-mail address for Homer Simpson from `Homer@springfield.com` to `Homer.Simpson@springfield.com` by using the `REPLACE` statement.

Because two records exist (one for Homer Simpson and one for Marge Simpson), you need to specify which record you want to change. You do this with the following partial code. The [1] indicates you're modifying the first contact record.

```
(/Root/Contact[1]/
```

To modify the second record, you would change this to

```
(/Root/Contact[2]/
```

You also must specify the node you want to modify, the data type of the node, and the instance of the node. The following partial code identifies the first instance of the email node and states that it's a text data type. Even though there's only one email node in the contact record, it must be specified as [1].

```
(/Root/Contact[1]/ContactInformation/email/text())[1]
```

The following code creates the XML instance and then modifies it:

```
--Declare the variables for the XML instance
DECLARE @myXML xml
--Create the XML instance
SET @myXML = '
<Root>
  <Contact ContactID="101" ContactName="Homer Simpson">
   <ContactInformation>
     <email>Homer@springfield.com</email>
     <Cell>1-123-555-1234</Cell>
   </ContactInformation>
  </Contact>
  <Contact ContactID="102" ContactName="Marge Simpson">
   <ContactInformation>
     <email>Marge@springfield.com</email>
     <Cell>1-123-555-5678</Cell>
   </ContactInformation>
  </Contact>
</Root>'
--Modify the email node
SET @myXML.modify('
  replace value of
    (/Root/Contact[1]/ContactInformation/email/text())[1]
  with      "Homer.Simpson@springfield.com"
')
--Display the change
select @myXML
```

The result shows that the email value has been replaced.

Book IV

Database Programming

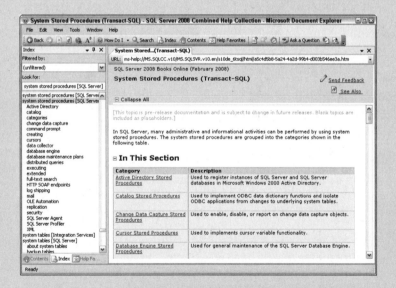

Using Books Online.

Contents at a Glance

Chapter 1: Understanding Transact-SQL

Transact-SQL is the primary language you use when communicating with your Microsoft SQL Server 2008 databases. T-SQL is derived from the ANSI/92 standard, which is 686 pages in length (not including the 76-page index).

Clearly, this chapter can't cover all the details of T-SQL, but it does cover some of the basics, such as Data Definition Language (DDL) statements and Data Manipulation Language (DML) statements. You also learn when it's best to use T-SQL and when it's best to use another language.

Key Language Concepts

Microsoft's flavor of Structured Query Language (SQL) is Transact-SQL (T-SQL). T-SQL is the primary language used to interact with Microsoft's SQL Server databases.

T-SQL is based on the ANSI/92 standard for SQL with extensions added from Microsoft. These extensions improve the language's functionality with SQL Server databases, but also make it different from other versions of SQL. Generally, scripts written to run with one version of SQL won't run on another version without modifications.

For such a popular database language, you'd think its name would be well known. Not necessarily true. It's pronounced in two ways:

✦ **Es-que-el (as the letters S, Q, and L):** The ANSI specification states that it should be pronounced this way.

✦ **Sequel (as a word):** The overwhelming majority of database professionals we work with pronounce it this way.

Transact-SQL (T-SQL) is Microsoft's flavor of SQL, though other flavors exist. Oracle uses Procedural Language / SQL (PL/SQL), and IBM uses SQL Procedural Language (SQL PL). All the different versions have their own extensions designed to meet the needs of the individual databases and their users.

SQL statements fall into two primary categories:

✦ **Data Definition Language (DDL) statements:** Used to add, delete, and modify objects within the database. Objects are entities within the database used to hold or manipulate data. They include tables, views, stored procedures, functions, and triggers.

✦ **Data Manipulation Language (DML) statements:** Used to add, delete, and modify data within the database. Data is held within tables.

Using Data Definition Language (DDL) statements

Data Definition Language (DDL) statements are used to manipulate objects. The three DDL statements are

✦ **CREATE:** Used to make new objects in SQL Server 2008.

✦ **ALTER:** Used to modify existing objects in SQL Server 2008.

✦ **DROP:** Used to remove existing objects from SQL Server 2008.

To create a database and a table within the database, follow these steps:

1. Launch SQL Server Management Studio (SSMS).

Choose Start➪All Programs➪Microsoft SQL Server 2008➪SQL Server Management Studio.

2. On the Connect to Server screen, click Connect.

3. Click the New Query button to create a new query window.

4. Enter and execute the following DDL statement to create a database:

```
CREATE DATABASE Practice
```

When additional details are not provided with the CREATE DATABASE statement, the database is created by making an exact copy of the Model database. The CREATE DATABASE statement can be as simple (as shown) or much more complex.

5. **Enter and execute the following code to create a table in your Practice database:**

```
USE Practice;
GO
CREATE TABLE Employee
(
  EmployeeID int IDENTITY(1,1) NOT NULL,
  FirstName varchar(50) NULL,
  LastName varchar(50) NULL,
  Phone varchar(20) NULL
  CONSTRAINT PK_Employee_EmployeeID
     PRIMARY KEY CLUSTERED (EmployeeID)
)
```

Many more details can be added when creating a table. If you want to review more of the possibilities, review Book II, Chapter 4.

6. **Use the following code to modify the table by adding a column for the e-mail address:**

```
ALTER TABLE Employee
ADD Email varchar(50) NULL
```

7. **Leave the query window open.**

Using Data Manipulation Language (DML) statements

Data Manipulation Language (DML) statements are designed to interact with the data. The four available statements are:

✦ **INSERT:** Adds new rows of data in tables.

✦ **SELECT:** Retrieves data from tables and views.

✦ **UPDATE:** Modifies existing data.

✦ **DELETE:** Deletes rows from tables.

Inserting data with the INSERT statement

Data is added to a table with the DML INSERT statement. The basic syntax of the INSERT statement is:

```
INSERT INTO table name
(column list)
VALUES
(values to be inserted into column list)
```

Use the following steps to add data to the Employee table:

1. **Using the open query window, enter and execute the following code:**

```
INSERT INTO Employee
(FirstName, LastName, Phone, Email)
VALUES
('Darril', 'Gibson', '755-555-1234',
    'darril@home.com'),
('Robert', 'Schneider', '215-555-4321',
    'robert@home.com')
```

2. **Add a row to the table with your name and information. Use the following code as a guide:**

```
INSERT INTO Employee
(FirstName, LastName, Phone, Email)
VALUES
('yourFirstName', 'yourLastName', 'yourPhoneNumber',
    'yourEmailAddress'),
```

3. **Leave the query window open.**

Retrieving data with the SELECT statement

The basic syntax of the SELECT statement is:

```
SELECT column list
FROM table or view name
WHERE search condition
```

For example, to locate the record of an employee with a first name of Darril in your database, you could use the following query:

```
SELECT FirstName, LastName, Phone, Email
FROM Employee
WHERE FirstName = 'Darril'
```

The columns that you want to display are listed in the column list. The table you're retrieving the data from is in the FROM clause. The WHERE clause is optional and can be used to filter the search.

Many more search conditions are possible with the query. For more details on the WHERE clause, refer to Book III, Chapter 5.

Modifying data with the UPDATE statement

Individual columns within any row are modified by using the UPDATE statement. The basic syntax of the UPDATE statement is

```
UPDATE table name
SET column name = new value
WHERE search condition
```

For example, if you need to change the phone number for one of the employees, you could use the following query:

```
UPDATE Employee
SET Phone = '757-555-6789'
WHERE FirstName = 'Darril' and LastName = 'Gibson'
```

Deleting data with the DELETE statement

One of our favorite stories is when an employee wins the lottery and leaves the company. What a wonderful event! In this case, you might choose to delete their employee record from the database. The basic syntax for the DELETE statement is

```
DELETE FROM table name
WHERE search condition
```

BE careful with the DELETE statement. If you don't include a WHERE clause, the command deletes all the records in the table. This becomes either an opportunity to test your backup strategy, or an opportunity to update your resume.

Use the following query to delete the employee that has won the lottery. Feel free to pick yourself!

```
DELETE FROM EMPLOYEE
WHERE FirstName = 'Darril' and LastName = 'Gibson'
```

Situations Where It Makes Sense to Use Transact-SQL

The primary purpose of the T-SQL language is to interact with Microsoft SQL databases. Some of the more common reasons to use T-SQL include

✦ **Retrieving data from a Microsoft SQL database:** The SELECT statement is used within SQL Server Management Studio (SSMS) or embedded in many different types of applications.

✦ **Manipulating data in a Microsoft SQL database:** The INSERT, UPDATE, and DELETE statements are used within SSMS or embedded in many different types of applications.

✦ **Creating databases and database objects with archive scripts:** SSMS provides the capability to easily script any object by right-clicking the object and choosing SCRIPT Object As⇨CREATE To⇨File.

Although many programmers would argue that T-SQL isn't a full programming language, it does include many of the common programming constructs. This includes the following:

✦ **Use of variables**

✦ **IF ... ELSE blocks**

✦ **WHILE loops**

✦ **BEGIN ... END blocks**

✦ **CASE statements**

✦ **Built-in functions**

✦ **User-defined functions**

✦ **System stored procedures**

✦ **User-defined stored procedures**

All the different T-SQL programming constructs can be included in batch or script files.

Scenarios When It's Time to Use Another Programming Language

While T-SQL is well suited to interact with Microsoft SQL databases, T-SQL is not a full-fledged programming language like Microsoft's Visual Basic .NET or C# .NET.

.NET programming languages, such as Visual Basic .NET and C# .NET, are diverse and are used to create a wide variety of applications, from accounting applications to games to Widgets. Trying to use T-SQL for any of these applications just isn't possible. However, it's very likely that any of these applications will have T-SQL code embedded within them to interact with Microsoft SQL databases.

Times to consider using a different language than T-SQL are

✦ **When an interface needs to be created:** T-SQL doesn't have the tools needed to create an interface, such as a Windows form or a Web form.

✦ **When complex calculations need to be performed:** While T-SQL can perform these calculations, you can usually get better performance by using a .NET language.

When deciding whether to use T-SQL or .NET CLR, consider the data that will be accessed and what will be done with the data. If you're performing calculations based on data from multiple rows, T-SQL usually performs better. However, if you're performing complex calculations or comparisons of data within the same row, .NET CLR performs better.

✦ **When sophisticated string comparisons need to be done:** While T-SQL can perform these comparisons, you can usually get better performance by using a .NET language.

One of the strengths of T-SQL, in SQL Server 2008, is the ability to integrate assemblies created in a .NET language with T-SQL. .NET applications use Microsoft's .NET Framework and are executed in the Common Language Runtime (CLR).

CLR assemblies can be integrated into T-SQL objects (such as stored procedures, functions, and more) and when the object is executed, the external CLR assembly is executed.

The steps required to integrate a .NET assembly into a T-SQL object are

1. Create and compile an assembly by using a .NET language.

2. Register the assembly in SQL Server.

3. Create an object (such as a stored procedure or a function) in SQL Server that uses the assembly.

The steps in the following section show how to create a simple CLR integrated stored procedure.

Creating an assembly using a .NET language

Use the following steps to create a simple assembly in Visual Basic .NET:

1. **Launch Notepad.**

2. **Within Notepad, enter the following text:**

```
Imports System
Imports System.Data
Imports Microsoft.SqlServer.Server
Imports System.Data.SqlTypes
Public Class CLRClass
  <Microsoft.SqlServer.Server.SqlProcedure()> _
  Public Shared Sub GetDay()
    Dim strWeekDay As String
    strWeekDay = WeekdayName(Weekday(Today()))
```

```
SqlContext.Pipe.Send("Today is " & _
    strWeekDay & ".")
End Sub
End Class
```

This code creates a subroutine that will determine the weekday and return that information in a string.

3. Press Ctrl+S to save the file.

4. Create a new folder named CLR in the root of C: (C:\CLR).

In the Save As dialog box, browse to the root of C:\ and click the Create New Folder button. Rename the new folder **CLR**.

5. Save the file as ReturnDay.vb.

In the Save As dialog box, click in the File Name box. Enter **ReturnDay.vb** and then click Save.

Ensure you enter the period between ReturnDay and vb. This ensures that it is saved as a Visual Basic file and not as a text file.

6. Launch a command prompt.

7. Enter the following command at the command prompt to compile your assembly:

```
cd c:\WINDOWS\Microsoft.NET\Framework\v2.0.50727
vbc /target:library c:\clr\ReturnDay.vb
```

At this point, you have a .NET assembly named ReturnDay.dll in the C:\CLR directory. Next, you register this assembly with SQL Server and enable SQL Server to use assemblies.

Registering the assembly in SQL Server

Use the following steps to register an assembly in SQL Server and configure SQL Server to use assemblies. This assumes you've created the ReturnDay.dll assembly in the previous steps.

1. Launch SQL Server Management Studio (SSMS).

Choose Start⇨All Programs⇨Microsoft SQL Server 2008⇨SQL Server Management Studio.

2. On the Connect to Server screen, click Connect.

3. Click the New Query button to open a new query window.

4. If you don't have a database named Practice in your server, create one now with this command:

```
CREATE DATABASE Practice
```

Press F5 to execute the code.

5. **In the query window, enter the following code and execute it:**

```
USE Practice;
GO
CREATE ASSEMBLY assyReturnDay
FROM 'c:\clr\ReturnDay.dll'
WITH PERMISSION_SET = SAFE
```

Press F5 to execute the code.

6. **Browse to the Practice | Programmability | Assemblies container.**

A display similar to Figure 1-1 appears. You'll see the assembly you just created from the ReturnDay.dll. Your assembly is named assyReturnDay and is in the Assemblies container.

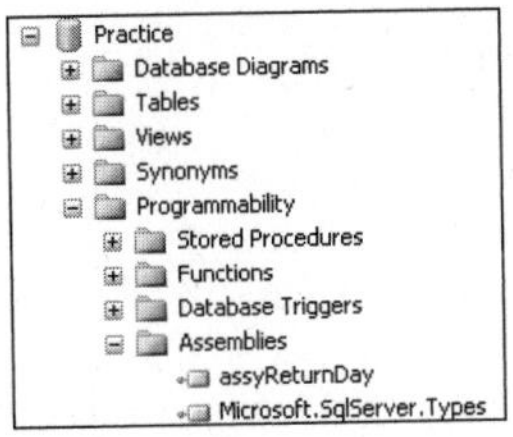

Figure 1-1:
The
assyReturn
Day
assembly.

7. **Enter the following code to enable the usage of CLR assemblies:**

```
sp_configure 'show advanced options', 1;
GO
RECONFIGURE;
GO
sp_configure 'clr enabled', 1;
GO
RECONFIGURE;
```

Press F5 to execute the code.

8. **Leave the query window open for the next set of steps.**

With an assembly created and added to SQL Server, you can now integrate it with a SQL Server object, such as a stored procedure.

Creating a CLR integrated stored procedure

Use the following steps to create and execute a CLR integrated stored procedure.

1. **In the query window, enter the following code and execute it:**

```
CREATE PROCEDURE uspReturnDay
AS
EXTERNAL NAME assyReturnDay.CLRClass.GetDay;
```

**Book IV
Chapter 1**

Understanding
Transact-SQL

Press F5 to execute the code.

2. **To verify that the stored procedure works as you expect it to, enter the following command and execute it:**

```
EXEC uspReturnDay
```

Press F5 to execute the stored procedure. A display similar to Figure 1-2 appears.

Figure 1-2:
Executing
the CLR
integrated
stored
procedure.

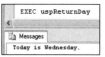

Creating a Script

A T-SQL script is nothing more than several T-SQL statements strung together in a single file or window. Generally, when people refer to *scripts,* they're talking about files that can be saved and retrieved, but technically what you've been entering throughout this chapter are also referred to as scripts.

Scripts are saved as files for archive purposes. You might have a database and a need to document all its details. By creating a script of the database creation, you can view the options from the script and, if necessary, rebuild the database.

Within a script are batches. *Batches* are snippets of code that are run together. Often, a script will have many batches. Only one batch can run at a time, and the next batch can't start until the previous batch has finished. T-SQL uses the GO keyword to signify the end of a batch.

For example, the following code shows a partial script separated into two batches:

```
CREATE DATABASE Practice
GO
USE Practice
CREATE Table Employee
. . .
```

The CREATE DATABASE statement is the only statement in the first batch. The USE statement starts the second batch after the GO statement.

Separating the batches this way allows one batch to complete before another batch begins.

Without the GO statement, the system would try to create a table in the Practice database before the Practice database was created. It wouldn't work; instead, it would result in an error.

Creating a script to create a database

Imagine that you have a database on one server and you need to create a copy of the database on another server (without any data). The simplest way to do so would be by creating a script on the first server and running the script on the second server.

The following steps lead you through the process of creating a script to create a database from an existing database.

These steps assume that you have the Adventureworks2008 database. If you don't have it installed, you can use the steps on any other database you've installed. If you want to install AdventureWorks2008, full details are included in Book III, Chapter 5.

1. **Launch SQL Server Management Studio (SSMS).**

   Choose Start⇨All Programs⇨Microsoft SQL Server 2008⇨SQL Server Management Studio.

2. **On the Connect to Server screen, click Connect.**

3. **Right-click the AdventureWorks2008 database and choose Script Database As⇨Create To⇨New Query Editor Window.**

   A new query window opens with the script to create a database with the same properties and settings as the AdventureWorks2008 database. This won't create the objects in the database (such as the tables and views) but only the database structure itself.

4. **Press Ctrl+H to access the Quick Replace dialog box.**

5. **Replace all instances of *AdventureWorks2008* with *Adventureworks2008Copy*.**

   In the Find What text box, enter **Adventureworks2008**. In the Replace With text box, enter **Adventureworks2008Copy**. Ensure the Look In is set to Current Document. Click Replace All.

6. **On the Microsoft SQL Server Management Studio dialog box, click OK. Close the Find and Replace dialog box.**

7. **Press Ctrl+S to access the Save File As dialog box.**

8. **Create a new folder named MySQLScripts.**

Browse to the root of C:\ and click the Create New Folder icon. In the New Folder dialog box, enter **MySQLScripts** and click OK.

9. **In the FileName box, enter** CreateAdventureworks2008CopyDB **and click Save.**

10. **Leave SSMS open.**

Creating a script to create database objects

Use the following steps to create a script that creates the Adventureworks2008 objects:

1. **With SSMS open, right-click the Adventureworks2008 database and choose Tasks⇨Generate Scripts.**

The Generate SQL Server Scripts Wizard appears.

2. **On the Script Wizard welcome page, click Next.**

3. **On the Select Database page, select Adventureworks2008. Select the check box next to Script All Objects in the selected database. Click Next.**

4. **On the Choose Script Options page, click Next.**

5. **On the Output Option page, leave the default of Script to New Query Window selected and click Next.**

6. **On the Script Wizard Summary page, click Finish.**

This takes a moment to complete. When done, it will indicate success. Additionally, a new query window opens, and the script to create the objects appears in the query window.

7. **When the task is completed and success is indicated, click Close on the Generate Script Progress page.**

8. **Press Ctrl+H to access the Quick Replace dialog box.**

9. **Replace all instances of** *Adventureworks2008* **with** *Adventureworks2008Copy.*

In the Find What text box, enter **Adventureworks2008**. In the Replace With text box, enter **Adventureworks2008Copy**. Ensure the Look In is set to Current Document. Click Replace All.

This replaces all instances of *Adventureworks2008* with *Adventureworks2008Copy.*

10. **Replace all instances of *Documents* with *DocumentsCopy*.**

In the Find What text box, enter **Documents**. In the Replace With text box, enter *DocumentsCopy*. Ensure the Look In is set to Current Document. Click Replace All.

This replaces *FileStreamDocuments* with *FileStreamDocumentsCopy*, and replaces the *Documents* filename with *DocumentsCopy*. You can then run the script on the same system without problems.

11. **On the Microsoft SQL Server Management Studio dialog box, click OK. Close the Find and Replace dialog box.**

12. **Press Ctrl+S to access the Save As dialog box.**

13. **In the Save File As dialog box, browse to the `c:\MySQLScripts` directory. In the File Name text box enter** Adventureworks2008CopyObjects **and click Save.**

14. **Close all the tabbed windows holding scripts but leave SSMS open.**

Running a script

When a script is created and saved, it's rather easy for you to retrieve and run it. The biggest thing to remember is where you saved it.

Use the following steps to retrieve and run the scripts created in the previous steps:

1. **With SSMS open, click the New Query button to open a blank query window.**

2. **Press Ctrl+O to open a new file.**

3. **In the Open File dialog box, browse to `C:\MySQLScripts`.**

4. **Click the CreateAdventureworks2008CopyDB script file and click Open.**

5. **Press F5 to run the script.**

You've created a database named Adventureworks2008Copy.

6. **Right-click the Databases container and click Refresh.**

You'll see your new database named Adventureworks2008Copy. However, if you open the database, you'll see that there are no objects (such as tables and views) within the database.

7. **Press Ctrl+O to open a new file.**

8. **In the Open File dialog box, browse to `C:\MySQLScripts`.**

9. **Click the Adventureworks2008CopyObjects script file and click Open.**

10. **Press F5 to run the script.**

You've created all the objects within the Adventureworks2008Copy database.

If you run the objects script on the same server where the Adventureworks2008 database exists, you'll receive a couple of errors when the script runs. However, the script is still successful. The errors are related to the names used for extended properties on the database.

11. **Right-click the Adventureworks2008Copy database and click Refresh. Open the different containers to see that the objects have been added.**

Although you probably ran the script on the same system that you created the script on, you could just as easily run the script on a different system. You'd just need to get a copy of the script (perhaps copied to a USB drive) and bring it to the new server and open it from there.

Modifying a Script

Any script that you create can be opened, modified, and saved again just as easy as you can rewrite your resume or a letter to your Mom.

The query window within SQL Server Management Studio (SSMS) is the best choice for modifying scripts because you have IntelliSense and color coding to help you quickly and easily see anything that might be wrong. However, any text editor can be used.

IntelliSense provides you with a choice of several valid options to help you easily complete queries. It can complete parameters, find the information you need, insert language elements, and more. The best thing is that it's free and always available in the SSMS editor.

Color coding helps you identify different elements in your scripts just by the color of the text. Keywords (such as SELECT) are in blue, comments are green, SQL strings are red, and identifiers are black. To make writing a script more meaningful, imagine that you want to check the structural integrity of databases in your system. The following command can be used:

```
DBCC CHECKDB(databasename)
```

When executed against the Adventureworks2008 database, the command provides a lot of details on the internal storage of the database and then ends with a very important message showing zero errors.

```
CHECKDB found 0 allocation errors and 0 consistency
    errors in database 'Adventureworks2008'.
DBCC execution completed. If DBCC printed error
    messages, contact your system administrator.
```

Creating a script to check databases manually

If you have three databases named Sales, Accounting, and Personnel, you could use the following steps to create a script that checks these three databases.

1. **Launch SQL Server Management Studio (SSMS).**

   Choose Start⇨All Programs⇨Microsoft SQL Server 2008⇨SQL Server Management Studio.

2. **On the Connect to Server screen, click Connect.**

3. **Click the New Query window to open a query window.**

4. **In the query window, enter the following code:**

   ```
   DBCC CHECKDB(Sales)
   DBCC CHECKDB(Accounting)
   DBCC CHECKDB(Personnel)
   ```

5. **Press Ctrl+S to save the script file.**

6. **In the Save File As dialog box, click My Projects. Enter CheckDB in the File Name box and click Save.**

7. **Leave the query window open.**

Modifying your script to automatically identify databases and check them

The previous script works fine for only three databases, but if you have many databases on your server (and especially if they sometimes change), the script simply isn't automated enough.

Use the following steps to modify your query to automatically identify each database on your server instance and run the CheckDB command against each of them:

1. **With the query window open, press Ctrl+O to open a script file.**

2. **If not already selected, click the My Projects icon and select the CheckDB script file. Click Open.**

3. **Delete all the lines displayed from the script file.**

4. **Enter the following script into the query window:**

```
--Declare variables
DECLARE @dbid integer
DECLARE @DBName nvarchar(50)
DECLARE @mySQL nvarchar(200)
--Start with first database
SET @dbid = 1
--Loop through all databases
WHILE @dbid < (SELECT MAX(dbid)
  FROM master.dbo.sysdatabases)
BEGIN
  SELECT @DBName = name
  FROM master.dbo.sysdatabases
  WHERE dbid = @dbid
  --Dynamically build DBCC CHECKDB for database
  SET @mySQL = 'DBCC CHECKDB(' + @DBName + ')'
  EXEC sp_executesql @statement = @mySQL
  --Increment to do the same for
  --the next database
  SET @dbid = @dbid + 1
END
```

5. **Press F5 to execute the query. The script may take a while to complete. On my system with five user databases it took 23 seconds.**

6. **Press Ctrl+S to save the script.**

You now have a script that can be used to check the integrity of all the databases on this server. You can run this same script on any other server to check the integrity of all its databases.

Chapter 2: Stored Procedures and Functions

In This Chapter

✔ Why you need stored procedures and functions

✔ Creating stored procedures and functions

✔ Using stored procedures and functions

Stored procedures and functions are invaluable tools that are available within database management systems. The stored procedures and functions that are installed when you install SQL Server 2008 allow you to do complex tasks without the need to program the complex details.

As a database developer, you can also create your own stored procedures and functions. These allow your users to do complex tasks without the need to program the complex details. However, in this case, you're the expert because you're the one who does the behind-the-scenes programming.

Why You Need Stored Procedures and Functions

Both stored procedures and functions can significantly add to the performance and usability of SQL Server 2008. By mastering these objects, you go a long way toward mastering programming within SQL Server.

Out of the box, SQL Server 2008 includes many system stored procedures and built-in functions. These are already optimized, and they provide two significant benefits:

✦ **They're ready to use without any programming by you.** All you have to do is identify the object that you want to use and plug it into your code. You don't have to understand the underlying code, and you especially don't have to program the underlying code. All you need to know is what's available and how to use it.

✦ **They're optimized.** Microsoft has already optimized the code for the built-in objects, which means that they run quicker and use the least possible amount of resources.

There will be times when the existing stored procedures and functions don't meet your needs. In these instances, you can create your own objects. These are referred to as *user-defined* (such as user-defined stored procedures and user-defined functions).

Understanding stored procedures

Stored procedures are groups of T-SQL statements put together into a single object. They can be composed of a single T-SQL statement, such as a SELECT statement, or hundreds of lines of T-SQL.

For example, you might need to write a T-SQL batch file that makes the appropriate entries in a database when a sales order is placed. In addition to updating the appropriate tables, the batch file could also check inventories and send an e-mail to personnel in purchasing when any inventories of the products are low. Because this is a repeatable task, you could easily convert this batch file into a stored procedure.

Stored procedures have a lot of versatility. They can

✦ **Accept parameters:** Parameters can be any valid T-SQL data type, such as char() or varchar() for text type data and integer or decimal for numeric data types.

✦ **Output data in many different formats:** Data can be in the form of a derived table (as would be displayed from a SELECT statement), a single value (as the result of a calculation), or a message indicating success or failure.

✦ **Output custom error messages:** Error messages can be created to output any desired text.

✦ **Include transactions:** Transactions can be used within stored procedures to ensure groups of T-SQL statements either succeed or fail as a whole.

✦ **Include TRY ... CATCH blocks for sophisticated error checking:** TRY ... CATCH blocks within T-SQL allow you to try some action (such as an UPDATE or DELETE) and, if an error occurs, catch the error and handle it gracefully.

✦ **Raise errors internally:** The RaiseError function can be used within a stored procedure to cause a specific error to occur. This is often used to provide feedback to the user or used when the SQL Server Agent is programmed to respond to a specific error.

Almost any T-SQL statement that you can write and execute in the new query windows in SQL Server Management Studio (SSMS) can be included within a stored procedure. One of the primary benefits of a stored procedure is that once you create it, you no longer have to enter all the code into the query window to run the procedure. Instead, you simply execute the stored procedure and all the code runs.

Other benefits of stored procedures include that they

✦ **Improve performance of SQL Server:** Stored procedures are parsed, optimized, compiled, and placed in cache when they're run. If executed again (and the compiled stored procedure is still in cache), the stored procedure doesn't have to be parsed, optimized, and compiled again. Instead, the compiled plan is executed directly from cache.

✦ **Shield database complexity:** A stored procedure can be very complex with hundreds of lines of code. A user doesn't need to understand all the internal code; instead, he needs to know only how to execute the stored procedure.

✦ **Allow business logic to be shared:** No one likes to reinvent the wheel. If someone has written the code and put it into a stored procedure, other users can use the stored procedure to perform the same task.

✦ **Enhance security:** Frequently, database administrators and database developers want to prevent users from manipulating tables directly. For example, a `usp_RecordSale` stored procedure could be used to modify a Sales table in a database. A user who is granted Execute permission on the stored procedure but zero permissions on the Sales table could use the stored procedure to update the Sales table but couldn't access the Sales table directly.

✦ **Reduce vulnerability to SQL Injection attacks:** SQL Injection attacks take advantage of Web sites that dynamically build SQL statements. Instead of dynamically building a SQL statement, parameters could be collected from the Web page and passed into the stored procedure. This is a primary prevention strategy for preventing SQL Injection attacks.

✦ **Reduce network traffic:** A stored procedure can include hundreds of lines of code. However, to execute the stored procedure, only one line of code needs to be sent over the network to execute it. Sending one line of code over the network instead of hundreds of lines of code can reduce network traffic.

Stored procedures can receive an input (in the form of parameters) and can return an output. They can be created to perform a specific task (such as rebuilding specific databases) without having any input or output, though it's generally good practice to have at least some type of output to indicate success or failure.

Stored procedures cannot be embedded within a SELECT statement. This is a significant difference between functions and stored procedures. Functions can be embedded within a SELECT statement.

Understanding system stored procedures

System stored procedures are included when you install SQL Server. Primarily, system stored procedures are used to interact with the SQL Server engine as opposed to data within user databases. All system stored procedures start with the sp_ prefix.

Some of the more commonly used categories are

✦ **Database Engine stored procedures:** These are used for general maintenance of SQL Server, and they include queries to retrieve general information on SQL Server and the databases.

For example, the sp_helpdb reports general information on all databases on the server or a single database if the database name is included.

✦ **Database Mail stored procedures:** These are used for e-mail operations from within SQL Server.

For example, the sp_send_dbmail system stored procedure can be used to send an e-mail when Database Mail has been enabled and configured.

✦ **Log Shipping stored procedures:** *Log shipping* is used to create and maintain a standby server with the same data as a primary server. These stored procedures are used to configure, modify, and monitor log shipping.

For example, the sp_add_log_shipping_primary_database stored procedure is used to set up a primary database for a log shipping configuration.

✦ **Replication stored procedures:** Replication is used to create full or partial copies of databases on multiple servers by identifying data that is to be replicated, which server(s) will replicate the data, and which server(s) will receive the data.

The sp_addpublication system stored procedure is used to identify data that will be replicated.

✦ **Security stored procedures:** These are used for various security purposes, such as adding or removing users, logins, and roles.

The sp_addlogin stored procedure can be used to add a login to the server so that a user can access the server.

✦ **XML stored procedures:** These are used to manage XML documents.

For example, the `sp_xml_preparedocument` stored procedure is used to read and parse an XML documents and ensure it's in a state that allows it to be consumed (or used) within SQL Server.

Microsoft has included literally hundreds of system stored procedures within SQL Server. They are all well documented in SQL Server's help feature — *Books Online.* You can launch SQL Server Books Online by choosing Start⇨All Programs⇨Microsoft SQL Server 2008⇨Documentation and Tutorials⇨SQL Server Books Online.

Figure 2-1 shows Books Online with the Index tab selected (at the bottom left). Typing in *system stored procedures* brings you to all the entries for system stored procedures. You can then select the categories section under system stored procedures [SQL Server] to show all the categories.

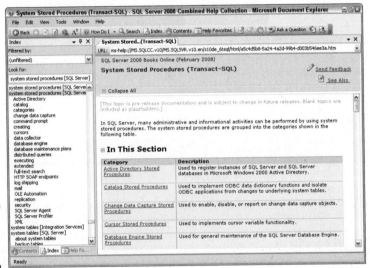

Figure 2-1: Using Books Online.

Understanding functions

Functions are similar to stored procedures in that they are used to encapsulate frequently performed logic and can accept parameters. However, functions are different from stored procedures in these ways:

✦ **Functions always return a value.** This is a core purpose of a function: to perform some type of calculation or data retrieval and return data. Data can be in the format of a derived table or a single value.

✦ **Functions always include parentheses.** As an example, the MONTH(date) function includes the date value in parentheses and returns the month of the given date. The date can be any valid date. The GETDATE() function returns the current date. Even though parentheses are included (and must be included), the GETDATE() function doesn't accept parameters.

✦ **Functions can be used within SELECT statements.** Stored procedures cannot be used within a SELECT statement. Scalar functions (those that operate on a single value and return a single value) can also be executed with the EXEC statement just like a stored procedure.

✦ **Functions can also be used anywhere a single value is expected.** Functions can be used anywhere in a query where a single value is expected. This includes the SET clause in an UPDATE statement, and the VALUES clause of an INSERT statement. They can be used in other functions, in stored procedures, in CHECK constraints, and DEFAULT definitions. In short, a function that returns a single value can be used just about anywhere a single value is expected in a T-SQL statement.

✦ **Many functions are built-in to SQL Server.** SQL Server includes system stored procedures, which are available when you install SQL Server. Functions that are available when you install SQL Server are *built-in functions*. If a function doesn't exist to meet your needs, you can create your own — referred to as *user-defined functions*.

Understanding built-in functions

Almost any programming language you use today includes *built-in functions*. These are designed to perform some of the common tasks that you can expect to need when using the language for application development.

As a common example, you might need to get an average of a group of numbers. Thinking back to grade school (a long time for me!), you probably remember that the average is calculated by adding a group of numbers together and then dividing the sum by how many numbers you added. The average of two numbers (8 and 10) is 18 (8 + 10) divided by 2, which is 9.

Knowing how to calculate the average and programming code to calculate the average are two different things. Yes, you could probably do it, but it'd be a whole lot better if you didn't have to perform such a tedious task. In T-SQL, the AVG() function is available for this.

Built-in functions exist in four primary categories:

✦ **Rowset functions:** A rowset function returns data in a table format. When a rowset function is used within a SELECT statement, the result is referred to as a derived table. The table doesn't actually exist in the database; it's derived from the function.

As an example, the `OPENQUERY()` function can be used to create a derived table from an external server that has been created as a linked server. An `OPENQUERY()` function is shown in the following code:

```
SELECT *
FROM OPENQUERY(SQLServer2, 'SELECT Lname, Phone FROM
    dbo.Customers')
```

Normally, a table name would immediately follow the `FROM` keyword. Instead, the `OPENQUERY()` function is being used to query the Customers table from a linked server named SQLServer2. This does require that SQLServer2 be created as a linked server.

✦ **Aggregate functions:** Aggregate functions work on a group of data and return a single value.

For example, you might be interested in knowing the maximum list price of products listed in your Products table. The following query could be used:

```
SELECT MAX(ListPrice) FROM Production.Product
```

✦ **Ranking functions:** Ranking functions add a column with a ranking value for each row. This can be useful in identifying where a row falls in comparison with the other rows. Four different ranking functions are available: `RANK`, `DENSE_RANK`, `NTILE`, and `ROW_NUMBER`. Each of the functions has subtle differences, such as how they handle a tie between two rows.

✦ **Scalar functions:** Scalar functions work on a single value and return a single value. These are the most popular built-in functions and include ten separate categories.

For example, consider the possibility that data names were entered into the database with leading spaces. The `LTRIM()` function could be used to retrieve the names but omit the leading spaces. A query with the `LTRIM()` function may look like this:

```
SELECT LTRIM(LastName), Phone From Person.Contact
```

Books Online documents all the built-in functions available within SQL Server 2008. The *Functions (Transact-SQL)* article includes links to all the categories and individual functions within the categories. In addition to finding the available built-in functions, you'll also find excellent examples of how to use the functions.

Understanding user-defined functions

There's sure to be a time when you need a specific functionality within your code, but your searches for a suitable built-in function turn up empty. No problem, you can create your own.

User-defined functions are created with the `CREATE` statement, modified with the `ALTER` statement, and removed with the `DROP` statement.

**Book IV
Chapter 2**

**Stored Procedures
and Functions**

The RETURNS clause within the function identifies the data type of the function. The data type can be a single value, such as varchar(20), or it can be a table.

You can create three different types of user-defined functions. The different types are categorized based on the data that is returned.

+ **Scalar functions:** Scalar functions accept a single parameter and return a single value.

+ **Inline table-valued functions:** These return a derived table created from a single statement.

+ **Multi-statement table-valued functions:** These return a derived table created from multiple statements within the function. These are easily identified by the use of the BEGIN...END statements within the function.

Creating Stored Procedures and Functions

Both stored procedures and functions can be created within SQL Server. Because system stored procedures affect the server and the databases (and not the data), you will very likely be creating your own user-defined stored procedures. However, because so many built-in functions exist that can be used to work on your data, the need to create user-defined functions isn't as great.

However, the successful database developer knows how to create both — or at least knows where to look when the need arises to create a user-defined stored procedure or function.

Creating user-defined stored procedures

Creating user-defined stored procedures is a skill that most database administrators need in day-to-day operations. If you say you can work with SQL Server, you're expected to know how to create basic stored procedures.

Darril recently went to a job interview for an application developer where this was given as one of the few questions the company asked: "Our applications frequently access databases, and we commonly create stored procedures to access the databases. Tell us about your knowledge related to creating stored procedures."

Knowing how to create and use stored procedures is often considered a core skill requirement. Your knowledge and skill set in this area may be the difference between getting a job offer or not. (By the way, Darril did get the job offer based on that interview.)

When you first start creating stored procedures, use the following steps:

1. **Start with the code that you'd write to perform the job function without worrying about the stored procedure.**

This might be something as simple as a SELECT or INSERT statement.

2. **After the code is tested, add the CREATE PROC statement.**

The general syntax is

```
CREATE PROC procedureName
AS
tested code
```

3. **Execute the procedure to verify it works as you expect.**

The syntax to execute a stored procedure is

```
EXEC procedure name
```

4. **Add parameters to your stored procedure.**

Parameters can be used as variables within your stored procedure and are identified with a leading @ symbol. Zero or more parameters can be used. They should be separated with a comma. The data type of the parameter also needs to be specified. Generally, this matches the same data type used in the table. The general syntax is

```
CREATE PROC procedureName
    @variablename datatype
AS
. . .
```

5. **Use the parameter variables in your script.**

For example, if your script used a SELECT statement, you could use a WHERE clause to check for the existence of the variable. The general syntax is

```
SELECT *
FROM table
WHERE columnName = @variableName
```

6. **Modify the stored procedure with the ALTER command.**

With the addition of the parameter and usage of the variable in the script, change the CREATE keyword to ALTER and press F5 to execute the script.

```
ALTER PROC procedureName
    @variablename datatype
AS
. . .
```

7. **Execute the stored procedure with the following command:**

```
EXEC procedureName parameter
```

What Darril has found when teaching stored procedures to students in the classroom who haven't written them before is they often want to jump right to Step 6, creating a stored procedure with parameters. They often struggle with typos that come with any type of scripting or programming. However, because they started with a complex step, they have a lot of difficulty troubleshooting the script and experience more than their fair share of frustration.

When starting out, go slow. Perform only one step at a time. Count each step that you finish as a mini-victory. Move to the next step only after succeeding with the current step.

Use the following steps to create an actual user-defined stored procedure that retrieves employee data from the AdventureWorks2008 database.

These steps assume you have the AdventureWorks database installed on your system. If you haven't installed it, download and install the AdventureWorks 2008 database. This file can be found by going to the Microsoft CodePlex site (`www.codeplex.com/MSFTDBProdSamples`) and clicking the Releases tab. Book III, Chapter 5 provides the complete steps on how to install AdventureWorks2008.

1. **Launch SQL Server Management Studio.**

   Choose Start⇨All Programs⇨Microsoft SQL Server 2008⇨SQL Server Management Studio.

2. **Create a new query window by clicking the New Query button.**

3. **Enter the following code to test a simple query.**

   Press F5 to execute the query. This returns 290 rows.

   ```
   USE AdventureWorks2008;
   GO
   SELECT *
   FROM Person.Person p
   INNER JOIN HumanResources.Employee e
   ON e.BusinessEntityID = p.BusinessEntityID
   ```

4. **Modify the query to create a stored procedure.**

   Press F5 to execute the query. The lines that are added are in bold.

   ```
   CREATE PROC usp_GetEmp
   AS
   SELECT *
   FROM Person.Person p
   INNER JOIN HumanResources.Employee e
   ON e.BusinessEntityID = p.BusinessEntityID
   ```

5. **Execute the stored procedure with the following line:**

```
EXEC usp_GetEmp
```

Highlight the line and press F5 to execute it. This returns 290 rows.

6. **Modify the stored procedure to add a parameter.**

The parameter is used within a WHERE clause to retrieve information on employees with a specific last name. The modifications are shown in bold.

```
ALTER PROC usp_GetEmp
    @LastName varchar(50)
AS
SELECT *
FROM Person.Person p
INNER JOIN HumanResources.Employee e
ON e.BusinessEntityID = p.BusinessEntityID
WHERE LastName = @LastName
```

Press F5 to execute the ALTER statement.

7. **Execute the stored procedure with the following statement:**

```
EXEC usp_GetEmp 'Gilbert'
```

This returns one row.

Creating user-defined functions

If a built-in function doesn't exist to meet your needs, you can simply create your own. The following three sections show the steps necessary to create each of the different types of functions.

The basic syntax to create a user-defined function is

```
CREATE FUNCTION functionName
    (input parameter and data type)
RETURNS
    (identifies the data type returned by the function)
AS
    Function definition
```

Creating a scalar function

Scalar functions work on a single value and return in a single value.

For example, you might want to modify the output of a query on the Production.Product table so that NULL is not used for colors. Any time the value of NULL is encountered, instead of outputting NULL in the query, you can use a function to substitute the value of Not Available for the color.

The following steps can be used to create a function that changes NULL values to Not Available.

1. **Launch SQL Server Management Studio.**

   Choose Start⇨All Programs⇨Microsoft SQL Server 2008⇨SQL Server Management Studio.

2. **Create a new query window by clicking the New Query button.**

3. **Enter the following query and execute it by pressing F5 to view how the Color column is displayed.**

   ```
   USE AdventureWorks2008;
   GO
   SELECT Name, ProductNumber, Color FROM
       Production.Product
   ```

4. **Enter the following code and execute it to create a user-defined scalar function:**

   ```
   CREATE FUNCTION fn_NULL_to_NA
    (@inputString nvarchar(30))
    RETURNS nvarchar(15)
   AS
   BEGIN
     If @inputString IS NULL
        SET @inputString = 'Not Available'
     -- At this point, the value of the @inputString
     -- variable is either the
     -- original color or it has been changed to Not
     -- Available if it was NULL
     Return @inputString
   END
   ```

5. **Enter the following query and execute it to view the way the Color column is displayed when the function is used.**

   ```
   SELECT Name, ProductNumber, dbo.fn_NULL_to_NA(Color)
       FROM Production.Product
   ```

When executing functions, the two-part name is used as in *schema. functionname*. Schemas can be used to organize and specify ownership of objects. If not specified when the object is created, it defaults to dbo, which indicates the database owner owns the object.

6. **Leave the query window open in SSMS for the next steps.**

One great thing about this function is that it's generic. In other words, although it was created specifically to change the value of NULL to Not Available for the Color column, nothing stops it from being used on other columns with a NULL value.

Once created and in the database, you can use the same function to change the value of NULL in the Phone column, the Fax column, the EmailAddress column, or any other column where you see a use.

Creating a table-valued function

Both inline table-valued functions and multi-statement table-valued functions return a derived table. The derived table can be used within a SELECT clause in place of an actual table.

The only real difference between an inline table-valued function and a multi-statement table-valued function is how the returned table is created. In a multi-statement table-valued function, the table is defined with multiple statements. In an inline table-valued function, the table is defined with a single statement.

You can compare a table-valued function with a view. A view can be created to show specific columns from one or more tables. However, a weakness with a view is that it can't accept parameters. By creating an inline table-valued function, you can mimic the functionality of a view with the added capability of using parameters.

As an example, imagine that you need to create the capability to retrieve e-mail addresses and phone numbers. The user has the person's last name. Use the following steps to create an inline table-valued function that returns this information with the last name as a parameter:

1. **With the query window open in SSMS, use the following query to return information on a person with the last name of Alameda:**

```
USE AdventureWorks2008;
GO
SELECT p.FirstName, p.LastName, em.EmailAddress,
    ph.PhoneNumber FROM Person.Person p INNER JOIN
        Person.PersonPhone ph
        ON p.BusinessEntityID = ph.BusinessEntityID
        INNER JOIN Person.EmailAddress em
        ON p.BusinessEntityID = em.BusinessEntityID
WHERE LastName = 'Alameda'
```

You use the same query in your function, but instead of identifying the name in the WHERE clause, you use a parameter to allow the name to be changed.

2. **Enter and execute the following code to create the function named `fn_PhoneEmail`:**

```
CREATE FUNCTION fn_PhoneEmail
  (@LastName nvarchar(50))
RETURNS table
AS
RETURN (
    SELECT p.FirstName, p.LastName, em.EmailAddress,
           ph.PhoneNumber
    FROM Person.Person p INNER JOIN
       Person.PersonPhone ph
       ON p.BusinessEntityID = ph.BusinessEntityID
       INNER JOIN Person.EmailAddress em
       ON p.BusinessEntityID = em.BusinessEntityID
    WHERE LastName = @LastName )
```

3. **Use the following query to use the function:**

```
SELECT * FROM dbo.fn_PhoneEmail ('Alameda')
```

The function is used right after the FROM clause. The FROM clause expects a table, and the function provides a derived table.

4. **Leave the query window open in SSMS for the next steps.**

Creating CLR integrated functions

A *CLR integrated function* is one that includes a program created in a .NET language. This can be quite powerful. Now you can use a fully featured language, such as Visual Basic .NET or C# .NET to write a complex subroutine. After the subroutine is compiled, you can then integrate it within a SQL Server object, such as a stored procedure or a function.

The steps to create CLR integrated stored procedures and CLR integrated functions are very similar. If you'd like to see the steps to create a CLR integrated stored procedure, check out Book IV, Chapter 1.

The high-level steps required to create CLR integrated objects are

1. Use a .NET language to create a Dynamic Link Library (DLL) assembly.

2. Register the assembly in SQL Server.

3. Create a SQL object (such as a stored procedure or function) that uses the assembly.

Imagine that you have a need to determine the day of the year. Each year has 365 or 366 days, and you want to determine the day of the year for the current date. You can use the following steps to create a CLR integrated object that returns the day of the year:

1. **Click Start⇨Run and enter** Notepad. **Press Return.**

This opens an instance of the Notepad text editor.

2. Enter the following code into Notepad:

```
Imports Microsoft.SqlServer.Server
Imports System.Data.SqlClient
Public Class DateFunctionsClass
    <SqlFunction(DataAccess:=DataAccessKind.Read)> _
        Public Shared Function fn_DayOfYear(ByVal dt _
    As System.Data.SqlTypes.SqlDateTime) As Integer
        Dim dtPassed As Date = dt.Value
        fn_DayOfYear = _
            DatePart(DateInterval.DayOfYear, dtPassed)
    End Function
End Class
```

This Visual Basic code creates a Visual Basic class (named `DateFunctionsClass`) that can be compiled into a DLL file. It includes only one function (named `fn_DayOfYear`) but could easily include many functions. The code returns the day of the year (from 1 to 366).

3. Save the file as `myCLR.vb` in the C:\CLRAssembly folder.

Press Ctrl+S to access the Save As dialog box. Browse to the root of `C:\` and create a folder named CLRAssembly. Enter **myCLR.vb** as the name of the file.

4. Click Start➪Run and enter cmd to launch the command line.

5. At the command line, change the directory to the directory holding the .NET Framework compiler by using the following command.

```
CD c:\Windows\Microsoft.NET\Framework\v2.0.50727
```

Several versions of the .NET Framework are available. Most current systems include at least version 2, build 50727 (v2.0.50727). If the change directory (CD) command doesn't work with the path of v2.0.50727, double-check to ensure that you don't have any spaces in the path. If it still doesn't work, use Windows Explorer to browse to the Windows\ Microsoft.NET\Framework folder to determine the version of the .NET Framework that you have on your system. Use the CD command to change the path to that directory.

6. Compile your assembly by using the Visual Basic Compiler (vbc). Use the following command from the command line:

```
vbc /target:library c:\CLRAssembly\myCLR.vb
```

If you use Windows Explorer to browse to the c:\CLRAssembly folder, you'll see that the `myCLR.dll` file has been created. You need to register this assembly in SQL Server.

7. With the query window open in SSMS, enter and execute the following code to create a database named CLRTest:

```
CREATE DATABASE CLRTest
```

**Book IV
Chapter 2**

**Stored Procedures
and Functions**

8. **Using the SSMS Object Explorer, browse to the Databases | CLRTest | Programmability | Assemblies container.**

   Figure 2-2 shows the empty Assemblies container within the Object Explorer in SSMS. Assemblies can be created via T-SQL code or by right-clicking the Assemblies container.

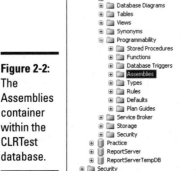

Figure 2-2: The Assemblies container within the CLRTest database.

9. **Right-click the Assemblies container and choose New Assembly.**

10. **Click the Browse button and browse to the C:\CLRAssembly directory. Select the myCLR.dll file and click Open. Enter DBO as the Assembly Owner. Click OK.**

    Before you click OK, your display looks similar to Figure 2-3. The Assembly name is filled in with the name of the assembly (myCLR). The Permission Set option defaults to Safe, which prevents the assembly from accessing anything other than what's in the database, and Path to Assembly is filled in with the name and path of the DLL file.

11. **Click OK in the New Assembly dialog box.**

    When you click OK, the assembly is registered within SQL Server. You need to create a stored procedure that will use it.

12. **In the query window, enter the following code to create a stored procedure that uses the myCLR assembly:**

    ```
    USE CLRTest;
    GO
    CREATE FUNCTION udf_DayOfYear(@dt as datetime)
    RETURNS integer
    AS EXTERNAL NAME myCLR.DateFunctionsClass.fn_DayOfYear;
    ```

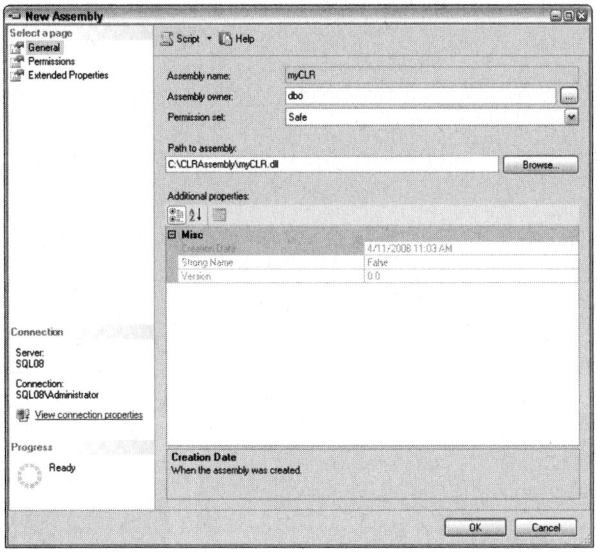

Figure 2-3:
The New
Assembly
dialog box.

The EXTERNAL NAME is created as the three-part name in the following format: assembly name (that you registered in SQL Server), class name (identified in the Visual Basic file that you created in Notepad), and the function name (within the class). Although our assembly includes only one class and only one function in the class, assemblies can be created with multiple classes within them, and multiple subroutines or functions within the classes.

13. **Enter the following code in the query window to enable the usage of CLR assemblies:**

```
sp_configure 'show advanced options', 1;
GO
RECONFIGURE;
GO
sp_configure 'clr enabled', 1;
GO
RECONFIGURE;
```

Press F5 to execute the code.

14. **Use the following code to execute your CLR integrated function:**

```
SELECT dbo.udf_DayOfYear('02/27/2008') AS [Day of Year]
SELECT dbo.udf_DayOfYear(GetDate()) AS [Day of Year]
```

The first SELECT statement shows how to use a given date in the function. The second statement shows how to use the current date in the function.

**Book IV
Chapter 2**

**Stored Procedures
and Functions**

Chapter 3: Triggers

In This Chapter

✔ **DML triggers: Letting your database look after itself**

✔ **DDL triggers: Letting your server look after itself**

✔ **Creating triggers**

✔ **Maintaining triggers**

Triggers are powerful tools that you can use to automate control of your server and databases. Three categories of triggers are available in SQL Server 2008: Data Manipulation Language (DML) triggers, Data Definition Language (DDL) triggers, and logon triggers.

To control data modifications within your database, you use a DML trigger. To control modifications of objects (such as databases or tables), you use a DDL trigger. To audit or control logins, you create a logon trigger.

The great thing about a trigger is that you create it once, and it manages your server or database forever more. You could be vacationing in Hawaii or the Swiss Alps, and the trigger will still do your bidding.

DML Triggers: Letting Your Database Look After Itself

Triggers are often referred to as a special type of stored procedure. Just as stored procedures can be programmed to perform just about anything within a database, so can triggers. Data Manipulation Language (DML) triggers are often used to

+ Make changes to other columns (in the same table or other tables within the database) in response to a data modification.

+ Perform auditing by recording who made a data modification and when.

+ Roll back or undo data modifications.

+ Provide specialized error messages.

Although a stored procedure can be executed with the EXEC command, Data Manipulation Language (DML) triggers can't be called directly. Instead, they are configured on individual tables or views and respond to the following DML commands:

✦ **INSERT:** When an `INSERT` command is executed on a table, an `INSERT` trigger on the table fires.

For example, when an order is placed (inserting data into the Orders table), you might like to update the on-hand inventory column in the Products table. You could create an `INSERT` trigger on the Orders table to do this. When someone orders five glossy widgets, the `INSERT` trigger would fire and would reduce the on-hand inventory value by five.

✦ **UPDATE:** When an `UPDATE` command is executed on a table, an `UPDATE` trigger on the table fires.

For example, management might want to know if anyone ever modifies data (such as the Salary column) in the Employees table. You could create an `UPDATE` trigger on the Employees table to record into an Auditing table who made the change and when he made the change. Now, if someone enters the database and updates his salary (perhaps by doubling it), the `UPDATE` trigger on the Employees table would fire and record in the Auditing table who did it and when.

✦ **DELETE:** When a `DELETE` command is executed on a table, a `DELETE` trigger on the table fires.

For example, the company you work at might not want to ever delete a customer from the Customers table. Instead, customers should be marked as inactive. You could create a `DELETE` trigger on the Customers table to roll back the deletion, and change the value of the Status column to `Inactive`. If someone ever tried to delete a customer, the `DELETE` trigger would fire and undo the deletion (by rolling back the `DELETE` statement) and changing the value of the Status column.

DML triggers can be programmed to perform either after the data modification or instead of the data modification. When a trigger is created, one of these choices is specified:

✦ **AFTER:** An `AFTER` trigger fires after the data modification. In other words, the data modification occurs, and then the trigger fires in response to the data modification. Therefore, an after trigger that rolls back a data modification becomes an expensive operation because the data is changed twice when it shouldn't be changed at all.

`AFTER` is the default for triggers. `AFTER` triggers can only be specified on tables; they can't be specified on views.

✦ **INSTEAD OF:** An `INSTEAD OF` trigger fires before the data modification. In other words, the data modification is prevented from occurring, and instead, the trigger is executed.

`INSTEAD OF` triggers are commonly created on updateable views. For example, if a view is created by using the `UNION` clause, an `UPDATE` on the view would fail because the UPDATE statement won't be able to determine which table to update.

The INSTEAD OF trigger can include logic to determine which table to update, and instead of updating the view, it would update the underlying table.

Triggers use two special tables that are only accessible to triggers. The data in these tables is available immediately after an INSERT, UPDATE or DELETE statement.

✦ **Inserted table:** The inserted table holds data from the last INSERT or UPDATE statement.

✦ **Deleted table:** The deleted table holds data from the last DELETE or UPDATE statement.

The use of INSERT and DELETE statements in these tables is straightforward. If one or more rows are added with an INSERT statement, the row(s) are held in the inserted table. If one or more rows are deleted with a DELETE statement, the row(s) are held in the deleted table.

However, an UPDATE statement isn't so clear. Notice an updated table doesn't exist.

When an UPDATE statement is executed, the database engine actually deletes the existing row (and holds it in the deleted table) and then adds a new row (and holds it in the inserted table). The new row has all the same column data as the deleted row, except for the column (or columns) that were modified. Although it appears as though the existing row was modified, it was actually deleted and inserted with the modified data.

An INSERT trigger has access to only the inserted table; a DELETE trigger has access to only the deleted table; however, an UPDATE statement has access to both the inserted table and the deleted table.

Understanding DML trigger benefits

A significant benefit of DML triggers is that they capture the data modification no matter how the data modification is accomplished. Although you could create a stored procedure to perform the same actions as the trigger, the actions of the stored procedure would occur only if the stored procedure is executed. If a user chose to bypass the stored procedure and modify the data directly, the actions wouldn't occur.

In contrast, a trigger can't be bypassed. That is, an UPDATE trigger on a table fires when data is modified from an UPDATE statement issued from an application, from a stored procedure, or even from a direct modification within SQL Server Management Studio.

Triggers can also provide sophisticated error messages. If you want to provide detailed feedback to the user, or log specific information in log files, you can use a trigger. Compared to constraints that provide system-defined feedback, triggers provide whatever information that you, the programmer, want to provide.

Understanding DML trigger drawbacks

The biggest drawback to triggers is that they execute after the data modification. Any time data is rolled back within a trigger, additional processing power is used. Instead of rolling back data within a trigger, you should consider other alternatives.

One alternative to triggers is the use of CHECK or DEFAULT constraints.

For example, you might want to ensure that a phone number is entered in the format of *(xxx)xxx-xxxx* where *x* is a number between 0 and 9. A CHECK constraint would check the data before it's entered in the database and prevent the data entry if it didn't comply with the CHECK. In contrast, a trigger would allow the data entry, and then roll it back if the phone number wasn't in the proper format. The CHECK constraint would be much more efficient.

Another alternative is to use an INSTEAD OF trigger rather than an AFTER trigger.

DDL Triggers: Letting Your Server or Your Database Look After Itself

Data Definition Language (DDL) triggers have been in SQL Server since SQL Server 2005. Like Data Manipulation Language (DML) triggers, DDL triggers can't be called directly. Instead, they respond to DDL events. DDL events are created when DDL statements are executed. DDL statements that can fire triggers include

- ✦ **CREATE:** The CREATE statement is used to create objects, such as tables, databases, and logins.
- ✦ **ALTER:** The ALTER statement is used to make modifications to objects.
- ✦ **DROP:** The DROP statement is used to remove objects.
- ✦ **GRANT:** The GRANT statement is used to grant permissions.

When you're removing data, you use the DELETE statement. When you're removing objects, you use the DROP statement. UPDATE is used to modify data, whereas ALTER is used to modify objects. It's a subtle difference, but the statement being used (DML or DDL) helps you identify whether you're working on data or working on objects.

DDL triggers have two possible scopes: database and server. The scope identifies the type of objects that the trigger will monitor.

+ **Database scope:** A trigger with a database scope monitors objects within a specific database. These include tables, views, stored procedures, functions, or any other object within a database that can be manipulated.

+ **Server scope:** A trigger with a server scope monitors any objects within the server (except objects within a database). These include databases, logins, messages, or any other object that can be created within a server instance.

DDL triggers are commonly used to

+ **Audit database operations:** Any changes to database objects (such as tables, views, or stored procedures) can be captured by a DDL trigger and recorded in a separate auditing table. For example, by modifying a table that is used by a view, it's possible to break the view. Imagine that this has happened one time too many where you work. By creating an ALTER trigger on the database, you can record exactly when any object was changed, what it was changed from, what it was changed to, and who changed it.

+ **Regulating database operations:** With DDL triggers, you can prevent database changes by capturing the change and rolling back what you don't want to occur. For example, you might want to prevent any changes to the database schema, such as altering the structure of a table.

+ **Audit server operations:** Any changes to server objects (such as the creation, deletion, or modification of databases) can be captured. The statement that caused the change can then be logged in to an auditing table including what was done, by whom, and when.

Logon Triggers: Monitoring and Controlling Login Events

Logon triggers are used to audit and control server sessions. When configured, a user-defined stored procedure fires in response to a login event. Some examples of how a logon trigger is used include:

+ **Track or audit all login activity:** You can use a logon trigger to capture logon information (such as who logged in and when they logged in) into an audit table.

✦ **Restrict logins:** Logon triggers can be used to restrict logins to the SQL Server during certain times. For example, you might want to restrict logins during maintenance periods.

✦ **Restrict logins for specific users:** You can use logon triggers to restrict a user from having more than a specific number of active sessions, or restrict a user's total monthly logon time.

The timing of when logon triggers fires gives you insight into how they can be used.

1. **User authenticates:** A user initiates a session with SQL Server. Credentials are passed and the user is authenticated.

2. **Logon trigger fires:** After the user authenticates (but before the session begins), the logon trigger fires. The logon trigger can capture information about the user. This information can be logged, or used to rollback the login and prevent the session.

3. **Session begins (or is prevented by logon trigger):** If the login doesn't rollback, the user's session begins.

Creating Triggers

Triggers are created using T-SQL code. Although they're viewable within the SQL Server Management Studio (SSMS) after they've been created, you can't create them in the graphical user interface.

Creating a DML trigger

The following basic syntax creates a DML trigger:

```
CREATE TRIGGER triggername
ON table or view
AFTER or INSTEAD OF
INSERT or UPDATE or DELETE
AS
trigger code
```

The trigger will be created in the current database. Because the default database is Master when you open SSMS, you would usually change the context of the database with a USE command immediately preceding the trigger code.

In the following steps, you create a Sales database, a Customers table, an UPDATE trigger, and a DELETE trigger. By manipulating the data within the Customers table, you'll see the triggers being fired.

1. **Launch SQL Server Management Studio.**

Choose Start➪All Programs➪Microsoft SQL Server 2008➪SQL Server Management Studio.

2. **Open a new query window by clicking the New Query button.**

3. **Enter and execute the following code to create a database named Sales with a table named Customers:**

```
USE Master;
GO
CREATE DATABASE Sales;
GO
USE Sales;
GO
CREATE TABLE Customers (
 CustomerID int NOT NULL,
 LName varchar(50) NOT NULL,
 FName varchar(50) NULL,
 Status varchar (10) NULL,
 ModifiedBy varchar(30) NULL
 )
```

4. **Add a customer with the following code:**

```
INSERT INTO Customers (CustomerID, LName, FName,
    Status)
VALUES (101, 'Dangerously', 'Johnny', 'Active')
```

Notice that the ModifiedBy column is left NULL.

5. **View your customer data with the following query:**

```
SELECT * FROM Customers
```

You should see the row you added and a blank ModifiedBy column.

6. **Add an UPDATE trigger on the Customers table with the following code:**

```
CREATE TRIGGER trgRecordModifyDate
ON Customers
AFTER UPDATE
AS
DECLARE @CustomerID int
SET @CustomerID = (SELECT CustomerID FROM inserted)
UPDATE Customers
  SET ModifiedBy = suser_sname()
  WHERE CustomerID = @CustomerID
```

The @CustomerID variable used to capture CustomerID was modified from the last UPDATE statement. Then the suser_sname() function captures the identity of the user that executed the UPDATE statement and stores it in the ModifiedBy column.

7. **Modify the customer data with the following query:**

```
UPDATE Customers
    SET FName = 'Johnathan'
    WHERE CustomerID = 101
```

This causes the UPDATE trigger to fire and add data to the ModifiedBy column.

8. **View your new customer data with the following query:**

```
SELECT * FROM Customers
```

You should see that the ModifiedBy column is no longer NULL.

9. **Add an INSTEAD OF DELETE trigger to prevent the deletion of customers with the following code:**

```
CREATE TRIGGER trgNoDelete
ON Customers
INSTEAD OF DELETE
AS
RAISERROR ('Customers can''t be deleted.  Customer
    changed to inactive instead.', 16, 10) WITH LOG
UPDATE Customers
  SET Status = 'Inactive'
  FROM Customers as c INNER JOIN deleted as d
  ON c.CustomerID = d.CustomerID
```

The trigger is an INSTEAD OF trigger, so the actual DELETE statement doesn't fire.

10. **Try to delete a customer with the following code:**

```
DELETE FROM Customers
Where CustomerID = 101
```

Instead of deleting the customer, the message *Customers can't be deleted. Customer changed to inactive* is displayed.

11. **View your new customer data with the following query:**

```
SELECT * FROM Customers
```

The status has been changed to Inactive.

12. **Leave the query window open in SSMS for the next set of steps.**

Creating a DDL trigger

The following basic syntax creates a DDL trigger:

```
CREATE TRIGGER triggername
ON DATABASE or SERVER
FOR event
AS
trigger code
```

A powerful tool that can be used when creating DDL triggers is the EVENTDATA() function. Any time a DDL trigger fires, the information about the trigger is captured in the EVENTDATA() function as XML data.

By copying the EVENTDATA into an XML variable, you can then query the data and store the pieces that you want or need.

Different event types hold different data. The two pieces of data used in the following steps are

✦ **EventType:** The EventType value holds the value of the event type that caused the trigger to fire. For example, a DDL trigger can be created to capture all DDL database events (DDL_DATABASE_LEVEL_EVENTS). The EventType value would be CREATE_TABLE for a CREATE TABLE statement or ALTER_VIEW for an ALTER VIEW statement.

✦ **TSQLCommand:** The TSQLCommand value holds the actual command that was executed. For example, if an ALTER TABLE command was issued, it would hold the full syntax of the command so that you could easily identify exactly what was altered.

It's important to realize that the EVENTDATA() function holds only the data for the trigger and is accessible only by the trigger. After the trigger has fired, you no longer have access to the data from the EVENTDATA() function.

In the following steps, you create and test several DDL triggers. Two have database level scope, and one has server level scope. The first provides feedback to the user that tables can't be modified. The last two triggers log the activity into a table within a database.

The following steps assume the Sales database has been created in the previous steps. If you haven't done so, create the Sales database and the Customers table.

1. **Add a trigger to prevent the modification of any tables within the Sales database with the following code:**

```
USE Sales;
GO
CREATE TRIGGER trgNoChange
ON DATABASE
FOR ALTER_TABLE
AS
  PRINT 'Tables may not be modified'
  ROLLBACK;
```

The ON clause identifies the scope. In this case, the scope is for the database. The USE statement set the context to the Sales database; therefore, the trigger is set on the Sales database.

2. Try to modify the Customers table with the following **ALTER** statement:

```
ALTER TABLE Customers
   ADD ZipCode varchar(10) NULL
```

3. Use the following command to verify that the table hasn't been modified.

```
SELECT * FROM Customers
```

4. Add a table called Audit with the following command:

```
USE Sales;
GO
CREATE TABLE Audit (
 DBUser varchar(50) NOT NULL,
 ExecutionTime datetime NOT NULL,
 EventType varchar (50) NULL,
 TSQLCmd varchar(500) NULL
 )
```

This table logs who executed the DDL command, what command was executed, and when it was executed.

5. Create the DDL trigger with the following command:

```
CREATE TRIGGER trgAuditDB
ON DATABASE
FOR DDL_DATABASE_LEVEL_EVENTS
AS
DECLARE @Event XML
SET @Event = EVENTDATA()
INSERT Audit
    (DBUser, ExecutionTime, EventType, TSQLCmd)
    VALUES
    (suser_sname(),GETDATE(),
    @Event.value('(/EVENT_INSTANCE/EventType)[1]',
    'nvarchar(50)'),
    @Event.value('(/EVENT_INSTANCE/TSQLCommand)[1]',
    'nvarchar(500)') ) ;
```

This trigger captures all database-level DDL events. The @Event variable captures the data from the Event function, such as the type that was captured and the actual T-SQL command that was executed, and inserts this information into the Audit table.

6. Use the following command to create a table within the database:

```
USE Sales;
GO
CREATE TABLE NoCreate (
 DBUser varchar(50) NOT NULL
 )
```

The DDL trigger doesn't stop the command from being executed, but it does log the information into an Audit table.

7. **You can observe the details of who created the table, when they created it, and what command they issued to create it by querying the Audit table with the following command:**

   ```
   SELECT * FROM Audit
   ```

8. **You can create a DDL trigger with a server scope with the following command:**

   ```
   CREATE TRIGGER trg_CreateDatabase
   ON ALL SERVER
   FOR CREATE_DATABASE
   AS
   DECLARE @Event XML
   SET @Event = EVENTDATA()
   INSERT Sales.dbo.Audit
       (DBUser, ExecutionTime, EventType, TSQLCmd)
       VALUES
       (suser_sname(), GETDATE(),
       @Event.value('(/EVENT_INSTANCE/EventType)[1]',
       'nvarchar(50)'),
       @Event.value('(/EVENT_INSTANCE/TSQLCommand)[1]',
       'nvarchar(500)') ) ;
   ```

   This trigger is similar to the trigger designed to capture database-level events. The exception is that you must identify the Audit table in the Sales database with a three-part name (Sales.dbo.Audit) because the trigger has a server scope (defined with ON ALL SERVER).

9. **Create a database named LogMe with the following command:**

   ```
   CREATE DATABASE LogMe
   ```

10. **The creation of the database is captured and logged by executing the following command:**

    ```
    USE Sales;
    GO
    SELECT * FROM Audit
    ```

Maintaining Triggers

During the life of a trigger, you'll likely need to make some changes.

For example, you might have originally created a trigger that provided feedback to a user stating that tables shouldn't be modified in a database. Instead of just informing users that it shouldn't be done, you decide that you want to audit whenever it's done by logging the change into the database.

With this situation, you don't have to re-create the trigger from scratch. Instead, you can use the ALTER statement to make the change.

The following basic syntax modifies a DML trigger:

```
ALTER TRIGGER triggername
ON table or view
AFTER or INSTEAD OF
INSERT or UPDATE or DELETE
AS
trigger code
```

This basic syntax modifies a DDL trigger:

```
ALTER TRIGGER triggername
ON DATABASE or SERVER
FOR event
AS
trigger code
```

The syntax is exactly the same except that the CREATE keyword is replaced with the ALTER keyword.

Chapter 4: Working with Visual Studio

In This Chapter

✔ **Visual Studio: the development companion to SQL Server**

✔ **Navigating SQL Server databases with Visual Studio**

✔ **Common Visual Studio and SQL Server tasks**

*W*e admit it. We think databases are cool. Call us nerdy if you like, but we love working with databases and helping to make them sing. However, we're aware that not everyone is like that and not everyone has SQL Server installed on his desktop.

You might be a developer using Visual Studio (or even one of the Visual Express editions of your favorite programming language) but without an SQL Server installed on your system. You might still need to access the databases. Thankfully, you can do so with Visual Studio.

In this chapter, you get a mini-introduction to Visual Studio and you find out how to connect to a SQL Server database. You also discover how to browse the database objects, view the data, and debug stored procedures.

Introducing Visual Studio

Microsoft Visual Studio is a full-featured development environment that can be used to create Windows applications, console applications, Web sites, Web applications, Web services, and more. It supports developing applications in a wide variety of programming languages including:

+ Visual Basic
+ Visual C#
+ Visual C++

Within the context of SQL Server, Visual Studio can be used to browse databases, debug stored procedures, develop Web services, and create SQL Server Management Object (SMO) applications. In Chapter 7 of this minibook, steps are included that show you how to create a basic SMO application by using Visual Basic.

Developers who are creating applications that access SQL Server databases can use Visual Studio to connect to databases (either as stand-alone files, or hosted on remote servers), and browse through the databases. Often, a developer needs to know details of a database, such as specifics of a table including column names, constraints, and data types.

The *Server Explorer* within Visual Studio can be used to browse through databases hosted on SQL Server. Figure 4-1 shows Visual Studio launched with the Server Explorer displayed. It has one connection to a database file, and also has a connection to a SQL Server named SRV08.

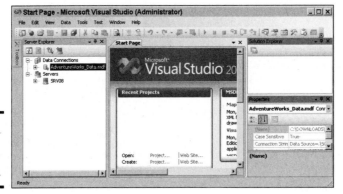

Figure 4-1:
Creating a
Data
Connection.

If you're using one of the Visual Studio Express editions, you won't have Server Explorer. Instead, you have the Data Explorer, which can do most of what Server Explorer can.

On the right, the Solution Explorer is blank. When developing applications, you use Visual Studio to create a solution that would include one or more projects. However, to browse databases, you don't have to create a project. You can simply launch Visual Studio, access the Server Explorer, and connect to the database you want to explore.

Below the Solution Explorer is the Properties pane. The Properties pane displays the properties of the object that is currently selected. If it disappears, it can be brought back by pressing F4.

You don't need the full version of Visual Studio to use Visual Studio with SQL Server. When you install SQL Server, you also get the Business Intelligence Development Studio (BIDS). BIDS is used for many of the development projects within SQL Server.

BIDS can be used with the following:

+ **SQL Server:** BIDS can be used to connect to databases, browse through databases objects, and even debug stored procedures.

+ **SQL Server Analysis Services (SSAS):** SSAS is used to reorganize data in a different format, allowing decision makers access to the data they need to make better-informed decisions.

+ **SQL Server Integration Services (SSIS):** SSIS projects are used to extract, transform, and load (ETL) data from a wide variety of sources. By using SSIS, you can create complex packages designed to cleanse and sanitize data for better consistency and data quality.

+ **SQL Server Reporting Services (SSRS):** SSRS projects are used to create and deploy reports, allowing users easy access to data via a familiar Web browser.

One of the differences between BIDS and Visual Studio is that Visual Studio allows you to connect to other SQL Servers, but BIDS doesn't give you that option. You can connect to database files only.

Get a free trial edition of Visual Studio

No doubt about it, Visual Studio is an expensive product. If you're a rich developer, it's just a cost of doing business, but most of us aren't rich. Yet.

If you want to try Visual Studio, you can download a free Trial Edition. Microsoft has a 90-day evaluation version of Visual Studio 2008 Professional Edition available for download. It's a fully functioning product, but it stops working after 90 days. You can download it from here:

```
http://msdn2.microsoft.com/en-us/vs2008/products/
cc268305.aspx
```

We've seen developers download the past editions of Visual Studio, play around with it, and then show management some of the magic they can perform with the product. It becomes a great "proof of concept" tool that justifies the cost. Of course, trial editions are great for those of us who just like to play, too.

When you download this, beware. It's a single ISO image that's almost 4GB in size. Even with a broadband connection, it'll take a while to download. We wouldn't want to try this with a dial-up connection. After you download the ISO image, burn it to a DVD, and then you're ready to start.

Remember though, BIDS is installed when SQL Server is installed. BIDS might be enough for you without having to install the full version of Visual Studio.

Launching Visual Studio

Whether you're using a full version of Visual Studio, or BIDS that installs by default with SQL Server, you'll want to launch it. Use the following steps to launch Visual Studio and connect to the AdventureWorks2008 database.

These steps assume that you have a copy of the AdventureWorks2008 database available on a SQL Server. If you don't have a copy, you'll need to download a copy. Start with an Internet search on *download AdventureWorks*. Full details on how to install AdventureWorks2008 are covered in Book III, Chapter 5.

1. **Launch Microsoft Visual Studio 2008.**

   Choose Start⇨All Programs⇨Microsoft Visual Studio 2008⇨Microsoft Visual Studio 2008.

2. **Choose View⇨Server Explorer to make the Server Explorer visible.**
   Alternately, you could press Ctrl+Alt+S.

3. **Right-click Data Connections and choose Add Connection.**

4. **On the Choose Data Source page, select Microsoft SQL Server and click Continue.**

5. **On the Add Connection dialog box, enter the name of the server that is hosting the AdventureWorks2008 database.**

   You can use **localhost** if SQL Server 2008 is installed on the same system.

6. **In the Connect to a Database section, enter** AdventureWorks2008 **(or choose it from the drop down list).**

   Your display looks similar to Figure 4-2. The server used for the screen-shot is named MCITP1, but your server might have a different name.

7. **Click Test Connection. A Microsoft Visual Studio dialog box appears indicating success. Click OK.**

The TCP/IP protocol must be enabled on the SQL Server 2008 server you are connecting to for this to succeed. You can access this by launching the SQL Server Configuration Manager; click Start⎮Microsoft SQL Server 2008⎮Configuration Tools⎮SQL Server Configuration Manager. In the SQL Server Network Configuration, you'll see protocols for MSSQL Server. If TCP/IP is set to Disabled, right-click it and select Enabled. You'll then need to restart the SQL Server service for the change to take effect.

8. **Click OK to close the Add Connection dialog box.**

   Your display looks similar to Figure 4-3. It shows the connection to the remote server with AdventureWorks opened up. You can browse the database objects from here, similar to how you can browse it with SQL Server Management Studio (SSMS).

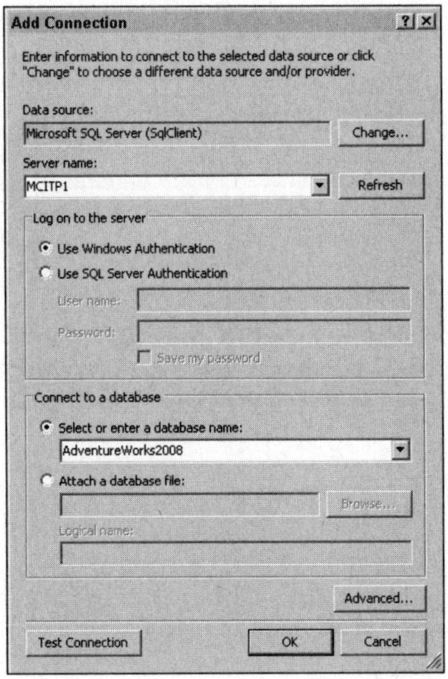

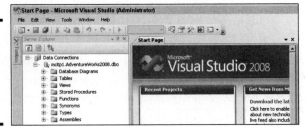

Figure 4-2:
Connecting to a database hosted on a SQL Server.

Figure 4-3:
Connecting to a remote server from Visual Studio.

Navigating an SQL Server Database with Visual Studio

One of the primary reasons you connect to an SQL Server database is to explore it. While exploring a database in Visual Studio you can

✦ **View the objects:** This includes database objects, such as tables, views, stored procedures, functions, and more.

✦ **Modify data:** By opening tables and views you can add, modify, and delete data in the database.

✦ **Execute, test, and debug stored procedures:** If a stored procedure accepts input variables, you're prompted to provide the input. You can test the stored procedures capability of handling different inputs and enter the debugger if your stored procedure isn't functioning as desired.

By using the Server Explorer in Visual Studio, you can easily explore a database and see all the elements. It avoids the need to install SQL Server on a development system just to explore the database.

Exploring tables and views from Visual Studio

The Visual Studio Solution Explorer works very similar to the Object Explorer in SQL Server Management Studio (SSMS). The best way to see this is by doing it.

While the following steps show you how to access a table, modify data in the table, and build a query, feel free to look around at any objects to see what you can do. As long as you're working with the AdventureWorks2008 database, the worst that can happen is the database could become corrupt, and you'd need to download another copy.

If you have any trouble connecting to the AdventureWorks2008 database, review the steps in the previous section. Those steps are a little more detailed than here.

1. **Launch Microsoft Visual Studio 2008.**

Choose Start➪All Programs➪Microsoft Visual Studio 2008➪Microsoft Visual Studio 2008.

2. **Choose View➪Server Explorer to make the Server Explorer visible.**

Alternately, you could press Ctrl+Alt+S.

3. **Select the data connection to AdventureWorks on a SQL Server that you created in the previous exercise.**

4. **Browse to AdventureWorks | Tables | Person (Person) table by clicking the + next to each category.**

The table name is Person, and Person also identifies the schema that owns the table.

5. **Right-click the Person (Person) table and choose Show Table Data.**

This opens the table and allows you to modify the data. To give you more room to see the table, you can click the X at the top right of the Solution Explorer and at the top right of the Properties windows. To bring back the Solution Explorer, select View➪Solution Explorer, as shown in Figure 4-4. The Solution Explorer and the Properties pages aren't displayed, giving much more room for the Person table. Leave the Solution Explorer closed.

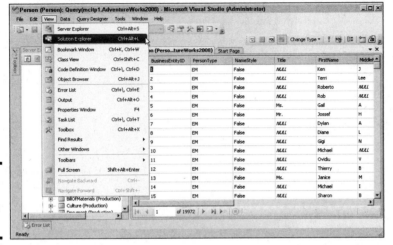

Figure 4-4:
Restoring the Solution Explorer.

6. **Scroll to the last row in the Person table.**

7. **In the row with all the NULL values, enter Elmer for the FirstName and press Enter.**

   This fails because some columns don't allow NULL data.

8. **Click OK to dismiss the information box indicating the row wasn't updated. Press Esc to abort the data entry.**

9. **Right-click the Person table and choose Open Table Definition.**

   The table definition allows you to see at a glance what columns can be NULL and what columns can't.

10. **Scroll to the rowguid column and select it. The pane below the table definition is the Column Properties pane. Scroll to the Default Value or Binding property.**

    Your display looks similar to Figure 4-5. This shows that the rowguid column can't be NULL, but it has a default value that is generated by the newid() function. By looking at all the columns, you can identify those that can't be NULL (BusinessEntityID, PersonType, NameStyle, FirstName, LastName, EmailPromotion, PasswordHash, PasswordSalt, rowguid, and ModifiedDate).

    By looking at the Column Properties, you can see the columns that don't have a default value or binding that must have a value are BusinessEntityID, PersonType, FirstName, and LastName.

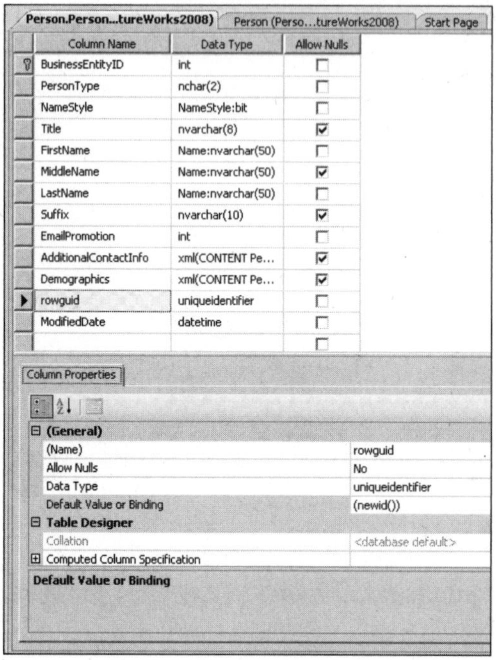

Figure 4-5:
Viewing the
definition of
a table.

11. **Select the Person(Person):Query tab that displays the data. If you're not at the first row, scroll to the first row.**

12. **You can modify the data in this window. Change the FirstName from Ken to Kenneth. Press Enter and your modifications are complete.**

13. **Delete the row by right-clicking in the left margin to the left of the row and choosing DELETE. A warning dialog box appears indicating that you're about to permanently delete the row. Click No to cancel the deletion.**

14. **Right-click the Views container in the Server Explorer and select New Query.**

The query window opens, allowing you to build a query.

15. **In the Add Table dialog box, select the Person(Person) table. Click Add. Select the EmailAddress(Person) table and click Add. Click Close.**

16. **In the top pane, select the check boxes next to the FirstName and LastName columns in the Person(Person) table. Select the check box for the EmailAddress column in the EmailAddress(Person) table.**

17. **In the middle pane, scroll to the Filter column and enter** Kenneth **on the FirstName row.**

The query adds the single quotes around Kenneth, with the letter N at the beginning. The N indicates that the data is displayed in Unicode format.

18. **Right-click anywhere in the query window and choose Execute SQL.**

Your display looks similar to Figure 4-6 — the same format as the Query Designer (explored in Book III, Chapter 3). The top pane is the *Diagram pane* (where your selected tables are shown), the next pane is the *Criteria pane* (where you entered the filter information), the next pane is the *SQL pane* (where your T-SQL statement is built), and the bottom pane is the *Results pane.*

Figure 4-6:
Building a
query in
Visual
Studio.

Exploring stored procedures from Visual Studio

You can also explore, execute, test, and debug stored procedures from within Visual Studio.

If you have SQL Server 2008 installed, you can execute and test stored procedures within a query window by using SQL Server Management Studio (SSMS).

But, if you don't have SQL Server installed, you can perform similar testing with Visual Studio.

If your stored procedure is complex and you're having trouble identifying the problem in the logic, you can use the debugger available in Visual Studio to slow the stored procedure. By using the debugger, you can step through the stored procedure one statement at a time.

If you've used SQL Server 2000, you might remember that the Query Analyzer had a built-in debugger. However, SQL Server 2005 SQL didn't include Query Analyzer; it included a query window within SSMS but that window didn't include a debugger. A welcome addition in SQL Server 2008 SSMS is the debugger. You can use SSMS as the debugger by simply clicking the green button or by pressing CTRL+F5.

When you *step into* a stored procedure, you begin the debugging process. The Debug toolbar includes several icons that can be used when debugging.

✦ **Continue:** Instructs the debugger to complete the remainder of the code. The icon is a green arrow.

✦ **Stop Debugging:** Instructs the debugger to exit without running any more code. The icon is a blue square.

✦ **Step Over:** Instructs the debugger to execute the next line of code. The icon is a line arrow simulating stepping over lines of code.

Figure 4-7 shows the debugging window. At the top, you can see the debugging toolbar. The middle pane displays the text of the stored procedure. While you step through the stored procedure, a yellow arrow points to the current statement. A breakpoint has been created on the WITH line so that the procedure always stops there. The bottom two panes are additional windows that can be displayed to give you information as you step through the stored procedure.

Some of the additional windows that can be used are

✦ **Autos:** Displays the value of variables used in the current line of code, and the preceding line of code. The Autos window can be displayed by selecting the Autos tab in Windows group 1 in Figure 4-7.

✦ **Locals:** Displays the visible variables from the current procedure. For example, when executing a stored procedure that requires input that will be used as a variable, the variables can be viewed here. In Figure 4-7, the two variables provided as input for the `uspGetBillOfMaterials` stored procedure are shown in Windows group 1.

Stored procedure text ─────   Debugging buttons

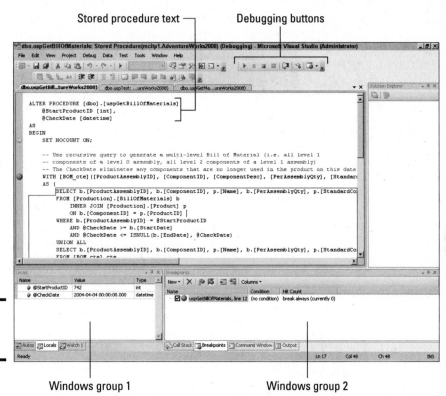

Figure 4-7:
The Debug
toolbar.

Windows group 1   Windows group 2

✦ **Watch:** Allows you to set *breakpoints* (points where the code will stop so that you can view the values of different variables) based on the value of a specific variable. In other words, you can task the debugger to watch a variable, and when it reaches a threshold, the code will stop. You can then view the value of other variables. The Watch 1 window is displayed as a tab in Windows group 1 in Figure 4-7. Multiple Watch windows can be configured.

✦ **Call Stack:** Displays procedures and functions that are executing. The Call Stack window is displayed as a tab in Windows group 2 in Figure 4-7.

✦ **Breakpoints:** Allows you to create breakpoints based on certain conditions. The Breakpoints window is displayed as a tab in Windows group 2 in Figure 4-7.

✦ **Command:** Used to execute commands while your code is running or paused. The Command window is displayed as a tab in Windows group 2 in Figure 4-7.

✦ **Output:** Displays debugging-specific output as the stored procedure is executed.

**Book IV
Chapter 4**

**Working with
Visual Studio**

The following steps show the basics of launching the debugger in Visual Studio to step through a stored procedure:

1. **Launch Microsoft Visual Studio 2008.**

Choose Start⇨All Programs⇨Microsoft Visual Studio 2008⇨Microsoft Visual Studio 2008.

2. **If the Server Explorer is not visible, choose View⇨Server Explorer to make it visible.**

3. **Connect to the AdventureWorks2008 database file stored on a SQL Server 2008 server.**

4. **Browse to Adventureworks2008 | Stored Procedures | uspGetBillOfMaterials. Right-click the `uspGetBillOfMaterials` stored procedure.**

Your display looks similar to Figure 4-8.

Note: You can add new stored procedures, open a stored procedure (to view the text and alter it), execute a stored procedure, or step into a stored procedure (for debugging).

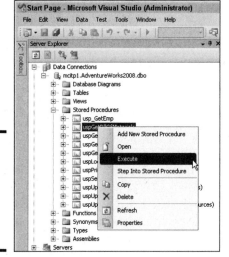

Figure 4-8:
Accessing the Stored Procedure menu in Visual Studio.

5. **Right-click the `uspGetBillOfMaterials` stored procedure and choose Open.**

The text used to create the stored procedure appears. This view helps you find out more about what the stored procedure is doing.

6. **Right click the `uspGetBillOfMaterils` stored procedure and choose Execute.**

Execute allows you to enter different parameters and ensure that the stored procedure works as expected.

7. **In the Run Stored Procedure window, enter** 742 **as the value of the @StartProductID, and** 2000-04-04 **as the @CheckDate.**

Your display looks similar to Figure 4-9. You would need to know valid values for the stored procedure, but if you're testing the stored procedure, it's expected that you would know what the valid values are. You can also use this for *edge testing.* In other words, if you want to see how your stored procedure responds when data is entered at the edge of valid values, you can easily enter the values here.

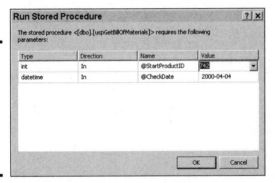

Figure 4-9: Entering variable values when executing a stored procedure.

8. **In the Run Stored Procedure window, click OK.**

The stored procedure runs, and the output displays in the Output pane at the bottom of Visual Studio.

The SQL Server Business Intelligence Studio will allow you to explore objects in a SQL Server database, but it won't allow you to debug stored procedures. If you don't have the Step Into Stored Procedure, verify you are running an instance of Visual Studio.

9. **You can also debug the stored procedure by stepping through it line by line. Right-click the stored procedure and choose Step Into Stored Procedure. In the Run Stored Procedure window, enter** 742 **as the value of the @StartProductID, and** 2000-04-04 **as the @CheckDate. Click OK.**

10. **Click the Step Over button.**

The stored procedure starts the common table expression (CTE) statement.

11. **Click the Step Over button again.**

The stored procedure finishes the execution.

Admittedly, this stored procedure is rather simplistic because it has only one common table expression (CTE). (It's probably a stretch to call any CTE simplistic though.) If the stored procedure had more complexity, executed functions, or called other stored procedures, the debugging process would be much more involved.

Using Visual Studio for other SQL Server tasks

Visual Studio is used when working on other SQL Server projects but not as a full-featured version of Visual Studio.

When we first installed SQL Server 2008 and saw that it included Visual Studio, our hearts jumped a beat. (Could it be true? Visual Studio for free with SQL?).

It wasn't true. You only get a subset of Visual Studio — the Business Intelligence Development Studio (BIDS).

However, one good thing about BIDS is that if you're familiar with the Visual Studio interface, it doesn't take much more time to use BIDS for SQL Server projects. As we mention earlier in this chapter, BIDS is used to create and manipulate the following:

✦ **SQL Server Reporting Services (SSRS):** SSRS is covered in more depth in Book V.

✦ **SQL Server Integration Services (SSIS):** SSIS is covered in more depth in Book VIII, Chapter 4.

✦ **SQL Server Analysis Services (SSAS):** SSAS is covered in more depth in Book VI.

Chapter 5: Web Services

In This Chapter

✔ The new way of distributed programming: Web services

✔ Using Web services in conjunction with SQL Server

*W*eb services are commonly used on networks to transfer data between computers. An application sends a request, and the Web service answers with the required data. The biggest usage is on the biggest network — the Internet. However, Web services can also be used to pass data on networks internal to a company.

SQL Server 2008 can easily be configured to directly serve data as a Web service. A benefit of providing data this way is that the code can be embedded in an application (such as a Windows application or a Web application) and ran on one computer, while the data is retrieved from the SQL Server on a completely separate system.

In SQL Server 2008, Microsoft deprecated the usage of Native XML Web Services. Deprecated does not mean that the services are not supported, but it does mean that support may become an issue in future SQL Server releases. Steering clear of the feature in new development projects (and modifying applications that currently use it) is a good idea. Native XML Web Services may be in use in existing projects however, so you may want to make modifications to the code in the short term as you plan for switching the code to ASP.NET over the longer haul.

Using Web Services to Distribute Data

A *Web service* is a software system used to transfer data across a network. That network could be the Internet, an intranet, or even an extranet. A Web service is designed to accept requests for information and return information based on the request.

The requests can be very simple or complex. Some common data returned by Web services include

+ **Weather data:** A ZIP code is passed into the service, and weather information (such as current temperature and future predictions) is passed back.

+ **Order status:** An order ID is passed into the service, and the current status of the order (such as *shipped* or *being processed*) is passed back.

+ **Shipping status:** A tracking number is passed into the service, and the current location or other shipping information is passed back.

Web services have several key elements:

+ **Provider:** The Web services provider gives the data that's requested from the Web services requestor. This could be a compiled application, or it could simply be SQL Server.

+ **Requestor:** The requestor queries the provider for specific information. The requestor is often a Web application that's used to embed information into a Web page.

+ **Web Services Description Language (WSDL):** WSDL (pronounced *Wizz-dull*) can be thought of as a contract. It identifies specifically what can be requested and what will be returned. For example, a WSDL for a Web service designed to provide order statuses would specify how a valid order ID could be provided and then identify what would be included in the answer (and what that answer means).

+ **Simple Object Access Protocol (SOAP):** SOAP is used to transfer both requests and data in an XML format. Because XML is simple text, it's easily transported over networks and it commonly uses HTTP and HTTPS.

+ **Universal Description Discovery and Integration (UDDI):** The UDDI is a registry that businesses can use to publish WSDLs. When the WSDL is published to the UDDI, it can then be retrieved by requestors.

Figure 5-1 shows how these elements are used together. A Web services provider is created that can send information to applications that request it. The specifics on how to request the information is contained in the WSDL. The WSDL is published to the UDDI. A requestor can then query the UDDI for Web services as long as they follow the requirements specified in the WSDL. The requestor then sends its request to the provider by using SOAP. The provider replies with the data by using SOAP.

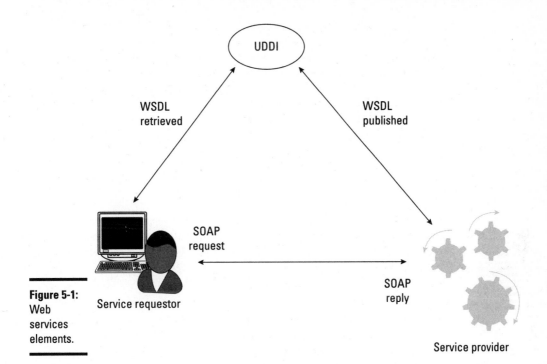

Figure 5-1:
Web
services
elements.

Although the public UDDI was originally intended to be a registry for all businesses and to include services information for these businesses, it was actually more often used for testing. The result was that a lot of the data published to the public UDDI was bogus data. In January 2006, IBM, Microsoft, and SAP discontinued hosting the public UDDI registries. Currently, large enterprises can host their own UDDI registry, but the demise of the public UDDI registries is on the horizon.

You don't have to use UDDI. For example, if you're creating a Web service in-house to be used by in-house developers only, you don't need to publish the WSDL to a UDDI. Instead, you can just tell the developers how to use your Web service.

Requesting data and getting a response

The Web service works by accepting a Web service request and sending back a Web service response.

**Book IV
Chapter 5**

Web Services

Both the request and the response are sent in an XML envelope using Simple Object Access Protocol (SOAP). The requirements for the SOAP message are quite stringent. It needs to be well-formed XML and must include specifically what the Web service expects.

A well-formed XML document conforms to several XML formatting requirements. For example, each opening tag (`<tagName>`) must have a corresponding closing tag (`</tagName>`).

As long as the request is formatted properly for the Web service, it will respond with the appropriate response. The application that called the Web service can then format the data as desired.

For example, a Web service that returns information on cloud conditions might return *clear, partially cloudy, cloudy, sprinkles, rain,* or even *raining cats and dogs.* A Web site can then display a different graphic depending on what's returned. For a clear condition, a bright sun could be shown. For raining cats and dogs, the graphic could show . . . well, you get the idea.

Seeing a Web service in action

Consider a Web service that you might use regularly when you access a news site, such as MSN.com, CNN.com, or your local newspaper. You can personalize most news sites by adding your ZIP code into a weather section.

If you've never done this, try it now. Go to `http://msn.com` and look for the weather link. On the weather page, enter your ZIP code (or if you like, enter Darril's: 23462).

After adding your ZIP code, local weather information appears. While it seems simple on the surface, there's a lot of activity that makes this happen.

Figure 5-2 shows accessing a news site via the Internet. When the Web server receives a request for weather information, it sends a SOAP request to the weather server that's hosting one or more Web services. Weather data is returned to the Web server and included in the page that is returned.

Of course, the weather service probably doesn't provide this information for free. Instead, the service is provided based on some type of subscription basis.

More than likely, the SOAP request includes a subscriber code that verifies the requestor as a valid subscriber in good standing (with his account paid).

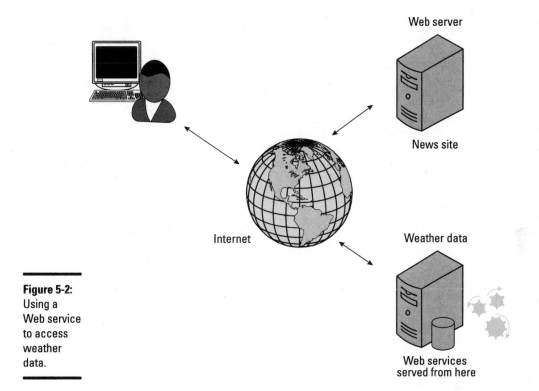

Figure 5-2:
Using a
Web service
to access
weather
data.

Using Web Services in Conjunction with SQL Server

SQL Server can be used to provide Web services directly. To support Web services in SQL Server, you need to create the following elements:

✦ **Stored procedure:** A stored procedure used in a Web service is the same as any stored procedure created within SQL Server. The only difference is that it will be called from a Web Method.

✦ **HTTP endpoint:** An *HTTP endpoint* is a designated port that SQL Server listens on for specific traffic. The HTTP endpoint includes a Web method.

✦ **Web method:** A *Web method* identifies a stored procedure within SQL Server that will be executed when the HTTP endpoint is queried. A Web method would commonly accept parameters, execute a store procedure with the parameters, and then return the results.

Creating HTTP endpoints to support Web services

Within SQL Server, a Web service can be created by creating an HTTP endpoint. The HTTP endpoint identifies the port that SQL Server will use to listen for Web service requests and the Web method that will be executed in response to a valid request.

To better understand how HTTP endpoints work, it helps to understand how IP addresses and ports are used by computers.

When data travels from one computer to another, it finds the destination computer using an IP address. If your long lost uncle wanted to send you an inheritance check from your other long lost uncle, he'd put the check in an envelope, stamp it, and hand it to the post office. An IP address works like the address on the envelope and gets the packet to the computer.

When you receive the envelope, you'd open it and realize you need to cash the check, so you place it somewhere safe until you can make it to the bank. The same day you receive the check, you might receive several pieces of junk mail. The junk mail will probably be placed somewhere different than the check (perhaps the trash). However, by opening each piece of mail, you know what to do with it.

Similarly, computer traffic includes a port that tells the computer what to do with it when it receives it. Port 25 sends this to the Simple Mail Transport Protocol (SMTP) service. Port 80 sends this to the HTTP service.

When you create an HTTP endpoint, you designate the port that the Web service will listen on. The default port is HTTP, but if another service is using port 80, you can designate another port as long as it doesn't conflict with yet another port in use on the computer.

When traffic is received by the computer, the packet is opened, and the port is identified. If the port is in use, the packet is passed to the service listening on that port.

You don't need a Web server (such as Internet Information Services) to listen on the HTTP endpoint. SQL Server listens on this port and services the HTTP endpoint without a Web server.

In addition to identifying the port that the HTTP endpoint will listen on, the HTTP endpoint also identifies the Web method that will be called.

The following basic syntax is used to create an HTTP endpoint:

```
CREATE ENDPOINT endPointName
STATE = { STARTED | STOPPED | DISABLED }
AS HTTP (
```

```
PATH = 'url'
        , AUTHENTICATION =( { BASIC | DIGEST | INTEGRATED
      | NTLM | KERBEROS } [
...n ] ),
      PORTS = ( { CLEAR | SSL} [ ,... n ] )
    [ SITE = {'*' | '+' | 'webSite' },]
    [, CLEAR_PORT = clearPort ]
    [, SSL_PORT = SSLPort ]  )
FOR SOAP(
    [ { WEBMETHOD [ 'namespace' .] 'method_alias'
        (   NAME = 'database.schema.name'
          [ , SCHEMA = { NONE | STANDARD | DEFAULT } ]
          [ , FORMAT = { ALL_RESULTS | ROWSETS_ONLY } ]
      )
    }
      [ , WSDL = { NONE | DEFAULT | 'sp_name' } ]
    [ , DATABASE = { 'database_name' | DEFAULT }
    [ , NAMESPACE = { 'namespace' | DEFAULT } ] )
```

The following steps create an HTTP endpoint that includes a Web method. You first create a database named Weather, and a table named CurrentConditions with some data. Then, you create a stored procedure that will be called from the Web method. With the database set up, you then create the HTTP endpoint.

1. **Launch SQL Server Management Studio.**

Choose Start➪All Programs➪Microsoft SQL Server 2008➪SQL Server Management Studio.

2. **Create a new query window by clicking the New Query button.**

3. **Create a database named Weather and a table named CurrentConditions by using the following T-SQL code:**

```
USE Master;
GO
CREATE DATABASE Weather;
GO
USE Weather;
GO
CREATE TABLE CurrentConditions (
 CurrentConditionsID int NOT NULL,
 ZipCode varchar(10) NOT NULL,
 Temperature int NOT NULL,
 CloudCondition varchar(20) NOT NULL
)
```

4. **Insert some data into the CurrentConditions table with the following INSERT statement:**

```
INSERT INTO CurrentConditions
VALUES (101, 23462, 78, 'Clear')
```

5. **Create a stored procedure that will retrieve current weather conditions for a specific ZIP code with the following code:**

```
CREATE PROC usp_GetWeather
    @Zip varchar(10)
AS
SELECT Temperature, CloudCondition
FROM CurrentConditions
WHERE ZipCode = @Zip
```

At this point, you have everything within your database that you need. You can now create the HTTP endpoint with the Web method to retrieve the data.

6. **Test your stored procedure with the following code:**

```
EXEC usp_GetWeather '23462'
```

This stored procedure accepts the ZIP code and returns the current temperature (78) and the current cloud conditions (clear). It's a beautiful day.

7. **Create the HTTP endpoint with the Web method by using the following code:**

```
CREATE ENDPOINT Weather_CurConditions
    STATE = Started
AS HTTP
    (
        PATH = '/CurrentConditions',
        AUTHENTICATION = (INTEGRATED),
        PORTS = (CLEAR), CLEAR_PORT = 8080,
        SITE = '*'
    )
FOR SOAP
    (
        WEBMETHOD 'GetWeather'
            (NAME = 'Weather.dbo.usp_GetWeather'),
        WSDL = DEFAULT,
        DATABASE = 'Weather',
        NAMESPACE = DEFAULT
    )
```

The endpoint is enabled with the STATE = Started clause. The default port is port 80, and to use port 80 you would omit the CLEAR_PORT = 8080 clause. The PATH clause is the URL for the endpoint. The WEBMETHOD includes the three-part name of the stored procedure that will be called.

8. **To view the Web Services Description Language (WSDL) of the endpoint, launch a Web browser and enter the following URL:**

```
http://localhost:8080/CurrentConditions?WSDL
```

The WSDL is quite lengthy with a lot of default XML nodes included. Thankfully, you don't have to create this from scratch. Although beyond the scope of this book, it can be modified.

With the HTTP Endpoint created and including a Web method, the database is now configured as a Web service. Web service calls to port 8080 and including the ZIP code as a parameter will return the current temperature and the current cloud conditions. This is referred to as *consuming* the Web service.

Although this example accepted only one parameter and passed back two values, your Web services can be as complex as you need them to be. Stored procedures can accept multiple input values and can pass back multiple outputs. As long as the developers of the Web service know what is expected, they can easily create the Web service to your specifications.

Note: You haven't actually created the SOAP request that calls the Web method. The SOAP request would be created in an application created externally from SQL Server.

Exploring the SOAP request and the SOAP response

The application that calls the Web service would typically use a Simple Object Access Protocol (SOAP) request. The Web service would respond with a SOAP response. Both the SOAP request and the SOAP response are sent as XML text files.

Although we just use the name *Localhost* when creating and exploring the HTTP endpoint, to access it we'd need an actual name. Imagine that the Web service is hosted on a Web site named SQLisEasy.com. The two SOAP messages would look similar to the XML code shown in Listings 5-1 and 5-2.

Listing 5-1: SOAP Request

```
<SOAP-ENV:Envelope
  xmlns:SOAP-
    ENV="http://schemas.xmlsoap.org/soap/envelope/"
  SOAP-
    ENV:encodingStyle="http://schemas.xmlsoap.org/soap/
    encoding/">
  <SOAP-ENV:Body>
    <m:GetWeather xmlns:m="http://SQLisEasy.com:8080">
      <ZipCode>23462</ZipCode>
    </m:GetWeather>
  </SOAP-ENV:Body>
</SOAP-ENV:Envelope>
```

Note: The ZIP code is embedded in the SOAP request. This is the parameter that will ultimately be passed to the stored procedure.

Listing 5-2: SOAP Response

```
<SOAP-ENV:Envelope
  xmlns:SOAP-
    ENV="http://schemas.xmlsoap.org/soap/envelope/"
  SOAP-
    ENV:encodingStyle="http://schemas.xmlsoap.org/soap/
    encoding/">
  <SOAP-ENV:Body>
    <m:GetWeatherResponse
    xmlns:m="http://SQLisEasy.com:8080">
      <Temperature>78</Temperature>
      <CloudCondition>Clear</CloudCondition>
    </m:GetWeatherResponse>
  </SOAP-ENV:Body>
</SOAP-ENV:Envelope>
```

The two values (temperature and cloud condition) are being passed back from the stored procedure called from the Web method.

Chapter 6: Developing Remote Applications

In This Chapter

✔ **Data everywhere: remote applications to the rescue**

✔ **Scenarios where it makes sense to access data remotely**

✔ **Using linked servers**

Remote applications are commonly used when interacting with SQL Server. In other words, SQL Server is rarely hosted on the same system as the applications that use them. Instead, the applications access the data remotely.

Additionally, tools are available that allow you to access data from the SQL Server to just any other data source. This allows applications to access a remote SQL Server which in turn accesses another remote data source. The three primary tools you'll use are OPENDATASOURCE, OPENROWSET, and linked servers.

Data Everywhere: Remote Applications to the Rescue!

When running SQL Server, it's highly unlikely that you'll be running it on your desktop system. Instead, you'll run SQL Server 2008 on a server product (such as Windows Server 2003 or Windows Server 2008) and access your SQL Server 2008 database over the network.

Moreover, you're not limited to only the data held on a single SQL Server. A *distributed query* is used to access data from different data sources through SQL Server. In other words, the distributed query is executed against SQL Server, but pulls data from somewhere else.

By using distributed queries, you allow your applications to be remote applications. The applications can run from anywhere and can access data from any other data source as long as they can establish connectivity with a single SQL Server. Of course, the SQL Server must have access to the other data source; that is, there must be connectivity and permissions must be granted.

Figure 6-1 shows how a distributed query works. The client application queries SQL Server. SQL Server then uses an Object Linking and Embedding Database (OLE DB) provider to query data from another data source, such as another SQL Server, Oracle, or Microsoft Access database — any data source with an Open Database Connectivity (ODBC) driver. This is by no means a complete list. Just about any data source that enjoys some level of popularity has either an OLE DB or ODBC provider that can be used.

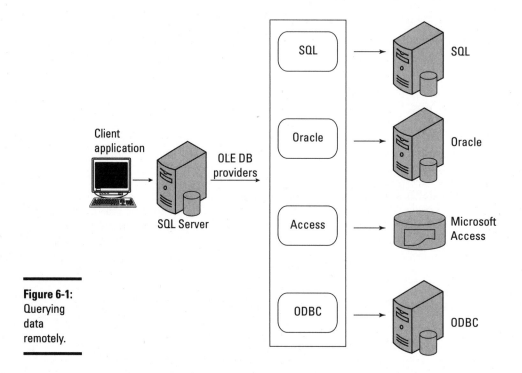

Figure 6-1:
Querying
data
remotely.

SQL Server 2008 includes several providers that are used to connect to external sources. Each of these providers is used to connect to specific data sources. The following are some of the more common providers:

- ✦ **ADsDSOObject:** Connects to Microsoft Directory Services (Active Directory).

- ✦ **Microsoft.JET.OLEDB.4.0:** The Joint Engine Technology (JET) provider allows SQL Server databases to connect to both Microsoft Access databases and Microsoft Excel spreadsheets.

- ✦ **MSDAORA:** The MSDAORA provider is used to connect to Oracle databases. In order to connect to an Oracle data source, you need to install the Oracle client. The Oracle Net component isn't included in SQL Server.

✦ **MSDASQL:** MSDASQL is used to connect to any data source that requires the legacy Open Database Connectivity (ODBC) provider.

✦ **MSIDXS:** Use the MSIDXS OLE DB provider to connect to a Microsoft indexing service data file.

✦ **MSOLAP:** The MSOLAP provider is used to connect to a Microsoft Analysis Services data source. OLAP represents Online Analytical Processing.

✦ **SQLNCLI10:** The SQLNCLI10 provider is the SQL Server (SQL) Native (N) client (CLI) included with SQL Server 2008. This is often shortened to SQLNCLI in provider strings. SQLNCLI automatically identifies the most current version of the Native client. For example, if SQLNCLI was used in SQL Server 2005 and then the server was upgraded to SQL Server 2008, everywhere that SQLNCLI was used would automatically use the newer SQLNCLI10 provider.

The 10 in SQLNCLI10 refers to the version of SQL. Although you know SQL Server 2008 as SQL Server 2008, internally, the version is identified as version 10. SQL Server 7.0 was version 70, sometimes annotated as 7.0. SQL Server 2000 was version 80, or sometimes 8.0. SQL Server 2005 was version 90, or 9.0, and SQL Server 2008 is identified as version 10 (but never 1.0).

✦ **SQLOLEDB:** SQLOLEDB is Microsoft's OLE DB provider for SQL Server. It has been used since SQL Server version 6.5.

✦ **SQLXMLOLEDB:** The SQLXMLOLEDB provider is used to expose Microsoft's SQLXML functionality through ActiveX Data Objects (ADO).

Three primary methods of connecting to remote data sources are

✦ **OPENDATASOURCE:** The OPENDATASOURCE function is used to specify connection information for a remote data source by specifying the OLE DB provider and an initialization string. OPENDATASOURCE can be used directly within a SELECT, INSERT, UPDATE, or DELETE statement.

✦ **OPENROWSET:** The OPENROWSET function is used to specify connection information for a remote data source and the name of an object that will return a result set (such as a stored procedure) or a query that will return a result set. Like OPENDATASOURCE, OPENROWSET can be used directly within a SELECT, INSERT, UPDATE, or DELETE statement.

✦ **Linked servers:** A *linked server* is an object within SQL Server that defines the connection properties of another SQL Server. When defined, queries can connect to the remote server using a four-part name, such as

```
SQLSrv1.AdventureWorks.person.Contact
```

**Book IV
Chapter 6**

**Developing Remote
Applications**

The four-part name identifies the server (SQLSrv1), the database (AdventureWorks), the schema (Person), and the object (Contact table). Linked servers are explored in more depth in the final section of this chapter.

Enabling ad hoc queries

An *ad hoc query* is one that is issued no more than a few times. Both the OPENDATASOURCE and OPENROWSET functions are used for ad hoc queries. If the query will be issued more frequently, linked servers are usually created.

However, ad hoc queries are not enabled by default. They must be enabled by using the sp_configure system stored procedure.

Enabling the use of ad hoc queries allows any authenticated login to execute both OPENROWSET and OPENDATASOURCE functions. You should enable this feature only if it's considered safe to be accessed by any SQL Server login.

To enable ad hoc queries, follow these steps:

1. **Launch SQL Server Management Studio.**

Choose Start➪All Programs➪Microsoft SQL Server 2008➪SQL Server Management Studio Center.

2. **Create a new query window by clicking the New Query button.**

3. **In the query window, enter the following command:**

```
sp_configure 'show advanced options', 1;
GO
RECONFIGURE;
GO
sp_configure 'Ad hoc Distributed Queries', 1;
GO
RECONFIGURE;
```

Before the Ad hoc Distributed Queries option can be changed, it must first be visible by changing the value of Show Advanced Options from a 0 to a 1 (or from false to true). The value of the Ad hoc Distributed Queries option is then set to a 1 (or true) so that they are allowed.

4. **Press F5 to execute the command.**

With the Ad hoc Distributed Queries option set to 1, both OPENDATASOURCE and OPENROWSET functions can be used.

Using OPENDATASOURCE

OPENDATASOURCE can be used instead of creating a linked server to access an external data source.

The basic syntax of OPENDATASOURCE is

```
OPENDATASOURCE ( provider_name, init_string )
```

Both the provider name and the initialization string have very specific syntax requirements. The easiest data source to connect to is another SQL Server. The provider name of SQLNCLI automatically uses the latest version of the SQL Server Native Client OLE DB provider.

For example, if you wanted to retrieve information from the Customers table using the default schema (dbo) in the Sales database from the SQL08 server, you could use the following query. Notice that the four-part name is SQL08. Sales.dbo.Customers.

```
SELECT *
FROM OPENDATASOURCE('SQLNCLI',
    'Data Source=SQL08;Integrated Security=SSPI')
    .Sales.dbo.Customers
```

In this example, the provider name is SQLNCLI. SSPI is the Security Support Provider Interface, which allows an application to use different security models. Integrated Security simply means that the connection will use the credentials of the user executing the statement.

Using OPENROWSET

OPENROWSET is similar to OPENDATASOURCE. The primary difference is that OPENROWSET always returns a result set, whereas OPENDATASOURCE typically returns a result set, but can also be used to simply execute a stored procedure.

The basic syntax of OPENROWSET is:

```
OPENROWSET ( provider_name, provider_string )
```

Just as OPENDATASOURCE has very specific syntax, OPENROWSET does also. However, a similarity between the two is that SQLNCLI automatically uses the latest version of the SQL Server Native Client OLE DB provider in both.

If you wanted to retrieve information from the same Customers table using the default schema (dbo) in the Sales database from the SQL08 server, you could use the following query.

```
SELECT rs.*
FROM OPENROWSET('SQLNCLI',
    'Server=SQL08;Trusted_Connection=yes;',
     'SELECT *
       FROM Sales.dbo.Customers') AS rs;
```

**Book IV
Chapter 6**

**Developing Remote
Applications**

Notice the subtle differences between OPENDATASOURCE and OPENROWSET. In the OPENROWSET function, a SELECT statement is embedded in the function. A trusted connection works similar to integrated security. It's also possible to include the username and password of a trusted login.

Determining When It Makes Sense to Access Data Remotely

One of the visions of SQL Server 2008 during its development was "Your Data, Any Place, Any Time." The idea was to meet the needs of companies of all sizes and provide support for many different types of data.

In Chapter 5 of this mini-book, Web services are covered. Web services aren't new, but they are popular examples of how data can be stored in one place and be accessible just about anywhere in the world via an Internet connection.

When SQL Server is configured with a Web service, applications anywhere can be used to retrieve information. Web services are enjoying widespread use and will continue to grow because of the convenience they provide.

By using distributed queries, you can access data from other data sources held on remote servers. Remote servers won't necessarily be available anywhere in the world, but they can be accessible anywhere on your network.

Darril currently works in a large enterprise environment spread across 10 states with 17 physical locations. All the locations are accessible to each other via redundant wide area network (WAN) connections. One group of database administrators manages the majority of the SQL Servers in this environment, and they can access the servers from a central location.

Admittedly, distributed queries aren't used for all the servers. Many servers are managed remotely using traditional system administration tools, such as Remote Desktop Connection (RDC), to remotely connect to the servers. However, they also use their fair share of distributed queries to access data.

Chapter 7 of this mini-book covers Service Broker. Service Broker can be used to create asynchronous communication "conversations" between servers. One server sends a message to a second server. The second server processes the message and sends an answer.

Even without reliable communications links, Service Broker can be used to provide reliable data transfer between servers.

Any time you need access to data that is located somewhere else, it makes sense to use a remote application rather than recreating the data on a local server. The hardest part is determining which method you'll use to access the data remotely.

Using Linked Servers

If you plan on querying an external data source more than a couple times, it makes sense to create a linked server. Creating the linked server does take some time and effort, but once created, you can refer to the data source on the remote server with a four-part name in Data Manipulation Language statements (such as SELECT, INSERT, UPDATE, and DELETE).

Creating and configuring a linked server is a two-step process:

1. **Create the linked server.**

The linked server identifies the details of the remote server, such as the name of the server and the provider to use when connecting.

2. **Create linked server logins.**

A login is a mapping between a login on the local server and a security account on the linked server.

It's easy to confuse the context of linked servers. You actually create a linked server object on a local server to connect to a remote server.

Let us say something obvious to avoid any confusion: When you create the linked server, you are not magically creating another physical server. Of course, that's ridiculous. Instead, the remote server already exists. By creating a linked server object in the local SQL Server, you are teaching SQL Server about the remote server.

Figure 6-2 shows the relationship between the local SQL Server, the remote server, and the linked server. It shows that you're creating the linked server object on the local SQL Server. The linked server object points to the remote server.

**Book IV
Chapter 6**

**Developing Remote
Applications**

SQL Server   Remote server

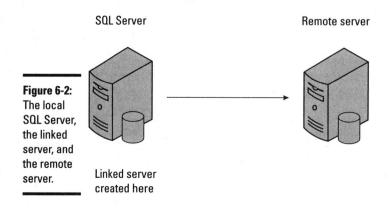

Figure 6-2:
The local
SQL Server,
the linked
server, and
the remote
server.

Linked server
created here

Creating a linked server

Linked servers can be created with the graphical user interface (GUI) in SQL Server Management Studio (SSMS) by using the `sp_addlinkedserver` system stored procedures.

The basic syntax of the `sp_addlinkedserver` system stored procedure is:

```
sp_addlinkedserver [ @server= ] 'server' [ , [
    @srvproduct= ] 'product_name' ]
        [ , [ @provider= ] 'provider_name' ]
        [ , [ @datasrc= ] 'data_source' ]
        [ , [ @location= ] 'location' ]
        [ , [ @provstr= ] 'provider_string' ]
        [ , [ @catalog= ] 'catalog' ]
```

The arguments for the stored procedure can be identified with a *variable = value* string (such as `@server = 'SQLSrv3'`). Or, if all arguments are being used, you can just enter the value and omit the variable name. However, if the variable name is omitted, you must enter values in the same order as the preceding syntax.

The only required argument is the server name. Other arguments have default values. While the arguments have the same name for any linked server, they have different values depending on the provider being used.

For example, when creating a linked server to SQL Server, the `@srvproduct` is SQL Server, and the `@provider` is SQLNCLI. When creating a linked server to an Oracle server, the `@srvproduct` can be anything, and the `@provider` is MSDAORA.

✦ **@server:** The @server argument holds the name of the linked server. @server is the only argument that can't be omitted.

✦ **@srvproduct:** @srvproduct holds the name of the product (such as SQL for a SQL Server, or Oracle for an Oracle server). The default is NULL. When SQL Server is specified, the rest of the arguments do not have to be provided.

✦ **@provider:** A unique programmatic identifier is entered into the @provider argument. The @provider argument corresponds to the @datasource argument. When SQLNCLI is used, SQL Server redirects to the most current version of SQL Server Native Client OLE DB provider.

✦ **@datasource:** The @datasource argument has different meanings depending on the provider. For example, for SQL Server, it can identify the server name or the server name and the instance. For Oracle, it can identify the actual database.

✦ **@location:** Some data providers require a location string (such as the location on a physical drive).

✦ **@provstr:** The provider string is entered into the @provstr argument. Different providers require different strings in this argument.

✦ **@catalog:** The @catalog argument means different things to different providers. For SQL Server, the @catalog argument identifies the default database that's used when the provider connects to the server.

For example, the following code could be used to create a linked server to a server named SQLSrv3:

```
USE master;
GO
EXEC sp_addlinkedserver
    @server = 'SQLSRV3',
    @srvProduct = N'SQL Server'
```

The name of the server (SQLSrv3) is included in the first argument, and the provider (SQL Server) is included in the second argument. The rest of the arguments are omitted. The N preceding the provider name identifies the string value as being stored as Unicode data and can be omitted if the characters are standard English characters.

Because the first two arguments are being used in the same order as the system stored procedure expects them, you can omit the name of the arguments. The following script will do just as well as the preceding script:

```
USE master;
GO
EXEC sp_addlinkedserver
    'SQLSRV3', 'SQL Server'
```

**Book IV
Chapter 6**

**Developing Remote
Applications**

As another example, the following code could be used to create a linked server to an Oracle server named OraSrv1 with a database named Sales.

```
USE master;
GO
EXEC sp_addlinkedserver
    @server = 'ORASRV1 ',
    @srvproduct = 'Oracle',
    @provider = 'MSDAORA',
    @catalog = 'Sales'
```

In this script, the name of the server is included as OraSrv1, the server product is included as Oracle, and the provider is MSDAORA. The MSDAORA provider expects the next argument to be the @catalog string.

If desired, this script can be rewritten without the argument names as follows:

```
USE master;
GO
EXEC sp_addlinkedserver
    'ORASRV1 ','Oracle',' MSDAORA', 'Sales'
```

Imagine that you have a SQL Server named SQLSrv3, an Oracle server named ORASRV1, and a need to configure both as linked servers. You can use the following steps to create the linked servers by using the GUI in SSMS and the sp_addlinkedserver system stored procedure.

1. **Launch SQL Server Management Studio.**

Choose Start➪All Programs➪Microsoft SQL Server 2008➪SQL Server Management Studio Center.

2. **Browse to the Linked Servers container within the Server Objects container in the SSMS Object Explorer.**

Your display looks similar to Figure 6-3. This shows where the Linked Servers container is and also shows that the Linked Servers container is currently empty except for the providers included with SQL Server.

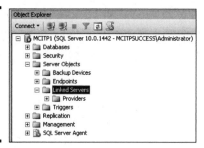

Figure 6-3: Viewing the Linked Servers container in SSMS's Object Explorer.

3. **Right-click the Linked Servers container and choose New Linked Server.**

4. **On the New Linked Server page, enter** SQLRV2 **in the Linked Server text box.**

   This is the actual host name of the server hosting the SQL Server database.

5. **Select SQL Server as the Server Type.**

   Because you've selected SQL Server as the server type, the default SQL Server provider (SQLNCLI10) will be used. Your display looks similar to Figure 6-4. The only two options that have been configured are the name of the linked server (SQLSRV2) and the server type (SQL Server).

Figure 6-4:
Creating a
linked
server using
the GUI.

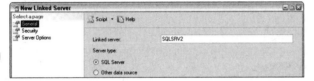

6. **Click OK to create the linked server.**

   As part of the creation process, SQL Server tries to connect to the linked server. Because the server doesn't exist, the connection test fails, and you receive an error stating:

   ```
   The linked server has been created but failed a
   connection test. Do you want to keep the linked server?
   ```

7. **On the Microsoft SQL Server Management Studio warning dialog box, click Yes to create the linked server despite the warning.**

   You've created the first linked server.

   It's also possible to create a linked server using the sp_addlinkedserver system stored procedure. Use the following steps to create a linked server named ORASRV1 by using a system stored procedure.

8. **Create a new query window by clicking the New Query button.**

9. **Enter the following query to create a linked server by using the sp_addlinkedserver system stored procedure:**

   ```
   USE master;
   GO
   EXEC sp_addlinkedserver
       'ORASRV1 ','Oracle',' MSDAORA', 'Sales'
   ```

10. **Press F5 to execute the system stored procedure.**

At this point, you've created both linked servers.

11. **Browse to the Linked Servers container in the SSMS Object Explorer.**

Your display looks similar to Figure 6-5. It shows two linked servers. SQLSRV2 was created with the GUI, and ORASRV1 was created with the system stored procedure.

Figure 6-5: Viewing the linked servers in the SSMS Object Explorer.

Creating logins for a linked server

With a linked server created, you can now create logins for the remote server. A *linked server login* maps a login on the local SQL Server with a security account on the remote server.

Logins can be created by using the GUI in SSMS or by using the sp_addlinkedsrvlogin system stored procedure.

The basic syntax of the sp_addlinkedsrvlogin is

```
sp_addlinkedsrvlogin [ @rmtsrvname = ] 'rmtsrvname'
      [ , [ @useself = ] 'TRUE' | 'FALSE' | 'NULL']
      [ , [ @locallogin = ] 'locallogin' ]
      [ , [ @rmtuser = ] 'rmtuser' ]
      [ , [ @rmtpassword = ] 'rmtpassword' ]
```

✦ **@rmtsrvname:** The remote server name identifies the name of the linked server where this login is applied. This argument must be supplied.

✦ **@useself:** By specifying true for the @useself argument, you don't need to add a local login name. Instead, the credentials for the user that is executing a command with the linked server is used. TRUE is the default. When FALSE is specified, the @locallogin must be specified. If @useself, @rmtuser, and @rmtpassword are all set to NULL (or not specified), then a login and password are not used to connect to the linked server.

✦ **@locallogin:** The `@locallogin` is used to specify a login account on the local SQL Server that's used to connect to the remote server. The login can be a SQL Server login, a Windows account, or a Windows group.

✦ **@rmtuser:** The `@rmtuser` identifies an account on the remote server that's used to connect to the remote server.

✦ **@rmtpassword:** The `@rmtpassword` identifies the password to be used with the `@rmtuser`.

Figure 6-6 shows how the login and user accounts interact. The user connects to the SQL Server that is the same place where you create the linked server object. When connecting to the remote server, the local login is used. The local login is mapped to the remote user account on the remote server.

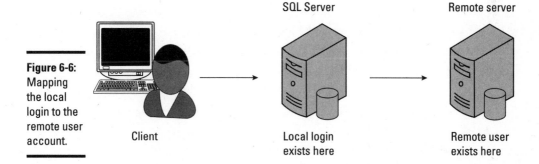

Figure 6-6: Mapping the local login to the remote user account.

Client — Local login exists here — Remote user exists here

SQL Server   Remote server

In the following steps, you create a SQL Server login. You then modify the linked server object that you created in the previous steps and map it to a fictitious remote account in the remote server.

1. **If not already open, launch SQL Server Management Studio.**

Choose Start➪All Programs➪Microsoft SQL Server 2008➪SQL Server Management Studio Center.

2. **Browse to the Security | Logins container in the SSMS Object Explorer.**

3. **Right-click Logins and choose New Login.**

4. **On the Login New page, enter** LnkSrvLogin **as the Login Name.**

5. **Select SQL Server Authentication.**

Although this step creates a SQL Server login, you could also use a Windows account or a Windows group.

6. **Enter** P@ssw0rd **in the Password and Confirm Password text boxes.**

7. **Clear the check box next to Enforce Password Policy.**

Your display looks similar to Figure 6-7. When the Enforce Password Policy box is cleared, the other password policy selections are dimmed. For security purposes, you should still use strong passwords and regularly change them.

Figure 6-7:
Creating a
SQL Server
login.

8. **Click OK to create the SQL Server login.**

9. **Browse to the Server Objects | Linked Servers container in the SSMS Object Explorer.**

10. **Right-click the SQLSRV2 linked server and choose Properties.**

11. **At the top left of the Linked Server Properties page, select the Security page.**

12. **Click the Add button to add a local server login.**

13. **Click the empty box under Local Login. Enter** LnkSrvLogin **as the name of the local server login you just created.**

14. **Click the empty box under Remote User and enter** RmtUser. **Click the empty box under Remote Password and enter** P@ssw0rd.

These entries assume that the remote server has an account named RmtUser with a password of P@ssw0rd. In practice, you'd use an actual account that was created on the remote server for this purpose.

Your display looks similar to Figure 6-8. This mapping causes the LnkSrvLogin from the local system to be used for the linked server. When connecting to the remote server, the RmtUser account (and its related permissions) on the remote server is used.

Figure 6-8:
Mapping
the local
login to the
remote
account.

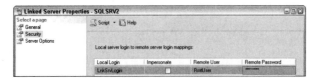

15. **Click OK.**

You get a warning reading the linked server has been updated but failed the connection test and asking if you want to edit the linked server properties. Click No.

Remember, you're mapping a login to a fictitious account on a fictitious server. If you have unlimited money, you can create another SQL Server to actually connect to in your test environment. The previous connection step would then succeed.

Querying data from a linked server

With the linked server created and mappings added, you can now create queries by using the linked server.

Using a linked server is significantly easier than using the OPENDATASOURCE or OPENROWSET functions. While creating the linked server does take some time, you create a linked server only once.

After the linked server is created, you can use a four-part name to access the linked server. With OPENDATASOURCE and OPENROWSET functions, you have to enter the syntax each time you use the function.

Imagine that you've created a linked server and login mappings for a server named SQLSRV2. Now you want to query a view named vwEmployees in the default schema (dbo) of the Sales database. The following query can be used:

```
SELECT * from SQLSRV2.Sales.dbo.vwEmployees
```

As long as the remote user account has permissions, you can use any SELECT, INSERT, UPDATE, or DELETE statement against any object in the remote server.

Chapter 7: Advanced Development Topics

In This Chapter

✔ **Better messaging through SQL Server Service Broker**

✔ **Automating administration with SQL Server Management Objects**

✔ **Integrated application development with the .NET Framework (CLR)**

*A*fter you master the basics of programming in SQL Server 2008, you might want to spread your wings and take on some of the more advanced development topics. In this chapter, we take a look at the possibilities you can achieve with the following advanced tools:

✦ **Service Broker** provides you with some sophisticated messaging without all the messy development work to manage messaging.

✦ **SQL Server Management Objects (SMO)** can be used to automate many of the administration tasks.

✦ **CLR integrated objects** (such as triggers and stored procedures) allow you to take advantage of the strengths of managed code by using any .NET programming language within SQL Server.

Better Messaging through SQL Server Service Broker

In days of yore (well, maybe only a few years ago), many database administrators and database developers yearned for databases that could talk to each other. Developers wanted one database to query another and, based on the response, take some specific action.

Because that capability didn't exist, developers wrote their own programs but still wished for databases that could talk to each other without requiring so much work on the developer's part.

With the release of SQL Server 2005, Microsoft released SQL Server Service Broker that filled this need. SQL Server 2008 includes some minor improvements of Service Broker.

Service Broker is a messaging service that is integrated into SQL Server. It allows database applications to easily exchange messages in a simple one-way conversation or a complex two-way dialog composed of as many messages as needed.

The two most important benefits of Service Broker are

✦ **Asynchronous messages:** As soon as a message is sent to Service Broker, the database can consider the task done and move on to other things. For example, you might want a stored procedure to send a message in the middle of a couple other processes. The message can be sent to Service Broker, and then the stored procedure can move directly onto the rest of the processes. With synchronous messaging, the stored procedure wouldn't be able to continue until the message was actually sent. With Service Broker's asynchronous messaging capability, the stored procedure doesn't need to wait until the message is actually sent before completing its work.

✦ **Guaranteed delivery:** Service Broker guarantees that messages will be delivered. More, it ensures the messages will be delivered only once and in the proper order. Even if a destination database has been taken offline temporarily or the network infrastructure has problems, you're still assured that the message (or messages) will be delivered when everything is working again.

Understanding the Service Broker elements

Service Broker includes several components that interact with each other. Take a look at Figure 7-1 as you review the following component definitions. By creating the different components, you define how the Service Broker service communicates with other Service Broker services.

✦ **Contract:** Just like a contract in the real world is an agreement between two entities, a *Service Broker contract* is an agreement between two Service Broker services. It defines the message sent between the databases, who sends the message (the initiator), and who receives the message (the target). Any contract can be used by more than one service.

✦ **Service:** A *Service Broker service* is composed of one or more steps in a defined process. Each service can have one or more contracts with each contract representing a specific task. Any service can have one or more contracts.

✦ **Queue:** *Queues* are used to accept messages for Service Broker services. Any service will have a single queue. Messages placed in a queue can be retrieved using the RECEIVE command. For example, a stored procedure could read the message and then perform some activity based on the content.

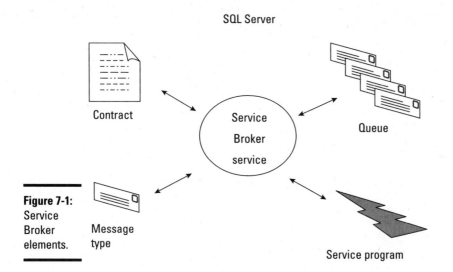

SQL Server

Figure 7-1:
Service
Broker
elements.

Contract

Service
Broker
service

Queue

Message
type

Service program

✦ **Message type:** Messages hold the information used in the conversation and can be composed of different data types. You can think of the message type as defining the language used in the conversation. Two common types of messages are well-formed XML, and typed or valid XML (conforming to a schema). Messages can also be binary (allowing just about any desired file type) or empty.

✦ **Service program or service application:** The service application provides the logic for the Service Broker service. It can be an external stored procedure (such as a .NET application) or an internal stored procedure.

Service Broker applications communicate through conversations. In the real world, a conversation is when two people communicate. One person sends a message. Another person receives the message and replies.

Within Service Broker, a *conversation* is a reliable asynchronous exchange of messages using a contract, queue, and service. In short, Service Broker conversations are created from sending and receiving messages.

You can see this in Figure 7-2. Two separate databases each have a defined Service Broker service. The services are able to send and receive messages between each other, effectively creating a two-way conversation.

The messages sent between two Service Broker applications can be one-way or two-way.

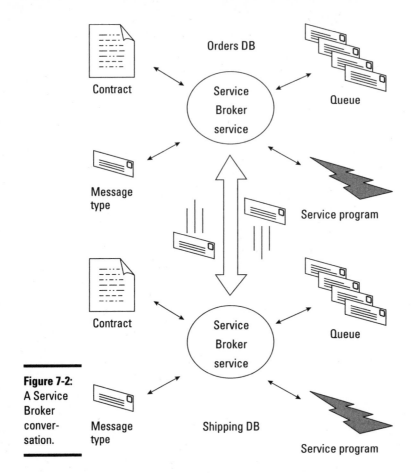

Figure 7-2:
A Service
Broker
conver-
sation.

In a one-way conversation, an application sends messages to another application. Think of this as someone leaving a message on your answering machine to remind you of an appointment. No reply is required.

A two-way conversation can be simple (a query and a response) or complex (several messages passed back and forth). For example, an Orders database could send a message to a Shipping database saying an order has been received and confirmed. The Shipping database could respond with a confirmation indicating the order is being processed and another message later when the order actually ships.

Service Broker can be configured to automatically launch the service program when a message is in queue, or the program can be configured to periodically check the queue for messages. Service Broker is flexible enough to work with different business needs.

Enabling Service Broker

Microsoft has gotten into the admirable habit of developing secure applications. It hasn't always been this way, but a few years ago, they adopted the mantra of SD^3+C, commonly known as

✦ Secure by Design

✦ Secure by Default

✦ Secure in Deployment and Communications

What this means within SQL Server is that anything that might be a security vulnerability is disabled by default. The SQL Server administrator must then enable certain functions before they can work — including Service Broker.

The Trustworthy database property affects much more than just Service Broker. It indicates that the SQL Server instance trusts the database to access resources beyond the scope of the database. For example, this property would be changed to allow the use of CLR integrated objects (programs integrated with a .NET assembly).

You can view the current state of the Trustworthy property by right-clicking the database, selecting Properties, and then selecting Options in the left pane. On the Options page, scroll to the Trustworthy property. As shown in Figure 7-3, the Trustworthy property is `True`, indicating it's been enabled. However, the property is dimmed — it can be viewed from the Options page but not changed from there.

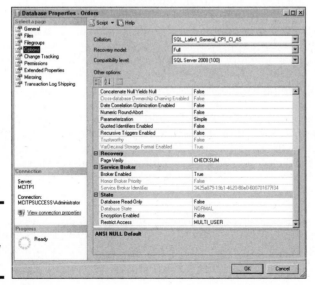

Figure 7-3: Viewing the Trustworthy property.

To modify the Trustworthy database property, you set it to ON. Yes, the Trustworthy database property shows `True` when you turn it on. You might be asking yourself, "Which is it, true or on?" Although the property is displayed as `True` in the Database Properties page, you can't change it here. You can only view it. If you try to set it to `True` (instead of ON), the T-SQL statement fails, and a syntax error occurs. The syntax to set the Trustworthy property to ON is

```
ALTER DATABASE database name
SET TRUSTWORTHY ON;
```

Using Service Broker

To create a Service Broker application, you must take the following high-level steps:

1. Enable Service Broker in the databases that use Service Broker. This is done by setting the Trustworthy property to ON.

2. Create Service Broker message types. The message type will have a name and a data type (such as well-formed XML).

3. Create Service Broker contracts. The contract includes the message types that will be used (identified by the name), the initiator (who sends the message), and the target (who receives the message).

4. Create Service Broker queues. The queue name and the status (OFF or ON) are specified. The queue holds the messages until they are retrieved.

5. Create the Service Broker service. The Service Broker service identifies the queue to be used and the contract.

After Service Broker is enabled and created, you can then use it to create a conversation between two databases. As an example, consider an Orders database and an Inventory database. The Orders database is used to accept and process orders, and the Inventory database is used to manage the inventory and the shipping details.

It's certainly reasonable that you would want the Orders and Inventory databases to talk to each other. For example, you might want the Orders database to query the Inventory database to determine whether a product is available. The Inventory database could respond with a specific location, as shown in Figure 7-4.

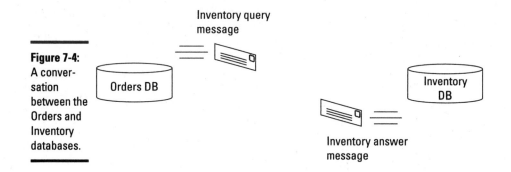

Inventory query
message

Figure 7-4:
A conver-
sation
between the
Orders and
Inventory
databases.

Orders DB

Inventory
DB

Inventory answer
message

Other uses and benefits of Service Broker include the following:

✦ **Asynchronous programming:** Consider the following scenario. You want
to create a trigger that will send a message to another database when
the on-hand inventory level of any product reaches a certain threshold.
If you program the trigger to send the message without Service Broker
and the message is held up, the trigger won't complete until the message
is sent. Until the trigger completes, locks on the data associated with the
trigger will prevent the data from being accessed by any other processes
in your database. This might result in significant delays.

Comparatively, if you use Service Broker to send the message, as soon
as the message is sent to Service Broker, the trigger considers it complete. The transaction associated with the trigger is complete, any locks
are released, and Service Broker guarantees delivery.

✦ **Detailed conversations with messages in a specific order:** Some applications require messages to be sent back and forth and depending on
the answer to one query, another query might be sent. For example, an
application might query the existence of a product that meets specific
characteristics (such as *tricycle* and *red*). The answer might include a list
of products with product IDs. The next query might request quantities
or locations of the product. Instead of an external application managing
these queries, Service Broker can be programmed to ensure that each
part of the conversation is executed in the proper order.

With Service Broker, the conversation can be as long and detailed as the
application requires. Service Broker guarantees the developer delivery
of each message in the proper order.

✦ **Sophisticated messaging without lengthy development time:** In the
past, developers were often forced to create their own messaging applications, which could take a significant amount of time. Service Broker
provides complex messaging within a database without the complex
programming.

Automating Administration with SQL Server Management Objects

SQL Server Management Objects (SMO) can be used to provide management of SQL Server with applications outside of SQL Server. In other words, they're designed to manage and access SQL Server beyond the capabilities of SQL Server Management Studio (SSMS).

SMO objects are built in to the Microsoft .NET Framework. Different name-spaces provide different capabilities.

In past versions of SQL Server, SQL Distributed Management Objects (SQL-DMO) were used to provide some of the functionality of SMO. SQL-DMO used a COM object model and was deprecated in SQL Server 2005. SMO is a .NET assembly and supersedes SQL-DMO in SQL Server 2008.

Some of the common database administration tasks that SMO objects can be used to do include

✦ **Backups and restores:** Many third-party tools use SQL Server Management Objects to simplify common backup and restore tasks.

✦ **Index maintenance:** In addition to traditional index maintenance, you can also manage index table partitioning. With partitioning you can opti-mize the performance of the database by dividing data from a large index or table so that the data is stored on more than one physical disk.

✦ **Integrity checks:** The Database Base Console Command (DBCC) includes many commands, such as CHECKDB, that can be periodically executed against a database to ensure the logical and physical integrity of the database including all database objects.

SMO can also be used to manage replication (by using Replication Manage-ment Objects, or RMO), SQL Server Agent, Database Mail, Service Broker, and more.

An important point to realize with SMO is that you can do the same tasks within SSMS as you can do with applications developed using SMO. Depending on your budget and application development expertise, you can choose any of the following methods to perform the same tasks.

✦ **Using SSMS:** Often, tasks (such as backup and restore) can be accom-plished by using either T-SQL statements or pointing and clicking within the SSMS graphical user interface. Obviously, using SSMS is cost-effective. However, it might require you providing more training to some adminis-trators who aren't familiar with SSMS.

✦ **Creating your own SMO application:** If you're a developer, you can create applications that automate specific administration tasks that are needed in your environment. The tasks can be as complex as you desire; your application can make launching the task as simple as clicking a button.

✦ **Purchasing a third-party application that uses SMO:** A wealth of third-party applications have popped up to support all the recent SQL Server versions. The most common applications help administrators automate backup and restore operations, but some are much more sophisticated.

Installing SMO

SMO is installed automatically when SQL Server is installed on a system. If you want to develop an SMO application on a system that doesn't have SQL Server installed, you can install the SQL Server client tools. All the SMO assemblies are automatically installed in the following directory:

```
C:\Program Files\Microsoft SQL Server\100\SDK\Assemblies\
```

Tools used to create an SMO application

Several development tools can be used to create your own SMO application. However, it's important to realize that the SMO program is a compiled application. Within Microsoft's family, the logical choice is to use Visual Studio.

Visual Studio is a full-featured development tool that you can use to create applications with any of the .NET applications, such as Visual Basic or C#. Microsoft also includes slimmed down products, such as products for some languages.

For example, you can download free Express Editions of Visual Basic 2008, Visual C# 2008, and Visual C++. Although Express Editions don't have the full functionality of Visual Studio, they often have enough capabilities to satisfy many people.

**Book IV
Chapter 7**

**Advanced
Development Topics**

To download the Visual Studio Express Editions, search on the Internet for *Download Visual Studio 2008 Express*. You can install the edition of your choice from the Web, or download the entire ISO image and burn it to DVD. No product keys are required. And, Express Editions are free!

Creating a simple SMO application

Remember, just about anything you can do with T-SQL statements, you can also program into an SMO application. However, the syntax isn't the same.

When creating an SMO application that issues commands against a database, you create a database object that references the actual database. This SMO database object then has several methods that can be executed against the database.

For example, if you want to execute the DBCC CheckDB command against a database using SMO, you connect to the server, identify the database, and then use the following syntax:

```
myOutput = db.CheckTablesDataOnly()
```

In this example, CheckTablesDataOnly() is a method in the SMO database object that mimics the functionality of the DBCC CheckDB command. If you're using a query window in the SQL Server Management Studio, you enter the following command:

```
DDBCC CheckDB(Master)
```

To create a simple SMO application, we downloaded and installed the Microsoft Visual Basic 2008 Express edition. If you download and install it on your system, you can follow these steps to create a simple SMO application that checks the integrity of the Master database and outputs the results:

1. **Launch Microsoft Visual Basic 2008 Express Edition.**

   Choose Start⇨All Programs⇨Microsoft Visual Basic 2008 Express Edition.

2. **Create a new project.**

   Choose File⇨New Project.

3. **In the New Project window, ensure Windows Forms Application is selected. Enter** SMO **as the Name and click OK.**

4. **Select the form. Change the value of Text from** Form1 **to** Easy SQL Admin.

5. **Drag a button onto the form from the Toolbox. Rename the button** btnCheck **and change the text of the button to** Check.

6. **Drag a text box onto the form from the Toolbox. Rename the text box** txtOutput. **Change the value of Multiline to** True. **Change the value of Scrollbars to** Vertical. **Resize the text box so that if fills the form.**

7. **On the right side of the window is the Solution Explorer. Change the name of** Form1.vb **to** AdminTasks.vb.

8. **Right-click SMO and select Add Reference. Scroll down and select Microsoft.SqlServer.SMO (Version 10.0.0.0 for SQL Server 2008).**

This adds the SQL Server Management Objects for SQL Server 2008. Your display looks similar to Figure 7-5. If you want to manage SQL Server 2005, you select the version that starts with 9 (shown as 9.0.242.0 in the figure).

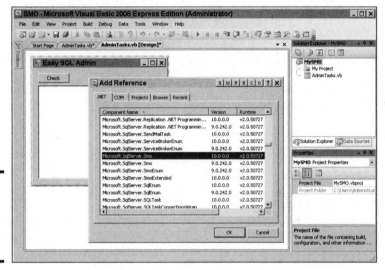

Figure 7-5: Adding references to the SMO project.

9. **Repeat the previous step to add the following references.**

You can use the Ctrl key to add multiple references at the same time.

```
Microsoft.SqlServer.ConnectionInfo.dll
Microsoft.SqlServer.Smo.dll
Microsoft.SqlServer.SmoEnum.dll
Microsoft.SqlServer.SqlEnum.dll
Microsoft.SqlServer.WmiEnum.dll
```

10. **Double-click the Check button on the form to access the underlying code. Add the following Imports lines as the very first and second lines above the `Public Class` statement:**

```
Imports Microsoft.SqlServer.Management.Smo
Imports Microsoft.SqlServer.Management.Common
```

11. **Enter the following code in the `btnCheck` event.**

```
'Connect to server
Dim Srv As Server
Srv = New Server

'Identify database that will be checked
Dim db As Database
```

**Book IV
Chapter 7**

**Advanced
Development Topics**

```
        db = Srv.Databases("Master")

        'Run DBCC CheckDB equivalent SMO command on
Master Database
        ' and collect the results in a string
collection
        Dim sc As Specialized.StringCollection
        sc = db.CheckTablesDataOnly()

        'Output results from string collection to text
box
        For i As Integer = 0 To (sc.Count - 1)
            If sc(i).Length > 0 Then
                txtOutput.Text = txtOutput.Text &
CStr(sc(i)) & vbCrLf
            End If
        Next
```

12. **Press F5 to run your program.**

13. **Click the Check button.**

> After a moment, the DBCC CheckDB command completes, and the results are output to the text box. Your display looks similar to Figure 7-6. Notice that the DBCC CheckDB command has a lot of output. I've scrolled to the bottom of the check box.

Figure 7-6:
Running
your SMO
program.

Obviously, a lot can be done to improve the usability and appearance of this program, but it does show the basics of connecting to a database and running a basic check. You could add the ability to select different databases to check from a drop-down box, and allow the user to select specifically what checks to run. You could even add the ability to create schedules so that when the database administrator identifies what he wants to do, the program automatically runs on a regular basis.

Integrated Application Development with the .NET Framework

Although you can do a lot using Transact-SQL, T-SQL isn't a full-featured development language. You might want your database application to do more complex operations than what T-SQL can do alone.

Therefore, you can create an assembly with a .NET language, such as Visual Basic or C#, and then integrate the assembly into a database object. This is referred to as *using managed code*.

A CLR integrated object is one that is using an external assembly. An *assembly* is a compiled Dynamic Link Library (DLL). The following database objects can be CLR integrated:

✦ Stored procedures

✦ Triggers

✦ User-defined functions

✦ User-defined types

✦ User-defined aggregates

CLR objects excel in the following situations:

✦ **String comparisons and manipulation:** For example, if you need to check to see whether a valid e-mail address is entered, you wouldn't be able to easily by using only T-SQL. An e-mail address may look like name@place.com. You need to check for one or more text characters, the @ symbol, one or more characters ending with a period, and a valid top-level domain, such as com or net. However, by using a high-level language, such as Visual Basic or C#, this could be reduced to a relatively simple string comparison.

✦ **Complex calculations:** Although T-SQL includes access to many built-in functions, managed code provides access to the full .NET Framework Library. The capabilities within the .Net Framework Library combined with the ease of use provided by a full-featured language streamline your ability to perform complex calculations with any CLR integrated objects.

Enabling CLR integration

Since the programming possibilities are endless when creating any assembly, it's also possible for malicious assemblies to be integrated into a database. By default, CLR integrated assemblies are not allowed, and it takes an administrator to enable CLR integration in a database.

To enable CLR integration, you change the value of `'clr enabled'` from a 0 to a 1. However, before this can be done, you have to enable the ability to view and modify advanced options.

The following code shows how to enable CLR integration on a database:

```
sp_configure 'show advanced options', 1;
GO
RECONFIGURE;
GO
sp_configure 'clr enabled', 1;
GO
RECONFIGURE;
```

Creating a CLR integrated stored procedure

The high-level steps required to create CLR integrated objects are

1. Enable CLR integration in your database.

2. Use a .NET language to create a Dynamic Link Library (.DLL) assembly.

3. Register the assembly in SQL Server.

4. Create a SQL object (such as a stored procedure or function) that uses the assembly.

You might remember that CLR integrated objects were covered in Book IV, Chapter 2. If you want to see the detailed steps needed to create a CLR integrated function, review that chapter.

The following steps show how to create a CLR integrated stored procedure.

1. **Launch SQL Server Management Studio (SSMS).**

Choose Start⇨All Programs⇨Microsoft SQL Server 2008⇨SQL Server Management Studio.

2. **Create a new query window by clicking the New Query button.**

3. **Enter and execute (by pressing F5) the following code to create a database named CLRTest and enable CLR integration in the database:**

```
USE Master;
GO
CREATE DATABASE CLRTest;
GO
sp_configure 'show advanced options', 1;
GO
RECONFIGURE;
GO
```

```
sp_configure 'clr enabled', 1;
GO
RECONFIGURE;
```

4. **Launch Windows Explorer by pressing the Windows key and the E key at the same time.**

5. **Browse to the root of C:\ and create a folder named CLR. Browse to the C:\CLR folder.**

6. **Right-click the C:\CLR folder and choose New⇨Text Document. Double-click the text document to open it in Notepad.**

Instead of using Notepad, you can create the assembly in Visual Studio or one of the free Visual Studio Express Editions. For example, if you downloaded and installed Visual Basic Express Edition to create a simple SMO application in the previous section, you can use it instead of Notepad. Downloading and installing Visual Basic Express takes some time, but it makes entering code a lot easier.

7. **Enter the following code in Notepad (or Visual Studio if you have it):**

```
Imports System
Imports System.Data
Imports Microsoft.SqlServer.Server
Imports System.Data.SqlTypes
Public Class myCLR
    <Microsoft.SqlServer.Server.SqlProcedure()> _
    Public Shared Sub HappyHappy()
        Dim strWeekDay As String =
WeekdayName(Weekday(Today()))
        SqlContext.Pipe.Send _
            ("Ren and Stimpy say: Happy " & strWeekDay
    & "!" )
    End Sub
End Class
```

This code includes one class named myCLR and one subroutine named HappyHappy. When the subroutine is called, it determines the name of today's date (such as Monday or Tuesday) and returns a string that includes the name.

8. **Choose File⇨Save As. In the File Name box, enter "HappyHappy.vb" (including the quotes) and click Save.**

By using the quotes around the name, you ensure the file is saved as a .vb file and not as a .txt file. If it's saved as a .txt file, it won't compile in the following steps.

9. **Press the Windows key and the R key at the same time to access the Run line. Enter cmd to launch the command line.**

10. **At the command line, enter the following two commands to change to the directory holding the Visual Basic compiler that compiles your assembly:**

```
CD c:\Windows\Microsoft.NET\Framework\v2.0.50727
vbc /target:library c:\CLR\HappyHappy.vb
```

Visual Basic compiles the program and creates a file named `HappyHappy.dll`

11. **Return to the query window in SSMS. Enter and execute (by pressing F5) the following code to create an assembly in the CLRTest database that you created earlier:**

```
USE CLRTest;
GO
CREATE ASSEMBLY CLR_Happy
FROM 'c:\CLR\HappyHappy.dll'
```

At this point, you've added the assembly to your database, but nothing is using it. In the next few steps, you create a stored procedure to access the assembly.

12. **Using the SSMS Object Explorer, browse to the CLR_Happy assembly located in the Databases | CLRTest | Programmability | Assemblies container.**

Your display looks similar to Figure 7-7. The assembly is named CLR_ Happy, but you can't determine from here what's actually inside the DLL file. In other words, just because someone knows the name of the assembly doesn't mean he can use it. The names of the class and the subroutines are also needed.

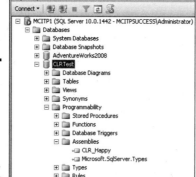

Figure 7-7:
Viewing your assembly in SQL Server Management Studio.

13. **Enter and execute (br pressing F5) the following code to create a stored procedure that uses your assembly:**

```
CREATE PROCEDURE uspMyCLR
AS
EXTERNAL NAME
   CLR_Happy.myCLR.HappyHappy;
```

The external name is expressed as assembly (that was added to SQL Server), the class is within the DLL file, and the subroutine is within the class. It's possible your assembly has multiple subroutines within the class and even multiple classes.

14. **Execute your stored procedure with the following code and pressing F5:**

```
EXEC uspMyCLR
```

Darril executed this on a Saturday, and the output was

```
Ren and Stimpy say: Happy Saturday!
```

Book V

Reporting Services

The 5th Wave   By Rich Tennant

"It's a solid ID management and tracking system, Ted. Over 15 years on the Kalahari and we never lost a single lion."

Contents at a Glance

Chapter 1: Introduction to SQL Server Reporting Services

In This Chapter

✔ **What Reporting Services provides to you and your users**

✔ **Understanding Reporting Services components**

✔ **Installing Reporting Services**

Reporting Services has come a long way since it was first introduced in 2004 as an add-on to SQL Server 2000. Back in those days, many people (your authors included) were using tools like Microsoft Access or Crystal Reports to pull data out of SQL Server and present it in a meaningful way.

Today, with Reporting Services, you can create reports and have them served from a report server as Web pages accessible to anyone with a Web browser (which is just about everyone these days).

For your sophisticated users, you can create report models and let them turn their creative juices loose and create their own reports. Of course, this leaves database developers like you free to do more important things, like . . . well, you fill in the blank there. We'll be playing more games.

What Reporting Services Provides to You and Your Users

SQL Server Reporting Services (SSRS) is a server-based tool used to provide end users with data reports that are derived from SQL Server databases. SSRS has been around for several years. It first appeared in 2004 and worked with SQL Server 2000. It was improved in SQL Server 2005 and improved even more in SQL Server 2008.

Figure 1-1 shows a typical configuration using SSRS. A server is configured as a report server, and reports are created and published to the SSRS server. When a user wants to view a report, he can use Internet Explorer (or some other Web browser) to send an HTTP request. The data for the report is retrieved from the SQL Server; the report is formatted and returned to the user as an HTML page.

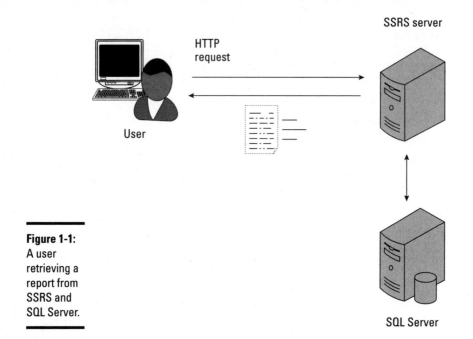

Figure 1-1:
A user
retrieving a
report from
SSRS and
SQL Server.

It's also possible to configure the SQL Server as an SSRS server. In other words, instead of having two servers, you could have only one. It depends on the load and the capabilities of the servers.

One of the great benefits of SSRS is that the reports become dynamic. A database developer can create the reports and publish them to the server once. When a user retrieves the data from the SSRS server, it retrieves data that is up-to-date. Users have the capability of running the reports when they need, and the data is accurate up to the moment it's updated.

Reports can also be configured to accept parameters. For example, managers might want to retrieve sales information from different stores, different sales people, and even different dates. By adding parameters, you can develop reports that change what's displayed based on what a user requests.

Figure 1-2 shows a sample report that accepts parameters. The report will show a year's worth of data ending in the month and year selected. December 2003 is selected, and a drop-down box is used to select an employee, David Campbell.

Figure 1-2:
Selecting
parameters
for a report.

With the employee selected, the report is generated. Figure 1-3 shows part of the report. As you can see, reports don't have to be boring. You can add graphics, charts, and more to spice them up to meet the needs of the audience.

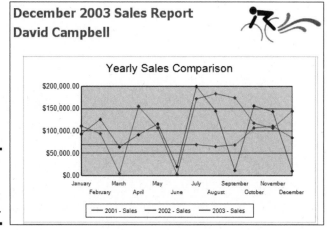

Figure 1-3:
A sample
employee
sales report.

Understanding Reporting Services Components

SQL Server Reporting Services (SSRS) has several components that are intertwined like a big jigsaw puzzle. Before getting too far, it's best to have an understanding of all the pieces of the SSRS puzzle.

Reports can be created by a developer or by an end user.

✦ **Reports created by developers:** These reports are created in the Business Intelligence Development Studio (BIDS) as a report server project. Figure 1-4 shows the process of building a report using the Report Designer in BIDS. All the details of the report are specified in the Report Designer. The Report Designer specifies the data source, query, filters, and specifically how the report is displayed. After the report is published to the SSRS server, end users only need to query these reports to retrieve the data. The Report Designer is explored in greater depth in Chapter 3 of this mini-book.

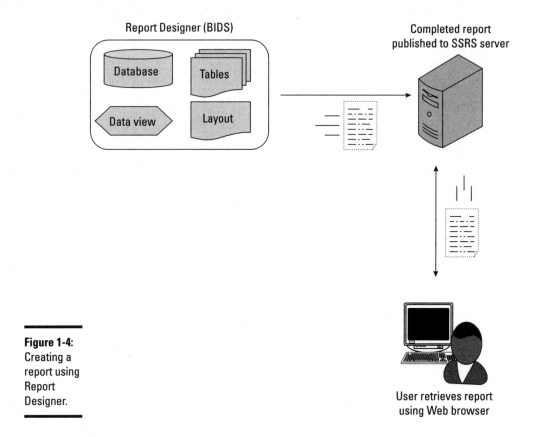

Report Designer (BIDS)

Completed report
published to SSRS server

Database

Tables

Data view

Layout

Figure 1-4:
Creating a
report using
Report
Designer.

User retrieves report
using Web browser

✦ **Reports created by end users:** A report model project is first created in BIDS by a database developer. Figure 1-5 shows the process of building a report from a report model. The developer creates a report model that works like a blueprint; the data source is specified, which identifies what data can be displayed. However, just as you can't live in a blueprint of a house, you can't view a report with a report model. Instead, users use the report model to create their own reports using the Report Builder. After a report is built from the report model, it can be published to the SSRS and server. Report models and the Report Builder are explored in greater depth in Chapter 2 of this mini-book.

The different elements that can be used to create reports are:

✦ **Business Intelligence Development Studio (BIDS):** BIDS is used to create projects used for Reporting Services. It uses the same interface as Visual Studio but is only used for Business Intelligence projects, such as SQL Server Reporting Services or SQL Server Analysis Services projects. Both complete reports (by using the Report Designer) and report models can be created in BIDS.

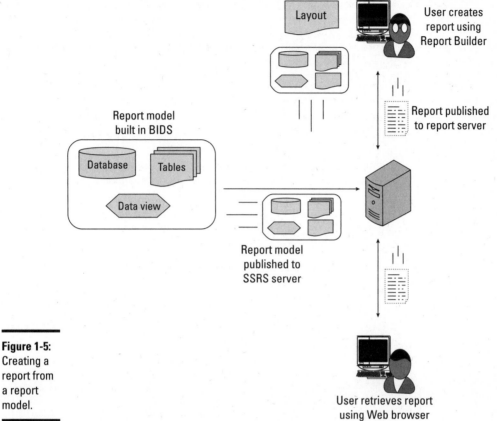

Figure 1-5:
Creating a
report from
a report
model.

+ **Report model:** The report model identifies the data source and the data view used to create a report. A report model won't actually display any data in a report, but instead identifies the data that can be added to a report. As an example, the report model may include the AdventureWorks database as the data source and the Person.Contact and HumanResources.Employee tables as the data view. A user can then choose any columns within the two tables to include in his report by using the Report Builder tool.

+ **Report Builder:** The Report Builder is used to create reports from a report model or from published data sources. The Report Builder is launched from the SSRS Web site that has a report model. When reports are created, they're available to users via the Report Manager.

+ **Report Builder 2.0:** The Report Builder 2.0 is a free download that functions as a stand-alone report creation tool. Users that can access data sources can create their own reports with this tool.

✦ **Report Manager:** The Report Manager is a Web interface served by the Reporting Services Web server and is the primary interface for reports. Any data source, report model, or reports that are published to the SSRS server are available via the Report Manager. Users can launch the Report Builder from the Report Manager.

✦ **Report server:** The report server is the Web server that serves reports as Web pages. The server hosts any published reports, report models, and data sources.

✦ **Model Designer:** The Model Designer is the tool used to create report models within a report model project. The Model Designer doesn't create actual reports; instead, it specifies the data source and data view that can be used to create a report within the Report Builder.

✦ **Report Designer:** The Report Designer is available in a BIDS report project. The Report Designer is used to create fully functional reports that can be viewed by end users when the report is published to a report server.

✦ **Reporting Services Configuration:** The Reporting Services Configuration tool is used to configure a Reporting Services installation. It can be used to configure both a local or remote report server instance. Figure 1-6 shows the Reporting Services Configuration Manager. After Reporting Services is installed, this tool can be accessed to manipulate many of the Reporting Services properties.

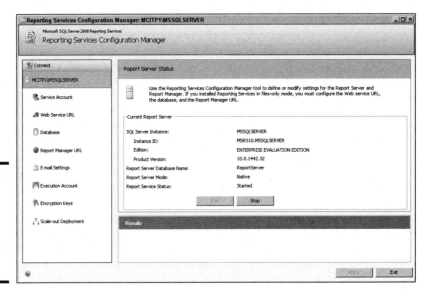

Figure 1-6:
The Reporting Services Configuration Manager.

Planning a deployment mode for SSRS

SQL Server 2008 supports two modes of deployment for a report server:

✦ **Native mode:** In Native mode, the report server runs as an application server and provides all processing and management capability only through Reporting Services components.

✦ **SharePoint Integrated mode:** In SharePoint Integrated mode, the report server is deployed as part of SharePoint. SharePoint provides much of the processing and management of the report server.

The report server can be in Native mode, or SharePoint Integrated mode, but not both at the same time. You can change modes on a deployed server after installation by using the Reporting Services Configuration Manager.

Using Native mode

When deployed in Native mode, a report server is a stand-alone application that performs all the work for reporting. This includes viewing reports, managing reports, processing reports, and delivering reports.

Native mode is the default mode when deploying a report server instance.

When the report server is deployed via Native mode, the URL for the Reporting Services Web server is `http://servername/ReportServer`.

✦ **Default Instance URL:**

> `http://servername/ReportServer`

For example, if the servername is SSRS, the URL will be:

> `http://ssrs/ReportServer`

✦ **Named Instance URL:**

> `http://servername/ReportServer_instancename`

For example, if the servername is SSRS and the named instance is SQL08, the URL will be:

> `http://ssrs/ReportServer_SQL08`

The well-known port for HTTP is 80. Normally, when you use HTTP, you don't include port 80 because port 80 is assumed. On most installations of SQL Server 2008, port 80 is used (unless IIS is installed). If you install it on Windows XP SP2, it will default to port 8080, and you'll need to include it in the address. For example, if your Windows XP system was named SQLXP, the address would be:

`http://SQLXP:8080/ReportServer`

Using SharePoint Integrated mode

When deployed in SharePoint Integrated mode, the report server is part of the SharePoint application. SharePoint manages all the content and operations of the report server.

To use SharePoint Integrated mode, you must be using Windows SharePoint Services version 3.0 or greater, or Office SharePoint Server 2007 or greater.

The URL used to access the report server is dependent on the configuration of either the Windows SharePoint services or the SharePoint server.

Installing Reporting Services

Use the following steps to install the default instance of SQL Server 2008 with Reporting Services in Native mode. This will result in a server with both SQL Server 2008 and Reporting Services installed.

1. **Launch the SQL Server installation program.**

Insert the DVD you used to originally install SQL Server 2008. If autoplay doesn't launch the program automatically, browse to the root directory and double-click the setup program.

2. **If the SQL Server setup program detects that you don't have the required Microsoft .NET Framework version or an updated Windows Installer version, it will prompt you to install them. Click OK to begin the installation.**

After the installation of the required components completes, the installation of SQL Server continues.

3. **On the SQL Server Installation Center page, click the Installation link.**

4. **Select New SQL Server Stand-Alone Installation or Add Features to and Existing Installation.**

5. **The Setup Support Rules page appears and runs some basic checks to see whether your system is ready to install SQL Server. If actions are needed (such as a reboot), follow the onscreen instructions. Click OK after the checks are complete.**

6. **The Setup Support Files page appears. Click Install.**

This will take some time as several support files are installed before the actual installation of SQL Server.

7. **The Setup Support Rules page appears again and runs some more advanced checks. After the checks complete, review the information and click Next.**

8. **On the Product Key page, either enter the product key or specify Enterprise Evaluation as the free edition. Click Next.**

9. **On the License Terms page, review the license, select the check box next to I Accept the License Terms, and then click Next.**

10. **On the Feature Selection page, select Database Engine Services and Reporting Services in the Instance Features section. In the Shared Features section, select Business Intelligence Development Studio, Client Tools Connectivity, SQL Server Books Online, Management Tools - Basic, and Management Tools - Complete.**

Your display looks similar to Figure 1-7.

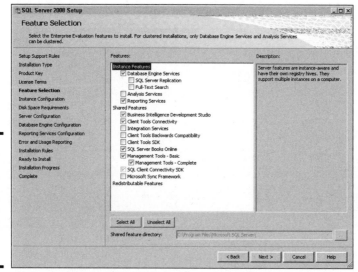

Figure 1-7:
Instance
features
selected to
install SQL
Server with
Reporting
Services.

11. **On the Feature Selection page, click Next.**

12. **On the Instance Configuration page, ensure Default Instance is selected, and click OK.**

13. **On the Disk Space requirements page, review the information and then click Next.**

14. **On the Server Configuration page, click the button to Use the Same Account for All SQL Server Services. Enter a username in the Account Name text box, and the user's password in the Password text box. Click OK and then click Next.**

The account can be an account from your local system (created in Computer Management), or an account from your domain (created in Active Directory). If this is a test bed, you can use the administrator account for your system. For a production server, ask your system administrator for an account with the appropriate permissions.

15. **On the Database Engine Configuration page, ensure Windows Authentication mode is selected, and click the Add Current User button. Click Next.**

16. **On the Reporting Services Configuration page, ensure that Install the Native Mode Default Configuration is selected.**

Your display looks similar to Figure 1-8.

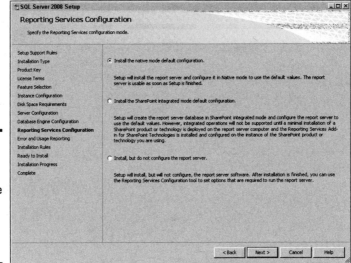

Figure 1-8:
Selecting
Native
mode for the
Reporting
Services
Configu-
ration.

17. **On the Reporting Services Configuration page, review the information and then click Next.**

18. **On the Error and Usage Reporting page, click Next.**

19. **On the Installation Rules page, review the information and then click Next.**

20. **On the Ready to Install page, review the summary and then click Install.**

The remaining installation takes several minutes to complete.

21. **When the install completes, the Installation Progress indicates status for each of the installed services and features. Click Next.**

22. On the Complete page, click Close.

23. If the Computer Reboot Required dialog box appears, indicating that you must reboot the system, click OK.

24. After your system reboots, log in.

25. Download and install the AdventureWorks2008 database.

If you don't recall how to download and install AdventureWorks2008, review Book III, Chapter 5 for the steps to do so. AdventureWorks2008 is useful as a populated database for creating practice or sample reports.

The previous steps install and configure SQL Server 2008 and Reporting Services. However, you might want to verify the installation using the Reporting Services Configuration Manager. The following steps lead you through the process of verifying the installation of Reporting Services by using Reporting Services Configuration Manager.

1. Launch the Reporting Services Configuration Manager.

Click Start⇨All Programs⇨Microsoft SQL Server 2008⇨Configuration Tools⇨Reporting Services Configuration Manager.

2. On the Connect to a Report Server Instance page, ensure your server name and instance are accurately listed.

A display similar to Figure 1-9 appears. The server name for this exercise is MCITP1, and the default instance is MSSQLSERVER.

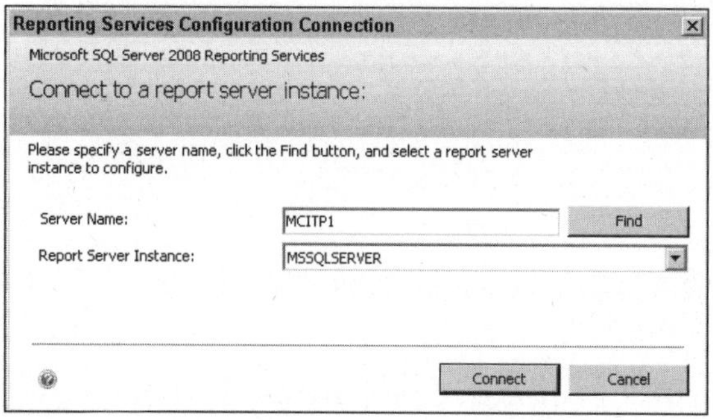

Figure 1-9: Connecting to a report server instance.

> **Reporting Services Configuration Connection**
>
> Microsoft SQL Server 2008 Reporting Services
>
> Connect to a report server instance:
>
> Please specify a server name, click the Find button, and select a report server instance to configure.
>
> Server Name: `MCITP1`   Find
>
> Report Server Instance: `MSSQLSERVER`
>
> Connect   Cancel

3. After verifying the server name and instance, click Connect.

After a moment, the Reporting Services Configuration Manger connects and reports the status of the report server.

4. Verify the Report Services Status reads *Started*. If not, click the Start button.

5. **Click Service Account in the Connect pane (on the left) of the Configuration Manager.**

   This shows the service account used to start SQL Server Reporting Services. For our controlled lab environment, we used the administrator account. If you want to change the account used to start the report server service, you can do so on this page.

   On a production server, you would want to give this service account the minimum permissions needed to perform the job. It's very unlikely you would need to grant full administrative permissions for a regular deployment of SQL Server Reporting Services.

6. **On the Reporting Services Configuration Manager page, click the Web Service URL.**

   You can view the URL for your report server here. TCP port 80 is the well-known port for HTTP. If this port is shown, you won't need to include the port number in the URL. If a different port number is selected (such as 8080), you will need to include it in the URL (for example, `http://servername:8080/ReportServer`).

7. **Click the URL for your report server.**

   A display similar to Figure 1-10 appears. Notice the URL is `http://MCITP1/ReportServer` because the server name is MCITP1. As reports are published to your Web server, they become available here.

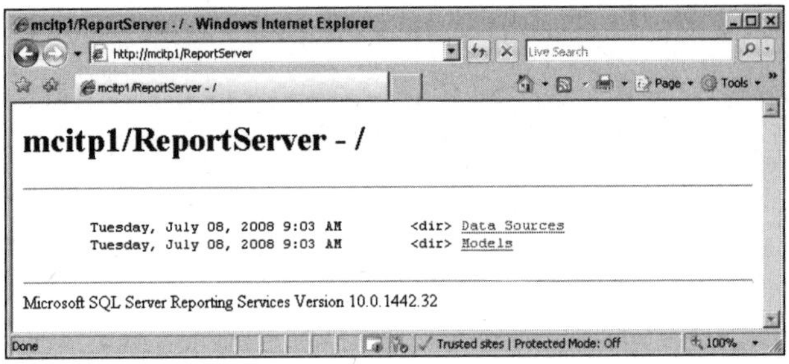

Figure 1-10:
An empty
Reporting
Services
Web site.

8. **On the Reporting Services Configuration Manager page, click the Database link in the Connect page.**

   You can change the database and credentials from this page, but the report server database was created as part of the installation.

9. **Click the Report Manager URL. Click the URL shown to launch the Report Manager.**

A display similar to Figure 1-11 appears. On our system, the URL is `http://MCITP1/Reports`, which changes to `http://MCITP1/Reports/Pages/Folder.aspx` as soon as the connection is established. At this point, the report server doesn't have any content, so the site is empty. After reports and report models are published to the report server, they appear in the appropriate folder, and their properties can be manipulated.

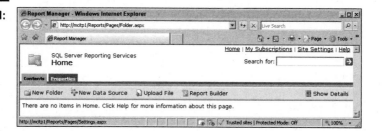

Figure 1-11:
Report
Manager
managing
the
Reporting
Services
Web site.

10. **Click the E-mail settings link in the Reporting Services Configuration Manager.**

    If you want your report server to use e-mail, you can configure the properties on this page.

11. **Click the Execution Account link.**

    If your reports require access to external data sources or images, you can specify the account name and credentials here.

12. **Click the Encryption Keys link.**

    Reporting Services uses encryption to protect credentials, connection strings, and other sensitive data. You can use this screen to back up and restore the key used for encryption.

13. **Click the Scale-out Deployment link.**

    This page allows you to view information on servers that are participating in a scale-out deployment.

14. **Close the Reporting Services Configuration Manager tool.**

In Chapters 2 and 3 of this mini-book, you have an opportunity to create and publish reports to the report server. After the reports are published, you can return to the Report Manager and the Reporting Services Web site to see how these pages appear with reports to manage and view.

Chapter 2: Creating Reports with Report Builder

In This Chapter

✔ Developing reports faster with Report Builder

✔ Designing a new report

✔ Publishing reports

✔ Maintaining reports

*T*he Report Builder is a relatively simple graphical user interface (GUI) that you can make available to end users to build their own reports. The difficult part is identifying what types of reports the users might want to create and including the available data in a report model.

After a report model has been created and deployed to the Report Manager within a Reporting Services Web site, users can create their own reports. Although creating a report with the Report Builder is fairly easy, predicting what reports your users might want and creating the report models might take a little more time and energy.

Developing Reports Faster with Report Builder

Report Builder is an easy-to-use tool that enables end users to create their own reports on an as-needed (or ad hoc) basis. Reports can be quite complex, so the goal of the Report Builder tool is to hide some of that complexity.

The overall steps required to build reports using Report Builder are

✦ **Install and configure Reporting Services:** If SQL Server Reporting Services (SSRS) wasn't installed with SQL Server 2008, it needs to be installed. The Reporting Services Configuration Manager is used to configure SQL Server Reporting Services. This tool is covered in Chapter 1 of this mini-book.

✦ **Create a report model from within Business Intelligence Development Studio (BIDS):** Report model projects include one or more data sources, data views, and report models.

✦ **Install and launch Report Builder from Report Manager:** Figure 2-1 shows the Report Manager, a Web-based tool that allows you (and your users) to access the Report Builder, deployed report models, and deployed reports.

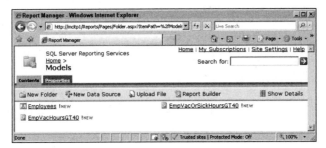

✦ **Create the report using the Report Builder:** Clicking the Report Builder button installs and launches the Report Builder. Figure 2-2 shows a report being built in the Report Builder. Reports are created mostly by dragging and dropping the desired components onto the report. The data available for a report is derived from the report model. In Figure 2-2, several entities related to the Person.Person table in the AdventureWorks database are shown. Each of these entities is derived from other tables and is defined in the report model.

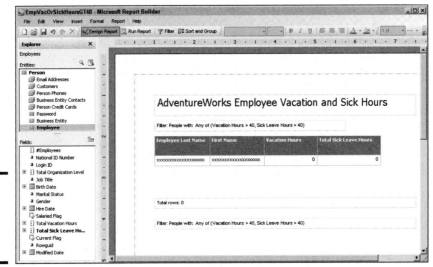

Figure 2-2:
A report
being built
in Report
Builder.

By using Report Builder to create reports, you're extending the ability to create reports to the decision makers. Instead of relying on database developers to create all the desired reports, end users can easily create and modify their reports as the business requirements change.

Designing a New Report

To create a report with Report Builder from a report model, you must do some preliminary steps:

1. Create a report model project in Business Intelligence Development Studio (BIDS).

2. Add a data source and a data source view to your report model project.

3. Create a report model within your report model project.

4. Deploy the report model to your SQL Server Reporting Services Web site.

5. Access the Report Manager Web site to launch the Report Builder.

6. Create the report by using the report model from within the Report Builder.

Figure 2-3 shows the flow of creating a report with the Report Builder. First, a data source and data view are identified and linked with a report model within BIDS. Any reports created from this report model can then use data from the tables and views from the identified database. Next, the report model is published or deployed to the reporting server. The Report Builder can be launched from the Report Manager and used to create a report. After a report is created in the Report Builder, it can be deployed to the reporting server.

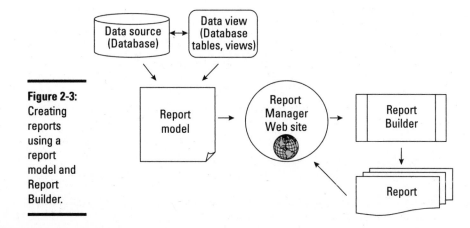

Figure 2-3:
Creating reports using a report model and Report Builder.

The following groups of steps lead you through each stage of the process.

The following steps assume that you have an instance of SQL Server 2008 installed with Reporting Services installed and configured in Native mode. If necessary, you can use the steps in Chapter 1 of this mini-book to install and configure Reporting Services. Additionally, it assumes you have a copy of the AdventureWorks2008 database hosted on this server. If you don't have AdventureWorks2008 installed, see Book III, Chapter 5 for details on how to download and install it.

In this first set of steps, you create a report model project within BIDS:

1. **Launch SQL Server Business Intelligence Development Studio (BIDS).**

Choose Start⇨All Programs⇨Microsoft SQL Server 2008⇨SQL Server Business Intelligence Studio.

2. **Click File⇨New⇨Project to create a new project within Visual Studio.**

3. **On the New Project page, ensure Business Intelligence Projects is selected, and select Report Model Project.**

As shown in Figure 2-4, you can change the name, location, and solution name of your project if necessary, or you can accept the defaults.

New Project		? X
Project types:	**Templates:**	.NET Framework 3.5
Business Intelligence Projects	**Visual Studio installed templates**	
Other Project Types	Analysis Services Project	Import Analysis Services 2008 Dat...
	Integration Services Connections P...	Integration Services Project
	Report Server Project Wizard	Report Model Project
	Report Server Project	
	My Templates	
	Search Online Templates...	
Create an empty Report Model project.		
Name:	Report Model Project1	
Location:	C:\ReportingServices	Browse...
Solution Name:	Report Model Project1	☑ Create directory for solution
		OK Cancel

Figure 2-4:
Creating a new report model project.

4. **Click OK to create your solution. Press CTRL+ALT+L to ensure the Solution Explorer is showing.**

The Solution Explorer holds three containers for your project: Data Sources, Data Source Views, and Report Models.

With a report model project created, you can now add the components needed in the report model. In the following steps, you create a data source and a data source view to use within your project.

1. Create a new data source by right-clicking Data Sources and choosing Add New Data Source.

2. On the Welcome to the Data Source Wizard page, click Next.

3. On the Select How to Define the Connection page, ensure the Create a Data Source Based on an Existing or New Connection is selected. Click New.

4. On the Connection Manager page (shown in Figure 2-5), enter the server name where you've installed SQL Server 2008.

   For this chapter, we installed it on the default instance of a server named MCITP1, so it is entered as MCITP1 in this box. If you used a named instance, enter **ServerName\NamedInstance**.

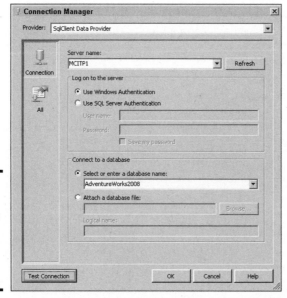

Figure 2-5:
Creating a data source connection with the Connection Manager.

5. In the Connect to a Database section, choose AdventureWorks2008 from the drop-down box. Click Test Connection to ensure you can access the server and database.

6. After clicking Test Connection, a dialog box appears indicating the test connection succeeded. Click OK. Click OK again on the Connection Manager page.

7. On the Select How to Define the Connection page, click Next.

8. On the Completing the Wizard page, click Finish.

9. **In the Solution Explorer, right-click Data Source Views and choose Add New Data Source View.**

10. **On the Welcome to the Data Source View Wizard page, click Next.**

11. **On the Select a Data Source page, select the Adventure Works2008 data source created in the previous steps. Click Next.**

12. **On the Select Tables and Views page, select the Employee (HumanResources) and Person(Person) tables. Click the Add Related Tables button to add all the related tables for these two tables.**

The default order that the tables and views are displayed in seems to be as logical as "alphabetical by height," but if you click over the Name column, the order changes to alphabetical. It's much easier to locate the tables this way.

Figure 2-6 shows that Person(Person), Employee (HumanResources), and related tables have been added to the data source view.

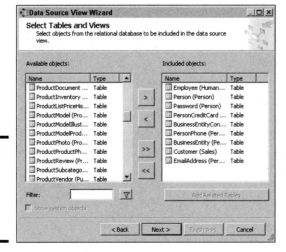

Figure 2-6:
Selecting
tables for
the data
source
view.

13. **Click Next on the Select Tables and Views page.**

14. **On the Completing the Wizard page, change the name to Employees and click Finish.**

At this point, you've created the report model project, added a data source (the AdventureWorks database), and added a data source view (the vEmployees view).

In this next set of steps, you create your report model within your project by using the data source and data source view. After the report model is created, you deploy it so that users can use the report model to create their own reports.

1. **Create a report model by right-clicking Report Models and choosing Add New Report Model.**

2. **On the Welcome to the Report Model Wizard page, click Next.**

3. **On the Select Data Source View page, select the data source view (`Employees.dsv`) that you created in the previous steps. Click Next.**

4. **On the Select Report Model Generation Rules page, accept the default rules and click Next.**

5. **In the Collect Model Statistics page, review the information, select Use Current Model Statistics Stored in the Data Source View, and then click Next.**

6. **On the Completing the Wizard page, accept the default name (Employees) and then click Run.**

7. **On the Completing the Wizard page, click Finish.**

Similar to Figure 2-7, the Solution Explorer (at the far right) shows all the elements you've created. With the `Employees.smdl` report model selected, the tables added to the report model are shown as report model entities.

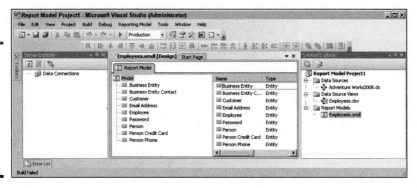

Figure 2-7:
A report model created within a report model project.

The Report Model is similar to the blueprints of a house. The blueprints will help you build a house, but you can't live in the blueprints. Similarly, the Report Model will help you build a report once you deploy the Report Model, but you can't view a report with the Report Model itself.

8. **Right-click the `Employees.smdl` report model and choose Deploy.**

   After a moment, the `Deploy succeeded` message appears in the bottom left of the page.

At this point, you've finished the heavy lifting for your report. ***Remember:*** One of the primary goals of the report model is to hide the complexity of the underlying data from the end user — the actual creator of the report.

Because the report hasn't been created, end users have the capability of creating reports based on the specific data they need. If it turns out they need additional data, they can easily modify their report, or create another report. It doesn't require waiting several days (or more) until a developer can create the new report.

For example, imagine your boss has asked you to create a report that lists all employees who have more than 40 hours of accrued vacation time.

The following steps show how this report can be created by using the Report Builder from the report model created in the previous steps:

1. **Launch Internet Explorer and use the address that is configured for your Report Manager home page.**

   On our system, the address is `http://MCITP1/Reports/`, which redirects to `http://MCITP1/Reports/Pages/Folder.aspx`. Similar to Figure 2-8, the Report Manager page now shows that Data Sources and Models (report models) exist within the site as new items.

Figure 2-8: Report Manager showing data sources and models.

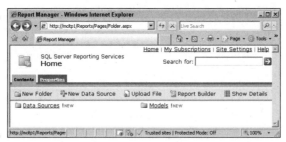

2. **Click Models.**

   You see the Employees report model created earlier.

3. **Click the Report Builder link in the toolbar above the Employees link.**

4. **If a security warning appears, click Run to run the Report Builder.**

   This downloads and runs the Report Builder.

In the Microsoft Report Builder application, you see a Getting Started pane at the far right.

5. **Under Select a Source of Data for Your Report, click Employees. For Report Layout, accept the default of Table (columnar). Click OK.**

   Similar to Figure 2-9, the Entities and Fields boxes are on the far left. The entities of the report model (the tables) appear in the Entities box. The Fields box shows the fields that are available for the selected table. The report is in the center of the window. The report is built when you drag and drop fields onto the page.

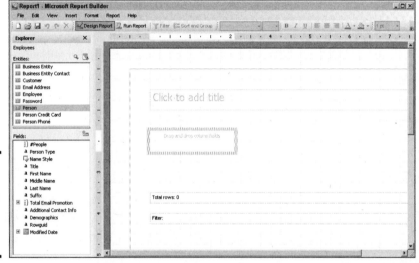

Figure 2-9:
Report Builder with the report model added.

6. **Select the Person entity. Drag and drop the Last Name field into the box in the report window.**

7. **Drag and drop the First Name field to the right of the Last Name field.**

   While you drag the First Name field, the cursor icon changes. When the cursor changes to an I-shaped cursor, the field can be dropped. Position your cursor within the same box as the Last Name field, but at the far right. When the cursor changes, release it.

8. **Select the Employee entity. In the Fields section, click the plus (+) next to Total Vacation Hours.**

   Under Vacation Hours are several functions that you can apply to the report. The # Vacation Hours shows the current vacation hours available to an employee.

9. **Drag and drop the # Vacation Hours field to the right of the First Name field in the report.**

10. **Click the Filter button on the toolbar.**

    This opens the Filter Data window.

11. **Select the Employee entity and within the Fields section, double-click the # Vacation Hours.**

    This creates a filter in the main part of the window showing `Vacation Hours Equals (unspecified)`. You need to change this so that it reads `Vacation Hours Greater Than 40`.

12. **Click Equals and select Greater Than. In the text box reading (unspecified), enter 40. Click OK.**

    Similar to Figure 2-10, this filter restricts the report to list only employees who have more than 40 hours of accrued vacation time.

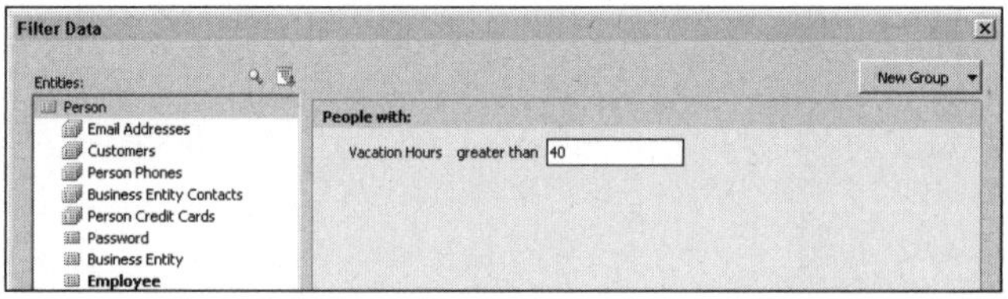

Figure 2-10: Creating a filter.

13. **(Optional) Clean up the report.**

    You might want to rename the column headers or resize the columns. For example, instead of Last Name, you may want to change the column header to Employee Last Name. Any of the columns can be resized by hovering over an edge until the cursor changes into a cross with two arrows. You can also add text within the Click To Add Title text box.

14. **Click Run Report from the Report Builder toolbar.**

    The report builds and displays. If you click to the last page (page 5), you'll see that 178 rows were returned.

15. **Click the Save button.**

16. **In the Save As Report dialog box, change the name of the report to** EmpVacHoursGT40. **Click Save.**

17. **Close the Report Builder by choosing File➪Exit.**

    If you look at the Report Manager, you'll see that your report has been added as a report within the Models folder.

18. **Click the report from within the Report Manager.**

Any user with access to this report via Report Manager will see the report as it's displayed for you. *Note:* This is the same way it was displayed within the Report Builder Design View.

Although this report shows you exactly what you originally needed, imagine your boss now asks you to add in sick hours, too. Specifically, she asks that the report list employees with more than 40 vacation hours *or* more than 40 sick hours. Because you saved the report, you can easily open it and make the required modifications.

In the next set of steps, you open the report to modify it and save it with a different name. This allows both reports to be accessible to users within the Report Manager.

1. **If Report Manager isn't showing, launch Internet Explorer and run the Report Manager. Click the Report Builder button.**

2. **After Report Builder launches, choose File⇨Open.**

3. **In the Open Report dialog box, open the Models container and select the EmpVacHoursGT40 report created in the previous steps. Click Open.**

4. **Select the Employee table from the Entities section. In the Fields section, click the plus (+) next to the Total Sick Leave Hours field.**

5. **Double-click the # Sick Leave Hours selection.**

By double-clicking the selection, the field is added to the report. If necessary, you can resize the field in the report.

6. **Click the Filter button on the toolbar. In the Filter Data dialog box, select the Employee entity and then double-click the # Sick Leave Hours field to add it to the Filter. Change *equals* to greater than and enter 40 in the text box.**

This modifies the filter so that only employees who have more than 40 vacation hours and more than 40 sick hours are listed. However, our boss asked for the report to list employees who have more than 40 vacation hours or more than 40 sick hours.

7. **Click the word *and* on the line between Vacation hours and Sick Leave Hours and select *or*.**

8. **Click OK in the Filter Data dialog box. Right click under the title and select Insert — Filter Description. Resize the text box so the text fits on one line.**

Similar to Figure 2-11, the filter is displayed in the report design in two places — under the title and at the bottom of the page. If you run the report, you'll see that the filter text added under the title is displayed on every page. The filter text at the bottom of the page is displayed only at the end of the report.

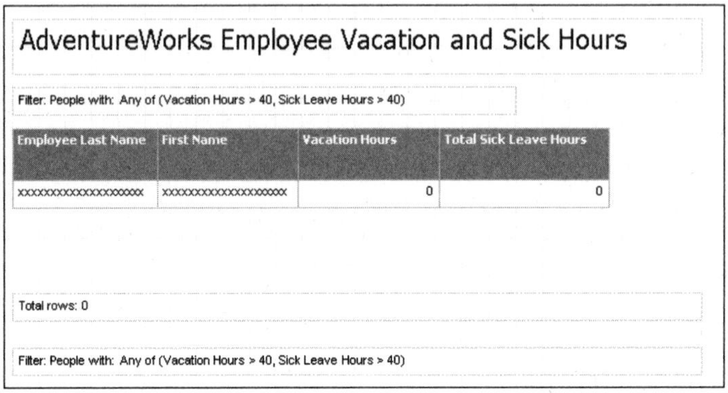

Figure 2-11:
A report with both vacation and sick hour filters applied.

AdventureWorks Employee Vacation and Sick Hours

Filter: People with: Any of (Vacation Hours > 40, Sick Leave Hours > 40)

Employee Last Name	First Name	Vacation Hours	Total Sick Leave Hours
xxxxxxxxxxxxxxxxxx	xxxxxxxxxxxxxxxxxx	0	0

Total rows: 0

Filter: People with: Any of (Vacation Hours > 40, Sick Leave Hours > 40)

9. **Click the Run Report button on the Report Builder toolbar.**

The report now lists 179 employees in 5 pages. If you're satisfied with the report, you can save it with a different name, such as EmpVacOrSickHoursGT40.

Publishing Reports

Reports are accessible to users only when they're published or deployed to the SQL Server Reporting Services (SSRS) Web site. A report is considered published when it's accessible to users. Often, this is done from within any of the tools used to create reports, report models, and data sources.

For example, Figure 2-12 shows how a report model is published from within the Business Intelligence Development Studio (BIDS). You right-click the report model and choose Deploy.

SSRS can be installed in one of two modes; both affect how reports are published:

✦ **Native mode:** In Native mode (the default), the SSRS Reporting Server runs as an application providing all processing and management functions through SSRS components.

Reports can be published via standard SSRS tools, such as Report Designer, Report Builder, and Model Designer.

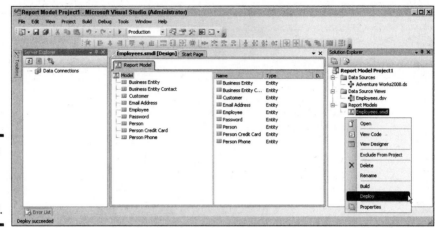

Figure 2-12:
Deploying
a report
model from
within BIDS.

✦ **SharePoint Integrated mode:** In SharePoint Integrated mode, the Reporting Services server still provides all the report processing, but the SharePoint site acts as a front end for report access.

In addition to the standard SSRS tools used for publishing reports, content can also be uploaded to the SharePoint site by using SharePoint tools.

When using SSRS in Native mode, you need to know the addresses to access both the default Web server and the Report Manager. If you're using the SharePoint Integrated mode, the addresses will be defined through the SharePoint hierarchy.

For Native mode, the URL addresses are

✦ **SSRS Reporting Server default instance:**

```
http://servername/ReportServer
```

For example, if the server name is SQL08, the URL will be

```
http://SQL08/ReportServer
```

✦ **SSRS Report Manager default instance:**

```
http://servername/Reports
```

For example, if the server name is SQL08, the URL will be

```
http://SQL08/Reports
```

✦ **SSRS Reporting Server named Instance:**

```
http://servername/ReportServer_instancename
```

For example, if the server name is SQL08 and the named instance is SSRSInstance, the URL will be

```
http://SQL08/ReportServer_SSRSInstance
```

✦ **SSRS Report Manager named instance:**

```
http://servername/Reports_instancename
```

For example, if the server name is SQL8 and the named instance is SSRSInstance, the URL for the Report Manager will be

```
http://SQL08/Reports_SSRSInstance
```

As soon as a report is published or deployed to SQL Server Reporting Services, it is available on both the Reporting Server Web site and the Report Manager Web site.

Maintaining Reports

Maintenance of reports consists mainly of updating the reports or report models to match the changing needs of users.

When a report is run, data is retrieved from the data source. In other words, as data is updated in the database, the reports show the updated data. No additional maintenance on the data is required.

Advanced implementations of SSRS allow you to create snapshots of reports and maintain a history of reports. It's also possible to cache reports so that they remain in memory for a specified time without the need to query the database again for the data. When using snapshots, history, and cached reports, the data isn't queried each time the report is retrieved. Instead, the report shows what the data was at a moment in time.

Reports can be updated by using the same tools used to create them. For example, if a report was created from a report model by using Report Builder, you can launch the Report Builder again, open the report, and then make any modifications desired. If you want to save the original report, simply save the report with a different name.

Chapter 3: Creating Reports with Report Designer

In This Chapter

✓ Generating sophisticated output with Report Designer

✓ Understanding Report Definition Language (RDL)

✓ Designing, publishing, and maintaining reports

Databases are great at storing data, but what we really want is to be able to see the data. Admittedly, SQL Server hasn't always been great at this, but things have been significantly changing over the years.

Today, you can easily create reports and deploy them to a report server. Users can use any Web browser (including Internet Explorer) to view reports with up-to-the-minute data. You can use two primary tools to create reports. The Report Designer is part of the Business Intelligence Development Studio and includes wizards to make your job easier. The Report Builder 2.0 is an easy-to-use stand-alone tool that you can download and install separately from SQL Server 2008.

In this chapter, you learn some basics about these tools, follow steps to create reports, and deploy reports to a reporting server.

Generating Sophisticated Output with Report Designer

The Report Designer is part of the SQL Server Business Intelligence Development Studio (BIDS) and is used to create reports. A *report* is a formatted output from your database.

If you remember running queries by using T-SQL statements in the SQL Server Management Studio, you know those outputs are rather plain and simple. With Report Designer, not only can you spice up your reports with graphics and different layouts, but you can also create interactive reports by using sophisticated tools, such as a matrix (described in the following paragraphs).

For example, Figure 3-1 shows a sample report retrieving company sales data from the AdventureWorks2008 database. It shows total sales for the years 2002 and 2003. Additionally, it breaks down the sales based on product categories.

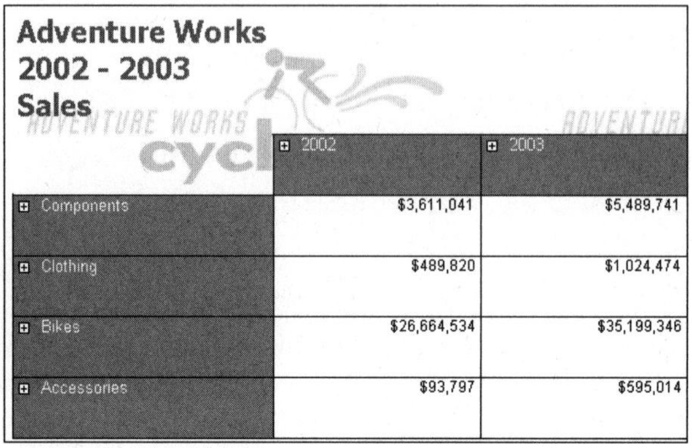

Adventure Works
2002 - 2003
Sales

	2002	2003
Components	$3,611,041	$5,489,741
Clothing	$489,820	$1,024,474
Bikes	$26,664,534	$35,199,346
Accessories	$93,797	$595,014

Figure 3-1:
Adventure
Works sales
report.

However, an executive, manager, or other decision maker, might have the following questions based on this report:

✦ Which quarter had the most sales?

✦ Which quarter had the least sales?

✦ Which bikes bring in the most revenue?

✦ Are there any noticeable trends in any of the categories?

A *matrix report* presents the data in an intersecting format. The matrix report starts with summary data, but allows you to interact with the report and drill down into the more detailed data. A matrix report is also known as a *cross-tab report.*

When you run a matrix report, you notice a plus next to data that can be expanded. By clicking the plus, the columns or rows expand.

Figure 3-2 shows a report with the matrix manipulated through user interaction. The plus next to 2003 was clicked to expand the year data and show the quarters. The Clothing and Bikes categories are expanded to show the sales values of individual items within the categories.

Adventure Works 2002 - 2003 Sales		2002	2003			
			Q1	Q2	Q3	Q4
Components		$3,611,041	$459,086	$1,111,521	$2,527,699	$1,391,434
Clothing	Bib-Shorts	$102,183	$21,544	$43,458	$351	
	Caps	$9,467	$1,782	$2,940	$8,676	$8,519
	Gloves	$90,897	$25,692	$41,876	$26,945	$23,619
	Jerseys	$110,846	$18,205	$31,335	$173,041	$140,703
	Shorts	$49,384	$11,230	$21,424	$97,610	$84,192
	Socks	$3,173			$6,969	$6,183
	Tights	$123,871	$27,588	$51,601	$780	$244
	Vests				$81,086	$66,883
Bikes	Mountain Bikes	$10,893,468	$2,517,500	$2,908,659	$3,617,012	$3,808,656
	Road Bikes	$15,771,066	$3,584,255	$4,119,659	$3,844,124	$3,734,892
	Touring Bikes				$3,298,006	$3,766,585
Accessories		$93,797	$15,628	$32,845	$262,613	$283,928

Figure 3-2:
Adventure Works sales report using a matrix.

By adding a matrix, you allow decision makers to click on the report and gain deeper insight into the data. With this insight, decision makers can explore both problem areas and potential opportunities that might not otherwise be apparent. Some things that jump out while looking at this report are

✦ The two quarters with the highest sales are the third and fourth quarters. If this is a repeatable trend, it makes sense to ensure additional resources are available for those periods.

✦ Sales of bib-shorts and tights have significantly fallen off. Perhaps another product could be added to replace the products that are no longer popular.

✦ Socks sold in 2002 but had zero sales in Q1 and Q2 of 2003. Is there a reason for this that can be prevented in the next year?

✦ Touring bikes were added, which significantly increased sales without influencing sales on other bikes. Are there other product lines that could be added to expand the market?

Figure 3-3 shows a sales report organized by territory that can also be used to drill down into the detailed data. By clicking Canada, the two employees with sales appear. The plus next to each salesperson tells you that you can get detailed information on the salesperson.

In addition to matrices, you can add graphics to your reports to highlight what's important. Adding a company logo or other pictures makes a report more appealing and easier to read, but you can also add charts and graphs to your report.

Figure 3-3:
Adventure
Works
territory
report using
a matrix.

Territory	Sales Person	Order Number	Total Sales
⊞ Australia			$1,943,016.45
⊟ Canada			$12,808,458.05
	⊞ Garrett Vargas		$4,840,689.25
	⊞ José Saraiva		$7,967,768.80
⊞ Central			$13,434,509.55
⊞ France			$6,083,690.96
⊞ Germany			$2,476,530.47
⊞ Northeast			$12,433,502.84
⊞ Northwest			$12,593,458.38
⊞ Southeast			$9,629,926.90
⊞ Southwest			$22,737,468.75
⊞ United			$11,384,512.99

Figure 3-4 shows a partial report with charts and graphs. To borrow from an old saying, a graph is worth a thousand numbers. By glancing at the graph, you can easily identify that Michael Blythe had the most sales. Looking at the numbers in the Employee Name and Sales table, this doesn't jump out as easily. Similarly, the pie chart shows that the top stores have relatively the same sales.

Figure 3-4:
Adventure
Works sales
report using
charts and
graphs.

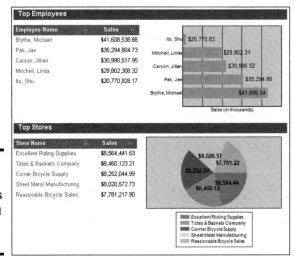

The two primary tools that you can use to create reports are

✦ **Report Designer:** The Report Designer is a part of the Business Intelligence Development Studio (BIDS). The Report Designer is used to create report server projects that can include multiple reports.

✦ **Report Builder 2.0:** The Report Builder 2.0 is a stand-alone graphical user tool that creates one report at a time. It is a free download as part of the Microsoft SQL Server 2008 Feature Pack and can be installed completely separate from SQL Server 2008.

The Report Builder 2.0 was previously called Report Designer Preview. There was some confusion because BIDS also included a Report Designer but both were completely separate applications. In Book V, Chapter 2, we cover the Report Builder that is used to create reports from report models in the Report Manager. Although similarly named, these are two completely separate applications. Aren't you glad they renamed it to clear up the confusion?

Exploring the Report Designer

Using the Report Designer in BIDS, you can create and manipulate reports that can then be deployed to a report server and served to users who have the appropriate access. Visual Studio includes three templates for report projects that use the Report Designer:

✦ **Report server project:** Report server projects are used to create reports. Once created, your reports can be deployed to your report server. You can add shared data sources, and multiple reports to a report server project.

✦ **Report Server Project Wizard:** This is similar to the report server project, but it immediately launches a wizard to simplify the creation of the first report.

✦ **Report model project:** Report model projects are used to create report models. Once deployed to a report server, a report model is used to create an actual report using the Report Builder.

Report model projects are covered in Chapter 2 of this mini-book. Steps included in that chapter show how to create a report model, build a report model, and deploy it to a report server. Once deployed, the Report Manager Web site launches the Report Builder and builds a report.

To launch the Report Designer, follow these steps:

1. **Choose Start⇨All Programs⇨Microsoft SQL Server 2008⇨SQL Server Business Intelligence Development Studio (BIDS).**

This launches BIDS, but to create reports, you need to create a report project.

2. In BIDS, choose File⇨New⇨Project.

In this section, you create a blank project to explore the Report Designer. In the "Designing a New Report" section later in this chapter, you have an opportunity to create an actual report.

3. On the New Project page, select Report Server Project and then click OK.

You can give your project a new name and new location or accept the defaults, as shown in Figure 3-5. Figure 3-5 also shows that you can select Report Model Project or Report Server Project Wizard. Report model projects are explored in Chapter 2 of this mini-book.

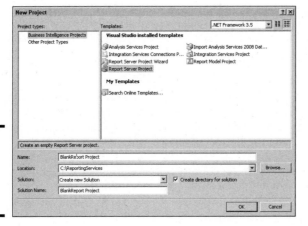

Figure 3-5: Creating a new report server project.

4. Solution Explorer is in the far right pane. Right-click your project and choose Add⇨New Item.

This allows you to add new reports (with or without using the report wizard) or data source items from templates either installed as part of SQL Server Reporting Services or available online.

5. Under Visual Studio Installed Templates, select Report and click Add. This accepts the default name of Report1.rdl.

A display similar to Figure 3-6 appears. Although the report is blank, you have an opportunity to see the Report Designer. The left pane is used to manipulate report data items, such as data sources, datasets, parameters, and images. The center pane has two tabs (Design and Preview). The Design tab is used to lay out your report, and the Preview tab allows you to view the report the end-user would see. Your overall project, which can include multiple reports, is shown in the Solution Explorer in the far right pane. The Output pane at the bottom displays results when you build and deploy reports to a reporting server. The Properties pane shows the properties of any item that is selected.

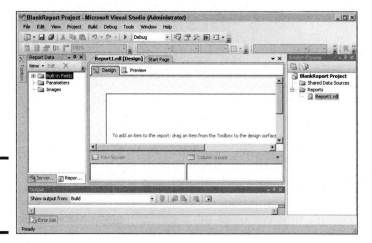

Figure 3-6:
Exploring
the Report
Designer.

Figure 3-6 shows the view with the Toolbox added. To make the Toolbox visible, select View➪Toolbox or simultaneously press Ctrl+Alt+X.

The elements available to you within your report project have the following purposes and uses:

✦ **Toolbox:** The Toolbox appears in the same place as the Report Data pane. When both the Toolbox and the Report Data panes are added (as shown in Figure 3-6), they can be chosen by a tab under the pane. When selected, the Toolbox allows you to drag and drop several different elements to your report, such as a text box, line, table, matrix, rectangle, list, subreport, chart, or an image.

✦ **Report Data:** The Report Data section is used to identify the data source and dataset for your report. You can also add additional fields, parameters, and images to your report from here. By selecting New Dataset, a dialog box appears that allows you to pick a data source (or create a new one if one doesn't exist), and then enter a query or execute a stored procedure to retrieve data for your report.

✦ **Datasets:** A *dataset* identifies the data source (the type of database and its location) and the data to be retrieved from the data source (from a specific query). Datasets are created in the Report Data section in the far left pane.

✦ **Design tab:** You can manipulate how your report looks from within the Design view. Objects are placed onto the page by dragging them from the Toolbox. Objects on the page in this view can be moved around (by dragging and dropping with the mouse) or resized (by clicking the handles and resizing just as you'd resize a Window), if desired. Additionally, object properties can be easily manipulated from this page.

✦ **Preview tab:** After you click the Preview tab, your report is generated, and you see how it will look when deployed to a report server. If you're like most people, your reports are never perfect the first time. However, the Preview tab allows you to see quickly what you want to fix. You can click back and forth between the Design and Preview tabs until your report looks exactly how you want it.

✦ **Solution Explorer:** The Solution Explorer shows all the data sources and reports that have been added to your project. You can also add additional data sources and reports from here.

✦ **Output:** The Output pane shows the results of building or deploying a report. Each time you preview your report, the report is built with output messages displayed in the Output pane. What you want to see here is `Build complete -- 0 errors, 0 warnings`. When things go wrong, you see error messages that might give you some insight into the problem.

✦ **Properties:** All objects (including reports and objects you place onto your reports) have properties. You can use the Properties pane to view and manipulate some of the properties of your reports and objects. Pressing F4 brings the Properties page into view if it isn't currently showing.

Exploring the Report Builder 2.0

This section is based upon a pre-release version of Report Builder and is subject to change. The Report Builder was a part of SQL Server 2008 during the beta stage, moved to the feature pack during the release candidate stage, but was not included when SQL Server 2008 was released. When a final version is released, this section will be updated and available for download at www.dummies.com/go/sqlserver2008aio.

The *Report Builder 2.0* is a stand-alone client used to create, preview, and publish reports. A primary significant difference between the Report Designer and the Report Builder 2.0 is that the Report Builder 2.0 can only work on a single report at a time, while a Report Designer Project allows you to manage several reports in a single project.

To launch the Report Builder 2.0, choose Start➪All Programs➪Microsoft SQL Server 2008 Report Builder➪Reporting Builder 2.0.

If you've used Microsoft Office 2007, you notice something familiar — the Ribbon. The Ribbon (integrated into Microsoft Office 2007 products) replaces the drop-down menus within the Report Builder 2.0.

Figure 3-7 shows the Report Builder 2.0 with the Home tab of the Ribbon displayed. Report Designer Preview includes three primary panes: the Ribbon, the Data section, and the report you're working on:

✦ **Ribbon:** The Ribbon is at the top of your page. Based on what is selected, it allows you to add or manipulate different objects in your page.

✦ **Data:** The Data pane includes several different fields that you can add to your report. For example, by dragging the PageNumber and TotalPages fields onto your report, you can easily have your report display *Page 4 of 56* on page 4 of a 56-page report. Additionally, after you add a data source and dataset, additional capabilities appear. You can add parameters and images to your report from this section also.

✦ **Report:** Here's where you see your report being built. In the Design view, you can drag and drop and manipulate objects. By clicking the Preview button from the Home or View tabs of the Ribbon, you can see what your final report will look like. When in the Preview view, you can click the Design button on the Ribbon to return to the Design view.

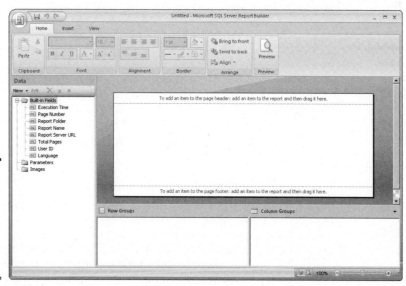

Figure 3-7:
Report
Builder 2.0
with the
Home tab of
the Ribbon
shown.

If you haven't worked with the Ribbon before, it's useful to know how to use it. In short, Microsoft received a lot of feedback saying that users were having trouble finding what they needed in the menus. So, to help those users, Microsoft created the Ribbon, which organizes the tasks into different groups. Unfortunately, for those of us that were able to find what we needed through the menus, we're now confused with the Ribbon. In time, maybe this will be easier.

The three Ribbon tabs available within the Report Builder 2.0 are

✦ **Home:** The Home tab of the Ribbon is primarily used to manipulate how objects appear on your page. The Font group allows you to select different text characteristics, such as Times New Roman, Arial, bold, italics, or underline. The Alignment group allows you to justify the text. In the Border group, you can add a border and manipulate the size and color of the border. The Arrange group's buttons allow you to place items in front of or behind other items, which can provide some cool image effects, and be used to arrange text.

✦ **Insert:** Figure 3-8 shows the Insert tab of the Ribbon, which gives you access to different objects you can add to your report. In the Data Regions group, you can add a table, matrix, chart, gauge, or list. The Report Items group offers objects that can be added to give your report some creative pizzazz. The Subreports group has the Subreport button. A *subreport* is a report that's embedded within a report page. Most items can be added by double-clicking the button on the Ribbon and then dragging and dropping the item within your report. You can also toggle the appearance of the header and footer by using the Header and Footer buttons in the Header & Footer group.

Figure 3-8:
Report
Builder 2.0
with the
Insert tab of
the Ribbon
shown.

✦ **View:** The View tab of the Ribbon is shown in Figure 3-9. You can toggle between the Design view and Preview view by clicking the appropriate button in the Report Views group. When in Design view, the Show/Hide group allows you to select additional items to display within the window. For example, when you're finished adding data, you can choose to deselect the Data pane to give you more room to view your report.

Figure 3-9:
Report
Builder 2.0
with the
View tab of
the Ribbon
shown.

In the upcoming "Using Report Builder 2.0" section, you can follow the steps
to create and manipulate a report within the Report Designer Preview.

Understanding Report Definition Language (RDL)

Reports are defined with the *Report Definition Language* (RDL). RDL is the
XML representation of a SQL Services Reporting Services (SSRS) report definition. It includes information on what data to retrieve and what way to display it.

The report definition can also include custom functions that spice up your
reports. This includes adding simple items, such as pictures, page numbers,
and dates — formatting them by modifying fonts and margins.

The report is created by using one of the tools, such as Report Designer,
Report Builder 2.0, or Report Builder (creating a report from a report model).
When the report is built, the RDL file is created. An *RDL file* is a text file that
follows a specific XML schema required by the report server. When rendered, the report server interprets the RDL to display the report accurately.

Although it's possible to modify the RDL file directly, it's unlikely you'll do
so. The graphical tools available make this much easier to do. However, if
you're a developer, you might create third-party tools that programmatically
create or modify RDL files. In that case, you need to learn the specifics of the
RDL file.

Designing, Publishing, and Maintaining Reports

Chapter 2 of this mini-book shows you how to create report models and publish them to the report server. You then use the Report Builder to create and
publish a report to the report server.

In this section, you find out how to design, publish, and maintain reports by using the Report Designer within the Business Intelligence Development Studio (BIDS) and the stand-alone Report Builder 2.0.

The following two sections show you exactly how to create reports. You create a report by using the Report Designer in BIDS. You then create a similar report by using the Report Builder 2.0.

The steps in the following two sections assume you have AdventureWorks2008 installed on your SQL Server 2008 server. If you don't have it installed, review Book III, Chapter 5 for the steps.

Using the BIDS Report Designer

In the following steps, you create a matrix report used to analyze sales within the Adventure Works Company.

1. **Choose Start➪All Programs➪Microsoft SQL Server 2008➪SQL Server Business Intelligence Development Studio (BIDS).**

   This launches BIDS.

2. **In BIDS, choose File➪New➪Project.**

   With Business Intelligence Projects selected, several Visual Studio installed templates are available including the Report Server Project.

3. **On the New Project page, select Report Server Project. Change the name to** Employees **and change the location to** C:\MyReports. **Ensure Create New Solution is selected for the Solution and ensure the check box for Create Directory for Solution is checked. Click OK.**

4. **In the Solution Explorer pane (at the far right of Visual Studio), right-click Reports and select Add New Report.**

   This launches the Report Wizard.

5. **On the Weleecome to the Report Wizard page, click Next.**

6. **The Select the Data Source page will appear. Click Edit.**

7. **On the Connection Properties page, enter** Localhost **as the Server Name. In the Connect to a Database section, choose AdventureWorks2008 from the drop-down list.**

   Your display looks similar to Figure 3-10. If you're connecting to a remote server, you can enter the name of that server in the Server Name box. Localhost can be used for the server where you are creating your report. Additionally, you can connect to any database you desire by selecting it here.

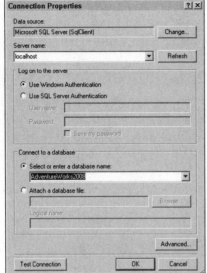

Figure 3-10:
Configuring
the
Connection
Properties
for your
data source.

8. **Click the Test Connection button.**

A Microsoft Visual Studio dialog box appears stating whether the test connection succeeded. If this doesn't succeed, double-check your spelling of *localhost.*

9. **Click OK on the Microsoft Visual Studio dialog box. Click OK on the Connection Properties dialog box.**

10. **A connection string is now present in the Select the Data Source page. Click Next.**

The Query Designer window opens, allowing you to enter a query for your dataset.

11. **Click the Query Builder button.**

12. **In the Query Designer, right click within the top pane and select Add Table.**

13. **Click the Views tab. Select the vEmployee(HumanResources) view. Click Add. Click Close to close the Add Table dialog box.**

14. **On the vEmployee view, select the checkbox next to the following columns: LastName, FirstName, PhoneNumber, EmailAddress.**

This query retrieves a listing of employees with their e-mail address and phone number.

15. **Press the exclamation mark to run your query. When you're satisfied with the query, click OK. On the Design the Query page, click Next.**

16. **On the Select the Report Type page, ensure Tabular is selected and click Next.**

17. **On the Design the Table page, click Next.**

18. **On the Choose the Table Style page, choose a table style that appeals to you and click next.**

19. **On the Completing the Wizard page, enter** EmployeeContact **in the Report Name box. Select the checkbox to Preview Report. Click Finish.**

Your display looks similar to Figure 3-11. The Report Data pane on the left includes the data source created by the wizard from the vEmployee view. The report is previewed in the middle pane, and the Solution Explorer shows you've added the Employee Contact report.

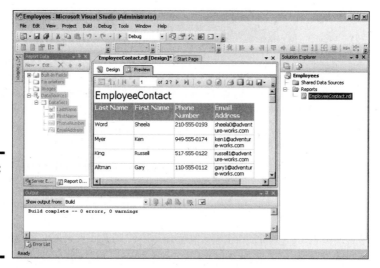

Figure 3-11:
Viewing your Employee Contact report.

20. **Click the Design Tab. Change the title name to** AdventureWorks Employee Contact Information.

21. **Click in the EmailAddress column. Hover over the right side of the gray bar until the two arrows appear. Drag the right of the EmailAddress column to the right to make it larger.**

You can resize any of the columns this way. Some of the employees have long last names causing them to take two lines. You can make the Last Name column larger to accommodate for this.

Although the previous steps show you how to create a report, we must stress that you can do quite a bit to spice it up. You can add graphics, add data to the header and footers, resize and manipulate any of the cells with color or formatting, and more.

The hardest part is getting the report to work and the wizard makes most of that work easy. When you're satisfied with a report you created, you can deploy it to a report server. If you created the report in the previous steps, follow these steps to publish it:

1. **Open the project's Properties page by selecting the Project drop-down menu and choosing Employees Properties.**

2. **Enter the URL of your reporting server in the TargetServerURL text box of your report server.**

   Depending on how you installed and configured SQL Server Reporting Services on your system, this is likely `http://localhost/report server` or `http://localhost:8080/reportserver`.

3. **Click OK to set the URL.**

4. **Select the Build drop-down menu and choose Deploy Employees.**

   In the Output pane, you see the report being deployed to your report server.

5. **Launch Internet Explorer and go to `http://localhost/report server` to access your reports.**

6. **Select the Employees directory and then select the Employee Contact report.**

   Your report is generated and displayed, as shown in Figure 3-12.

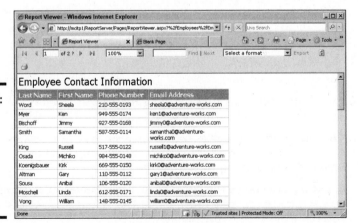

Figure 3-12:
Viewing your deployed report on your reporting server.

7. **You can also view your report via the Report Manager by using the following URL: `http://localhost/reports`.**

   Again, depending on how you installed and how you configured SQL Server Reporting Services on your system, the URL could also be `http://localhost:8080/reports`.

8. **In the Report Manager, select the Employees folder and then select the EmployeeContact report.**

   Figure 3-13 shows your report within the Report Manager.

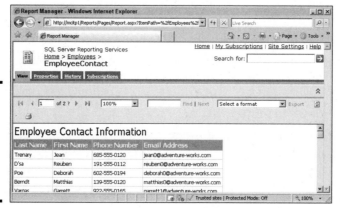

Figure 3-13: Viewing your deployed report via the Report Manager.

Using Report Builder 2.0

In the following steps, you create a report with the Report Builder 2.0. These steps assume you've downloaded and installed the Report Builder 2.0 and the AdventureWorks 2008 database.

1. **Launch the Report Builder 2.0 by choosing Start⇨All Programs⇨ Microsoft SQL Server 2008 Report Builder⇨Report Builder 2.0.**

2. **Select the Insert tab of the Ribbon and click the Table button from the Data Regions group.**

3. **On the Data Source Properties page that appears, enter** AdventureWorksEmployees **as the Name.**

4. **Click the New button. On the Data Source Properties page, enter** AdventureWorks2008 **as the Name. With Embedded Connection selected, click Edit.**

5. **On the Connection Properties page, enter** Localhost **as the Server Name. Choose the AdventureWorks2008 database from the drop-down list. Click the Test Connection button.**

A Test Results dialog box appears indicating whether the test succeeded.

6. **Click OK on the Test Results dialog box. Click OK on the Connection Properties page.**

7. **On the Data Source Properties page, click Next.**

8. **In the Query Designer window, enter the following query:**

```
SELECT * FROM HumanResources.vEmployee;
```

9. **Click the exclamation mark to run and test the query. Click Finish when the query is entered successfully.**

You've created the datasource for your report. Now you need to pick which columns from the data source you want to add to your report.

10. **Drag and drop the FirstName, LastName, PhoneNumber, and EmailAddressfields to the second row of the table.**

Make sure you put the fields on the second row, not the top row. The top row of the table is the header and the second row is for the data. If you drag any of the fields (FirstName, LastName, and so on) to the top row, each page of the report will hold only one row. In other words, an Employee report of 290 employees would take 290 pages.

11. **Click the View tab of the Ribbon and then click the Preview button.**

Notice that both the Phone Number and Email Address columns are wrapping within the cell. You can resize these columns so that they only take one line, allowing more rows per page.

12. **Click within the Phone Number column, and a gray bar appears above the columns. Hover over the line in the gray bar between Phone Number and Email Address. Click and drag the double arrow to the right to resize the Phone Number column. Do the same with the Email Address column.**

This might take some experimentation. You resize the column and then preview the results. If the column still isn't a single row, repeat the process.

13. **Change the header name of the Phone Number column to Telephone by clicking in the header and typing** Telephone.

You can modify the text and display of any of the headers or leave them how they are.

14. **Click the Insert tab. Double-click Text Box to add a text box to your report. Drag the text box to the header and enter Employee Contact Information. Resize it to ensure it doesn't wrap.**

You can also manipulate the font settings from the Home tab.

15. **Select the PageNumber field from the Built-in Fields section of the Data pane. Drag and drop it to the footer of the report.**

You use this to add *1 of 290* or *4 of 290,* depending on which page is displayed. This field will show the page number of the displayed page.

16. **With the Insert tab of the Ribbon displayed, double-click the Text Box button. This creates a blank text box in the report area. Drag the text box to the footer and enter the word** of.

The text box appears directly over the First Name header. If you have trouble finding the text box, you can move the table away and then add the text box. After you position the text box, move the table to where it was.

17. **Select the TotalPages field from the Built-in Fields section of the Data pane. Drag and drop it to the footer of the report to the right of the text box.**

Your display looks similar to Figure 3-14. The header is empty (though you can add pictures or text here), the report data and header are in the middle, and the page information is added to the footer.

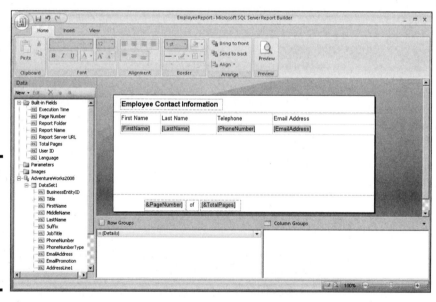

Figure 3-14:
The Employees phone and e-mail report in Design view.

18. **Select the View tab of the Ribbon and click the Design button to view your report.**

You might notice that the footer doesn't look quite right. You might want to adjust the justification of the three boxes in the footer to make them look more natural.

19. **(Optional) To adjust the justification of any of the boxes in the footer, select the Home tab of the Ribbon.**

   a. *Select the PageNumber box in the footer and then click the right justification button in the Alignment group.*

   b. *Select the text box in the report area and then select the center justification button.*

   c. *Select the TotalPages box and then select the left justification button.*

With the report created, you can deploy it from the Report Builder 2.0 to your report server by using the following steps.

1. **Select the Windows Jewel icon (at the top left of the Report Bulder 2.0 window) and then select Publish.**

2. **On the Deployment Settings dialog box that appears, enter** http://local host/reportserver **as the Report Server URL.**

3. **Change the Report Name to Employee Phone Email Listing.**

   Your display looks similar to Figure 3-15. The Report Folder field has a slash (/) in it. This indicates the report will be deployed to the root of the report server. If desired, you can add a report folder name, and it automatically will be created on the report server.

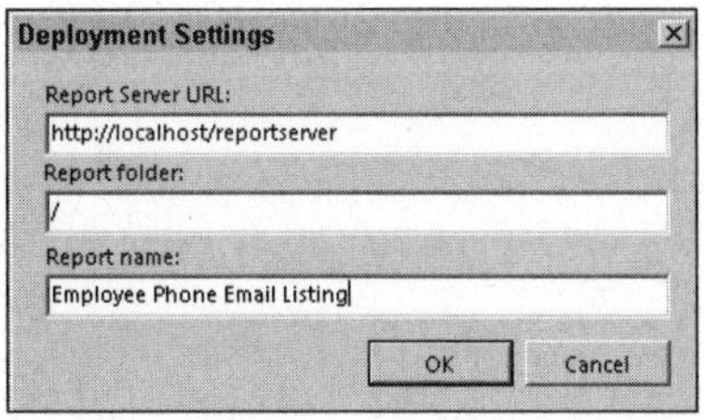

Figure 3-15:
The
Deployment
Settings
dialog box.

Deployment Settings	✕
Report Server URL:	
http://localhost/reportserver	
Report folder:	
/	
Report name:	
Employee Phone Email Listing	
OK	Cancel

4. **Click OK. A Deploy dialog box appears indicating whether the report was deployed successfully. Click OK.**

5. **Launch Internet Explorer and go to** `http://localhost/report server` **to access your reports.**

   Depending on how your report server is set up, you might need to use port 8080 to access the report server. You can use this URL address: `http://localhost:8080/reportserver`.

6. Select the Employee Phone Email Listing to view the report.

7. You can also view your report via the Report Manager by using the following URL: `http://localhost/reports`.

   The Employee Phone Email Listing report is available as shown in Figure 3-16. Notice how the system changes the URL to `http://localhost/Reports/Pages/Folder.aspx`.

8. In the Report Manager, select the Employee Phone Email Listing report.

Figure 3-16:
Accessing
your
deployed
report via
the Report
Manager.

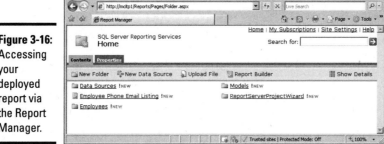

Chapter 4: Integrating Reports

In This Chapter

✓ Sharing reports through SharePoint

✓ Viewing reports with familiar Microsoft Office tools

✓ Allowing access to report information through Web Services

*U*sing SQL Server Reporting Services enables users to retrieve reports *when* — and *from where* — they want. Additionally, by using SharePoint or by discovering how to export reports, your users can grab data *how* they want.

If you integrate Reporting Services into SharePoint, developers can add reports into a Web page with Web Parts. By using a Web Part, SQL Server Reporting Services reports can be embedded into a Web page just as easily as developers could add graphics to a page.

Several different tools, such as BIDS and Report Manager, render reports. Although you can look at the report through these tools, you might need to send the report to others, perhaps as an e-mail attachment.

Any rendered report can be exported into one of several formats, such as a PDF file or an archive Web page, with just a couple clicks.

In this chapter, you learn a little about integrating Reporting Services with SharePoint and the different formats for exporting reports.

Tying Reports Together with SharePoint

SharePoint is a group of technologies tied together that is gaining quite a bit of popularity in enterprises today. Users can easily share information with SharePoint.

A common question is, "What is SharePoint?" Depending on whom you ask, expect different answers. It isn't that people are confused; it's that SharePoint is so versatile that it fills many different needs, on many different levels.

Two SharePoint families exist, and people might be referring to either one when they say, "SharePoint."

✦ **Windows SharePoint Services (WSS):** This is a free product available as a download. It can be installed on a server product, such as Windows Server 2008 or Windows Server 2003.

✦ **Microsoft Office SharePoint Server (MOSS):** This is a full server product just like SQL Server 2008. It builds on WSS and adds significant functionality and capabilities.

SQL Server 2008 Reporting Services can be integrated into either WSS or MOSS.

Understanding Web Parts

SharePoint displays Web pages, but it puts the Web pages together as separate *Web Parts*. Web Parts can be a task list, news item, discussion pane, or even a SQL Server Reporting Services report.

Developers are able to lay out Web pages by adding Web Parts to the page and even making them user selectable.

You've probably seen the same Web Part concept on the Internet. Some Web sites allow you to customize what you see. If you're interested in news headlines, you can add the news Web Part. If you're interested in horoscopes, you can add the horoscope Web Part.

Of course, they don't label them as Web Parts on the Web sites. That type of wording is reserved for techies who seem to want to confuse us with convoluted language.

Similarly, SharePoint developers can add a report viewer Web Part to view reports from a report server. The report server does need to be configured for SharePoint integration. Both report definition files (RDL) and Report Builder reports can be displayed in a report viewer Web Part.

Reports displayed in a Web Part allow users to navigate pages, search, zoom, export, and print the report. The report viewer Web Part can only be used with RDL files processed by a Microsoft SQL Server Reporting Services report server.

Integrating SQL Server and SharePoint

From a SQL Server Reporting Services point of view, the biggest requirement when you integrate reports with SharePoint is to choose the SharePoint Integrated mode. This can be done during installation or later by using the Reporting Services Configuration Manager.

As a reminder, SQL Server Reporting Services supports two deployment modes:

✦ **SharePoint Integrated mode:** In SharePoint Integrated mode, SharePoint does most of the processing and management of the Report Server. SharePoint Integrated mode requires at least Windows SharePoint Services version 3.0 or Office SharePoint Server 2007 or greater. You must use this if you want to run your reports on the SharePoint site.

✦ **Native mode:** In Native mode, SQL Server Reporting Services (SSRS) runs as an application server and does all the processing and management for reporting. If running in Native mode, reports cannot be displayed on a SharePoint Web site.

If you install SQL Server Reporting Services in Native mode, you can switch to SharePoint Integrated mode later. However, it's much easier to do the complete installation in SharePoint Integrated mode from the start. If you want to install Reporting Services in Integrated mode, you need to install SharePoint before installing Reporting Services.

After SQL Server is configured in SharePoint Integrated mode, the report viewer Web Part can be used within SharePoint Web pages by the SharePoint developers. The report viewer Web Part uses the report definition (RDL) files.

Using Familiar Microsoft Office Tools to View Reports

Reports created with SQL Server Reporting Services can be exported and saved in several different formats after the report is rendered. As a reminder, SQL Server reports can be rendered from multiple tools:

✦ **Report Builder 2.0:** The Report Builder 2.0 is a stand-alone tool that is used to create and preview reports without installing SQL Server Reporting Services. While in the Preview view, you can click the disk icon to export the report.

✦ **Business Intelligence Development Studio (BIDS):** BIDS can be used to create reports. Reports are rendered by selecting the Preview tab. After the report is rendered, you can right-click within the report to access the Export options shown in Figure 4-1. You have seven options to choose from when exporting your report.

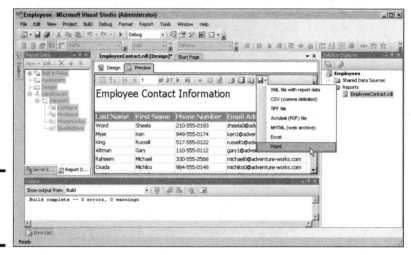

Figure 4-1:
Exporting a
report from
BIDS.

+ **Reporting Services report server:** Reports can be selected from the
report server by using the default URL of `http://servername/
Reportserver` and browsing to the desired report. After a report is
rendered, you can use the Select a Report drop-down box to choose the
format, and then click the Export link.

+ **Reporting Services Report Manager:** Reports can be selected from the
Report Manager by using the default URL of `http://servername/
Reports` and browsing to the desired report. After a report is rendered,
you can use the Select a Report drop-down box to choose the format,
and then click the Export link. The order shown in Figure 4-2 is a little
different from what you see in BIDS, but the choices are the same.

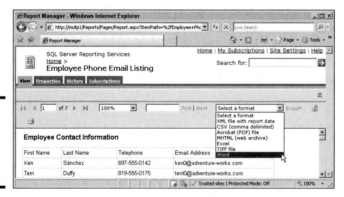

Figure 4-2:
Exporting a
report from
Report
Manager.

Exporting reports

When a report has been rendered with one of the Reporting Services tools, you can choose to export the report. An exported report can be in one of several formats.

Of course, the format you choose depends on your needs. The following formats are supported:

+ **XML file with report data:** Saves the report as an XML file. XML files are very useful for importing data into other databases, applications, or XML messages. For example, you might need to import the data into another database application, such as Microsoft Access. You can export the data to an XML file and then import it into Microsoft Access.

+ **CSV (comma delimited):** Comma Separated Value files (CSV) are plain-text data files. Each line in the file relates to a record and commas separate cells within the records, such as FirstName, LastName, Phone. A CSV file is often used when the contents of the report need to be imported into an external application that can't read the actual report file. Additionally, CSV files are often used in spreadsheet programs, such as Microsoft Excel.

+ **Acrobat (PDF) file:** This is the file type that Adobe created and made available as an open standard. PDF stands for *Portable Document Format* and the title fits. PDF files are great if you want to share files with others and ensure the formatting stays the same.

+ **MHTML (Web archive):** The MIME Encapsulation of Aggregate HTML Documents (MHTML) standard captures an entire HTML page (including pictures and other resources) as a single file. The MHTML file can easily be copied or added as an attachment to an e-mail.

+ **Microsoft Excel:** Reports saved in Excel format try to retain the report's layout and design. Each page of the report is saved in a separate worksheet. If the layout isn't important or you want all the data in a single worksheet, you can consider exporting the report as a CSV file and then opening it in Microsoft Excel.

+ **TIFF file:** A TIFF is an image formatted file. Image files default to TIFF (`.tiff`) files; they can also be exported as BMP (`.bmp`), EMF (`.emf`), GIF (`.gif`), and JPEG (`.jpeg`) files. To save an image in a different format, you just need to add the extension to the filename, and the export takes care of the rest.

+ **Word file:** Saves the file in a Word 97-2003 format with a .doc extension.

Viewing exported reports

After you have exported your reports, how can you view them? It depends on the format.

✦ **TIFF file:** Double-clicking any image file opens the file in an image viewer. The Microsoft Office Document Imaging program opens by default unless your system has another graphics program installed. A cool feature is that each page of the report is viewable, which allows you to scroll through the entire report.

✦ **MHTML (Web archive):** Double-clicking the MHTML archive file opens the Web page in the Web browser installed on your system. For example, if you have Internet Explorer, the MHTML file automatically opens in Internet Explorer.

✦ **Acrobat (PDF) file:** You need Adobe Acrobat Reader or another third-party PDF viewer installed on your system to view the PDF file. If a PDF viewer is installed, the file opens when you double-click it.

✦ **Microsoft Excel:** No surprise here. You need Microsoft Excel to open a report exported to Excel. What may be surprising is that each page in the report is a separate worksheet in Excel. For a two-page report, separate worksheets are no big deal, but for a 100-page report, the report can be difficult to work with. Additionally, Microsoft Excel has a limitation on the number of colors it displays, so the report might not look exactly the same.

✦ **CSV (comma delimited):** A CSV file opens in Microsoft Excel if Microsoft Excel is installed on your system. You can also import CSV files into databases, such as Microsoft Access or Microsoft SQL Server. Additionally, because CSV files are simple text files with values separated by commas, you can open them in any text editor, such as Notepad or Microsoft Word.

✦ **XML file with report data:** Data in XML format isn't often used by end users. Instead, the XML file is imported into another application and then presented in a more meaningful way. However, if you double-click an XML file, it displays in your Web browser, XML tags and all.

✦ **Word:** Data in Word format can be viewed in any version of Microsoft Word from 97 to Word 2007.

Exposing Report Information with Web Services

SQL Server Reporting Services includes the Report Server Web service. Using the Report Server Web service, any client or application can communicate with the report server by using Simple Object Access Protocol (SOAP) messages.

Book IV, Chapter 5 covers Web services in more depth including Web Services being deprecated in SQL Server 2008. The chapter gives an overview of how Web services are used and includes steps on how a stored procedure is made available via Web services.

The Report Server Web service is an XML Web service. The service passes XML Web messages (containing report data) by using a standard SOAP over HTTP interface.

Figure 4-3 shows one possibility for a Report Server Web service. A user is accessing a Web server over the Internet. The Web server requests the data from the Report Server Web service, which is returned in XML format. The Web server then populates pages with the relevant retrieved data.

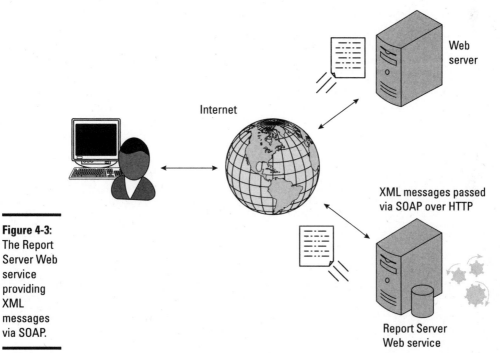

Figure 4-3:
The Report Server Web service providing XML messages via SOAP.

One of the great benefits of passing XML messages using SOAP over HTTP is that the messages can easily pass through firewalls. The HTTP interface uses the well-known port 80. Because almost every network has port 80 open to allow users to access the Internet, additional firewall ports don't need to be open. If you've ever tried to get a firewall administrator to open another port, you know that can be about as difficult as herding cats.

The Report Server Web service has several methods that can be used from external applications. However, that's an important point. It's an external application that needs to be developed to take advantage of the Report Server Web service.

Three paths are available to create applications that can use the Report Server Web service:

+ **Use Microsoft Visual Studio:** The Microsoft .NET Framework includes all the high-level programming constructs to allow you to create a Web service application. You would create a Web service proxy, authenticate with the report server, and then call the appropriate Web method.

+ **Use the Reporting Services script environment:** The rs utility allows you to write scripts in Visual Basic .NET. Reporting Services scripts can be used to run any of the Report Server Web service operations.

+ **Develop applications using any SOAP-enabled tool:** Because the Reporting Services Web service is SOAP-based, any third-party tool can be used. The Reporting Services Web service receives the SOAP request and responds with the XML data.

Book VI

Analysis Services

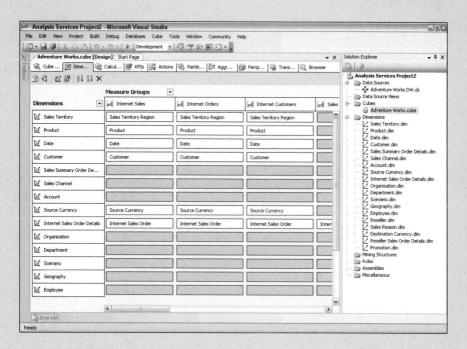

Business Intelligence Development Studio (BIDS).

Contents at a Glance

Chapter 1: Introduction to SQL Server Analysis Services

In This Chapter

✔ Introducing SQL Server Analysis Services

✔ Leveraging the power of multidimensional data

✔ Choosing an environment for Analysis Services

SQL Server Analysis Services is one of the key components of a business intelligence (BI) solution. Historically, BI has been a tool only for larger enterprises; however, the usability of many of the BI tools emerging today is helping many smaller enterprises implement business intelligence into their company's database structure.

In this chapter, you discover some of the basics of SQL Server Analysis Services (SSAS). A great benefit of SSAS is its ability to convert huge amounts of raw data into actionable intelligence. In short, SSAS provides the answers to key business questions almost as quick as the decision makers can ask the questions.

Introducing SQL Server Analysis Services (SSAS)

The core purpose of SQL Server Analysis Services (SSAS) is to present data in a more meaningful way for decision makers. When implemented, SSAS enables users to ask complex questions and quickly receive actionable insight.

Actionable insight is information that can be used to make sound business decisions. Instead of just collecting huge amounts of data, business intelligence (BI) methods and technologies allow you to convert this raw data into actionable intelligence.

BI within SQL Server 2008 is composed of several components:

✦ **SQL Server Analysis Services (SSAS):** SSAS provides an Online Analytical Processing (OLAP) solution that includes data mining solutions. Specialized algorithms are used to help decision makers identify patterns, trends, and associations in business data.

✦ **SQL Server Reporting Services:** SSRS provides a sophisticated solution to bring the data to the users. With SSRS, users can create, publish, and distribute detailed business reports.

✦ **SQL Server Integration Services:** SSIS is used for extract, transform, and load (ETL) operations. In other words, data can be retrieved from other data sources (extract), modified or manipulated to conform to requirements in the receiving database (transform), and imported into the receiving database (load).

SSAS is only one component of business intelligence, but it's certainly an important component.

SQL Server Analysis Services uses Online Analytical Processing (OLAP) as opposed to Online Transaction Processing (OLTP). OLAP and OLTP differ in how the database is used, and in how the database is constructed:

✦ **Online Analytical Processing (OLAP):** The database is highly queried with SELECT-type statements. An OLAP database is denormalized to optimize for the queries and is often reconfigured by using cubes and dimensions.

✦ **Online Transaction Processing (OLTP):** An OLTP database is highly modified (using INSERT, UPDATE, and DELETE statements). For optimization of the transactions, an OLTP database is typically normalized as a relational database.

Understanding key OLAP terms

Key terms to grasp when talking about an OLAP database are cubes, dimensions, measures, and Key Performance Indicators (KPIs). In the following sections, we discuss each of these terms in turn.

Cubes

A *cube* is a denormalized version of the database, which is an extension of the two-dimensional tables found in typical OLTP databases.

Consider Figure 1-1. Imagine you have such a cube on your desk and that within the cube is a detailed three-dimensional representation of the city you live in. You can pick up the cube and view the city from the east. You might be interested in what the eastern view looks like from above, therefore, you can immediately turn the cube and view it from that perspective. For any view, you can rotate the cube and see the data from a different angle. The model doesn't have to be rebuilt each time a different view is desired.

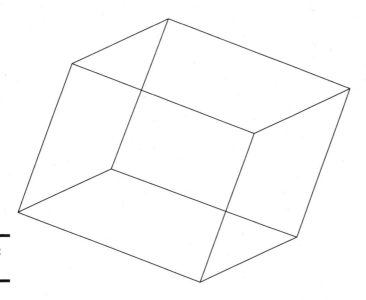

Figure 1-1:
A cube.

Similarly, database cubes allow you to look at the data from different perspectives. Database cubes are derived from two-dimensional OLTP databases, but a cube adds dimensions so that the data can be viewed from different perspectives. Moreover, because the cube is built in advance, the entire database doesn't need to be queried each time a different view is desired.

Multiple cubes can be created within a single SSAS database.

Dimensions

A *dimension* in a cube is a method used to compare or analyze the data. As an example, a product dimension within a cube could be created using the following product attributes: product name, product cost, product list price, product category, and product color.

By adding additional dimensions (such as sales over a time period, or sales by individual stores), the product data can easily be presented in a different way. Consider a sales analyst that is interested in a specific product. After viewing the product attributes, she might want to know sales information. Because additional dimensions have been created within the cube, this sales data can be presented quickly and easily in a different format.

When a dimension is created within a cube, it's a *cube dimension*.

Measures

A *measure* in a cube is a column that measures quantifiable data (usually numeric). Measures can be mapped to a specific column in a dimension and can be used to provide aggregations (such as SUM or AVG) on the dimension. For example, a measure can be used to identify how many products sold during a given time period.

Typically, the summary data derived from the dimension is presented in such a way that the user is able to easily drill down into the details of the data, often just by clicking on the summary data.

For example, total sales of a given product might be derived from a time period dimension. The measure shows the total sales for the time period, but the data could be presented as total sales for given years, quarters, or months.

Key Performance Indicator (KPI)

Business decision makers define a Key Performance Indicator (KPI). By identifying certain thresholds that management might be interested in, they can easily measure performance of the company, or certain elements of the company, against these thresholds. For example, if a retailer has several stores and expects each store to exceed $1 million in retail sales each quarter, you could create a KPI with this definition.

SSAS includes a full KPI framework to support KPIs with a great deal of flexibility in defining key metrics and scorecards. With this framework, the KPIs can be built in to external performance management applications.

Improvements in Analysis Services

SQL Server Analysis Services (SSAS) 2008 provides many new improvements over SSAS 2005. However, many of these improvements are under the hood. They include:

+ **Improved scalability:** Larger databases can be accessed by more users concurrently.

+ **Improved performance:** Data refresh rates within OLAP databases, and query times are improved. The goal is to give end users access to up-to-date data as quickly as possible.

+ **Improved data mining:** Improved algorithms used to create data mining models provide better insight and control to the underlying data.

One of Microsoft's goals with SSAS 2008 was to ensure that no significant surprises occur between SQL Server 2005 and SQL Server 2008. Although SQL Server 2008 does improve some of the performance under the hood, the implementation of SSAS is largely unchanged.

Additionally, SQL Server 2008 had a design goal of "no breaking changes." In other words, an upgrade from SQL Server 2005 to SQL Server 2008 shouldn't cause anything to break.

Interacting with Microsoft Office products

Part of the goal of business intelligence (BI) solutions using SQL Server Analysis Services is the ability to bring the data to the users easily. The following Microsoft Applications can be used as interfaces for back-end SQL Server 2008 BI databases:

✦ **Microsoft Office Excel 2007:** Microsoft Office Excel is a powerful spreadsheet on its own, but can also be used as an interface for OLAP analysis and data mining. Both SQL Server 2008 and Microsoft Excel 2007 are designed to work together. Excel includes an enhanced Reporting Services Excel renderer that enables Excel to receive reports directly in Excel.

✦ **Microsoft Office Word 2007:** Word includes a report renderer that can be used to render Reporting Services reports obtained from analytical data.

✦ **Microsoft Office Visio 2007:** Visio can be used to present the data mining views in an enhanced graphical format. Visio drawings provide significantly more graphical capabilities than SQL Server 2008.

✦ **Microsoft Office SharePoint Server:** SQL Server 2008 is tightly integrated with Office SharePoint Server 2007 allowing the capability of easily rendering reports.

Leveraging the Power of Multidimensional Data

To leverage the power of SQL Server Analysis Services (SSAS), very often a separate database is created. However, it's also possible to combine the data from multiple data sources. This is *unifying the data.*

After you create an SQL Server Analysis Services database (by using cubes, dimensions, and measures), you can begin to query that data. Although a typical relational database is queried with Transact-SQL statements, an SSAS database is queried with its own query language: Multidimensional Expressions.

Unifying your business data

A strength of SQL Server Analysis Services is that it can access data from different sources and present it as a single data source.

In a perfect world, large enterprises would have a single database that met the needs of everyone in the enterprise. However, the perfect world scenario is rarely achieved. Instead, many different databases are used by different departments.

One of the benefits of an SSAS solution is that it has the capability of unifying data access by creating a separate data warehouse or a data source view.

✦ **Data warehouse:** A data warehouse is a separate database that receives its information from several different data sources. The data sources can be from SQL Server 2005, or from different vendors, such as Oracle or IBM. Figure 1-2 shows an example of a data warehouse. The key difference between a data warehouse and a data source view is that a data warehouse is a completely separate database.

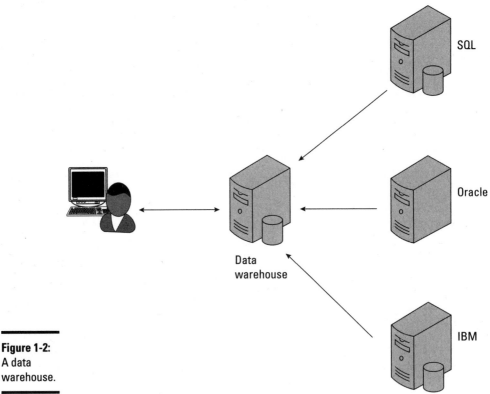

Figure 1-2:
A data
warehouse.

A data warehouse can also be derived from a single database. For example, the AdventureWorksDW database contains the same information as the AdventureWorks database. However, it's been highly denormalized. OLTP databases work best with a normalized database, but cubes work best with a highly denormalized database.

✦ **Data source view:** A data source view is similar to a data warehouse from an end-users perspective, but it creates views based on the source databases instead of using a completely separate database. Figure 1-3 shows how the data source view would look. The key point is that even though the source data is derived differently, it appears the same to the end user.

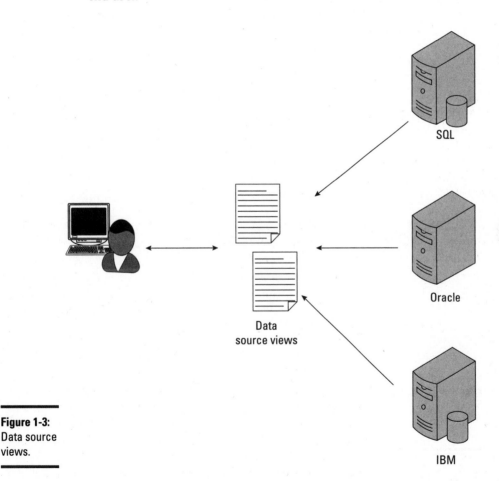

Figure 1-3:
Data source
views.

A key advantage to using a data warehouse is that it provides the best performance for querying the analytical data with minimal impact on the source databases. The only time the source databases are impacted is when data needs to be retrieved.

Additionally, extract, transform and load (ETL) methods can be used to ensure that data is presented consistently in the data warehouse, even when the data isn't presented consistently in the source databases.

The key advantage to using a data source view is that it provides you with access to real-time data.

Data mining

Actionable insight is derived by using data mining techniques. *Data mining* is the process of extracting valid, authentic, and actionable information from a database.

Data mining uses a data model to create an analysis cube. The *data model* is used to derive patterns and trends that can be collected together. An effective data model allows managers to make intelligent decisions based on the existing data. Often, the data model answers common questions that a decision maker might have.

Some examples of data mining include

✦ **Predicting future sales:** By looking at past sales, future sales patterns can be predicted. For example, Black Friday (the day after Thanksgiving) is widely known as the day that many retailers come out of the red and start to make a profit. Retailers know this by analyzing sales. Data mining can also help them answer other business questions, such as what other days are high volume days, what the best selling product is, and which products have the highest profit margins.

✦ **Conducting mass mailings (or mass e-mail mailings):** Customer buying habits can be identified to target customers with specific buying habits for sales. For example, Nightingale Conant sells audio recordings on a wide variety of topics. If you purchase recordings from them, they frequently send you advertisements, but almost exclusively on topics related to your purchases. How do they know what advertisements to send? They clearly are using a business intelligence solution.

✦ **Identifying products that can be bundled together:** As customers, we see Amazon do this very effectively. When we purchase a product, it often has a similar product that can be purchased with the first at a discounted price. We're often intrigued enough to look. Without this recommendation, we find the product we want, we purchase it, and we're done. Without the implementation of a business intelligence solution, the result is a lost add-on sale.

✦ **Identifying products that customers add to the shopping cart first:** Admittedly, this is for online sales only, but it allows a company to identify what a customer decided to buy first. For us, we know that it takes a lot to add the first item to the shopping cart; we're committing to making a purchase. After that first commitment is made, it's easier to add additional items. By identifying the products that are being added first, companies know what enticements are helping users make the decision to purchase.

✦ **Identifying buying patterns online:** Do customers typically purchase one product or more than one? Again, using Amazon as an example, we imagine that it looked at how many products a majority of customers purchased, it was often just a single book, and the single book cost was rarely more than $25. Therefore, it added free shipping for any purchases over $25, and now many customers (us included) think of adding a second book to get free shipping.

Querying multiple dimensional data

Multiple dimensional data has its own query language for working with SQL Server Analysis Services (SSAS): Multidimensional Expressions (MDX).

MDX is based on the XML for Analysis Services specification. It can be used to

✦ **Return data from an SSAS cube to a client application.**

✦ **Format the results of the query as needed by the client application.**

✦ **Perform cube design tasks, such as defining calculated members and key performance indicators.**

✦ **Perform administrative tasks.**

MDX has some similarities to T-SQL; however, it's not the same and has its own set of rules.

Learning the key MDX elements

Before you can build MDX expressions, you need a basic understanding of the MDX syntax elements listed in the following bullets:

✦ **Axis:** Within a query, you have one axis or multiple axes. An axis directly relates to a dimension. Two types of axes exist: a query axis and a slicer axis. A *query axis* is an embedded SELECT statement; multiple query axes returns multiple data sets within the query. A *slicer axis* is used as a filter to restrict the returned data.

✦ **Comments:** Comments are notes inserted into the code. Comments aren't executed. Commenting characters can be double forward slashes (//), double hyphens (–), or block character comments starting with /* and ending with */.

✦ **Functions:** Similar to T-SQL, functions can accept one or more input values and return either a scalar value or an object. Many categories of built-in functions are available to use within SSAS.

✦ **Identifiers:** Identifiers are the names of objects within an Analysis Services database, such as cubes, dimensions, members, and measures. For example, a cube could be called Sales. `Sales` would be the identifier.

✦ **MDX expressions:** Expressions are used within a query to identify single values or objects. They can include functions that return a single value or calculations that return a single value. For example, a query could be used to show a discount and include the MDX expression of `Measures.Discount Amount * .1` to represent a 10-percent discount.

✦ **Operators:** Operators allow you to assign values to data, or search for data based on certain expressions. As an example, values can be assigned with the = operator. The same = operator could also be used to compare the value of two expressions.

✦ **Query axis:** This identifies the data that will be returned by the query. An MDX query can have multiple axes. Each axis has a number: 0 for the x-axis, 1 for the y-axis, 2 for the z-axis, and so on. The x-axis is the first dimension; the y-axis is the second dimension, and so on. The query axis is mandatory in an MDX query and can include as many as 128 axes, although it's uncommon to have more than five.

✦ **Slicer axis:** The slicer axis is used to filter the data returned by the MDX SELECT statement. A slicer axis works similar to how the WHERE clause in a T-SQL query works and is included in the WHERE clause of an MDX query.

There's a great deal of depth to the MDX language, and this section only scratches the surface. If you want to find out more about it, check out the MDX Language Reference on Microsoft's TechNet Web site. At this writing, it's located here: `http://technet.microsoft.com/en-us/library/ms145595.aspx`. As you know though, things change on the Internet. If the link has changed, use your favorite search engine and search on *MDX Language Reference*.

Building a basic MDX query

The syntax for a basic MDX query is shown in the following code. The code surrounded in brackets is optional.

```
SELECT [ * | ( <SELECT query axis clause>
          [ , <SELECT query axis clause> ... ] ) ]
FROM <SELECT subcube clause>
[ <SELECT slicer axis clause> ]
[ <SELECT cell property list clause> ]
```

You can compare this to the basic syntax for a SELECT statement by using T-SQL:

```
SELECT select_list [ INTO new_table ]
[ FROM table_source ]
[ WHERE search_condition ]
```

Book VI
Chapter 1

Introduction to SQL
Server Analysis
Services

✦ Both have a SELECT clause but identify the output differently. MDX identifies the output as one or more axes.

✦ Both have a FROM clause but identify the source differently.

✦ The MDX uses a slicer axis clause (that includes a WHERE statement) to filter the results, and the T-SQL statement uses a WHERE clause to filter the results.

A query will have one or more axes. Take a look at the following query. It includes three axes, two query axes, and one slicer axis.

```
SELECT
    { Route.Path.Members } ON COLUMNS,
    { Time.[1st half].Members } ON ROWS
FROM TestCube
WHERE ( [Measures].[Packages] )
```

The first query axis is Route.Path.Members, which will be displayed as columns. The second query axis is the Time.[1st half].Members, which will be displayed as rows. The cube being queried is Test.Cube. The Measures.Packages is the slicer axis used to filter the query.

The result is shown in Table 1-1. Notice the first half of the year is broken into the first two quarters.

Table 1-1	Result of MDX Query	
	Air	*Sea*
1st Quarter	650	540
2nd Quarter	330	320

Choosing an Environment for Analysis Services

SQL Server 2008 provides two environments for working with SQL Server Analysis Services (SSAS):

✦ **Business Intelligence Development Studio**

✦ **SQL Server Management Studio**

Using Business Intelligence Development Studio

The Business Intelligence Development Studio (BIDS) is the primary tool you use for most of the development of an SQL Server Analysis project.

Figure 1-4 shows BIDS open with a SQL Server Analysis Services (SSAS) project. The project is derived from the AdventureWorksDW database, which was developed by Microsoft for business intelligence examples. If you're familiar with Visual Studio, many of these elements will look familiar to you.

Project tabs

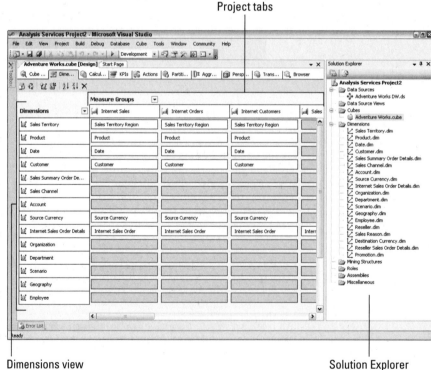

Figure 1-4:
Business
Intelligence
Development
Studio
(BIDS).

Dimensions view

Solution Explorer

Figure 1-4 shows three key elements of a SSAW project.

On the far right are all the objects that have been developed within the project. These include data sources, data source views, cubes, dimensions, and others. The AdventureWorks BI project includes the AdventureWorksDW database, the AdventureWorks cube, and several dimensions.

Beneath the toolbar are several tabs that appear when a cube is opened. Each of the elements is associated with the cube. They include

+ **Cube:** Used to build or edit the measures or measure groups of the cube.

+ **Dimensions:** Used to define how dimensions are used within the cube.

+ **Calculations:** Used to build or edit calculations for the cube.

+ **KPIs:** Used to build or edit Key Performance Indicators for the cube.

+ **Actions:** Used to build or edit actions for the cube.

+ **Partitions:** Used to build or edit partitions of the cube.

+ **Aggregations:** Used to build aggregations for the cube.

+ **Perspectives:** Used to build or edit perspectives of the cube.

+ **Translations:** Used to build or edit translations of the cube.

+ **Browser:** Used to browse the deployed cube.

Figure 1-4 also shows that the primary pane of the BIDS window is viewing the Dimensions tab. Both dimensions and measure groups can be viewed and manipulated from this view.

Using SQL Server Management Studio (SSMS)

The second tool that can be used to manage SQL Server Analysis Services (SSAS) databases is SQL Server Management Studio (SSMS). The primary purpose of SSMS for SSAS projects is to administer instances of Analysis Services objects (such as performing back-ups, monitoring processing, and so on).

SSMS can also be used to recreate objects and cubes, although you generally find that these tasks are easier to accomplish with the Business Intelligence Development Studio.

Querying data from an Analysis project is done with scripting. SSMS provides an Analysis Services Scripts project that can be used to develop, test, and save scripts. Multidimensional Expressions (MDX) scripts, Data Mining Extensions (DMX) scripts, and XML for Analysis (XMLA) scripts can be developed and tested within SSMS.

Chapter 2: Creating Business Intelligence Solutions with BIDS

In This Chapter

✔ **Understanding business intelligence**

✔ **Understanding Analysis Services Scripting Language (ASSL)**

✔ **Creating a SQL Server Analysis Project**

✔ **Exploring Your Project**

*B*usiness intelligence translates raw data into usable information — exactly what business managers need to make intelligent decisions. Whether a manager is overseeing 100 different projects, or 100 different retail stores, she must be able to view the key information. By creating cubes from databases, you can convert raw data into usable information.

The Business Intelligence Development Studio (BIDS) is the central tool used to create SQL Server Analysis Services (SSAS) projects. You can use it to create, modify, and manage cubes. In this chapter, you create a cube and gain a better understanding of the details that can be added to a cube from within BIDS.

Understanding Business Intelligence

Business intelligence (BI) is a group of applications used together to improve the decision making process. With the availability of databases and the huge amount of data they contain, the problem facing executives isn't that they don't have enough data, but instead that they have too much data.

BI tools are used to compile and present the data in a more meaningful way so that executives and decision makers can focus on what's important. BI provides *actionable insight* — information useful enough to take action on.

SQL Server 2008 includes three BI applications. All three are available within the Business Intelligence Development Studio (BIDS). They are

+ **SQL Server Reporting Services (SSRS):** SSRS provides a means to retrieve relevant data from databases and present it to users in a meaningful way without requiring users to know things like SELECT, FROM, and WHERE. Instead, a user can launch his Web browser, and simply point and click to retrieve the needed data.

+ **SQL Server Integration Services (SSIS):** When data needs to be combined, SSIS can extract, transform, and load (ETL) data. Sophisticated SSIS packages can be created within BIDS to integrate databases.

+ **SQL Server Analysis Services (SSAS):** SSAS allows you to design, create, and manage multidimensional structures that allow decision makers the ability to view data easily from different perspectives. Cubes are denormalized versions of the database (the multidimensional structures) used to provide different views and help decision makers focus on what's important.

While each of the applications can be used separately, in sophisticated BI applications, they're tied together to improve the decision making process.

Microsoft Project Server 2007 provides an excellent example of how different elements can be tied together to provide better business intelligence. The BI tools are used by an external application (Project Server) to provide decision makers with the in-depth knowledge they need to make intelligent decisions.

First, consider a single project. A Project Manager (PM) may use a tool, such as Office Project Professional 2007, to create and manage a project. He would create a timeline, milestones, tasks, and other details on the project. This project could then be published to Project Server 2007. All this information is held in a database on the Project Server. Then others who are interested or involved in the project can view and provide entries into the project via their Web browser.

For example, project team workers are assigned tasks and as they complete the tasks, they access the project on Project Server to mark the tasks complete. The PM can easily track the progress of the project and make adjustments as needed.

Now consider a company that has 100 different projects occurring simultaneously. The CEO needs to know what's going on with the projects. Are any projects behind? Are any projects over budget? Should resources be reallocated? Although the CEO does need to know about problem areas, she can't afford to be engulfed with the details of every project.

Because PMs publish their projects to the Project Server and the data is held within databases, cubes can be created by using SQL Server Analysis Services to compile this information. Measures and dimensions can be used within the cubes to give the CEO the focused information she needs. Key performance indicators (KPIs) can be used to define thresholds, such as 10 percent over budget or 10 percent behind schedule. Now, with just a few clicks, the CEO can call up reports that quickly identify problem areas.

Microsoft Project Server is just one of many different applications that can pull together the different information.

The AdventureWorks2008 database focuses on the Adventure Works Cycles business. Instead of projects, timelines, and budgets, the focus is on products and sales. Cubes created on the AdventureWorks2008 database would have different measures, dimensions, and KPIs.

Understanding Analysis Services Scripting Language (ASSL)

Using the Business Intelligence Development Studio (BIDS) is an excellent way to build, manage, and modify cubes; however, advanced developers and programmers can use the Analysis Services Scripting Language (ASSL).

ASSL is an XML-based scripting language, and ASSL scripts are executed from different applications. They're actually executed from within BIDS after you complete a wizard, although you won't see the ASSL script. If desired, ASSL scripts can be executed from within fully developed applications (such as Project Server) to modify or manipulate cubes.

ASSL commands are divided into two parts:

✦ **Data Definition Language (DDL):** These commands define and describe an instance of SQL Server Analysis Services (SSAS) including the databases and data contained in the instance.

✦ **Command language:** The command language is used to send action commands (such as `Create`, `Alter`, and `Process`) to SSAS.

How you interact with SSAS and how you use ASSL depends largely on which role you have within your organization. Generally, three database roles exist related to business intelligence (BI) specialists. The three roles are

✦ **Database administrator:** The database administrator (DBA) generally ensures the SSAS server remains operational. The DBA might occasionally tweak SSAS objects, but generally uses SQL Server Management Studio to interact with SQL Server Analysis Services objects.

✦ **Database developer:** The database developer designs the cubes (including dimensions and measures) from the ground up based on business needs. The Business Intelligence Development Studio (BIDS) includes many tools to help the developer. The developer can edit the ASSL XML files directly, but usually uses the graphical tools to accomplish the necessary tasks.

✦ **Business intelligence developer:** The business intelligence (BI) developer is more specialized in developing BI solutions for companies. A BI developer might do the majority of the building of the SSAS solution in BIDS, but can also create applications in high-level languages, such as C# or Visual Basic, to interact with SSAS.

To be a BI developer, you need a solid understanding of the syntax and rules of ASSL. However, most of us can use BIDS to accomplish required tasks.

As a simple example (really, this is a simple example for ASSL), the following code creates a data source by using the `Create` command. Notice that it follows the rules of XML with XML tags and nested tags.

Steps are included in the next section ("Creating a SQL Server Analysis Project") to create a data source view after you've created a BIDS project. The bold items in the following script show what you enter or configure with the wizard.

The following script uses the `xmlns` tag extensively to identify XML namespaces that are used to define schemas. An *XML schema* (also known as an *XML schema definition* or *xsd*) is used to define what tags are acceptable and unacceptable. They can be very valuable in helping a developer avoid typos.

```
<Create
    xmlns="http://schemas.microsoft.com/analysisservices
    /2003/engine">
-- This is the end of the Create tag.
    <ParentObject>
        <DatabaseID>AdventureWorks</DatabaseID>
    </ParentObject>
    <ObjectDefinition>
        <DataSource
xmlns:xsd="http://www.w3.org/2001/XMLSchema"
xmlns:xsi="http://www.w3.org/2001/XMLSchema-
instance"
xmlns:ddl2="http://schemas.microsoft.com/analysisser
vices/2003/engine/2"
xmlns:ddl2_2="http://schemas.microsoft.com/analysiss
ervices/2003/engine/2/2"
xmlns:ddl100_100="http://schemas.microsoft.com/analy
sisservices/2008/engine/100/100"
xsi:type="RelationalDataSource">
```

```
         <ID>Adventure Works DW 2008</ID>
         <Name>Adventure Works DW 2008</Name>
         <ConnectionString>Provider=SQLNCLI10.1;Data
   Source=localhost;Integrated Security=SSPI;Initial
   Catalog=AdventureWorksDW</ConnectionString>
           <ImpersonationInfo>
     <ImpersonationMode>ImpersonateServiceAccount</Impers
     onationMode>
           </ImpersonationInfo>
           <Timeout>PT0S</Timeout>
       </DataSource>
     </ObjectDefinition>
   </Create>
```

**Book VI
Chapter 2**

**Creating Business
Intelligence
Solutions with BIDS**

The previous code was created by right-clicking the data source of a deployed project in SQL Server Management Studio (SSMS) and choosing Script Data Source As⇨Create To⇨New Query Editor Window. However, it could just as easily be executed from a third-party application used to create a connection to a data source. Chapter 3 in this mini-book shows you how to use SSMS to explore a deployed SSAS project.

Creating a SQL Server Analysis Project

The Business Intelligence Development Studio (BIDS) is used to create SQL Server Analysis Services (SSAS) projects. SQL Server 2008 uses the Visual Studio 2008 shell, so if you're familiar with Visual Studio, you'll notice many similarities.

The overall steps that you need to follow to create and use a cube are

1. Create a project

2. Define a data source

3. Define a data source view

4. Create a cube using measures and dimensions

The following sets of steps lead you through each process.

These exercises use the AdventureWorksDW2008 database available as a free download from Microsoft's CodePlex site. CodePlex is Microsoft's open source project hosting Web site. The SQL Server database samples are found here:

www.codeplex.com/MSFTDBProdSamples

At the site, click the Releases tab and download the AdventureWorksDW2008 database. Run the executable on your SQL Server system and follow the installation wizard to install the AdventureWorksDW2008 database. Be sure to select Restore AdventureWorksDW2008 to be installed on your local hard drive.

Use the following steps to create an SSAS project within BIDS. You use this project to create a SQL Server Analysis cube. These steps assume you've installed SQL Server Analysis Services on your server.

1. **Launch the Business Intelligence Development Studio by choosing Start⇨All Programs⇨Microsoft SQL Server 2008⇨SQL Server Business Intelligence Development Studio.**

BIDS launches but is blank. A project needs to be either opened or created.

2. **Choose File⇨New⇨Project.**

3. **On the New Project page, select Analysis Service Project. Enter** AdventureWorks **as the name and set the location to** C:\AdventureWorks.

You might have to create a folder named AdventureWorks on your C:\ drive for this project, but you can do so with the Browse button. At this point, your display looks like Figure 2-1. The Name, Location, and Solution Name should be the same on your screen.

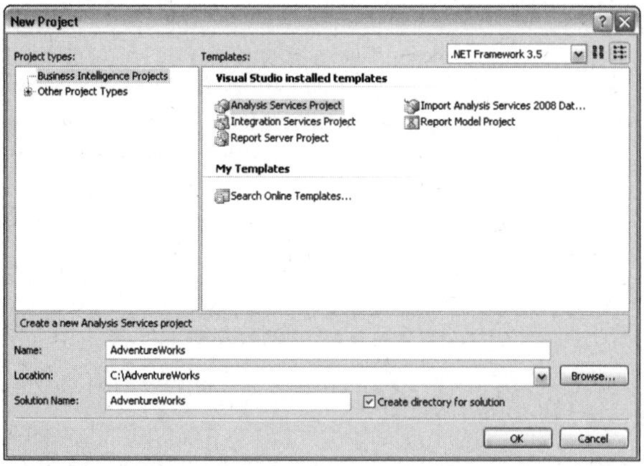

Figure 2-1:
Creating
an SSAS
project
in BIDS.

4. **Click OK. Your project is created and displayed in Visual Studio.**

On the far right of Visual Studio, is the Solution Explorer. Your project (AdventureWorks) is shown here. It includes containers for all your SSAS objects used within the project. (Although at this point, all the containers are empty.)

5. **Leave BIDS open for the next steps.**

Creating a data source

After you create your project, you need to connect to a database and pick the tables or views you want to use within your SSAS cube.

For this project, you use the AdventureWorksDW2008 database. If you haven't downloaded and installed the AdventureWorksDW2008 database yet, now's the time.

The following steps add the AdventureWorksDW2008 database to the project as your data source. You then add tables and views that are used as data source views within your project.

1. **If not already open, launch BIDS by clicking Start⇨All Programs⇨ Microsoft SQL Server 2008⇨SQL Server Business Intelligence Development Studio. Open the AdventureWorks project created in the previous steps.**

2. **In Solution Explorer, right-click Data Sources and choose New Data Source.**

   The New Data Source Wizard launches.

3. **On the Welcome to the Data Source Wizard page, click Next.**

4. **On the Select How to Define the Connection page, ensure the Create a Data Source Based on an Existing or New Connection option is selected. Click the New button.**

5. **On the Connection Manager page, ensure the Provider is set to Native OLE DB/SQL Server Native Client 10.0. In the Server Name text box, enter** Localhost. **In Select or Enter a Database Name, select AdventureWorksDW2008 from the drop-down box.**

   Your display looks like Figure 2-2. The Provider, Server Name, and Database Name should be the same on your screen.

6. **On the Connection Manager page, click OK.**

7. **On the Select How to Define the Connection page, click Next.**

8. **On the Impersonation Information page, select Use the Service Account and then click Next.**

9. **On the Completing the Wizard page, accept the Data Source of Adventure Works DW2008 and then click Finish.**

10. **Leave BIDS open for the next steps.**

At this point, you have a project with a data source (the AdventureWorks DW2008 database), but need to create a data source view and a cube.

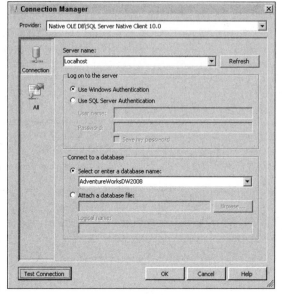

Figure 2-2:
Configuring
the
Connection
Manager for
your data
source.

Creating a data source view

The *data source view* defines the tables and views you use within your cube. In order to pick the best tables and views, you really need to know your data.

Fortunately, in this section, we use the AdventureWorksDW2008 database and name the tables within the steps. However, in a real-life environment, you spend a lot of time trying to determine what data the end users want so that you can accurately pick the correct tables. You add these tables to the data source view to use within your cubes.

The good news is that these aren't final decisions. If you need to change your data source view later, you can. You must ensure, however, that you don't remove tables that are being used within any cubes in your project.

The following steps show you how to create a data source view. These steps assume you created the data source in the previous steps; however, you can also create the data source and the data source view at the same time by launching the Data Source View Wizard.

1. **If not already open, launch BIDS by choosing Start➪All Programs➪ Microsoft SQL Server 2008➪SQL Server Business Intelligence Development Studio. Open the AdventureWorks project created in the previous steps.**

2. **Right-click Data Source View and select New Data Source View.**

3. **On the Welcome to the Data Source View Wizard page, click Next.**

4. **On the Select a Data Source page, ensure the AdventureWorks DW2008 data source is selected and then click Next.**

5. **On the Select Tables and Views page, hold down the Ctrl key and select the following tables: DimCustomer, DimGeography, DimProduct, DimDate, and FactInternetSales. Click the > button to add the tables to the list of included objects.**

   Your display looks like Figure 2-3. You should have the same five items in the Included Objects area.

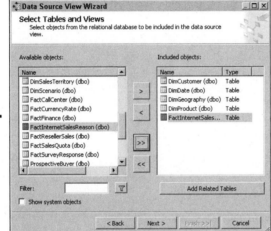

Figure 2-3:
Selecting tables and views for your data source view.

6. **On the Select Tables and Views page, click Next.**

7. **On the Completing the Wizard page, accept the name of Adventure Works DW2008 and then click Finish.**

   Your display looks similar to Figure 2-4. This is a graphical representation of the data source showing the selected tables and the relationships among the tables. The primary key for each table is identified with they key icon.

   The FactInternetSales fact table is central to all the tables through the primary key and foreign key relationships. A *fact table* (also known as a *measure group table*) contains the measures that are important to your user (such as the number of units sold).

8. **Leave BIDS open for the next steps.**

With the data source and data source view created, you can create the cube.

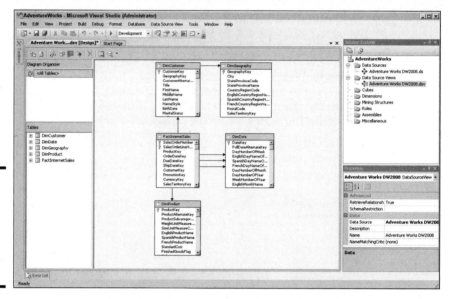

Figure 2-4:
Viewing tables and views in your data source view.

Creating a cube

A cube includes the dimensions and measures used within the cube. Depending on the tables you add, the Cube Wizard suggests which tables to use for measures and dimensions.

After it's configured, you can think of a cube as a complex view. You can observe and manipulate the cube properties just as you can observe and manipulate a view. Additionally, you can observe the data retrieved from the cube just as you can observe the data retrieved from the view. Unlike the view, the cube can allow multiple perspectives of the data depending on the dimensions and measures you add.

In the following steps, you use the data source view created from the previous steps. That data source view includes the FactInternetSales table. The wizard will analyze the tables you've selected and accurately suggest that you use the FactInternetSales table as a measure group table.

1. **If not already open, launch BIDS by clicking Start⇨All Programs⇨ Microsoft SQL Server 2008⇨SQL Server Business Intelligence Development Studio. Open the AdventureWorks project created in the previous steps.**

2. **Right-click Cubes and choose New Cube.**

3. **On the Welcome to the Cube Wizard page, click Next.**

4. **On the Select Creation Method page, ensure Use Existing Tables is selected and then click Next.**

5. **On the Select Measure Group Tables page, click the Suggest button.**

   The `FactInternetSales` table is selected as a measure group table.

6. **Click Next on the Select Measure Group Tables page.**

   The Select Measures Page appears. Notice that all the measures from within the fact table (`FactInternetSales`) are checked. However, not all of these measures are valid; therefore, you don't need to add all the measures to your cube.

7. **On the Select Measures page, clear the check box for the following columns within the `FactInternetSales` table: `Promotion Key`, `Currency Key`, `Sales Territory Key`, and `Revision Number`. Click Next.**

8. **On the Select New Dimensions page, deselect the check box next to Fact Internet Sales and leave the rest of the check boxes checked. Click Next.**

   This adds dimensions for `Product`, `Date`, and `Customer`.

9. **On the Completing the Wizard page, click Finish.**

   Before you can browse the cube, you need to build and deploy it.

10. **From the Build drop-down menu, choose Build AdventureWorks.**

11. **From the Build drop-down menu, choose Deploy AdventureWorks.**

    In the bottom-right pane (under the Properties pane), the Status pane indicates that the deployment succeeded. This may take a minute or so. You can launch SQL Server Management Studio (SSMS), connect to the Analysis Services instance, and browse the database you deployed.

That's it. You've created, built, and deployed a cube. Don't be misled though. Although the wizard has done a lot of the work and made it look rather easy, a lot has gone on. If you created this by using the Analysis Services Scripting Language (ASSL), you'd have pages and pages of scripts.

At this point, you might want to explore the project. BIDS gives you several tools that can be used to view, test, and modify your project. In the next section, each of the tabs associated with a cube are explained and explored.

Exploring a SQL Server Analysis Services Project

You can use the Business Intelligence Development Studio (BIDS) to explore, test, and maintain a SQL Server Analysis Services (SSAS) project. By exploring a project, you can identify what cubes are available, how each cube is created, and what data is available. The actual data presented by any cube can be explored and tested with the Browser feature within BIDS.

BIDS is the tool you, as the developer, use to view and test your project, but it isn't what the end-user uses. Instead, the end-user views the project's cube data from an external application.

For example, your company might develop an application that reads cube data and displays it via SharePoint. End users could access the application via their Web browser. However, before you deploy the cubes, you'd need to view and test them to ensure that the appropriate data is available. Viewing and testing your project within BIDS saves a lot of development time.

Figure 2-5 shows Solution Explorer open with a solution named Adventure Works. A data source and data source view has been created from the AdventureWorksDW database. The AdventureWorksDW cube is selected, and right below it, you can see all the dimensions that are included within the cube.

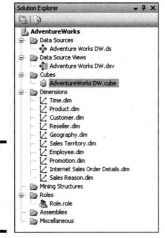

Figure 2-5:
An
Adventure
Works
solution.

You can view and test any element of this solution within BIDS by double-clicking the element in the BIDS Solution Explorer. For example, to view the `AdventureWorksDW` cube, you double-click the cube. This opens a window with several panes showing the details of the cube. The measures and dimensions used within the cube identify the key information the cube will exploit. However, a cube has several more elements that can enhance the capabilities of the cube. All these are shown when the cube is open. By clicking the Browser tab of an open cube, you have the capability of testing the cube to verify you're getting the data you expect.

One of the great things about BIDS is that additional features become available based on the type of project you're working with. For example, with a SQL Server Analysis Project (SSAS), the primary pane in BIDS includes multiple tabbed documents.

Of course, this can be an intimidating aspect of BIDS. Suddenly, all these extra windows are available. For example, Figure 2-6 shows a cube open and being browsed. To allow all the tabs to be shown, we unpinned the Toolbar, Solution Explorer, and Properties panes. The Browser tab is selected, and dimensions from the cube have been dragged into the primary pane to view the data.

**Book VI
Chapter 2**

**Creating Business
Intelligence
Solutions with BIDS**

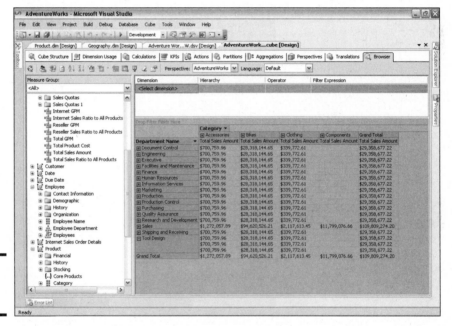

Figure 2-6:
Viewing
a cube.

Any pane can be pinned or unpinned in BIDS. A pushpin icon at the top-right of the pane allows you to "pin" the pane to the window, just as you pin a note to a note board. If you "unpin" the pane, it slides to the edge of the window but can be retrieved by hovering over the tab. Figure 2-6 shows the panes unpinned, but each tab is still showing. Each tab shows a different element of the cube. The tabs that are available when you work with cubes are described in the following sections.

The Cube Structure tab

You use the Cube Structure tab to build and edit the measures and dimensions of a cube.

Figure 2-7 shows the cube structure of a sample cube. It lists all the measures and dimensions of the cube. *Note:* Each measure and each dimension are preceded with a plus (+). You click the + to drill into the details of any measure or dimension to give you better insight into the underlying data.

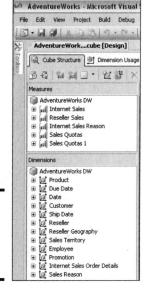

Figure 2-7: Viewing the Cube Structure tab.

Measures are usually numbers like quantities or dollar amounts, and in a business, sales are frequently measures. A *dimension* holds a collection of related objects (also called *attributes*) such as different properties of a product.

The Dimension Usage tab

The Dimension Usage view shows the relationships between measures and dimensions. Measures are grouped together in *measure groups*.

A dimension is related to one or more measures; however, a dimension doesn't need to be related to all the measures in a cube. Similarly, any measure can be related to one or more dimensions but doesn't need to be related to all dimensions.

Figure 2-8 shows a view of the Dimension Usage tab. The Product dimension is related to both the Internet Sales and Reseller Sales measure groups. Other dimensions are also available (though not shown in the figure) that relate to other measures.

Often dimensions are tied together with hierarchies to allow users of the cube to drill down into more-detailed data. For example, a product can be within a category and subcategory. To show these relationships, the dimension hierarchy would be created as Category, Subcategory, Product.

**Book VI
Chapter 2**

Creating Business
Intelligence
Solutions with BIDS

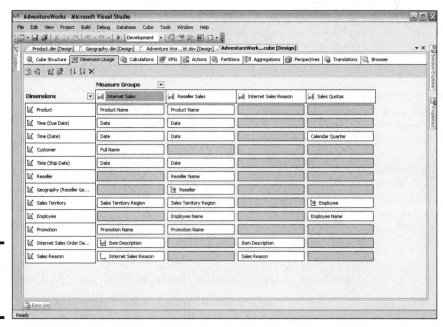

Figure 2-8:
Viewing the
Dimension
Usage tab.

The Calculations tab

You build and edit calculations for the cube in this view. Calculations are used to combine different members of a dimension or measure. For example, you can create a calculated member that multiplies two dimension values within the cube. The calculated definition is stored in the cube, but the values are actually calculated at query time.

Figure 2-9 shows the Calculations tab for a cube. The Script Organizer pane shows the calculations that have been created, with the Total Sales Amount calculation selected. The primary pane shows the expression used to create the calculation.

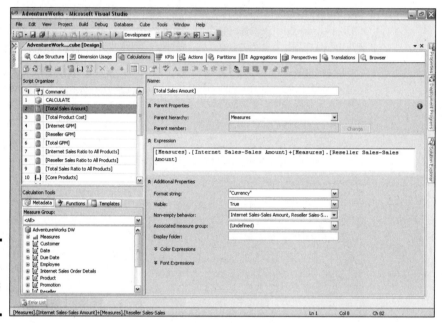

Figure 2-9:
Viewing the Calculations tab.

The Sales Amount for the Internet Sales is added to the Sales Amount for the Reseller Sales to give the Total Sales Amount. You can add as many calculations as needed for your cube.

The Key Performance Indicators (KPIs) tab

The KPIs tab is used to build or edit key performance indicators for the cube. KPIs are created to identify key company specific measures such as gross sales, net profit (or loss), or sales growth.

A company's progress toward meeting overall strategic objectives can be measured with KPIs. Figure 2-10 shows the KPIs tab. The Reseller Revenue KPI is selected with the value, goal, and status showing. The trend would be available by scrolling down.

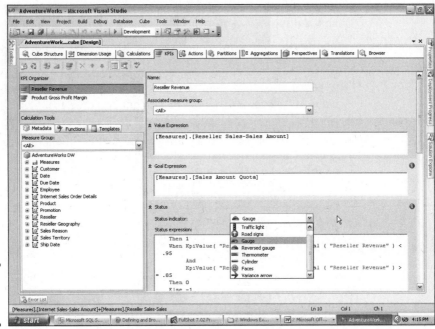

Figure 2-10:
Viewing the
KPIs tab.

To understand KPIs better, you need to understand how they are created.
A KPI includes at least a value, but can also include a goal, status, and trend.
Each of these elements is explained in the following list:

Book VI
Chapter 2

Creating Business
Intelligence
Solutions with BIDS

✦ **Value:** The current value of the KPI is represented in the Value Expression
box. In Figure 2-10, the expression points to the Sales Amount for Reseller
Sales. In other words, the actual sales amount for resellers is used.

✦ **Goal:** The goal is matched to the strategic goals of the company. For
example, resellers might have a specific sales quota for a given time
period. In Figure 2-10, the Goal Expression box shows that the goal is
expressed as the value from the Sales Amount Quota measure. It's also
possible to use a calculated value within the goal. For example, a goal
for a quarterly sales KPI could be expressed as 1.2 * the value of the
same quarter last year. This indicates a goal of a 20-percent increase in
sales.

✦ **Status:** The KPI status is used to compare the value to the goal. Status
can be displayed as three or five values. With three values, 1 is good or
high performance, 0 indicates acceptable or medium performance, and
–1 is poor or low performance.

When using five values, a risk value is added between bad and acceptable. Additionally a raising value is added between acceptable and high.

The status expression is used to identify ranges for each of these values and is created in the Status box. For example, a value that meets or exceeds the goal could be assigned a value of 1. A value that is between 85 percent and less than 100 percent of the goal could be assigned a value of 0. A value less than 85 percent could be assigned a value of −1.

Going with the old saying that an icon is worth a thousand words, icons are used to represent the status. In Figure 2-10, the icon is shown as a gauge. The gauge could use the low zone to indicate the value −1, the middle zone for the value 0, and the high zone for the value 1.

✦ **Trend:** The KPI trend is used to show how well the KPI value is doing over a specific period. For example, you might want to compare last year's quarterly sales with this year's quarterly sales.

The trend indicates whether the performance is degrading, staying the same, or increasing.

The Actions tab

You build or edit actions in this view. *Actions* are used to associate methods of displaying data when the cube is browsed. Three types of actions can be specified to occur when different areas of the cube are selected:

✦ **Standard actions:** Standard actions are used to return data, such as data from a URL, an HTML page, a dataset, or a rowset.

✦ **Drillthrough actions:** A drillthrough action returns a set of rows representing the underlying data of a selected cell. In other words, the source of the data is shown instead of the derived data result. For example, imagine that total annual sales are derived by adding sales for each month. Instead of showing an annual sales figure, the individual monthly sales figures can be shown.

✦ **Reporting actions:** A reporting action specifies that a report will be displayed in this section of the cube. The report is retrieved from SQL Server Reporting Services (SSRS).

Figure 2-11 shows the Actions tab with a single action (Internet Sales Details Drillthrough Action) defined. When selected, it displays the five columns from the Internet Sales Order Detail dimension in the Drillthrough Columns box of the primary pane.

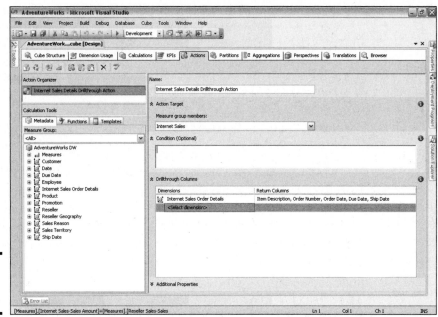

Figure 2-11:
Viewing the
Actions tab.

Actions are often used to show data outside of the cube. For example, individual invoices might not be available in a cube that aggregates sales data. However, if your cube allows the user to drill that low into the data, an SSRS report could be retrieved and shown instead.

The Partitions tab

Partitions can be built or edited within this view. Except for very large cubes, a single partition is usually all that you see here.

Every cube has at least one partition, but you can create multiple partitions if desired. A *partition* holds the data and aggregations for a measure group. If desired, you can add additional fact tables and store them in different partitions within the cube.

When using large cubes, creating additional partitions can make your job of managing the cubes much easier. For example, instead of a single partition to hold sales data for the past 15 years, you can create a separate partition for each year.

Figure 2-12 shows the Partitions tab. Five partitions are shown (Internet Sales, Reseller Sales, Internet Sales Reason, Sales Quotas, and Sales Quotas 1). The Internet Sales partition is open.

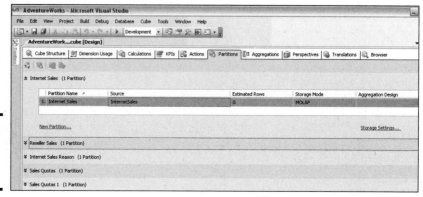

Figure 2-12: Viewing the Partitions tab.

Additional partitions can be created by clicking the New Partition link and following the New Partition Wizard.

The Aggregations tab

Use this view to build or edit aggregations for the cube. *Aggregating* data is the process of gathering data and presenting it in summary form. Aggregations within the cube are pre-calculated summaries.

Most data that you view within a cube is summarized, or *aggregated*. However, not all possible aggregations are created when the cube is built. If an aggregation isn't available when data is queried, SSAS is able to compute the value on the fly.

By creating aggregations in advance, frequently queried values can be ready when queried, which speeds up the process.

SQL Server 2008 includes an Aggregation Manager that can view existing aggregations and create additional aggregations.

The Perspectives tab

This view is used to build or edit perspectives for the cube.

A cube *perspective* is a subset of the cube. Think of a cardboard box; it has several different sides. By moving the box in different ways, you change the perspective and change what is viewable.

A cube might be much larger and more complex than a user needs. Creating perspectives reduces the complexity of the cube. For example, a cube that holds all the sales data can be presented as an Internet Sales perspective or a Reseller Sales perspective. Now the VP of Internet Sales can look at exactly what's important to her.

Figure 2-13 shows the Perspectives tab. Three perspectives are shown (Internet Sales, Reseller Sales, and Sales Summary). You can see how different perspectives include different measures. For example, the Internet Sales perspective includes the Total Product Cost, Sales Amount, Tax Amount, Freight, and Count measures.

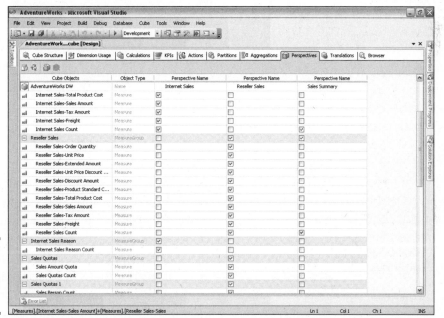

Figure 2-13:
Viewing the Perspectives tab.

If you want to modify the measures available within a perspective, it's as easy as simply checking or unchecking the box for the measure. If you want to omit the tax amount from the Internet Sales perspective, you uncheck the box for the Internet Sales-Tax Amount measure.

The Translations tab

Translations are built or edited in the Translations view.

"Translations" sounds like something fancy, such as translating a 4-dimensional dimension into a 12-sided cube, but it's not that complex. With the Translations tab, you can have captions displayed in different languages.

Captions of cubes, dimensions, measures, measure groups, KPIs, and actions are referred to as *cube metadata*. All metadata can be displayed in different languages by creating translations. If it was a perfect world, you could name a cube *Sales* to have it display in French, Greek, or Latin automatically when you are in a country that uses French, Greek, or Latin.

Perhaps someday, but we aren't there yet. Instead, you need to enter each caption manually. Figure 2-14 shows the Translations tab. Translations in both Spanish and French are entered for Internet Sales and Internet Sales - Sales Amount.

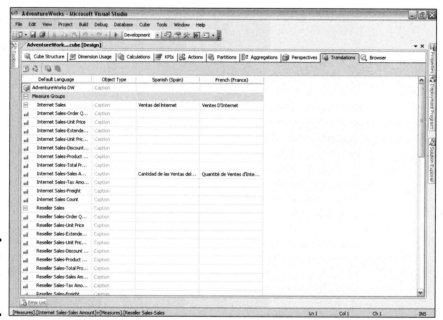

Figure 2-14: Viewing the Translations tab.

You can add as many translations as you need, but translations aren't needed if everyone using your cube speaks the same language.

Viewing cube data

To view the cube, you click the Browser tab. This allows you to test the cube to ensure it's accessing the data you expect. In other words, you can browse the data within the cube.

When you first click the Browser tab, you don't see any data. Instead, a blank slate allows you to choose what data you want to view. You can drag dimensions for the rows and columns and a measure for the center pane to give you either totals or summary details.

Figure 2-15 shows a cube being browsed using a measure of the Sales Amount for Internet Sales. The rows are populated with customer data, and the columns are populated with product data. Notice all the + signs. A user can interact with this data by pressing the plus and drilling into more-detailed data.

Figure 2-15:
Browsing
Internet
Sales data.

Category ▾			
⊞ Accessories	⊞ Bikes	⊞ Clothing	Grand Total
Country-Region ▾	Internet Sales-Sales Amount	Internet Sales-Sales Amount	Internet Sales-Sales Amount	Internet Sales-Sales Amount
⊞ Australia	$138,690.63	$8,852,050.00	$70,259.95	$9,061,000.58
⊞ Canada	$103,377.85	$1,821,302.39	$53,164.62	$1,977,844.86
⊞ France	$63,005.65	$2,523,523.04	$26,793.77	$2,613,322.46
⊞ Germany	$62,232.59	$2,808,514.35	$23,565.40	$2,894,312.34
⊞ United Kingdom	$75,155.42	$3,231,209.26	$31,788.65	$3,338,153.33
⊞ United States	$258,297.82	$9,081,545.60	$134,200.22	$9,474,043.64
Grand Total	$700,759.96	$28,318,144.65	$339,772.61	$29,358,677.22

For example, if an executive was interested in more than the total sales of bikes, but, more specifically, what bikes generated the most revenue, she could click the plus next to Bikes and expand the data.

Additionally, more detail can be gained on the customer data. Instead of just viewing the total data on a per country basis, a manager might want to know which locations in Australia were generating the most revenue.

Figure 2-16 shows the same report as Figure 2-15 but with more user interaction to show more detail on Bikes and more detail on Australia. This shows that New South Wales has the most Internet sales of bikes with almost $4 million in sales. It also shows that, globally, road bikes sell the most at more than $14 million with mountain bikes at almost 10 million.

Figure 2-16:
Drilling into
Internet
sales data
for bikes
sold in
Australia.

		Category ▾ Subcategory					
		⊟ Bikes					⊞ Clot
		⊞ Mountain Bikes	⊞ Road Bikes	⊞ Touring Bikes	Total		
Country-Region ▾	State-Province	ount Internet Sales-Sales Amount	Internet Sales-Sales Amount	Internet Sales-Sales Amount	Internet Sales-Sales Amount	Interne
⊟ Australia	⊞ New South Wales	$1,219,303.19	$2,203,910.30	$420,648.03	$3,843,861.53	$30,78
	⊞ Queensland	$642,064.76	$1,062,536.81	$238,081.08	$1,942,682.65	$14,17
	⊞ South Australia	$200,785.95	$344,305.36	$59,964.30	$605,055.60	$4,361
	⊞ Tasmania	$70,702.14	$135,212.45	$27,282.60	$233,197.18	$2,699
	⊞ Victoria	$720,963.41	$1,258,583.50	$247,706.13	$2,227,253.04	$18,23
	Total	$2,853,819.45	$5,004,548.42	$993,682.14	$8,852,050.00	$70,25
⊞ Canada		$615,440.40	$935,616.29	$270,245.70	$1,821,302.39	$53,16
⊞ France		$890,030.75	$1,298,262.60	$335,229.69	$2,523,523.04	$26,79
⊞ Germany		$1,003,800.98	$1,380,342.85	$424,370.52	$2,808,514.35	$23,56
⊞ United Kingdom		$1,142,822.30	$1,572,770.69	$515,616.27	$3,231,209.26	$31,78
⊞ United States		$3,446,845.68	$4,329,043.19	$1,305,656.73	$9,081,545.60	$134,2
Grand Total		$9,952,759.56	$14,520,584.04	$3,844,801.05	$28,318,144.65	$339,7

Book VI
Chapter 2

Creating Business
Intelligence
Solutions with BIDS

With this cube data, decision makers can easily view summary data and also drill into as much detail as they need to answer key business decisions. Clearly, this data shows that road bikes sell the most. "Which road bike is the best seller?" Click the plus next to Road Bikes, and the data is expanded. "How many locations are in New South Wales?" Click the plus, and it shows 17 locations.

Depending on how the database and cube is configured, you can drill into the stores and even the employees to determine which employees are selling which bikes.

Chapter 3: Data Mining and Maintaining Analysis Services Objects

In This Chapter

✔ Discovering data mining

✔ Integrating with Business Intelligence Development Studio

✔ Creating new scripts

✔ Managing existing Analysis Services objects

*T*he majority of your work with SQL Server Analysis Server (SSAS) projects is within the Business Intelligence Development Studio (BIDS). However, you can also use the SQL Server Management Studio (SSMS) to work with your SSAS objects.

SSMS provides access to the tools you use to create ASSL scripts easily for your objects. You can use these scripts for archives, or as templates to create additional objects using ASSL. You can also write DMX, MDX, or XMLA scripts against the SSAS project to retrieve project data. Of course, you can also use the SSMS graphical user interface to view and modify object properties.

If you don't know what all these acronyms mean — ASSL, DMX, MDX, and XMLA — don't worry. You find out about them in this chapter.

An Introduction to Data Mining

Data mining is another element of Business Intelligence (BI) available within SQL Server 2008. BI is a group of tools and technologies used to extract actionable information from a large database. Data mining is one of the BI tools.

In addition to traditional Business Intelligence analysis, data mining looks at the data and performs predictive analysis. Predictive analytics are designed to identify patterns and trends that exist in the data, and as the name implies, predict what will happen next.

Some of the benefits of predictive analysis are

+ Forecasting sales (of specific products, in specific locations, from specific customers, and so on)
+ Targeting mailings to specific customers
+ Identifying products to bundle
+ Tracking customer activity in a Web site

Some of the terms associated with data mining are

+ **Data mining:** Data mining is the process of retrieving the relevant data from a database and then using that data to perform predictive analysis. Within SSAS, data mining is achieved by retrieving the data from a data mining structure.

+ **Data mining structure:** A data mining structure identifies the database schema shared by all mining models. It includes the data source, the data source view, and the number and types of columns that can be used from within the data source view. It can include one or more mining models.

+ **Data mining model:** A data mining model is used to describe the business problem you're trying to solve through data mining. You can choose the tables desired from the data source view, and then identify the specific attributes (columns) that you want the data mining model to analyze. After the data mining model is created, it is trained, and then can be explored.

+ **Data Mining Wizard:** The Data Mining Wizard is available within the Business Intelligence Development Studio (BIDS). The wizard can be used to create a data mining structure and data mining models using that structure.

+ **Training the model:** Before you can use a data mining model for predictions, you must train the model. This is a fancy way of saying that you load it with data. Training the model is also referred to as *model processing.* After the model is trained, it is able to analyze the data and determine trends and patterns.

+ **Prediction queries:** Data mining attempts to go beyond just reporting what happened. By using prediction queries on data mining structures or data mining models, you're able to identify trends of what will likely occur in the future.

After a data mining model is created from a data mining structure, it is deployed. You then use SQL Server Management Studio (SSMS) to explore and view the data mining models. SSMS includes a query editor that executes Data Mining Extensions (DMX) queries.

Easy Integration with Business Intelligence Development Studio

To get a good feel for what a SQL Server Analysis Services (SSAS) project looks like within SSMS, you need to build and deploy a project from within BIDS. We cover BIDS in depth in the previous chapter; however, the following steps guide you through the basics of how to get an application into SSAS that you can explore.

For this procedure, you need the following installed:

✦ **SQL Server Database Services:** A typical SQL Server installation allows you to add the `AdventureWorks DW2008` file.

✦ **SQL Server Analysis Services:** After the cubes and data mining structures are built, you deploy them to SQL Server Analysis Services.

✦ **AdventureWorks DW BI 2008 file:** This file includes the AdventureWorksDW2008 database and can be obtained from this page:

`www.codeplex.com/MSFTDBProdSamples`

On the Microsoft CodePlex site, click the Releases tab to access the `AdventureWorksDWBI2008` file. After downloading the file, double-click it to launch the installation wizard and install the AdventureWorksDW2008 database on your SQL Server system. You should be able to see this database when connected to SQL Server in SQL Server Management Studio.

If you have the prerequisite files, follow these steps to build and deploy a SQL Server Analysis project that already has most of what you need. You browse to the project and launch BIDS by double-clicking the solution file. From within BIDS, you build and deploy the project.

1. **Launch the Business Intelligence Development Studio (BIDS) by choosing Start⇨All Programs⇨Microsoft SQL Server 2008⇨ SQL Server Business Intelligence Development Studio (BIDS).**

2. **Within BIDS, choose File⇨New⇨Project.**

3. **On the New Project page, ensure that Analysis Services Project is selected. Enter** Customer **in the Name text box and enter** C:\Adventureworks **in the Location box. Click OK.**

4. **Right-click Data Sources in the Solution Explorer and choose New Data Source.**

5. **On the Welcome to the Data Source Wizard page, click Next.**

6. **On the Select How To Define the Connection page, select the Adventureworks DW2008 connection. If a connection doesn't exist, follow these steps to create one.**

   a. **Select New**

   b. **Enter** localhost **for the Server Name.**

   c. **Choose AdventureWorksDW2008 from the Select or Enter a Database Name drop-down box.**

   d. **Click OK.**

7. **Click Next after you've selected the data source.**

8. **On the Impersonation Information page, select Use the Service Account and click Next.**

9. **On the Completing the Wizard page, click Finish.**

10. **Right-click Data Source Views and choose New Data Source View.**

11. **Click Next on the Welcome to the Data Source View Wizard page.**

12. **Ensure that the AdventureWorks DW2008 data source is seleced and then click Next on the Select a Data Source page.**

13. **Select the DimCustomer(dbo) table and click the right arrow to move the table to the Included Objects column. Click the Add Related tables button to add tables related to the DimCustomer table.**

    Your display will look similar to Figure 3-1. The Included Objects column will have the DimCustomer table you added, and the other three tables that were added when you clicked the Add Related Tables button.

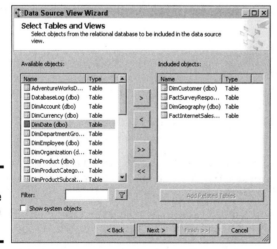

Figure 3-1: Creating the data source view.

14. **Click Next to move to the Completing the Wizard page. Click Finish.**

    The data source and the data source view is created. In the next steps, you create a mining structure and then deploy the entire project to SSAS.

15. **Right-click Mining Structures and choose New Mining Structure.**

    The Data Mining Wizard launches.

16. **On the Data Mining Wizard Welcome page, click Next.**

17. **On the Select the Definition Method page, ensure that From Existing Relational Database or Data Warehouse is selected and then click Next.**

18. **On the Create the Data Mining Structure page, ensure that Create Mining Structure with a Mining Model is selected with Microsoft Decision Trees as the data mining technique.**

    Your display looks similar to Figure 3-2. If you want to use a different data mining technique, the drop-down box provides many additional choices.

Figure 3-2:
Selecting the data mining structure and data mining technique.

19. **Click Next to access the Select Data Source View page. Accept the Adventure Works DW2008 data source view included with the project and then click Next.**

20. **On the Specify Table Types page, select the Case check box for the Customer table. Click Next.**

21. **On the Specify the Training Data page, ensure the Key check box is selected for the CustomerKey column.**

22. **Scroll to YearlyIncome and select the Prediction column. Click the Suggest button.**

    The suggest button suggests recommended inputs for the YearlyIncome Prediction column.

23. **On the Suggest Related Columns page, click OK. On the Specify the Training Data page, click Next.**

24. **On the Specify Columns' Content and Data Type page, click the Detect button to detect the content types accurately. Click Next.**

25. **On the Create Testing Set page, accept the defaults and then click Next.**

26. **On the Completing the Wizard page, click Allow Drill Through and then click Finish.**

    At this point, the project is completed and can be built and deployed to your server running SQL Server Analysis Server.

27. **Right-click the name of the project (Analysis Services Tutorial) in the Solution Explorer.**

    A contextual menu similar to the one shown in Figure 3-3 appears. Note that you have several choices from this menu including Build and Deploy.

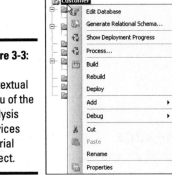

Figure 3-3:
The contextual menu of the Analysis Services Tutorial project.

28. **Choose Deploy from the contextual menu.**

    If you watch the bottom left, you'll see that the build starts and completes and then the deployment starts and completes. The build is quick, but the deployment takes a little time. Additionally, you'll see a Status window appear in the bottom right. When the deployment is complete, a green message indicates that the deployment completed successfully.

29. **Close BIDS.**

You've deployed the full project to SQL Server Analysis Services. At this point, we bet you're anxious to find out what that means.

Use the following steps to launch SQL Server Analysis Services (SSAS) in SQL Server Management Studio (SSMS):

1. **Launch the SQL Server Management Studio by choosing Start⇨ All Programs⇨Microsoft SQL Server 2008⇨SQL Server Management Studio.**

2. **On the Connect to Server dialog box, set the Server Type to Analysis Services. Enter your server name in the Server Name text box. Click Connect.**

This launches SQL Server Management Studio.

3. **To open the view, click the plus (+) next to Databases and then click the plus (+) next to Analysis Services Tutorial.**

Your display looks similar to Figure 3-4. This shows the deployed SQL Server Analysis Services Tutorial project from within SSMS. You can browse through the deployed project to view and analyze the data.

Figure 3-4:
Viewing the
deployed
Analysis
Services
Tutorial
project in
SSMS.

Understanding the DMX Language

When working with SSAS databases within SSMS, you can use the Data Mining Extensions (DMX) language.

DMX is similar to T-SQL statements, but DMX has enough differences that it requires you to spend some time to master it. If you understand T-SQL, you probably can pick up a book and learn enough of the DMX language in one sitting to get around. However, that book will be much thicker than this short chapter. All we can give you here is a short introduction.

DMX statements are used to work with mining structures and mining models. With DMX statements you can

+ Create mining structures and mining models
+ Process mining structures and mining models
+ Delete or drop mining structures or mining models
+ Copy mining models
+ Browse mining models
+ Predict against mining models

Two types of DMX statements exist:

+ **DMX DDL:** Data Definition Language statements used to create and define new mining structures and models, import and export mining models and structures, and drop existing models. DMX DDL statements include CREATE, ALTER, EXPORT, IMPORT, SELECT INTO, and DROP.

+ **DMX DML:** Data Manipulation Language statements used to work with mining models, browse the models, and create predications against them. DMX DML statements include INSERT INTO and SELECT. Just as in regular T-SQL statements, SELECT statements in DMX DML have a lot of depth in the available options.

DMX statements can be issued by using the SSMS query window while connected to a SQL Server Analysis Services instance.

Creating New Scripts

When working with SQL Server Analysis Services (SSAS) projects in SQL Server Management Studio (SSMS), you have the ability to create different types of scripts.

Using the tools within SSMS, you can generate Analysis Services Scripting Language (ASSL) scripts, or you can create your own DMX, MDX, or XMLA queries.

The Analysis Services Scripting Language is described briefly in Book 6, Chapter 2. In short, it is an XML-based scripting language used to create and modify SQL Server Analysis objects.

Generating ASSL scripts

One of the benefits of using SQL Server Management Studio is the ability to create new scripts easily from existing SQL Server Analysis Services projects. It's as easy as right-clicking the SSAS object you want to script and selecting the output target.

For example, Figure 3-5 shows how you can create an Analysis Services Scripting Language (ASSL) script for a mining structure. By right-clicking any object, you can generate a script to a New Query Editor Window, an external file, or the Clipboard so that you can paste the script into another document.

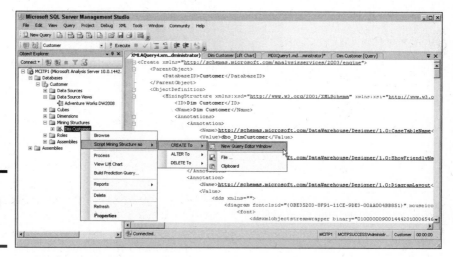

Figure 3-5: Generating an ASSL script.

Any of the objects within an SSAS project can be scripted by using this process. This includes the entire database, data sources, data source views, cubes, dimensions, measure groups, and data mining structures.

Creating queries

Within SSMS, you can create and execute three types of queries. Figure 3-6 shows how to create any of the query windows. To execute queries against the database, you right-click the database. Choosing New Query creates an MDX query window, shown behind the New Query⇨DMX selection.

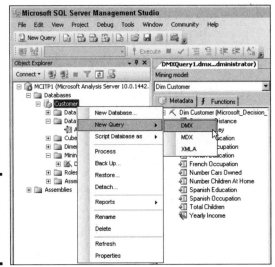

Figure 3-6:
Creating an
SSAS query
window in
SSMS.

As shown in Figure 3-6, the three types of queries you can create within
SSMS are

+ **DMX:** Data Mining Extensions (DMX) are used to query and work with
  data mining models. For example, prediction queries are created in DMX
  to retrieve data. DMX statements are also used in SQL Server Reporting
  Services reports.

+ **MDX:** Multidimensional Expressions (MDX) are used to query multidimensional data or create MDX expressions within a cube. The MDX language
  references tuples and sets. A *tuple* identifies a single cell within the cube
  by using a multidimensional coordinate. A *set* is a collection of tuples.

+ **XMLA:** XML for Analysis (XMLA) queries are used to query data sources
  that exist on the World Wide Web or that are accessible using traditional
  World Wide Web protocols, such as HTTP within a network. XMLA is an
  open standard, but Microsoft has extended the specification with additional commands used for data definition, data manipulation, and data
  control support.

Managing Existing Analysis Services Objects

All the SQL Server Analysis Services (SSAS) objects have properties and set-
tings that can be viewed and manipulated by using SQL Server Management
Studio. Some of the properties pages allow you to view only the properties.
The only way to change these properties is to go back into the Business
Intelligence Development Studio (BIDS), make the modification, and re-
deploy the database.

However, most objects can be manipulated within SSMS. For example, Figure 3-7 shows the Proactive Caching property page of the Customer dimension within a deployed SSAS database. These settings determine how the data is stored, and how much latency is acceptable.

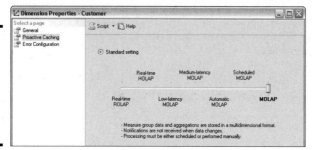

Figure 3-7: Business Intelligence Development Studio (BIDS).

The Proactive Caching settings can be manipulated on cubes, measures, and dimensions to affect both the storage type and latency. Remember, the SSAS database and objects are built from a regular SQL Server database. As the SQL Server database changes, the SSAS database becomes out of date.

How often the core data changes and how up-to-date the data needs to be for the end-users determine the caching settings that you need. The choices are

✦ **Real-time ROLAP (Relational Online Analytical Processing):** Updates to the data happen in real time and both the data and aggregations are stored in a relational format (instead of a multidimensional format).

✦ **Real-time HOLAP (Hybrid OLAP):** Updates to the data happen in real time. The data is stored in a relational format, and the aggregations are stored in a multidimensional format.

✦ **Low-latency MOLAP (Multidimensional OLAP):** Updates to the data are targeted to occur within 30 minutes of the change. Both the data and the aggregations are stored in a multidimensional format.

✦ **Medium latency MOLAP:** Updates to the data are targeted to occur within four hours of the change. Both the data and the aggregations are stored in a multidimensional format.

✦ **Automatic MOLAP:** Updates to the data are targeted to occur within two hours of the change. Additionally, automatic MOLAP retains data in the current MOLAP cache when new cache data is being rebuilt. This causes automatic MOLAP to perform better than other MOLAP choices and would be chosen when query performance is most important. Both the data and the aggregations are stored in a multidimensional format.

✦ **Scheduled MOLAP:** Updates to the data are targeted to occur automatically every 24 hours. Scheduled MOLAP is most useful in situations where only daily updates are required. Both the data and the aggregations are stored in a multidimensional format.

✦ **MOLAP:** Updates to the data source are not tracked, and updates to the OLAP data must be done manually or scheduled. MOLAP provides the best possible performance, and it can be used when updating data isn't critical. Both the data and the aggregations are stored in a multidimensional format.

Book VII

Performance Tips
and Tricks

The 5th Wave   By Rich Tennant

"They can predict earthquakes and seizures,
why not server failures?"

Contents at a Glance

Chapter 1: Working with the SQL Server Optimizer

In This Chapter

↙ **Understanding how a query optimizer works**

↙ **Communicating with the Optimizer**

↙ **Helping your Optimizer to help you**

Modern, sophisticated relational database management systems like SQL Server rely on core technology known as *query optimizers*. This key component is tasked with planning the most efficient course to achieve your data goals. To do so, it must weigh many factors, such as table size, indexes, query columns, data distribution metrics, and so on, before it can generate an accurate plan.

In this chapter, you gain a good understanding of SQL Server's Query Optimizer, and you help it do the best possible job for you. We begin by showing you what an optimizer does, using a real-world analogy as a guide. Next, you see how to interpret reports and other guidance offered by the Optimizer. Finally, you discover how to provide the Optimizer with the most up-to-date information so that it can make the best decisions.

Understanding How an Optimizer Works

Whenever you present a request to SQL Server, it must choose one of many possible approaches to give you your requested results. These strategies often employ very different processing steps; however, each strategy must achieve the same results.

A good real-world analogy is beginning a trip by car. If you need to drive from your house to the one across the street, you don't need much trip planning: You really have only one way to get there. However, what if you want to visit three other friends, each of whom lives in a different city, all of which are spread hundreds of kilometers apart? When planning your route, it doesn't matter which friend you visit first, but you must somehow see them all. Dozens of streets and roads interlace these cities. Some are high-speed freeways; others are meandering country lanes. Unfortunately, you have very limited time to visit all these friends, and you've heard rumors that traffic and construction are very bad on some of these roads.

If you were to sit down and map all the potential routes from the thousands of possible combinations, it's likely that it would take you longer to complete your mapping than if you simply picked one friend to visit at random, followed by another, and so on. Alas, you do need some sort of plan. It makes sense to get the most recent maps and construction reports and then do your best to chart an optimal course that visits all three friends as quickly as possible. If you didn't have any details about traffic and construction, you'd likely choose the high-speed freeways over the alternate routes.

Switching modes to the database world, it's the job of the optimizer to do just that: pick the right route to get you to your information as quickly as possible. When the optimizer does its job, it needs to look at all sorts of details to help it make a decision. Before arriving at the optimal outcome, the optimizer weighs such factors as the index availability, the columns you're querying, the size of the tables, and the distribution of the data.

Continuing with the database-driven example, imagine that you issue a simple query that joins data from a table containing customer records with data from a table containing payment entries. You ask the engine to find all the customers who live in Canada (the `country` field in the `customer_records` table) who have made a payment within the last six months (the `date_paid` field in the `payments` table). Furthermore, assume that an index is in place on the `customer` table's `country` field but none on the `payment` table's `date_paid` field.

How should the query proceed? Should it first scan all the rows in the `payments` table to find records with `date_paid` in the last six months and then use the index to search the `customer` table on the `country` field? Or should it do the opposite by first finding Canadians, and then finding appropriately time-stamped records from that group? How does the fact that only a few Canadian records are in the database affect the decision?

This is the work of an optimizer. By using all the available information about the table(s), it picks an action plan that correctly and efficiently satisfies the user's request. The designated course is a *query plan*. However, optimizers aren't flawless; they often require assistance and maintenance from database administrators, and can take suggestions from developers on how to determine the best query plan.

Communicating with the Optimizer

If your goal is to design and maintain a high-performance database-driven application, you're wise to invest a little time to learn how to interpret some of the many details offered by the SQL Server Query Optimizer.

Chief among these aspects are query plans, which offer a comprehensive description of how SQL Server plans to satisfy your requests. In this section, we show you the kinds of information that you find in a query plan, as well as how you can use this intelligence as guidance toward improving performance. To keep things simple, we start with some basic illustrations of query plans and then explore examples that are more intricate.

First, using the SQL Server Management Studio we created a simple header table to hold details about orders. Initially, no indexes or other performance aids are in place on this table.

```
CREATE TABLE order_header
(
    order_id INTEGER NOT NULL,
    order_date DATETIME NOT NULL,
    order_total DECIMAL(5,2) NOT NULL,
    order_instructions VARCHAR(50)
)
```

Next, we filled it with 50,000 rows of data. With the table loaded, we can start evaluating some query plans.

There are several ways to view query plans, including in XML and plain-text format. However, in keeping with this book's philosophy of leveraging powerful graphical tools, such as the SQL Server Management Studio, we focus on showing you query plans via that avenue.

To view query plans in the SQL Server Management Studio, click the Display Estimated Execution Plan icon, located along the top menu bar. In addition, consider clicking the neighboring Include Actual Execution Plan icon to see the actual resource consumption from your query.

The first query is about as simple as you can get:

```
SELECT * FROM order_header
```

Figure 1-1 shows a query execution plan generated by SQL Server.

**Book VII
Chapter 1**

Working with the
SQL Server
Optimizer

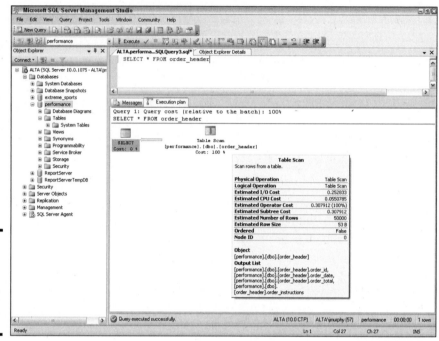

Figure 1-1:
A query execution plan for a very simple query.

In reviewing its output, a few relevant details jump out:

✦ **Physical Operation: Table Scan** — To satisfy the query, SQL Server had to read (that is, scan) all the rows to return its results.

   Table scans can be extremely costly, especially when encountered on tables containing copious data.

✦ **Estimated Costs (I/O, CPU, Operator, Subtree)** — These indicators provide guidance on SQL Server's internal estimates of its expected workload to return your results. *Note:* These numbers don't mean much in isolation; they're interesting only when compared against other query plans.

✦ **Estimated Number of Rows: 50,000** — Because we asked to see all the rows, SQL Server accurately reports that it estimates a return result set size of 50,000 rows.

The next query uses filtering to return a specific subset of rows in this table:

```
SELECT * FROM order_header WHERE order_total = 50
```

Figure 1-2 displays the new execution plan.

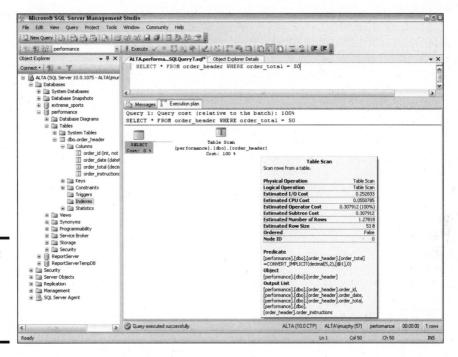

Figure 1-2:
A query execution plan for a filtered query.

SQL Server has reduced the number of estimated rows, as well as filled in the Predicate field with details about the query syntax. It's still using a table scan, so we added an index on the `order_total` column:

```
CREATE INDEX order_header_ix1 ON order_header(order_total)
```

Figure 1-3 shows what happens when the query is re-run from Figure 1-2.

This is much better: SQL Server can now use an index to return results more quickly and efficiently. Next, to make things more interesting, we created a table containing line item details about orders:

```
CREATE TABLE order_detail
(
    order_detail_id INTEGER NOT NULL PRIMARY KEY,
    order_id INTEGER NOT NULL REFERENCES order_header,
    part_number INTEGER NOT NULL,
    part_quantity SMALLINT NOT NULL
)
```

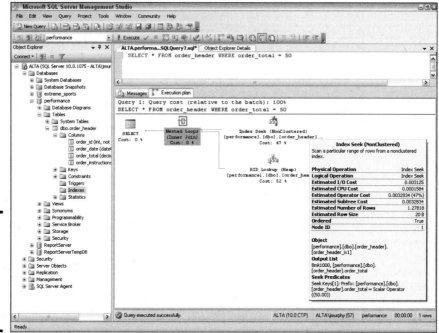

Figure 1-3:
A query
execution
plan for a
filtered
query using
an index.

Note: To enable the foreign key relationship between these two tables, we
had to create a primary key on the order_header table's order_id
column. We then inserted 250,000 rows of sample data into this new table.

With these two related tables in place, the next query is a simple join, as
shown below:

```
SELECT order_header.*, order_detail.*
FROM order_detail INNER JOIN
order_header ON order_detail.order_id = order_header.order_id
```

Figure 1-4 displays the query plan.

You can see from the execution plan that SQL Server is building an internal,
temporary table to process the results of this join. The plan also shows clustered index access to both tables, indicating an efficient strategy.

Whenever you create a primary key constraint on a table, SQL Server automatically generates an index and physically stores your table in this index
order. This is known as *clustering,* which we cover in Book VII, Chapter 3.

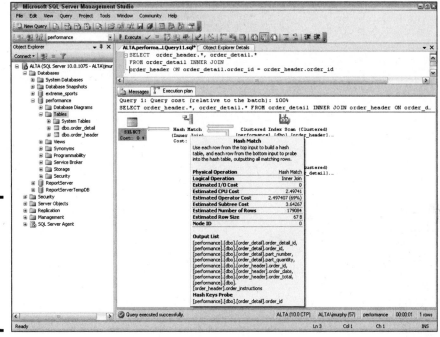

Figure 1-4:
A query
execution
plan for
a join
between
two related
tables.

Finally, we created a more complex query that includes sorting, indexed filtering, joins, and non-indexed filtering:

```
SELECT order_header.*, order_detail.*
FROM order_detail INNER JOIN
order_header ON order_detail.order_id = order_header.order_id
WHERE order_header.order_date = '12/30/2009'
AND order_detail.part_number = 1793
OR order_detail.part_quantity BETWEEN 1 AND 10
ORDER BY order_header.order_date
```

Figure 1-5 displays the SQL Server's plan to deliver the results.

If metrics and statistics are your thing, you'll have a great time interpreting execution plans for these kinds of queries.

Experience is the best teacher — feel free to create sample databases, populate them with data, and then create and evaluate the query execution plans.

Execution plans aren't just for queries. SQL Server generates these plans for any operations that interact with your database.

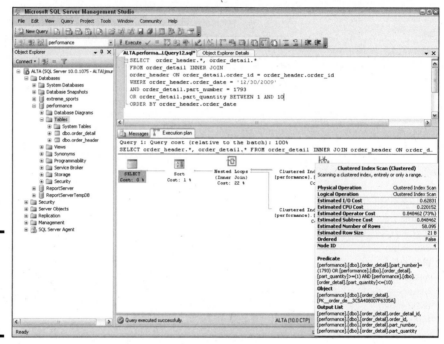

Figure 1-5:
A more
complex
query
execution
plan.

Helping Your Optimizer Help You

The SQL Server Query Optimizer is quite adept at using all available resources to execute your database tasks as quickly and efficiently as possible. However, you can take specific steps to make the Optimizer more productive, which translates into better performance for you and your users.

Create effective indexes

In the absence of a well-thought-out indexing strategy, the Query Optimizer can do only so much: Table scans and other sub-optimal accommodations will always be time-consuming and sluggish. Remember this fact when you design and configure your SQL Server database.

Write well-designed queries

Even if you've created effective indexes, unfortunately, you're still free to create poorly conceived queries that might prove too challenging for an efficient query execution plan. To combat this undesirable outcome, Chapter 3 of this mini-book furnishes you with some tips to make your queries run more quickly.

Enable and maintain statistical information

To pick the optimal query execution plan, SQL Server employs statistical details about all the tables that are participating in the query. When you define an index, SQL Server automatically creates statistics for any columns present in that index.

To get an idea of what SQL Server tracks about your data, Figure 1-6 shows the output of the DBCC SHOW_STATISTICS command.

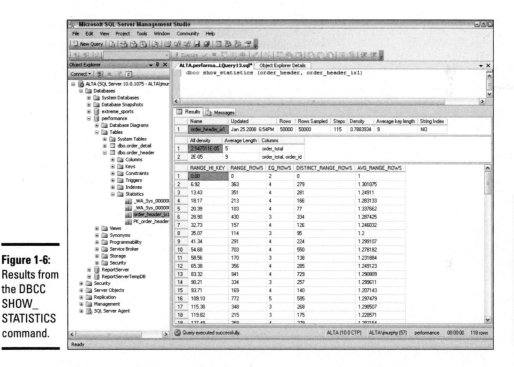

Figure 1-6: Results from the DBCC SHOW_STATISTICS command.

These metrics were generated when we placed an index on the order_amount column from the order_header table. Even though much of this statistical information is automatically generated and maintained, there might be times when you explicitly want to create a set of statistics, such as on a non-indexed column. Follow these steps to do so:

1. **Launch SQL Server Management Studio.**

2. **Connect to the appropriate SQL Server instance.**

3. **Expand the connection's entry in the Object Explorer view.**

4. **Expand the Databases folder.**

5. **Expand the folder for the database containing the table where you want to create new statistics.**

6. **Expand the folder for the appropriate table.**

7. **Right-click the Statistics folder, and choose New Statistics.**

   A dialog box where you configure the new statistics appears.

8. **Provide a name for the statistics.**

   This can be anything you like, as long as it doesn't conflict with an already existing name.

9. **Click the Add button, and select all the columns that should be part of this statistics group.**

   Figure 1-7 shows the Select Columns dialog box.

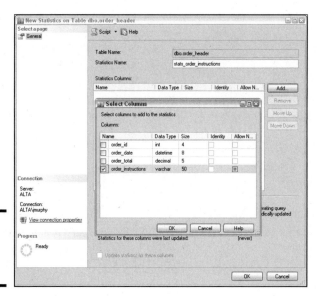

Figure 1-7:
Creating
new
statistics.

In this case, we've asked SQL Server to track statistical details about the `order_instructions` column.

10. **Click OK to complete the task.**

    SQL Server creates new statistics that use the chosen column(s).

If you want SQL Server to stay on top of maintaining its statistical oversight of your database, don't disable automatic statistic updating for the server.

Chapter 2: Using Performance Monitoring Tools

In This Chapter

✔ Getting a complete picture with Windows Task Manager

✔ Administering performance monitoring with Microsoft Management Console System Monitor

✔ Taking advice from the Database Engine Tuning Advisor

✔ Viewing graphical performance information with SQL Server Profiler

✔ Enforcing control with the Resource Governor

*I*n the old days (circa 1990) of deciphering the root causes of performance problems, database administrators were often in the dark about what exactly was happening on their systems. There were collections of relatively primitive tools, but understanding how to use these aids was often more trouble than it was worth. Fast forward to today, and things have improved tremendously. This chapter shows you the excellent collection of performance monitoring technologies that are at your disposal and how to use the technologies most effectively.

We begin the chapter by describing some best practices for your performance monitoring. We then examine the *Windows Task Manager* — a great tool for understanding the high-level performance landscape of your SQL Server system. Next, you find out about the Microsoft Management Console System Monitor, the highly effective Database Engine Tuning Advisor, and the SQL Server Profiler. Finally, as part of a good performance-optimization strategy, you use the Resource Governor to bring order to key resources.

Laying the Right Foundation for Performance Monitoring

Before getting started with a detailed performance monitoring tool review, here are a few tips that you can use to make this important effort as productive as possible.

Change one variable at a time

For overworked administrators facing performance nightmares, it's often tempting to rush ahead and make many optimizations at one time. Unfortunately, this makes it nearly impossible to figure out which of the alterations worked. Consequently, you're always better off changing one setting at a time, and then monitoring the results of your modification.

Focus on graphical tools

While SQL Server has matured over the years, Microsoft has done an excellent job of providing increasingly sophisticated graphically based management and monitoring tools. Still, many character-based techniques are available that you can use to stay on top of performance, but currently, you'll get the most mileage by focusing on these graphical tools (which the balance of the chapter describes). Of course, if you're curious, you're free to look at the output of performance-related stored procedures and other character-based utilities.

Set performance policies

SQL Server ships with a collection of highly capable system management best practices. Known as *policies* (accessible through the SQL Server Management Studio's Management folder), implementing these recommendations can give you a leg up on performance. For example, Figure 2-1 shows one of these performance-related policies (focused on setting the maximum degree of parallelism).

As with many of SQL Server's administrative capabilities, feel free to experiment with these performance monitoring and management tools by using a sample database and projected workload. This can go a long way toward giving you the necessary experience and confidence to support your production users.

Collect performance statistics

Book I, Chapter 4 shows you how to gather and store performance-related metrics. If you haven't considered this approach, it bears investigation: It's the foundation for conducting performance research even if a given problem might have been spurious and occurred in the past.

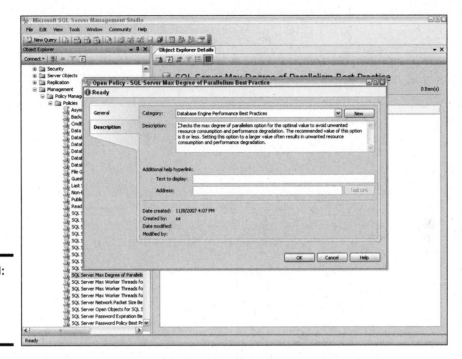

Figure 2-1:
A perfor-
mance-
related
policy.

Getting a Complete Picture with Windows Task Manager

Chances are, if you spend any time administering a Windows-based computer, you've probably gotten to know the Windows Task Manager and its
ability to give you an overview of everything that's happening on your computer. What you might not realize, however, is that this tool is also helpful in
determining high-level causes of SQL Server performance degradation. Take
a brief look at this beneficial utility.

Launch the Windows task manager by simply right-clicking the taskbar and
choosing the Task Manager option. As shown in Figure 2-2, it features several
tabs of statistics and details of interest to SQL Server administrators:

✦ **Applications:** This tab informs you which programs (usually launched
  by a user) are running on the server.

✦ **Processes:** Unlike the relatively few user-launched programs that are
  typically active at one time, this tab shows you a full list of specific
  processes that are currently running. Pay special attention to this tab.
  Often, many more processes are running than you might have realized.

Windows servers are notorious for having extraneous, memory-draining processes hanging around.

If you don't see the SQL Server processes within the Windows Task Manager, you might need to check the box (or button, depending on the version of Windows you're running) that tells the utility to display all running processes.

✦ **Performance:** Here, you find a collection of helpful statistics about the overall load on your server. Be especially cognizant of the Page File Usage History graph — paging is one of the most expensive operations your computer can perform.

✦ **Networking:** On this tab, you find specialized graphs that inform you about current communication activities for each network connection.

✦ **Users:** This tab itemizes details about all the users currently connected to your server. You can even disconnect or logout a specific user session.

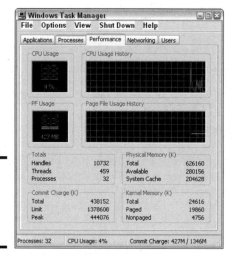

Figure 2-2:
The
Windows
Task
Manager.

If you're a statistics maven, don't forget to look at the View menu for each tab. Often, many additional performance-related indicators are available.

The Windows System Monitor

The Windows Task Manager is a great place to start when trying to understand the current performance profile of your system. However, when it's time to get more serious about gaining a deeper understanding of your performance metrics, it's hard to beat the *Windows System Monitor* — a sophisticated tool that tracks massive data amounts, including SQL Server-specific information. What's also especially useful is that it works for your local machine as well as remote machines. This means that you can monitor multiple servers at one time from within one user interface.

Depending how your server is configured, there are several ways to launch this utility. One fail-safe approach is to open the Control Panel, and drill into the Administrative Tools folder. When you're in this folder, double-click the Performance shortcut. Figure 2-3 shows a rudimentary example of this utility.

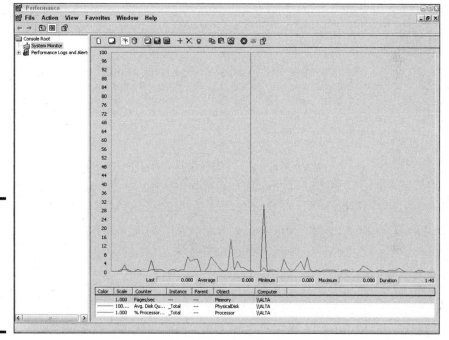

Figure 2-3:
The Microsoft Management Console System Monitor.

One of the most compelling capabilities for this monitor is its ability to incorporate reams of information from various classes of system metrics into a holistic, easy to understand user experience. A list of all available objects and their related statistics would fill many pages; therefore, here's a look at several of the most relevant objects from the perspective of a SQL Server system administrator:

✦ **Processor:** As part of this performance object, you find numerous indicators related to the health of your computer's central processing unit.

✦ **System:** This performance object rolls up a number of system-wide performance metrics.

✦ **Physical disk:** Because optimal disk performance is vital to the overall health of your SQL Server installation, examine all of the statistics available as part of this performance object.

✦ **Logical disk:** This group of statistics takes physical performance indicators and maps them to any logical disks that have been enabled for your system.

✦ **SQL Server:** More than three dozen performance objects are dedicated solely to SQL Server. Within each performance object are collections of related statistics.

Don't be intimidated by all these performance objects and counters. If you're unsure of what value a specific statistic provides, highlight the counter, and then click the Explain button to learn about it.

After you have the system monitor running, it's quite simple to add statistics of interest to your graph. Clicking the + symbol above the graph shows you a list of all performance objects. Highlight the performance object of interest to see a group of counters for that object. Figure 2-4 gives you an idea of just how many performance objects are available.

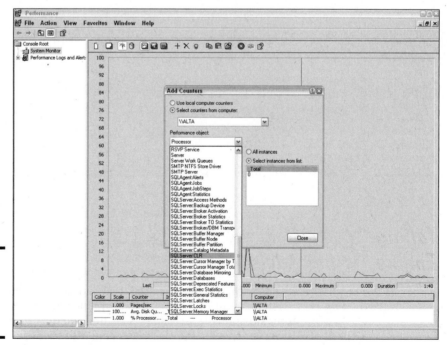

Figure 2-4:
Selecting a performance object.

After you've chosen your performance object, you can identify one or more counters to include on your graph. *Remember:* Hold down the Ctrl key to select multiple counters. For example, in Figure 2-5, we chose the `SQLServer:Databases` performance object and are now selecting from the counters list.

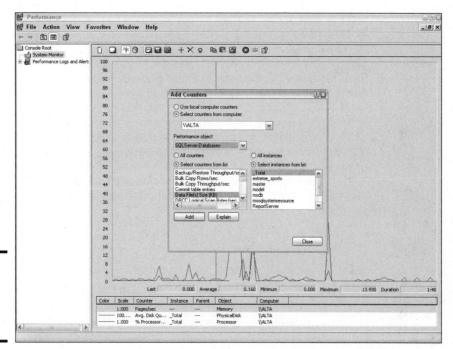

Figure 2-5:
Selecting performance counters.

**Book VII
Chapter 2**

**Using Performance
Monitoring Tools**

When you've finished picking your counters, click Add to place them on your graph. If you no longer want to see a given counter, highlight it and click the X icon.

Taking Advice from the Database Engine Tuning Advisor

The chapter begins with an explanation of the Windows Task Manager and the Windows System Monitor — performance utilities that allow you to check SQL Server's responsiveness. In this section, we turn your attention to a group of SQL Server-specific utilities, beginning with the Database Engine Tuning Advisor.

Given their busy schedules, database administrators often don't have the time to explore fully all the performance ramifications for the databases under their control. This results in well-administered (yet unnecessarily sluggish) database and application performance. This is where the *Database Engine Tuning Advisor* comes into the picture — it harnesses the power of a sophisticated rules engine that delivers customized performance recommendations based on your database structures and predicted workloads. In fact, you can even include an exact, real-world series of Transact-SQL statements for this utility to evaluate. This realism takes out much of the guesswork of administering and tuning your SQL Server instance, especially with regard to important decisions involving indexes, indexed views, and partitioning. This results in more predictable, optimal responsiveness. Here's how to launch and use this extremely capable technology.

For the purposes of this example (and the others yet to come in this chapter), we're continuing with the database introduced in Book II, Chapter 6. To refresh your memory, this sample database was created to support a new business that focuses on teaching extreme sports. As to workload, we've created a rather complex SQL statement that aims to identify all the courses that generated at least $1,200 in tuition during 2007. Here's how that query appears:

```
SELECT SUM(payment_amount) as 'Total Payments',  c.course_name
FROM payments p JOIN student_courses sc ON (p.student_id = sc.student_id),
courses c JOIN student_courses sc1 ON (c.course_id = sc1.course_id)
WHERE p.payment_date BETWEEN '2007-01-01' AND '2007-12-31'
GROUP BY c.course_name
HAVING SUM(payment_amount) > 1200
```

We're using this query to show you the value of managing real-world style workloads with the powerful analytical capabilities of the Database Engine Tuning Advisor. Here's how to get started:

1. **Launch the SQL Server Management Studio.**

2. **Choose Tools⇨Database Engine Tuning Advisor.**

   A New Connection dialog box appears.

3. **Choose the server you want to analyze, your authentication method, and then click Connect.**

   An empty session monitor appears, as shown in Figure 2-6.

4. **Right-click the server name and choose the New Session option.**

   This opens a specialized dialog box where you enter all the information necessary for SQL Server to perform the analysis. (The next series of steps explores these necessary details.)

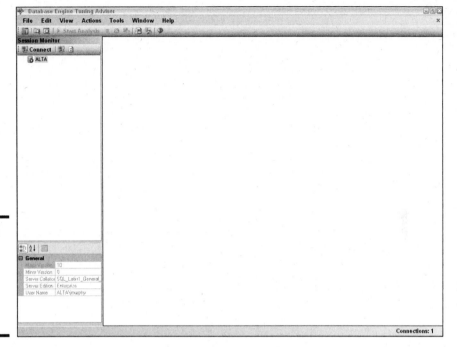

Figure 2-6:
The initial
Database
Engine
Tuning
Advisor
screen.

5. **(Optional) Provide a name for the session.**

   If you don't give it a name, SQL Server uses a combination of your user-name with the date and time.

6. **Identify either a file or a table where the workload can be found.**

   There's no need to type the exact path to the workload. Regardless of whether you choose a file or a table, SQL Server allows you to browse for the workload contents. For the purposes of this example, a stand-alone SQL query file contains the Transact-SQL statement from earlier in this chapter.

7. **Choose a database to hold the results of the workload analysis.**

8. **Pick a database and the tables that you want SQL Server to tune.**

   Figure 2-7 shows that SQL Server will analyze the `extreme_sports` database and all its tables.

9. **Configure your tuning options.**

   Figure 2-8 illustrates all the tuning options at your disposal and the advanced options as well.

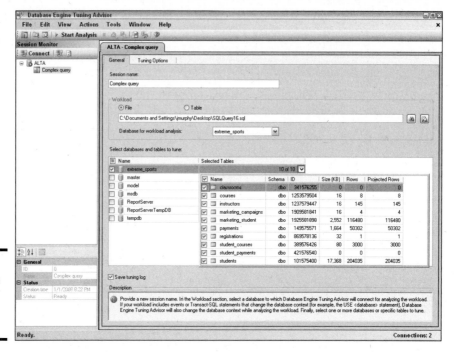

Figure 2-7:
Choosing a
database
and tables
for tuning.

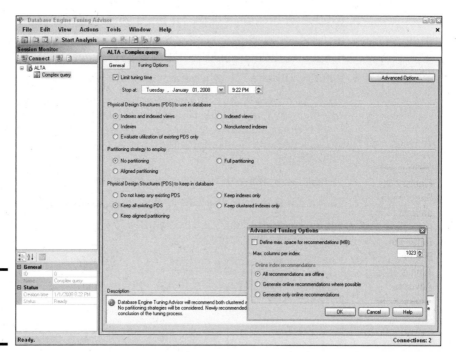

Figure 2-8:
Setting
tuning
options.

For this example, we're placing a limit on the amount of time SQL Server can tune the database, and we're requesting guidance on indexes and indexed views. For this session, we don't want any advice on partitioning, and we're electing to keep all physical design structures in the database.

10. **When you've finished setting tuning targets and options, click the Start Analysis button at the top of the screen.**

SQL Server gets to work running your analysis. This might take some time depending on the complexity of your workload and database structure.

After the Database Engine Tuning Advisor finishes its work, output similar to Figure 2-9 appears. In this case, SQL Server has recommended that we create two indexes on both the `payments` and `student_courses` tables.

It's also worthwhile to look at one of the many reports that SQL Server generates as part of this operation. Figure 2-10 shows one of these reports. *Note:* You can get to these reports by clicking the Reports tab at the top of the screen.

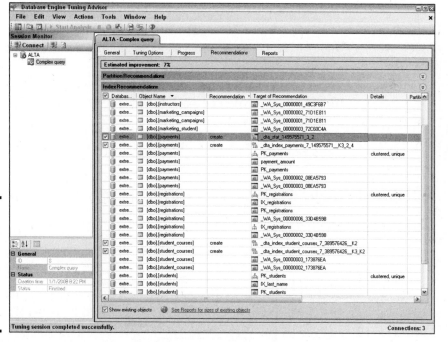

Figure 2-9: Recommendations from the Database Engine Tuning Advisor.

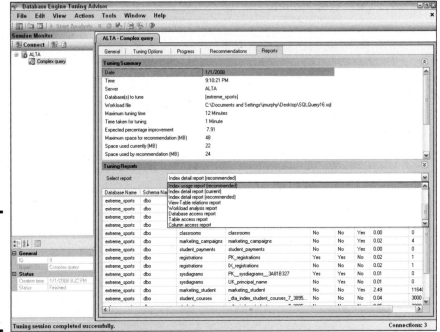

Figure 2-10:
Reports
from the
Database
Engine
Tuning
Advisor.

11. **Implement the suggestions made by the Database Engine Tuning Advisor.**

It's quite easy to put these recommendations into play — choose the Apply Recommendations option from the actions menu. You have the flexibility of applying the recommendations right now or setting a date and time in the future. Figure 2-11 shows the output of applying these recommendations to the database.

Viewing Graphical Performance Information with SQL Server Profiler

If you could predict the exact date, time, and type of performance problems in advance, chances are you could solve them before anyone is the wiser. Unfortunately, these issues rarely give much notice when they arise. This is where the *SQL Server Profiler* comes in — it enables you to collect all sorts of performance-related (and other) administrative information that you can then view to identify trouble spots. This makes it much easier to enhance your SQL Server throughput.

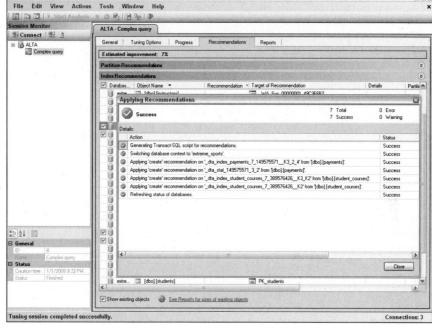

Figure 2-11:
Results from applying Database Engine Tuning Advisor recommendations.

Gathering trace information

In this section, we show you how to launch this important tool, as well as gather and analyze performance metrics. Here's how to get the ball rolling:

1. **Launch the SQL Server Management Studio.**

2. **Choose Tools⇨SQL Server Profiler.**

You can also launch this utility from the Windows SQL Server performance tools submenu. Regardless of how you launch this tool, a New Connection dialog box appears.

3. **Choose the server you want to profile, your authentication method, and then click Connect.**

The Trace Properties dialog box appears, where you set all the parameters necessary to conduct your trace. Figure 2-12 shows the initial Trace Properties dialog box.

This dialog box contains two tabs: General and Events Selection. On the General tab, you provide the name of your trace, whether to use a template, where you want output to go, and whether you want to set an end time for your trace. The Events tab is where you select the database activity you want to trace.

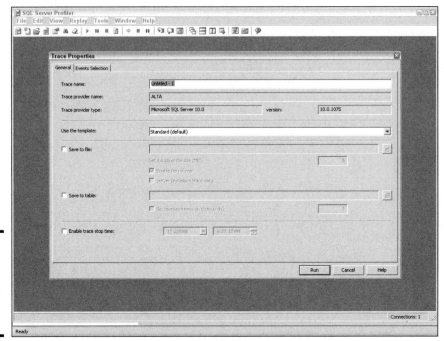

Figure 2-12:
The initial window for tracing SQL Server activity.

The amount of information generated by this utility can be quite large. If you're concerned about consuming massive amounts of disk space, give some thought to placing a stop time on your trace.

4. **Switch to the Events tab and then select one or more event classes to trace.**

SQL Server offers a truly massive number of event classes. To see a full list of these event classes, remember to select the Show All Events check box. You can get a better idea of what's tracked within each event class by rolling your cursor over the event name. Finally, within each event class are numerous individual types of events to track, as you'll see shortly.

Here's a list of all the available event classes that you can trace with a brief summary of their purpose:

- **Broker:** Events related to SQL Server's service broker, which is used for messaging, integration, and distributed computing purposes.

- **CLR:** Details about the SQL Server common language runtime.

- **Cursors:** Events that track usage of these data management structures.

- **Database:** Information regarding database and log file activity.

- **Deprecation:** A gathering of metrics regarding soon-to-be-obsolete capabilities.

- **Errors and Warnings:** Alerts you when faults of varying severity are generated.

- **Full text:** Details regarding searches and other manipulation of full-text based data.

- **Locks:** Messages about lock-related activities.

- **OLEDB:** Reports of calls to this API.

- **Objects:** Events related to creation, alteration, and deletion of database objects.

- **Performance:** Metrics and indicators related to throughput-based events.

- **Progress Report:** Updates regarding online index operations.

- **Query Notifications:** Details about query-driven publications and subscriptions.

- **Remote Activation:** Traces of activities that are initiated from other computers.

- **Scans:** Indicators about when table/index scans are started and stopped.

- **Security Audit:** Details about activities from a security perspective.

- **Server:** Events that affect server-wide resources.

- **Sessions:** Messages regarding new sessions.

- **Stored Procedures:** Indicators related to the preparation and execution of these server-based components.

- **TSQL:** Activities regarding Transact-SQL statement compilation and execution.

- **Transactions:** Events of interest about the creation, successful completion, and rollback of transactional activities.

- **User Configurable:** A set of events that you, the administrator, can define and trace.

5. **For each event class, choose one or more event types.**

To get a full list of event types for each event class, click on the + symbol for the event class. The complete inventory of events that can be traced appears, as shown in Figure 2-13.

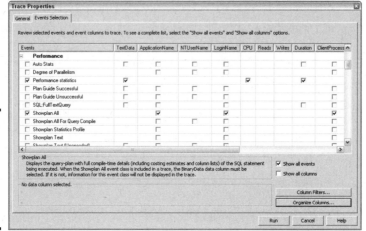

Figure 2-13:
An expanded view of the Performance event class.

In this example, we've expanded the Performance event class, and have begun choosing individual events for inclusion in the trace. Again, if you're interested in what each event type means, roll your mouse over the event name to see a description.

6. For each event, select one or more columns to trace.

We aren't kidding when we say that the SQL Server Profiler can track massive amounts of runtime activity. As an administrator, however, you can select which details to track for each event. This is important because if you just take all the available columns, you run the risk of being overwhelmed with details. Figure 2-14 provides an example of the rich variety of columns at your disposal.

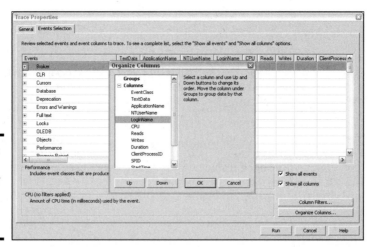

Figure 2-14:
Available columns for the SQL Server Profiler.

If you're a glutton for information, and want to see all the potential columns that can be tracked, select the Show All Columns check box.

7. Decide whether you want to filter any column values. If so, click the Column Filters button. Click OK when you've finished your filter settings.

If left to its own devices, the SQL Server Profiler will generate tons of data. With that amount of metrics, finding the source of your performance problem is akin to finding a needle in a haystack. Fortunately, you have the option of instructing the SQL Server Profiler to filter your results based on meaningful criteria. This greatly reduces the amount of generated data and makes it much easier for you to identify any throughput bottlenecks. Figure 2-15 shows the Edit Filter dialog box.

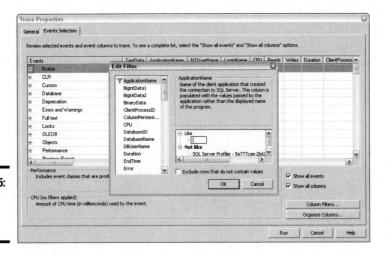

Figure 2-15: Editing column filters.

Book VII
Chapter 2

Using Performance
Monitoring Tools

8. Click the Run button to launch the trace.

This opens a window where you can monitor your results. Figure 2-16 shows an example of real-time, query plan monitoring. Figure 2-17 shows the same results in an XML format. With a little imagination, there's no limit to what you can track using the SQL Server Profiler.

9. When you're ready to stop the trace, click the Stop icon at the top of the window.

If you want to halt the trace temporarily, click the Pause icon located at the top of the window. Clicking the Run icon restarts the trace.

10. If you want to preserve your trace for future analysis or replay, choose File⇨Save.

The next section shows you how to open an existing trace and even replay the action.

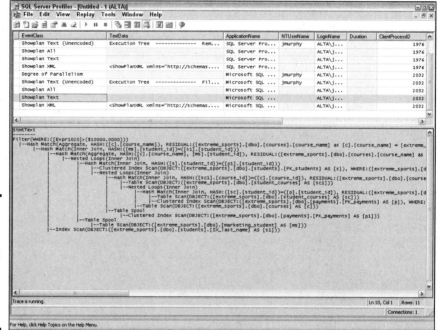

Figure 2-16:
Viewing text-based SHOWPLAN output from the SQL Server Profiler.

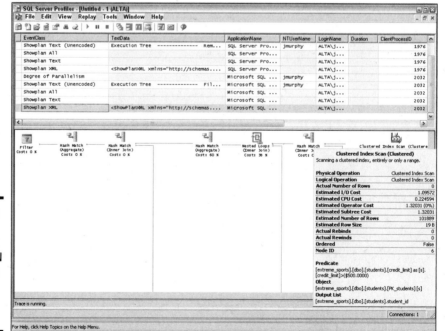

Figure 2-17:
Viewing XML-based SHOWPLAN output from the SQL Server Profiler.

Opening and replaying existing traces

If all this information gathering wasn't enough, the SQL Server Profiler gives you the option of saving and then replaying your trace at a future date. Here's all you need to do:

1. **Launch the SQL Server Management Studio.**

2. **Choose Tools⇨SQL Server Profiler.**

3. **Choose File⇨Open.**

Select a trace file, table, or a script.

4. **Set your replay options.**

If you're familiar with development tools, such as Visual Studio, you're probably comfortable replaying traces. Under the Replay menu are several valuable debugging options, including:

- **Step**
- **Start**
- **Run to Cursor**
- **Pause**
- **Stop**
- **Set a Breakpoint**

Certain types of commands can't be replayed. If the SQL Server Profiler encounters one of these commands, it will display an error message and halt the replay action.

Enforcing Control with the Resource Governor

The previous sections of this chapter show you how to monitor your SQL Server performance passively. In this section, you get proactive and implement a set of throughput-related guidelines that SQL Server can enforce for you via the *Resource Governor,* a new feature available in SQL Server 2008.

The SQL Server Resource Governor delivers several key benefits to database administrators like you. These include

- ✦ **Increased predictability and reliability of your SQL Server installation**
- ✦ **CPU and memory-based resource rationing**
- ✦ **Prevention of excessive resource consumption**
- ✦ **Activity prioritization**

Using the Resource Governor to derive these advantages could easily consume its own dedicated chapter. Because space is limited, we focus on showing you how to set up the Resource Governor, along with how to best integrate it into your environment. As with many other topics in this book, we suggest that you explore this capability in more detail by using sample database and workload profiles. When you gain the understanding of how to use the Resource Governor, you'll be in great shape to deploy it in your environment. Finally, as with most of SQL Server's other administrative capabilities, you're free to use either the SQL Server Management Studio or direct entry via Transact-SQL. In keeping with the philosophy of this book, we emphasize using the graphically based SQL Server Management Studio because that provides a consistent and easier to understand approach.

Key Resource Governor concepts and architecture

For this capability, there are three interrelated system structures — resource pools, workload groups, and classifications — each of which affects the other. After illustrating these structures, we show you how to enable, use, and monitor the Resource Governor.

Resource pools

Think of these components as several distinct, virtual groupings of SQL Server's physical resources (such as CPU and memory). The product ships with two resource pools already defined:

+ **Internal:** This resource pool is dedicated to resources consumed by internal database processing, and cannot be modified by the administrator.

+ **Default:** This resource pool is for you, the administrator, to use as a container for your workload groups. You might also create additional resource pools.

Resource pools let you configure two settings:

+ **CPU:** Within this setting, you are able to adjust two values:
  • The minimum amount of CPU resources (expressed in percentages) that workloads assigned to this resource pool may consume. *Note:* The sum of these values across your SQL Server instance may not exceed 100.
  • The maximum amount of CPU resources consumed by workloads in this resource pool.

+ **Memory:** As you probably expect, this setting is aimed at controlling memory utilization within the resource pool. It also has the minimum and maximum parameters as described above.

Workload groups

From the perspective of database processing, consider workload groups as birds of a feather. In other words, you use workload groups to help gather and monitor similar types of jobs and activities. These are grouped together for control and prioritization. As with the resource pools, SQL Server ships with two workload groups already defined:

✦ **Internal:** This workload group is associated with the internal resource pool.

✦ **Default:** This workload group is for you, the administrator, as a generic container for any requests that can't be identified with a classification formula. You're free to create additional workload groups.

Classifications

SQL Server uses these formulas (either defined by the system based on connection attributes or by a function written by the administrator) to help associate any new incoming requests with a given workload (and related resource pool). Connection attributes include

✦ **Host name**

✦ **Application name**

✦ **Username**

✦ **Group membership**

Before leaving this topic, it's worth noting that the Resource Governor may be used only for managing and monitoring the database engine. It can't be used for any of the following types of activity:

✦ **Analysis Services**

✦ **Integration Services**

✦ **Reporting**

Enabling Resource Governor

Despite the rich capabilities and limitless number of performance management permutations offered by the Resource Governor, setting it up and maintaining it is actually quite easy. Here's all you need to do:

1. **Launch the SQL Server Management Studio.**

2. **Connect to your SQL Server instance.**

3. **Expand the Management folder in the Object Explorer.**

You then see the Resource Governor. Before going any further, note that by right-clicking this entry, you can enable or disable the Resource Governor. If it's not already enabled, please do so.

4. **Expand the Resource Pools folder.**

You're shown a folder containing existing system resource pools, as well as a list of user-defined resource pools (if any exist).

5. **Right-click the main Resource Governor entry, and choose the Properties option.**

The Resource Governor Properties dialog box appears, as shown in Figure 2-18. It's worth pointing out that you can expand the Resource Governor folder to see its resource pools and their related workload groups. However, unlike many other SQL Server user interface conventions, the Resource Governor allows you to manage everything from a single properties page.

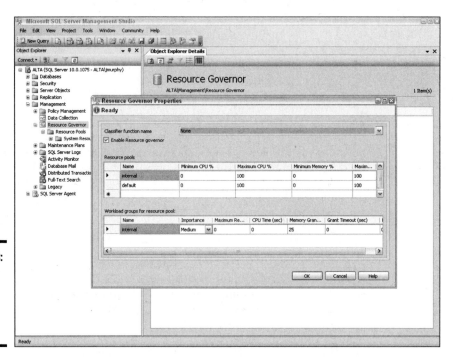

Figure 2-18:
The
Resource
Governor
Properties
page.

6. **By using the grid control, create any new resource pools and their associated workload groups.**

   If you're familiar with Microsoft Access-style grid controls, you'll be comfortable using the Resource Governor's data entry template. If not, you might want to spend a little time getting acquainted with this style of interaction with SQL Server. Alternatively, it might make sense in this situation to use direct SQL entry via your favorite query tool. We show you how to script this later in this chapter.

7. **When creating a new resource pool, provide values for the minimum and maximum settings for CPU and memory utilization.**

8. **For workload groups, provide values to help guide the Resource Governor in controlling resource consumption.**

   These settings include

   - *Importance*
   - *Maximum requests*
   - *CPU time (in seconds)*
   - *Memory grant %*
   - *Grant timeout (in seconds)*
   - *Degree of parallelism*

9. **Select a classifier function to help SQL Server identify and associate an incoming request to a workload group.**

   Recall from earlier in this chapter that SQL Server uses classifier functions to link any inbound requests with relevant resource pools. If you don't have a classifier function in place, you need to write it and then associate it with this workload group. An example of a classifier function is covered in the next part of this chapter.

10. **When you're finished making your changes, click OK.**

Resource Governor in action

After all this time examining how the Resource Governor works, how about seeing a real-world example? In this case, suppose that you're running a mission-critical SQL Server database yet must grant access to a specific user that has the potential to overload your server. Ideally, you'd simply replicate your production database to another server and let this user run queries to their heart's content. However, budget cuts have prevented you from fully realizing your vision, so it's the Resource Governor to the rescue.

For the purposes of this example, assume that this user has an already-existing login, FredCDobbs. Here's how to write and execute SQL statements to set up the necessary SQL Server structures that let the Resource Governor prevent runaway queries.

1. **Launch the SQL Server Management Studio or any other direct-entry SQL tool.**

2. **Connect to your SQL Server instance and use the master database.**

   Obviously, you need to have administrative privileges to perform the upcoming tasks.

3. **Run an SQL statement to create the resource pool.**

   Here's an example that creates a resource pool with a maximum CPU utilization of 50 percent:

   ```
   create resource pool RP_50_CPU
   with
       MAX_CPU_PERCENT = 50);
   ```

4. **Run an SQL statement to create the workload group.**

   Here's how this appears:

   ```
   create workload group WG_50_CPU
   using RP_50_CPU;
   ```

   Notice that we reference the just-created resource pool when setting up the workload group.

5. **Run an SQL statement to create the classifier function.**

   This function compares the login name with the resource-hungry user we identified at the start of the example. If there's a match, then it associates this session with the workload group. Otherwise, this session is part of the 'Default' workload group.

   Also, observe the link between this function and the workload group we created in Step 4.

   ```
   create function F_50_CPU() returns SYSNAME
   with schemabinding
   as
   begin
       declare @workload_group_to_assign as SYSNAME
       if (SUSER_NAME() = 'FredCDobbs')
           set @workload_group_to_assign = 'WG_50_CPU'
       return @workload_group_to_assign
   end;
   ```

6. **Tell the Resource Governor about the new classifier function.**

All this takes is a simple SQL statement:

```
alter resource governor with
(CLASSIFIER_FUNCTION = dbo.F_50_CPU);
```

7. Start the Resource Governor.

This also needs a basic SQL statement:

```
alter resource governor reconfigure;
```

That's all it takes to put the Resource Governor to work on your behalf. If you want to disable this classifier function, just re-run Steps 6 and 7, replacing Step 6's dbo.F_50_CPU with NULL.

Tracking Resource Governor activity

Earlier in this chapter, we show you the many statistics and other metrics that you can gather from the Microsoft Management Console System Monitor. As you might expect, the Resource Governor is very well integrated with this vital administrative tool. Figure 2-19 shows an example of configuring the tool to gather these metrics.

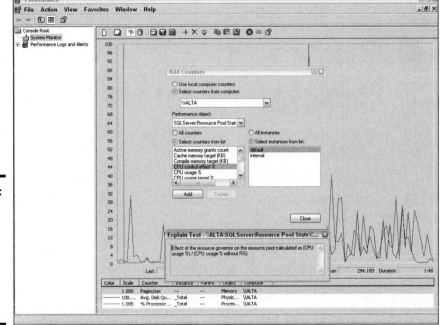

Figure 2-19:
The Resource Governor, as viewed in the Windows System Monitor.

Here's a brief itemization of the types of statistics that you can follow for each resource pool and workload group. To begin, you can examine the following for the SQLServer:Resource Pool Stats performance object:

+ **CPU usage %**
+ **CPU usage target %**
+ **CPU control effect %**
+ **Compile memory target (KB)**
+ **Cache memory target (KB)**
+ **Query exec memory target (KB)**
+ **Memory grants/sec**
+ **Active memory grants count**
+ **Memory grant timeouts/sec**
+ **Active memory grant amount (KB)**
+ **Pending memory grant count**
+ **Max memory (KB)**
+ **Used memory (KB)**
+ **Target memory (KB)**

If you're not sure about what purpose a given metric serves, simply click on the Explain button beneath the list of counters, and SQL Server will give you more insight.

Next, you can monitor the following for the SQLServer:Workload Group Stats performance object:

+ **Queued requests**
+ **Active requests**
+ **Requests completed/sec**
+ **CPU usage %**
+ **Max request CPU time (ms)**
+ **Blocked requests**
+ **Reduced memory grants/sec**
+ **Max request memory grant (KB)**

✦ **Query optimizations/sec**

✦ **Suboptimal plans/sec**

✦ **Active parallel threads**

Finally, the Resource Governor introduces several events that can be watched in the SQL Server and system event log. They include

✦ **CPU Threshold Exceeded Event Class**

✦ **PreConnect:Starting Event Class**

✦ **PreConnect:Completed Event Class**

Chapter 3: Data Access Strategies

In This Chapter

✔ Setting a good foundation for speedy data access

✔ Using indexes to enhance performance

✔ Designing high-velocity queries

✔ Changing data quickly

*B*elieve it or not, users are often more accepting of the occasional application bug than they are of a consistently sluggish system. If you think about it, this makes sense: A periodic, spectacular crash can liven up an otherwise boring day, whereas an always-lethargic application gets annoying very quickly. This chapter shows you some common tips and tricks for getting the most speed from your SQL Server database. However, this chapter focuses exclusively on database and query-level suggestions, so if you're interested in engine tuning and disk layout concepts, check out the next chapter. Moreover, if you're curious about good database design practices, make sure to peruse Book II, which focuses on these important foundations.

We start the chapter by pointing out that it's imperative to lay the groundwork for a well-running system, as well as take advantage of all the tools and technologies at your disposal for monitoring and tuning your SQL Server installation. After that, we show you how to employ indexes as an important aid in coaxing the most speed from your database. With that out of the way, it's time to see how to design queries for maximal throughput. Finally, we close the chapter with a discussion of some techniques that you can follow to make data alterations as peppy as possible.

Setting a Good Foundation

Designing and developing a high-performance database is challenge enough; there's no need to be a hero and try to figure out everything yourself. In this section, we give you a few easily implemented ideas that you can use as the underpinning for all the performance-enhancing work that you'll be undertaking. Microsoft, as well as the other vendors cited in this section, has done great work in bringing to market a collection of powerful (yet easy-to-understand) tools and technologies that can help the database administrator or application developer deliver the fastest possible solution.

Design your database with performance in mind

Conceptually, delivering a high-performance database isn't that different from many other technology design and delivery situations: It's always better to take performance considerations into account during the design phase rather than waiting until after the solution has been created and the related application code has been developed. Unfortunately, many database architects and application developers are under time constraints and forced to cut corners during the design and delivery phases of their projects. The resulting solution often has major structural inefficiencies that are difficult, (if not impossible) to correct after the project has been delivered to the users.

With this in mind, as a database designer or application developer, any performance-related effort you expend up front pays you back with interest when you get to production. If you're interested in more details about how to design your database for performance, see Book II; its chapters are tailored to help you design the most efficient database possible. Also, examine Book III, Chapter 1, which is dedicated to explaining solid normalization techniques.

Use graphical tools to assist in monitoring throughput

There's no need to operate in the dark when it comes to trying to decipher what's going on in your active SQL Server environment. As described at length in the previous chapter, Microsoft offers an excellent spectrum of tools and technologies that give the database administrator unprecedented visibility into the inner workings of the SQL Server environment. It's well worth your time to get to know each of the technologies described in that chapter. Even if you don't think you'll ever use a specific performance-related tool, you might be surprised to find that this utility provides the exact metrics that you need to understand what's slowing down your system.

For example, check out Figures 3-1 and 3-2, where you can sample the valuable results served up by the Database Engine Tuning Advisor and SQL Server Profiler, respectively.

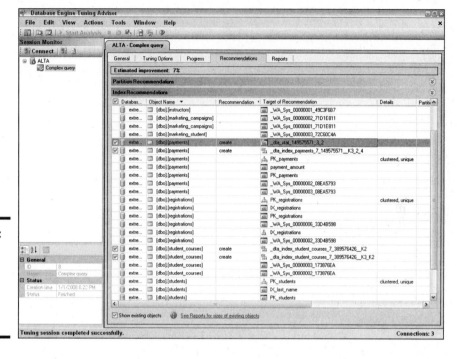

Figure 3-1:
Results
from the
Database
Engine
Tuning
Advisor.

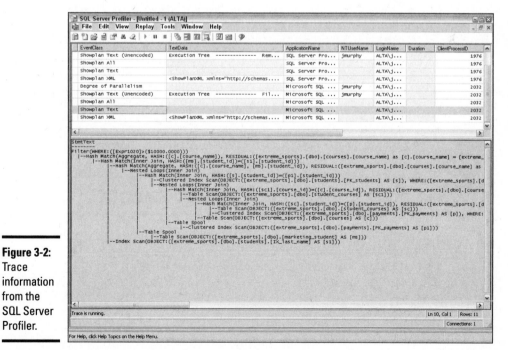

Figure 3-2:
Trace
information
from the
SQL Server
Profiler.

Take advantage of virtual machines

Microsoft does many things well. Unfortunately, as anyone who has administered a Windows system for any length of time can attest, its registry has a tendency to get cluttered and clogged with extraneous information, leading to a noticeable slowdown of your computer. This registry architectural problem is exacerbated when it comes to installing and then removing software. In fact, in many cases, barring a full scrub of your disk, it's just not possible to return your system to the pristine state it was in prior to the installation or modification. This is where virtual machines can be a lifesaver. You can easily use them to set up test environments where you can conduct experiments, confident in the knowledge that it's trivial to restore your computer to its original condition.

On the Windows platform, you have two commercial choices for virtual machine technology:

✦ **Microsoft Virtual PC:** Available for free download from Microsoft's Web site, this technology allows you to create and then run multiple separate instances of your Windows operating system on one computer. You can run as many concurrent virtual machines as you like; your only limitations are the amount of available memory, disk, and CPU capacity. This product is designed from a desktop perspective; if you're more interested in a server-side viewpoint, check out the next product.

✦ **Microsoft Virtual Server:** This product also protects your bank account: It's free! Virtual Server 2005 R2 SP1 lets you run multiple virtual instances on your computer, and sports more server-friendly capabilities than the desktop-centric Virtual PC.

✦ **VMWare Server:** Also available for free download, this is a competitive alternative to Microsoft's offerings. VMWare is compelling in that it's more adept at running different operating systems than Windows. Comparatively, you'll likely run into Microsoft license restrictions for this platform that are absent from the Virtual PC technology.

If you're running the 64-bit version of Windows Server 2008, you might want to look into Microsoft's Hyper-V technology, which is included with the operating system and offers better performance than any of the software packages I just described.

A number of open source, virtual machine alternatives are out there. However, given Microsoft and VMWare's dominance and low (or free) price points, it's wise to stick with either of these vendors.

Use data loading tools to simulate realistic information volume

Given their crushing workloads, many database architects and designers fall into the trap of populating their new creations with only small samples of data and then conducting rudimentary performance tests. Unfortunately, this small, unrealistic subset of data is an insufficient foundation upon which to build a set of meaningful performance tests. As described in Chapter 1 of this mini-book, the SQL Server Query Optimizer makes performance-related decisions based on the amount and distribution of data. Consequently, having a tiny, unworkable volume of data means that you won't be able to predict the decisions the Query Optimizer will make in production.

Other administrators or developers, facing the same need for sample data, devote scarce resources to creating their test data generation tools. Unfortunately, this isn't the best use of anyone's time. A better approach is to purchase one of the many inexpensive data generation applications available on the market. We use the DTM Data Generator (available from www. sqledit.com) to fill our newly created database with large, realistic data samples. We then evaluate the Query Optimizer's plans for the most common queries, knowing that the runtime execution plans will likely match our test cases. The combination of a data generation tool and virtual machines is unbeatable. You can create carbon copies of your runtime environment and test them to your heart's content without ever affecting a production user. As you'll see in a moment, adding a testing tool to the mix makes your experiments even more rational.

Use testing tools to simulate realistic usage

Some database designers and architects yield to the temptation to use small subsets of data in an attempt to explore their database's performance. This tiny data set results in meaningless throughput metrics. Things get worse when it comes to running application performance test cases. In many cases, no formalized testing is ever done! This omission leads to unpleasant surprises at runtime, when errors, sluggish response, data corruption, and other nasty bombshells make themselves known.

With the rise of open source, low-cost testing software, there's no reason to skimp on this important step. Instead, prescient database and application designers make the investment to implement and use these new tools to help increase the quality of their overall solution. PushToTest is an excellent example of one of these innovative technologies. You can use it to set up functional, performance, and quality of service tests without having to write any code.

Use replication to spread the workload

Database and system administrators occasionally ask too much of their computers. CPU, disk, and memory resources are finite, yet users' requirements and performance demands are limitless. The resulting response quagmire can be difficult to overcome. However, distributing the processing load can make a huge difference. As shown in Book VIII, Chapter 5, SQL Server offers a set of powerful data distribution capabilities known as *replication*.

By replicating your data, you share the workload among multiple computers. For example, suppose you're running a SQL Server database that supports a retail point-of-sale (POS) solution. Given the real-time performance demands of such an application, it's imperative that this database experience no throughput bottlenecks. At the same time, however, management also needs to run decision support reports to help run the business optimally. These reports must also be delivered quickly. At first glance, this would appear to be a no-win situation. However, this is an ideal example of where replication makes sense. You can use this feature to synchronize data between your production server (which supports the POS application) and a server dedicated for reporting. Users of the secondary server can run all the reports they like; users on the production server will never be impacted by this workload. In fact, you can set up ever-more sophisticated replication architectures, and spread the workload to more and more computers. This is a proven recipe for increasing throughput, and it's also economical given the constant drop in computer pricing.

Using Indexes to Enhance Performance

A comprehensive indexing strategy, which is often overlooked by harried database designers and application developers, is often all that's needed to supercharge a sluggish database solution. It's common to see performance improve by orders of magnitude simply by creating a new index or correcting an erroneous one. In this section, we give you some concrete, easy-to-implement index-related suggestions that can have a dramatic impact on performance.

Book II, Chapters 4 and 6 are focused on all things related to creating tables, including considerations regarding indexes.

Always define a primary key

It's easiest to think of a primary key as a unique identifier that guarantees a row's individuality. In some cases, your data already contains one or more candidate columns for primary keys. In other situations, SQL Server can generate a primary key for you. For example, take a look at Figures 3-3 and 3-4.

In Figure 3-3, we created a table and defined a primary key on an existing column. In Figure 3-4, we used the combination of the `uniqueidentifier` data type and the `NEWID()` function (used when inserting new rows) to have SQL Server create a dedicated column that will hold a unique, binary key value. As an alternative approach, we could have chosen the `identity` property for the primary key column, and SQL Server would have added new values to that field as well.

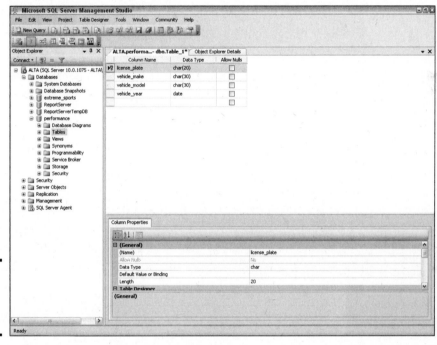

Figure 3-3:
A DBA-defined primary key.

**Book VII
Chapter 3**

**Data Access
Strategies**

The reason we chose to use our own primary key in Figure 3-3 was that we were confident that there would not be two vehicles with the same license plate. In Figure 3-4, we elected to have SQL Server create the primary key because we couldn't guarantee that there would never be a duplicate value. What's especially nice is that this value is guaranteed to be unique not only on our computer, but on any other computer in the world.

In addition to helping protect the integrity of your information, primary keys make it possible for SQL Server to perform only one read operation to find a match for a given search criteria. For example, imagine that you've defined a table that holds street address and phone number information for your customers. Further, assume that each customer has a unique phone number. By placing a primary key on the column containing the phone number, and then looking for rows based on a given phone number, SQL Server returns your result extremely quickly. In the absence of an index, SQL Server is forced to examine each row to find a match for you. And in the absence of a defined primary key, SQL Server needs to continue to look for other phone numbers that match, even though there will be at most one row with that phone number value.

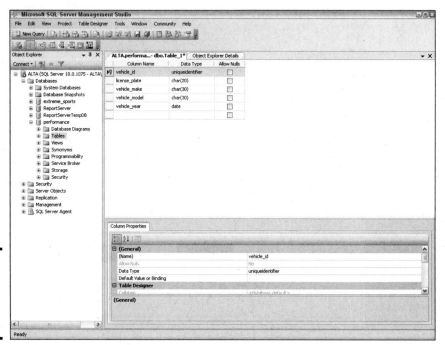

Figure 3-4:
A SQL
Server-
defined
primary key.

Use foreign key indexes when appropriate

SQL Server uses foreign keys to help safeguard related information that happens to be stored in two or more tables. In addition to the safety-related benefits provided by foreign keys, you can also boost performance by creating your indexes on these foreign key fields.

Index filter columns

You use filter columns to help SQL Server narrow the range of results for your queries. For example, you might want to return a list of customers who reside in a certain state or country. Without a filter, a query will return all the rows from the table, no matter where the customer lives. If you employ filters as part of your queries (or as part of UPDATE and DELETE operations as well), you should plan to index your most frequently used filter columns, especially if the underlying table has many rows.

Place indexes on join columns

Join columns are the mechanism that SQL Server uses to establish equivalency among two or more tables, which makes it possible to retrieve a unified view of your data. In most cases, it's a good idea to ensure that both sides of the join are indexed.

Understand clustered indexes

As with many modern relational database management systems, SQL Server gives database administrators the opportunity to store their information in the order specified by a given index. This capability, known as a *clustered index,* makes sequential access to the table very fast as long as you're using the column(s) that make up the clustered index. It's important to note that you can have only one clustered index for a table, and that SQL Server automatically uses your primary key to create the clustered index. You have the ability to change the clustering to use a different index, however.

Clustered indexes can deliver a powerful performance punch in any of the following situations:

- ✦ Queries that return large amounts of information
- ✦ Queries that return ranges of data
- ✦ Queries that join information to other tables
- ✦ Sorted (ORDER BY, GROUP BY) result sets

Don't forget to index temporary tables

If you explicitly create a temporary table and then fill it with a significant number of rows, remember that even temporary tables merit indexing, assuming that you'll be conducting operations that might benefit from supporting indexes.

Avoid highly duplicate indexes

Sometimes, in an effort to be as performance-minded as possible, administrators travel in the opposite direction and create far too many indexes on columns that never should be indexed in the first place. For example, suppose that you have a table that tracks survey results. One of the columns contains either a Yes or No value — never anything else. In this situation, it's generally unwise to create an index. Indexes consume disk space, and they also require SQL Server to perform routine maintenance whenever a row is created, modified, or deleted. This overhead can add up, and in the case of a highly duplicate index there's very little benefit to having such an index in place.

SQL Server makes optimal use of indexes when there is some variability of values contained in the index. If this column contained several other values (say, Maybe, Perhaps, and No Way), it might make more sense for you to utilize an index. You could also create a multi-column index that includes more selective, distinct data from other columns.

Take advantage of index-only access

If you frequently query groups of columns, you might benefit from a composite index to reduce the amount of disk interaction. For example, suppose that you repeatedly query a table to retrieve a customer's city, last name, and first name. If you place a composite index on these three fields and then run a search to get this information from these three columns for a particular city, SQL Server can scan the index itself to bring back your results without having to consult the underlying table.

This technique only works when the index contains all columns of interest for the query, and the search criteria include the left-most index columns.

Support your local Optimizer

As shown in the previous chapter, the SQL Server Query Optimizer works hard on your behalf, examining queries and available data metrics to determine the optimal execution plan for your database interactions. To help the Optimizer help you, remember to configure the right set of statistics to support your processing profile. After the statistics are configured, don't forget to let SQL Server update them for you periodically. For example, Figure 3-5 shows a list of statistics we created for the `payments` table, along with extensive details about one of them.

Designing High-Velocity Queries

The previous sections of this chapter give you some recommendations on how to create a positive environment for high-performance databases, as well as some guidelines for implementing a responsive indexing infrastructure. This section looks at how you can speed up your interactions with your data and how to construct the most efficient queries possible. We also give you some tips on how to streamline your data-modifying interactions.

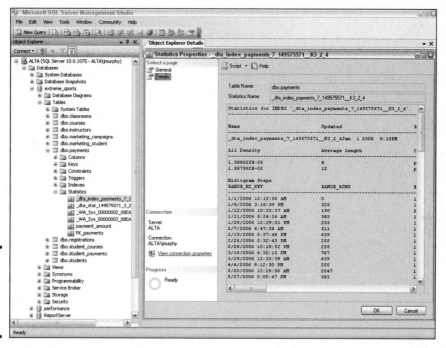

Figure 3-5:
A collection
of statistics,
along with
details.

Understand query execution plans

The previous chapter is devoted to helping you come to grips with the SQL Server Query Optimizer and how to take advantage of its power. One suggestion we make is for you to learn how to interpret execution plans because SQL Server uses these reports to tell you exactly how it plans to process your query. Armed with this information, you can take steps to remedy any queries that don't quite measure up. For example, Figure 3-6 shows an execution plan for a moderately complex query.

In addition to providing all these helpful details about the upcoming execution plan, SQL Server also notifies you of any potential trouble spots.

Avoid leading wildcards

As a database designer or application developer, you always strive to take advantage of indexes for queries against large tables. Otherwise, SQL Server is forced to scan the entire table for the rows that will make up your result set. These table scans are extremely costly and time-consuming. Unfortunately, you can construct a query that forces SQL Server to bypass your well-designed indexes and perform a brute force table scan. One way to trigger a costly table scan is to use a leading wildcard in your query.

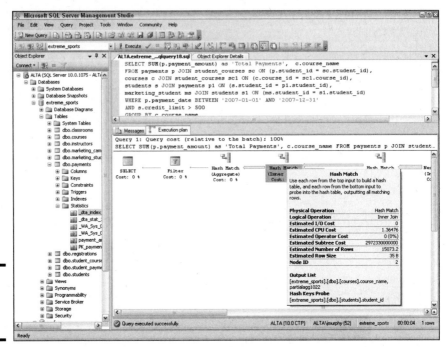

Figure 3-6:
A query
execution
plan.

For example, suppose that you have a table that contains 100 million rows of customer information. To speed access to this table, you've placed an index on the last_name column. In most situations that use this column as the query criteria, SQL Server dutifully uses this index to quickly retrieve records that match a given last name. So far, so good. What happens, however, when you ask SQL Server to look for records based on a subset of the values contained in this column, as shown here?

```
SELECT * FROM Customers WHERE last_name LIKE '%ilson'
```

Because indexes (for Western-based character sets) store information from left to right, SQL Server will be unable to take advantage of the index and will then require a row-by-row perusal of the table. For a table with only a few thousand rows, this isn't a problem. For a table with millions or billions of rows, it's a big deal.

This is most easily illustrated with a real-world scenario. Imagine that we handed you the white pages for a large city and asked you to find all the entries with a last name of Jones. Faced with this request, you'd quickly turn to the section beginning with *Jo,* and in a matter of seconds have the entire list of Jones entries identified. However, what would happen if we asked you to find all the entries with a last name ending in *nes*? Assuming that you didn't throw the phone book in disgust, you'd be forced to go through every entry in the book, trying to identify candidates. This would take much longer than a few seconds would to complete, and you wouldn't be able to stop working until you went through the entire phone book.

Keep this real-world example in mind when you're tempted to create a query that searches for a subset of data from an indexed column.

Take advantage of views

Views, which are discussed in several sections of this book (especially Book III, Chapter 7), improve database administrators' lives in many ways. From a purely performance perspective, a view can help reduce the number of rows and columns returned by a query. By reducing the size of an overall result set, a view lightens the load on the database server while easing the networking burden.

Put stored procedures and functions to work

In addition to all their security and logic centralization benefits, stored procedures and functions have the potential to boost performance as well. This benefit is largely delivered by offloading processing work from the database client to the database server. Network traffic is also reduced because there's generally less data to ship from the server to the client. However, be aware that heavily employing centralized server objects, such as stored procedures and functions, does run the risk of placing an excessive load on your server, thus degrading performance. As with many performance-related techniques, this approach requires administrators and developers to weigh many variables when determining their tactics.

Use the TOP clause to preview large result sets

SQL Server offers a handy feature — the TOP clause — that allows you to preview information from large result sets. You can limit the number of rows that you want to see, either as an absolute number or as a percentage. For example, look at the following two queries:

```
SELECT TOP 150 * FROM payments
SELECT TOP 20 PERCENT payment_amount FROM payments
```

In the first example, we asked SQL Server to retrieve all the columns from the top 150 rows in the payments table. In the second example, we requested only the payment_amount column from the top 20 percent of the rows in the payments table.

The SQL Server Management Studio also offers the `TOP` clause to limit the number of rows that are returned from a table. Figure 3-7 shows the top 1,000 rows being returned from a large table.

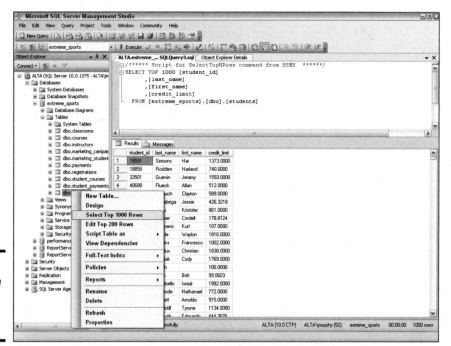

Figure 3-7: Viewing the top 1,000 rows for a table.

Changing Data Quickly

Typically, users perceive a slow-running database application when they're attempting to retrieve information. However, many circumstances exist where database performance might bog down on operations that actually create, change, or remove data. This final section furnishes you with some tips that you can use to coax additional performance from any data-altering operations. We begin by discussing techniques for speeding up data insert activities. Next on the agenda are some guidelines for boosting performance for operations that change data. Finally, we show you how to say goodbye to your data as quickly as possible.

Insert optimization

Normally, inserts performed by user-driven applications happen quite quickly: The user provides the program with some data, and the program writes this data into SQL Server in the blink of an eye. However, other occasions occur where inserting data can be much more of a performance burden, chiefly when loading large amounts of information in a batch. These events can degrade responsiveness for all users and lead to a general perception of system sluggishness even though it's been caused by a special situation. In this section, we offer some suggestions that you can use to make these hefty inserts less taxing on your SQL Server system.

Take advantage of SQL Server's specialized bulk loading capabilities

SQL Server offers two helpful tools that simplify and speed this previously challenging task. You can use the BULK INSERT statement from SQL or the bcp utility from the command line.

The BULK INSERT statement

This statement is very useful when you have a file that you want to insert all at once, and you want to use direct SQL entry to launch the insert operation.

For example, imagine that you've built a point-of-sale system. Each day, your cash registers generate a large file (Register.txt), and you want to load this into your Sales table. Suppose that the raw file looks like this:

```
3422,3,6/10/2009,9.00
3423,8,6/10/2009,3.50
3424,1,6/10/2009,2.75
3425,15,6/10/2009,12.25
3426,22,6/10/2009,10.00
3427,30,6/10/2009,18.00
```

Loading this file requires a simple SQL statement:

```
BULK INSERT Sales FROM 'C:\Register.txt'
WITH (DATAFILETYPE = 'char', FIELDTERMINATOR = ',')
```

This command loads the information found in the file and reports on the number of rows it processed:

```
(114 rows processed)
```

 Pay attention to the layout of your raw data files. It's very easy to get confused about the exact character that separates each field. The fields themselves might be in the wrong order, which causes no end of aggravation as you try to decipher what's happening when you insert information.

The bcp utility

Just as the BULK INSERT statement makes it possible to take a text file and load it into SQL Server via the SQL interface, the bcp utility does the same from the command line. Here's how you'd invoke bcp to load the sales information from your database:

```
C:\>bcp Westbay.dbo.Sales in Register.txt -S
DBSERVER\sqlexpress
```

A lot can go wrong with a bulk insert process. Problems can range from syntax errors, data issues, and so on. It's a good idea to test this type of operation with a small data file before attempting a massive upload. The alternative is to potentially damage your database, which is not much fun.

Format file

Ideally, your raw data files will match the layout of your tables exactly. Unfortunately, things are rarely this simple in the real world. It's more likely that there will be significant differences between what you're given and what you need. Fortunately, you can create a format file that tells SQL Server exactly what to expect from these data files.

To generate a format file easily, just run the bcp utility as shown in the following code. SQL Server walks you through the specified table and file, and gives you the option to create a format file at the end.

```
C:\>bcp Westbay.dbo.Sales in Register.txt -S
DBSERVER\sqlexpress
Password:

Enter the file storage type of field SaleID [int]:
Enter prefix-length of field SaleID [0]:
Enter field terminator [none]:

Enter the file storage type of field FlavorID [smallint]:
Enter prefix-length of field FlavorID [0]:
Enter field terminator [none]:

Enter the file storage type of field DateofSales [datetime]:
Enter prefix-length of field DateofSales [0]:
Enter field terminator [none]:

Enter the file storage type of field Amount [decimal]:
Enter prefix-length of field Amount [1]:
Enter field terminator [none]:

Do you want to save this format information in a file? [Y/n]
Host filename [bcp.fmt]:
```

When you've finished defining this file, you can use it for all future bcp runs.

XML Bulk Load

Given the often-enormous size and complex structure of XML documents, it can be a significant challenge to efficiently load a large one into a SQL Server table. In many cases, you can simply get by with the `INSERT` statement and the `OPENXML` function. Fortunately, in situations where there's too much data to load via the standard mechanism, you can employ the XML Bulk Load COM object, found in the SQLXML 4.0 utility, to streamline these costly activities. ***Note:*** This approach requires you to create an XML schema and write code or script.

Consider dropping indexes before loading large volumes of information

In certain cases, typically, when you have a heavily indexed table and the proportion of rows to be loaded is large when compared with the number of rows already present in that table, it makes sense to first drop any indexes, load the data, and then re-create the indexes after the load has finished. The reason is because each time you load a row, SQL Server must update its indexes for that table. When there are many rows to insert, it can be more efficient to load the rows into a non-indexed table, and then construct the indexes after the insert operation has completed.

If you drop indexes on an active table, other users who are working with that table might experience significant performance degradation until you've rebuilt the indexes.

Book VII
Chapter 3

Update optimization

When faced with sluggish update responsiveness, one of the first things you should do is review the statement's execution plan to ascertain that indexes are indeed being used to quickly locate those rows that are candidates for the update operation. When you've put that doubt to rest, another possible cause for this degraded performance also relates to indexes. However, in this case, it could be that you've set up too many indexes. It's quite common for SQL Server to bog down when updating unnecessary indexes during a large update operation. As a database administrator, you must always walk a fine line between providing enough indexes to keep query performance coming and not employing so many indexes that `INSERT`, `UPDATE`, or `DELETE` throughput is damaged.

Data Access
Strategies

Consider employing replication when faced with a seemingly unsolvable conflict between the needs of real-time, transactional users and those of reporting-focused users. You could easily configure SQL Server to maintain a fresh, continually updated copy of your database on another server. With the alternate computer available, you can then steer users interested in resource-intensive reporting tasks to that server.

Delete optimization

As any database administrator who's ever tried to delete millions of rows from a table can attest, removing data from your database can take much longer than you ever thought possible. In this section, we describe two techniques you can follow to avoid this possible bottleneck.

Dropping a table versus using the DELETE statement

When you're faced with a situation that requires you to delete a significant percentage of the rows in a given table, you might be better off exporting any rows that need to remain, and then simply dropping the table. After the table is dropped (which takes only milliseconds to complete), you can then re-create the table and re-import the rows that you exported prior to dropping the table. This bypasses the potentially time consuming and resource intensive logging operations that SQL Server normally performs on any data modification.

Dropping any table should be done carefully. Make sure you have truly exported all the rows necessary to reconstitute the table to your requirements.

Taking advantage of the TRUNCATE TABLE statement

When faced with the need to perform a massive delete operation, another alternative is to employ the TRUNCATE TABLE statement. The DELETE statement creates a record of all removed rows in the transaction log, whereas the TRUNCATE TABLE statement records only page deallocation events, which takes a fraction of the time.

The TOP clause, described earlier in this chapter, can also be very helpful when deleting rows.

Chapter 4: Tuning SQL Server

In This Chapter

✔ Improving performance with tuning

✔ Adjusting memory and processor settings

✔ Adjusting disk and communication settings

*I*f you've been a database administrator for a while, chances are that you're accustomed to tinkering with the settings of your relational database platform in an attempt to squeeze out some additional performance. Some administrators even enjoy this often tedious, but frequently necessary chore. If this kind of experimentation appeals to you, we have good news and bad news. The bad news is that SQL Server 2008 automatically adjusts many of its internal settings so that you don't have to. The good news is that you can still have an impact on SQL Server's performance, which is what this chapter is all about.

To begin, we remind you that tweaking database server settings is no substitute for a solid performance foundation, including database design, indexing, optimal queries, and so on. With that admonition out of the way, the next task is to explore memory and other processor-related properties that you can set to augment system speed. We then explore how disk-related settings can shape your server's overall responsiveness. Finally, because communication protocols and other topics are important, too, the chapter closes with an examination of what these settings mean to you from a performance vantage.

This chapter doesn't focus on optimal ways to interact with your data: That essential theme is covered in the previous chapter. Also, although you can make many of these changes using a script, stored procedure, or other character-based technique, we continue the graphically driven focus of the book and use the SQL Server Management Studio as the primary mechanism for implementing these performance-setting alterations. Finally, when undertaking any performance analysis or optimization exercise, remember that you're never without SQL Server's excellent set of performance monitoring tools and wizards. To learn more about these helpful assistants, drop by Book VII, Chapter 2.

Tuning: The Last Resort for Improving Performance

It might sound a bit melodramatic, but if your performance-enhancing strategy relies on tuning SQL Server's internal settings, chances are it's too late to make much of a difference. The reason for this overarching assumption is that unless something is drastically wrong with your database server's settings, other attributes have a much bigger impact on performance.

If you do your best to deliver on all the requirements listed here, and things are still stumbling along, then it may indeed be time to take more-advanced measures to squeeze some additional throughput from your SQL Server environment. The balance of this chapter is dedicated to that subject.

In keeping with the book's philosophy of using graphical tools wherever possible, SQL Server Management Studio is the mechanism to implement these tuning-related changes. You find this tool under the main SQL Server menu.

Solid database design

When creating a highly responsive SQL Server-based application, there's no substitute for an intelligent, realistic database design that accurately models your real-world requirements and proven normalization guidelines. If this topic is of interest, Book III, Chapter 1 delves into the intricacies of normalization, including those situations where it's okay to bend (or break) the rules.

Good indexing strategy

After you design an efficient database, your next goal is to create a collection of useful, well-planned indexes. Seeing sluggish query times reduced by 99 percent after you create the right kind(s) of index is common. SQL Server can help you fill any gaps in your indexing strategy; take a look at Book VII, Chapter 2 to get to know the Database Engine Tuning Advisor. For guidance on the theories behind SQL Server indexes, stop by Book VII, Chapter 3.

Well-planned data interaction

After constructing a solid database platform, and all of its supporting indexes, your next major responsibility is to ensure that every interaction (SELECT, INSERT, UPDATE, DELETE, and so on) is written as efficiently as possible. You can find more about effective SQL statements as part of Book VII, Chapter 3.

Memory and Processor Settings

Database-driven applications have the potential to be extremely memory intensive. Sophisticated relational database management systems, such as SQL Server, offer caching algorithms that are highly efficient at leveraging available memory to reduce the need for disk interaction. Because disk interaction is roughly ten times slower than memory, anything you can do to reduce the amount of communication with the disk will have a dramatic performance benefit.

One of the easiest things you can do to address a memory problem is . . . buy more memory! With memory prices at an all-time low, it might be less of a hassle to stuff the server with more RAM than to wrack your brain trying to coax a bit more performance from your applications or database engine. However, by default 32-bit operating systems can only address roughly 3.2GB of memory, so anything above that is wasted. An exception to this rule is that Windows Server 2003 and 2008 will address more than 3GB of RAM if you employ the /3GB switch in the boot configuration. Windows Server 2003 R2 can address up to 32GB of RAM, all of which can be leveraged by SQL Server provided the boot switches have been properly configured. Comparatively, a 64-bit operating system can address much more memory without any special settings.

Determining if there's a problem

Before you try to fix a memory problem, wouldn't it be useful to first figure whether there's an issue? Fortunately, you can employ a host of operating system– and SQL Server–provided tools to determine whether you need to take action on any performance-related anomaly.

From a memory-problem diagnosis perspective, two tools stand out:

✦ **Windows Task Manager:** To launch this tool, simply right-click the taskbar and select the Task Manager option. As shown in Figure 4-1, the Task Manager features several tabs of statistics and details of interest to SQL Server administrators. For the purposes of diagnosing a memory problem, the following two are especially relevant:

  • **Processes:** This tab itemizes all active processes. Review the names and memory footprints of each process — there might be some that aren't necessary that can be halted and prevented from starting again.

   If you're running Windows Server 2003 or 2008, you might need to select the "Show All Processes" option to see every running process.

- **Performance:** This tab tells you about the overall load on your server. The most important statistic here is the Page File Usage History graph. Like borrowing money at 20-percent interest per week from a loan shark, *paging* (which uses the disk drive as a surrogate for RAM) is one of the most expensive operations your computer can perform. If you see an active page file, chances are that your system can't handle the memory demands placed on it.

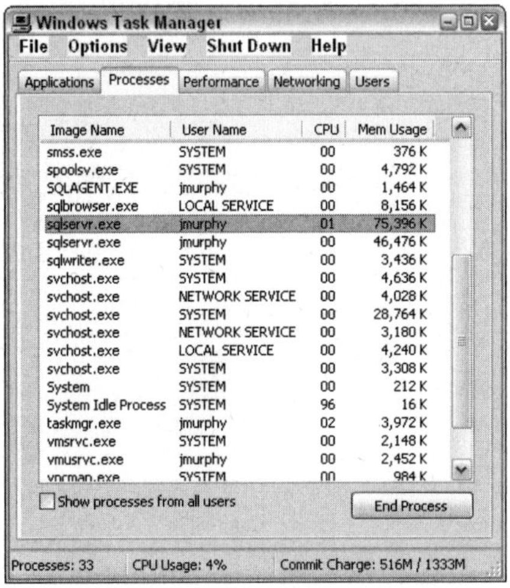

Figure 4-1:
The
Windows
Task
Manager.

✦ **Windows System Monitor MMC snap-in:** This utility offers a much more detailed view into your systems' overall performance profile. The easiest way to launch it is to open the Control Panel, and drill into the Administrative Tools folder. After you enter this folder, simply double-click the Performance shortcut. Inside are dozens of groups of statistical indicators, many of which offer visibility into memory-related problems. Figure 4-2 shows an example of this utility in action.

These are two of the excellent tools at your disposal; Book VII, Chapter 2 describes many others.

If either of these diagnostic utilities indicates a memory issue, you still need to determine whether anything can help resolve the problem. For instance, maybe you're trying to do more on your database server computer than its capable of handling; you might be better served by distributing information and related processing tasks onto multiple computers. If you're interested in this topic, be sure to explore Book VIII, Chapter 6 to get the lowdown on replication.

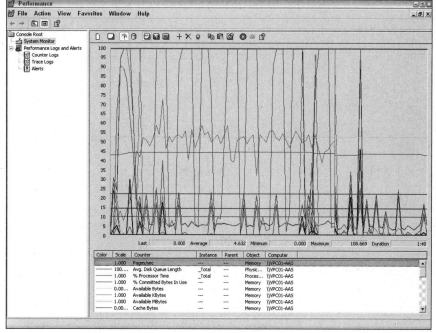

Figure 4-2:
Memory
indicators in
Windows
System
Monitor.

Adjusting memory parameters

If you want to experiment with SQL Server's memory settings, remember that SQL Server 2008 requires much less memory tuning on the part of its administrators — significant amounts of this work are now handled automatically by the database engine. If you're interested in this topic, however, here are some of the most common memory- and CPU-related settings.

✦ **Use AWE to allocate memory:** For 32-bit x86 servers running with more than 3.2GB of memory, you can direct SQL Server to take advantage of Address Windowing Extensions (AWE) to employ up to 64GB of memory. This isn't necessary on a 64-bit server.

✦ **Minimum server memory (in MB):** This setting controls the minimum amount of buffer pool memory available to SQL Server. The default setting of zero should suffice.

✦ **Maximum server memory (in MB):** This setting determines the maximum amount of memory available to SQL Server for its buffer pool. Generally, it's wise to leave this setting at its default value.

✦ **Index creation memory (in KB):** This setting determines how much memory SQL Server can take advantage of when creating an index. By using the default of zero, SQL Server will automatically determine the right value — see what I mean about letting the database engine do the hard work?

✦ **Minimum memory per query (in KB):** This setting provides a baseline for the memory that SQL Server consumes for each running query. It can be set from 512KB to 2GB. To get more throughput for applications that feature numerous small queries, try lowering this amount.

As with any experiment, change only one variable at a time and then measure the results.

Figure 4-3 shows how this page appears.

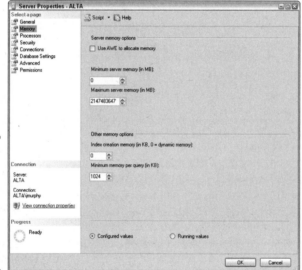

Figure 4-3: The Memory properties page in SQL Server Management Studio.

Adjusting processor parameters

Modern server technology supports multiple central processing unit (CPU) configurations; SQL Server is designed to take advantage of these high-performance environments. Figure 4-4 shows the Processors properties page, which is where you find a collection of settings aimed at optimizing how SQL Server interacts with your computer's CPU.

If your database server has only one CPU, many of these settings don't apply; they're relevant only in a multi-processor environment. If the options are grayed in your environment, you don't need to consider them.

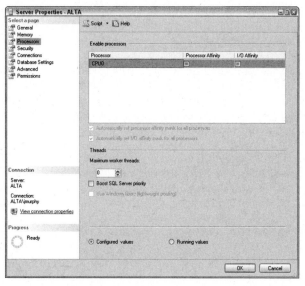

Figure 4-4:
The Processors properties page in SQL Server Management Studio.

Here's more about each section on this page:

+ **Enable processors:** This grouping of settings specifically aims at getting the most from multi-processor environments. By default, SQL Server binds to all the processors on your server. If you want to limit the number of these bindings (to let other applications have their fair share of these valuable resources), enable these check boxes. On the other hand, if the multi-processor computer running SQL Server is earmarked as a dedicated database server, there's no need to restrict SQL Server's access to your processors.

+ **Threads:** For the majority of SQL Server environments, the default values in this section will suffice. If you decide to experiment, do so carefully — a mistake here can have major ramifications.

Disk Settings

Before getting started with SQL Server-specific disk optimization suggestions, it's worth noting that when it comes to disk storage, you get what you pay for. Disk drive manufacturers continue to deliver ever-faster drives in larger capacities. However, you should be aware of major performance differences among various products. Generally, a faster RPM rating translates into faster database performance, assuming that your applications are disk-intensive. Additionally, storage technologies, such as RAID (Redundant

Array of Inexpensive Disks), can improve throughput and increase the safety of your valuable information. Specialized storage appliances offer their own sets of disk-related features.

RAID takes advantage of multiple hard disks to improve performance, scalability, and reliability. It offers administrators a number of configurations (also known as *levels*). While a detailed analysis of this technology is beyond this book's scope, here's a brief look at some of the levels of primary interest to the SQL Server administrator.

+ **RAID 0:** This approach enhances performance by *striping* (distributing) information across multiple disk drives. The operating system is then able to take advantage of parallel processing to return results more quickly. However, if any of the disk drives fail, the entire array is destroyed. This vulnerability makes this level unacceptable for a relational database application.

+ **RAID 1:** This technique uses two or more disks to enable a mirroring configuration. If one disk should fail, its data is preserved on the partner mirror. Although this approach isn't specifically targeted to performance optimization, it's a valid choice for storing database logs safely.

+ **RAID 5:** This option leverages disk striping to distribute information across multiple disks. It improves performance, but is vulnerable to failure if more than one disk drive fails. For this reason, consider it only for relatively static data warehouse applications.

+ **RAID 1+0:** This combines the responsiveness of level 0 with the data assurance features of level 1, and is an excellent choice for performance and protection for SQL Server.

Disk defragmentation

Disk drives are not immune from the universal law of entropy. Over time, even the fastest disk will contain a patchwork of scattered file segments. These fragments place a heavy load on your database server, because even the simplest operation can require multiple physical reads of the disk. With disk reads being roughly 10 times slower than memory reads, this imposes a severe performance tax on your applications.

Fortunately, Microsoft makes it easy to reorganize your disk drives, thereby removing a major throughput impediment. Here's how to proceed:

1. **Open the Control Panel.**

2. **Open the Administrative Tools folder.**

3. **Double-click the Computer Management icon.**

4. **Expand the Storage folder.**

5. **Highlight the disk volume you want to defragment and then click the Analyze button.**

The utility gets to work reviewing all the files on your disk to see whether it's a good candidate for defragmentation. When the work finishes, you see a report similar to the one shown in Figure 4-5.

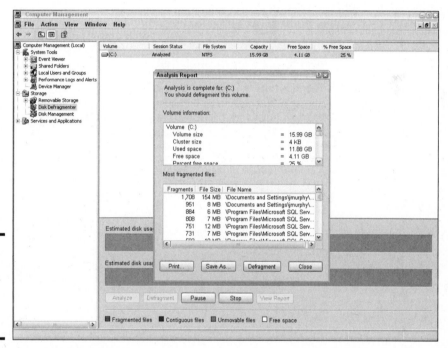

Figure 4-5:
Disk
defragmen-
tation
analysis
report.

6. **If the utility recommended it, click the Defragment button.**

This launches the actual defragmentation software. Depending on the amount of information present on the drive, this may take quite some time. When it finishes, you receive a summary report.

Data compression

If disk space is at a premium in your environment, you might find it necessary to compress your data. This is a very easy task for SQL Server, and it can be performed on a table-by-table basis, offering fine-grained control over your compression implementation. Here's what to do:

1. **Launch SQL Server Management Studio.**

2. **Connect to the appropriate database server.**

3. **Expand the Databases folder in the Object Explorer.**

4. **Open the folder for the database that contains the table you want to compress.**

5. **Open the Tables folder.**

6. **Right-click the table and then choose the Manage Compression option from the Storage submenu.**

   This launches the aptly named Data Compression Wizard that walks you through the process of squeezing any excess space from the table.

7. **Choose a compression type for the table.**

   You can compress at either the row or the page level. Additionally, you may assign different compression techniques to each partition, or may use one technique for all partitions.

8. **Click on Calculate button to see your projected savings and then click Next when you're ready to proceed.**

   Figure 4-6 illustrates the compression savings for one table.

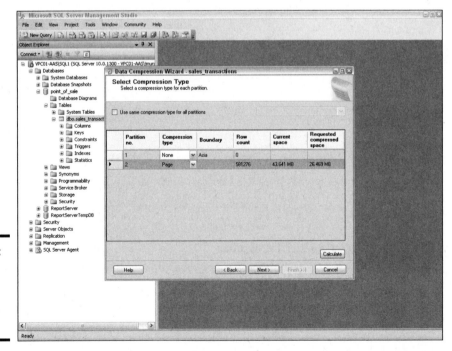

Figure 4-6: Projected space savings from compression.

9. **Decide how you want the wizard to deliver its output and then click Next.**

Options range from running the compression immediately to creating a script that you can run later.

10. **Review the upcoming compression details and then click Finish when you're ready to proceed.**

11. **If you've elected to generate a script, review its content.**

Here's an example of how one of these compression scripts appears:

```
USE [point_of_sale]
ALTER TABLE [dbo].[sales_transactions]
REBUILD PARTITION = 2 WITH(DATA_COMPRESSION = PAGE )
```

Because SQL Server must first decompress any information that has been stored in a compressed format, data compression negatively affects performance. You might find it advantageous to acquire more disk storage and avoid these costs.

Encryption

Transparent encryption is one of the most compelling "what's new" features in SQL Server 2008. Application developers no longer have to write two versions of the solutions (one for encrypted data, and one for non-encrypted data). Instead, they can focus on delivering their best code, and SQL Server can manage encryption internally and transparently.

In this context, *encryption* refers to physically encrypting data files on disk, not the data that SQL returns in response to a query. If you want to encrypt a column's information, you need to do this via the SQL Server Management Studio specifically. You can also combine disk-based encryption with column-based encryption.

To enable encryption, follow these simple steps:

1. **Launch SQL Server Management Studio.**

2. **Connect to the appropriate database server.**

3. **Expand the Databases folder in the Object Explorer.**

4. **Right-click the database that you wish to encrypt.**

5. **Choose the Manage Database Encryption option from the Tasks menu.**

This opens a dialog box where you can select an encryption algorithm, select either a server certificate or asymmetric key, and enable encryption.

6. After setting your encryption preferences, click OK.

That's all there is to it! Your database is now encrypted.

Just as data compression imposes a performance tax, encryption also places some additional burdens on your processor.

Partitioning

Some tables contain so much information, and are so dynamic in their processing profile, that they impose an extraordinary burden on your disk storage mechanisms. In an effort to address these significant bottlenecks, SQL Server offers a sophisticated information distribution capability. *Partitioning* allows you to spread the workload onto multiple disk devices, and can yield dramatic performance enhancement in circumstances where one or more of the following conditions are true for a given table:

✦ **Large amount of data**

✦ **Predictable data loads**

✦ **Dynamic data**

✦ **Archival-capable information**

✦ **Multiple disk drives available**

If you're interested in applying this to your environment, make sure to read Book VIII, Chapter 6.

Communication Settings

To achieve optimal communication-related performance, administrators need to consider two primary factors: achieving the best possible network speed and selecting the right communication protocol.

Network speed

Normally, other than pleading for better networks with less latency, database administrators don't have much interaction with, or impact on, network speeds. However, a SQL Server administrator can still have a positive impact on network-related performance.

Reducing network traffic via stored procedures and functions

One way to guarantee poor performance (and overload your network to boot) is to transmit massive amounts of data between SQL Server and its clients. Fortunately, SQL Server offers capabilities that you can use to process more information on the server, thereby dramatically reducing the amount of data sent between client and server.

Stored procedures and functions are server-side logic that clients of your database server can use to automate operations. Aside from their proven traffic-reduction benefits, they also help simplify client-side application code, increase security, and centralize business logic.

Using high-performance subnets

Wherever possible, place database servers, Web servers, and application servers on a high-speed subnet. These lightning-fast connections can do wonders for response time.

Communication protocol

When connecting with SQL Server, you have several choices of communication protocol at your disposal. Here's a look at each of these protocols, along with situations where you use them.

✦ **TCP/IP:** This is the underlying communication protocol that much of the Internet uses. When communicating between database servers and their clients, this is the most logical protocol.

✦ **Named pipes:** This protocol is generally used for communication between clients and servers, as well as server-only traffic. It's not nearly as common for Internet traffic as TCP/IP, and is somewhat less secure.

✦ **Virtual Interface Adapter (VIA):** As a protocol that is reliant on specialized hardware, the odds are that most readers aren't likely to encounter VIA as much as they'll experience TCP/IP or named pipes.

✦ **Shared memory:** For processes that reside on the same server as the database, this protocol can leverage a fast, dedicated section of memory that SQL Server uses for communication. However, there's the rub; unless both the database application and the database server are on the same computer, this protocol isn't applicable.

Book VIII

Database Administration

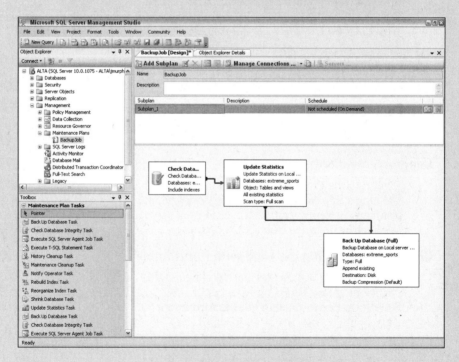

The Maintenance Plan Editor.

Contents at a Glance

Chapter 1: Configuring SQL Server

In This Chapter

✔ SQL Server configuration tools

✔ Adjusting server parameters

✔ Generating configuration scripts

*W*ith each new release of SQL Server, Microsoft continues to improve and simplify the daily tasks of the database administrator. However, it's still not possible to run the database on autopilot, or replace the DBA with a robot. Given that reality, this chapter aims to help administrators make sense of all the server-wide settings and properties that they encounter each day.

We begin by giving you a brief overview of a collection of SQL Server's configuration tools and technologies. However, from the day-to-day perspective of a database administrator, most configuration tuning is controlled via the SQL Server Management Studio. Consequently, the lion's share of this chapter is dedicated to understanding how that tool allows you to fine-tune the dozens of parameters that influence SQL Server's behavior. Finally, we show you how to generate scripts so that you can further automate the maintenance and administration of your SQL Server environment.

SQL Server Configuration Tools

If you're new to SQL Server, the sheer number of available tactics that achieve the same goal might confuse you. Part of this is because SQL Server has been around for many years, and still ships with several legacy technologies. However, Microsoft has been steadily moving in the direction of becoming 100-percent graphical, so it's worthwhile to become familiar with these tools. Consequently, throughout this book, we devote the majority of our attention to making the most of the SQL Server Management Studio. We also point out, however, that character-based approaches to getting the job done still exist. These same rules apply to many administrative tasks. We look at each of the major technologies available for performing administrative work.

If you want to get a holistic view of how these tools work together, see Book I, Chapter 2.

SQL Server Configuration Manager

This graphical tool (launched from within the SQL Server Configuration Tools menu) is primarily meant to let administrators enable or disable SQL Server's system services as well as client/server communication protocols. Figure 1-1 shows this tool in the context of managing services.

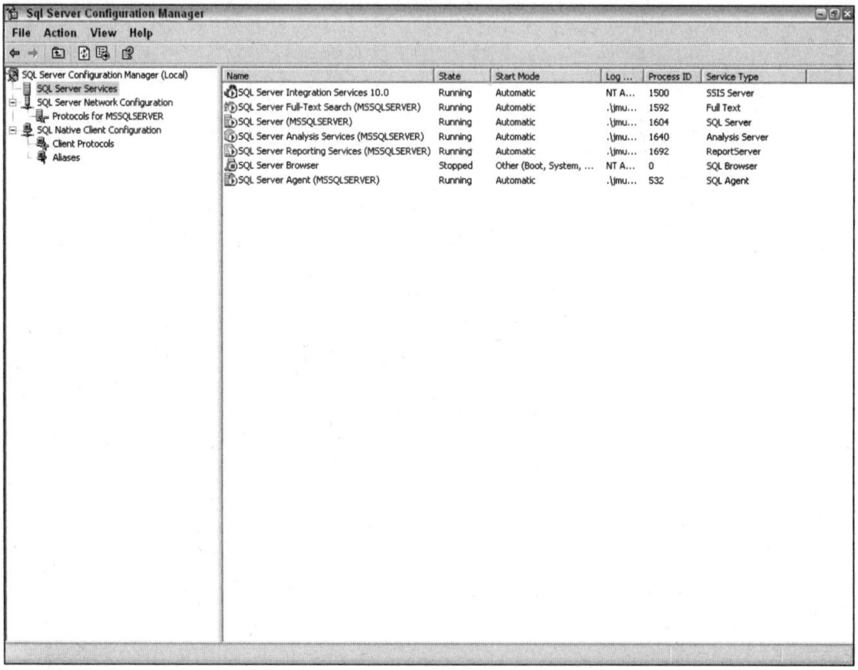

Figure 1-1:
The SQL
Server
Configu-
ration
Manager.

SQL Server Surface Area Configuration Tool

This graphical tool (also launched from within the SQL Server Configuration Tools menu) allows the administrator to determine which features and capabilities will be available to users. Given the very real security risks and dangers faced by administrators, this tool is meant to help minimize the areas (or services) for a potential attack.

sp_configure

Before there were graphical tools, there was the `sp_configure` stored procedure. Administrators have used this powerful procedure for many years to control SQL Server's behavior, and many DBAs still perform all their configuration tasks this way.

This procedure can be launched at least two ways. The first uses the character-based SQLCMD utility, and the second allows you to use a query window within the SQL Server Management Studio.

SQL Server Management Studio

This graphical tool, which ships with every edition of SQL Server, gives the database administrator unprecedented control over the behavior of his SQL Server environment. We spend the rest of the chapter showing you how to use this tool to manage your server configuration settings.

One of the most exciting features (especially from the perspective of the DBA) found in SQL Server 2008 is Policy-Based Management. This new capability, tasked with simplifying and making SQL Server management more consistent, is explored in Book I, Chapter 2. We then show you how to use it later in that mini-book as part of Chapter 4. Book VII, Chapter 2 shows how Policy-Based Management can play a big role in performance optimization and management.

Adjusting Server Properties

In this section, we show you how to configure a wide variety of SQL Server properties. These settings affect all databases, so think carefully when going down this road.

Be as scientific as you can in your efforts. Whenever possible, change only one setting at a time. This makes it much easier to weigh the impact of any alterations.

We begin by illustrating how to use the SQL Server Management Studio to make these configuration parameter changes. Here's how to get started:

1. **Launch SQL Server Management Studio.**
2. **Connect to the appropriate SQL Server instance.**
3. **Right-click the connection's entry in the Object Explorer view, and choose Properties.**

   This opens the Server Properties dialog box, as shown in Figure 1-2.
4. **Choose the appropriate properties page that contains the setting you want to change.**

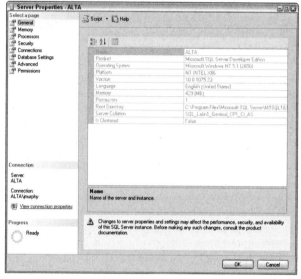

Figure 1-2:
The General
Server
Properties
page in SQL
Server
Management Studio.

You can select among eight different pages, including:

General   Connections

Memory   Database settings

Processors   Advanced

Security   Permissions

We walk you through each of these pages and their associated settings in a moment.

5. **Make your change, and click OK.**

Note: Certain alterations require you to restart SQL Server for them to take effect.

When it comes to tuning and optimizing your SQL Server instance's performance, server settings are among the least effective mechanisms to use. Modern database environments (such as SQL Server) do a great job of real-time engine performance and throughput management. You'll get much better mileage by focusing on your database design, indexing strategy, and how queries and other operations will interact with SQL Server. If performance is something that interests you, Book VI is dedicated to this important topic.

General properties

This page (refer to Figure 1-2) contains a collection of read-only settings and summaries. Although you can't change them, it's a good idea to familiarize yourself with these parameters:

✦ **Memory:** This is the total memory on the database server, not just the amount allocated to SQL Server.

✦ **Processors:** The number of physical central processing units (CPU) on the database server.

✦ **Server Collation:** Regionally driven settings that determine how data is compared and sorted.

✦ **Is Clustered:** Specifies whether this instance of SQL Server has been included in a failover cluster.

Memory properties

As you might surmise from its name, this is the page where you control SQL Server's usage of memory. Its parameters include

✦ **Use AWE to Allocate Memory:** If your database server is running on a 32-bit version of Windows and sports more than 4GB of memory, you can instruct SQL Server to take advantage of Address Windowing Extensions (AWE) to employ up to 64GB of memory.

✦ **Minimum Server Memory (in MB):** This setting controls the minimum amount of buffer pool memory that's available to SQL Server.

✦ **Maximum Server Memory (in MB):** This setting determines the maximum amount of memory that's available to SQL Server for its buffer pool. Generally, it's wise to leave both these memory settings at their default values.

✦ **Index Creation Memory (in KB):** This parameter gives SQL Server a guideline on how much memory it can take advantage of when creating an index. The default of 0 (zero) means that SQL Server automatically determines the right value.

✦ **Minimum Memory per Query (in KB):** This setting provides a baseline for the memory that SQL Server consumes for each running query. It can be set from 512KB to 2GB.

Figure 1-3 shows how this page appears.

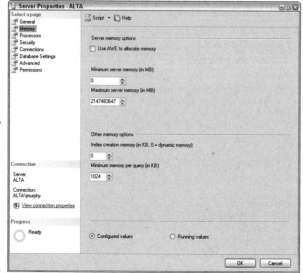

Figure 1-3:
The
Memory
Server
Properties
page in
SQL Server
Manage-
ment Studio.

Processor properties

Figure 1-4 shows the Processors Server Properties page where you find a collection of settings aimed at optimizing how SQL Server interacts with your computer's central processing unit (CPU). Additionally, deploying multiprocessor servers is an increasingly popular way to derive added performance from your SQL Server database environment. This page includes settings specifically tailored for those types of environments.

Several of these settings are meaningful only if you're running a multiple processor database server. If the options are grayed-out in your environment, then you don't need to consider them.

Here's a look at each of these sections:

+ **Enable Processors:** This grouping of settings is aimed specifically at getting the most from multiprocessor environments. You can request that SQL Server bind itself to, and take advantage of, one or more of these processors by checking the processor affinity and I/O affinity boxes.

+ **Threads:** This grouping of settings should be approached with caution. They let the SQL Server administrator dictate specialized, operating system–level performance requirements.

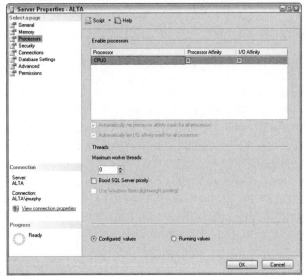

Figure 1-4:
The
Processors
Server
Properties
page in
SQL Server
Manage-
ment Studio.

Security properties

Chapter 3 in this mini-book is dedicated to a complete overview of all SQL
Server considerations, including logins and permissions. At this point, we
examine how to set some server-wide security settings, as shown in Figure 1-5.

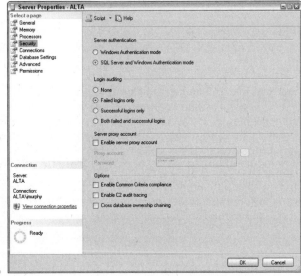

Figure 1-5:
The Security
Server
Properties
page in
SQL Server
Manage-
ment Studio.

The Security Server Properties settings include

✦ **Server Authentication:** You can choose between Windows Authentication mode, which relies on the operating system for its account information, and SQL Server and Windows Authentication mode, which requires coordination between the database and operating system. In many cases, the former option is simpler for administrators to maintain. In fact, the default setting is Windows Authentication Mode.

✦ **Login Auditing:** SQL Server allows you to audit (that is, create log entries) for failed logins, successful logins, or both. You can also elect not to audit logins at all.

✦ **Server Proxy Account:** If you want to designate a specific login for major SQL Server administration tasks (that is, a "proxy"), you can fill in those details here.

✦ **Enable Common Criteria Compliance:** By checking this box, you instruct SQL Server to enforce behavior and collect information that is used in support of the security standards (the *Common Criteria*) specified by a multinational IT security organization.

✦ **Enable C2 Audit Tracing:** If you need to comply with C2 auditing, and its associated logging, check this box to begin collecting these detailed statistics.

✦ **Cross Database Ownership Chaining:** SQL Server allows you to manage multiple database objects by setting permissions on only one of them. This concept is *ownership chaining,* and enabling this check box makes it possible for this behavior to span multiple databases.

Connection properties

This page, as shown in Figure 1-6, is where you customize SQL Server's behavior with regard to its handling of connections. Major settings include

✦ **Maximum Number of Concurrent Connections:** With a default value of 0, SQL Server allows as many connections as it can support with available system resources. If you want to limit the number of concurrent connections, manually provide your own setting for this parameter.

✦ **Use Query Governor to Prevent Long-running Queries:** If you're concerned about users or programs that might generate a seemingly never-ending query, check this box and provide a value (in seconds) that serves as a limit on how long a query can take to return results.

✦ **Default Connection Options:** Here, you find a group of options (each with its own check box) that determines how a connection to your server behaves. See Book II, Chapter 1 if you're interested in understanding these options in more detail.

✦ **Remote Server Connections:** This check box gives you the choice to let remote users and computers connect to this database server. If you elect to make this possible, you also have the ability to set a timeout value for how long it takes a remote query to complete execution. If you're concerned about remote operations running for extended amounts of time, provide a maximum value.

✦ **Require Distributed Transactions for Server-to-Server Communication:** The Microsoft Distributed Transaction Coordinator (DTC) helps ensure that transactions that span multiple computers complete successfully. Transactions are a big part of Book III, Chapter 8. For now, if you expect to run many distributed transactions, consider enabling this check box, especially if you have concerns either about the complexity of the transaction or the quality of the underlying network infrastructure.

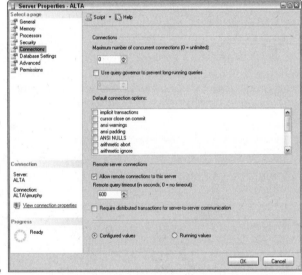

Figure 1-6: The Connections Server Properties page in SQL Server Management Studio.

Book VIII Chapter 1

Configuring SQL Server

Database Setting properties

This page allows an administrator to define behavior for SQL Server's backup, restore, and recovery capabilities. As shown in Figure 1-7, you can set the following parameters for your environment:

✦ **Default Index Fill Factor:** Book VII, Chapter 3 focuses heavily on proper index techniques for SQL Server. For now, this setting instructs SQL Server how full each index page should be when it creates a new index from existing data. A value of 0 (which behaves the same as a value of 100) tells SQL Server to fill these pages as much as possible. In most cases, the default value is fine.

✦ **SQL Server New Tape Behavior:** If your backup operations rely on tape, here's where you tell SQL Server how long it should wait for you to provide a new tape.

✦ **Default Backup Media Retention:** As part of its backup safeguards and capabilities, SQL Server doesn't overwrite an existing backup tape until that tape has expired. Here's where you provide details on how long you want a tape to be retained.

✦ **Compress Backup:** If you're concerned about available space on your backup media, you can use this check box to tell SQL Server to compress the archive.

✦ **Recovery Interval:** In most cases, SQL Server is perfectly capable of managing the time it takes to recover a database. The default value of 0 allows SQL Server to make its own determinations on how to proceed. However, if you're concerned that a recovery might take too long, provide your own value for this parameter. This places an upper limit on the time a recovery may take.

✦ **Database Default Locations:** To manage your information, SQL Server uses two types of files: data and log. Here's where you can set default values about where these files are located. *Note:* You always have the freedom to specify individual file locations when creating or updating a database; this value merely sets a default location.

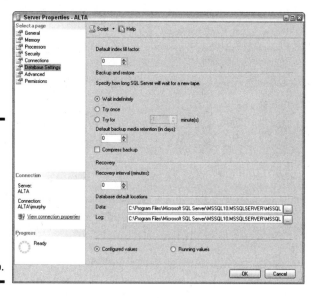

Figure 1-7:
The Database Settings Server Properties page in SQL Server Management Studio.

Advanced properties

This page is the kitchen sink of SQL Server properties — you find a little bit of everything on it. Figure 1-8 highlights how this page appears. Before we look at each of these settings, note that (in most cases) the default values provided by Microsoft are sufficient:

✦ **Filestream Configurable Level:** Recall that SQL Server allows you to use filestreams as a way of leveraging operating system disk storage in conjunction with the database. This setting determines the *granularity* (that is, scope) of filestream operations. SQL Server takes your configuration value and reports on it in the read-only Effective Level field.

✦ **Filestream Share Name:** If you've elected to enable filestreams, you can provide a reference name for the share here.

✦ **Allow Triggers to Fire Others:** Enabling this option allows one trigger to launch another trigger.

✦ **Cursor Threshold:** To enhance throughput, SQL Server can take advantage of asynchronous operations. This value guides SQL Server on when to enable this performance-enhancing capability. The default value of –1 is a good choice.

✦ **Default Full-Text Language:** This numeric code identifies the language to be used for full-text searches.

✦ **Default Language:** SQL Server uses this default language for any new login.

✦ **Max Text Replication Size:** You can place a cap on the amount of text that SQL Server replicates. Consider changes to this field carefully. You must balance performance considerations with the information preservation offered by replication.

✦ **Scan for Startup Procs:** As an administrator, you can instruct SQL Server to run one or more stored procedures when the database engine starts. This field controls whether SQL Server undertakes this operation.

✦ **Two Digit Year Cutoff:** Remember the Y2K crisis? This value allows you to specify the final year that will work with a two-digit year value.

✦ **Network Packet Size:** This parameter allows you to tweak the size of network packet messages. Only experienced database and network administrators should change this from its default value.

✦ **Remote Login Timeout:** This value, specified in seconds, sets the time that SQL Server waits before responding to a failed remote login attempt. If you're concerned about denial of service or other remote attacks on your database, keep this setting high. If this is not a concern, you can safely lower it.

✦ **Cost Threshold for Parallelism:** This option tweaks the SQL Server behavior for *parallel* operations (that is, taking advantage of multi-processors), based on query plans generated from the Optimizer. With a range from 0 to 32767, you have leeway to experiment, but make these changes carefully.

✦ **Locks:** For operations that employ parallel processing, this parameter determines the maximum number of locks employed as part of the procedure. Leaving it at 0 is a good idea. This allows SQL Server to manage this important behavior.

✦ **Max Degree of Parallelism:** You can cap the number of processors that participate in a parallel operation by using this setting.

✦ **Query Wait:** You can tell SQL Server how many seconds you want the query to wait for resources before giving up and timing out. Unless you have special needs or complications, using the default of –1 is a good idea.

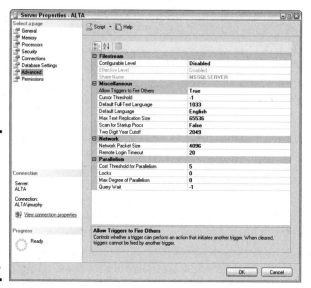

Figure 1-8:
The Advanced Server Properties page in SQL Server Management Studio.

Permission properties

This page gives the administrator the ability to set explicit permissions for individual users (both logins and roles). If you're looking for a detailed exploration of the entire security topic, see Chapter 3 in this mini-book.

Generating Configuration Scripts

Microsoft subscribes to the database administration philosophy that wizards and graphical tools are good, and repetitive, tedious hand coding is bad. Despite this natural preference toward wizard-driven automation, circumstances still exist where database administrators might need to create or modify scripts that manage their databases. Some DBAs even prefer to work this way, rather than always using graphical tools. For this important constituency, SQL Server makes it easy to generate, and then edit, all kinds of administrative scripts. We close this chapter by seeing how this is done.

To get started, launch the SQL Server Management Studio. You'll soon be in an excellent position to generate all the scripts you need. Here's how:

1. **Launch SQL Server Management Studio.**

2. **Connect to the appropriate SQL Server instance.**

3. **Expand the connection's entry in the Object Explorer view.**

4. **Expand the Databases folder.**

5. **Right-click the database that you want to administer.**

6. **Choose Tasks.**

7. **Choose Generate Scripts.**

   This launches the Generate SQL Server Scripts Wizard. For the purpose of this example, we show you how to generate a simple script that creates a table. When you start to use this wizard, however, you can do much more.

8. **Highlight the database where the object(s) that you want to script can be found, and click Next.**

9. **Customize the script options that you want an SQL Server to employ, and click Next.**

   More than two dozen ways to tweak your script exist, ranging from error handling to the types of objects you want scripted. As is the case with many of SQL Server's wizards, feel free to experiment with sample databases before trying this on production information.

10. **Identify the types of objects that you want to script, and click Next.**

    These objects can include defaults, rules, tables, user-defined data types, and views.

11. **Identify the specific objects that you want to script, and click Next.**

    Your available choices are dependent on what types of objects you select in Step 10.

12. **Decide where you want the output to be placed, and click Next.**

SQL Server dutifully creates the output in a file, on the Clipboard, or in a new query window.

13. **Review your script generation choices, and click Finish.**

SQL Server gives you one more chance to look over the options it will use when creating your script. For this simple example, Figure 1-9 shows how this script will be generated.

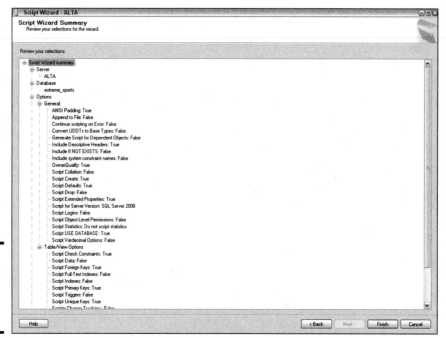

Figure 1-9:
A summary
of Script
Wizard
settings.

SQL Server takes a few moments to generate your script. You can monitor the progress and view or edit your script when things are done. Figure 1-10 shows the results of this simple example.

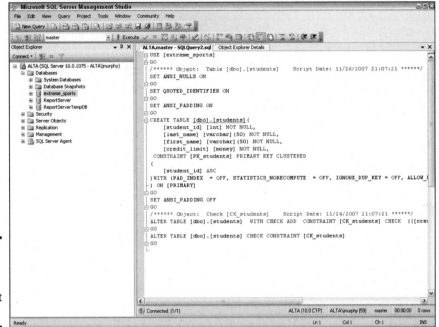

Figure 1-10:
A script
generated
by the Script
Wizard.

Chapter 2: Performing Major Administrative Tasks

In This Chapter

- ✔ Controlling database state
- ✔ Managing disk space
- ✔ Moving databases
- ✔ Backing up and restoring information
- ✔ Automating tasks with Maintenance Plans

A database administrator's work is never done: Just when you think you're caught up, a completely new series of demands arises. Fortunately, if you've chosen SQL Server 2008 as your database platform, many shortcuts, wizards, and tools are at your disposal. In this chapter, we look at each major administrative task, along with ways to simplify, automate, and otherwise make your life easier.

We start by seeing how to take databases off-line and bring them back online, as well as view the database logs generated by SQL Server 2008. After that, you discover how to conserve valuable disk space by shrinking databases. Next, we discuss moving databases between servers — an important topic, which includes import and export considerations. Because safeguarding your information is vital, we then provide a detailed discussion of backing up, and then restoring, databases. Finally, SQL Server offers an extremely potent and flexible set of capabilities known as *maintenance plans*. We close the chapter with a brief example of how you can make the most of this labor-saving technology.

The SQL Server Management Studio is a powerful tool provided by Microsoft to help you manage your SQL Server 2008 instances. Additionally, you can perform some of these tasks by using the character-based SQLCMD utility. However, that's a much more cumbersome way to administer your database, so we focus on the friendlier, graphically based SQL Server Management Studio.

Here's how to fire up the SQL Server Management Studio and get ready for the important work we describe throughout the chapter:

1. **Launch the SQL Server Management Studio.**

2. **Connect to the appropriate SQL Server instance.**

3. **Expand the connection's entry in the Object Explorer view.**

4. **Expand the Databases folder.**

5. **Right-click the database you want to administer.**

6. **Choose the Tasks menu option.**

Figure 2-1 shows how this menu looks in SQL Server Management Studio. Get to know it because as an administrator you'll be spending a lot of time on this menu.

The tasks that you read about in this chapter generally affect only a single database. Other databases that reside on your server are unaffected by these types of operations unless you explicitly include them.

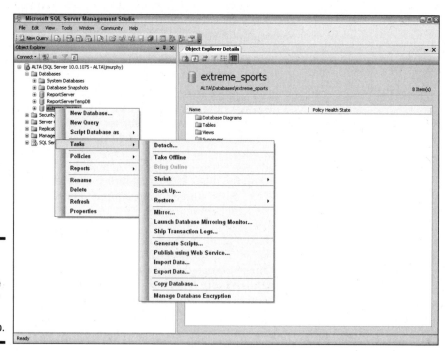

Figure 2-1:
The Tasks menu in the SQL Server Management Studio.

Controlling Database State

Before we get started on how to take a database offline and then bring it back online, a short detour is in order to get a good understanding of the many different states that your SQL Server 2008 database can be in. These states include:

- ✦ **Online:** You hope to see this state most frequently for your database. It means that the database is ready for action.

- ✦ **Off-line:** This generally refers to a database that has been deliberately taken off-line, usually for actions, such as moving it to a new disk or new server.

- ✦ **Recovering:** SQL Server is attempting to recover the database, usually after a restore or system restart.

- ✦ **Recovery pending:** This state generally happens when SQL Server is missing a resource or other key component during the database recovery process. When you see this state, it's likely that an administrator will have to take some further action to help things work right.

- ✦ **Suspect:** You don't want to see this state. It means that something has gone wrong with your database (either during startup or recovery), and SQL Server considers your database (or one of its underlying data files) to be damaged.

- ✦ **Emergency:** As you might expect, this database state means that some serious administrative work needs to be done before the database is ready for general consumption. Typically set when an administrator is trying to figure out why a database was placed into the suspect state, the database is only in single-user mode until the problem is resolved.

To get a list of all your databases and their current states, run the following statement within your favorite SQL editor:

```
SELECT name, state_desc from sys.databases;
```

Now that you've seen the different states you might encounter for your database, we look at how you would take a database off-line.

Taking a database off-line

Generally, most administrators rarely need to take a database off-line. The most common situations that require such action typically are related to restoring portions of a database because of complications during a backup, or other operational problems.

As with most of the tasks in this chapter, you must first locate the Tasks menu from within the database you wish to alter. The beginning of this chapter explains how to get to this menu. Assuming that you're on the Tasks menu, choose the Take Offline option.

After you've chosen this command, SQL Server displays a dialog box that shows the progress of your request. Figure 2-2 shows this dialog box, along with the new icon and message indicating that your database is off-line.

Figure 2-2:
Taking a
database
off-line in
SQL Server
Manage-
ment Studio.

If you're inclined to use an SQL command to achieve this result (rather than the graphical SQL Server management studio), look at the `ALTER DATABASE` command; it's very useful for these types of administrative tasks.

Bringing a database online

Assuming there's nothing wrong with your database that would prevent a successful operation, bringing it back online is quite easy. Again, you need to find your way to the Tasks menu for the database in question. After you arrive, choose the Bring Online option. As when you take the database off-line, SQL Server displays a dialog box that shows the progress of returning your database to its desired state.

Viewing database logs

The most successful database administrators bring a broad range of inter-personal and technical skills to the job. In fact, database administrators and detectives often share similar traits. Both jobs require the ability to analyze mounds of information to gain a true picture of reality. Luckily, SQL Server 2008 provides a powerful logging utility that helps database administrators find the underlying cause of difficult problems.

To view your logs, follow these simple steps:

1. **Launch the SQL Server Management Studio.**
2. **Connect to the appropriate SQL Server instance.**
3. **Expand the connection's entry in the Object Explorer view.**
4. **Expand the Management folder.**
5. **Expand the SQL Server Logs folder.**
6. **Double-click the log file you want to view.**

   This opens the SQL Server Log File Viewer.
7. **Check the available boxes to see any additional logs.**

These log files provide tremendous amounts of information. Here's a quick summary of the data available to you as an administrator. *Note:* Some of these columns are context-sensitive; you might not see them in all cases.

✦ **Date:** The date and time that the logged event occurred.

✦ **Source:** The origination service for the logged event.

✦ **Message:** A detailed description of what is being logged.

✦ **Log Source:** The actual file that contains the message.

✦ **Log Type:** The class of logged information. Values can include SQL Server, SQL Server agent, database mail, and the operating system.

✦ **Category:** Additional details to help you identify the source of the log entry.

✦ **Event:** The operating system's numeric identifier for this log entry.

✦ **User:** The login ID that created or caused this log event.

✦ **Computer:** The host identifier for the computer that generated this log event.

Figure 2-3 shows the SQL Server Log File Viewer. Notice that we're looking at the SQL Agent, SQL Server, and Windows NT logs.

The Log File Viewer's filtering feature is a powerful capability. It's extremely helpful in teasing out the exact information you seek. Figure 2-4 displays this useful dialog box in action.

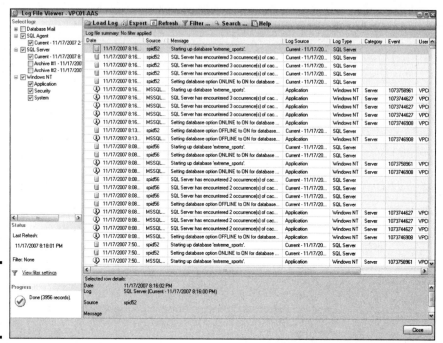

Figure 2-3:
The SQL
Server Log
File Viewer.

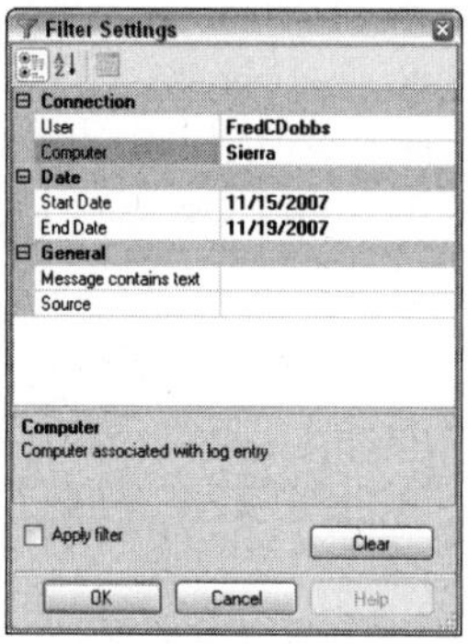

Figure 2-4:
Filtering log
file records.

Managing Disk Space

SQL Server administrators typically face two major disk space management
challenges: providing sufficient disk space so that the database can do its
job, and conversely reclaiming space used by the database when some of
that storage is no longer necessary. In this section, you perform both of
these important tasks.

Adding new disk storage

To store its information, SQL Server employs a collection of database files that are stored on your Windows file system. These files can contain *primary information storage* (data and indexes) or *log details* (used by SQL Server to maintain the database's integrity). It's very easy to set up these important database components. Here's what you do:

1. **Launch the SQL Server Management Studio.**

2. **Connect to the appropriate SQL Server instance.**

3. **Expand the connection's entry in the Object Explorer view.**

4. **Expand the Databases folder.**

5. **Right-click the database you want to administer.**

6. **Choose the Properties option.**

7. **Select the Files page.**

   This opens the dialog box shown in Figure 2-5.

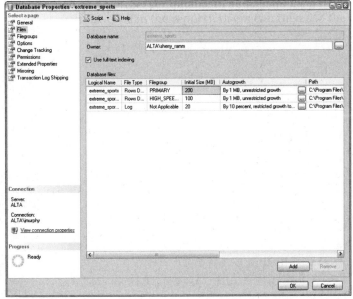

Figure 2-5: Adding new data storage files in the SQL Server Management Studio.

8. **Click the Add button and fill in the details about your new data storage.**

These details include:

- A logical name for the file. Try to make this meaningful for your environment.

- The kind of information to be stored in the file (rows or log).

- The filegroup in which you want to store the new file.

  Filegroups are a handy way of organizing your disk storage in a logical manner. If you're interested in this topic, Book II, Chapter 1 covers this in much more detail.

- The initial size of the file in megabytes.

  Try to resist the temptation to allocate an enormous initial amount of disk space to the file. As you see in a moment, you can instruct the SQL Server to grow the file automatically when needed.

- The growth plan for the file. The Autogrowth option instructs SQL Server to expand the file as necessary.

- The path for the file. There is no need to provide a filename; SQL Server takes care of this for you.

9. **When you've finished making your entries, click OK to save your work.**

Removing disk storage

Sometimes, it's necessary to place your database on a diet. It's quite common for a database administrator to over-allocate storage space, which ends up wasting valuable disk resources. Although disk drives are getting cheaper by the minute, they're still not free. Fortunately, it's quite easy to remove unneeded disk storage space, thereby liberating it for other purposes.

Two main mechanisms are at your disposal to free disk space. You can remove unneeded data files from SQL Server's control, which is the opposite of the steps just described (adding new files to SQL Server). All you need to do is follow Steps 1 through 7 in the previous section. Then, instead of clicking the Add button in Step 8, click the Remove button.

SQL Server enables the Remove button only for those files that are candidates for elimination. A file is a candidate for elimination when it no longer contains any information; SQL Server won't even enable the Remove button if doing so would damage your data.

Another way to free disk space is to shrink the size of already-existing data files without actually removing them. To do that, follow the steps at the beginning of the chapter to reach the SQL Server Management Studio database's Tasks menu. When you arrive at this menu, choose the Shrink option. You're presented with a submenu that allows you to shrink either the database or its constituent data files. After you're finished, click OK. SQL Server does the rest.

TIP

If you're unsure about the distribution of information in a database's underlying files, you're probably better off choosing the Shrink Database menu option. Comparatively, if you know that a given file is under-utilized, select the Shrink Files option. Figure 2-6 shows how it looks to shrink a database. Figure 2-7 illustrates the same work for a file.

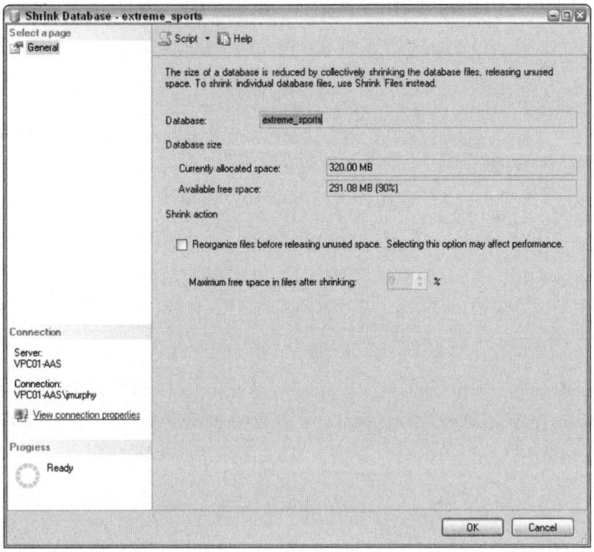

Figure 2-6:
Shrinking a database in the SQL Server Management Studio.

Regardless of which approach you follow, taking these important steps allows you to utilize this newly freed disk space for purposes that are more productive.

Moving Databases

This next section takes you on a tour of the different options at your disposal for moving databases and their associated information. To begin, you see how to detach and then reattach a database. The next step helps you understand how to copy a database between SQL Server instances. Finally, you get the hang of importing and exporting data while also understanding when to ship transaction logs to different servers.

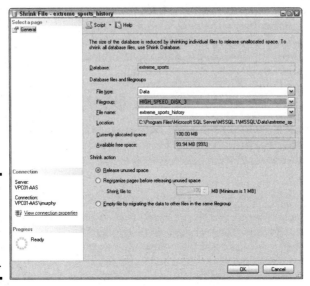

Figure 2-7:
Shrinking
files in the
SQL Server
Manage-
ment Studio.

As with many of SQL Server's administrative options, it's a good idea to familiarize yourself with these tasks by using a test or sample database. After you've mastered these techniques, you'll be in great shape to try them on live data.

All the operations described in this section can be launched from the SQL Server Management Studio database's Tasks menu. See the beginning of this chapter if you don't remember how to access this menu.

Detaching databases

SQL Server offers a number of helpful mechanisms to move information between different locations. These locations can be on the same computer, on different computers in the same building, or even halfway around the world. One of the easiest ways to pick up and copy an entire database with a minimal amount of fuss is to detach it from its original instance and then reattach it to another instance. Here's how to make that happen:

1. **Choose the Detach option from the database's Tasks menu.**

You're presented with a simple dialog box, as shown in Figure 2-8. While on this page, you can also choose to drop existing connections, update the database's statistical profile, and preserve any full-text catalogs.

If you elect to encrypt your database, make sure to export your encryption keys before detaching your database.

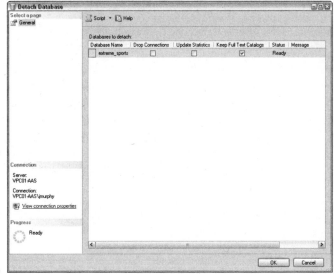

Figure 2-8:
Detaching a
database in
the SQL
Server
Manage-
ment Studio.

2. **When you're ready, click OK.**

The database detaches from its current server. To move it to another
server, copy its data and log files and then reattach the database on the
new instance.

After you detach a database, you'll no longer see it in the list of active databases on your SQL Server instance. Don't worry, it hasn't been deleted; it's
available to be reattached on this instance or on a different instance.

A few caveats to detaching databases do exist. If any of the following conditions apply, you won't be able to detach your database:

✦ An active database snapshot is in the database.

✦ The database is being mirrored.

✦ Problems with the database exist, and it's been placed in a suspect
state.

✦ The database is identified as a system database.

✦ The database is replicated and has been published.

Attaching databases

Attaching an existing database to a SQL Server instance is very simple.
Here's what you need to do:

1. **Copy all relevant files to the new server.**

This includes all the data and log files that were used by the database.

Try to have a list of these files ready before you begin the detach-and-attach process. This is much easier than trying to figure out later all the files that supported the database.

If you're attempting to attach an encrypted database, you'll first need to import its encryption keys.

2. **Choose the Attach option from the SQL Server Management Studio Database menu.**

To get to this menu, right-click the Databases folder in the SQL Server Management Studio Object Explorer.

3. **Click the Add button to open a dialog box that allows you to select the appropriate data and log files.**

Figure 2-9 shows this file-selection dialog box.

4. **Click OK after you've found the file.**

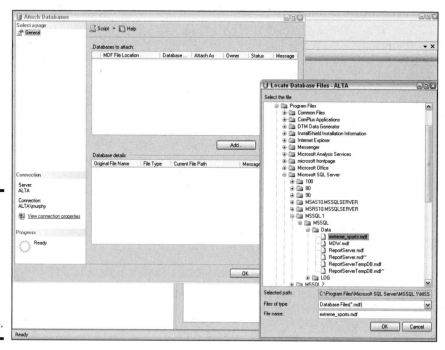

Figure 2-9: Choosing a database file for attaching in the SQL Server Management Studio.

After choosing the data file, SQL Server populates the Attach Databases dialog box with a list of all the constituent files that are needed to support the database. Figure 2-10 gives you an idea of what this dialog box looks like.

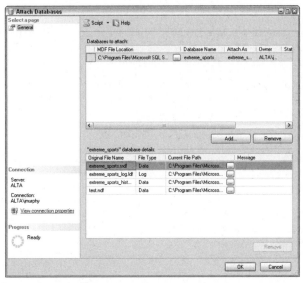

Figure 2-10: A list of associated files for attaching a database in the SQL Server Management Studio.

5. **Click OK when you're satisfied with the list of files.**

SQL Server reattaches your database.

Copying databases

As described in the preceding sections, you can use the Detach and Attach database maintenance options to copy a SQL Server database between instances. As is the case with many of SQL Server's administrative responsibilities, there is an alternate way to make this happen: the Copy Database Wizard, which is the subject of the next portion of this chapter.

You can't copy or move any of SQL Server's system databases.

To launch this helpful wizard, choose the Copy Database option from the database's Tasks menu. You're presented with the launch screen for this wizard. When you're past the launch screen, here's what to do next:

1. **Identify the source server (that is, the server that holds the database you wish to copy).**

You're prompted for a login to this database server, and you must decide between Windows or SQL Server-style authentication.

2. **Select the destination server (that is, the server where the database will be copied).**

   You're prompted for a login to this server. Again, you must decide between Windows or SQL Server-style authentication.

3. **Choose whether you want SQL Server to use the detach-and-attach method (similar to the steps described in the preceding sections) or the SQL Management Object method.**

   The advantage of the latter approach is that SQL Server can remain online while the change is underway. This approach is slower than the detach-and-attach method, however.

4. **Select one or more databases to copy.**

   Figure 2-11 illustrates a dialog box that provides details on the affected files for the upcoming database copy operation.

Figure 2-11: A list of associated files for copying a database in the SQL Server Management Studio.

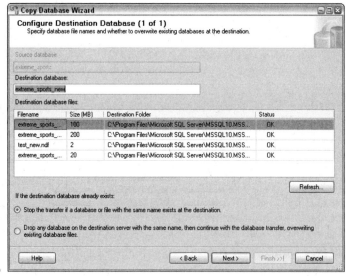

5. **Configure the Integration Services package with details, such as the package's name, its logging options, and so on.**

   See Chapter 4 of this mini-book if you'd like to gain more insight into the powerful capabilities of SQL Server's Integration Services.

6. **Determine when you want this job to run, along with which Integration Services proxy account you want to use.**

7. Launch the operation.

The time SQL Server takes to complete the work depends on the size of your database. While the job is running, you see a progress report that allows you to track exactly where things stand. Should anything go awry, you're notified via this dialog box.

Importing and exporting data

Despite the rapid advances made in real-time integration, the fact remains that a major part of a database administrator's role revolves around loading and unloading data from information repositories (such as SQL Server). To address this need, SQL Server offers a highly sophisticated set of integration services. The lion's share of Chapter 4 in this mini-book provides a detailed analysis of how you can make these services work for you. For now, it's time to take a brief look at how easy it is to use SQL Server Management Studio to import and export information.

To illustrate these examples in as clear a manner as possible, we focus on importing data from a simple text file, and then exporting data to an Excel spreadsheet. Obviously, you can construct much more sophisticated data movement patterns than the ones described here, but understanding these examples will help build a solid foundation for you. For both of these illustrations, you use the SQL Server Import and Export Wizard to streamline these tasks.

Importing from a text file

In this example, we create a simple text file that contains three columns of information. Each column is separated from its neighbor by a comma. We also have a destination table in the database that awaits its new information.

1. To initiate the import process, begin by choosing the Import option from the database's Tasks menu.

This launches the Import and Export Wizard. Use the Next button to advance through this utility; the Back button takes you back one panel.

2. Choose the source of your imported information, along with the server name.

For the data source, a drop-down box allows you to select from one of many data access methods. For this example, use the Flat File Source. You also need to provide details on a number of other context-sensitive settings. In the case of a flat file, you must instruct SQL Server on the file's location and format, whether there's a header row, what delimiter to use, and so on. You can also preview the soon-to-be-imported data at this point.

3. **Select the destination for your information.**

If there's not a table already in place, don't worry; SQL Server will create a new one for you.

Before launching a massive import job, you'd be wise to preview the information.

4. **Review the data type mappings for your upcoming import.**

At this point, SQL Server gives you the ability to determine what should happen in the case of an error.

5. **Schedule the job.**

You can elect to have the export task run immediately, or schedule it using the SQL Server Integration Services package. For the purposes of this example, run the job right away.

6. **Review your choices from the wizard.**

SQL Server gives you one more chance to check the details of the upcoming import job.

7. **Run the job.**

As with many administrative tasks, SQL Server displays a dialog box that summarizes the job's progress. Pay close attention to the details contained in this dialog box because errors are prominently displayed here. Figure 2-12 shows that the import process finished successfully.

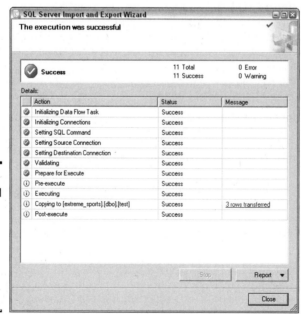

Figure 2-12: A successful import process in the SQL Server Import and Export Wizard.

Exporting to a spreadsheet

To extract information from your SQL Server database:

1. Initiate the export process by choosing the Export option from the database's Tasks menu.

This launches the Import and Export Wizard. Use the Next button to advance through this utility; the Back button takes you back one panel.

2. Choose the source of your exported information, along with the server name.

For the data source, a drop-down box allows you to select from one of many data access methods. For this example, use the SQL Server Native Client 10.0. You also need to decide the style of authentication to follow, along with the database name from which you wish to export information.

3. Select the destination for your information.

Figure 2-13 shows the wide variety of possible destinations. Microsoft Excel is the destination for the data. You also see that context-sensitive connection settings are dependent on the type of export that you're performing.

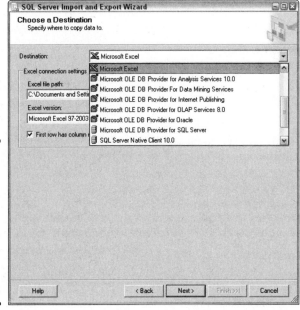

Figure 2-13: A list of associated files for copying a database in the SQL Server Management Studio.

4. **Decide whether you want to copy information, or construct a query to retrieve a subset of all available data.**

In many cases, you'll simply want to copy information from your SQL Server database. However, you have the flexibility to create a specialized query if need be.

5. **Select one or more tables and views from which to export data.**

You can also edit your column mappings, as well as preview the upcoming export from this dialog box. Figure 2-14 shows how the table selection and data preview dialog boxes appear.

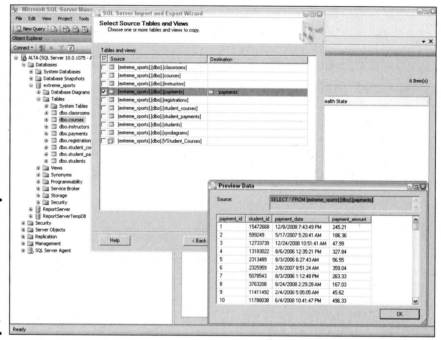

Figure 2-14:
Previewing
export
information
in the SQL
Server
Manage-
ment Studio.

Before executing a massive export job, take a few moments to preview the information. It's a good opportunity to double-check what is about to happen and a great time to correct any mistakes.

6. **Review the data type mappings for your upcoming export.**

At this point, SQL Server gives you the ability to determine what should happen in the case of an error.

7. **Schedule the job.**

You can elect to have the export task run immediately, or schedule it using the SQL Server Integration Services package. For the purposes of this example, run the job right away.

8. **Review your choices from the wizard.**

   SQL Server gives you one more chance to check the details of the upcoming export job.

9. **Run the job.**

   As with many administrative tasks, SQL Server displays a dialog box that summarizes the job's progress. Pay close attention to the details contained in this dialog box because errors are prominently displayed here.

Backing Up and Restoring Information

Although we save this topic for last, in many ways the most important job of a database administrator is to provide a solid information backup and restore strategy. In this section, you see how to make the most of SQL Server's powerful built-in utilities to protect your information and restore your system in the event of a disaster or other data-damaging event. Also, stay tuned for the next section, where we show you how to use the SQL Server Maintenance Plan Wizard to automate many of the tasks shown in this segment.

We begin by exploring the backup utility. When you know that your data is safely archived, you can turn your attention to restoring a backed-up database. As you might imagine, the topic of data archiving and restoration could (and does) fill an entire book. In fact, there's an entire industry focused solely on information backup and restoration. Consequently, given the amount of available space in this book for this important topic, we focus only on relatively simple data backup and restoration scenarios.

 Before designing and implementing a backup and restoration architecture for your production data, spend some time experimenting with sample databases. It's always better to make mistakes with test data than with live data.

Backing up data

As with many of the tools and utilities described throughout this chapter, you launch SQL Server's backup capabilities from the SQL Server Management Studio database's Tasks menu. See the beginning of this chapter if you're unsure about where this menu is located. When you arrive at this menu, follow these steps:

1. **Select the Back Up menu option.**

   You're presented with a dialog box similar to the one shown in Figure 2-15.

Book VIII
Chapter 2

Performing Major
Administrative
Tasks

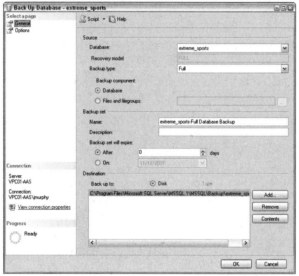

Figure 2-15:
The initial database backup dialog box in the SQL Server Management Studio.

2. **Fill in values for all the relevant fields.**

   Here's a brief explanation of these fields:

   - **Database:** Choose the database you want to back up from the drop-down list.

   - **Recovery model:** This setting (configured when creating the database and unchangeable here) describes your options when faced with a server outage as well as what steps you can take during backup and restore.

   - **Backup Type:** Your choices here are full, differential, and transaction log. As you might expect, the *full database backup* archives all the information found in the database. The *differential backup* archives only data that has changed since the last full backup. Finally, the *transaction log backup* archives only information that has been written into the transaction log by SQL Server.

   - **Backup Component:** You can elect to back up the entire database, or only a subset of the database's supporting files.

   Unless disk space is at a premium or there are other unique requirements (such as certain database files being offline), it's a good idea to back up the entire database rather than only a subset of your files.

   - **Name:** This is a name that helps identify the backup set. SQL Server will provide one for you if you don't generate your own.

- **Description:** This is an optional administrator-generated summary of the backup set.

- **Backup Set Will Expire:** This optional field allows you to determine when the information that you archive will expire. You can choose a set date or a number of days after this backup.

- **Destination:** If you have a tape drive installed, SQL Server offers you the option of backing up your information to that drive. Comparatively, many administrators simply back up their data to a disk.

3. **If necessary, fill in additional information on the options page.**

   Navigate to this page by clicking Options on the left of this dialog box. On the Options page, shown in Figure 2-16, you can set additional criteria about the upcoming backup.

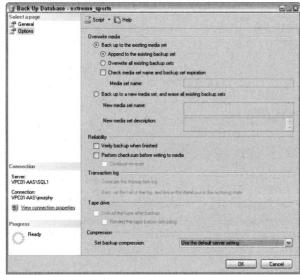

Figure 2-16: The Options backup dialog box in the SQL Server Management Studio.

Here's an explanation of these fields:

- **Overwrite Media:** You can instruct SQL Server whether it should append, overwrite, or create a new set of media in support of your backup.

- **Reliability:** These two settings help provide additional assurance that your backup has been done correctly.

   Although it takes more time, it's a good idea to verify the backup and perform a checksum prior to writing to media. One day, you might be happy that you took the time to perform both of these safeguards.

- **Transaction Log:** If you're backing up the transaction log, you can choose whether to *truncate* (that is, delete) backed up transactions from the log, or simply back up the very end of the transaction log.

- **Tape Drive:** If you've elected to back up your information to a tape drive, these two settings help control the physical device.

- **Compression:** Because backups can be quite large, SQL Server allows you to specify whether you want these archives to be compressed.

4. When you've finished setting your backup options, click OK.

SQL Server launches the backup. Depending on how much information is being archived, this can take some time to complete. When the backup finishes, SQL Server displays a message stating that the work is done. SQL Server also writes a record of this backup into the system log. If you're interested in reading system logs, the earlier "Viewing database logs" section discusses this in more detail.

When a backup finishes, you're free to look at the contents of the media that you just created. To do so, click the Contents button from the General page within the Back Up utility (you access it from the SQL Server Management Studio Tasks menu). Figure 2-17 shows how this looks for a recently completed backup.

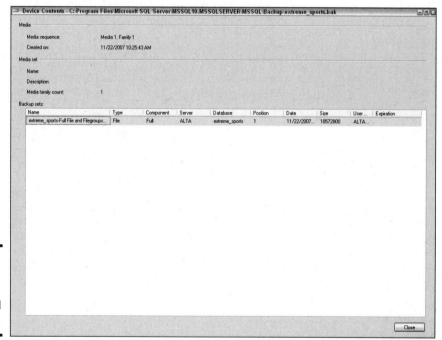

Figure 2-17:
Media contents for a completed backup.

Restoring a backup

Backing up information is only half the fun; the real excitement begins when you find yourself needing to restore a database. Perhaps you've experienced a virus, hardware failure, or simple user error that has damaged your organization's vital information. These kinds of situations are where your hard work can pay off.

To begin the restore process, follow these steps:

1. **Launch the SQL Server Management Studio.**

2. **Connect to the appropriate SQL Server instance.**

3. **Expand the connection's entry in the Object Explorer view.**

Assuming that you need to restore an entire database that is no longer present, right-click the Databases folder and choose either the Restore Database or Restore Files and Filegroups option. For the purposes of this example, imagine that you've lost the entire database and need to restore the full set of information. Comparatively, if you haven't lost the entire database, you can also access restore functionality by right-clicking the database and choosing the same two options from the Tasks menu.

4. **Fill in values for all relevant fields.**

Two pages' worth of options are at your disposal. This section describes the General page; thereafter, the Options page is covered. The following fields require your attention:

- **Destination for Restore:** You can instruct SQL Server about which database should receive the restored information. If an original database has been damaged, a good strategy is to restore the archive into a brand-new database, rather than trying to overlay the already-damaged database.

  You can also specify whether you want your restore to be as recent as possible, or to a specific date and time. The SQL Server transaction log makes this possible. This capability is handy when you know that a particular database-damaging event occurred at a precise date and time. You can restore your archive just prior to the problematic incident.

- **Source for Restore:** You can point SQL Server at the archived information. Your choices are to select an archive by database name, or from a backup device. In most cases, you should be able to use the From Database drop-down list to identify the database for recovery. Figure 2-18 shows this page in more detail.

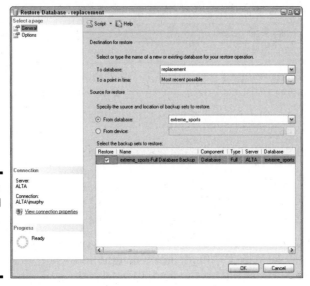

Figure 2-18:
The General properties page for restoring a database.

5. **If necessary, fill in additional information on the Options page.**

> *Note:* SQL Server doesn't permit you to view the Options page until you've successfully filled in the appropriate fields on the General page. Figure 2-19 shows the Options page.

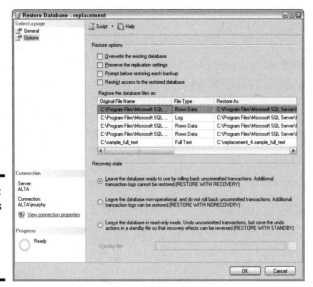

Figure 2-19:
The Options properties page for restoring a database.

When you arrive at the Options page, the following fields are at your disposal:

- **Overwrite the Existing Database:** As you might surmise from the name of this option, you can instruct SQL Server on whether you want an existing database overlaid with restore data. Until you're very sure of what you're doing, it's not a bad idea to leave this option unchecked.

- **Preserve the Replication Settings:** We cover replication in detail as part of Chapter 5 in this mini-book. For now, this setting simply determines whether SQL Server enables full replication settings upon restoration.

- **Prompt before Restoring Each Backup:** This option requests that SQL Server pass the administrator before proceeding on the restoration.

- **Restrict Access to the Restore Database:** You can instruct SQL Server on whether the database should be immediately available upon restoration. Given that you're probably restoring because of a serious issue, you might want to restrict access until you're sure that the restore has gone according to plan.

- **Restore the Database Files As:** SQL Server automatically creates file-names for you. If you want to alter these system-generated names, you can do so. However, in most cases, this won't be necessary.

- **Recovery State:** You have three choices for the recovery state of your database. In most cases, you'll want to leave the database in a ready to use state. This rolls back any uncommitted transactions. The additional states provide additional control over uncommitted transactions.

6. **When you've finished setting your restore options, click OK.**

    SQL Server launches the restore operation. Depending on how much information is being archived, this can take some time to complete. When the restore finishes, SQL Server displays a message stating that the work is done. SQL Server also writes a record of this into the system log. If you're interested in reading system logs, see the earlier "Viewing database logs" section.

Automating Things with Maintenance Plans

Setting up and managing all the maintenance jobs that we've shown you in this chapter demands a significant amount of work on the administrator's part. If you've stuck with us this far, you're about to see how managing these sometimes-mundane responsibilities can be made easier with maintenance plans.

It's probably simplest to think of *maintenance plans* as a collection of events that helps guide SQL Server in automatically executing the administrator's maintenance requirements. Microsoft has made it easy to create and maintain maintenance plans via a collection of graphical tools and wizards. We spend some time to help you understand these helpful assistants.

For the purposes of this simple example, assume that you want to automate a series of steps that culminates in a full backup of a particular database. We show you how to use the SQL Server Maintenance Plan Wizard to make this happen, and then show you how to fine-tune the automatically generated maintenance plan.

1. **Launch the SQL Server Management Studio.**

2. **Connect to the appropriate SQL Server instance.**

3. **Expand the connection's entry in the Object Explorer view.**

4. **Expand the Management folder.**

5. **Right-click the Maintenance Plans folder.**

6. **Choose the Maintenance Plan Wizard menu option.**

This launches the SQL Server Maintenance Plan Wizard where you specify your requirements.

7. **Give your maintenance plan a name, along with an optional description, and click Next.**

You can also create separate schedules for each task, or a single schedule to execute all tasks. For the purposes of this basic example, we use a single schedule. As you become more familiar with this wizard, you can certainly set up automated runs for your new job.

8. **Select one or more maintenance tasks, and click Next.**

SQL Server presents you with a collection of important maintenance operations, as shown in Figure 2-20. Highlighting each option brings up a helpful description at the bottom of this dialog box. For this example, we've selected the Check Database Integrity, Update Statistics, and Full Backup options.

9. **Order your maintenance tasks, and click Next.**

You can tell SQL Server in which order you want your tasks to run.

10. **For each of the tasks, select the target database, and click Next.**

You have the option of choosing a specific database, or requesting that this task be performed for all databases. *Note:* The specific options that you're shown will depend on the kind of task you're performing.

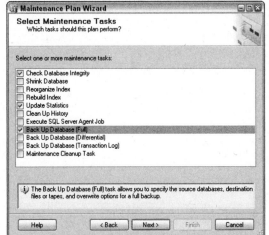

Figure 2-20:
Selecting
database
mainte-
nance tasks.

11. **Tell SQL Server where you want reports about this job to go, and click
Next.**

You can have the output written to a text file, or even e-mailed to an
operator.

12. **Review your choices, and click Finish.**

Figure 2-21 shows the proposed series of steps in this simple maintenance plan. After you click Finish, SQL Server launches your maintenance plan and reports on its results. ***Remember:*** You can also schedule
this maintenance plan to run whenever you like.

After you've run your maintenance plan, SQL Server adds it to its list of
available maintenance plans. You're then free to edit the maintenance plan
and customize it to your heart's content by right-clicking the maintenance
plan, and choosing the Modify option. Figure 2-22 shows how the maintenance plan editor looks for the plan.

Space constraints in this book don't permit a detailed exploration of this
extremely powerful tool; however, you can use this editor to set up more
sophisticated workflow, handle conditional logic, and further customize your
job scheduling.

**Book VIII
Chapter 2**

**Performing Major
Administrative
Tasks**

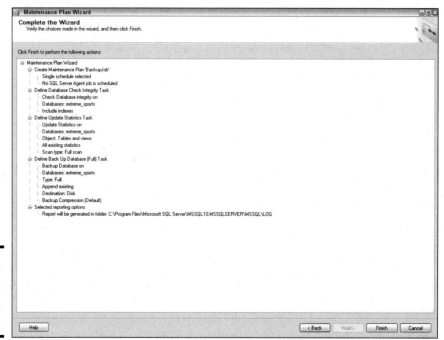

Figure 2-21:
Reviewing the steps in the maintenance plan.

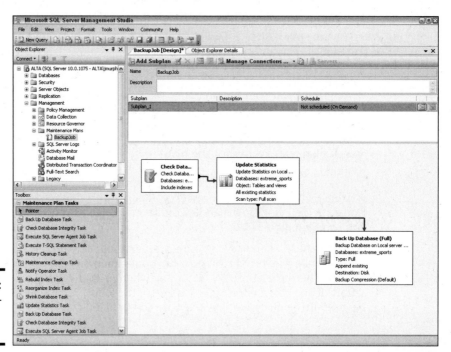

Figure 2-22:
The maintenance plan editor.

Chapter 3: Security: Keeping SQL Server Safe

In This Chapter

✔ SQL Server's security model

✔ Setting up a well-thought-out security plan

✔ Granting and revoking access to SQL Server

✔ Integrating database and operating system security

For harried administrators faced with keeping users happy on an ever-tightening schedule (while simultaneously grappling with shrinking budgets), setting up and managing database security are often the last things that come to mind. Unfortunately, the damages that result from lapses in security can wreak havoc on an organization (and those stressed administrators, too), usually at the most inopportune time. Fortunately, SQL Server ships with a collection of powerful yet easy-to-configure security capabilities, which is what this chapter is all about.

To begin, because securing your database does add to your workload, we point out why you should care about this important topic. We then cite the broad range of database objects that you can lock down. When the overview is complete, we show you how to perform some of the most commonplace security tasks.

Before getting started, keep in mind that this isn't a comprehensive guide to all the possible SQL Server security permutations. That would fill a book! Instead, the focus is on getting productive quickly and handling the most common types of security-related tasks.

The Value of Security

To a database administrator already overwhelmed with daily tasks, setting up a well-designed security plan can sometimes seem more trouble than it's worth. Therefore, it's quite fair to ask whether there's value in making the effort. If you can answer, "Yes" to any of the following questions, then you'll eventually be glad you took the time and implemented a decent security plan:

✦ Will your database hold sensitive information?

✦ Will multiple people work with your data?

✦ Might any of the people who interact with your data ever part ways with your organization in a less-than-amicable manner?

✦ Will other computers connect to your database?

✦ Might any of these external computers be compromised?

✦ Will your database server be available over a local network or the Internet?

Chances are that at least one of these will apply to most readers. With that in mind, it's time to see how to get started setting up the right security plan for your database.

What Can You Secure?

If you can store it or represent it in SQL Server, chances are that you can secure it. Microsoft has done a great job in creating fully integrated security architecture. All security-capable objects are *securables.* One securable might in turn enclose additional securables, thereby producing an encapsulated group of objects. These are *scopes,* and by setting security at the scope level, all securables contained within the scope receive the same security settings. Many securables can make up each scope; however, for the purposes of this chapter we focus on a few of the object securables within the schema scope.

To give you an idea of how many security options you have, the following list is categorized by SQL Server's three securable scopes:

1. **Server.**

This scope in turn contains three securables:

Endpoint

Login

Database

2. **Database.**

User	Remote service binding
Role	Full-text catalog
Application role	Certificate
Assembly	Asymmetric key

Message type	Symmetric key
Route	Contract
Service	Schema

3. Schema.

Type

XML Schema Collection

Object

The Object securable is of most interest for this chapter, and will likely be the focus of most readers of this book. It contains the following components:

Aggregate	Statistic
Constraint	Synonym
Function	Table
Procedure	View
Queue	

If some of the items in the preceding lists look a little unfamiliar to you, don't worry. The balance of the chapter focuses on securing the more recognizable objects, such as tables and views.

Who Can You Let Use Your Database?

The preceding section shows all the items that you can secure. The next question to answer is what kind of users can work with your database. In fact, some of these users aren't people; they're application programs and processes. Regardless of whether the entity accessing your database ingests food or electricity, SQL Server uses the term *principal* to describe them.

The three major classifications of principal, which in turn contain resources, are as follows:

1. Operating system-based principals

Windows domain login

Windows local

2. SQL Server-based principals

SQL Server login

3. **Database-based principals**

> Database user
>
> Database role
>
> Application role

SQL Server also supports the *pre-packaged permissions* concept. These are known as *roles,* but you can think of them as a one-stop shop that allows you to grant permissions en masse. Table 3-1 lists all the fixed server-level roles along with their purposes. Table 3-2 lists the same for fixed database-level roles.

Table 3-1	SQL Server Fixed Server Roles
Name	*Permission Available*
bulkadmin	Run the BULK INSERT command
dbcreator	Create, change, restore, or drop a database
diskadmin	Administer disk files
processadmin	End SQL Server processes
securityadmin	Set server and database-level permissions; set password
serveradmin	Shut down the server; modify server configuration values
setupadmin	Manage linked servers; run system stored procedures
sysadmin	Perform any administrative task on the server

Table 3-2	SQL Server Fixed Database Roles
Name	*Permission Available*
public	Default role for all database users
db_accessadmin	Maintain access permissions to the database
db_backupoperator	Archive the database
db_datareader	Read all data from any user table
db_datawriter	Make any modifications to any user's data
db_ddladmin	Execute any DDL command in any database
db_denydatareader	Blocked from reading data in a database
db_denydatawriter	Prevented from making any data modifications
db_owner	Perform all setup and database maintenance
db_securityadmin	Administer permissions and roles

It's important to understand that all new database users are associated with the `public` database role. If you don't explicitly set permissions for a given securable, these users automatically inherit the permissions that have been granted to the `public` database role for the securable in question. Later in this chapter, we show you how to define permissions, including permissions for the `public` database role.

What Can You Let Users Do?

Until this point, you've seen the type of objects that you can secure, and the types of users and roles that you can support. The next step in realizing your security vision is to decide who you want to work with your database, and then grant them the appropriate permissions.

Who gets to use the database?

Having seen all the configurable security options at your fingertips, you might be tempted to rush out, start setting up profiles and granting access to your database server. However, because no two enterprises will have the same security profile, it's worth taking a little more time and getting a better handle on exactly what you need to do for your own organization.

A great start is to figure out the types of users who you'll need to support. The next section lists some of the typical SQL Server user profiles that you're likely to encounter, in increasing order of responsibility. Your site might not have all of these functions; you might also have the same person handling multiple jobs, or you might be faced with additional roles and responsibilities. Nevertheless, use this handy list as a starting point:

✦ **Reporting user:** This kind of user typically connects to your database via a third-party reporting tool and runs reports or other data analysis. Generally, you can safely restrict the ability to make changes to the database because reporting users are primarily interested in reading data, not altering it.

✦ **Application user:** This type of SQL Server user often doesn't even know that a database server is part of the picture. Instead, he generally logs in to an application and performs work that just happens to get registered in your database. Mostly, you don't need to give tremendous power to this class of user; in fact, you can usually look to your application developer or vendor for guidance on the right security profile. Certain types of applications handle their own security, which usually translates into a smaller set of SQL Server-based logins.

✦ **Database user:** Akin to reporting users, database users are generally interested in the raw contents of your database, rather than information filtered by any third-party applications.

✦ **Application power user:** These sophisticated users often need to have higher levels of database privileges for tasks, such as creating views, new tables, or even granting access to additional users. Nevertheless, you would be wise to concede only as few additional privileges as possible. They can always request more control if it's necessary.

✦ **Operator:** Normally, operators are concerned only with routine (but essential) database administration tasks, such as backup and restore operations. Unless it's necessary for them to have higher authority, you can generally limit their access to your database to these purely administrative tasks.

✦ **Application developer:** It's common for these folks to want broad security power, which can trigger an adversarial relationship with the database administrator. Developers themselves are often subject to the changing whims of their application users, whose requests often require changes to the database or underlying server.

   However, by setting up development and test servers, you can have your cake and eat it, too. The developers can have wide-open security permissions on these non-production servers, and you can sleep better knowing that your production environment is safe.

✦ **System administrator:** It's quite understandable if a system administrator views database administration as a bit of a nuisance. After all, his primary job is ensuring the health of the server computer. However, it's important that these overseers be given sufficient permission to fill in or otherwise assist the person with the ultimate responsibility for the database's health: the database administrator.

✦ **Database administrator:** This profile represents the alpha and omega of SQL Server security. Typically, the database administrator can perform any task on a SQL Server computer. However, all this power comes neatly packaged with a great deal of responsibility, so be careful about handing out this role.

Choosing from the permissions menu

You use permissions to grant or remove privileges to a principal on one or more securables. For example, you might want to give a certain user full privileges for table 1, read-only privileges for table 2, and no privileges for table 3. We show you how to set permissions as part of the next section.

Implementing Security

Because you're up to speed on all the clever SQL Server security possibilities, it's time to put them to the test. To begin, you figure out who can already access your server and databases. After you know that, you can grant access to your database server and databases and then set specific permissions on particular objects.

While you're free to use the character-based SQLCMD utility in concert with SQL Server's numerous administrative stored procedures, the graphical SQL Server Management Studio is a much more productive venue for this type of work. Consequently, that's where we illustrate our examples for the balance of the chapter.

Getting a login list

Just as a login allows you to access a computer, a SQL Server login allows people (or processes) to connect to your database system. Here's how to get a full list of authorized logins:

1. **Start the SQL Server Management Studio.**

2. **Connect to your database server.**

3. **Expand the Security folder.**

4. **Open the Logins folder.**

That's all there is to it. All these people or processes can log in to your system.

Getting a user list

It's not enough to just log in to a SQL Server system. You also need permission to connect to, and work with, one or more databases. The following steps show how you can tell who is allowed to do this:

1. **Start the SQL Server Management Studio.**

2. **Connect to your database server.**

3. **Expand the Databases folder.**

4. **Open the specific folder for the database that you want to check.**

5. **Open the Security folder for the database.**

6. **Expand the Users folder.**

You can see everyone who is authorized to connect to this particular database.

Granting access

Authorizing people and applications to work with your SQL Server system is the most common, security-related administrative task that you're likely to face. In this next section, we show you the sequence of events you need to follow to make that happen.

Creating logins

To begin, anyone who wants to talk with your SQL Server database server needs a login. Here's how to create one:

1. **Start the SQL Server Management Studio.**

2. **Connect to your database server.**

3. **Expand the Security folder.**

You find a group of interesting folders beneath the security folder. These folders include:

- *Logins:* Individuals or processes that can connect to your SQL Server instance.

- *Server roles:* A collection of pre-defined groups of permissions.

- *Credentials:* Authentication details that let a SQL Server-validated user gain access to resources and services outside the SQL Server environment.

- *Cryptographic Providers:* If you've elected to include any third-party cryptographic capabilities, here's where you'll find a list.

4. **Right-click the Logins folder, and choose New Login.**

This opens a dialog box where you can enter details about your new login, as shown in Figure 3-1.

5. **Decide whether you want to use Windows or SQL Server authentication.**

When you choose Windows authentication, you're instructing SQL Server to obtain its login information directly from the operating system. This integrated security approach, which is the default, makes sense especially if you're using the same login architecture for other applications. You can search your computer or others on your network for login details.

Comparatively, choosing SQL Server authentication means that you're creating a login that is meaningful only within the confines of your database server; it has no relationship with the operating system. You set your server authentication behavior via the Server Properties page within the SQL Server Management Studio. You can elect to allow Windows Authentication Mode only, as well as authorize SQL Server Authentication.

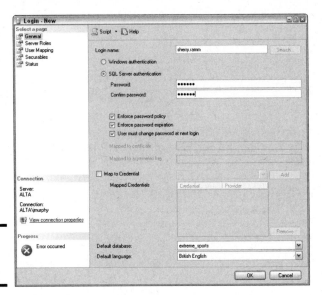

6. **Fill in additional general properties.**

   Here's where you can set the security policy for this login as well as its default database and language. You might also take the opportunity to associate one more credentials with this login. A credential contains information necessary to work with non–SQL Server-based resources.

7. **Switch to the Server Roles page, and authorize any server roles that you want this login to have.**

   Available server roles are listed in the earlier "Who Can You Let Use Your Database?" section. Be careful about giving new logins broad capabilities.

8. **Switch to the User Mapping page, and enable connectivity to all relevant databases.**

   By enabling database connectivity here, SQL Server automatically creates a user with this name in each database, which saves you time later. You can also set his default schema and database role membership on this property page.

9. **(Optional) Switch to the Securables page and associate the login.**

   You can have a group of logins inherit the security settings of the `public` role, which is much faster than setting them on an object-by-object basis.

10. **Switch to the Status page, and grant the login permission to connect to the database.**

    You can also disable active logins on this page.

11. **After you've finished setting the properties for this login, click OK to save it.**

    This login is ready to connect to your database server. Additionally, if you associated the login with one or more databases and those databases have public permissions set, this login works with those databases.

Creating users

A database user is someone who not only has permission to connect to your SQL Server instance, but also has the ability to work with one or more databases. As just described, you can make this happen by simply associating a login with one or more databases. Comparatively, here's how to get the job done if you want to do this manually:

1. **Start the SQL Server Management Studio.**

2. **Connect to your database server.**

3. **Expand the Databases folder.**

4. **Expand the folder for the specific database where you want to create the user.**

5. **Expand the Security folder.**

    Although our focus is on the Users folder, beneath the Security folder you can find details about all roles, schemas, encryption keys, and certificates for this database. You can also create new instances of roles and schemas by right-clicking the appropriate folder.

6. **Right-click the Users folder, and choose New User.**

    This opens a dialog box with a series of different pages, as highlighted in Figure 3-2.

7. **Associate the new user with any owned schemas.**

8. **Assign the new user to any database roles.**

9. **Switch to the Securables page, and set up authorization for the new user.**

    You can set security permissions by user, or you can set them for the `public` database role (which is faster and more convenient). If you want to set them by user, use the Securables page. You can search for the specific types of securables from within this page.

Figure 3-2:
Creating a
new user.

10. **After setting the security profile for the new user, click OK to save the record.**

Your user can now work with all authorized objects in this database.

Setting permissions by securable

So far, we've described security from the perspective of the user. However, a different (and often better) way to implement your security architecture is available. In this case, you set your security at the securable level, granting or revoking permissions for users, database roles, or application roles.

For example, suppose that you want to set permissions on a given table. Here's how to make this possible:

1. **Start the SQL Server Management Studio.**

2. **Connect to your database server.**

3. **Expand the Databases folder.**

4. **Expand the folder for the specific database where you want to set the permissions.**

5. **Expand the Tables folder.**

6. **Right-click the table in question, and choose Properties.**

7. Switch to the Permissions page.

8. Click the Search button.

This opens a dialog box that allows you to locate users, application roles, and database roles.

9. Click Browse to see a list of candidates.

10. Choose at least one candidate for permission granting, and click OK.

11. Set permissions for the candidate, and click OK.

With your candidates identified, you can now set their permissions (even to the column level) according to your security policies. Figure 3-3 gives you an idea of what this dialog box looks like.

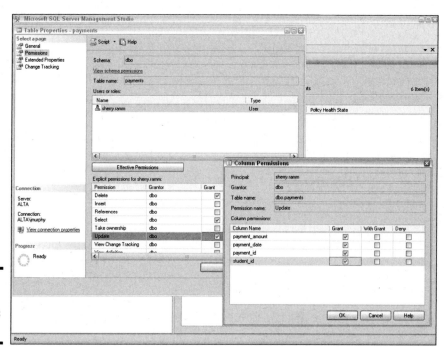

Figure 3-3:
Granting
permissions
on a table.

Modifying or revoking permissions

Altering or denying permissions is a relatively straightforward affair. In the case of SQL Server Management Studio, you generally use the same sequence of steps to make these changes; the main difference is that instead of adding permissions, you remove them.

With SQL Server 2008, Microsoft introduced a collection of administrator-centric technologies known as *Policy-Based Management.* While many DBAs primarily use these capabilities to configure and tune their database environment, this strategy can also play an important role in helping to secure SQL Server. If this interests you, visit Book I, Chapters 2 and 4 because enforcing good security standards is a significant part of that discussion.

To whet your appetite, Figure 3-4 shows a simple example of running one of SQL Server's built-in security-focused policies (in this case, checking for Guest permission violations). This is a very small example of the kind of security operations that you can automate by using Policy-Based Management.

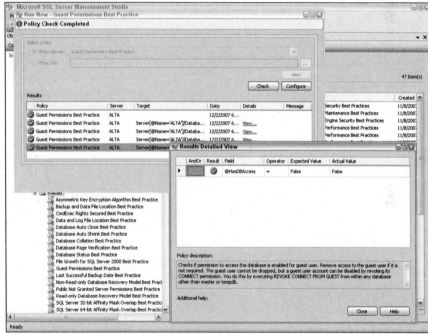

Figure 3-4: Running a security policy check in the SQL Server Management Studio.

Chapter 4: Integration and Your Database

In This Chapter

✔ Addressing common integration challenges

✔ Tying Integration Services all together

✔ Using SQL Server Integration Services

Although proud SQL Server administrators like to think that their databases occupy a cherished location in the enterprise, most organizations store information in a wide variety of venues and formats. This disparity, along with the ever-present need to tie all this data together, has traditionally caused database administrators no end of aggravation. Fortunately, SQL Server 2008 includes some very powerful integration tools that help remove much of the pain from these never-ending exercises, which is what this chapter is all about.

We get the ball rolling by citing a handful of the most common integration challenges that liven up the existences of SQL Server administrators. After these examples, I take you on a brief tour of the SQL Server Integration Services technology, which is the mechanism at your disposal to address these needs. Finally, I show you how to use these features to build and deploy a simple integration project.

Integration is a very rich topic, with a virtually limitless quantity of complexities and permutations. Given space restrictions, the goal of this chapter is to give you a solid foundation upon which you can construct your customized integration solution. Comparatively, if you're simply looking for how to import and export data, check out Chapter 2 of this mini-book.

Common Integration Challenges

Overcoming integration-based problems has always tested the skills and patience of database administrators. While technology continues to proliferate, however, the number of integration touch-points expands exponentially. Here are a few examples of some common integration scenarios. Fortunately, SQL Server Integration Services can help you address each one of them.

✦ Periodic exporting of information to flat files (text, comma-separated, and so on)

✦ Periodic importing of information from flat files

✦ Setting up a Web services/XML interface

✦ Consolidating multiple data sources into one

✦ Distributing a single data source to multiple locations

✦ Feeding information into a packaged enterprise application (such as SAP, Oracle, and so on)

✦ Interacting with multiple relational database platforms (such as Oracle, MySQL, and so on)

✦ Creating a data warehouse

✦ Using FTP to send and receive data

✦ Integrating data with desktop productivity tools (such as Microsoft Excel, Word, and so on)

These are just a few examples; chances are that most readers are faced with several additional, specialized integration requirements of their own.

How SQL Server Integration Services (SSIS) Ties It All Together

If you run a Web search for *Extract, Transform, and Load Tools* (also known as ETL), be prepared to spend a while evaluating your results. Dozens of products (of varying quality and depth) that specialize in moving information among disparate systems are available. If that prospect doesn't excite you, you'll probably be pleasantly surprised to know that the SQL Server Integration Services (SSIS) technology that comes with your database provides a robust set of capabilities to help you get the job done.

In this section, I briefly summarize how SSIS works and what it's used for. In the next section, I show you how to put it to work solving your own data integration challenges.

SSIS and the rest of the SQL Server platform

With SQL Server 2008, Microsoft has done an excellent job of delivering a seamless data platform. For example, SSIS integrates with the data mining capabilities of the SQL Server Analysis Services (described in Book VI). It also uses the Visual Studio development platform, as does both Analysis and Reporting Services (described in Book V). Therefore, investing in learning one part of the SQL Server platform pays you dividends when you research the other parts of the technology.

SSIS architecture

Given the potentially enormous data volumes found in modern integration projects, SSIS was designed for high performance. It uses the following techniques to drive throughput:

✦ **Threading**

✦ **Buffer-oriented architecture**

✦ **Caching/persistent lookups**

✦ **Change Data Capture (CDC)**

The last capability is very useful in identifying only data that has been changed; performance increases by updating only altered information. Also, an interim staging database is unnecessary; everything is handled in memory.

SSIS uses adapters to connect to the wide variety of formats shown in the following list:

✦ **ADO.NET**

✦ **OLE DB**

✦ **ODBC**

✦ **Flat file**

✦ **Excel**

✦ **XML**

✦ **3rd party formats**

As shown in the next section, SSIS is able to handle complex data flows, including splitting, merging, and combining data streams. It's also adept at handling XML data, "shredding" it into tabular form.

By integrating with the Visual Studio development environment, SSIS doesn't force the developer to learn a new platform. In terms of programming languages, SSIS easily leverages code written in

✦ **C#**

✦ **C++**

✦ **Visual Basic .NET**

✦ **Scripts**

SSIS also includes a debugger, which is extremely helpful in deciphering the inevitable data and logic issues encountered during integration.

Using SQL Server Integration Services

Now that you're up to speed on some of the capabilities offered by SQL Server Integration Services, the balance of the chapter walks you through a practical integration example. In this scenario, you load a Microsoft Excel spreadsheet containing new customer and payment transaction records into a database. What makes this exercise a little more challenging than a basic import operation is that the records found in the spreadsheet need to be split and then placed into two different tables. The tables' structures are defined here:

```
CREATE TABLE [dbo].[students]
(
    [student_id] [int] NOT NULL,
    [last_name] [varchar](50) NOT NULL,
    [first_name] [varchar](50) NOT NULL,
    [credit_limit] [money] NOT NULL
)


CREATE TABLE [dbo].[payments]
(
    [payment_id] [int] NOT NULL,
    [student_id] [int] NOT NULL,
    [payment_date] [datetime] NOT NULL,
    [payment_amount] [money] NOT NULL
)
```

After the integration project is created, the next step is to deploy it to the server where it was created.

This example is extremely simple; in reality, you face complex requirements for data formatting, transformation, exception handling, publishing to multiple servers, and so on. As described in the previous section, SQL Server Integration Services is designed to support these types of real-world constraints gracefully.

To make this section more readable, the instructions are broken into several step groups. In keeping with the philosophy followed throughout the book, you use SQL Server's excellent graphical tools to accomplish these tasks.

Creating the project

First things first, right? To start, you create the project and give it a name, as shown in the following steps:

1. **Launch SQL Server Business Intelligence Development Studio.**

You find this under the SQL Server 2008 menu. Depending on your configuration, you might see a summary page, or a blank screen.

2. **Choose File⇨New Project.**

You see a dialog box where you can pick the type of project you want to create, as shown Figure 4-1.

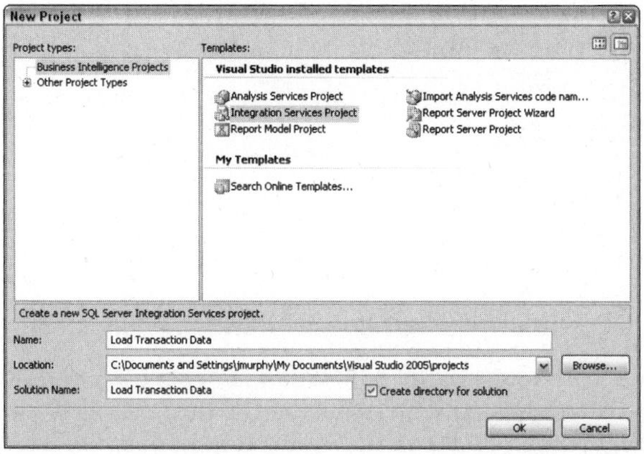

Figure 4-1: Creating a new project.

3. **Click the Integration Services Project option.**

4. **Fill in the name of the project, its working directory, and the name you want for the finished solution; then click OK.**

Adding connections for all data sources

With the project created and named, you next set up and configure connections to all the participants in the upcoming integration.

Adding a connection to Microsoft Excel

To begin with the connection to the Microsoft Excel spreadsheet that contains the transaction data, follow these steps:

1. **Make sure that the Control Flow tab is selected.**

2. **Right-click the Connection Managers tab.**

3. **Choose the New Connection option.**

4. **Choose Excel from the drop-down list and then click Add.**

   We weren't kidding when we described how flexible SQL Server Integration Services is; Figure 4-2 shows some of the varied connection types at your disposal.

Figure 4-2: Available types of connection.

5. **Enter details about your spreadsheet and then click OK.**

   You're prompted to provide a filename, an Excel version, and whether the spreadsheet has column names in the first row. If you're connecting to a different type of information source, you fill in different options.

   After you click OK, the new connection is listed in the Connection Managers area of the Control Flow tab.

When working with flat files (including spreadsheets), you find things more pleasant when you include column names at the top of the file.

Adding a connection to the database

It takes two to tango. The connection to the Excel spreadsheet is ready to go; the following steps set up a connection to the database:

1. **Make sure that the Control Flow tab is selected.**

2. **Right-click the Connection Managers tab.**

3. **Choose the New Connection option.**

4. **Choose ADO.NET from the drop-down list and then click Add.**

   Other connector technologies can be used to interact with a SQL Server database, but ADO.NET is the latest-and-greatest technique, so that's what we've chosen.

5. **Fill in the ADO.NET Configuration Manager dialog box.**

   If there was an already existing connection to SQL Server, I could simply select it from the list of available connections shown on the left side of this dialog box under Data Connections. Because there isn't, I've clicked the New button, which brings up the Configuration Manager dialog box.

6. **Provide details to identify the new connection and then click OK.**

   You're asked to choose a provider (just use the default value), enter a server name, enter login details, and pick a database where your data will go. You can even test the connection to ensure everything works, which is what we've done, as shown in Figure 4-3.

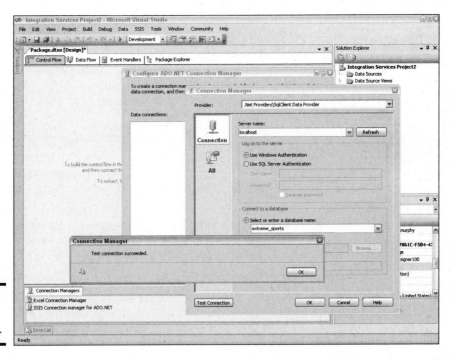

Figure 4-3:
Testing a
connection.

Book VIII
Chapter 4

Integration and
Your Database

7. **Review the details for your new connection and then click OK.**

   You see both of your connections (Excel and SQL Server) on the Connection Managers tab.

Creating a data flow task

With both sides of the integration job represented with connections, you next set up a conversation between the two parties.

1. **Click the Data Flow tab.**

2. **Click the link in the middle of the screen to create a new Data Flow Task.**

   Note: If there aren't any defined data flow tasks, the link reads, 'No Data Flow Tasks have been added to this package. Click here to add a new Data Flow task.'

3. **Click on the Toolbox icon in the upper left of the screen.**

   This collection of tools supports Data Flow tasks.

4. **Drag the Excel source icon from the Data Flow Sources section of the Toolbox onto the palette.**

5. **Drag the ADO.NET destination icon from the Data Flow Destinations section of the Toolbox onto the palette. Do this twice.**

   Your palette (found on the Data Flow tab) now has an Excel source and two ADO.NET destinations (one per destination table: `students` and `payments`). At this point, you're free to rename these graphics to something more meaningful for your environment. Just click the icons and enter your selection.

   Leave some room among the icons; in a moment, we'll add a connection graphic.

6. **Drag the Multicast icon from the Data Flow Transformations section of the Toolbox onto the palette.**

   Position the Multicast icon between the Excel object and the two ADO.NET objects; in a moment, we'll draw lines between them. We've selected Multicast because this example shows portions of a spreadsheet being copied into two different tables.

7. **Drag the green line from the Excel object to the Multicast object.**

   This represents a flow of information from Excel to the Multicast object; the red line is used for error handling (which isn't part of this example).

8. **Drag a green line from the Multicast object to each of the two ADO.NET objects.**

   This indicates that information will be distributed to each of the two database connections. Figure 4-4 shows the completed connection diagram.

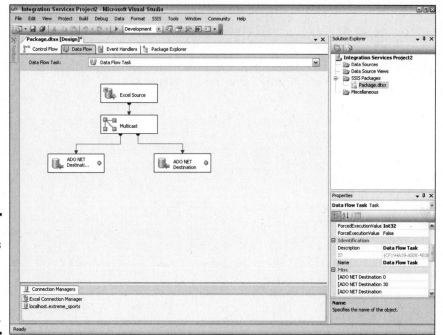

Figure 4-4:
Connections
between
source,
multicast,
and
destinations.

This simple example just scratches the surface of the potential for sophisticated information flow. You have many more transformation options in the Toolbox.

Associating connections with the data flow

At this point, you have two connections (one for Excel, one for the database), as well as a data source (for Excel) and two data destinations (one per table). The next task is to associate the connection with the members of the data flow.

1. **Double-click the Excel icon on the palette.**

This opens a dialog box where you can

- **Choose a connection manager.** In this case, you select the Excel connection manager we created earlier in this chapter.

- **Decide upon the data access mode.** For this example, we've chosen Table or View, which means that the spreadsheet is treated like a table.

- **Select the worksheet.**

- **View all columns in the spreadsheet.** This is why it's a good idea to have formalized names at the top of your text files.

- **Configure exception handling.**

You're even able to get an advance look at your data by clicking the Preview button, as shown in Figure 4-5.

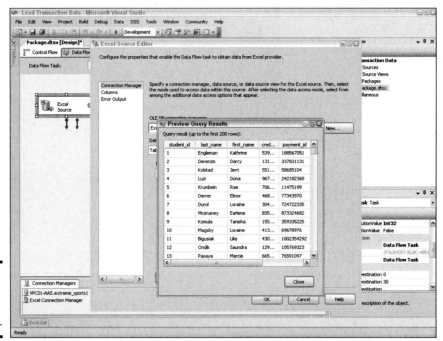

Figure 4-5:
Previewing
the spread-
sheet's data.

2. **After you've finished associating the Excel connection with the Excel data source, click OK.**

The next order of business is to perform the same type of configuration for each database destination.

3. **Double-click either of the two ADO.NET icons on the palette.**

This opens a dialog box where you can select the destination table, the mappings between the source and destination columns, and how you want errors to be handled. Figures 4-6 and 4-7 show how this dialog box appears, for the students and payments table, respectively.

If you'd like an idea of how things might turn out, you can click on the preview button to see more. After you've finished configuring the connection, click OK to save your work.

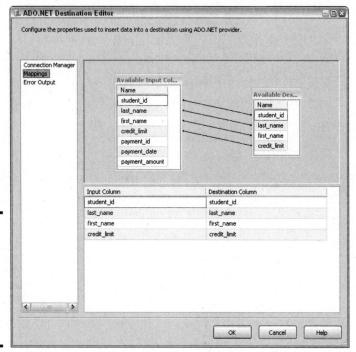

Figure 4-6:
Configuring
the
database
connection
for the
students
table.

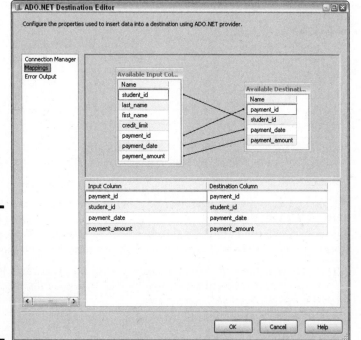

Figure 4-7:
Configuring
the
database
connection
for the
payments
table.

4. **Repeat Step 3 for the other ADO.NET icon.**

   You need to configure every destination.

5. **Test the project to ensure everything works correctly.**

   Click the Run icon and monitor your results.

   Save your work — you don't want all that effort to be wasted!

Congratulations! You've set up your integration project. Figure 4-8 shows how the completed diagram appears during a test run.

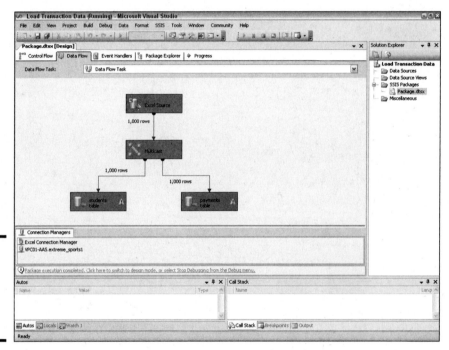

Figure 4-8:
Performing a test run of your integration project.

Your work isn't complete, however. You still need to build and deploy the project.

Building the project

The next step in implementing a SQL Server Integration Services project is to set properties and then build the project. Here's how to make that happen:

1. **Right-click the project's name in the Solution Explorer window and then choose Properties.**

   This opens a dialog box where you can set several important attributes for the project, including:

   - *The output directories for the build process*
   - *Whether you want the build process to create deployment files*
   - *Debugging options*

   Choose `True` for the `CreateDeploymentUtility` property so that SQL Server generates the files necessary to run the project outside of the development environment.

2. **When you've finished making your configuration changes, click OK to save your work.**

3. **Construct the project by choosing the Build option from the SQL Server Business Intelligence Development Studio menu.**

   SQL Server uses the options you set in Step 1 to generate the files necessary to support your integration project. You can double-check the output directory to ensure that everything was done correctly.

Running the project

Now the fun begins — you run the project in the real world. To keep this example simple, assume that you're running the project manually. Of course, you can also set it to run via the Windows Scheduler utility, as well as other more sophisticated deployment options, such as distributing the project to multiple servers, setting configuration options, and reporting results.

1. **Open Windows Explorer in the directory where you deployed the project.**

2. **Double-click the SQL Server Integration Services package file.**

   This file has a `.dstx` suffix; you set its name during the development process.

3. **Fill in any desired settings in the Execute Package Utility and then click Execute to run the integration.**

   This utility (shown in Figure 4-9) offers several pages of properties, including:

   - **General:** Here's where you tell SQL Server the name of the package (it's already filled in by default), whether the package will be run from a file or the database, and any necessary login details.

   - **Configurations:** This page allows you to import any customized configuration details.

- **Command files:** If you want to use a command line-based execution statement, you enter it here.

- **Connection Managers:** This displays the connection managers that you defined as part of the project.

- **Execution Options:** Here's where you set runtime behavior for the package, including whether you want validation, checkpoints, and so on.

- **Reporting:** This page's purpose is to allow you to determine which console events and console-logging attributes will be reported on.

- **Logging:** If you wish to add logging to your package, here's where you can do so.

- **Set Values:** This page establishes runtime values for any properties of your package.

- **Verification:** You have significant control over whether SQL Server will verify the package build, package ID, and version ID for this project.

- **Command Line:** This displays an editable command line for launching the package.

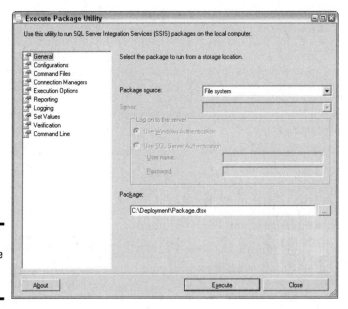

Figure 4-9:
The Execute Package utility.

4. **Review your results.**

SQL Server reports on your project's outcome. Figure 4-10 shows how this appears.

Figure 4-10:
Results from executing an integration package.

Chapter 5: Replication

In This Chapter

✔ **Exploring the publisher metaphor**

✔ **Defining a replication publishing model**

✔ **Configuring replication**

✔ **Replicating between different hosts**

*V*ery often, you need to have all or some of your data in more than one place at the same time. If the data is never modified, you could just make a copy of it as you would make a copy of a piece of paper on a Xerox copier. However, databases are rarely static. They change. Although it's impossible to update the copied piece of paper when the original changes (at least it's impossible today), replicating the changes from one database to another database is possible.

The goal of *replication* is to make copies of the data and ensure those copies are kept up to date. How often the data is updated depends on how often the data changes and how up to date the data needs to be. Some of the reasons to replicate data are to offload the reporting workload to another SQL Server, replicate the data to dedicated backup server so backups can occur without interfering with the online server, and keeping data centralized from several branch office databases.

Exploring the Publishing Metaphor

Replication is based on a publishing metaphor. In the publishing world, there are publishers, distributors, and subscribers. Replication defines different roles based on the real-world example of publishing.

✦ **Publishers:** Publishers maintain the source database that will be replicated.

✦ **Distributors:** Distributors send the desired portions of the database to subscribers. Often, the publisher also fulfills the role as a distributor, but this isn't required. When a large number of subscribers exist, distributors take some of the load off the publisher.

✦ **Subscribers:** Subscribers receive the replicated data in the form of a publication.

Figure 5-1 shows the relationship between publishers, distributors, and sub-scribers. Remember though, it's very common for the publisher to also fulfill the distributor role.

The data that is published and distributed isn't necessarily the entire data-base. Instead, portions of the database (such as tables and indexes) are identified to be published. The published data are referred to as articles and publications:

✦ **Articles:** Articles are the individual database objects that are published. These objects are typically tables, indexes, and stored procedures, but can be any object within the database.

✦ **Publication:** A publication includes one or more articles. Subscribers can subscribe to publications (but not individual articles).

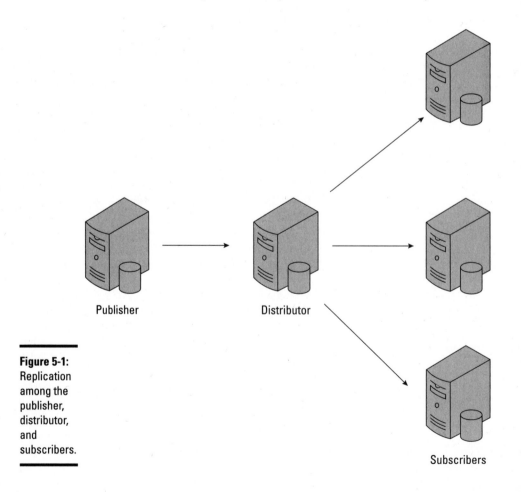

Publisher   Distributor

Figure 5-1:
Replication
among the
publisher,
distributor,
and
subscribers.

Subscribers

This works similarly in the real world. *Newsweek* magazine, which is published internationally, has one central publisher that creates all the content. After a magazine is published, it's handed over to distributors who send the copies to subscribers.

Each magazine has articles within it based on the publication. The Asian publication has different articles than the U.S. publication. The publication you subscribe to determines which articles you receive.

It's not possible to subscribe to only certain articles (at least not in the print version). Instead, you subscribe to the publication and receive all the articles in the publication.

Subscriptions can either be push subscriptions or pull subscriptions:

✦ **Push Subscription:** A *push subscription* is initiated by the distributor. Push subscriptions are sent either continuously as changes occur or on a preset schedule.

✦ **Pull Subscription:** A *pull subscription* is initiated by the subscriber. Sticking with the publishing metaphor, this would be when you go to the magazine newsstand and pick up a copy of *Newsweek*.

Defining a Replication Publishing Model

With replication, three different models exist. These models define whether the entire database is replicated (or only the changes), how often the replication occurs, and who can make changes to the source database.

✦ **Snapshot replication:** Snapshot replication involves making a copy of the publication at a moment in time. The entire publication is then replicated to the receiving database. Snapshot replication is the easiest to implement, but takes the most bandwidth.

✦ **Transactional replication:** Transactional replication is used to constantly update and publish the articles. This is used when the subscribers need access to changes as they occur. All changes to the database are recorded in the transaction log. The log reader agent then reads the transaction log to replicate the changes to the receiving database. These changes are then applied to the receiving database.

✦ **Peer-to-peer transactional replication:** Peer-to-peer replication is used for applications that might read or modify data at any of multiple databases participating in replication. It's built on the foundation of transactional replication, but peers in transactional replication can both read and modify changes; subscribers in transactional replication can only receive the changes.

✦ **Merge replication:** Merge replication is used when multiple locations need to be able to update the data. For example, a retail chain might have multiple stores that all need to submit sales and inventory data to the headquarters location. If they don't have a product in stock, they check other locations for customers, so they need access to inventory data at other locations. Merge replication allows each of the retail stores to be publishers.

In other words, instead of changes made at only one central location, changes can be made in databases at multiple locations and then merged.

Figure 5-2 shows how different servers could communicate in Merge replication. Each server holds all three roles of publisher, distributor, and subscriber. For changes to their database, each retail store server would be a publisher and a distributor, sending their changes to the HQ database. The HQ server would be a subscriber to each of the retail store servers. Additionally, the HQ server would be a publisher and subscriber to each of the retail store servers.

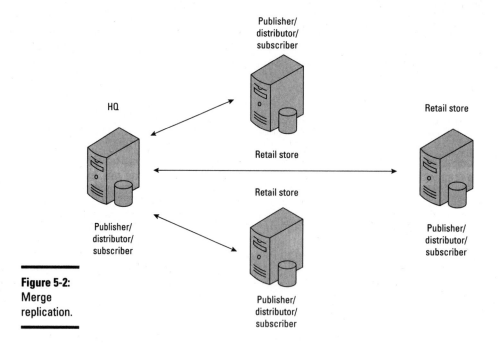

Figure 5-2:
Merge
replication.

Reasons to use Snapshot replication

Snapshot replication is most useful when subscribers don't need the data to be completely up to date.

All replication types start with a snapshot. Transactional and Merge replication use different methods to keep the replicated data up to date. In contrast, the Snapshot replication simply creates another snapshot to update the second database.

The primary reasons to use Snapshot replication include

✦ **Data rarely changes:** If the data is relatively static, the added overhead of other types of replication isn't needed. For example, consider a database that includes product information used to produce a catalog. If the catalog is produced quarterly, then snapshot replication could be used to create a snapshot of the database on only a quarterly basis.

✦ **Subscribers can be out of date with the publisher:** In situations where the subscriber doesn't have to be up to date with the publisher, snapshot replication can be used. For example, the marketing department of a company might need access to past sales to do marketing analysis. Giving the marketing department a new snapshot of data on a monthly basis might provide data as much as 30 days out of date, which is completely acceptable.

✦ **Small amounts of data are replicated:** A database could be over 20GB in size. However, publications can be very small. In a situation where the publication is only 5MB, creating a snapshot replication would cause little overhead. Different factors, such as bandwidth (replicating over 100MB LAN, or replicating over 56K demand-dial connection) and resource usage (CPU, Memory, and Disk) on the source database determine what's considered small amounts of data.

✦ **Bulk changes occur on a schedule:** Consider a product database that holds products that your company sells. The product changes once a month. On a monthly basis, products are added, deleted, and modified via a bulk import and modification process. Immediately after the changes are implemented, you can use snapshot replication.

The primary benefit of using Snapshot replication is that you don't have the additional overhead required by Transactional and Merge replication.

Reasons to use Transactional replication

Transactional replication keeps the replicated database up to date by copying the transaction log and applying the transactions that apply to the publication.

The primary reasons to use Transactional replication include

✦ **Subscribers need the changes as they occur:** In other words, subscribers need their data to be as up to date as possible. Consider a company that sells products that are housed in three different warehouses via an online Web application. Prior to a sale, customers want to know if the product is in stock. The databases at the warehouses could be replicated to a central database accessible by the Web application and kept up to date with Transactional replication.

✦ **Latency must be minimized:** Similarly, the data must be up to date. With Transactional replication, the data can be replicated much more often than snapshot replication.

✦ **The publisher has a high volume of data changes:** If the database is highly active (with many INSERT, UPDATE, and DELETE statements), using snapshot replication would cause only the data to be out of date quickly. Transactional replication would allow the data to stay up to date.

The primary benefit of Transactional replication is ensuring that the subscriber's data is kept up to date.

Reasons to use Peer-to-peer replication

Peer-to-peer replication maintains multiple copies of the same data across multiple servers. Applications that need access to the data can query any one of the copies, or query multiple copies simultaneously.

In peer-to-peer replication, servers are referred to as *nodes*. Each of the nodes can accept changes (inserts, updates, and deletions) and replication ensures the changes are made at the other nodes.

The primary reasons to use peer-to-peer replication include

✦ **Load Balancing:** With the database stored on multiple nodes, applications can be programmed to query the data from different locations.

   A single application can perform queries across multiple nodes simultaneously providing significant improvements in read performance. Or, multiple servers can query different nodes. For example, a Web application running on a Web farm can have multiple Web servers. Servers in the Web farm can be programmed to query different nodes.

✦ **High Availability:** A single node can fail and the other nodes can take over the load. This can also be used to take nodes offline for maintenance purposes.

The primary benefit of peer-to-peer replication is the ability to spread multiple copies of the database across multiple nodes. Additionally, both reads and writes can occur on any of the nodes.

Reasons to use Merge replication

Merge replication allows each subscriber to be a publisher/distributor also. In other words, each server involved in Merge replication can receive changes from other replication partners, and send changes to other replication partners.

The primary reasons to use Merge replication include

✦ **Subscribers need to be able to update their own data:** In other words, the subscribers need to be able to make changes to the database. Instead of only being subscribers, they also need to be publishers.

✦ **Subscribers need their own partition of data:** Databases can be horizontally partitioned so that each location owns some of the data. For example, consider a database that records sales from four different stores. The database could have four million rows (one million rows for each store). By horizontally partitioning the data, each store would own their rows and could host them on their server. However, other servers could access all the data. If subscribers need their own partition of data, Merge replication is useful.

✦ **Conflict resolution and detection is needed:** When multiple publishers are allowed to update the same database, conflicts can occur. For example, if five cases of a certain red wine are in stock and two stores both sold one case at the same time, the possibility exists for the inventory to be decremented by one case, instead of two. Merge replication has methods in place to detect and resolve this conflict.

The primary benefit of Merge replication is allowing the subscribers to update data (or also act as publishers).

Configuring Replication

Replication primarily occurs between two different systems (such as a server to a server or a server to a client), but it's also possible to replicate data between one database and another.

From a big picture perspective, replication is configured in three steps:

1. Configure the publisher and distributor.

2. Choose articles and create publications.

3. Configure the subscriber.

We discuss each of these in turn throughout the rest of this section.

Configuring the publisher and distributor

In the following steps, you create a database and then configure the replication distributor and publisher.

1. Launch SQL Server Management Studio (SSMS).

Choose Start⇨All Programs⇨Microsoft SQL Server 2008⇨SQL Server Management Studio.

2. On the Connect to Server screen, click Connect.

3. Click the New Query button to create a new query window.

4. Enter and execute the following code to create a new database named ReplicateMe:

```
USE Master;
GO
CREATE DATABASE ReplicateMe;
```

5. Enter and execute the following code to create a table in your database:

```
USE ReplicateMe;
GO
CREATE TABLE Employee
(
    EmployeeID int IDENTITY(100,1) NOT NULL,
    LastName varchar(35) NULL,
    FirstName varchar(35) NULL,
   CONSTRAINT [PK_Employee_EmployeeID]
      PRIMARY KEY CLUSTERED
      (
   EmployeeID
       )
)
```

6. Enter and execute the following code to add a couple of rows of data to your database:

```
INSERT INTO Employee (LastName, FirstName)
VALUES
        ('Herman', 'Munster'),
        ('Sally', 'Fields')
```

7. Enter and execute the following code to create a stored procedure in your database:

```
USE ReplicateMe;
GO
CREATE Proc dbo.usp_ShowHelp
AS
EXEC sp_help Employee
```

This creates a stored procedure that provides information on the Employee table. When you configure replication, you can configure whether this stored procedure will be replicated.

8. **Find the Replication container in the SSMS Object Explorer, as shown in Figure 5-3.**

   This is below Server Objects and contains Local Publications and Local Subscriptions.

Figure 5-3: The Replication container in SSMS.

9. **Right-click the Replication container and choose Configure Distribution.**

10. **On the Configure Distribution page, click Next.**

    Note: It is possible to click Finish at this point. The following steps (up to Step 15) simply show you the screens that you can modify if you choose.

11. **On the Distributor page, accept the default showing the same computer will act as its own distributor. Click Next.**

12. **On the SQL Server Agent Start page, accept the default saying Yes, configure the SQL Server Agent service to start automatically. Click Next.**

13. **On the Snapshot Folder page, accept the default snapshot folder. Click Next.**

14. **On the Distribution Database page, accept the defaults. Click Next.**

15. **On the Publishers page, accept the default showing your computer will be a publisher. Click Next.**

16. **On the Wizard Actions page, ensure Configure Distribution is checked. Click Next.**

17. **On the Complete the Wizard page, click Finish.**

    After a moment, the Configuring page indicates that the publisher has been enabled, the distributor has been configured, and SQL Server Agent has been set to start automatically.

18. **On the Configuring Success page, click Close.**

At this point, you've configured a publisher and a distributor. However, you haven't identified articles to include in a publication, or any subscribers, so replication won't actually start yet.

19. **Leave SSMS open for the next part of the exercise.**

Creating a publication

In the following steps, you create a publication using Snapshot replication. You add the table created earlier as an article to your publication but omit the stored procedure.

1. **With SSMS Open, right-click Local Publications and choose New Publication.**

2. **On the New Publication Wizard page, click Next.**

3. **On the Publication Database page, select the ReplicateMe database and click Next.**

4. **On the Publication Type page, select Snapshot Publication and click Next.**

5. **On the Articles page, click the check box next to Tables. Click the plus (+) next to Tables.**

Similar to Figure 5-4, your display shows only the objects that are available within the database, allowing you to choose which objects to replicate.

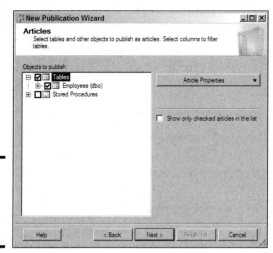

Figure 5-4:
Selecting articles for the publication.

6. **On the Articles page, click Next.**

7. **On the Filter Table Rows page, click Next.**

   If desired, you can choose to filter the table so that only some of the rows appear.

8. **On the Snapshot Agent page, select both check boxes.**

   One is to create a snapshot immediately and keep the snapshot available to initialize subscriptions. The second is to schedule when the Snapshot Agent runs.

9. **Click the Change button to change the schedule.**

   The schedule page allows you to change the schedule from Daily to Weekly to Monthly. Currently, it's scheduled to run once per hour every day.

10. **On the Schedule page, click Cancel to accept the default schedule.**

11. **On the Snapshot Agent page, click Next.**

12. **On the Agent Security page, click Security Settings.**

13. **On the Snapshot Agent Security page, select Run Under the SQL Server Agent Account.**

    Note: As a security best practice, it's recommended to create an account specifically for the replication agent.

    The SQL Server Agent needs to be running for this to succeed. You can check the status of the SQL Server Agent in SSMS. If it has a red down arrow, it's not running. Right-click it and select Start.

14. **On the Snapshot Agent Security page, click OK. On the Agent Security page, click Next.**

15. **On the Wizard Actions page, accept the default of Create the Publication. Click Next.**

16. **On the Complete the Wizard page, enter** ReplicateMe Employees **as the name of the publication. Click Finish.**

17. **Leave SSMS open.**

At this point, you've created a publication that includes the Employees table as an article. However, it won't replicate until a subscriber is added.

Creating a subscriber

The last step required to configure replication is to create a subscriber. In a real-world situation, this would be done on a separate server. However, for our example, we just create it on the same server, in the same instance of SQL Server.

1. With SSMS open, right-click Local Subscriptions and choose New Subscriptions.

2. On the New Subscription Wizard page, click Next.

3. On the Publication page, ensure that your server is selected as the publisher and the ReplicateMe Employees publication is selected from the ReplicateMe database. Click Next.

4. On the Distribution Agent Location page, accept the default of running all agents at the distributor. Click Next.

   This causes push subscriptions to be pushed from the distributor to the subscriber.

5. On the Subscribers page, select your computer name as the subscriber.

6. On Subscription Database, select the drop-down box and scroll to the top. Choose <New database>.

7. On the New Database page, enter IAmReplicated as the database name. Click OK.

8. On the Subscribers page, click Next.

9. On the Distribution Agent Security page, click the ellipsis (. . .) to the far right of your server name.

10. On the Distribution Agent Security page, select Run Under the SQL Server Agent Service Agent. Accept the other defaults and click OK.

11. On the Distribution Agent Security page, click Next.

12. On the Synchronization Schedule page, accept Run Continuously (the default) and click Next.

13. On the Initialize Subscriptions page, accept the defaults and click Next.

14. On the Wizard Actions page, accept the default to create the subscription and click Next.

15. On the Complete the Wizard page, click Finish.

16. When the wizard completes, click Close.

17. To verify the Employee table in the database has been replicated, execute the following script:

    ```
    USE IAmReplicated;
    GO
    SELECT * FROM Employee
    ```

    You should see the same employees you entered into the ReplicateMe database retrieved from the IAmReplicated database.

18. **To verify that only the data specified in the publication was replicated, execute the following script:**

```
USE IAmReplicated;
GO
EXEC usp_ShowHelp
```

This fails because the stored procedure wasn't specified in the publication.
This verifies that only the items that you specified in the publication were
replicated.

Exploring the replication agents

When the wizards are run to publishers, publications, and subscribers, several SQL Server Agent jobs are created. Figure 5-5 shows the jobs created as
part of the previous steps. These jobs were all created by the wizards used
to enable replication. Some of the jobs are for publications, some for distri-
butions, and some for subscriptions.

Figure 5-5:
SQL Server
Agent jobs
created for
replication.

You can right-click any of these jobs and choose properties to show the
details of the job. The Steps tab shows what is actually being done by the
job, and the Schedules tab shows how often the job is being executed.

Replicating between Hosts

Replication between hosts is grouped into two categories:

✦ **Between server and clients:** Replication between server and clients
can be from the server to the clients or from the clients to the server.
It's often done to exchange data with mobile users or point-of-sale
applications.

✦ **Between servers and servers:** Data is replicated in one or more servers
either for data integration or for offloading processing.

Replicating between servers and clients

When replicating data between servers and clients, the clients can fill any of several roles. For example, clients can be desktop computers, laptops, tablets, or other portable devices.

Some of the scenarios where data can be replicated between servers and clients are

✦ **Exchanging data with mobile users:** As an example, Darril's father used to sell and deliver bread and similar products to grocery stores (he called it "peddling bread"). He had a handheld client device he'd take into the stores to create the store's order based on what they needed (and what the device showed he had in the truck). He'd plug it into a printer in his truck to print invoices. On a nightly basis, he would connect his client device to the company computer via a dial-up line. It would upload current sales data and download the next days order. Of course, hundreds or more other "bread peddlers" were also doing the same thing.

✦ **Point-of-sale applications:** The day of the simple cash register is long gone. Instead, point-of-sale (POS) devices are used that tie into POS applications. Often, multiple cashiers run POS applications that all tie into a main database in another area of the store.

✦ **Integrating data from multiple sites:** This allows multiple stores to interact with the main office. In this scenario, the retail stores are acting as clients. Not too long ago, Darril bought an item at a warehouse store where a rebate was offered. He waited a day and then went to its online site and entered information from the receipt that identified the store (and even the cash register where he made the purchase) and showed the items that had a rebate. In this situation, each warehouse store is replicating its data daily to the main office, and then the main office is making some of that data available online.

You might be thinking that the explanation for integrating data from multiple sites sounds like it'd be from a server to another server. And you'd be right. However, in this context, the retail stores are acting as clients to the primary database at a central location. Admittedly, it's a fuzzy distinction.

Replication between servers and servers

Replication between servers and servers is generally done for some type of offloading of the workload. The following scenarios show some common situations where data is replicated between servers:

✦ **Improved scalability:** *Scalability* is serving more and more clients without any degradation of service. SQL Server can be *scaled up* (adding additional processors and memory) or *scaled out* (adding additional servers). Network Load Balancing can be used to add multiple servers with the identical data. Replication can be used to ensure each of the servers holds the same data.

✦ **Improved availability:** *Availability* is whether the server is available to serve the data when the server is queried. By replicating data to a standby server, you can plan for the possible failure of an online server. In the case of a failure, you can easily bring the standby server online with up-to-date data.

✦ **Offloading processing:** Some processing is too time and resource intensive to run on the online server. Instead, you can replicate the data to a secondary server, run your processing there, and if necessary, replicate any results from the processing to the online server. For example, in one environment where Darril worked, backups were taking too long on the production server. Replication was used to replicate the data to a secondary server, and backups were then run on the secondary server.

✦ **Reporting and data analysis:** Often, data needs to be accessible to clients in other formats than the raw database. For example, SQL Server Reporting Services (SSRS) can be enabled to serve reports based on the data, and SQL Server Analysis Services (SSAS) can be used to make the data more accessible for decision support systems. If SSRS and SSAS are run on the same server as the online server, it might overwhelm the resources. Instead, replication can be used to send the data to a server dedicated to reporting or analysis.

Chapter 6: Spreading the Load with Partitioning

In This Chapter

✔ Understanding how SQL Server uses partitioning

✔ Partitioning key terms and concepts

✔ Setting up partitioning in your environment

S QL Server is designed to support very large databases and heavy transaction loads. When combined with modern server hardware, which often features multiple CPUs, fast disk drives, and so on, SQL Server provides a potent information-processing infrastructure that is able to solve most computing challenges. However, data volumes can be so large at times, that SQL Server administrators are forced to explore different options to increase performance. Partitioning is one of the most popular techniques available, delivering significant performance optimizations for disk-intensive operations.

In this chapter, I help you understand how to make the most of partitioning in your environment. I get started by illustrating how partitioning actually works. When you've gotten the hang of that, the next order of business is to get you familiar with key partitioning-related terms and concepts, forming a solid foundation for the last part of the chapter where I show you how to implement partitioning in your SQL Server installation.

Understanding SQL Server Partitioning

In most cases, database application performance barriers can be linked to a CPU-, memory-, or disk-based resource challenge. When faced with a disk-based resource obstacle, partitioning is one technique that you can use to distribute the workload and thereby boost throughput. When partitioning is in place, SQL Server is also more likely to take advantage of hardware that features multiple CPUs.

Generally speaking, to *partition* data (or an index) is to spread the information across multiple physical disk objects. Typically, these objects are found on separate disk drives, although this isn't mandatory. Disk drives and related information storage technology performance continue to advance; combining these with the sophisticated partitioning algorithms present in SQL Server can yield some dramatic improvements in responsiveness.

When setting up a partitioning plan, the database administrator is called upon to identify criteria that will help SQL Server determine how to distribute data onto multiple disk objects. It's important that the database administrator work closely with business and other technology domains to better understand the expected information workflows, making it possible to design an accurate and efficient partitioning strategy.

Before heading down the partitioning path, make sure that your performance bottlenecks (either current or expected) are due to disk-related volume issues; partitioning can't add any value to a resource-bound CPU or memory server.

Determining the correct candidate tables for partitioning is more of an art than a science. Generally, a given table can benefit from partitioning when more than one of the following conditions is true:

✦ **Large amount of data:** Does the table contain millions or even billions of records? Partitioning really shines when the table holds hefty amounts of information. However, if you're running on sluggish hardware with relatively small data sets, you might still realize some benefits from partitioning.

✦ **Predictable distribution of data:** Partitioning requires that you identify criteria upon which to spread information. Ideally, this means that the table is loaded and modified in a predictable way. One of the most common scenarios for partitioning involves a table that contains sales transactions that are more-or-less evenly distributed throughout the year.

✦ **Dynamic data:** Typically, a highly dynamic table (such as one that holds sales transactions) benefits from partitioning more than a relatively static table (such as one that contains unchanging product codes).

✦ **Archival information:** Partitioning may also add value in situations where significant amounts of data can be safely archived. For example, a given table may contain an enormous amount of information. However, upon further examination, you learn that much of this data is accessed relatively infrequently. Partitioning allows you to keep the smaller set of active data on the fastest disk drives, while shunting lesser-accessed information onto inexpensive, more leisurely disk drives.

✦ **Supporting hardware:** Partitioning, generally, makes sense only when appropriate hardware is available to support the distributed workload. If all your data resides on one disk, the benefits of partitioning this information diminish significantly. In general, partitioning and modern, high-speed distributed disk arrays go hand-in-hand.

✦ **Low downtime tolerance:** Does your data processing environment require you to maintain very high levels of SQL Server uptime? If so, using partitioning to spread data among multiple disk objects might help reduce the amount of administrative downtime.

Partitioning Key Terms and Concepts

Before getting started on a simple partitioning example, it's worth understanding some underlying architectural concepts and terminology.

✦ **Partition type:** An administrator might partition tables based on data or index values. Partitions based on data are *range partitions*. Database designers typically use an easy-to-understand factor when creating a range partition. For example, dates, regions, and other easily explained values are ideal for distributing information to multiple destinations. You might also associate indexes with your partition, which streamlines access to your data and related indexes. In fact, if you create an index on an already partitioned table, SQL Server automatically places the index into the appropriate partition.

✦ **Partition key:** This is a column that SQL Server uses as input to a partition function (described in a moment). The database administrator identifies this column and cites it when creating the partitioning scheme and associated table definition. When new rows are created, or existing rows are modified, the partition function examines the value contained in this column to decide where its associated row is placed.

✦ **Partition functions:** These specialized functions, defined by a SQL Server database administrator, serve as logical filters that help identify the appropriate destination for a given row.

Writing an effective partition function requires that the database administrator have significant insight into the expected operational patterns encountered by the application. This would be an excellent time to involve business or other users in the discussion.

✦ **Filegroups:** These are logical names used to associate one or more disk-based files with administrator-defined categories. This helps organize a potentially unwieldy set of disk files into easily-understood groups for the purposes of administration or other management-related activities.

✦ **Partition schemes:** This internal SQL Server structure relates a partition function with associated filegroups. A database can contain multiple partition schemes; each one applies different partitioning criteria for distinct purposes. For example, there might be one partition scheme for transaction history records, another for order management details, and so on.

Setting Up Partitioning in Your Environment

Previously in this chapter, I briefly describe SQL Server's partitioning architecture along with details about some of the most relevant terms and concepts you're likely to encounter. Here, I show you how easy it is to set up partitioning for your database.

First, a little background: Assume that you've been tasked with designing and developing an application to store point-of-sale information. Because creativity isn't your organization's strong suit, the database is named `point_of_sale`. Furthermore, imagine that you're designing a specific table (`sales_transactions`) that you expect will receive hundreds of millions of records each year. Your organization has grown, and now supports customers in Europe and Asia. Sales transactions will arrive from both of these regions, and you're concerned that they will overwhelm your primary disk drive. Consequently, you purchase and install a high-speed disk array. For the purposes of this simple example, assume that the disk array offers a `C:` drive and a `D:` drive, and that you want to place European sales data on drive C, and Asian sales transactions on drive D.

Although you can use SQL Server Management Studio to enable partitioning (see the wizard shown in Figure 6-1), it's actually easier to understand by using a combination of graphical- and character-based techniques.

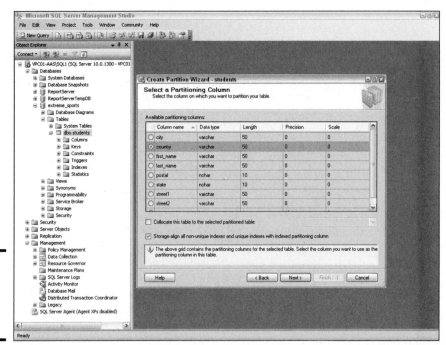

Figure 6-1:
The SQL Server Partition Wizard.

Because partitioning is somewhat complex to comprehend fully, before getting started on a production-ready partitioning plan, try implementing a simple example from this chapter. Here's what to do:

1. **Launch the SQL Server Management Studio.**

You find this utility under the main SQL Server menu.

2. **Connect to the database that holds the table that you wish to partition.**

3. **Click the New Query icon to open a dialog box where you type your partitioning instructions.**

Make sure that you're connected to the database where you want to apply partitioning rather than the default Master database.

4. **Create a function that SQL Server will use to determine where a given row should be placed.**

Here's the SQL that you execute to make this happen:

```
CREATE PARTITION FUNCTION PF_Region(char(10))
AS RANGE RIGHT FOR VALUES ('Asia');
```

This brief statement instructs SQL Server to use the value of `Asia` as the determining criteria for where a given row is placed. Additionally, this function expects to receive a data type of `char(10)`.

5. **Create two filegroups (one dedicated to Europe, one dedicated to Asia).**

Here's the SQL to accomplish this:

```
ALTER DATABASE point_of_sale ADD FILEGROUP FG_EUROPE;
ALTER DATABASE point_of_sale ADD FILEGROUP FG_ASIA;
```

You're free to use any names you like for your filegroups; if possible, however, try to use a consistent naming convention and meaningful filegroup names.

6. **Associate a disk file with the new filegroups.**

Here's the SQL that makes this association:

```
ALTER DATABASE point_of_sale ADD FILE
(name = 'Europe', filename = 'c:\europe.ndf')
TO FILEGROUP FG_EUROPE;

ALTER DATABASE point_of_sale ADD FILE
(name = 'Asia', filename = 'd:\asia.ndf')
TO FILEGROUP FG_ASIA;
```

Notice that the two files are on separate disk drives. Additionally, remember that you may name these files anything you like. Generally, it's a good idea to use meaningful names for both filegroups and associated files.

Book VIII Chapter 6

Spreading the Load with Partitioning

7. Create a partition scheme to associate the partition function with the filegroups.

This requires a single SQL statement:

```
CREATE PARTITION SCHEME PS_REGION
AS PARTITION PF_REGION TO (FG_EUROPE, FG_ASIA);
```

Observe how this statement ties the partition function, scheme, and filegroups together. All that remains is to associate the table with this scheme.

8. Write the SQL to create the table that will benefit from this partitioning scheme.

Here's the SQL to set up partitioning for this table:

```
CREATE TABLE sales_transactions(
    sales_transaction_id int NOT NULL,
    sales_transaction_date datetime NOT NULL,
    sales_transaction_amount money NOT NULL,
    sales_transaction_product smallint NOT NULL,
    sales_transaction_region char(10) NOT NULL
CONSTRAINT C_sales_transaction_region
CHECK (sales_transaction_region = 'Europe' OR
    sales_transaction_region = 'Asia'),
) ON PS_REGION(sales_transaction_region)
```

If you want to partition based on a column's values, you must create a constraint that restricts its potential entries to match the entries you've defined for the partition. In this case, this means that the sales_transaction_region column can only contain values of Europe or Asia.

9. Adjust your indexes accordingly.

In most cases, SQL Server is quite clear about external requirements for its features. Unfortunately, this isn't so with regard to partitioning, which can be a little confusing, especially with regard to indexes. For example, to complete this sample partitioning scenario successfully, we had to run the following SQL statement:

```
CREATE UNIQUE INDEX ix_01 ON
sales_transactions(sales_transaction_id,
sales_transaction_region)
```

That's all there is to it. Any data insertions or modifications to your table will now use this partitioning scheme to distribute the data between drive C and drive D, based on the contents of the sales_transaction_region column.

The small screenshot shown in Figure 6-2 has a lot of information. Notice the constraint present under the `sales_transactions` table. Look at the Partition Schemes and Partition Functions folders on the left side of the screen. Finally, observe the Storage page of the table properties, which tells that the table has two partitions, which partition scheme is in use, and the column upon which the partition is defined.

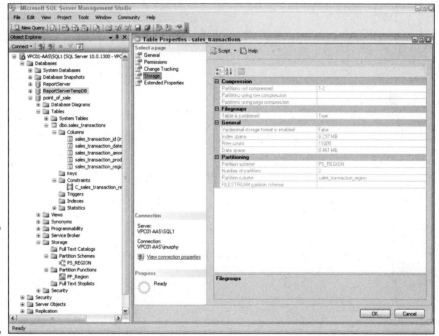

Figure 6-2:
The results of setting up partitioning for a given table.

This has been a simple example; you could easily set up much more sophisticated partitioning scenarios to meet the exact needs of your data processing environment.

Book IX

Appendixes

The 5th Wave   By Rich Tennant

SCIENTISTS FROM *SETI GO TO LUNCH
*Search for Extraterrestrial Intelligence.

"We're still at the restaurant. We've been signaling for a waitress for several hours now, but still haven't made contact."

Contents at a Glance

Appendix A: Ten Sources of Information on SQL Server 2008

In This Chapter

- ✔ Microsoft SQL Server Web site
- ✔ Microsoft Developer Network
- ✔ Wikipedia, newsgroups, and user groups
- ✔ Magazines and books
- ✔ Design, administrative, and data generation tools

Given the popularity of Microsoft SQL Server, it should come as no surprise that tons of helpful resources are available for SQL Server database designers, developers, and administrators. In this section, we humbly suggest a few of our favorites.

Microsoft SQL Server Web Site

Here's a great place to get started learning more about SQL Server. Aside from the usual marketing-flavored imagery, you find a variety of valuable product and technical details that you can use to further your understanding of all things SQL Server. You can find it at

```
www.microsoft.com/sql/2008
```

Note: You might have to tweak the URL to get to SQL Server 2008; at the time of this writing, the URL pointed at SQL Server 2005.

Microsoft SQL Server Developer Center

In an effort to support software developers, Microsoft offers a comprehensive set of services known as the Microsoft Developer Network (MSDN). In addition to the broad suite of software available for purchase, an extremely content-rich Web site is available to anyone, not just subscribers. It contains white papers, technical briefs, and a deep knowledge base that you can search to get answers to your questions. You can find it at

```
http://msdn.microsoft.com/sql
```

Wikipedia

This Internet-based, open source encyclopedia (`www.wikipedia.org`) is a great source of information about all technology topics, including relational database theory and practical application. For example, here's a link to a very comprehensive article on database normalization in theory and practice:

`http://en.wikipedia.org/wiki/Database_normalization`

Newsgroups

These collaborative spaces are an immense help when you're struggling with a technical problem. Chances are that someone here can address your question. In the past few years, Google has done a great job helping to organize and rescue Usenet. It's easier than ever to access these groups via your browser. Here's a shortcut to 32 (at last count) newsgroups focused solely on SQL Server:

`http://groups.google.com/groups/dir?lnk=gh&hl=en&sel=33606733`

Alternatively, you can search Google Groups (`www.groups.google.com`) for groups with SQL Server in their names.

Magazines

Several well-written magazines are available that provide significant coverage of database topics. Some are database-agnostic, while others focus specifically on SQL Server. These periodicals include

- *SQL Server Magazine* — `www.sqlmag.com`
- *SQL Server Solutions* — `www.pinpub.com/spec_sql.htm`
- *Databased Advisor* — `www.databasedadvisor.com`

As an added bonus, many magazines maintain online community message boards that let you interact with other readers.

User Groups

These gatherings of like-minded individuals are a great place to enhance your understanding of SQL Server 2008. Some groups meet virtually, while others have physical events; some groups span both realms. The following list highlights two of the better and most relevant, Internet-focused user groups:

✦ SQL Server Worldwide User Group — www.sswug.org

✦ Professional Association for SQL Server — www.sqlpass.org

On the other hand, if you want to meet and greet your counterparts face-to-face, chances are that an Internet search can locate a good user group not too far from you.

Books

This book helps you get started with SQL Server 2008, but many other titles can give you a broader understanding of how to build high-quality database applications. Look for well-regarded books that cover any of these topics (which are all pertinent in the context of SQL Server 2008):

✦ Relational database design theory and practice

✦ Best practices for user interface design

✦ Distributed computing

Database Design Tools

If you're building a simple application, chances are that you won't need to perform any extensive database design and modeling to realize your goals. However, if you face a more daunting task, you're wise to look into specialized tools that focus on this portion of the application development lifecycle. Embarcadero Technologies makes a collection of products that add value throughout the entire process. You can find them at

www.embarcadero.com/products/products.html

Administrative Tools

As we've shown throughout the book, Microsoft's SQL Server Management Studio is a great tool for administering your SQL Server 2008 database. However, you might also be interested in one of the available third-party tools. We've used Toad for SQL Server by Quest Software; versions of this product are available for all the major database platforms. You can find Toad for SQL Server at

www.toadsoft.com/toadsqlserver/toad_sqlserver.htm

Data Generation Tools

Generating sample data by hand is one of the more tedious tasks you face when building and testing an application for your SQL Server 2008 installation. Fortunately, tools are available that can automate this for you, freeing you to spend time developing and then tuning your application. We've had great success with the DTM Data Generator, which is located at

`www.sqledit.com/dg/index.html`

Appendix B: Troubleshooting SQL Server 2008

In This Chapter

✔ Solving installation problems

✔ Handling administration headaches

✔ Resolving data inconsistencies

✔ Setting up automated operations

✔ Simplifying complicated data structures

✔ Interchanging information

✔ Securing your database

✔ Speeding up a sluggish server

✔ Locating and installing the sample databases

✔ Finding reports on your report server

Given all the things you can do with SQL Server 2008, it's natural that you might get confused from time to time. Never fear: This entire appendix is dedicated to helping you rise above some of the most common predicaments that you're likely to encounter.

I Can't Install the Software!

Having some cool new software and not being able to get it installed isn't much fun. Luckily, SQL Server 2008 usually gets up and running without a hitch. If you do encounter an obstacle, use the following checklist to help you avoid hot water:

1. **Make sure you have sufficient permissions to add or remove software.**

Generally, a good idea is to install or remove software as an administrator. Otherwise, the operating system might block you from making these changes.

2. **Ascertain that your computer is powerful enough to support the product.**

   SQL Server gobbles memory, CPU, and disk resources. Trying to install it on a lightweight machine guarantees frustration. If you want to learn more about its exact requirements, head to Book I, Chapter 3.

3. **Remove any previous versions (such as beta installations) of SQL Server 2008 via the Add/Remove Programs application within the Control Panel.**

   If you skip this step, a good chance exists that the installer will complain loudly and then keel over. Even though it's tedious, take the time to clean things up before trying to install.

4. **Make sure you have all necessary supporting software.**

   Generally, the SQL Server installer is quite intelligent and diligently acquires whatever is missing (for example, Windows Installer, .NET Framework 2.0, SQL Server Native Client, and so on). However, you might need to obtain these components yourself. Book I, Chapter 3 has the full list of supporting characters.

If you want to get some more ideas about the overall installation experience, check out Book I, Chapter 4.

How Can I Administer My Database?

A database administrator's work is never done. Fortunately, Microsoft didn't skimp on the supporting tools. Here are two good choices to get the job done quickly and easily:

✦ **SQLCMD utility:** This character-based tool ships with every copy of SQL Server. You can run just about any administrative task using direct Transact-SQL or one of the hundreds of built-in system stored procedures. However, you're better served by the SQL Server Management Studio, which I describe next.

✦ **SQL Server Management Studio:** If you have more of a hankering for graphical tools when it comes to administration, you want to look at this utility. You can perform just about any administrative chore you might ever face. And, whatever isn't possible can be handled with direct Transact-SQL or system stored procedures.

My Data Is Messed Up!

Unless you believe in gremlins or other supernatural entities that descend from the ether and wreak havoc on your data, chances are that any information problem is because of an error or omission. Here's what to watch out for:

✦ **Referential integrity issues:** To help keep all your data synchronized, SQL Server offers referential integrity features. These prevent you or your applications from inadvertently altering rows from one table without making corresponding changes in another table. To get a better idea of how to use referential integrity to your advantage, take a look at Book II, Chapter 6.

✦ **Failure to use transactions:** Transactions help certify that your database interactions happen in logically consistent groups. Without proper transactions, an operation may update one table but fail to do the same for other tables. The result is damaged data integrity. Book III, Chapter 9 is designed to help you make the most of transactions.

✦ **Incorrectly defined columns:** Believe it or not, sometimes database designers choose the wrong data type when setting up their tables. For example, a particular field might need to contain currency amounts, which include decimals. Yet when designers write the SQL to create the table, they choose the INTEGER data type — SQL Server discards any fractional amounts from the column.

✦ **Not enough space for character-based fields:** Another common problem is database designers not providing enough space for character-based fields. Again, SQL Server cheerfully tosses away any extra data, which leads to damaged information and unhappy users.

I Want to Automate Some Operations

SQL Server offers two very helpful features that you can use to help streamline common database tasks:

✦ **Stored procedures and functions:** Stored procedures and functions are bits of logically grouped application software that you can write in a variety of programming languages, including Transact-SQL, Visual Basic, Visual C#, and so on. After you create them, you then place these procedures inside the SQL Server engine, where anyone with the right permission can run them. This centralizes your application logic, and generally helps performance. If you're curious about stored procedures and functions, check out Book IV, Chapter 2.

✦ **Triggers:** Think of a trigger as a very specialized stored procedure, one that is run when a certain event happens. For example, you might want to send an e-mail alert when inventory drops below a certain level. That's a great use of a trigger; you can probably think of many more that apply in your organization. You can also use triggers to help you administer your database server and run administrative operations. If you want to get a better handle on triggers, have a look at Book IV, Chapter 3.

How Can I Simplify My Data?

For database administrators, making sense of information can be confusing, especially if the environment sports a substantial number of tables with complex interrelationships. If you find it difficult, imagine how laborious it is for your users and application developers. Luckily, none of you have to suffer in silence. One way to create a more transparent picture of your data is to take advantage of views.

Think of a view as a window into your information, one that can span the entire database to retrieve results. By pre-building all the joins and stripping any extraneous details, you can make this window much simpler than the underlying data. The end result is that your users and developers can work with the view, rather than the base database tables. To see how views can make things better for your enterprise, take a look at Book III, Chapter 8.

How Can I Load Information into SQL Server?

Things would be so much simpler if your SQL Server database held all the information that your organization cares about. Because you need to integrate SQL Server with data from external systems, this isn't likely. In some cases, you're tasked with loading data from these other information silos, while at other times you're called to take data from SQL Server and send it to other repositories.

No matter what the integration task, Microsoft has you covered. If your import or export task is relatively simple, a wizard is waiting to help you. (You read about the Import and Export Wizard in Book VIII, Chapter 2.) Comparatively, if you're faced with a more complex integration project, perhaps one that involves repetitive or sophisticated workflow, SQL Server Integration Services is just what the doctor ordered; see Book VIII, Chapter 4.

My Data Is Unprotected!

Don't worry about bad folks crashing your database party. SQL Server has excellent, easy-to-use security features that can help you lock down and protect your data. You can configure your security settings through the simple but powerful SQL Server Management Studio. Here are just a few of the database objects that can have their own security settings:

✦ **Table**

✦ **View**

✦ **Function**

✦ **Procedure**

✦ **Constraint**

✦ **Queue**

✦ **Statistic**

✦ **Synonym**

Book VIII, Chapter 3 is where you find the fascinating security details.

My Database Server Is Too Slow!

Before you toss your slow-running database server out the window, you can run a few effortless checks to identify and remedy the source of the headache.

✦ **Are your tables indexed correctly?** Without a doubt, improper or missing indexes cause most of the performance problems that plague the average database application. Take the time to ensure that you've placed indexes in the right places. Book VII, Chapter 3 is a great place to start on the path to good indexing.

✦ **Is there enough memory?** Don't shortchange your database server by denying it the memory it needs to get the job done quickly. You can tell if you're running out of memory by launching the Windows Task Manager and viewing the amount of available physical memory. If this number is approaching zero, you're asking your server to do too much work with too little memory.

✦ **Are there too many users and applications?** Sometimes, no matter how much memory you install, or how well your tables are indexed, you approach the limit of what a database server can handle. There's no hard-and-fast way to tell whether you're on the brink, but if you've exhausted all your options and you can't coax any more speed from your server, then distribute your workload among multiple servers.

✦ **Are you taking advantage of SQL Server's performance tools?** There's no need to guess about what's causing a responsiveness problem because SQL Server offers a collection of excellent performance monitoring and management tools. Take a look at Book VII, Chapter 2, which itemizes all these technologies and shows you how to use them.

Where Is AdventureWorks?

AdventureWorks2008 is the primary sample database used with SQL Server 2008; you'll see quite a bit of documentation within Books Online on AdventureWorks. AdventureWorks was included with SQL Server 2005 but the version for SQL Server 2008 must be downloaded.

The different variations of AdventureWorks2008 are

✦ **SQL2008.AdventureWorks_OLTP_DB_v2008:** The primary OLTP sample database for the company Adventure Works Cycles.

✦ **SQL2008.AdventureWorks_LT_DB_v2008:** A scaled-down version of the Adventure Works Cycles database.

✦ **SQL2008.AdventureWorks_DW_BI_v2008:** The Adventure Works Cycles Data Warehouse and the Analysis Services database project.

Each of the variations of the AdventureWorks2008 database has three hardware platform versions. The x86 platform is for x86-based 32-bit systems, the x64 platform is for x86-based 64-bit platforms, and the ia64 platform is for Intel Itanium 64-bit systems. Download the version that matches your hardware.

You can download the AdventureWorks2008 databases from Microsoft's open source project hosting Web site, CodePlex. In addition to the sample databases, you can find a lot of different code samples and tutorials. Point your browser to the following URL to get current versions of the databases and samples:

```
http://www.codeplex.com/MSFTDBProdSamples
```

For detailed steps on how to install the AdventureWorks2008 OLTP database, check out Book III, Chapter 5.

Where Are My Reports?

After setting up an SQL Server Reporting Services (SSRS) server, it's common to "lose" the URL you need to access the reports. The actual URL you use depends on whether SSRS is installed in the default instance of SQL Server or a named instance.

You can access both the report server (which lists all your reports) and the Report Manager (which allows you to manage many of your reports) via Web browsers.

✦ **Finding SSRS on a default instance:** To access the SSRS report server (which lists all your reports) on a server named SRV1, use the following URL:

```
http://SRV1/ReportServer
```

To access the Report Manager (which allows you to manage your reports) on a server named SRV1, use this URL:

```
http://SRV1/Reports
```

✦ **Finding SSRS on a named instance:** When accessing an SSRS that's installed on a named instance, you need to add the instance name to the end of the URL preceded by an underscore.

For example, if your named instance were MyReports on a server named SRV1, the URL for the report server would be:

```
http://SRV1/ReportServer_MyReports
```

To access the Report Manager on a server named SRV1 with a named instance of MyReports, use this URL:

```
http://SRV1/Reports_MyReports
```

Appendix C: Glossary

ad hoc query: A query issued infrequently, or on an as-needed basis. Typically ad hoc queries are issued against remote data sources from a SQL Server, but can also be issued against SQL Server from a wide variety of sources. If you have a need to issue queries against a remote data source more often, linked servers are created to simplify the syntax of the ad hoc query. *See also* linked server.

article: A database object (such as a table, stored procedure, or view) that is contained within a publication. *See also* replication.

assembly: Application logic that is stored in, and managed by, the SQL Server database server, including objects like triggers, CLR software, and stored procedures. Assemblies are written in a .NET language, such a C# or Visual Basic. *See also* CLR.

attribute: Information, contained in the form of name-value pairs, located after the start tag of an XML element. *See also* element; content.

backup: The process of copying your database's information to another form of media, such as tape or disk. A good backup strategy is vital for any production SQL Server environment. *See also* full backup; full differential backup.

backup device: A hardware unit that hosts the media for your database backups. You configure your backup to work with this object. These devices are typically disk or tape drives. *See also* backup.

checkpoint: Like any modern relational database management system, SQL Server performs much of its work within high-performance memory. However, to make any data alterations permanent, eventually, memory must preserve data onto disk drives. The checkpoint process is how the database server accomplishes this synchronization.

column: Stored within tables, a column contains a particular piece of information. For example, if you're tracking details about a customer, you would likely place this data in a table. Within the table, you would have specialized columns to store things like name, address, and so on. *See also* table.

Common Language Runtime (CLR): When building a database application, many developers choose to use SQL Server's internal language, Transact-SQL. However, other programming languages, (such as Visual Basic, Visual C#, and so on) might offer better performance and functionality than Transact-SQL for certain situations. CLR is a Microsoft software development and integration technology that makes it possible to build software and store it within SQL Server using one of these other languages.

Composite index: An index that is made of two or more columns. *See also* column.

Constraint: A constraint is used to enforce the integrity of data in the column of a table, beyond the data type. Several specific types of constraints can be used within SQL Server 2008. *See also* primary key; foreign key.

content: All information contained between the start tag and end tag of an XML element. *See also* element; attribute.

cube: A multidimensional structure that contains dimensions and measures. Cubes are a denormalized version of either the entire database or part of the database and are used within SQL Server Analysis Services (SSAS). *See also* SQL Server Analysis Services; measure; dimension.

data mining: The process of retrieving relevant data to make intelligent decisions. SQL Server Analysis Services is used to create data mining models.

database server: A sophisticated software product that hosts a broad range of data, making it available for many concurrent clients. SQL Server is one example of a database server. Other vendors, such as Oracle and IBM, offer their versions of this type of product.

DELETE statement: `DELETE` is used to remove rows from tables or views.

DDL trigger: A Data Definition Language (DDL) trigger can be used to respond to DDL event statements, such as `CREATE`, `ALTER`, and `DROP`. DDL triggers can be configured with a server scope or a database scope. For example, a CREATE DATABASE trigger could be created with a server scope. The trigger would fire any time the `CREATE DATABASE` statement is executed on the server. *See also* trigger.

deprecated: Features that were supported in previous versions of SQL Server, but aren't recommended for use in the current version. Deprecated features will most likely not be supported in the next version of SQL Server.

dimension: A group of related objects within a cube that's used to provide information about related data. For example, a product dimension could include a product name, a product category, a product size, product cost, and product price. *See also* cube; measure.

distributor: A central database server that acts as an administrator and coordinator for replication. *See also* replication.

DML trigger: A Data Manipulation Language (DML) trigger can be used to respond to DML event statements, such as `INSERT`, `UPDATE`, and `DELETE`. DML triggers are configured on tables or views. For example, an INSERT trigger on the Sales table would execute any time a row was inserted into the Sales table. *See also* trigger.

Document Type Definition (DTD): A specification that describes the structure and format of an XML document. Generally included at the top of the XML document, it helps people and applications better understand and work with the XML-based information. *See also* XML.

element: Surrounded by a start tag and end tag, this is XML-based information that might also include attributes and content. Elements may contain other nested, child elements. *See also* attribute; content.

file backup: A type of backup relevant only when there are multiple filegroups. *See also* filegroup.

filegroup: Collections of SQL Server data files. For performance and administrative reasons, you can place user objects into dedicated filegroups. *See also* master data file; file backup.

first normal form: One of the three normal forms that make up relational database guidelines, this rule states that a table should not have any repeating fields. *See also* normalization; second normal form; third normal form.

foreign key: Information that establishes a relationship between two tables. By preventing erroneous data modifications, this association helps preserve data integrity. *See also* primary key.

full backup: As its name implies, this type of backup archives all information within a database. Should the database be lost or damaged, you can restore it to its state as of the time you created the full backup. *See also* full differential backup; partial backup; restore.

full differential backup: Identical to a full backup, with one major difference: A full differential backup archives only information that has changed since the last full backup. This can be very handy if only small portions of your database change on a regular basis; by running differential backups you don't need to incur the time and media costs of full backups. *See also* backup; full backup.

function: A centralized, server-based routine that can be included as part of your Transact-SQL statements. Typically used to streamline logic and reduce the amount of required programming effort, you can build your own functions. You can also take advantage of the many built-in functions offered by SQL Server. One difference between functions and stored procedures is that a function must return a value; it's optional with a stored procedure. *See also* stored procedure.

index: An internal database structure, sometimes defined by the database administrator, and sometimes automatically created by SQL Server. Indexes make it possible to speed access to information as well as perform integrity and other validations to safeguard data. *See also* unique index; composite index.

INSERT statement: `INSERT` is used to add rows to a table or view within a database.

isolation level: A configurable setting that affects how a transaction interacts with other SQL Server users and processes. Increasingly stringent isolation levels include

Read uncommitted

Read committed

Repeatable read

Snapshot

Serializable

These isolation levels interact with your application, allowing or denying visibility to modified data depending on the setting. *See also* transactions.

linked server: Database objects that provide the connection information for remote data sources housed on another server. The other server could be a SQL Server, an Oracle server, a Microsoft Access database, or one of many other data sources. Linked servers are created when the remote data source will be accessed more than once or twice. *See also* ad hoc query.

log file: A file-system–based, internal database construct that records data and table modifications, making it possible to restore information to its previous state should the application roll back a transaction.

logical design: The abstract design and structure of your relational database. Focusing on the high-level objects and their interrelationships, this is usually generated during the analysis phase of most projects. It then serves as a guideline for creating the actual implementation of your SQL Server database. *See also* physical design.

master data file (MDF): SQL Server databases contain two types of operating system files: MDF and log files. This class of file stores data and is dedicated to one-and-only-one database. *See also* log file, filegroup.

measure: A column of quantifiable data mapped to a dimension within a cube. Measures are often used to provide access to aggregations of data (such as annual sales of a product or a store), while also giving the ability to drill down into the details (such as quarterly or monthly sales). *See also* cube; dimension.

Model Designer: The Model Designer is used to create report models. Report models include the *data source definition* (the database where the data is coming from), and the *data view* (what tables and views to include in the report). Report models do not create actual reports that can be viewed. Instead, users can use the Report Builder to create reports from a report model. The Model Designer is available within BIDS.

named pipes: A communication method between two processes. In the context of SQL Server, this is a means for a database client to communicate with the database server. *See also* protocol.

namespace: A collection of element and attribute names designed to reduce confusion and ambiguity when dealing with XML documents. Generally available for consultation from a commonly available Internet address. *See also* XML.

normalization: A series of database design recommendations that dictate how information should be dispersed among tables as well as how these tables should relate. *See also* first normal form; second normal form; third normal form.

Optimizer: The Optimizer is an internal technology that is responsible for selecting the most efficient means to accessing or altering information. It uses detailed statistics about the database to make the right decision.

partial backup: An operation that archives a subset of your database, including

> Data from the primary filegroup
>
> Any requested read-only files
>
> All read-write filegroups

See also partial differential backup; full backup; full differential backup.

partial differential backup: Archives only those portions of the last partial backup that have changed since the partial backup was completed. *See also* partial backup; full backup; full differential backup.

permission: A privilege that you grant to a principle. When authorized, the principle may then interact with one or more securables. *See also* principal; securable.

physical design: The actual tables, columns, indexes, and other data structures used to store information in a SQL Server database. Development projects typically progress from a logical database design to a physical database design. *See also* logical design.

primary key: This column, or group of columns, provides a unique definition for a given row. By definition, no two rows in the same table can have the same primary key value. *See also* foreign key.

principal: Any user or process that you can authorize to interact with your SQL Server database. *See also* securable.

procedural language: A general-purpose programming language containing full logic and flow control capabilities. Typically compiled to binary code, these languages can usually handle more complex algorithms at a higher performance than interpreted database-centric languages, such as Transact-SQL. *See also* CLR.

protocol: To communicate effectively, client applications and database servers need a commonly agreed-upon approach. A protocol is a communication standard adhered to by both parties that makes these conversations possible. *See also* TCP/IP; named pipes.

publication: A single unit containing one-to-many articles, available for replication to other database servers. *See also* replication.

publish-and-subscribe: An architecture that allows easy interchange of information among distributed computers and processes. Data may be pushed by a publisher or pulled by a subscriber. *See also* replication.

publisher: A specific database server that offers information to other databases using replication technology. *See also* replication.

record: A grouping of information typically returned from a query or other database operation. It can consist of data from only one table or be an aggregation of information dispersed among many tables. *See also* row.

recovery model: A preset plan used by SQL Server when archiving and restoring information. *See also* backup; restore.

referential integrity: A set of rules, enforced by the database server, the user's application, or both, that protects the quality and consistency of information stored in the database.

replication: A process whereby information is published from a database server and sent to one or more subscribers. Data may be transferred proactively by the publisher or requested by the subscribers. *See also* publish-and-subscribe.

Report Builder: A tool launched from the report server that allows users to create reports from a report model.

Report Designer: The Report Designer is used to create reports from scratch. The reports will include the *data source definition* (the database where the data is coming from), the *data view* (what tables and views to include in the report), and the individual columns to show. Filters can be used to show only certain rows from the tables, and tools are available within the Report Designer. The Report Designer is available within BIDS.

Report Manager: A Web interface served by the report server. The Report Manager provides access and property pages for any data source, report model, and reports that are published to the report server. Users are able to launch the Report Builder from the Report Manager.

report model: A "blueprint" of a report. A report model includes the *data source* (such as a SQL Server database) and a *data view* (the tables and/or views that can be used in the report). Users can then use the report model to create their own reports, picking and choosing what data they want to include from the data view.

restore: The process of reinstating archived information onto your database server. *See also* backup; recovery model.

row: An individual entry from a given table. For example, a table may contain details about thousands of customers; a specific customer's data will be found in one row. *See also* record.

schema: A group of database objects that make up a given namespace. Objects include tables, views, and statements that grant or revoke access to other securable objects. No two objects in any namespace can have the same name.

second normal form: Data is said to be in the second normal form if it complies with the first normal form and has one or more columns in a table that uniquely identify each row. *See also* first normal form; third normal form.

securable: This represents any type of object that can be given its own security setting. Some examples of securables include tables, views, and users. *See also* principal.

SELECT statement: SELECT is used to read data from tables and views.

Service Broker: A messaging service integrated into SQL Server. It allows database applications to send messages in either one-way or two-way conversations.

Service Broker conversation: A reliable asynchronous exchange of messages using a Service Broker contract, queue, and service. Service Broker conversations are created from sending and receiving messages.

SQL Server Analysis Services (SSAS): A database engine within SQL Server that allows databases to be reconfigured in cubes. When properly configured, SSAS databases allow decision makers to easily drill into the information they need. Cubes are created within an SSAS database.

SQL Server Integration Services (SSIS): A collection of technologies designed for sophisticated information interchange and workflow between SQL Server and other information repositories, such as different relational database management systems, flat files, XML, and so on.

SQL Server Management Objects (SMO): A set of objects within the `Microsoft.SqlServer.Management.Smo` namespace used to manage and administer SQL Server. SMO is used in applications external to SQL Server Management Studio.

SQL Server Reporting Services (SSRS): A server-based tool used to provide easy reporting capability of data from a SQL Server. Reports are published to the server and users can retrieve the reports by using a Web browser, such as Internet Explorer. It's also possible to publish report models that can be used by end-users to create reports based on their specific needs.

SQL Server Management Studio: Provided by Microsoft, this tool allows you to perform common database administration tasks as well as run direct Transact-SQL statements.

stored procedure: Centralized, server-based application code. Typically used to standardize business logic and reduce the amount of required programming effort, you can build your own stored procedures or leverage the many built-in stored procedures offered by SQL Server. One difference between stored procedures and functions is that the latter must return a value; it's optional with the former. *See also* CLR; function.

Structured Query Language (SQL): Originally developed by IBM, this is a standards-based language that allows access to information stored in a relational database. *See also* Transact-SQL.

subquery: A nested query that returns information to an outer query, thereby helping the outer query correctly identify results.

subscriber: A database server that collects replicated, published information sent by one or more publishers. *See also* replication.

subscription: An appeal sent to a publisher requesting a publication to be sent via replication. *See also* replication.

table: These contain logical groupings of information about a given topic. For example, if you're interested in students and their grades, your application could have at least two tables: One to track details about students and one to monitor their test scores. *See also* column.

TCP/IP: An abbreviation for Transmission Control Protocol/Internet Protocol, this standard makes up the foundation of most computer-to-computer communication across the Internet and on local networks.

third normal form: Table data that complies with both the first and second normal forms and directly relates to each rows primary key. *See also* first normal form; second normal form.

transactions: To prevent data corruption or other inconsistent results, developers use transactions to logically group sets of related database access statements into one work unit. If something goes wrong during the processing of these statements, it's easy to cancel, or *roll back,* the transaction so that none of the changes takes place. Comparatively, if everything completes normally, the transaction ensures that all the alterations are made at the same time.

Transact-SQL: Microsoft's implementation of SQL. It includes a number of enhancements that make it easier to develop powerful database applications. These additions include conditional logic, variables, and error handling logic. *See also* SQL.

Transmission Control Protocol/Internet Protocol: *See* TCP/IP.

trigger: Stored in, and managed by, your database server, this software is executed when a certain event occurs. These events can range from information creation or modification to structural changes to your database. When the event occurs, the trigger is executed, causing a pre-determined set of actions to take place. These actions can encompass data validation, alerts, warnings, and other administrative operations. Triggers can invoke other triggers and stored procedures. *See also* stored procedures.

unique index: Sometimes created explicitly by the user, and sometimes created automatically by the database server. By guaranteeing one-and-only-one value for a given table, this structure speeds access to information and preserves data integrity. *See also* index.

UDPATE statement: UPDATE is used to modify existing rows in tables or views.

view: A virtual grouping of one or more tables, often done to reduce complexity while increasing security and reliability. An administrator defines the view, which is then available for developers and users to access instead of working with the underlying tables.

Visual Studio: Microsoft's flagship development environment, supporting a wide variety of programming languages with a full set of professional features and capabilities for the modern software developer. *See also* Visual Studio Express.

Visual Studio Express: An easy-to-learn, free, integrated collection of software development and data management tools provided by Microsoft. These tools are aimed at entry-level developers, students, and hobbyists.

Web services: A software system used to transfer data. A common use of a Web service is to transfer data across the Internet. A Web service provider receives requests for data and responds. For example, a weather Web service could accept a zip code as input and respond with weather data for the zip code.

XML: A standards-based, structured way of representing and working with information in easily readable text files. Consisting of nested elements that contain content and attributes, XML has become the de-facto standard for transmitting data among disparate systems. SQL Server supports storing and working with XML data. *See also* element; attribute; content.

XQuery: Designed to interrogate XML-based data, this standards-based query language also has some programming capabilities. *See also* XML.

Index

B

Q